# The Infographic Guide to Medicine

T0346328

# The Infographic Guide to Medicine

**Neeral Shah, MD, FACP, AGAF, FACG**

*Associate Professor*
*University of Virginia School of Medicine*
*Charlottesville, Virginia*

**Mc Graw Hill**

New York   Chicago   San Francisco   Athens   London   Madrid   Mexico City
Milan   New Delhi   Singapore   Sydney   Toronto

# The Infographic Guide to Medicine

1 2 3 4 5 6 7 8 9   DSS   26 25 24 23 22 21

ISBN 978-1-260-45397-3
MHID 1-260-45397-9

Book ISBN 978-1-260-45398-0
Book MHID 1-260-45398-7

Binder MHID H3.1025199

This book was set in Minion Pro by KnowledgeWorks Global Ltd.
The editors were Amanda Fielding, Julie Grishaw and Christina M. Thomas.
The production supervisor was Richard Ruzycka.
Project management was provided by Harleen Chopra, KnowledgeWorks Global Ltd.
The cover designer was W2 Design.

**Library of Congress Cataloging-in-Publication Data**

Names: Shah, Neeral L., editor.
Title: The infographic guide to medicine / [edited by] Neeral Shah.
Description: New York : McGraw Hill, [2020] | Includes bibliographical
   references and index. | Summary: "We all know millennial medical
   students are looking to ingest as much information as possible, in as
   little time as possible. These infographics take the top 200 diagnoses
   aligned with USMLE Steps 1 and 2, and present need-to-know information
   in a quick one page snap shot that leverages memorable visual elements,
   like color coding for topic groupings and text placement. To aid in
   combining clinical knowledge with clinical skills, the back of each
   infographic card will include the top 5 questions that should be asked
   or considered when evaluating a patient with the suspected diagnosis"—
   Provided by publisher.
Identifiers: LCCN 2020013676 | ISBN 9781260453973 | ISBN 9781260453997
   (ebook)
Subjects: MESH: Internal Medicine | Pictorial Work | Study Guide
Classification: LCC RC46 | NLM WB 17 | DDC 616.0022/2—dc23
LC record available at https://lccn.loc.gov/20200136/6

*Dedicated to my wife Paige Perriello, MD and our children.*

# Contents

# Associate Editors

### Cardiology
**Victor Soukoulis, MD, PhD**
*Assistant Professor*
*UVA Health, Heart and Vascular Center Fontaine*
*Charlottesville, Virginia*

### Dermatology
**Vinod Nambudiri, MD, MBA**
*Assistant Professor, Brigham Dermatology Associates*
*Harvard Medical School*
*Brigham and Women's Hospital*
*Boston, Massachusetts*

### Emergency Medicine
**Alicia Lydecker, MD**
*Emergency Medicine/Medical Toxicology Physician*
*Albany Medical Center*
*Albany, New York*

**Kathryn Mutter, MD, MPH**
*Assistant Professor of Emergency Medicine, Course Director of Internship*
*    Readiness and Transition Courses*
*University of Virginia, School of Medicine*
*Charlottesville, Virginia*

### Endocrinology
**Gregory Hong, MD**
*Assistant Professor*
*UVA Health, Multidisciplinary Pituitary Clinic*
*Charlottesville, Virginia*

### Gastroenterology/Hepatology, Nephrology, Psychiatry, and Pulmonology
**Neeral Shah, MD**
*Associate Professor, Course Director for Annual UVA GI/Hepatology Conference*
*University of Virginia, School of Medicine*
*Charlottesville, Virginia*

## Hematology/Oncology
**Michael E. Devitt, MD**
*Assistant Professor*
*University of Virginia, School of Medicine*
*Charlottesville, Virginia*

## Infectious Diseases
**Onyema Ogbuagu, MBBCh, FACP, FIDSA**
*Associate Professor of Medicine, AIDS Program*
*Yale School of Medicine*
*New Haven, Connecticut*

## Musculoskeletal System
**Brett R. Levine, MD, MS**
*Associate Professor, Hip & Knee Reconstruction and Replacement Specialist*
*Midwest Orthopedics at Rush University Medical Center*
*Chicago, Illinois*

## Nephrology
**Brendan T. Bowman, MD**
*Associate Professor*
*University of Virginia, School of Medicine*
*Charlottesville, Virginia*

## Neurology
**Aaron L. Berkowitz, MD, PhD**
*Director of Global Health, Professor*
*Kaiser Permanente Bernard J. Tyson School of Medicine*
*Pasadena, California*

## Obstetrics/Gynecology
**Dana L. Redick, MD**
*Associate Professor*
*University of Virginia, School of Medicine*
*Charlottesville, Virginia*

## Pediatrics
**Amy D. Thompson, MD**
*Associate Program Director*
*Nemours Children's Health System*
*Wilmington, Delaware*

**Carlos E. Armengol, Jr., MD, FAAP**
*Physician*
*Pediatric Associates of Charlottesville*
*Charlottesville, Virginia*

**Alaina Brown, MD, FAAP**
*Physician*
*Pediatric Associates of Charlottesville*
*Charlottesville, Virginia*

## Rheumatology
**Geeta Nayyar, MD, MBA**
*Executive Medical Director*
*Salesforce*
*Miami, Florida*

## Urology
**Ryan P. Smith, MD**
*Associate Professor*
*University of Virginia, School of Medicine*
*Charlottesville, Virginia*

# Student Contributors

## Cardiology

**Franck Azobou Tonleu**
*University of Virginia School of Medicine*
*2019*

**Lydia Luu**
*University of Virginia School of Medicine*
*2020*

**Simone Reaves**
*University of Virginia School of Medicine*
*2019*

**Shawn Shah**
*University of Virginia School of Medicine*
*2020*

**John Popovich**
*University of Virginia School of Medicine*
*2020*

**Corey Benjamin**
*University of Virginia School of Medicine*
*2020*

## Dermatology

**Joe Tung**
*Harvard Medical School*
*2020*

**Connie Zhong**
*Harvard Medical School*
*2020*

**Gabriel Molina**
*Harvard Medical School*
*2020*

**Kira Seiger**
*Harvard Medical School*
*2020*

## Emergency Medicine

**Rachel Le**
*Albany Medical College (Emergency Medicine Resident)*

**Cecily Swinburne**
*Albany Medical College (Emergency Medicine Resident)*

**David Loughran**
*Albany Medical College (Emergency Medicine Resident)*

**Spencer Lord**
*Albany Medical College (Emergency Medicine Resident)*

**Ashley Nelsen**
*Albany Medical College*
*2021*

**Jordan Sheehan**
*Albany Medical College*
*2021*

**Benjamin Miller**
*Albany Medical College*
*2022*

**Breann Litwa**
*Albany Medical College*
*2022*

**Kajol Doshi**
*Albany Medical College*
*2022*

**Danielle Stansky**
*Albany Medical College*
*2019*

**Nicholas Lang**
*Albany Medical College*
*2022*

**Richard Tartarini**
*Albany Medical College*
*2022*

**Kliment Todosov**
*Albany Medical College*
*2021*

**Nisha Khubchandani**
*Albany Medical College*
*2022*

**Christopher M. Tossing**
*University of Virginia (Emergency*
*Medicine Resident)*

**Lindsay Troyer**
*University of Virginia School of Medicine*
*2020*

**Jenna Milstein**
*University of Virginia School of Medicine*
*2021*

**Kayvon Izadpanah**
*University of Virginia School of Medicine*
*(Emergency Medicine Resident)*

**Aaron M. Blackshaw**
*University of Virginia School of Medicine*
*(Emergency Medicine Resident)*

**Azhar Ahmed**
*University of Virginia School of Medicine*
*(Emergency Medicine Resident)*

**Moira Smith**
*University of Virginia School of Medicine*
*2019*

**Matthew D. Eisenstat**
*University of Virginia School of Medicine*
*(Emergency Medicine Resident)*

**John P. Baker**
*University of Virginia School of Medicine*
*2019*

## Endocrinology
**Zachary Swenson**
*University of Virginia School of Medicine*
*2020*

**Ashley Bolte**
*University of Virginia School of Medicine*
*(Endocrinology Resident)*

**Nicholas Lucchesi**
*University of Virginia School of Medicine*
*2020*

**Elena Lagon**
*University of Virginia School of Medicine*
*2019*

**Ilana Green**
*University of Virginia School of Medicine*
*2020*

## Gastroenterology/Hepatology
**Martha Stewart**
*University of Virginia School of Medicine*
*2020*

**Haley Podeschi**
*University of Virginia School of Medicine*
*2019*

**Joseph Mort**
*University of Virginia School of Medicine*
*2020*

Joanna Odenthal
*University of Virginia School of Medicine*
*2020*

## Hematology/Oncology
Shannon May
*University of Virginia School of Medicine*
*2020*

Ryan Sutyla
*University of Virginia School of Medicine*
*2020*

Shan Guleria
*University of Virginia School of Medicine*
*2020*

Ashwini Tilak
*University of Virginia School of Medicine*
*2019*

Joseph Mort
*University of Virginia School of Medicine*
*2020*

Laura Walk
*University of Virginia School of Medicine*
*2020*

## Infectious Diseases
Christopher Radcliffe
*Yale School of Medicine*
*2023*

Natty Doilicho
*Yale School of Medicine*
*2023*

## Musculoskeletal
Elizabeth Terhune
*Rush University Medical Center*
*(Orthopedic Resident)*

Nabil Mehta
*Rush University Medical Center*
*(Orthopedic Resident)*

Michael Fice
*Rush University Medical Center*
*2019*

Robert Burnett
*Rush University Medical Center*
*(Orthopedic Resident)*

John Hamilton
*Rush University Medical Center*
*(Orthopedic Resident)*

Philip Locker
*UCSF Fresno (Orthopedic Resident)*

Kamran Movassaghi
*UCSF Fresno (Orthopedic Resident)*

Jefferson Li
*UCSF Fresno*
*2019*

## Nephrology
Claire Harrington
*University of Virginia School of Medicine*
*2019*

Merwise Baray
*University of Virginia School of Medicine*
*2020*

Josceyln Hodge
*University of Virginia School of Medicine*
*2020*

Kayvon Ghoreshi
*University of Virginia School of Medicine*
*2020*

Shan Guleria
*University of Virginia School of Medicine*
*2020*

## Neurology
Galina Gheihman
*Harvard Medical School*
*2019*

**Jaeho Hwang**
*Harvard Medical School*
*2019*

**Vihang Nakhate**
*Harvard Medical School*
*2019*

## Obstetrics/Gynecology
**Allison Bosch**
*University of Virginia School of Medicine*
*2020*

**Emily Schutzenhofer**
*University of Virginia School of Medicine*
*2019*

**Martha Stewart**
*University of Virginia School of Medicine*
*2020*

**Vicky Adele**
*University of Virginia School of Medicine*
*2019*

**John Baker**
*University of Virginia School of Medicine*
*2019*

**Aubrie Carroll**
*University of Virginia School of Medicine*
*2020*

**Elena Lagon**
*University of Virginia School of Medicine*
*2019*

**Raul Krishnan**
*University of Virginia School of Medicine*
*(Obstetrics/Gynecology Resident)*

## Pediatrics
**Joanna Odenthal**
*University of Virginia School of Medicine*
*2020*

**Logan McColl**
*University of Virginia School of Medicine*
*2020*

**Hitoshi Koshiya**
*University of Virginia School of Medicine*
*2019*

**Samantha Epstein**
*University of Virginia School of Medicine*
*2020*

**Erin Adonnino**
*University of Virginia School of Medicine*
*2020*

**Paul G. Mitchell**
*University of Virginia School of Medicine*
*2020*

**Lindsay Williams**
*Philadelphia College of Osteopathic*
*Medicine*
*2022*

**Dana Neuman**
*Alfred I. duPont Hospital for Children*
*Department of Pediatrics (Pediatric*
*Resident)*

**Amanda McCarthy**
*Alfred I. duPont Hospital for Children,*
*Department of Pediatrics (Pediatric*
*Resident)*

**Devika Locke**
*Alfred I. duPont Hospital for Children,*
*Department of Pediatrics (Pediatric*
*Resident)*

**Alyssa Zuziak**
*Alfred I. duPont Hospital for Children,*
*Department of Pediatrics (Pediatric*
*Resident)*

## Psychiatry

**Lindsey McClelland**
*University of Virginia School of Medicine
2020*

**Ziyi Fan**
*University of Virginia School of Medicine
2020*

**Alexandra Deal**
*University of Virginia School of Medicine
2020*

**Michaela Banks**
*University of Virginia School of Medicine
2019*

**Malcolm Roberson**
*University of Virginia School of Medicine
2020*

## Pulmonology

**Albert Chang**
*University of Virginia School of Medicine
2020*

**Chris Kaperak**
*University of Virginia School of Medicine
2020*

**Peter Liaw**
*University of Virginia School of Medicine
2020*

## Rheumatology

**Salim Najjar**
*University of Virginia School of Medicine
2019*

**Kara Harrison**
*University of Virginia School of Medicine
2020*

## Urology

**Ralph Grauer**
*University of Virginia School of Medicine
2020*

**Mark Sultan**
*University of Virginia School of Medicine
2020*

**Yates Congleton**
*University of Virginia School of Medicine
2020*

# Preface

As a medical student I always struggled reading numerous pages of text to try and pick out details of diseases and therapies. Trained as an engineer, I found images flowcharts and algorithms easier to understand. More recently, as a medical educator, I took notice that many of my students also favored visually based materials to help provide a basis for their learning. They often seek out these resources to provide them with quick snapshots and commit high yield details to memory. At the same time, I had encountered infographics that were being used to explain complex topics for the purpose of patient education. I was surprised to learn that while infographics were being used to convey information to patients, this modality was not being used in medical education.

With my specialty training in gastroenterology and transplant hepatology, I set out to develop a set of infographics for this field. With the help of two other physicians (Joseph Mort and Joanna Odenthal), who were medical students at the time, we developed an initial set of 29 infographics that covered major topics in gastroenterology and hepatology. We studied the literature in graphic design for optimal layouts, space to text ratios, and white space use. Keeping these guidelines in mind, we created and edited an initial set of infographics. The weeks after we released this initial set of infographics, many learners asked about their origin, inquired about access, and provided valuable feedback. Word of mouth spread quickly and learners beyond our institution and in other parts of the world were downloading our infographics. We surveyed some of the initial users and found that 93% of survey participants reported the infographics being useful. The top three reasons learners identified that they would use infographics were knowledge reinforcement prior to patient care (55%), exam preparation outside of patient care (26%), and knowledge reinforcement after patient care (10%). It seemed a graphical summary of high yield clinical pearls could be used for exams, but more importantly, to help improve patient care. The graphical nature allowed quick review of a topic, and provided cues to recall previously learned material.

From this initial concept, and a partnership with McGraw Hill, I decided to expand the topic areas beyond gastroenterology and hepatology. We enlisted the help of content experts from many different fields in medicine and many technologically savvy medical students (many from my own institution, the University of Virginia). With everyone's help, we were able to create this first edition, "The Infographic Guide to Medicine" that covers over 600 topics. Coordinating the work of more than 13 associate editors and over 75 students was challenging, but it was also rewarding to bring multiple viewpoints to the final design. Each card we know has been reviewed by at least 4-5 people looking to optimize the design and distill difficult concepts.

I am proud to say, to my knowledge, this is the first book dedicated to infographics for medical education. These clear and concise infographics provide a great overview as an adjunct to a learner's foundational learning, and helps to solidify concepts in their busy schedules. The culmination of this book would not have been possible without the innumerable hours dedicated by medical students and associate editors from around the United States. I also could not have completed this without the endless support of my wife. I hope you are able to use these infographics as you create your own culture and community of learning to ultimately provide better care to your patients.

Neeral L. Shah, M.D.

# Cardiology

*Victor Soukoulis, MD, PhD*

# Angina Pectoris

**①** **Etiology:**
**Myocardial $O_2$ Demand > Supply**

- Atherosclerosis
- Coronary vasospasm (rare)
- Severe anemia

**③** **Diagnosis**

- History consistent with angina
- ECG (usually normal)
- Stress testing
- Troponin if concerned for MI

**⑤ Treatment—Nonmedical Therapy**

- Medical therapy not always effective
- Cath + PCI/CABG if persistent symptoms

**Clinical Presentations** **②**

- Exertional substernal chest pressure
- May radiate to neck or arm
- Associated with shortness of breath (SOB)
- Improves with rest, nitroglycerin
- Symptoms last <10 min

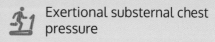

**Treatment—Medical Therapy** **④**

- β Beta-blockers 1st-line
- Calcium channel blockers 2nd-line
- Nitrates for acute symptoms
- ASA, statin to prevent MI
- Quit smoking

# Aortic Dissection

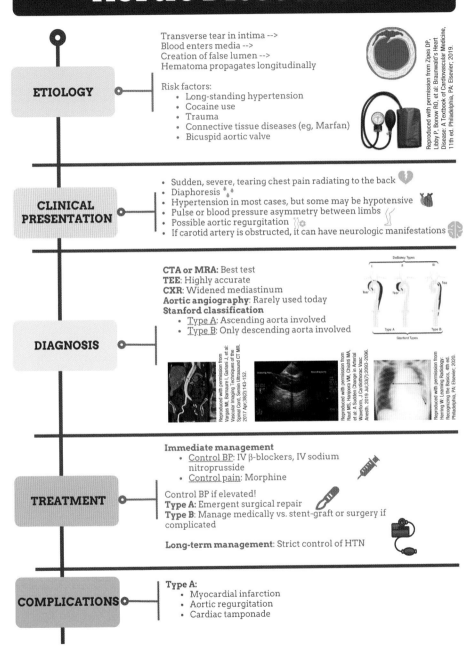

## ETIOLOGY

Transverse tear in intima -->
Blood enters media -->
Creation of false lumen -->
Hematoma propagates longitudinally

Risk factors:
- Long-standing hypertension
- Cocaine use
- Trauma
- Connective tissue diseases (eg, Marfan)
- Bicuspid aortic valve

## CLINICAL PRESENTATION

- Sudden, severe, tearing chest pain radiating to the back
- Diaphoresis
- Hypertension in most cases, but some may be hypotensive
- Pulse or blood pressure asymmetry between limbs
- Possible aortic regurgitation
- If carotid artery is obstructed, it can have neurologic manifestations

## DIAGNOSIS

**CTA or MRA:** Best test
**TEE:** Highly accurate
**CXR:** Widened mediastinum
**Aortic angiography**: Rarely used today
**Stanford classification**
- Type A: Ascending aorta involved
- Type B: Only descending aorta involved

## TREATMENT

**Immediate management**
- Control BP: IV β-blockers, IV sodium nitroprusside
- Control pain: Morphine

Control BP if elevated!
**Type A:** Emergent surgical repair
**Type B**: Manage medically vs. stent-graft or surgery if complicated

**Long-term management**: Strict control of HTN

## COMPLICATIONS

**Type A:**
- Myocardial infarction
- Aortic regurgitation
- Cardiac tamponade

# Aortic Regurgitation

## 1 Etiology

- Bicuspid aortic valve
- Connective tissue disorders (Marfan syndrome)
- Infective endocarditis
- Aortic dissection
- Syphilis
- Trauma

## 2 Pathophysiology

- Chronic aortic regurgitation leads to increased end diastolic volume and compensatory hypertrophy.
- Ultimately develop heart failure.
- Acute regurgitation (rare) leads to cardiogenic shock.

## 3 Clinical Presentation

- Asymptomatic
- Fatigue
- Exertional dyspnea
- Orthopnea
- Paroxysmal nocturnal dyspnea

- Soft, high-pitched diastolic decrescendo murmur along LSB at end expiration while sitting up and leaning forward.
- Austin Flint murmur at apex
- Wide pulse pressure: Corrigan pulse, de Musset's sign

## 4 Diagnosis

- Echocardiography: Modality of choice. If inconclusive, cardiac MRI can be used.

- Chest X-ray: Variable; cardiomegaly and pulmonary edema in late presentation.

## 5 Management

- If asymptomatic, follow up with regular echocardiograms.
- For HTN: Use vasodilators (ACE-Is or CCBs).
- Valve replacement when symptomatic or EF <50%.
- Acute regurgitation is a surgical emergency.

# Aortic Stenosis

 **Etiology**

1

- Age-related calcification of a normal (trileaflet) aortic valve (patient >60 years old)
- Early-onset calcification of a **bicuspid aortic valve** (younger patient)

2 **Pathophysiology**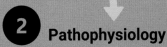

Obstructed aortic valve outflow due to calcified valve

↓

Increased pressure load on left ventricle

↓

LVH, low compliance --> dyspnea

↓

LVH, increased wall stress --> $O_2$ supply/demand mismatch and angina

3 **Clinical Presentation**

Often asymptomatic for years; once symptoms present: **"SAD"**

**S**yncope
**A**ngina
**D**yspnea on exertion

**Physical Exam:**

- **Crescendo-decrescendo systolic ejection murmur** radiates to carotids

- Pulsus parvus et tardus

5 **Treatment**

For symptomatic patients with severe stenosis: definitive treatment is **aortic valve replacement**

4

**Diagnosis**

- ECG: LVH
- **Echocardiogram**: calcified aortic valve with stenosis, LVH
- Cardiac catheterization: rarely used

# Atrial Fibrillation & Atrial Flutter

## Atrial Fibrillation

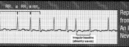

### Etiology

**Acute AFib**

- Electrolyte changes
- Alcohol
- Anemia
- Thyrotoxicosis
- Sepsis

- - - - - - - - - - - - -

**Chronic AFib**

Abnormal circular electrical currents around the atria.

- Hypertension (years)
- Heart failure
- Rheumatic heart disease
- Older age

### Signs & Symptoms

- Asymptomatic
- Shortness of breath
- Chest pain
- Palpitations

### Treatment

- Correct underlying disease (thyroid, etc.)
- Anticoagulation
- Rate control (try first): BBs or CCBs
- Rhythm control: amiodarone, flecainide, cardioversion

## Atrial Flutter

### Etiology

Abnormal circular electrical circuit in atrium

### Signs & Symptoms

- Asymptomatic
- Palpitations
- Shortness of breath

### Treatment

- Anticoagulation
- Same rate/rhythm control as AFib
- "Ablation" procedure to disrupt circuit

# AV Nodal Reentry Tachycardia & WPW

## Rhythm

Fast | Narrow | Regular

## Presentation

- Asymptomatic
- Palpitations
- Syncope
- Shortness of breath

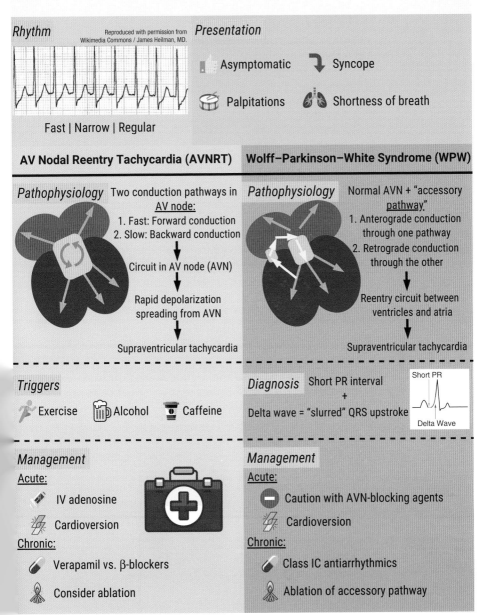

| AV Nodal Reentry Tachycardia (AVNRT) | Wolff–Parkinson–White Syndrome (WPW) |
|---|---|
| **Pathophysiology** Two conduction pathways in AV node: <br> 1. Fast: Forward conduction <br> 2. Slow: Backward conduction <br><br> Circuit in AV node (AVN) <br><br> Rapid depolarization spreading from AVN <br><br> Supraventricular tachycardia | **Pathophysiology** Normal AVN + "accessory pathway" <br> 1. Anterograde conduction through one pathway <br> 2. Retrograde conduction through the other <br><br> Reentry circuit between ventricles and atria <br><br> Supraventricular tachycardia |
| **Triggers** <br> Exercise   Alcohol   Caffeine | **Diagnosis** Short PR interval <br> + <br> Delta wave = "slurred" QRS upstroke <br><br> Short PR / Delta Wave |
| **Management** <br> Acute: <br> IV adenosine <br> Cardioversion <br> Chronic: <br> Verapamil vs. β-blockers <br> Consider ablation | **Management** <br> Acute: <br> Caution with AVN-blocking agents <br> Cardioversion <br> Chronic: <br> Class IC antiarrhythmics <br> Ablation of accessory pathway |

# Cardiac Tamponade

## Etiology

Pericardial effusion mechanically impairs diastolic filling -> decreased cardiac output

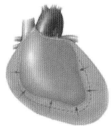

Causes:

- Acute pericarditis
- Iatrogenic
- Penetrating trauma
- Free wall rupture post-MI
- Malignancy
- Aortic dissection

## Clinical Presentation

- Dyspnea, anxiety, tachycardia, tachypnea
- **Beck triad:** Hypotension, distant heart sounds, JVD
- Pulsus paradoxus (10 mm Hg drop in BP with inspiration)
- Venous waveforms: Prominent x descent, absent y descent

## Diagnosis

- **Act quickly** if high clinical suspicion and unstable!!!

- **Echo:** Gold standard. Shows effusion and RV diastolic collapse
- **CXR:** Enlarged cardiac silhouette ("water-bottle-shaped heart"), clear lung fields
- **ECG:** Electrical alternans
- **Cardiac cath:** Equalization of pressures in all chambers of the heart

## Treatment

Aggressive volume expansion with **IV fluids**
**If nonhemorrhagic tamponade:**
Pericardiocentesis
**If hemorrhagic tamponade secondary to trauma:**
Emergent surgery to repair the injury

# Carotid Artery Stenosis

## Risk Factors

- HTN
- Smoking
- HL
- Older age
- DM
- CAD

## Pathogenesis

**Lipid and SMC proliferation cause stenotic plaque**

**Plaque rupture triggers thrombosis ± embolization**

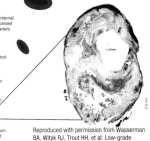

External carotid artery
Internal carotid artery
Emboli
Superior thyroid artery
Ulcer
Plaque
Common carotid artery

Reproduced with permission from Brunicardi FC, Andersen DK, Billiar TR, et al: Schwartz's Principles of Surgery, 11th ed. New York, NY: McGraw Hill; 2019.

Lumen
NC

Reproduced with permission from Wasserman BA, Wityk RJ, Trout HH, et al: Low-grade carotid stenosis: looking beyond the lumen with MRI, Stroke. 2005 Nov;36(11):2504-2513.

*Narrowed common carotid lumen due to large atheroma*
*NC = necrotic core*
*\* = focal calcification*

## ~20%
### of ischemic strokes
are caused by carotid artery disease

## Complications

| Amaurosis Fugax | TIA | CVA |
|---|---|---|

   **24 h**

## Diagnosis

**Duplex U/S**

**MRA**

Angiography (small risk of stroke)

Routine carotid screening <u>not</u> recommended

## Medical Therapy

Antiplatelet
Statin
Antihypertensive
Lifestyle modification

**+**
**−**

## Invasive Therapy

CEA (gold standard)
Stenting
Decision based on: Symptoms, % stenosis, and gender

# Complete (Third-Degree) AV Block

## Etiology

 Drug-induced (β-blockers, calcium channel blockers, digoxin, antiarrhythmics)

Myocardial infarction (inferior)

Infectious (viral myocarditis, Lyme carditis, endocarditis)

Infiltrative (amyloidosis, sarcoidosis)

## Clinical Presentation

 Fatigue

Dyspnea

Chest pain

Syncope

## Diagnosis

- ECG used for diagnosis
- Complete dissociation between atria and ventricles
- P waves and QRS complexes marching independently

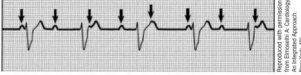

Reproduced with permission from Elmoselhi A: Cardiology: An Integrated Approach. New York, NY: McGraw Hill; 2018.

## Management

  Atropine (if unstable)

 Pacemaker

# Deep Vein Thrombosis

## Etiology

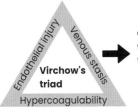

**Virchow's triad**
- Endothelial Injury
- Venous stasis
- Hypercoagulability

→ Clot formation in the large veins of the legs or pelvis

## Clinical Presentation

 Unilateral lower extremity pain and swelling

 Well's score

 Palpable cord

 Low-grade fever

## Diagnosis

 **D-dimer test:** High sensitivity, low specificity

 **Doppler ultrasound:** Noncompressible vein

## Treatment

 **Heparin or enoxaparin --> Warfarin or direct oral anticoagulant (DOAC)** eg, rivaroxaban

 **IVC filter** to prevent PE if patient has contraindication to anticoagulation

 **DVT prophylaxis** for hospital patients: Ambulate, pneumatic compression, heparin, or enoxaparin

## Complications

 Pulmonary embolism

 Post-thrombotic syndrome (chronic venous insufficiency)

 Phlegmasia cerulea dolens (compartment syndrome)

# Dyslipidemia & Atherosclerosis

## Pathophysiology

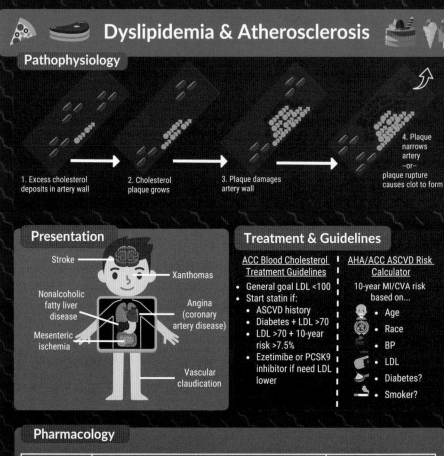

1. Excess cholesterol deposits in artery wall
2. Cholesterol plaque grows
3. Plaque damages artery wall
4. Plaque narrows artery
   --or--
   plaque rupture causes clot to form

## Presentation

- Stroke
- Xanthomas
- Nonalcoholic fatty liver disease
- Angina (coronary artery disease)
- Mesenteric ischemia
- Vascular claudication

## Treatment & Guidelines

### ACC Blood Cholesterol Treatment Guidelines

- General goal LDL <100
- Start statin if:
  - ASCVD history
  - Diabetes + LDL >70
  - LDL >70 + 10-year risk >7.5%
  - Ezetimibe or PCSK9 inhibitor if need LDL lower

### AHA/ACC ASCVD Risk Calculator

10-year MI/CVA risk based on...
- Age
- Race
- BP
- LDL
- Diabetes?
- Smoker?

## Pharmacology

| Drug | Mechanism of Action | Side Effects |
| --- | --- | --- |
| Statins | HMG-CoA reductase inhibitors—decrease cholesterol synthesis | Hepatitis, myopathy |
| Ezetimibe | Decrease cholesterol absorption in gut | Diarrhea |
| PCSK9 inhibitors | Stop LDL receptor degradation—increase LDL uptake from blood | Flu-like symptoms |
| Fibrates | Upregulate lipoprotein lipase—decrease triglycerides | Myopathy, gallstones |

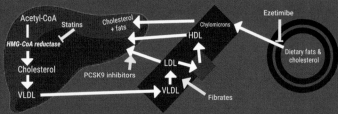

# Essential Hypertension

## 1 Risk Factors

**Modifiable**

 Obesity

 Increased salt intake

 Smoking

 Excess alcohol consumption

Stress

**Nonmodifiable**

 Age

Ethnicity (AA > white)

## 2 Diagnosis

**Classification**

Normal BP: **<120/80**
Stage 1 HTN: **130-139/80-89**
Stage 2 HTN: **>140/>90**
**Rule out white-coat hypertension**

**Workup**

 Blood glucose, metabolic panel, lipids

Urinalysis and albumin-to-creatinine ratio

 Electrocardiogram

## 3 Complications

 Coronary artery disease

 Congestive heart failure

 Aortic dissection

 Aortic aneurysm

 Stroke

 Chronic kidney disease

Retinopathy

## 4 Management

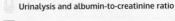 

Weight loss, **DASH diet**, less salt and alcohol, exercise, and no smoking

 **Pharmacotherapy**

- Consider **thiazide diuretics and CCBs**
- β-blockers in CAD and HF
- **ACE inhibitors/ARBs** in DM, CKD, and HF
- Start **combination therapy** in stage 2 HTN

# Heart Failure
## with Preserved Ejection Fraction (HFpEF)

## Etiology

Decreased ventricular compliance with normal systolic function (EF >50%)

Impaired active relaxation and/or passive filling

**Associated with:**

- HTN
- Obesity
- Older age
- CAD
- Diabetes
- Obesity

## Clinical Presentation

Exertional dyspnea, fatigue, orthopnea, PND, edema

**Exam:**
- JVD
- S4 gallop
- Rales
- Peripheral edema

## Diagnosis

**Clinical Diagnosis**

**CXR:** Pulmonary congestion

**ECG/Echo:** Normal EF (>50%), abnormal LV diastolic function, poss LVH

**BNP:** Elevated

## Treatment

**Treat Underlying Condition/Sx:**
- Diuretics
- BP control
- Weight loss

No proven mortality benefit to any treatments

**14**

# Heart Failure
## with Reduced Ejection Fraction (HFrEF)

## Etiology

 **Reduced EF (<40%)** leading to increased EDV and LV dilatation

**Causes:**

- CAD
- Viral myocarditis
- EtOH
- Pregnancy
- Untreated valve disease
- Idiopathic

## Clinical Presentation

 Exertional dyspnea (at rest if end-stage), orthopnea, PND, edema

 **Exam:**
- JVD
- Displaced PMI
- S3 gallop
- Rales
- Peripheral edema

**NYHA Heart Failure Classification**
I - No symptoms or activity limitations
II - Mild symptoms with slight limitations
III - Marked limitations due to symptoms
IV - Symptoms at rest; severe limitations

## Diagnosis

 **Clinical diagnosis primarily**

 **Echo:** Best test. Shows decreased EF (<40%) and ventricular dilatation. May help determine underlying cause (ie, old MI, valve dz)

 **ECG:** May show Q waves, arrhythmia

 **CXR:** Pulmonary congestion, cardiomegaly, pleural effusions

 **BNP:** Elevated

## Treatment

**Acute:**
- Lasix
- Oxygen
- Position (sit upright)

**Chronic:**
- <u>Lifestyle</u>: Limit sodium and fluid intake
- <u>Pharmacologic therapy</u>:
(* = mortality benefit)
  - BB* and ACEi*/ARB*
  - Spironolactone/eplerenone*
  - Hydralazine/nitrates if African American*
  - Diuretics
  - Digoxin

**Advanced Treatments:**
Consider ICD*
LVAD or transplant if unresponsive to maximum medical therapy

# Hypertensive Crises
## Urgencies & Emergencies

## Hypertensive Urgency

Severely elevated blood pressure (eg, >180/>120 mm Hg)...

...with NO symptoms.

## Hypertensive Emergency

Severely elevated blood pressure (eg, >180/>120 mm Hg)...

...with signs/symptoms of **end-organ damage.** Examples:

Stroke
Papilledema
Aortic dissection
Acute kidney injury

Encephalopathy
Retinal hemorrhages
Myocardial infarction

## Causes

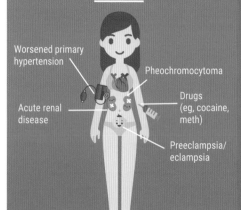

Worsened primary hypertension

Acute renal disease

Pheochromocytoma

Drugs (eg, cocaine, meth)

Preeclampsia/ eclampsia

## Management

- For urgency use oral meds
- For emergency use IV meds (usually do <u>not</u> decrease BP too quickly— can cause ischemic stroke):
  - β-blocker: Labetalol
  - Nitrate: Nitroprusside
  - Ca channel blocker: Nicardipine

# Hypertrophic Cardiomyopathy

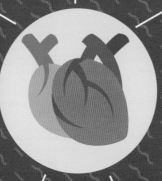

### Cause: Genetics
- Autosomal dominant
- Mutations in myosin-binding protein C or β-myosin heavy chain

### Pathology:
- Concentric LV hypertrophy
- Thickened interventricular septum (IVS)

### Hypertrophic **obstructive** cardiomyopathy:
- Subtype with more growth of septum and MV leaflet causing LV outflow tract obstruction

### Symptoms:
- Syncope
- Dyspnea
- Sudden cardiac death (athletes)

### Treatment:
- No competitive sports
- β-blockers
- Ca channel blockers
- Implantable defibrillator
- Surgery (septal myectomy; last resort)

### Diagnosis:
- ECG showing LVH
- Echocardiogram (gold standard)
- Genetic testing

### Signs:
- S4 gallop (thick LV)
- Systolic murmur (LV outflow tract obstruction)

# Long QT Syndromes

## Definition

- Prolonged QT interval leads to arrhythmias
- Acquired or congenital
- Increased risk of torsades de pointes (TdP)

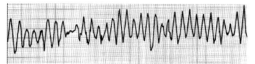

Reproduced with permission from Knoop KJ, Stack LB, Storrow AB, et al: The Atlas of Emergency Medicine, 4th ed. New York, NY: McGraw Hill; 2016.

*Torsades de Pointes*

## Presentation

Palpitations

 Syncope

 Sudden cardiac arrest

## Etiology

Genetics

Electrolyte imbalance (K, Mg)

Myocardial infarction

Drug-induced (ABCDE):
- AntiArrhythmics
- AntiBiotics
- Anti"C"ychotics
- AntiDepressants
- AntiEmetics

## Pathophysiology

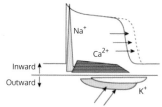

Reproduced with permission from Hammer GD, McPhee SJ: Pathophysiology of Disease: An Introduction to Clinical Medicine, 8th ed. New York, NY: McGraw Hill; 2019.

Dysfunction of sodium and potassium channels -> abnormal repolarization and QT prolongation

## Diagnosis

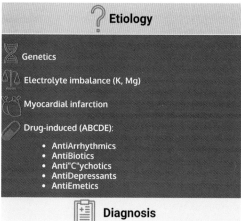

Reproduced with permission from Knoop KJ, Stack LB, Storrow AB, et al: The Atlas of Emergency Medicine, 4th ed. New York, NY: McGraw Hill; 2016.

- Obtain electrocardiogram (ECG)
- Calculate QTc = QT/$\sqrt{RR}$
- >450 ms is abnormal (highest risk when >500 ms)
- Consider event monitor

## Management

Ask family history of SCD or arrhythmias

Evaluate for secondary causes

Avoid QT-prolonging drugs

β-blockers

Magnesium and/or shock if torsades

ICD placement

# Mitral Valve Stenosis

## Etiology

- **Rheumatic fever (>60%)**
- Calcifications (elderly)
- Endocarditis

## Clinical Presentation

 Dyspnea (with faster HR/exercise)

 Stroke (embolism)

 Heart failure (elevated LA pressure)

 Atrial fibrillation (dilated left atrium)

## Exam—Murmur

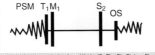

PSM $T_1M_1$    $S_2$   OS

Reproduced with permission from Kibble JD: The Big Picture Physiology: Medical Course & Step 1 Review, 2nd ed. New York, NY: McGraw Hill; 2020.

 Opening snap

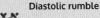 Diastolic rumble

 Best heard at apex

## Diagnosis

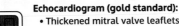 **Echocardiogram (gold standard):**
- Thickened mitral valve leaflets
- "Fish-mouth" valve opening
- Calcifications
- Enlarged left atrium

 **Possible ECG findings:**
- Left atrial abnormality (P mitrale)
- Atrial fibrillation

## Treatment

 No treatment if asymptomatic

 Consider BB or CCB to slow HR, warfarin if atrial fibrillation

 Balloon valvuloplasty or valve replacement if symptomatic

# Mitral Valve Prolapse (MVP)

## Etiology

 Primary

Secondary due to connective tissue disorders (eg, Marfan, Ehlers-Danlos)

## Clinical Presentation

Young woman

Usually asymptomatic

## Exam—Murmur

Mid-systolic click

### Diagnosis and Treatment

Echo shows prolapse of myxomatous mitral valve

⊘ No treatment if asymptomatic

Surgery if develop severe MR (rare)

 Late systolic crescendo murmur at apex

Earlier murmur with Valsalva and standing (decreased preload)

# Mitral Regurgitation (MR)

## Etiology

Acute—Papillary muscle rupture in MI

Chronic—Rheumatic fever, MVP

## Clinical Presentation

Dyspnea with exertion

Heart failure (elevated LA pressures)

Orthopnea

## Exam—Murmur

 Holosystolic

Blowing murmur

③ May hear S3

 Radiates toward left axilla

### Diagnosis and Treatment

Echo shows MR; possible LV/LA enlargement

Meds: Diuretics for symptoms, ACEi for HTN

Surgery if severe symptomatic MR or LV dysfunction

# Pericarditis

## Acute Inflammation of the Pericardial Sac

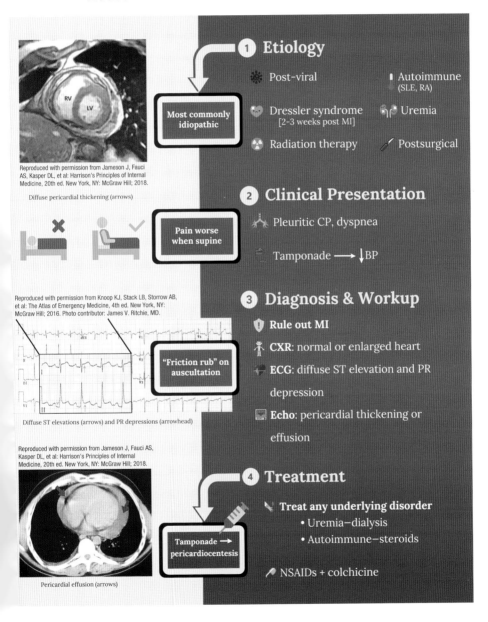

### 1 Etiology

**Most commonly idiopathic**

- Post-viral
- Autoimmune (SLE, RA)
- Dressler syndrome [2-3 weeks post MI]
- Uremia
- Radiation therapy
- Postsurgical

Reproduced with permission from Jameson J, Fauci AS, Kasper DL, et al: Harrison's Principles of Internal Medicine, 20th ed. New York, NY: McGraw Hill; 2018.

Diffuse pericardial thickening (arrows)

### 2 Clinical Presentation

**Pain worse when supine**

- Pleuritic CP, dyspnea
- Tamponade ⟶ ↓BP

Reproduced with permission from Knoop KJ, Stack LB, Storrow AB, et al: The Atlas of Emergency Medicine, 4th ed. New York, NY: McGraw Hill; 2016. Photo contributor: James V. Ritchie, MD.

### 3 Diagnosis & Workup

**"Friction rub" on auscultation**

- **Rule out MI**
- **CXR**: normal or enlarged heart
- **ECG**: diffuse ST elevation and PR depression
- **Echo**: pericardial thickening or effusion

Diffuse ST elevations (arrows) and PR depressions (arrowhead)

Reproduced with permission from Jameson J, Fauci AS, Kasper DL, et al: Harrison's Principles of Internal Medicine, 20th ed. New York, NY: McGraw Hill; 2018.

### 4 Treatment

**Tamponade ⟶ pericardiocentesis**

- Treat any underlying disorder
  - Uremia–dialysis
  - Autoimmune–steroids
- NSAIDs + colchicine

Pericardial effusion (arrows)

# Peripheral Artery Disease (PAD)

## Overview

- Narrowing of blood vessels in the extremities.
- Most commonly affects the iliac, femoral, and popliteal arteries.
- Risk factors: Older age, smoking, diabetes, hypertension, hyperlipidemia.
- Atherosclerosis accounts for 90% of cases. Other causes include embolism, thrombosis, vasculitis (Buerger disease), and iatrogenic (following invasive procedures).

## Clinical Presentation

- Presentation is dependent on the affected artery and degree of decreased blood flow.
- Most patients asymptomatic; others present with atypical leg pain.
- Some have classic **intermittent claudication** (muscle pain, cramping, fatigue associated with exertion that resolves within 5-10 min of rest).
- Physical exam: Hair loss, bruits, decreased pulses, and pallor/cyanosis.

## Diagnosis

- **Ankle-brachial index (ABI)** is the initial test. PAD when ABI <0.9.
- If symptoms consistent with PAD but ABI is normal, do exercise ABI.
- Duplex ultrasound and CTA/MRA can also be used.
- Angiography is the gold standard.

## Management

- Lifestyle modification: Smoking cessation is most important.
- Cardiovascular risk reduction: Maintain HbA1C <7%, BP <130/80, LDL <100.
- Antiplatelet therapy: Aspirin or clopidogrel.
- Symptomatic relief: Walking/exercise program, cilostazol.
- Intervention: Endovascular or surgical if refractory and/or critical limb ischemia.

## Complications

- **Chronic limb-threatening ischemia** due to long-standing PAD: Rest pain, cold/numbness in feet, nonhealing ulcers, tissue loss, and/or gangrene. Revascularization may be limb-saving.
- **Acute limb ischemia** due to sudden arterial occlusion: Pain, pulselessness, pallor, paresthesia, paralysis, and poikilothermia/coldness (the 6 P's). Surgical emergency.

# RESTRICTIVE CARDIOMYOPATHY

## Etiology

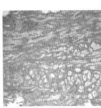

**5%** of all cardiomyopathy cases

*Diffuse infiltration of the myocardium by amyloid*

Purple = myocyte
*Green* = amyloid

Used with permission from Robert Padera, MD, PhD, Department of Pathology, Brigham and Women's Hospital, Boston.

### Infiltrative

- ★ **Amyloidosis**
- ⚘ Sarcoidosis
- Hemo-chromatosis

### Iatrogenic

- ☢ Radiation
- 💉 Chemo

### Idiopathic

- Endomyocardial fibrosis
- Loeffler endo-myocarditis

## Pathophysiology

| ↓ Myocardial compliance | ↔ (no change) Systolic function | ↑ LV thickness |

Diastolic function

"Stiff" ventricles
cause diastolic dysfunction

## Presentation

**R**
- 🧍 JVD (Kussmaul's)
- Hepatomegaly
- Ascites
- 🦶 Edema

**L**
- Dyspnea
- Pulmonary HTN
- Pulmonary edema
- Right-sided failure ⏮

## Diagnosis

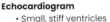

🖥 **Echocardiogram**
- Small, stiff ventricles
- Enlarged atria
- Diastolic dysfunction

*Grossly dilated atria (A) and small ventricles (V)*

Reproduced with permission from Fuster V, Harrington RA, Narula J, et al: Hurst's the Heart, 14th ed. New York, NY: McGraw Hill; 2017.

## Treatment

Diuretics ➤ **Offload the heart** 🔧

Consider CCB, BB

Treat underlying disease

Consider heart transplant or palliative care if advanced

🖤 Prognosis is poor

**⚠ Be careful of clinical mimickers**

*Constrictive pericarditis* has a similar clinical presentation and is surgically curable

**Cardiac MRI**

| Thickened pericardium | Normal pericardium |
| ↓ | ↓ |
| Constrictive pericarditis | **Endomyocardial biopsy** can be diagnostic |

# ST-Elevation Myocardial Infarction

##  Pathophysiology

- Atherosclerosis -> plaque rupture -> vessel occlusion

##  Acute Presentation

- **Crushing** chest pain, radiates to left arm & neck
- Diaphoresis
- Shortness of breath

##  Laboratory Diagnosis

- Troponin: Appears by 3 hours, peaks at 24 hours, elevated for 7-10 days

##  ECG Diagnosis and Localization

- ST-segment elevation in **2+ anatomically contiguous leads**

| MI Location | Vessel | Leads w/STE |
|---|---|---|
| Anterior | LAD | V1-V4 |
| Anterolateral | LCx | I, aVL, V5-V6 |
| Inferior | RCA | II, III, aVF |

| I<br>Antero-lateral | aVR | V1<br>Anterior | V4<br>Anterior |
|---|---|---|---|
| II<br>Inferior | aVL<br>Antero-lateral | V2<br>Anterior | V5<br>Antero-lateral |
| III<br>Inferior | aVF<br>Inferior | V3<br>Anterior | V6<br>Antero-lateral |

##  Acute Treatment

- Aspirin (immediately), anticoagulant, β-blocker
- Percutaneous coronary intervention (PCI)
- Thrombolytics (tPA) if can't do PCI

##  Long-Term Management

- Dual antiplatelet therapy
- β-blocker
- Statin
- ACEi + aldosterone antagonist (if low EF)

##  Post-MI Complications

| | | | | | | | |
|---|---|---|---|---|---|---|---|
| | Ventricular Septal Rupture | Ventricular Free-Wall Rupture | | | Dressler Syndrome | | |
| Arrhythmia | Papillary Muscle Rupture | | | Ventricular Aneurysm | Heart Failure | | |
| 1d | 3d | 5d | 7d | 10d | 14d | Mos | Yrs |

# Supraventricular Tachycardia

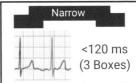

Narrow

<120 ms
(3 Boxes)

WPW

Delta wave

PR interval

- Most Common Ventricular Pre-Excitation Syndrome
- Bundle of Kent

## REGULAR

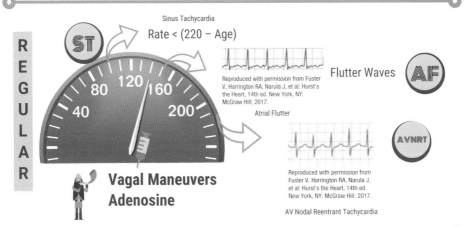

ST

Sinus Tachycardia

Rate < (220 – Age)

80   120   160
40            200

**Vagal Maneuvers**
**Adenosine**

Flutter Waves    AF

Atrial Flutter

AVNRT

AV Nodal Reentrant Tachycardia

## IRREGULAR

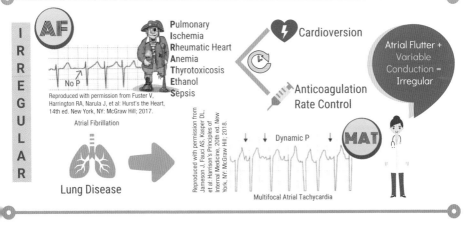

AF

**P**ulmonary
**I**schemia
**R**heumatic Heart
**A**nemia
**T**hyrotoxicosis
**E**thanol
**S**epsis

No P

Atrial Fibrillation

Lung Disease

Cardioversion

Anticoagulation
Rate Control

Atrial Flutter +
Variable
Conduction =
Irregular

Dynamic P    MAT

Multifocal Atrial Tachycardia

---

  Angina or MI →  Cardioversion ←  Low Pressure

# Syncope

| Pathophysiology: Decreased Brain Perfusion | Typical Presentation |
|---|---|

↓ Inadequate **blood volume**

 ↑ **Vasodilation**

↓ Blood **pumped** to brain

**Prodrome***—can include nausea, lightheaded, warm, cold/clammy, pale

⚠ *Except arrhythmias—no prodrome!*

Recovery within 15-30 sec

No postictal state

## Etiologies of Syncope

## 1 Neurocardiogenic (Vasovagal)

↑ Increased **vagus nerve** stimulation

**Hypotension** and **bradycardia**

Pain, blood draws, defecation, coughing, strong emotional stimulus

## Orthostatic Hypotension 2

**Volume-depleted** (**diarrhea**, vomiting, hemorrhage)

**Hypotension** when **changing position** (sitting to standing)

More common in the **elderly**

## 3 Mechanical (Cardiac)

Adolescents/young adults = **hypertrophic cardiomyopathy (HCM)***

⚠ *Can present with arrhythmia/sudden death also*

Elderly = **aortic stenosis**

Mechanical **obstruction** of blood flow

**Decreased** blood flow to brain with **exertion**

**Echo** important in diagnosis of mechanical syncope

## Arrhythmias 4

**Sudden** onset with **no prodrome**

Initial ECG may be **normal**

# Unstable Angina (UA) and Non-ST-Elevation Myocardial Infarction (NSTEMI)

## Spectrum of Ischemic Cardiac Disease

 Stable Angina |  Unstable Angina |  NSTEMI |  STEMI

**Definition**

| Pain with **exertion, resolves** with rest or nitroglycerin | **Increase in pain** (frequency or intensity) or pain at rest | Increase in pain **with elevated troponin** | **+ST elevations** in 2+ contiguous leads |

 |  |  |

**Pathophysiology**

| **Stable atherosclerotic plaque**—ischemia only with increased demand | **Possible thrombosis** with **incomplete** coronary occlusion | **Thrombosis** with **incomplete** coronary occlusion and **cardiac biomarker release** | **Thrombosis** (usually **plaque rupture**) with **complete** coronary occlusion |

## Diagnosis of Unstable Angina vs. NSTEMI

| | Change in Pain? | Elevated Troponin? | ECG Changes? |
|---|---|---|---|
| **Unstable Angina** |  ✓ | ✗ | • +/− ST depression or T wave changes<br>• No ST elevation |
| **NSTEMI** |  ✓ |  ✓ | • +/− ST depression or T wave changes<br>• No ST elevation |

## Risk Stratification and Management

### TIMI Risk Score
Estimates mortality of UA/NSTEMI from...

 • Age

 • CAD risk factors or history?

• ECG changes?

• + Troponin?

### Management

#### Acute
- Nitrates
- Aspirin
- β-blocker
- Statin
- Heparin
- Consider angiography +/− revascularization

#### Chronic
- Risk factor reduction (lifestyle changes, ACEi + statin + BB, etc.)

# Ventricular Septal Defect

## Etiology

 Most common congenital heart defect

**4** Four types, classified by location

No gender predilection

Can be isolated or part of syndrome:
Trisomies (13, 18, **21**)
Fetal alcohol syndrome
TORCH infections

## Clinical Presentation

Symptoms correlate with **size** (degree of L->R shunt)

Most small/medium VSDs are **asymptomatic** and close spontaneously

Children may exhibit dyspnea, lethargy, and failure to thrive

Blood from LV ("y") is shunted through VSD, causes pulmonary overcirculation & symptoms

Reproduced with permission from Jameson J, Fauci AS, Kasper DL, et al: Harrison's Principles of Internal Medicine, 20th ed. New York, NY: McGraw Hill; 2018.

## Diagnosis & Workup

 Prenatal: large VSDs may be detected in utero

 Physical exam: harsh, **holosystolic murmur** loudest at **LLSB** (smaller VSD = louder murmur)

 CXR: cardiomegaly, enlarged PA, **increased pulmonary vascular markings**

 **Echocardiography:** confirms diagnosis (visualize defect & shunt)

## Treatment

Asymptomatic patients can be **monitored** with an excellent prognosis

**Surgical closure** via sternotomy or endovascular techniques in eligible patients may reduce future pulmonary disease

**Degree of shunting** measured during cardiac catheterization dictates management

 Qp/Qs >1.5 with clinical evidence of CHF supports surgical closure

## Complications

Eisenmenger syndrome = R->L **shunt reversal** (poor prognosis)

Large untreated VSDs

 Pulmonary vascular changes **Pulmonary HTN**

 **CHF** Infective endocarditis AR if VSD located right below AV

# Ventricular Tachyarrhythmias
## Ventricular Tachycardia & Fibrillation

| Ventricular Tachycardia | Ventricular Fibrillation |
|---|---|
| **Rhythm** 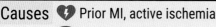 | **Rhythm**  |

Reproduced with permission from Jameson J, Fauci AS, Kasper DL, et al: Harrison's Principles of Internal Medicine, 20th ed. New York, NY: McGraw Hill; 2018.

Reproduced with permission from Jameson J, Fauci AS, Kasper DL, et al: Harrison's Principles of Internal Medicine, 20th ed. New York, NY: McGraw Hill; 2018.

## Causes

 Prior MI, active ischemia

 Long QT -> torsades

Cardiomyopathy

## Causes

 VTach degenerates to VFib (ischemia, long QT)

## Presentation

Palpitations  Cardiogenic shock

Dizziness  Sudden cardiac death

## Presentation

 Loss of consciousness
No pulse
No blood pressure
Sudden cardiac death

## Management

### Nonsustained VTach
(<30 sec, no symptoms)

✔ Check electrolytes     Echo esp if + history of CAD

- - - - - - - - - - - - - - - - - - -

### Sustained VTach
(>30 sec + symptoms)

Stable vitals -> pharmacologic treatment
(amiodarone, lidocaine)

Unstable vitals -> DC cardioversion
(then antiarrhythmic therapy)

## Management

Immediate CPR

Defibrillate ASAP

Epinephrine q3-5 min

Amiodarone (if no better with epi)

- - - - - - - - - - - - - - - - - - -

If in field, priorities are

Immediate CPR

Activation of EMS, transport to hospital

Prompt defibrillation

# References

**Angina Pectoris**
Le T, Bhushan V. *First Aid for the USMLE Step 2 CK*. 10th ed. New York, NY: McGraw Hill; 2018; 33-34.
Le T, Bhushan V, Sochat M. *First Aid for the USMLE Step 1 2019*. New York, NY: McGraw Hill; 2019:301, 314.

**Aortic Dissection**
Braverman AC, Thompson R, Sanchez L. Diseases of the aorta. In: Bonow RO, Mann DL, Zipes DP, Libby P, eds. *Braunwald's Heart Disease*. 9th ed. Philadelphia, PA: Elsevier; 2011:1309-1337.
Ferri FF. *Ferri's Best Test*. Philadelphia, PA: Elsevier; 2019:229-426.
Herring W. *Learning Radiology: Recognizing the Basics*. Philadelphia, PA: Elsevier; 2019:108-122.
Taut MS, Hanjoora VM, Chishti MA, et al. A sudden change in arterial waveform. *J Cardiothorac Vasc Anesth*. 2019;33(7):2093-2096.
Vargas MI, Barnaure I, Gariani J, et al. Vascular imaging techniques of the spinal cord. *Semin Ultrasound CT MRI*. 2017;38(2):143-152.

**Aortic Regurgitation**
Elmoselhi A, ed. *Cardiology: An Integrated Approach*. New York, NY: McGraw Hill; 2017.
Fuster V, Harrington RA, Narula J, Eapen ZJ, eds. *Hurst's The Heart*. 14th ed. New York, NY: McGraw Hill; 2017.
Le T, Bhushan V, Sochat M, et al. *First Aid for the USMLE Step 1 2017: A Student-to-Student Guide*. New York, NY: McGraw Hill; 2017.

**Aortic Stenosis**
Le T, Bhushan V. *First Aid for the USMLE Step 1 2016: A Student-to-Student Guide*. New York, NY: McGraw Hill Education; 2016:273.
Papadakis MA, McPhee SJ, Bernstein J, eds. *Quick Medical Diagnosis & Treatment 2019*. New York, NY: McGraw Hill; 2019. http://accessmedicine.mhmedical.com/content.aspx?bookid=2566&sectionid=206878374AV

**Atrial Fibrillation & Atrial Flutter**
Le T, Bhushan V, Sochat M, et al. *First Aid for the USMLE Step 1 2017: A Student-to-Student Guide*. New York, NY: McGraw Hill; 2017.
Le T, Bhushan V. *First Aid for the USMLE Step 2 CK*. 10th ed. New York, NY: McGraw Hill; 2018.

**AV Nodal Reentry Tachycardia & WPW**
Bashore TM, Granger CB, Jackson KP, Patel MR. Heart disease. In: Papadakis MA, McPhee SJ, Rabow MW, eds. *Current Medical Diagnosis & Treatment 2019*. New York, NY: McGraw-Hill; 2019. http://accessmedicine.mhmedical.com.proxy01.its.virginia.edu/content.aspx?bookid=2449&sectionid=194435482. Accessed March 28, 2019.
Stone P, VonAlvensleben J, Burkett D, Darst JR, Collins KK, Miyamoto SD. Cardiovascular diseases. In: Hay WW, Levin MJ, Deterding RR, Abzug MJ, eds. *Current Diagnosis and Treatment: Pediatrics*. 24th ed. New York, NY: McGraw-Hill; 2018. http://accessmedicine.mhmedical.com.proxy01.its.virginia.edu/content.aspx?bookid=2390&sectionid=189078621. Accessed March 28, 2019.
Le T, Bhushan V. *First Aid for the USMLE Step 2 CK*. 9th ed. New York, NY: McGraw Hill; 2015.
Valente A, Landzberg MJ. Congenital heart disease in the adult. In: Jameson J, Fauci AS, Kasper DL, Hauser SL, Longo DL, Loscalzo J, eds. *Harrison's Principles of Internal Medicine*. 20th ed. New York, NY: McGraw-Hill; 2018. http://accessmedicine.mhmedical.com/content.aspx?bookid=2129&sectionid=189405859. Accessed March 28, 2019.

Bashore TM, Granger CB, Jackson KP, Patel MR. Ventricular septal defect. In: Papadakis MA, McPhee SJ, Bernstein J, eds. *Quick Medical Diagnosis & Treatment 2019*. New York, NY: McGraw-Hill; 2019. http://accessmedicine.mhmedical.com.proxy01.its.virginia.edu/content.aspx?bookid=2566&sectionid=206897951. Accessed March 28, 2019.

### Cardiac Tamponade
Verlaan D, Veltman JD, Grady B. Total electrical alternans in a patient with malignant pericardial tamponade. *BMJ Case Rep*. 2018;2018:bcr2018224771. Published 2018 Jul 19. doi:10.1136/bcr-2018-224771

### Carotid Artery Stenosis
Altkorn D, Schulwolf E. Screening and health maintenance. In: Stern SC, Cifu AS, Altkorn D, eds. *Symptom to Diagnosis: An Evidence-Based Guide*. 4th ed. New York, NY: McGraw Hill; 2020. http://accessmedicine.mhmedical.com/content.aspx?bookid=2715&sectionid=228237646. Accessed November 27, 2019.

Le T, Bhushan V. *First Aid for the USMLE Step 2 CK*. 9th ed. New York, NY: McGraw Hill; 2015:39-41.

Lin PH, Bechara CF, Chen C, Veith FJ. Arterial disease. In: Brunicardi F, Andersen DK, Billiar TR, et al, eds. *Schwartz's Principles of Surgery*. 11th ed. New York, NY: McGraw Hill; 2019. http://accessmedicine.mhmedical.com/content.aspx?bookid=2576&sectionid=216209143. Accessed November 27, 2019.

### Complete (Third-Degree) AV Block
Elmoselhi A, ed. *Cardiology: An Integrated Approach*. New York, NY: McGraw Hill; 2017.
Fuster V, Harrington RA, Narula J, Eapen ZJ, eds. *Hurst's The Heart*. 14th ed. New York, NY: McGraw Hill; 2017.

### Deep Vein Thrombosis
Le T, Bhushan V, Sochat M, et al. *First Aid for the USMLE Step 1 2017: A Student-to-Student Guide*. New York, NY: McGraw Hill; 2017.

### Dyslipidemia & Atherosclerosis
American College of Cardiology/American Heart Association. *2018 Guideline on the Management of Blood Cholesterol*. https://www.acc.org/~/media/Non-Clinical/Files-PDFs-Excel-MS-Word-etc/Guidelines/2018/Guidelines-Made-Simple-Tool-2018-Cholesterol.pdf

Le T, Bhushan V, Sochat M, et al. *First Aid for the USMLE Step 1 2017: A Student-to-Student Guide*. New York, NY: McGraw Hill; 2017.

### Essential Hypertension
2017 ACA/AHA Guidelines. Guideline for the Prevention, Detection, Evaluation, and Management of High Blood Pressure in Adults: A Report of the American College of Cardiology/American Heart Association Task Force on Clinical Practice Guidelines. *J Am Coll Cardiol*. 2018;71:e127-e248.

Fuster V, Harrington RA, Narula J, Eapen ZJ, eds. *Hurst's The Heart*. 14th ed. New York, NY: McGraw Hill; 2017.

Le T, Bhushan V, Sochat M, et al. *First Aid for the USMLE Step 1 2017: A Student-to-Student Guide*. New York, NY: McGraw Hill; 2017.

Leonard SL. *Pathophysiology of Heart Disease: A Collaborative Project of Medical Students and Faculty*. Philadelphia, PA: Lippincott Williams & Wilkins, 2003.

### Heart Failure with Preserved Ejection Fraction (HFpEF)
Yanagisawa H, Saito N, Imai M, et al. Successful balloon aortic valvuloplasty as a bridge therapy to transcatheter aortic valve implantation during the proctoring period. *J Cardiol Cases*. 2015;12(4):113-116.

### Heart Failure with Reduced Ejection Fraction (HFrEF)
Muniz J. Functional Classification of Heart Failure. https://medcomic.com/medcomic/nyha-heart-failure/

## Hypertensive Crises

Aronow WS. Treatment of hypertensive emergencies. *Ann Transl Med.* 2017;5(Suppl 1):S5.

Le T, Bhushan V, Sochat M, et al. *First Aid for the USMLE Step 1 2017: A Student-to-Student Guide.* New York, NY: McGraw Hill; 2017.

## Hypertrophic Cardiomyopathy

Le T, Bhushan V, Sochat M, et al. *First Aid for the USMLE Step 1 2017: A Student-to-Student Guide.* New York, NY: McGraw Hill; 2017.

## Long QT Syndromes

Fuster V, Harrington RA, Narula J, Eapen ZJ, eds. *Hurst's The Heart.* 14th ed. New York, NY: McGraw Hill; 2017.

Le T, Bhushan V, Sochat M, et al. *First Aid for the USMLE Step 1 2017: A Student-to-Student Guide.* New York, NY: McGraw Hill; 2017.

## Mitral Valve Stenosis

Le T, Bushan V. *First Aid for the USMLE Step 1 2019.* New York, NY: McGraw Hill; 2018.

## Mitral Valve Regurgitation/Prolapse

Le T, Bushan V. *First Aid for the USMLE Step 1 2019.* New York, NY: McGraw Hill; 2018.

## Pericarditis

Bashore TM, Granger CB, Jackson KP, Patel MR. Acute inflammatory pericarditis. In: Papadakis MA, McPhee SJ, Rabow MW, eds. *Current Medical Diagnosis and Treatment 2020.* New York, NY: McGraw-Hill; 2020. http://accessmedicine.mhmedical.com.proxy01.its.virginia.edu/content.aspx?bookid=2683&sectionid=225041077. Accessed November 26, 2019.

Le T, Bhushan V. *First Aid for the USMLE Step 2 CK.* 9th ed. New York, NY: McGraw Hill; 2015:39-41.

## Peripheral Artery Disease (PAD)

Fuster V, Harrington RA, Narula J, Eapen ZJ, eds. *Hurst's The Heart.* 14th ed. New York, NY: McGraw Hill; 2017.

Jameson JL, Fauci AS, Hauser SL, Longo DL, Loscalzo J, eds. *Harrison's Principles of Internal Medicine.* 20th ed. New York, NY: McGraw Hill; 2018.

Leonard SL. *Pathophysiology of Heart Disease: A Collaborative Project of Medical Students and Faculty.* Philadelphia, PA: Lippincott Williams & Wilkins, 2003.

Williams BA, Chang A, Ahalt C, et al, eds. *Current Diagnosis & Treatment: Geriatrics.* 2nd ed. New York, NY: McGraw Hill; 2014.

## Restrictive Cardiomyopathy

Bashore TM, Granger CB, Jackson KP, Patel MR. Restrictive cardiomyopathy. In: Papadakis MA, McPhee SJ, Rabow MW, eds. *Current Medical Diagnosis and Treatment 2020.* New York, NY: McGraw-Hill; 2019. http://accessmedicine.mhmedical.com.proxy01.its.virginia.edu/content.aspx?bookid=2683&sectionid=225041010. Accessed November 26, 2019.

Goldstein JA. Restrictive cardiomyopathy. In: Crawford MH, ed. *CURRENT Diagnosis & Treatment: Cardiology.* 5th ed. New York, NY: McGraw-Hill; 2017. http://accessmedicine.mhmedical.com.proxy01.its.virginia.edu/content.aspx?bookid=2040&sectionid=152995977. Accessed November 26, 2019.

Le T, Bhushan V. *First Aid for the USMLE Step 2 CK.* 9th ed. New York, NY: McGraw Hill; 2015:39-41.

## ST-Elevation Myocardial Infarction

Le T, Bhushan V, Sochat M, et al. *First Aid for the USMLE Step 1 2017: A Student-to-Student Guide.* New York, NY: McGraw Hill; 2017.

Switaj TL, Christensen SR, Brewer DM. Acute coronary syndrome: current treatment. *Am Fam Physician.* 2017;95(4):232-240.

**Supraventricular Tachycardia**

Agabegi SS, Agabegi ED, Duncan MD, Chuang K. *Step-Up to Medicine.* 5th ed. Philadelphia, PA: Wolters Kluwer; 2020.

Le T, Bhushan V. *First Aid for the USMLE Step 2 CK.* 10th ed. New York, NY: McGraw Hill; 2018.

Le T, Bhushan V, Sochat M, et al. *First Aid for the USMLE Step 1 2017: A Student-to-Student Guide.* New York, NY: McGraw Hill; 2017.


**Syncope**

Le T, Bushan V. *First Aid for the USMLE Step 1 2019.* New York, NY: McGraw Hill; 2018.


**Unstable Angina (UA) and Non-ST-Elevation Myocardial Infarction (NSTEMI)**

Antman EM. TIMI Risk Score for UA/NSTEMI. https://www.mdcalc.com/timi-risk-score-ua-nstemi

Antman EM, Cohen M, Bernink PJLM, et al. The TIMI risk score for unstable angina/non–ST elevation MI: a method for prognostication and therapeutic decision making. *JAMA.* 2000;284(7):835-842. doi:10.1001/jama.284.7.835

Le T, Bhushan V, Sochat M, et al. *First Aid for the USMLE Step 1 2017: A Student-to-Student Guide.* New York, NY: McGraw Hill; 2017.


**Ventricular Septal Defect**

Gomella LG, Haist SA, eds. *Clinician's Pocket Reference: The Scut Monkey.* 11th ed. New York, NY: McGraw-Hill; 2007. http://accessmedicine.mhmedical.com.proxy01.its.virginia.edu/content.aspx?bookid=365&sectionid=43074905. Accessed April 01, 2019.

Le T, Bhushan V, Deol M, et al. *First Aid for the USMLE Step 2 CK.* New York: McGraw-Hill Education, 2019.

Le T, Bhushan V, Sochat M, et al. *First Aid for the USMLE Step 1 2019.* New York: McGraw-Hill Education, 2019.

McKean SC, Ross JJ, Dressler DD, Scheurer DB, eds. *Principles and Practice of Hospital Medicine.* 2nd ed. New York, NY: McGraw-Hill; 2017. http://accessmedicine.mhmedical.com.proxy01.its.virginia.edu/content.aspx?bookid=1872&sectionid=146944828. Accessed April 01, 2019.


**Ventricular Tachyarrhythmias**

Agabegi SS, Agabegi ED, Duncan MD, Chuang K. *Step-Up to Medicine.* 5th ed. Philadelphia, PA: Wolters Kluwer; 2020.

Le T. Bhushan V. *First Aid for the USMLE Step 2 CK.* 10th ed. New York, NY: McGraw Hill; 2018.

Le T, Bhushan V, Sochat M, et al. *First Aid for the USMLE Step 1 2017: A Student-to-Student Guide.* New York, NY: McGraw Hill; 2017.

# Dermatology

*Vinod Nambudiri, MD, MBA*

# Acanthosis Nigricans

## Localized skin disorder linked to medical comorbidities

### Clinical Appearance

- Symmetric velvety hyperpigmented plaques
- Most commonly on neck and axillae, as well as flexural and intertriginous areas

### Epidemiology

- Most commonly linked to diabetes mellitus and insulin resistance
- Rarely associated with malignancy

### Pathogenesis

- Insulin-like growth factor receptors on keratinocytes may be stimulated --> skin thickening and darkening

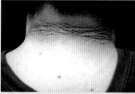

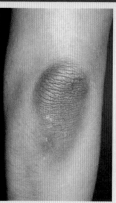

## Workup (Must treat underlying condition!)

### Hirsutism?
Check for PCOS and HAIR-AN syndrome.

### At birth?
Check for autosomal dominant genetic syndromes.

### Weight loss?
Check for malignancy, especially gastric carcinoma.

### Meds?
Check for niacin, OCPs, corticosteroids, human growth hormones, protease inhibitors --> Drug-induced!

### In a child?
Check for generalized or partial lipodystrophy.

### Obesity?
Check for insulin resistance and endocrinopathies, ie, diabetes mellitus, thyroid disease, & Addison's disease.

# Acne Vulgaris

## Common Disorder of the Pilosebaceous Follicle

### Pathogenesis

 1. **Follicular plug** forms from keratinocyte desquamation

 2. **_Propionibacterium acnes_** & sebum accumulate due to androgens

3. **Inflammatory response** and long-term scarring

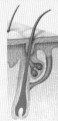   

**Early Comedo**
- Hyperkeratosis
- Corneocyte cohesion
- Sebum production

**Comedo**
- Shed keratin, corneocytes, and sebum accumulate

**Inflammatory Papule/Pustule**
- _P. acnes_ proliferates, stimulating mild inflammation (mostly neutrophils)

**Nodule**
- Inflammation (mostly T cells)
- Ruptured follicular wall
- Scarring in long term

**Open comedo** (dilated follicular ostium with darkened keratin plug from oxidized lipids & melanin)

**Closed comedo** (no follicular opening)

**Hormonal acne often found along the jawline and chin**

Reproduced with permission from Soutor C, Hordinsky MK: Clinical Dermatology. New York, NY: McGraw Hill; 2013.

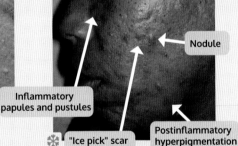

**Nodule**

**Inflammatory papules and pustules**

 **"Ice pick" scar**

**Postinflammatory hyperpigmentation**

Used with permission from Dr. Marcia Ramos-e-Silva.

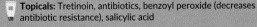

### Treatment

 **Topicals:** Tretinoin, antibiotics, benzoyl peroxide (decreases antibiotic resistance), salicylic acid

 **Orals:** Spironolactone (hormonal acne), antibiotics, isotretinoin (curative treatment; teratogen)

# Actinic Keratosis

## Overview

Actinic keratoses (AKs) are precancerous lesions of the keratinocytes. Up to 10% of AKs may ultimately become squamous cell cancers.

## Etiology

 →  p53 mutation →  Propagation of abnormal keratinocytes →  Faster division of cells

## Clinical Presentation

Reproduced with permission from Soutor C, Hordinsky MK: Clinical Dermatology. New York, NY: McGraw Hill; 2013.

Ill-defined scaly, rough lesion that will crust up when scratched

 On sun-exposed areas, such as face and distal extremities

 Usually asymptomatic, but can be sensitive to touch

## Histology

Partial-thickness atypia of epidermis of the skin; may involve appendageal structures such as hair follicles

## Treatment

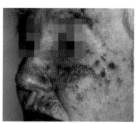

Reproduced with permission from Soutor C, Hordinsky MK: Clinical Dermatology. New York, NY: McGraw Hill; 2013.

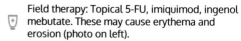 Cryotherapy: Typically liquid nitrogen

Field therapy: Topical 5-FU, imiquimod, ingenol mebutate. These may cause erythema and erosion (photo on left).

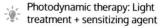 Photodynamic therapy: Light treatment + sensitizing agent

If no resolution, biopsy may be indicated to rule out squamous cell carcinoma or basal cell carcinoma.

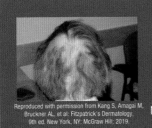

# Alopecia Areata

Non-Scarring Autoimmune Hair Loss

## Pathophysiology:

T-lymphocyte mediated peribulbar inflammation disrupts the normal hair cycle.

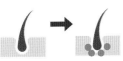

Follicles in anagen phase (active hair growth) prematurely transition to catagen and telogen phases (arrested hair growth).

## Clinical Presentation:

- Patchy round areas of hair loss that are non-scarring because hair follicles are not destroyed

- Nail pitting and ridging

**Alopecia totalis**—Loss of all scalp hair

**Alopecia universalis**—Loss of all scalp and body hair

## Diagnosis: Clinical! Biopsy only if equivocal

Trichoscopy may reveal hairs with tapered bases, called **exclamation mark hairs**.

**Yellow dots may also be seen.**

Consider testing for concurrent autoimmune disease (eg, hypothyroidism)

## Treatment:

- Very mild alopecia: Topical mid- to high-potency steroids

- Mild- to moderate-alopecia: Intralesional corticosteroid injections

- Severe disease (alopecia totalis or universalis): PUVA or immunomodulators

- All patients: Psychological support

# Benign Nevi
## ("Moles")

## Fast Facts

- May be acquired or congenital
- Adults typically have 10-40 nevi. Prevalence lower in darker skin types
- Sun exposure plays role in new formation
- Usually asymptomatic

## Classification

### Junctional
Cells at dermal–epidermal junction

### Compound
Portion of cells in papillary dermis

### Dermal
Cells exclusively in dermis. Usually raised and in adults

## Special Categories

### Halo Nevus
Sharply demarcated and depigmented border

### Nevus Spilus
Hairless lesion with darker speckles

### Spitz Nevus
Dome-shaped papule, typically in children

### Nevus of Ota
Dark brown nevus, commonly around eye or in sclera

### Nonmelanocytic Nevus
Becker nevus, nevus anemicus

## Management and Follow-Up

- Removed for cosmetic reasons or concern for melanoma
- Patients with sizable or multiple nevi should be routinely followed
- Remember the ABCDE's! (see Melanoma infographic)

**A**symmetry
**B**order (irregular)
**C**olor (variable)
**D**iameter (>6 mm)
**E**volution (shape, size, color)

# Bullous Impetigo

Localized staphylococcal toxin-mediated skin infection most commonly seen in children

## Pathophysiology

 **Staphylococcus aureus** infection

 Exfoliative **toxins** (A & B)

 **Desmoglein 1** cleavage

Superficial blister formation

## Epidemiology

**20%** of all impetigo cases

 Summer months & humid conditions

 Newborn **infants** & young **children**

## Clinical Presentation

 Vesicles or bullae
- **Superficial**
- **Flaccid**
- Thin-walled
- Serous **fluid-filled**
- Negative Nikolsky's sign

Reproduced with permission from Kang S, Amagai M, Bruckner AL, et al: Fitzpatrick's Dermatology, 9th ed. New York, NY: McGraw Hill; 2019.

Reproduced with permission from Kang S, Amagai M, Bruckner AL, et al: Fitzpatrick's Dermatology, 9th ed. New York, NY: McGraw Hill; 2019.

 Erosions
- **Honey-colored crust**
- Sharply demarcated

Reproduced with permission from Stern S, Cifu AS, Altkorn D: Symptom to Diagnosis: An Evidence-Based Guide, 4th ed. New York, NY: McGraw Hill; 2020.

 Rare constitutional symptoms

Fever, malaise, irritability

 Distribution
- **Extremities** > trunk

## Diagnosis

 History & physical exam

 Gram stain
**Gram-positive cocci in clusters**

 Culture
*S. aureus*

## Management

 Standard and contact precautions

 Topical antibiotics

 Oral antibiotics
Dicloxacillin
Cephalexin
Erythromycin
Clindamycin (MRSA)
Doxycycline (MRSA)

 Look out for:
Methicillin-resistant *S. aureus*

**Staphylococcal Scalded Skin Syndrome**

# Bullous Pemphigoid

Autoimmune bullous disease of the skin

## Pathophysiology

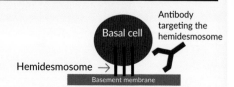

- Type 2 hypersensitivity reaction—IgG autoantibodies target hemidesmosomes, which hold basal cells to the basement membrane

Basal cell

Antibody targeting the hemidesmosome

Hemidesmosome →

Basement membrane

## Clinical Presentation

- Tense bullae (subepidermal blisters) and sometimes urticaria-like plaques typically in flexural and intertriginous regions

- Common: Pruritic prodrome; Uncommon: Mucosal lesions

- Older adults over age 60

*Clinical Pearl*

**Nikolsky's sign is NEGATIVE.**

Lateral pressure applied to the bullae does **NOT** cause skin shearing.

## Diagnosis & Histology

- Punch biopsy: Subepidermal blistering with eosinophils and dermal edema

- Direct immunofluorescence (DIF): Linear IgG and C3 deposition on the basement membrane zone

- Indirect immunofluorescence (IIF): IgG deposition on the epidermal side (roof) of salt-split skin

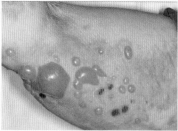

## Treatment

- Topical, intralesional, or oral **corticosteroids** based on severity
- Tetracyclines and immunosuppressive antimetabolites

### Remember:

- IgG antibodies target hemidesmosomes.
- Blistering is subepidermal (deeper than pemphigus vulgaris).
- Bullae are tense.

**42**

# Candidiasis

Common fungal infection caused by *Candida* yeast

## Risk Factors

 Obesity

 Diabetes mellitus

 Tight clothing

Hospitalization

 Antibiotics Steroids

 Surgery

 Radiation

 Very young Elderly

## Mucous Membranes

**Oral candidiasis ("Thrush")**

Painless, white papules and plaques on tongue, hard palate, and oropharynx

Reproduced with permission from Shah B, Lucchesi M: Atlas of Pediatric Emergency Medicine, 3rd ed. New York, NY: McGraw Hill; 2019. Photo contributors: Binita R. Shah, MD.

**Esophageal**

Odynophagia in HIV patients

**Vulvovaginal**

Vaginal itching and dysuria with thick, white curd-like discharge

Reproduced with permission from Kline MW: Rudolph's Pediatrics, 23rd ed. New York, NY: McGraw Hill; 2018.

# Cutaneous Candidiasis: Many Forms

## Intertrigo

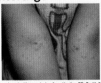

Reproduced with permission from Usatine RP, Smith MA, Mayeaux EJ, Chumley HS: The Color Atlas and Synopsis of Family Medicine, 3rd ed. New York, NY: McGraw Hill; 2019. Photo contributor: Richard P. Usatine, MD.

Central erythema with surrounding vesicles or pustules in moist, macerated, intertriginous folds (axillary, inframammary, gluteal, groin)

## Diaper dermatitis

Reproduced with permission from Usatine RP, Smith MA, Mayeaux EJ, Chumley HS: The Color Atlas and Synopsis of Family Medicine, 3rd ed. New York, NY: McGraw Hill; 2019. Photo contributor: Richard P. Usatine, MD.

Well-demarcated beefy red diaper area with occasional scale associated with antibiotics and diarrhea

## Paronychia

Erythema, edema, and tenderness of the nail folds with purulent discharge

Reproduced with permission from Bajwa ZH, Wootton RJ, Warfield CA: Principles and Practice of Pain Medicine, 3rd ed. New York, NY: McGraw Hill; 2017.

## Balanitis

Vesicles on the glans that cause itching and burning

Reproduced with permission from Usatine RP, Sabella C, Smith MA, et al: The Color Atlas of Pediatrics. New York, NY: McGraw Hill; 2015. Photo contributor: Richard P. Usatine, MD.

## Onychomycosis

Nail thickening with yellowish discoloration and onycholysis

Reproduced with permission from Hamm RL: Text and Atlas of Wound Diagnosis and Treatment, 2nd ed. New York, NY: McGraw Hill; 2019.

## Angular cheilitis

Erythema and fissuring of the labial commissures

Reproduced with permission from Kelly AP, Taylor SC, Lom HW, et al: Taylor and Kelly's Dermatology for Skin of Color, 2nd ed. New York, NY: McGraw Hill; 2016.

# Diagnosis

 **Wet mount**
Skin scrapings in 10% **KOH** will reveal **hyphae** and pseudohyphae

 **Other tests**
Periodic acid-Schiff

**Gram stain**
Methenamine silver

# Management

 **Topical Antifungals**
Nystatin
Azoles

**Systemic Antifungals**
Fluconazole (vulvovaginal/esophageal)
Clotrimazole (thrush)

# Carcinoma, Basal Cell

Most common type of skin cancer. Slow-growing localized with rare metastatic potential

## Etiology

UV Exposure

Mutations in Sonic Hedgehog, PTCH (patched), or p53 tumor suppressor

Cancer of keratinocytes of the basal layer of the epidermis

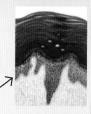

## Clinical Presentation

Commonly on sun-exposed areas

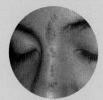
Reproduced with permission from Usatine RP, Smith MA, Mayeaux EJ, Chumley HS: The Color Atlas and Synopsis of Family Medicine, 3rd ed. New York, NY: McGraw Hill; 2019. Photo contributor: Richard P. Usatine, MD.

### Nodular BCC
"Pimple that doesn't heal"

Translucent, pearly papule with erythema, telangiectasia, well-defined rolled borders

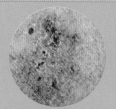
Reproduced with permission from Soutor C, Hordinsky MK: Clinical Dermatology. New York, NY: McGraw Hill; 2013.

### Superficial BCC
"Chronic eczema"

Erythematous patch or flat-topped plaque with well-defined borders

Reproduced with permission from Soutor C, Hordinsky MK: Clinical Dermatology. New York, NY: McGraw Hill; 2013.

### Sclerotic BCC
"Chronic scar"

Also known as morpheaform BCC
Ill-defined scar-like plaque

##  Histology

Basophilic cells in nests in the dermis and subcutis; "palisading" nuclei

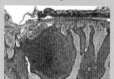
Reproduced with permission from Wikimedia Commons https://commons.wikimedia.org/wiki/File:Basal_cell_carci-noma_histopathology_(1).jpg

## Treatment

- Excision with 4 mm margins, Mohs surgery, electrodesiccation, and curettage
- Topical treatment: Imiquimod, 5% topical fluorouracil
- Photodynamic therapy
- Systemic therapy for advanced/metastatic disease: Vismodegib (Hedgehog pathway inhibitor)

# Carcinoma, Squamous Cell

Non-Melanoma Skin Cancer Derived from Suprabasal Epidermal Keratinocytes

## Population

More common in:
- Men
- Lighter skin tones
- Extensive UV exposure
- Older people

## Risk Factors

 UV exposure

 Environmental carcinogens

 Immunosuppression (transplant patients)

 On scars or burns

 Infection (human papillomavirus)

 Genodermatoses (albinism, xeroderma pigmentosum, porokeratosis, epidermolysis bullosa)

 Precursor lesions: Actinic keratosis, Bowen disease (SCC in situ)

## Clinical Findings

Occurs on sun-exposed areas.

Patients may complain of pimple-like lesion that grows and episodes of bleeding/tenderness.

Reproduced with permission from Goldsmith LA, Katz SI, Gilchrest BA et al: Fitzpatrick's Dermatology in General Medicine, 8th ed. New York, NY: McGraw Hill; 2012.
**Squamous cell carcinoma of lower lip**

Reproduced with permission from Soutor C, Hordinsky MK: Clinical Dermatology. New York, NY: McGraw Hill; 2013.
**Hyperkeratotic papule or plaque**

Reproduced with permission from Riordan-Eva P, Augsburger JJ: Vaughan & Asbury's General Ophthalmology, 19th ed. New York, NY: McGraw Hill; 2018.
**Ulcer**

Reproduced with permission from Goldsmith LA, Katz SI, Gilchrest BA et al: Fitzpatrick's Dermatology in General Medicine, 8th ed. New York, NY: McGraw Hill; 2012.
**Smooth nodule**

 **Marjolin's ulcer:** SCC that occurs in chronic wound

## Histopathology

Invasive SCC: Atypical keratinocytes beyond the basement membrane; foci of keratinization (**"keratin pearls"**)

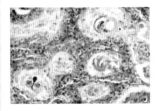

## Differential Diagnosis

- Wart

- Seborrheic keratosis

- Actinic keratosis

- Dermatitis

- Basal cell carcinoma

- Trauma

## Treatment

 **Topical therapy**, such as 5-fluorouracil or imiquimod (in situ disease only)

 **Surgery:** Standard excision, Mohs surgery, electrodesiccation, & curettage

 **Radiation**

 Patients should get regular follow-ups and be counseled on good sun protection

**45**

# Cellulitis
### Localized infection of deep dermis and sometimes subcutaneous fat

## Clinical Features

 **Rubor** (redness)
**Calor** (warmth)
 **Dolor** (pain)
**Tumor** (swelling)
**Poorly defined borders**
**Almost always unilateral!**

**Fever, chills, malaise, leukocytosis**

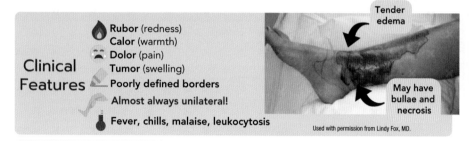

Tender edema

May have bullae and necrosis

## Pathogenesis

**Immunocompetent hosts:**
- *Streptococcus pyogenes* or *Staphylococcus aureus* most common
- Direct inoculation

**Immunocompromised hosts:**
- Mix of Gram-positive cocci and Gram-negative bacilli
- Hematogenous seeding

## Risk Factors

- History of deep vein thrombosis
- History of cellulitis with lymphangitis
- Immunosuppression
- Chronic edema, especially lower extremities
- Tinea pedis (compromised skin barrier)

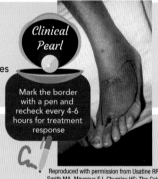

*Clinical Pearl*

Mark the border with a pen and recheck every 4-6 hours for treatment response

## Differential Diagnosis

**Diagnosis is clinical! Differential includes:**
- Stasis dermatitis
- Lipodermatosclerosis
- Erysipelas
- Necrotizing fasciitis (underline must rule out!)
- Pseudocellulitis

## Treatment

- Empiric oral or IV antibiotics depending on severity and host risk factors (eg, immunocompromised)
- Consider MRSA risk factors and clinical features (eg, bullae)

**46**

# Cherry Angioma

**Also known as:** Cherry Hemangioma    Senile Hemangioma    Campbell de Morgan Spots

## Presentation

Reproduced with permission from Usatine RP, Smith MA, Mayeaux EJ, Chumley HS: The Color Atlas and Synopsis of Family Medicine, 3rd ed. New York, NY: McGraw Hill; 2019. Photo contributor: Richard P. Usatine, MD.

Small cherry-red macule or papule

Most frequently on trunk and upper extremities

Increase in number with age

## Diagnosis

Reproduced with permission from Wolff K, Johnson RA, Saavedra AP, et al: Fitzpatrick's Color Atlas and Synopsis of Clinical Dermatology, 8th ed. New York, NY: McGraw Hill; 2017.

**Cherry angioma is a clinical diagnosis!**

### Differential diagnoses to consider:

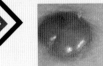

Reproduced with permission from Usatine RP, Smith MA, Chumley HS, et al: The Color Atlas of Family Medicine, 2nd ed. New York, NY: McGraw Hill; 2013. Photo contributor: Ashfaq Marghoob, MD.

**Nodular melanoma**

Reproduced with permission from Wolff K, Johnson RA, Saavedra AP, et al: Fitzpatrick's Color Atlas and Synopsis of Clinical Dermatology, 8th ed. New York, NY: McGraw Hill; 2017.

**Venous lake**

Reproduced with permission from Wolff K, Johnson RA, Saavedra AP, et al: Fitzpatrick's Color Atlas and Synopsis of Clinical Dermatology, 8th ed. New York, NY: McGraw Hill; 2017.

**Angiokeratoma**

## Management

No treatment required. Consider excision, electrodesiccation, or laser ablation if cosmetically undesirable or chronically traumatized.

## Pearl

Sudden onset of multiple cherry angiomas may accompany some internal malignancies. Can also consider POEMS syndrome (polyneuropathy, organomegaly, endocrinopathy, monoclonal protein, skin changes).

# Dermatitis, Atopic

Chronically relapsing skin disease that occurs most commonly in infancy or childhood

## Etiology

Complex interaction between genes affecting innate immune system, skin barrier function, and allergic response. Most common gene affected is **filaggrin**, a cornified envelope gene.

 **Scratch-itch cycle**: Mechanical injury from scratching induces cytokine and chemokine release, leading to more itch

## Atopic Triad

Asthma

Allergic rhinitis          Atopic dermatitis

## Clinical Features

- **Risk factors:** Personal or family history of atopic disease, xerosis/skin barrier dysfunction
- **Signs/symptoms:** Pruritus, rash on face and/or extensors in infants and young children, allergic shiners (darkening beneath eyes), hyperlinear palms and soles, ichthyosis vulgaris (thick, dry scales)
- **Labs:** Elevated serum immunoglobulin E

## Clinical Presentation

 **Atopic dermatitis is a clinical diagnosis**

Weeping and crusting of eczematous lesions in childhood atopic dermatitis

Reproduced with permission from Goldsmith LA, Katz SI, Gilchrest BA et al: Fitzpatrick's Dermatology in General Medicine, 8th ed. New York, NY: McGraw Hill; 2012.

**Hyperlinear palms**

Reproduced with permission from Goldsmith LA, Katz SI, Gilchrest BA et al: Fitzpatrick's Dermatology in General Medicine, 8th ed. New York, NY: McGraw Hill; 2012.

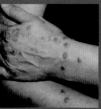

Reproduced with permission from Goldsmith LA, Katz SI, Gilchrest BA et al: Fitzpatrick's Dermatology in General Medicine, 8th ed. New York, NY: McGraw Hill; 2012.

**Prurigo papules** in patient with atopic dermatitis

**Eczema herpeticum:** Caused by HSV infection; confluent papules and vesicles with "punched-out" discrete erosions

Reproduced with permission from Kang S, Amagai M, Bruckner AL, et al: Fitzpatrick's Dermatology, 9th ed. New York, NY: McGraw Hill; 2019.

Sites of predilection by age: Extensor involvement in infancy, flexural involvement in adulthood

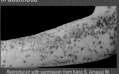

Reproduced with permission from Kang S, Amagai M, Bruckner AL, et al: Fitzpatrick's Dermatology, 9th ed. New York, NY: McGraw Hill; 2019.

## Evolution of Lesions

**Acute:** Intensely pruritic, papules, vesicles, serous exudate

**Subacute:** Erythematous, excoriated scaling papules

**Chronic:** Thickened plaques, fibrotic plaques (prurigo nodularis), accentuated skin markings

## Pathology

Not required for diagnosis, but will show intercellular edema (spongiosis) of the epidermis. Sparse epidermal infiltrate of T lymphocytes.

Reproduced with permission from Kang S, Amagai M, Bruckner AL, et al: Fitzpatrick's Dermatology, 9th ed. New York, NY: McGraw Hill; 2019.

## Treatment

 Moisturizers: Can also be preventative
Anti-inflammatory: Topical steroids, topical calcineurin inhibitor (eg, tacrolimus)

⊘ Eliminate triggers (eg, soaps, detergents)

Pruritus: Systemic antihistamines

If signs of infection: Topical/oral antimicrobial that covers *S. aureus*. Consider dilute bleach baths.

Phototherapy: UV treatment

Systemic therapy:
- Avoid oral glucocorticoids because that can cause rebound flare upon discontinuation
- Cyclosporine
- Antimetabolites (mycophenolate mofetil, methotrexate, azathioprine)
- Omalizumab (anti-IgE), Dupilumab (anti-IL4/13)

## Differential Diagnosis

- Seborrheic dermatitis
- Psoriasis
- Contact dermatitis
- Scabies

## Prognosis

 Variable, some continuing or recurring

# Dermatitis, Allergic Contact

## Pathophysiology

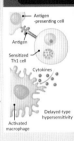

- Type 4 hypersensitivity reaction (delayed type)
- Requires repeated exposures before allergic response noted
- Symptoms 24-72 hours after exposure

## Common Causes

 Metals (eg, nickel, cobalt)

 Urushiol (eg, poison ivy, oak)

 Fragrances

 Topical antibiotics

## Presentation

- Often geometric shapes with well-demarcated borders corresponding to area of contact with allergen
- Acute: Erythema, vesicles, bullae
- Chronic: Scaling, lichenification, fissures
- Pruritus is common symptom

## Differential Diagnosis

- Irritant contact dermatitis
- Atopic dermatitis
- Cutaneous fungal infections
- Other eczematous skin conditions

## Tests

- Patch test to identify allergen
- Skin biopsy to rule out noneczematous conditions (if needed)
- Skin scraping to rule out fungal infections (if needed)

## Management

 **STOP** Avoid using offending agents.

 Topical steroids and calcineurin inhibitors have been used. Antihistamines may be used for pruritus.

Phototherapy can be considered for refractory disease.

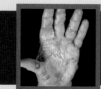

# Dermatitis, Irritant Contact

## Pathophysiology

- Direct cytotoxic damage to keratinocytes (non-immunologic)
- May occur even after short, first-time exposure
- Symptoms and skin eruptions may occur soon after exposure

## Common Causes

 Most common form of occupational skin disease

 Detergents and cleaning agents

 Cosmetics

Excessive exposure to water

## Presentation

- Well-demarcated erythema and superficial edema corresponding to area of contact with irritant
- Hands are most commonly affected area

- Vesicles and bullae form; in severe cases, erosions and frank necrosis may be seen
- Burning and stinging are common

## Differential Diagnoses

- Allergic contact dermatitis
- Palmoplantar psoriasis
- Cutaneous fungal infections
- Asteatotic eczema

## Tests

- Often diagnosis of exclusion
- Thorough history: High-risk jobs include cleaning, healthcare, food preparation, hairdressing (high risk in atopic dermatitis)
- Patch test (rule out allergic contact dermatitis)
- Skin scraping to rule out fungal infections (if needed)

## Management

 Beware of bacterial superinfection!

 Avoid irritant or caustic chemicals. Consider protective clothing.

 Topical steroids and calcineurin inhibitors have been used. Petroleum jelly or moisturizing cream should be applied.

 Phototherapy can be considered for refractory disease.

# Dermatitis, Seborrheic

## 1   What is it?

- Chronic inflammatory condition affecting sebum-rich areas, like the face and scalp
- Affects 5% of the population
- Also called "dandruff" or in babies "cradle cap"

## 2   What does it look like?

- Erythematous patches and plaques with loose, greasy scales
- Skin colored, yellow-white, or red-brown appearance
- Typically symmetrical distribution

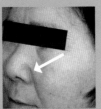

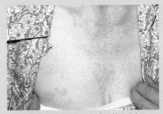

Reproduced with permission from Tenenbein M, Macias CG, Sharieff GQ, et al: Strange and Schafermeyer's Pediatric Emergency Medicine, 5th ed. New York, NY: McGraw Hill; 2019.

Reproduced with permission from Kang S, Amagai M, Bruckner AL, et al: Fitzpatrick's Dermatology, 9th ed. New York, NY: McGraw Hill; 2019.

Reproduced with permission from Murtagh J, Rosenblatt J, Coleman J, et al: Murtagh's General Practice, 7th ed. New York, NY: McGraw Hill; 2018.

## 3   What causes it?

- Immune response to *Malassezia* (*Pityrosporum*), a yeast commonly found on the skin
- Stress may exacerbate the condition
- More common and severe in immunocompromised patients and those with neurological disorders like Parkinson's disease

## 4   How do we confirm it?

- Clinical diagnosis
- Consider KOH preparation to rule out tinea
- Consider measuring zinc levels to rule out acrodermatitis enteropathica in patients with poor nutrition
- Consider HIV testing in those at risk and with severe disease

## 5   What can we do about it?

- No cure: Chronic condition
- Therapy should be restarted each time the condition flares
- Mild disease: Shampoos containing pyrithione zinc or selenium sulfide
- Topical ketoconazole, topical salicylic acid can also be used
- Topical steroids may be useful adjunct for inflammatory flares

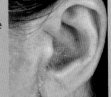

Reproduced with permission from Kang S, Amagai M, Bruckner AL, et al: Fitzpatrick's Dermatology, 9th ed. New York, NY: McGraw Hill; 2019.

# Dermatitis, Stasis

Eczematous Inflammatory Condition Affecting the Lower Legs Caused by Chronic Venous Insufficiency

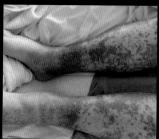

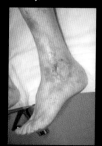

## Risk Factors

! Obesity

! Congestive heart failure

! Deep vein thrombosis

! Hypertension

! Varicose veins

! Venous insufficiency

## What to Look For

Erythematous, scaly plaques

May be exudative or lichenified

Distal lower leg and ankles

May cause an id reaction (autosensitization rash)

Often symmetric, bilateral

## Distinguishing From Cellulitis

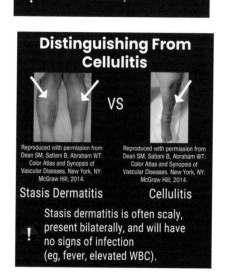

VS

Stasis Dermatitis          Cellulitis

! Stasis dermatitis is often scaly, present bilaterally, and will have no signs of infection (eg, fever, elevated WBC).

## Management

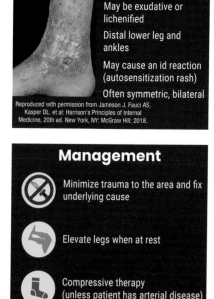

Minimize trauma to the area and fix underlying cause

Elevate legs when at rest

Compressive therapy (unless patient has arterial disease)

High-potency corticosteroids (decrease chronic inflammation)

# Dermatomyositis

Idiopathic Inflammatory Myopathy Associated with Malignancy

## Population

Bimodal distribution: Children (5-14 years old) and adults (45-64 years old)

DM is usually diagnosed from combination of clinical and laboratory findings (eg, elevated muscle enzymes). Skin biopsy may be warranted in nonspecific cases.

## Types of DM

- ✓ Classic: Skin involvement and weakness
- ✓ Hypomyopathic: Skin findings without clinical muscle weakness; however, evidence of myosis on laboratory studies, EMG, or MRI
- ✓ Amyopathic: Skin findings without evidence of myositis

## Extracutaneous Findings

Interstitial lung disease (leading cause of morbidity and mortality)

Cardiac involvement (ST-T changes)

Malignancy (10-20% of DM cases)

Myositis (symmetrical proximal muscle weakness)

Arthralgias (usually small joints)

Gastrointestinal involvement

## Clinical Findings

Reproduced with permission from Grippi MA, Elias JA, Fishman JA, et al: Fishman's Pulmonary Diseases and Disorders, 5th ed. New York, NY: McGraw Hill; 2015.

Heliotrope sign: Violaceous erythema and edema of upper eyelid

Reproduced with permission from Grippi MA, Elias JA, Fishman JA, et al: Fishman's Pulmonary Diseases and Disorders, 5th ed. New York, NY: McGraw Hill; 2015.

V-neck sign: Red telangiectatic patch on upper chest

Reproduced with permission from Kang S, Amagai M, Bruckner AL, et al: Fitzpatrick's Dermatology, 9th ed. New York, NY: McGraw Hill; 2019.

Gottron sign: Violaceous erythema on knees

Reproduced with permission from Grippi MA, Elias JA, Fishman JA, et al: Fishman's Pulmonary Diseases and Disorders, 5th ed. New York, NY: McGraw Hill; 2015.

Gottron papules: Papules over PIP and DIP

Reproduced with permission from Kang S, Amagai M, Bruckner AL, et al: Fitzpatrick's Dermatology, 9th ed. New York, NY: McGraw Hill; 2019.

Shawl sign: Pink patches and plaques on upper posterior back

Reproduced with permission from Zaoutis LB, Chiang VW: Comprehensive Pediatric Hospital Medicine, 2nd ed. New York, NY: McGraw Hill; 2018.

Dilated proximal nailfold capillary loops

Reproduced with permission from Kang S, Amagai M, Bruckner AL, et al: Fitzpatrick's Dermatology, 9th ed. New York, NY: McGraw Hill; 2019.

Holster sign: Ill-defined pink plaques with scale on lateral thigh

Reproduced with permission from Kang S, Amagai M, Bruckner AL, et al: Fitzpatrick's Dermatology, 9th ed. New York, NY: McGraw Hill; 2019.

Mechanic's hands: Hyperkeratotic papules on lateral second digits

## Histopathology

Vacuolar interface dermatitis, basement membrane thickening, perivascular lymphocytic infiltrate, increased dermal mucin

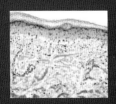

## Management

| | Skin Disease | Muscle Disease |
|---|---|---|
| First Line | Photoprotection Topical steroids Hydroxychloroquine or Chloroquine Quinacrine | Systemic corticosteroids |
| Second Line | Methotrexate Mycophenolate mofetil Intravenous immune globulin Azathioprine | |
| Third Line | Tofacitinib Leflunomide Dapsone Thalidomide Cyclosporine Cyclophosphamide | Rituximab Leflunomide Cyclosporine Cyclophosphamide |

Reproduced with permission from Kang S, Amagai M, Bruckner AL, et al: Fitzpatrick's Dermatology, 9th ed. New York, NY: McGraw Hill; 2019.

## DON'T FORGET:
- Cancer screening
- Monitoring for extracutaneous disease (eg, muscle testing, pulmonary function testing, troponin tests for cardiac damage)

## Prognosis

Presence of anti-MDA5 antibodies is a risk factor for death.

Major causes of death: Malignancy, pulmonary or cardiac disease, infection.

Long-term survival rate for adults is 65-75%. Remission rates are 20-40% at 5 years.

# Discoid Lupus Erythematosus (DLE)

- Form of chronic cutaneous lupus erythematosus
- Most common in women in the 3rd or 4th decade of life
- Increased risk in people of African or Hispanic descent

## Cutaneous Findings

Conchal fossa (bowl) plaque and scarring is pathognomonic

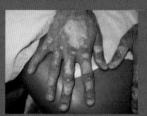

Atrophic, erythematous, photodistributed plaques with overlying scale, typically above the neck

Scarring alopecia with keratotic plugs

## Diagnosis

- Skin biopsy and direct immunofluorescence

- Autoantibody studies can be useful but not required

## Management

- Sun protection and avoidance of triggers such as excessive temperatures

- Topical steroids or calcineurin inhibitors
- Hydroxychloroquine or immunomodulators such as methotrexate

**25%** — **5%** — While 25% of patients with systemic lupus erythematosus (SLE) have a discoid rash, only 5% of patients with DLE progress to SLE.

# Drug Eruptions

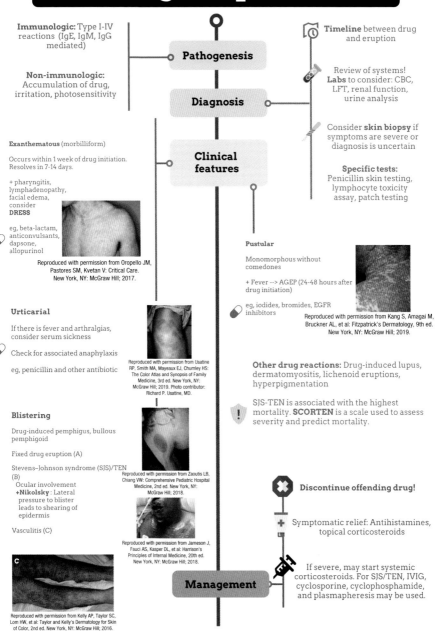

## Pathogenesis

**Immunologic:** Type I-IV reactions (IgE, IgM, IgG mediated)

**Non-immunologic:** Accumulation of drug, irritation, photosensitivity

## Diagnosis

**Timeline** between drug and eruption

Review of systems! **Labs** to consider: CBC, LFT, renal function, urine analysis

Consider **skin biopsy** if symptoms are severe or diagnosis is uncertain

**Specific tests:** Penicillin skin testing, lymphocyte toxicity assay, patch testing

## Clinical features

**Exanthematous** (morbilliform)

Occurs within 1 week of drug initiation. Resolves in 7-14 days.

+ pharyngitis, lymphadenopathy, facial edema, consider **DRESS**

eg, beta-lactam, anticonvulsants, dapsone, allopurinol

Reproduced with permission from Oropello JM, Pastores SM, Kvetan V: Critical Care. New York, NY: McGraw Hill; 2017.

**Urticarial**

If there is fever and arthralgias, consider serum sickness

Check for associated anaphylaxis

eg, penicillin and other antibiotic

Reproduced with permission from Usatine RP, Smith MA, Mayeaux EJ, Chumley HS: The Color Atlas and Synopsis of Family Medicine, 3rd ed. New York, NY: McGraw Hill; 2019. Photo contributor: Richard P. Usatine, MD.

**Blistering**

Drug-induced pemphigus, bullous pemphigoid

Fixed drug eruption (A)

Stevens–Johnson syndrome (SJS)/TEN (B)
  Ocular involvement
  **+Nikolsky**: Lateral pressure to blister leads to shearing of epidermis

Vasculitis (C)

Reproduced with permission from Zaoutis LB, Chiang VW: Comprehensive Pediatric Hospital Medicine, 2nd ed. New York, NY: McGraw Hill; 2018.

Reproduced with permission from Jameson J, Fauci AS, Kasper DL, et al: Harrison's Principles of Internal Medicine, 20th ed. New York, NY: McGraw Hill; 2018.

Reproduced with permission from Kelly AP, Taylor SC, Lom HW, et al: Taylor and Kelly's Dermatology for Skin of Color, 2nd ed. New York, NY: McGraw Hill; 2016.

**Pustular**

Monomorphous without comedones

+ Fever --> AGEP (24-48 hours after drug initiation)

eg, iodides, bromides, EGFR inhibitors

Reproduced with permission from Kang S, Amagai M, Bruckner AL, et al: Fitzpatrick's Dermatology, 9th ed. New York, NY: McGraw Hill; 2019.

**Other drug reactions:** Drug-induced lupus, dermatomyositis, lichenoid eruptions, hyperpigmentation

SJS-TEN is associated with the highest mortality. **SCORTEN** is a scale used to assess severity and predict mortality.

## Management

**Discontinue offending drug!**

Symptomatic relief: Antihistamines, topical corticosteroids

If severe, may start systemic corticosteroids. For SJS/TEN, IVIG, cyclosporine, cyclophosphamide, and plasmapheresis may be used.

# ⚕ Erythema Multiforme

Immune-mediated mucocutaneous disorder caused by drugs or infection that results in "target" lesions

## Population

Adolescents and young adults
2:1 Male:Female ratio

## Causes

 **Idiopathic**

 **Infection**
HSV
*Mycoplasma pneumoniae*
Epstein–Barr virus
Cytomegalovirus

 **Medications**
Sulfonamides
NSAIDs
Anticonvulsants

 **Medical Conditions**
Malignancies
Autoimmune disease

 **Other**
Menstruation
Immunizations

**EM major:** Mucous membrane involvement, systemic symptoms

**EM minor:** Less severe, no mucosal disease

## Morphology

 **"Target" lesions:**
Dusky center +/− blister
Pale ring
Erythematous halo

Reproduced with permission from Kane KS, Nambudiri VE, Stratigos AJ: Color Atlas & Synopsis of Pediatric Dermatology, 3rd ed. New York, NY: McGraw Hill; 2017.

Reproduced with permission from Prose NS, Kristal L: Weinberg's Color Atlas of Pediatric Dermatology, 5th ed. New York, NY: McGraw Hill; 2017.

Reproduced with permission from Kline MW: Rudolph's Pediatrics, 23rd ed. New York, NY: McGraw Hill; 2018.

**Mucosal lesions can be painful!**

Reproduced with permission from Soutor C, Hordinsky MK: Clinical Dermatology. New York, NY: McGraw Hill; 2013.

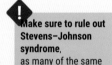 **Make sure to rule out Stevens–Johnson syndrome,** as many of the same drugs can cause both.

- Usually **asymptomatic**
- If associated with infection, may have **prodromal symptoms**
- Lesions occur over 3-5 days (**acutely**)
- Starts on extremities and spread **centripetally**
- **Symmetrical**
- **Palmoplantar** involvement common

## Histology 🔬

**Lymphocyte** accumulation in dermal–epidermal interface; subepidermal **cleft** formation

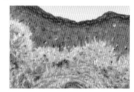

## Management

Usually self-resolving within 1-4 weeks

 **Chest X-ray if patient has respiratory symptoms**

 **Symptomatic treatment:** Oral antihistamines, cool compresses, wet dressings

 Treat underlying infection

 Remove offending drugs

 Steroids can suppress symptoms

 **Prevention:** If caused by HSV, may try antivirals (eg, acyclovir)

# Erythema Nodosum
## — Most Common Form of Septal Panniculitis —

## Causes/Associated Conditions

Idiopathic

Pregnancy

Infection (*streptococcal pharyngitis* in children)

Lymphoma

Autoinflammatory (Sarcoidosis & IBD)

Drugs (sulfonamides, oral contraceptives)

## Clinical Presentation

 5:1 Female predominance (in adults); ages 20-45

**Nodules & Plaques**

Tender
Erythematous
Deep-seated

**Distribution**

Anterior shins
Thighs
Buttocks

**Associated Symptoms**

Fever
Malaise
Arthralgia

**Progression**
Flattening
Color changes
No ulceration

**Löfgren syndrome:** Benign variant of systemic sarcoidosis with erythema nodosum (EN) and bilateral hilar lymphadenopathy.

## Workup

 **Laboratory Evaluation**
- **CBC, BMP, LFTs** (for various potential underlying infections)
- **ESR, ACE** (elevated in certain autoinflammatory conditions)
- **Rapid strep, ASO titers** (if strep infection is suspected)
- **hCG**

 **Imaging**
**Chest Radiograph** (for sarcoidosis or TB)

 **Histology**
- Septal panniculitis
- Lymphocytic predominance
- Occasional histiocytes in characteristic Miescher radial granuloma
- Thickened, fibrotic septa
- Occasional lobular involvement with fat necrosis

## Management

 **Prompt identification and treatment of underlying illness**
**Spontaneous resolution occurs within 6 weeks among most cases when no underlying illness is identified**

**EN recurs in ~1/3 of cases**

**Non-pharmacologic**

Bed rest
Elevation of involved extremities
Cool, wet compresses

**Pharmacologic**

NSAIDs
Colchicine
Potassium iodide

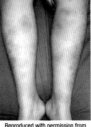

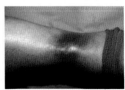

# Eyelid Lesions

## Common Benign Lesions

**Most eyelid lesions are benign and may be inflammatory, infectious, or neoplastic**

### Hordeolum ("stye")

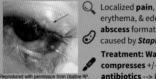

🔍 Localized **pain**, erythema, & edema with **abscess** formation, caused by **Staph aureus**

💊 **Treatment: Warm compresses** +/– topical **antibiotics** --> Incision & drainage

Reproduced with permission from Usatine RP, Smith MA, Mayeaux EJ, Chumley HS: The Color Atlas and Synopsis of Family Medicine, 3rd ed. New York, NY: McGraw Hill; 2019. Photo contributor: Richard P. Usatine, MD.

May be external (**black arrow**) or internal (white arrow)

### Chalazion

🔍 **Nontender**, rubbery nodule on the **inner eyelid**, caused by meibomian

🧀 **gland obstruction**

👁 Often resolves **spontaneously**; may require **warm compresses or rarely surgery if chronic**

Reproduced with permission from Riordan-Eva P, Augsburger JJ: Vaughan & Asbury's General Ophthalmology, 19th ed. New York, NY: McGraw Hill; 2018.

### Molluscum Contagiosum

🔍 Multiple, 2-5 mm, **flesh-colored, umbilicated papules**, caused by a **poxvirus**

⏱ Usually **self-limited** by 6-12 mo; may require **cryotherapy** or curettage

Used with permission from Dr. Morrell D, UNC Dermatology.

### Xanthelasma

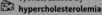
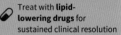

🔍 **Soft, yellow** plaques on the **medial** aspect of the eyelids, caused by **hypercholesterolemia**

💊 Treat with **lipid-lowering drugs** for sustained clinical resolution

Reproduced with permission from Gardner D, Shoback D: Greenspan's Basic and Clinical Endocrinology, 10th ed. New York, NY: McGraw Hill; 2018.

### Milia

🔍 **White**, firm, **pinpoint papules**, caused by **hair follicle keratin plugging**; very common in newborns

⏱ Usually **self-limited** but may be treated with thin **incision** or keratolytics

Reproduced with permission from Usatine RP, Smith MA, Mayeaux EJ, Chumley HS: The Color Atlas and Synopsis of Family Medicine, 3rd ed. New York, NY: McGraw Hill; 2019. Photo contributor: Richard P. Usatine, MD.

### Squamous Papilloma ("skin tag")

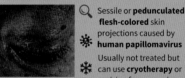

🔍 Sessile or **pedunculated flesh-colored** skin projections caused by **human papillomavirus**

❄ Usually not treated but can use **cryotherapy** or excision for cosmesis

Reproduced with permission from Riordan-Eva P, Augsburger JJ: Vaughan & Asbury's General Ophthalmology, 19th ed. New York, NY: McGraw Hill; 2018.

## Malignant Lesions

### Basal Cell Carcinoma

Reproduced with permission from Papadakis MA, McPhee SJ, Rabow MW: Current Medical Diagnosis & Treatment 2020. New York, NY: McGraw Hill; 2020.

### Squamous Cell Carcinoma

Reproduced with permission from Riordan-Eva P, Augsburger JJ: Vaughan & Asbury's General Ophthalmology, 19th ed. New York, NY: McGraw Hill; 2018.

### Sebaceous Carcinoma

Used with permission from Drs. Nahyoung Grace Lee, MD, and Fouad R. Zakka, MD, Boston, MA, USA.

# Folliculitis

## Inflammation of the Superficial Hair Follicle

## Common Causes

 **Infection**
- **Bacterial**—*Staph* & *Strep*
- Viral—VZV, HSV, molluscum
- Fungal—dermatophyte, *Candida*
- Parasitic

 **Medications**
- Steroids
- Androgens
- EGFR inhibitors
- Antipsychotics

 **Chemicals**

**Physical Injury**

## Risk Factors

 **Shaving**

 Hyperhidrosis

 Obesity

 Diabetes

 Friction

 HIV

 Occlusion

 Topical steroids

## Clinical Presentation

**Follicularly** centered erythematous **papules** and **pustules** +/− overlying crust

 **Furunculosis**

Involvement of **deeper** pilosebaceous unit leading to **painful nodules**

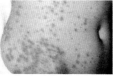

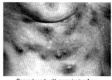

Reproduced with permission from Usatine RP, Smith MA, Mayeaux EJ, Chumley HS: The Color Atlas and Synopsis of Family Medicine, 3rd ed. New York, NY: McGraw Hill; 2019. Photo contributor: Richard P. Usatine, MD.

Reproduced with permission from Kelly AP, Taylor SC, Lom HW, et al: Taylor and Kelly's Dermatology for Skin of Color, 2nd ed. New York, NY: McGraw Hill; 2016.

Reproduced with permission from Murtagh J, Bird S: Murtagh's Cautionary Tales, 3rd ed. New York, NY: McGraw Hill; 2019.

Reproduced with permission from Wolff K, Johnson RA, Saavedra AP, et al: Fitzpatrick's Color Atlas and Synopsis of Clinical Dermatology, 8th ed. New York, NY: McGraw Hill; 2017.

##  Differential Diagnosis

- Acne
- Rosacea
- Keratosis pilaris
- Tinea infections
- Milia
- Candidiasis

## Management

**Avoid predisposing triggers** (hyperhidrosis, shaving, etc)

 Topical Antibiotics

eg, mupirocin, clindamycin

 Systemic Antibiotics

eg, dicloxacillin, cephalexin

# Gangrene

Tissue Death and Destruction Caused by Ischemia or Infection

## Risk Factors

 Obesity

 IV Drug Use

 Diabetes Mellitus

 Surgery

Smoking

 Trauma

 Hyperlipidemia

 Alcoholism

## Subtypes

### Dry Gangrene
Arterial obstruction following long-standing peripheral artery disease or vasculitis in the lower extremities of diabetic patients

### Wet Gangrene
Necrotizing soft tissue infection usually caused by invasion of bacteria into site of local trauma or skin breaches

### Gas Gangrene
Myonecrosis frequently caused by gas-producing anaerobe *Clostridium perfringens*.

## Clinical Findings

### Dry Gangrene

Features of **black eschar** located on the distal extremities:
- Clearly demarcated
- Hard, dry
- Foul odor
- Painful

Reproduced with permission from Usatine RP, Smith MA, Mayeaux EJ, Chumley HS: The Color Atlas and Synopsis of Family Medicine, 3rd ed. New York, NY: McGraw Hill; 2019. Photo contributor: Richard P. Usatine, MD.

Skin is **atrophic, shiny,** and free of hair. Limb is **pale, cold,** and pulseless.

Reproduced with permission from Knoop KJ, Stack LB, Storrow AB, et al: The Atlas of Emergency Medicine, 4th ed. New York, NY: McGraw Hill; 2016. Photo contributor: Lawrence B. Stack, MD.

### Wet Gangrene

Edematous, moist-appearing skin characterized by:
- Cyanosis
- Blistering
- Foul odor
- Painful

Reproduced with permission from Usatine RP, Smith MA, Mayeaux EJ, Chumley HS: The Color Atlas and Synopsis of Family Medicine, 3rd ed. New York, NY: McGraw Hill; 2019. Photo contributor: Javier La Fontaine, DPM.

Patient may also present with systemic signs and symptoms of infection.

Reproduced with permission from Knoop KJ, Stack LB, Storrow AB, et al: The Atlas of Emergency Medicine, 4th ed. New York, NY: McGraw Hill; 2016. Photo contributor: Robert Tubbs, MD.

### Gas Gangrene

Severe pain with evidence of gas (crepitus) on palpation

Reproduced with permission from Dean SM, Satiani B, Abraham WT: Color Atlas and Synopsis of Vascular Diseases. New York, NY: McGraw Hill; 2014.

Reproduced with permission from Knoop KJ, Stack LB, Storrow AB, et al: The Atlas of Emergency Medicine, 4th ed. New York, NY: McGraw Hill; 2016. Photo contributor: David Kaplan, MD.

 **Fournier's Gangrene**

Life-threatening necrotizing fasciitis involving the genital or perineal regions

Reproduced with permission from Hall BJ, Schmidt GA, Kress JP: Principles of Critical Care, 4th ed. New York, NY: McGraw Hill; 201

## Management

### Dry Gangrene

1. **Risk reduction strategies** (smoking cessation, diet, & exercise, routine foot exam)

2. **Revascularization**

3. **Amputation/debridement** once blood flow is optimized

### Wet/Gas Gangrene

 1. Aggressive surgical **debridement**
2. Systemic broad-spectrum **antibiotics**

 Wet: Carbapenem + MRSA agent + clindamycin
Gas: Clindamycin + piperacillin-tazobactam

# Guttate Psoriasis

## Pathophysiology

 **Environmental Exposure**
(eg, strep infection)

*triggers*

 **Immune Response**
(Th1-mediated IL2 release)

*in*

 **Genetically Susceptible Individual**
(HLA-Cw6 predisposition)

## Overlap with Psoriasis

Guttate exacerbation of general plaque psoriasis is less likely to be associated with streptococcal infection.

Guttate psoriasis may occasionally progress to general plaque psoriasis.

## Differential Diagnosis

**Tinea Corporis**
(Central clearing; use KOH prep to differentiate)

**Cutaneous T-Cell Lymphoma**
(Biopsy is necessary for diagnosis; CTCL onset typically slower)

**Nummular Dermatitis**
(Intensely pruritic; affects middle-aged individuals)

**Pityriasis Rosea**
(Herald patch precedes generalized eruption)

## Clinical Presentation

 Older children

 Young adults (under 30)

 Preceding streptococcal pharyngitis (2-3 weeks earlier)

 Acute onset

 Trunk and extremities (can be generalized)

 Small, discrete, raindrop-like papules

 Fine scale and associated pruritus

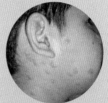

Reproduced with permission from Usatine RP, Smith MA, Mayeaux EJ, Chumley HS: The Color Atlas and Synopsis of Family Medicine, 3rd ed. New York, NY: McGraw Hill; 2019. Photo contributor: Richard P. Usatine, MD.

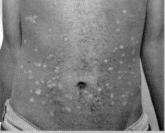

Reproduced with permission from Usatine RP, Smith MA, Mayeaux EJ, Chumley HS: The Color Atlas and Synopsis of Family Medicine, 3rd ed. New York, NY: McGraw Hill; 2019. Photo contributor: Richard P. Usatine, MD.

Reproduced with permission from Soutor C, Hordinsky MK: Clinical Dermatology. New York, NY: McGraw Hill; 2013.

## Management

 Treatment of streptococcal infection (if present)

 Spontaneous resolution (in weeks to months) is common

 Phototherapy (narrow-band UVB) for widespread disease

 Topical treatments (steroids +/− calcipotriene) for limited disease

# Herpes Simplex

Common, Highly Contagious Mucocutaneous Viral Infection

## Epidemiology & Virology

 Infections caused by **HSV-1** (orolabial, anogenital) and **HSV-2** (genital)

 Common in children and adults; globally prevalent

 90% adults seropositive to HSV-1
20% seropositive to HSV-2

## Transmission & Pathogenesis

 Transmission by **direct contact** with contaminated body fluids (HSV-2 is **sexually transmitted**)

 Latent virus settles in **dorsal root ganglia** and can reactivate to cause **episodic recurrences**

## Clinical Subtypes

### Common Features:

Grouped vesicles atop an erythematous base
+/− Prodrome of fever, malaise, and localized pain
Triggers: **Immunosuppression, stress**, local trauma

### Herpetic Gingivostomatitis

Shallow ulcers on lip and tongue with edematous gingiva

Can cause **pain with eating/drinking**

Reproduced with permission from Soutor C, Hordinsky MK: Clinical Dermatology. New York, NY: McGraw Hill; 2013.

### Herpes Labialis

Reproduced with permission from Centers for Disease Control.

AKA "cold sores"

### Herpetic Whitlow

Reproduced with permission from Knoop KJ, Stack LB, Storrow AB, et al: The Atlas of Emergency Medicine, 4th ed. New York, NY: McGraw Hill; 2016. Photo contributor: Selim Suner, MD, MS.

Painful; distal finger

### Herpes Genitalis

Reproduced with permission from Ryan K, Ahmad N, Alspaugh JA, et al: Sherris Medical Microbiology, 7th ed. New York, NY: McGraw Hill; 2018.

Reproduced with permission from Kang S, Amagai M, Bruckner AL, et al: Fitzpatrick's Dermatology, 9th ed. New York, NY: McGraw Hill; 2019.

Genital lesions are often **painful, erosive**, and may crust over.
Symptoms include **dysuria** and vaginal discharge.

## Diagnosis

 History & Physical Exam

Reproduced with permission from Public Health Image Library, Centers for Disease Control and Prevention. Photo contributor: Dr. Joe Miller.

 **Tzanck Smear**
Scrapings of lesion base reveal **multinucleated giant cells**

Other Tests
Direct fluorescence antigens
HSV DNA PCR testing

## Management

 Standard and contact precautions

 **Oral Antivirals**
Initiate **within 72 hours**
Treat for 7-10 days
Options include:
Acyclovir
Valacyclovir
Famciclovir

 **Immunocompromised patients**
Consider IV antivirals
Continue until lesions resolve
**Antiretroviral therapy** for HIV-positive patients

# Impetigo

Localized, Superficial Gram-Positive Bacterial Skin Infection Most Common in Children

## Pathophysiology

 **Predisposing Risk Factors**
Immunosuppression
**Atopic dermatitis**
**Trauma**/insect bite

 **Gram-Positive** Bacterial Infection
*Staphylococcus aureus*
Group A *Streptococcus*

## Epidemiology

 **Summer Months & Humid Conditions**

 Newborn **Infants** & Young **Children**

## Clinical Presentation

Reproduced with permission from Kelly AP, Taylor SC, Lom HW, et al: Taylor and Kelly's Dermatology for Skin of Color, 2nd ed. New York, NY: McGraw Hill; 2016.

 **Morphological Progression**
Small red **papules** evolve into **vesicular** or **pustular** lesions that rupture and coalesce to form **golden crusted plaques**

 **Characteristic Features**
**Honey-colored crust**
Surrounding erythema
Non-tender

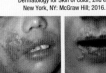

Reproduced with permission from Stern S, Cifu AS, Altkorn D: Symptom to Diagnosis: An Evidence-Based Guide, 4th ed. New York, NY: McGraw Hill; 2020.

Reproduced with permission from Tenenbein M, Macias CG, Sharieff GQ, et al: Strange and Schafermeyer's Pediatric Emergency Medicine, 5th ed. New York, NY: McGraw Hill; 2019.

 **Clinical Variants**
**Non-bullous** (70-80%)
Bullous (20-30%)
Ecthyma (deeper, ulcerative)

 **Distribution**
**Face** (perioral, perinasal)
Legs

## Diagnosis

 History & Physical Exam

 Gram Stain
**Gram-positive cocci in clusters or chains**

 Culture
*S. aureus* or *Streptococcus*

## Management

 **Standard and Contact Precautions**

 **Topical Antibiotics**
mupirocin, bacitracin, retapamulin

 **Oral Antibiotics**
Dicloxacillin
Cephalexin
Erythromycin
Clindamycin (MRSA)
Doxycycline (MRSA)

 **Look Out for:**
Methicillin-resistant *S. aureus*

# Kaposi's Sarcoma

## Vascular and Lymphatic Neoplasm Caused by Human Herpesvirus-8

### Pathophysiology

Caused by human herpesvirus-8. Proliferation and inflammation of endothelial-derived spindle cells.

### Subtypes

1. **AIDS-related KS:** Most common neoplasm associated with AIDS
2. **Classic/Mediterranean KS:** Eastern Europeans >50 years old; progress slowly; familial predisposition; M > F
3. **Endemic African KS:** Young men; rapidly fatal
4. **Transplant-associated KS:** Immunosuppressed patients

### Clinical Features

Red/purple plaques or nodules on skin or mucosal surfaces. Usually asymptomatic

### Common Locations
Classic KS:    HIV-associated:

### Diagnosis

**Skin biopsy.** Histology shows proliferation of spindle cells in dermis with inflammatory cells. Hemorrhage is common.

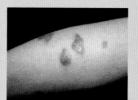

Reproduced with permission from Grippi MA, Elias JA, Fishman JA, et al: Fishman's Pulmonary Diseases and Disorders, 5th ed. New York, NY: McGraw Hill; 2015.

Reproduced with permission from Papadakis MA, McPhee SJ, Rabow MW: Current Medical Diagnosis & Treatment 2020. New York, NY: McGraw Hill; 2020.

---

**!**

Order an **HIV test** in patients with KS. Check mouth for mucosal involvement and oral leukoplakia.

Ask about cough, bloody stool, and fatigue for **systemic involvement.**

### Differential Diagnosis

1. Hemangioma
2. Bruise
3. Bacillary angiomatosis
4. Lichen planus
5. Psoriasis
6. Syphilis

### Treatment

❄ Cryotherapy
💊 Topical therapy (eg, imiquimod)
💉 Intralesional chemotherapy (eg, vinblastine)
☢ Radiation
🖊 Excision

**HIV/AIDS:** Antiretroviral therapy
**Iatrogenic immunosuppression:** Reduce dose of immunosuppression
**Systemic symptoms:** Systemic chemotherapy

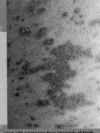

# Lichen Planus
## Idiopathic Disorder of the Skin, Mucosa, Nails, and Hair Follicles, Typically in Adults

## Clinical Features

**5P's**

Purple
Polygonal
Pruritic
Planar (flat-topped)
Papules

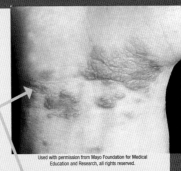

**Wickham striae:** Fine white lacy reticulate lines are pathognomonic.

**Koebner phenomenon:** Excoriation ➡ linear array of papules

## Pathogenesis

- May be T-cell-mediated immune reaction against keratinocytes
- Oral LP: May be associated with hepatitis C

## Treatment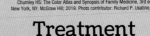

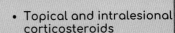

- Topical and intralesional corticosteroids
- Topical calcineurin inhibitors
- Phototherapy
- Oral corticosteroids or other systemic therapy

## Variants

- Variants: Hypertrophic (most common), exanthematous, bullous, annular

# Melanoma

## Cancer of Melanocytes

### Pathophysiology

- Most begin as de novo lesions
- Most common mutation in familial melanoma: CDKN2A

### Risk Factors

- Sunburns
- Blue/green eyes, blonde/red hair, fair complexion
- Prior personal or family history of melanoma
- >100 typical nevi
- Atypical nevi
- p16 mutation

### Population

Mean age of diagnosis: 63 years

### Most Common Locations

Back in men

Lower extremity in women

### Features of Melanoma (ABCDE)

**A**symmetry
**B**order (irregular)
**C**olor (variable)
**D**iameter (>6 mm)
**E**volution (shape, size, color)

**Ugly duckling sign:** Look for moles that are different from other moles

## Melanoma Subtypes

Common sites of metastasis:
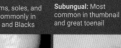

| Superficial spreading | Lentigo maligna | Nodular | Acral lentiginous | |
|---|---|---|---|---|
| Fast radial growth phase, good prognosis when detected early | Sun-damaged skin of elderly patients; in situ melanoma | Lack radial growth phase, progress quickly | On palms, soles, and nails; commonly in Asians and Blacks | **Subungual:** Most common in thumbnail and great toenail |

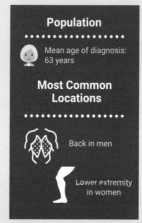

### Histopathology

Pagetoid growth pattern: Abnormal melanocytes in upper layers of the dermis

Tumor staging is based on **Breslow depth,** which is thickness of tumor.

### Management

Surgery +/− sentinel lymph node biopsy

Chemotherapy, targeted therapy, immunotherapy

Radiation

# Molluscum Contagiosum

A Cutaneous Infection
Caused by a Poxvirus, a DNA Virus

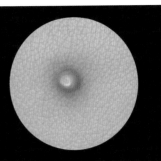

## Transmission

- Poxvirus infection spreads through **direct contact,** ie, sexual transmission, autoinoculation, and fomites.
- Transmission via fomites can occur by:

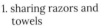

1. sharing razors and towels

2. trying on underwear and swimsuits before washing them

3. swimming in pools

## Diagnosis

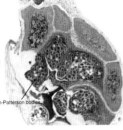

Henderson–Patterson bodies

- Generally determined by clinical appearance

- **Henderson–Paterson bodies**, basophilic intracytoplasmic inclusion bodies, can be seen on light microscopy

## Clinical Presentation

- Dome-shaped, smooth, firm 2-6 mm pink, white, or flesh-colored papules with **central umbilication**

Reproduced with permission from Hoffman BL, Schorge JO, Halvorson LM, et al: Williams Gynecology, 4th ed. New York, NY: McGraw Hill; 2020.

- Commonly occurs in **children** on the trunk and extremities
- **Anogenital** distribution is common in **adults** due to sexual transmission

- Characteristic papules in a linear pattern suggest **autoinoculation** from scratching or shaving

Reproduced with permission from Usatine RP, Smith MA, Mayeaux EJ, Chumley HS: The Color Atlas and Synopsis of Family Medicine, 3rd ed. New York, NY: McGraw Hill; 2019. Photo contributor: Richard P. Usatine, MD.

## Treatment

- Condition is **self-limited** in immunocompetent patients.
- Removal can be performed with **curettage** or **cryotherapy**
- Sexual partners should be screened.
- Precautions should be taken to decrease spread (ie, avoid shaving).

# Mycosis Fungoides (MF)

- Most common form of cutaneous T-cell lymphoma
- More common in males, older adults, and African-Americans
- Overall 5-year survival: 88%; staged from IA to IVB

## Progression over years to decades

Patch stage  Plaque stage  Tumor stage

- <u>Patch stage:</u> Typically on sun-protected body sites
- <u>Plaque stage:</u> Often annular or polycyclic
- <u>Tumor stage:</u> Ulceration may be present

## Other Variants

Hypopigmented — Folliculotropic — Granulomatous slack skin — Pagetoid reticulosis

## Diagnosis
- Biopsy: Atypical T-cells with epidermotropism and clonal T-cell proliferations
- Patients often have history of multiple nondiagnostic biopsies

## Treatment
- Topical therapies, systemic biologics, and/or systemic chemotherapy based on stage

## Sezary Syndrome
- Leukemic form of MF
- Triad of erythroderma, lymphadenopathy, and Sezary cells in the skin, blood, and lymph nodes

# Necrotizing Fasciitis

Localized Skin and Soft-Tissue Infection Leading to Rapidly Progressive Necrosis

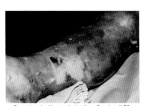

Reproduced with permission from Brunicardi FC, Andersen DK, Billiar TR, et al: Schwartz's Principles of Surgery, 11th ed. New York, NY: McGraw Hill; 2019.

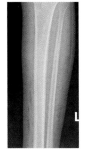

Reproduced with permission from Sherman SC, Weber JM, Schindlbeck MA, et al: Clinical Emergency Medicine. New York, NY: McGraw Hill; 2014.

## Clinical Features

 Necrosis down to fascia/muscle

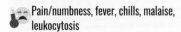 Pain/numbness, fever, chills, malaise, leukocytosis

 Foul-smelling discharge

Anogenital = Fournier's gangrene

## Pathogenesis

Polymicrobial; anaerobes, aerobes

10% due to Group A Strep

## Risk Factors

Trauma, diabetes mellitus, PVD, immunosuppression, older age, alcoholism

## Workup

 CBC, CRP, CPK, urea, Cr, electrolytes, blood, and wound cultures

 Rapid, frequent assessment

 Plain X-ray

## Treatment

 Surgical debridement

 Broad-spectrum IV antibiotics

 Fluids

Reproduced with permission from Yeomans ER, Hoffman BL, Gilstrap LC, et al: Cunningham and Gilstrap's Operative Obstetrics, 3rd ed. New York, NY: McGraw Hill; 2017.

Reproduced with permission from Hall BJ, Schmidt GA, Kress JP: Principles of Critical Care, 4th ed. New York, NY: McGraw Hill; 2015.

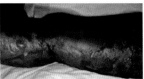

Reproduced with permission from Oropello JM, Pastores SM, Kvetan V: Critical Care. New York, NY: McGraw Hill; 2017.

Reproduced with permission from Hoffman BL, Schorge JO, Halvorson LM, et al: Williams Gynecology, 4th ed. New York, NY: McGraw Hill; 2020.

# Pediculosis

## Lice infestation (Head, Body, Pubic Hair)

---

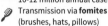
### Pediculosis Capitis
#### AKA "Head Lice"

**Epidemiology**

- Children **3-12 years**
  10-12 million annual cases
- Transmission via **fomites**
  (brushes, hats, pillows)

Reproduced with permission from Usatine RP, Smith MA, Mayeaux EJ, Chumley HS: The Color Atlas and Synopsis of Family Medicine, 3rd ed. New York, NY: McGraw Hill; 2019. Photo contributor: Richard P. Usatine, MD.

**Etiology**

*Pediculus humanus capitis*
Lives 30 days on **scalp hair**
Lays 5-10 eggs (**nits**) per day

Reproduced with permission from Centers for Disease Control and Prevention. Photo contributor: Dennis D. Juranek.

Maculae ceruleae: Bluish spots on the skin of infested individuals; likely from local anticoagulation.

**Clinical Findings**

Lice and nits (**1 mm gray specks**) in scalp hair, especially in **occipital** and **retroauricular** regions

+/– **maculae ceruleae**
+/– pruritus/excoriations
+/– lymphadenopathy

**Treatment**

| | |
|---|---|
| Permethrin | Ivermectin |
| Malathion | Spinosad |

---

### Pediculosis Corporis
#### AKA "Body Lice"

**Epidemiology**

- Affects **homeless**, refugees, victims of war/disasters
- Transmission via **clothing**/bedding

Reproduced with permission from Usatine RP, Smith MA, Mayeaux EJ, Chumley HS: The Color Atlas and Synopsis of Family Medicine, 3rd ed. New York, NY: McGraw Hill; 2019. Photo contributor: Richard P. Usatine, MD.

**Etiology**

*Pediculus humanus corporis*
Lives 20 days laying up to 300 eggs in **seams** of clothing

Reproduced with permission from Public Health Image Library, Centers for Disease Control and Prevention. Photo contributor: Dr. F. Collins

**Clinical Findings**

**Linear excoriations** on the back, neck, shoulders, and waist. Lice are **not easily visualized**.

Intense **pruritus**
+/– postinflammatory hyperpigmentation

**Treatment**

Clothing/bedding should be treated as **biohazard waste.** Patient treated with oral **ivermectin**

---

### Pediculosis Pubis
#### AKA "Pubic Lice"

**Epidemiology**

- Patients often have multiple **STIs**
- Transmission via **sexual contact** and clothing

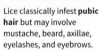
Reproduced with permission from Prose NS, Kristal L: Weinberg's Color Atlas of Pediatric Dermatology, 5th ed. New York, NY: McGraw Hill; 2017.

**Etiology**

*Phthirus pubis*
Lives 3 weeks, laying 25 eggs primarily in **pubic/perianal** region

Reproduced with permission from Public Health Image Library, World Health Organization.

**Clinical Findings**

Lice classically infest **pubic hair** but may involve mustache, beard, axillae, eyelashes, and eyebrows.

Reproduced with permission from Usatine RP, Smith MA, Mayeaux EJ, Chumley HS: The Color Atlas and Synopsis of Family Medicine, 3rd ed. New York, NY: McGraw Hill; 2019. Photo contributor: Luis Dehesa, MD.

Intense **pruritus**
+/– **maculae ceruleae**

**Treatment**

Oral **ivermectin** is first-line but same topical therapies as pediculosis capitis are effective.

---

# Pemphigus Vulgaris

Autoimmune Bullous Disease of the Skin and Mucous Membranes

## Pathophysiology

- Type 2 hypersensitivity reaction—IgG autoantibodies target desmoglein in desmosomes, which hold keratinocytes together in the stratum spinosum.
- Keratinocytes in the epidermis separate from one another (acantholysis).

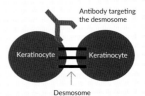

Antibody targeting the desmosome

Keratinocyte | Keratinocyte

Desmosome

## Clinical Presentation

- Shallow, flaccid bullae (acantholysis is superficial in the epidermis)
- Superficial erosions (ruptured blisters)
- Mucosal involvement (ie, vaginal, penile, anal, oral, conjunctival)
- Spares palms and soles

*Clinical Pearl*

Nikolsky's sign is POSITIVE.

Lateral pressure applied to the bullae causes skin shearing.

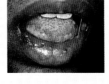

## Diagnosis & Histology

- Punch biopsy: Suprabasal epidermal acantholysis and intact adhesion of basal cells ("tombstoning")
- Direct immunofluorescence (DIF): IgG deposition

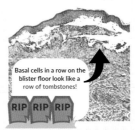

Basal cells in a row on the blister floor look like a row of tombstones!

RIP RIP RIP

## Treatment

- Corticosteroids (ie, prednisone) and other immunosuppressive agents

### Remember:

- IgG antibodies target desmosomes
- Cell adhesion is impaired in the epidermis
- Flaccid bullae
- Mucosal involvement

# Petechiae & Purpura

### Non-blanching macules and patches caused by extravasation of blood

## Definitions

**Petechiae:** Discrete, small (1-3 mm), non-blanching red or purple spots caused by minor mucocutaneous bleeding from platelet abnormalities or capillary wall disruption.

**Purpura:** Larger (3-10 mm), non-blanching red or purple discolorations caused by intradermal hemorrhage and may be palpable or retiform (angulated, netlike).

 Need to distinguish from **ecchymoses**, which are traumatic dermal hemorrhages that tend to be geometric or linear.

# Potential Etiologies

### Petechiae

Reproduced with permission from Kang S, Amagai M, Bruckner AL, et al: Fitzpatrick's Dermatology, 9th ed. New York, NY: McGraw Hill; 2019.

Reproduced with permission from Soutor C, Hordinsky MK: Clinical Dermatology. New York, NY: McGraw Hill; 2013.

**Low platelets (<150k)**
1. Immune thrombocytopenia
2. Disseminated intravascular coagulation
3. Meningococcemia
4. Drug-induced (quinine, bactrim)

**Normal platelets (>150k)**
1. Von Willebrand disease
2. Uremia
3. Drug-induced (ASA, NSAIDs)

### Retiform Purpura

Reproduced with permission from Soutor C, Hordinsky MK: Clinical Dermatology. New York, NY: McGraw Hill; 2013.

1. Chilblains
2. Rheumatic vasculitis
3. Heparin necrosis
4. TTP / PNH
5. Cholesterol embolus
6. Endocarditis
7. Calciphylaxis

### Palpable

Reproduced with permission from Usatine RP, Smith MA, Mayeaux EJ, Chumley HS: The Color Atlas and Synopsis of Family Medicine, 3rd ed. New York, NY: McGraw Hill; 2019. Photo contributor: Richard P. Usatine, MD.

### Purpura

Reproduced with permission from Oropello JM, Pastores SM, Kvetan V: Critical Care. New York, NY: McGraw Hill; 2017.

1. Leukocytoclastic vasculitis (distal legs)
2. Henoch–Schönlein purpura (age <20)
3. Urticarial vasculitis (preceding hives)
4. Mixed cryoglobulinemia (acral sites)
5. Wegener's granulomatosis (+ANCA)

# Evaluation

**History & Physical**
- Constitutional Sx
- Infectious signs

**Skin biopsy**
- Vessel occlusion
- Vessel inflammation
- Immunofluorescence

**Labwork**
- CBC (platelets)
- Coag. studies
- LFTs
- ESR / CRP
- ANA / ANCA

# Management

Supportive therapy: Local wound care and prevention of secondary infection

Treatment is directed at the underlying cause (infectious, immune-mediated, etc.)

# Pilonidal Disease
## Skin Infection of the Gluteal Cleft Overlying the Coccyx

## Pathophysiology

 Disruption of skin overlying coccyx leads to formation of a dimple ("pit")

 Pit draws in hair and debris leading to **follicular plugging**

 Ingrown hairs prevent drainage and promote **abscess formation** and **infection**

## Risk Factors

 Obesity

 Prolonged sitting

Hirsutism

## Epidemiology

 Male sex
(3:1 M:F ratio)

 **Young adults**
Peak incidence 16-20 yrs
Regression >40 yrs

## Differential Diagnosis

- Anal fistula (inferior to gluteal cleft)
- Hidradenitis suppurativa (off midline)
- Inflammatory bowel disease
- Tuberculosis

## Clinical Presentation

### Acute Exacerbation

 **Sudden onset** of pain and swelling in or along the **gluteal cleft** followed by development of warm, **tender**, erythematous **nodule** (abscess) over the sacrum.

 +/− purulent/blood drainage
+/− fever and malaise

### Chronic Disease

 Recurrent **drainage** and pain from one or more visible **midline sinus tracts**, usually containing **hair** and other  debris.

Constitutional symptoms are rare.

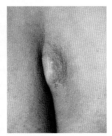

Reproduced with permission from Reichman EF: Reichman's Emergency Medicine Procedures, 3rd ed. New York, NY: McGraw Hill; 2019.

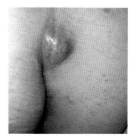

Reproduced with permission from Usatine RP, Smith MA, Mayeaux EJ, Chumley HS: The Color Atlas and Synopsis of Family Medicine, 3rd ed. New York, NY: McGraw Hill; 2019. Photo contributor: Richard P. Usatine, MD.

## Management

 Acute abscesses require prompt **incision and drainage** under local anesthesia, after which the wound is **cleaned** (hair and debris removed) and **packed** with gauze.

 Antibiotics are necessary only if there is evidence of **cellulitis** or the patient is **immunocompromised**.

 Chronic disease is managed with **conservative measures** (shaving and frequent washing) followed by pilonidal **cystectomy** if recalcitrant.

# Pityriasis Rosea

## Population

Mostly adolescents and young adults (peak incidence 10-35 years old)

More concerning in pregnant women—associated with fetal demise and miscarriage

## Presentation

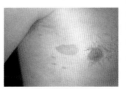

Reproduced with permission from McKean S, Ross JJ, Dressler DD, et al: Principles and Practice of Hospital Medicine, 2nd ed. New York, NY: McGraw Hill; 2017.

Discrete oval, erythematous, scaly plaques and patches

Pruritic or asymptomatic
Constitutional symptoms (fever, headache, cough) may precede

## Distribution

Reproduced with permission from of the Centers for Disease Control and Prevention.

Solitary "herald patch" appears first, often on trunk

Reproduced with permission from Kelly AP, Taylor SC, Lom HW, et al: Taylor and Kelly's Dermatology for Skin of Color, 2nd ed. New York, NY: McGraw Hill; 2016.

"Christmas tree" distribution

Reproduced with permission from Stern S, Cifu AS, Altkorn D: Symptom to Diagnosis: An Evidence-Based Guide, 4th ed. New York, NY: McGraw Hill; 2020.

Often oriented along skin lines
Face, palms, and soles usually spared

## Diagnosis

Clinical diagnosis. May be associated with reactivation of HHV-6 and HHV-7

syphilis

Reproduced with permission from Kang S, Amagai M, Bruckner AL, et al: Fitzpatrick's Dermatology, 9th ed. New York, NY: McGraw Hill; 2019.

Reproduced with permission from Soutor C, Hordinsky MK: Clinical Dermatology. New York, NY: McGraw Hill; 2013.

May run serologies to exclude secondary syphilis and KOH to exclude tinea

## Management

Usually self-limiting; resolves within 8 weeks. Education and reassurance of patients.

Symptomatic treatment for pruritus: Antihistamines and mid-potency steroids

# Plaque Psoriasis

## Common, Chronic Inflammatory and Immune-Mediated Skin Disorder

### Pathophysiology

 Foreign antigens stimulate **antigen-presenting cells** to release cytokines (IL-23)

 Dermal and helper T cells release **IL-17 & TNF-α**, leading to **keratinocyte hyperproliferation**

 Positive feedback loop maintains **heightened immune response** and psoriatic plaque formation

### Risk Factors

 **Obesity**      **Family history**

 Smoking      Medications
Lithium
Beta-blockers
Alcohol     Anti-malarials

### Epidemiology

 3% prevalence in USA
No sex predilection

 Bimodal peak incidence
Ages 30-39 and 50-69
Less common in children

### Differential Diagnosis

- Cutaneous T-cell lymphoma
- Nummular eczema
- Tinea corporis / cruris
- Lichen planus
- Pityriasis rosea
- Cutaneous candidiasis

### Clinical Presentation

**Characteristic description:** **Sharply demarcated**, **erythematous**, pruritic plaques with thick, **silvery scale** symmetrically distributed on **extensor surfaces** (elbows & knees) and trunk

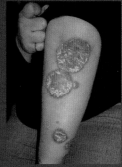

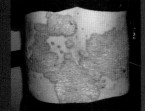

**Koebner phenomenon:** Occurrence of psoriasis plaques at sites of skin trauma

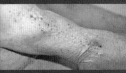

 **Auspitz sign:** Removal of plaque's scale results in **pinpoint bleeding**

**Psoriatic arthritis:** Seronegative inflammatory arthritis (**morning joint pain & stiffness**) that occurs in **~30%** of psoriasis patients and may be suggestive of severe disease

### Management

Topical therapies:
**High-potency topical corticosteroids**     Topical retinoids
Vitamin D analog (**calcipotriene**)     Tar-based therapy

Phototherapy:
UVB radiation     **Photochemotherapy (PUVA)**

Systemic therapies:
Immunosuppressants (**methotrexate**, cyclosporine, mycophenolate)
TNF-α inhibitors (etanercept, infliximab, **adalimumab**)
**IL-17A inhibitors** (secukinumab, ixekizumab, brodalumab)

# ⚕ Pressure Ulcers

## AKA Pressure Sores, Bedsore

## Etiology

**Pressure**    Shearing forces

Friction    **Moisture**

**Tissue compression**
between bony prominence
and external surface

→ Decreased blood flow

↓

Ischemia    Edema
Thrombosis

↓

Cell death &
ulcer formation

## Risk Factors

🛏 **Limited mobility**

⚖ Sudden weight changes

🍴 **Malnutrition**

🚬 Smoking

💊 Medications

🏹 **Advanced age**

🚽 Incontinence

☠ **Terminal illness**

# Clinical Presentation

## Common Sites

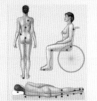

Reproduced with permission from Preventing
Pressure Ulcers: A Patient's Guide. Washington,
DC, US Department of Health and Human Services,
USGPO 617-025/68298, 1992.

**Sacrum**

**Calcaneus**

Ischial tuberosity

Trochanter

**65%**
Pelvic region

**30%**
Lower limbs

## Staging Classification

**Stage I**

Nonblanchable
erythema over
intact skin

Reproduced with permission from Goldsmith LA,
Katz SI, Gilchrest BA et al: Fitzpatrick's Dermatology in
General Medicine, 8th ed. New York, NY: McGraw Hill; 2012.

**Stage II**
Partial
thickness
skin loss
(epidermis and
some dermis)

Reproduced with permission from Knoop KJ, Stack LB,
Storrow AB, et al: The Atlas of Emergency Medicine, 4th ed.
New York, NY: McGraw Hill; 2016.
Photo contributor: Suzanne Dooley-Hash, MD.

**Stage III**

Full thickness
skin loss
down
to fascia

Reproduced with permission from Knoop KJ, Stack LB,
Storrow AB, et al: The Atlas of Emergency Medicine,
4th ed. New York, NY: McGraw Hill; 2016.
Photo contributor: David Effron, MD.

**Stage IV**

Full thickness
skin loss to
muscle/bone

Reproduced with permission from Knoop KJ, Stack LB,
Storrow AB, et al: The Atlas of Emergency Medicine,
4th ed. New York, NY: McGraw Hill; 2016.
Photo contributor: Lawrence B. Stack, MD.

 ❗ **Unstageable** — Ulcer covered with slough or
eschar such that depth cannot
be assessed.

# Complications

 **Local infection**
Erythema
Warmth
Pain
Purulent discharge

 **Osteomyelitis**

 **Squamous cell carcinoma**
(Marjolin's ulcer)

# Management

 **Pressure relief**
Repositioning
Support surfaces
(air/water mattress)

 **Wound care**
Cleansing
Debridement
Dressing

💊 Infection & pain control

# Rosacea

## Clinical Features

Chronic, inflammatory condition with a relapsing–remitting course

Reproduced with permission from Kelly AP, Taylor SC, Lom HW, et al: Taylor and Kelly's Dermatology for Skin of Color, 2nd ed. New York, NY: McGraw Hill; 2016.

Facial flushing and erythema, telangiectasia, papules, pustules on nose, cheeks, brow, and chin

## Epidemiology

Mostly in individuals between 30-50 years old

Reproduced with permission from Murtagh J, Rosenblatt J, Coleman J, et al: Murtagh's General Practice, 7th ed. New York, NY: McGraw Hill; 2018.

Primarily affects lighter skin phototypes
Less common in skin types IV-VI.

## Subtypes

Reproduced with permission from Usatine RP, Smith MA, Mayeaux EJ, Chumley HS: The Color Atlas and Synopsis of Family Medicine, 3rd ed. New York, NY: McGraw Hill; 2019. Photo contributor: Richard P. Usatine, MD.

### Erythemato-telangiectatic
Persistent erythema with flushing

Reproduced with permission from Baumann L: Cosmetic Dermatology: Principles and Practice, 2nd ed. New York, NY: McGraw Hill; 2009.

### Papulopustular
Acneiform papules and pustules

Reproduced with permission from Usatine RP, Smith MA, Mayeaux EJ, Chumley HS: The Color Atlas and Synopsis of Family Medicine, 3rd ed. New York, NY: McGraw Hill; 2019. Photo contributor: Richard P. Usatine, MD.

### Phymatous
Thickening of skin with sebaceous hyperplasia

Reproduced with permission from Usatine RP, Smith MA, Mayeaux EJ, Chumley HS: The Color Atlas and Synopsis of Family Medicine, 3rd ed. New York, NY: McGraw Hill; 2019. Photo contributor: Paul D. Comeau.

### Ocular
Conjunctivitis, blepharitis, hyperemia

## Diagnosis

Clinical diagnosis

rosacea

Reproduced with permission from Usatine RP, Smith MA, Mayeaux EJ, Chumley HS: The Color Atlas and Synopsis of Family Medicine, 3rd ed. New York, NY: McGraw Hill; 2019. Photo contributor: Richard P. Usatine, MD.

Reproduced with permission from Kelly AP, Taylor SC, Lom HW, et al: Taylor and Kelly's Dermatology for Skin of Color, 2nd ed. New York, NY: McGraw Hill; 2016.

Look for comedones to distinguish from acne!

## Treatment

Avoid triggers!

Topical Tx: Metronidazole, azelaic acid, erythromycin, calcineurin inhibitors
Systemic Tx: Tetracycline antibiotics, metronidazole

# Scabies

 Intensely pruritic    ● Extremely contagious

## The Human Itch Mite (*Sarcoptes scabiei* var. *hominis*)

- 8-legged parasite <0.5 mm in size
- Transmitted through person-to-person contact
- 10-20 mites in a typical infection, but in institutionalized patients or the immunocompromised, the mite burden can be >1000

## Diagnosis

- History: Intense itch, worse at night
- Physical exam: Burrows and erythematous papules along flexor wrists, around axilla, in interdigital web spaces, and in genitals
- Secondary lesions: Excoriations, crusting, and prurigo-like nodules
- Scabies prep: Visualize mites and eggs under microscopy. Negative prep does not rule out scabies!
- Important to check family members and caretakers

## Management

- Treat all family and close contacts
- Wash bed linen, clothing, and towels with hot water and dry on high heat
- Topical permethrin cream or oral ivermectin
- Extended treatment for crusted scabies

# Seborrheic Keratosis

## Benign Epidermal Growth Found in Older Adults

### Pathophysiology

Most are sporadic, though may have some genetic predisposition

### Epidemiology

Most common **benign epithelial tumor** of the skin. Usually found in older adults.

###  Histology

Acanthosis (thickening of epidermis), pseudo-horn cysts (keratotic invaginations), papillomatosis, and hyperkeratosis

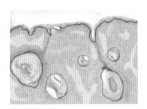

**i** **Leser-Trélat sign:** Multiple eruptive seborrheic keratosis may signify internal malignancy. Most common: GI malignancy and lymphoproliferative disease.

## Clinical Features

Verrucous, **stuck-on tan-brown papules** and plaques

Inflamed seborrheic keratosis with erythema

↓

On dermoscopy, you will see:
**horn cysts** and comedo-like openings

Comedo-like opening  Horn cysts

###  Differential Diagnosis

- Melanoma
- Solar lentigo
- Wart
- Lichen planus-like keratosis

 Biopsy rapidly changing, symptomatic, or atypical lesions to rule out malignancy!

## Management

Usually no treatment required, but if the lesion is cosmetically bothersome or irritated, can be treated with:

 Cryotherapy

 Shave biopsy

# Stevens–Johnson Syndrome (SJS)

## Etiology

- **Life-threatening** full-thickness epidermal necrosis and widespread keratinocyte apoptosis
- Mainly **induced by medications** within the first 8 weeks of treatment
- May be triggered by viral or bacterial **infections**

## Prodrome

**−1d**
- Fever, malaise, headache, rhinorrhea, odynophagia, dysuria, burning of the eyes
- 1-3 days prior to eruption

## Cutaneous Lesions

**Mucosal involvement occurs in >90% of cases**

- **Less than 10% of body surface area**
- Symmetric, proximal > distal involvement

Atypical target lesions
Reproduced with permission from Kang S, Amagai M, Bruckner AL, et al: Fitzpatrick's Dermatology, 9th ed. New York, NY: McGraw Hill; 2019.

Dusky, Nikolsky + bullae
Reproduced with permission from Kang S, Amagai M, Bruckner AL, et al: Fitzpatrick's Dermatology, 9th ed. New York, NY: McGraw Hill; 2019.

Erosions
Reproduced with permission from Kang S, Amagai M, Bruckner AL, et al: Fitzpatrick's Dermatology, 9th ed. New York, NY: McGraw Hill; 2019.

Reproduced with permission from Jameson J, Fauci AS, Kasper DL, et al: Harrison's Principles of Internal Medicine, 20th ed. New York, NY: McGraw Hill; 2018.

Reproduced with permission from Lueder G: Pediatric Practice Ophthalmology. New York, NY: McGraw Hill; 2011.

Mucosal lesions may be:
1. Oral (>90%)
2. Ocular (>80%)
3. Urogenital
4. Respiratory
5. Gastrointestinal

Reproduced with permission from Jameson J, Fauci AS, Kasper DL, et al: Harrison's Principles of Internal Medicine, 20th ed. New York, NY: McGraw Hill; 2018.

## Treatment

- **Identify and remove offending agent as early as possible**
- Admission for supportive care, often in a burn or critical care unit
- Long-term ocular and urogenital follow-up
- Avoidance of similar medication agents in future

# Tinea Capitis
Superficial Dermatophyte Infection of the Scalp

## Etiology

Caused by dermatophytes. In the United States, the most common dermatophyte is *Trichophyton tonsurans*.

## Population

Most common in pre-pubertal children. Tinea capitis is infectious.

## Clinical Features

 Occipital lymphadenopathy and pruritus are common!

Reproduced with permission from Shah S, Ratner AD, Kemper AR: Pediatric Infectious Diseases: Essentials for Practice, 2nd ed. New York, NY: McGraw Hill; 2019.

Reproduced with permission from Hamm RL: Text and Atlas of Wound Diagnosis and Treatment, 2nd ed. New York, NY: McGraw Hill; 2019.

Reproduced with permission from Kang S, Amagai M, Bruckner AL, et al: Fitzpatrick's Dermatology, 9th ed. New York, NY: McGraw Hill; 2019.

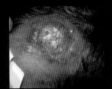

Reproduced with permission from Prose NS, Kristal L: Weinberg's Color Atlas of Pediatric Dermatology, 5th ed. New York, NY: McGraw Hill; 2017.

"Gray-patch" type: Hyperkeratotic plaque of alopecia with broken hair shafts

Black dots from broken hairs; +/− dandruff-like scale

Inflammatory pustules

Kerion = boggy plaque with pustules

## Diagnosis

Scalp fungal culture reveals hyphae. *Microsporum* infections will fluoresce under Wood's lamp.

 DDx: Alopecia areata, seborrheic dermatitis, psoriasis, bacterial infection

Reproduced with permission from Usatine RP, Smith MA, Mayeaux EJ, Chumley HS: The Color Atlas and Synopsis of Family Medicine, 3rd ed. New York, NY: McGraw Hill; 2019. Photo contributor: Richard P. Usatine, MD.

## Management

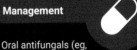

Oral antifungals (eg, griseofulvin, terbinafine)

 Topical treatments alone aren't recommended, but **ketoconazole or selenium sulfide shampoo** can be used in conjunction with oral therapy.

# Tinea Corporis

## Superficial Dermatophyte Infection of the Body

### Etiology

Caused by dermatophytes (eg, *Trichophyton rubrum* and *Microsporum canis*) of glabrous skin (except palms, soles, and groin). Transferred directly by contact; can also transmit by autoinoculation.

### Population

Common in active people (eg, wrestlers), hot and humid conditions, and crowded communities

### Clinical Features

Neck and back are most common locations

Annular plaque with scaly, active border and central clearing

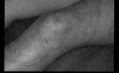
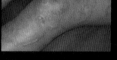

Tinea corporis affecting legs

**Majocchi granuloma:** Deep infection of dermal aspect of hair follicle

Often itchy and spreads outwards

### Diagnosis

KOH exam of active border shows branched septate hyphae. Can also do fungal culture of tissue.

DDx: Erythema annulare centrifugum, nummular eczema, psoriasis, subacute cutaneous lupus erythematosus

### Management

For isolated plaques, use topical antifungals (eg, clotrimazole)

For more widespread or inflammatory lesions, use oral antifungals (eg, griseofulvin)

Do not treat with topical steroids alone as that will make the infection worse!

# Tinea Cruris

Superficial Dermatophyte Infection of the Groin; "Jock Itch"

## Etiology

Caused by dermatophytes (*Trichophyton rubrum* is the most common) of the groin. Transferred by contact or fomites; can also transmit by autoinoculation from tinea pedis or onychomycosis.

## Population

More common in men than women; obesity and diabetes mellitus may be risk factors

## Clinical Features

Usually spares scrotum

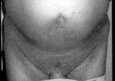

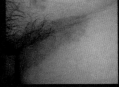

Sharp margins and active, spreading periphery

Postinflammatory hyperpigmentation from tinea cruris

Follicular pustules may be present

 Often itchy and spreads outward; can be recurrent

## Diagnosis

KOH exam of active border shows branched septate hyphae. Can also do fungal culture of tissue.

## Management

Drying powders and topical antifungals (eg, terbinafine cream)

 DDx: Candidiasis, seborrheic dermatitis, intertrigo, inverse psoriasis, and erythrasma

 For more widespread or failed topical treatment, use oral antifungals (eg, oral terbinafine)

# Tinea Pedis/Manuum

Superficial Dermatophyte Infection of the Palms and Soles ("Athlete's Foot")

### Etiology

Caused by **dermatophytes** (*Trichophyton rubrum* is the most common) of the palms and soles. Transferred by contact or fomites; can also transmit by autoinoculation.

### Risk Factors

**Tinea pedis:** Occlusive footwear; communal baths/pools
**Tinea manuum:** Transmitted by direct contact; typically one hand affected (from touching feet)

### Clinical Features

Itching, burning, stinging or may be asymptomatic

**Interdigital type:** Maceration with opaque white scale

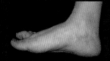

**Moccasin-Type:** Patchy erythema and scaling in moccasin distribution

**Vesiculobullous type:** Bullae or vesicles on soles

**"Two feet, one hand"** presentation (both feet, only one hand, are affected). On hand, there is dry scaling accentuated in creases.

Tinea pedis creates entry point for bacteria so it is the most common risk factor for lower extremity cellulitis in healthy individuals

### Diagnosis

KOH exam shows branched septate hyphae. Can also do fungal culture of tissue.

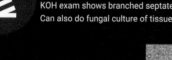

DDx: Psoriasis, contact dermatitis, pompholyx, scabies, candidiasis

### Management

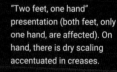

Drying powders and topical antifungals (eg, clotrimazole)

Bullous tinea pedis may not respond to topicals. Can use oral antifungals (eg, terbinafine)

Prognosis: Usually recurrent

# Tinea Versicolor

Superficial Skin Infection Caused by *Malassezia*

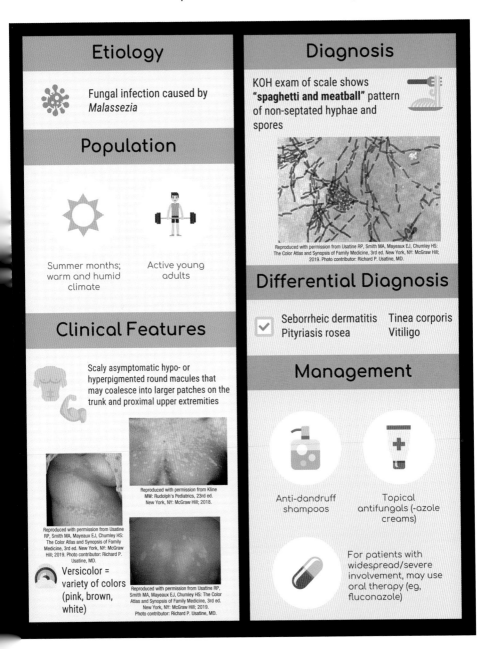

## Etiology

Fungal infection caused by *Malassezia*

## Population

Summer months; warm and humid climate

Active young adults

## Clinical Features

Scaly asymptomatic hypo- or hyperpigmented round macules that may coalesce into larger patches on the trunk and proximal upper extremities

Reproduced with permission from Kline MW: Rudolph's Pediatrics, 23rd ed. New York, NY: McGraw Hill; 2018.

Reproduced with permission from Usatine RP, Smith MA, Mayeaux EJ, Chumley HS: The Color Atlas and Synopsis of Family Medicine, 3rd ed. New York, NY: McGraw Hill; 2019. Photo contributor: Richard P. Usatine, MD.

Versicolor = variety of colors (pink, brown, white)

Reproduced with permission from Usatine RP, Smith MA, Mayeaux EJ, Chumley HS: The Color Atlas and Synopsis of Family Medicine, 3rd ed. New York, NY: McGraw Hill; 2019. Photo contributor: Richard P. Usatine, MD.

## Diagnosis

KOH exam of scale shows **"spaghetti and meatball"** pattern of non-septated hyphae and spores

Reproduced with permission from Usatine RP, Smith MA, Mayeaux EJ, Chumley HS: The Color Atlas and Synopsis of Family Medicine, 3rd ed. New York, NY: McGraw Hill; 2019. Photo contributor: Richard P. Usatine, MD.

## Differential Diagnosis

☑ Seborrheic dermatitis   Tinea corporis
Pityriasis rosea   Vitiligo

## Management

Anti-dandruff shampoos

Topical antifungals (-azole creams)

For patients with widespread/severe involvement, may use oral therapy (eg, fluconazole)

# Toxic Epidermal Necrolysis (TEN)

## Etiology

- TEN is a **more severe and life-threatening** form of Stevens–Johnson syndrome (SJS)
- Mainly **induced by medications**

## Symptoms

- Prodrome 1-3 days prior to eruption, similar to SJS
- Systemic symptoms are common

## Complications

- High risk of secondary infection and sepsis

- Genital adhesions
- Gastrointestinal strictures
- Nail dystrophy

- Corneal ulcerations

**TEN has a 25-35% mortality rate**

## Cutaneous and Mucosal Lesions

- **At least 30% of body surface area** (SJS/TEN overlap involves 10-30% of the body surface area)
- Large coalesced bullae and erosions with sloughing of skin and mucosal involvement

Reproduced with permission from Tintinalli J, Ma O, Yealy DM, et al: Tintinalli's Emergency Medicine: A Comprehensive Study Guide. 9th ed. New York, NY: McGraw Hill; 2020.

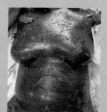

Reproduced with permission from Jameson J, Fauci AS, Kasper DL, et al: Harrison's Principles of Internal Medicine, 20th ed. New York, NY: McGraw Hill; 2018.

## Treatment

- **Identify and remove offending agent as early as possible**
- Admission for supportive care to a burn or critical care unit
- Treatment of complications and long-term ocular and urogenital follow-up

# Type 1 Hypersensitivity Reaction
## Allergic / Immediate Hypersensitivity

**1** Allergic  **2** Cytotoxic  **3** Immune Complex  **4** Delayed

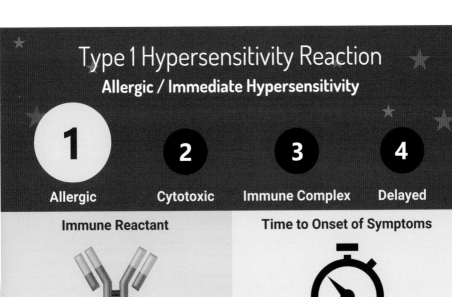

### Immune Reactant

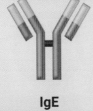

IgE

### Time to Onset of Symptoms

2-30 minutes

**Pathophysiology**

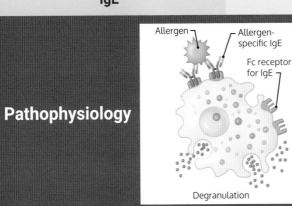

Allergen — Allergen-specific IgE

Fc receptor for IgE

Degranulation

Antigen induces cross-linkage of IgE bound to mast cells, leading to degranulation and release of vasoactive mediators

## Examples:

Asthma

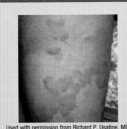

Used with permission from Richard P. Usatine, MD.

Urticaria/Hives

Food Allergies

# Type 2 Hypersensitivity Reaction
## Cytotoxic / Antibody–Mediated Hypersensitivity

**1** Allergic  **2** Cytotoxic  **3** Immune Complex  **4** Delayed

## Immune Reactant

J chain

**IgG or IgM**

## Time to Onset of Symptoms

**5-8 hours**

## Pathophysiology

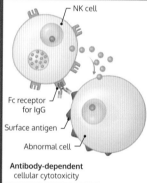

NK cell

Fc receptor for IgG

Surface antigen

Abnormal cell

**Antibody-dependent** cellular cytotoxicity

Antibody directed against cell surface antigens mediate cell destruction

## Examples:

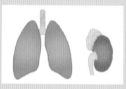

Reproduced with permission from Usatine RP, Smith MA, Mayeaux EJ, Chumley HS: The Color Atlas and Synopsis of Family Medicine, 3rd ed. New York, NY: McGraw Hill; 2019. Photo contributor: Richard P. Usatine, MD.

Reproduced with permission from Tintinalli J, Ma O, Yealy DM, et al: Tintinalli's Emergency Medicine: A Comprehensive Study Guide. 9th ed. New York, NY: McGraw Hill; 2020.

**Hemolytic Reactions**  **Goodpasture's Syndrome**  **Bullous Pemphigoid**  **Pemphigus Vulgaris**

# Type 3 Hypersensitivity Reaction

## Immune Complex Hypersensitivity

**1** Allergic   **2** Cytotoxic   **3** Immune Complex   **4** Delayed

### Immune Reactant

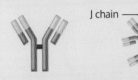

J chain

**IgG or IgM**

### Time to Onset of Symptoms

**2-8 hours**

### Pathophysiology

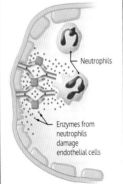

Neutrophils

Enzymes from neutrophils damage endothelial cells

Antigen–antibody complexes deposit in tissue and induce complement activation

## Examples:

Reproduced with permission from Prose NS, Kristal L: Weinberg's Color Atlas of Pediatric Dermatology, 5th ed. New York, NY: McGraw Hill; 2017.

**Systemic Lupus Erythematosus**

Reproduced with permission from Wolff K, Johnson RA, Saavedra AP, et al: Fitzpatrick's Color Atlas and Synopsis of Clinical Dermatology, 8th ed. New York, NY: McGraw Hill; 2017.

**Polyarteritis Nodosa**

Reproduced with permission from Stern S, Cifu AS, Altkorn D: Symptom to Diagnosis: An Evidence-Based Guide, 4th ed. New York, NY: McGraw Hill; 2020.

**Rheumatoid Arthritis**

Reproduced with permission from Kaushansky K, Lichtman MA, Prhal JT, et al: Williams Hematology, 9th ed. New York, NY: McGraw Hill; 2015.

**Serum Sickness**

# Type 4 Hypersensitivity Reaction
## Delayed / Cell-Mediated Hypersensitivity

**1** Allergic **2** Cytotoxic **3** Immune Complex **4** Delayed

| Immune Reactant | Time to Onset of Symptoms |
|---|---|
| **Th1** | |
| T cells | 24-72 hours |

**Pathophysiology**

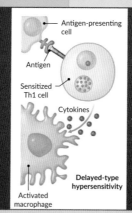

Antigen-presenting cell

Antigen

Sensitized Th1 cell

Cytokines

Delayed-type hypersensitivity

Activated macrophage

Sensitized T cells release cytokines that activate macrophages and cytotoxic T cells to mediate direct cell damage

## Examples:

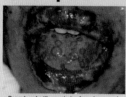

**Stevens–Johnson Syndrome**

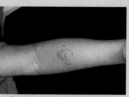

**PPD Test**

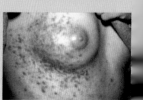

**Contact Dermatitis**

# Urticaria (Hives)

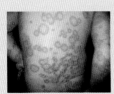

Reproduced with permission from Kane KS, Nambudiri VE, Stratigos AJ: Color Atlas & Synopsis of Pediatric Dermatology, 3rd ed. New York, NY: McGraw Hill; 2017.

- [ ] Well-circumscribed, erythematous, edematous papules or plaques

- [ ] Blanching with pressure

- [ ] May be annular, serpiginous, or irregularly shaped

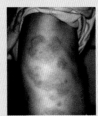

Reproduced with permission from Usatine RP, Sabella C, Smith MA, et al: The Color Atlas of Pediatrics. New York, NY: McGraw Hill; 2015. Photo contributor: Richard P. Usatine, MD.

## • Inciting Factors •

**Infection**

**Drugs**

**Food**

**Inducible stimuli**
(mechanical, temperature, solar)

## • Diagnostic Approach •

**Review of systems**

**Review of medications**

**Review of inducible triggers**

 If individual lesions persist for >24 hours, consider a biopsy to exclude urticarial vasculitis.

## • Management Options •

**H1 antagonist**
(antihistamines)

**Corticosteroids**
(for severe cases)

**Omalizumab**
(decreases IgE; for chronic urticaria)

 **Eliminate any triggers and counsel patients on trigger avoidance.**
**Look for signs of anaphylaxis! Immediately secure the airway if anaphylaxis is suspected.**

# Varicella-Zoster Virus (VZV)

**Primary infection causes varicella (chickenpox)**

VZV establishes **latency in the dorsal root ganglia**

VZV can **reactivate** due to stress, infection, medications, or immunosuppression

Reactivation causes **herpes zoster (shingles)**

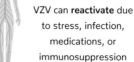

## Varicella (Chickenpox)

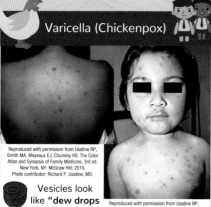

Reproduced with permission from Usatine RP, Smith MA, Mayeaux EJ, Chumley HS: The Color Atlas and Synopsis of Family Medicine, 3rd ed. New York, NY: McGraw Hill; 2019. Photo contributor: Richard P. Usatine, MD.

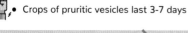

Vesicles look like **"dew drops on a rose petal"**

Reproduced with permission from Usatine RP, Smith MA, Mayeaux EJ, Chumley HS: The Color Atlas and Synopsis of Family Medicine, 3rd ed. New York, NY: McGraw Hill; 2019. Photo contributor: Richard P. Usatine, MD.

- Spread by respiratory droplets
- Fever and malaise (prodrome)
- Crops of pruritic vesicles last 3-7 days

## Herpes Zoster (Shingles)

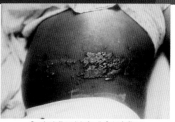

Reproduced with permission from the Centers for Disease Control and Prevention, Public Health Image Library.

- Pain along a dermatome (prodrome)
- Grouped vesicles
- Unilateral, typically on the trunk or face

Reproduced with permission from Riordan-Eva P, Augsburger JJ: Vaughan & Asbury's General Ophthalmology, 19th ed. New York, NY: McGraw Hill; 2018.

**Herpes zoster ophthalmicus (V1)**

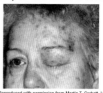

Reproduced with permission from Martin T, Corbett J: Practical Neuroophthalmology. New York, NY: McGraw Hill; 2013.

**Herpes zoster oticus (Ramsay–Hunt syndrome)**

**Disseminated zoster** (immunocompromised patients)

Reproduced with permission from Kang S, Amagai M, Bruckner AL, et al: Fitzpatrick's Dermatology, 9th ed. New York, NY: McGraw Hill; 2019.

## Prevention

- Immunity with prior infection or vaccine during childhood
- Post-exposure prophylaxis with vaccine if immunocompetent or with immunoglobulin if immunocompromised
- Zoster vaccine for adults age 50+

# Verrucae (Warts)

Verruca Vulgaris = Common Wart
Verruca Plana = Flat Wart
Verruca Pedis = Plantar Wart

## Basic Facts

### Appearance

- Hyperkeratotic
- Skin-colored papules
- Rough and irregular surface

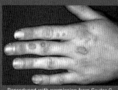

Reproduced with permission from Soutor C, Hordinsky MK: Clinical Dermatology. New York, NY: McGraw Hill; 2013.

### Etiology

- Caused by HPV 2 and 4
- Most often on hands & feet
- Most common in the immunocompromised or school-aged children

### Spread

- Spread by direct and indirect contact
- Auto-inoculation common

## Diagnosis and Management

### Clinical diagnosis!

Look for tiny black or red dots within the lesion, representing thrombosed capillaries

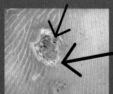

Look for interruption in normal skin lines (dermatoglyphics)

Reproduced with permission from Usatine RP, Smith MA, Mayeaux EJ, Chumley HS: The Color Atlas and Synopsis of Family Medicine, 3rd ed. New York, NY: McGraw Hill; 2019. Photo contributor: Richard P. Usatine, MD.

### Management

1. Benign and usually self-limited: Reasonable to not treat!
2. Destructive therapy (eg, salicylic acid)
3. Cryotherapy (liquid nitrogen)
4. Topical medications (eg, 5-fluorouracil, imiquimod)
5. Intralesional therapy (eg, *Candida* antigen, bleomycin)

 Lesions resistant to therapy should be biopsied to rule out squamous cell carcinoma!

# Vitiligo

A Condition Characterized by Melanocyte Destruction and Flat Depigmented Lesions

## Pathophysiology:

Hypothesized causes of **melanocyte destruction** include:

1. Autoimmune attack on normal melanocytes

2. Intrinsic melanocyte defects

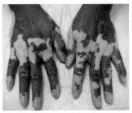

## Clinical Presentation:

- Well-circumscribed **depigmented** macules coalescing into confluent patches

- Location: Commonly **symmetric** and **periorificial** (ie, surrounding mouth, eyes, etc.). Predilection for sites of trauma/friction

- Patterns: 1. Localized, 2. Generalized, 3. Universal

- Patients are **asymptomatic**, though quality of life may be significantly affected

- No increased incidence by age, gender, or ethnicity

**Clinical Pearl**

Look for a **halo nevus**, a benign melanocytic nevus with a surrounding rim of depigmentation. A halo nevus can be a marker of vitiligo.

## Diagnosis:

- Clinical diagnosis based on appearance of depigmentation and absence of elevated lesions

- **Wood's lamp** uses UV light to confirm milk-white depigmentation, rather than hypopigmentation

- Skin biopsy will show **absence of melanocytes**

- Check for signs of autoimmune disease in workup: Thyroid disease, Addison's, diabetes (ie, TSH, TPO antibody, ANA, fasting blood glucose)

## Management:

- Topical calcineurin inhibitors (eg, tacrolimus) for local disease

- **Narrowband UVB phototherapy** for widespread disease

- Combination therapy of topical and oral steroids plus phototherapy may be indicated

- Sun protection

- Psychosocial support

Repigmentation after treatment may be **perifollicular**

# References _____

**Acanthosis Nigricans**

Bolognia J, Schaffer J, Duncan K, Ko C, eds. *Dermatology Essentials*. Philadelphia, PA: Saunders/Elsevier; 2014.

Cheng K, Burgin S, Tan B. Acanthosis nigricans in adult. VisualDx. https://www.visualdx.com/visualdx/diagnosis/acanthosis+nigricans?diagnosisId=51010&moduleId=101

**Acne Vulgaris**

Bolognia J, Schaffer J, Duncan K, Ko C, eds. *Dermatology Essentials*. Saunders/Elsevier; 2014.

Elbuluk N, David J, Barbosa V, Taylor SC. Acne vulgaris. In: Kelly A, Taylor SC, Lim HW, Serrano A, eds. *Taylor and Kelly's Dermatology for Skin of Color*. 2nd ed. New York, NY: McGraw-Hill; 2016.

Marks JG, Miller JJ. *Lookingbill and Marks' Principles of Dermatology*. 4th ed. Saunders/Elsevier; 2006.

**Actinic Keratosis**

Lee PK. Actinic keratosis, basal, and squamous cell carcinoma. In: Soutor C, Hordinsky MK, eds. *Clinical Dermatology*. New York, NY: McGraw Hill; 2017. http://accessmedicine.mhmedical.com/content.aspx?bookid=2184&sectionid=165460313. Accessed April 03, 2019.

**Alopecia Areata**

Messenger AG. Alopecia areata: Cclinical manifestations and diagnosis. *Uptodate*. https://www.uptodate.com/contents/alopecia-areata-clinical-manifestations-and-diagnosis?search=alopecia+areata&source=search_result&selectedTitle=2~61&usage_type=default&display_rank=2. Accessed August 26, 2019.

**Benign Nevi**

Kang S, Amagai M, Bruckner AL, et al, eds. *Fitzpatrick's Dermatology*. 9th ed. New York, NY: McGraw Hill; 2019.

Usatine RP, Smith MA, Mayeaux EJ Jr, Chumley HS, eds. *The Color Atlas and Synopsis of Family Medicine*. 3rd ed. New York, NY: McGraw Hill; 2019.

Wolff K, Johnson R, Saavedra AP, Roh EK, eds. *Fitzpatrick's Color Atlas and Synopsis of Clinical Dermatology*. 8th ed. New York, NY: McGraw Hill; 2017.

**Bullous Impetigo**

Goldsmith LA, Katz SI, Gilchrest BA, Paller AS, Leffell DJ, Wolff K, eds. *Fitzpatrick's Dermatology in General Medicine*. 8th ed. New York, NY: McGraw Hill; 2012.

Hay WW Jr, Levin MJ, Deterding RR, Abzug MJ, eds. *Current Diagnosis & Treatment: Pediatrics*. 24th ed. New York, NY: McGraw Hill; 2018.

Kang S, Amagai M, Bruckner AL, et al, eds. *Fitzpatrick's Dermatology*. 9th ed. New York, NY: McGraw Hill; 2019.

Papadakis MA, McPhee SJ, Rabow MW, eds. *Current Medical Diagnosis & Treatment 2019*. New York, NY: McGraw Hill; 2019.

Stern SC, Cifu AS, Altkorn D, eds. *Symptom to Diagnosis: An Evidence-Based Guide*. 3rd ed. New York, NY: McGraw Hill; 2014.

Tintinalli JE, Stapczynski J, Ma O, Yealy DM, Meckler GD, Cline DM, eds. *Tintinalli's Emergency Medicine: A Comprehensive Study Guide*. 8th ed. New York, NY: McGraw Hill; 2016.

**Bullous Pemphigoid**

Leiferman KM. Clinical features and diagnosis of bullous pemphigoid and mucous membrane pemphigoid. *Uptodate*. https://www.uptodate.com/contents/clinical-features-and-diagnosis-of-bullous-pemphigoid-and-mucous-membrane-pemphigoid?search=bullous+pemphigoid&source=search_result&selectedTitle=2~130&usage_type=default&display_rank=2. Accessed August 26, 2019.

**95**

## Candidiasis

Jameson JL, Fauci AS, Kasper DL, Hauser SL, Longo DL, Loscalzo J, eds. *Harrison's Principles of Internal Medicine*. 20th ed. New York, NY: McGraw Hill; 2018.

Kang S, Amagai M, Bruckner AL, et al, eds. *Fitzpatrick's Dermatology*. 9th ed. New York, NY: McGraw Hill; 2019.

Kelly A, Taylor SC, Lim HW, Serrano A, eds. *Taylor and Kelly's Dermatology for Skin of Color*. 2nd ed. New York, NY: McGraw Hill; 2016.

Usatine RP, Smith MA, Chumley HS, Mayeaux EJ Jr, eds. *The Color Atlas of Family Medicine*. 2nd ed. New York, NY: McGraw Hill; 2013.

## Carcinoma, Basal Cell

Chu DH. Development and structure of skin. In: Goldsmith LA, Katz SI, Gilchrest BA, Paller AS, Leffell DJ, Wolff K, eds. *Fitzpatrick's Dermatology in General Medicine*. 8th ed. New York, NY: McGraw Hill; 2012. http://accessmedicine.mhmedical.com/content.aspx?bookid=392&sectionid=41138700. Accessed April 20, 2019.

Kemp WL, Burns DK, Brown TG, eds. Dermatopathology. *Pathology: The Big Picture*. New York, NY: McGraw Hill; 2008. http://accessmedicine.mhmedical.com/content.aspx?bookid=499&sectionid=41568303. Accessed April 20, 2019.

Lee PK. Actinic keratosis, basal, and squamous cell carcinoma. In: Soutor C, Hordinsky MK, eds. *Clinical Dermatology*. New York, NY: McGraw Hill; 2017. http://accessmedicine.mhmedical.com/content.aspx?bookid=2184&sectionid=165460313. Accessed April 03, 2019.

## Carcinoma, Squamous cell

Grossman D, David JL. Squamous cell carcinoma. In: Goldsmith LA, Katz SI, Gilchrest BA, Paller AS, Leffell DJ, Wolff K, eds. *Fitzpatrick's Dermatology in General Medicine*. 8th ed New York, NY: McGraw Hill; 2012. http://accessmedicine.mhmedical.com/content.aspx?bookid=392&sectionid=41138831. Accessed April 22, 2019.

Lee PK. Actinic keratosis, basal, and squamous cell carcinoma. In: Soutor C, Hordinsky MK, eds. *Clinical Dermatology*. New York, NY: McGraw Hill; 2017. http://accessmedicine.mhmedical.com/content.aspx?bookid=2184&sectionid=165460313. Accessed April 22, 2019.

## Cellulitis

Bolognia J, Schaffer J, Duncan K, Ko C, eds. *Dermatology Essentials*. Saunders/Elsevier; 2014.

Nurmohamed S, Burgin S. Cellulitis in adult. VisualDx.

## Cherry Angioma

Kang S, Amagai M, Bruckner AL, et al, eds. *Fitzpatrick's Dermatology*. 9th ed. New York, NY: McGraw-Hill; 2019

Usatine RP, Smith MA, Chumley HS, Mayeaux EJ Jr, eds. *The Color Atlas of Family Medicine*. 2nd ed. New York, NY: McGraw Hill; 2013.

Wolff K, Johnson R, Saavedra AP, Roh EK, eds. *Fitzpatrick's Color Atlas and Synopsis of Clinical Dermatology*. 8th ed. New York, NY: McGraw Hill; 2017.

## Dermatitis, Atopic

Elenitsas R, Chu EY. Pathology of skin lesions. In: Kang S, Amagai M, Bruckner AL, et al, eds. *Fitzpatrick's Dermatology*. 9th ed. New York, NY: McGraw Hill; 2019. http://accessmedicine.mhmedical.com/content.aspx bookid=2570&sectionid=210415075. Accessed April 03, 2019.

Leung DM, Eichenfield LF, Boguniewicz M. Atopic dermatitis (atopic eczema). In: Goldsmith LA, Katz SI, Gilchrest BA, Paller AS, Leffell DJ, Wolff K, eds. *Fitzpatrick's Dermatology in General Medicine*. 8th ed. New York NY: McGraw Hill; 2012. http://accessmedicine.mhmedical.com/content.aspx?bookid=392&sectionid=41138709. Accessed April 03, 2019.

Simpson EL, Leung DM, Eichenfield LF, Boguniewicz M. Atopic dermatitis. In: Kang S, Amagai M, Bruckner A et al, eds. *Fitzpatrick's Dermatology*. 9th ed. New York, NY: McGraw Hill; 2019. http://accessmedicine.mhmedical.com/content.aspx?bookid=2570&sectionid=210417027. Accessed April 03, 2019.

**Dermatitis, Allergic Contact**
Le T, Bhushan V, Sochat Matthew, C et al. *First Aid for the USMLE Step 1 2019*. 29th ed. New York, NY: McGraw Hill, 2019.

Wolff K, Johnson R, Saavedra AP, Roh EK, eds. *Fitzpatrick's Color Atlas and Synopsis of Clinical Dermatology*. 8th ed. New York, NY: McGraw Hill; 2017.

**Dermatitis, Irritant Contact**
Kang S, Amagai M, Bruckner AL, et al, eds. *Fitzpatrick's Dermatology*. 9th ed. New York, NY: McGraw-Hill; 2019.

Wolff K, Johnson R, Saavedra AP, Roh EK, eds. *Fitzpatrick's Color Atlas and Synopsis of Clinical Dermatology*. 8th ed. New York, NY: McGraw Hill; 2017.

**Dermatitis, Seborrheic**
Jameson JL, Fauci AS, Kasper DL, Hauser SL, Longo DL, Loscalzo J, eds. *Harrison's Principles of Internal Medicine*. 20th ed. New York, NY: McGraw Hill; 2018.

Kang S, Amagai M, Bruckner AL, et al, eds. *Fitzpatrick's Dermatology*. 9th ed. New York, NY: McGraw Hill; 2019.

Kelly A, Taylor SC, Lim HW, Serrano A, eds. *Taylor and Kelly's Dermatology for Skin of Color*. 2nd ed. New York, NY: McGraw-Hill; 2016.

**Dermatitis, Stasis**
Jameson JL, Fauci AS, Kasper DL, Hauser SL, Longo DL, Loscalzo J, eds. *Harrison's Principles of Internal Medicine*. 20th ed. New York, NY: McGraw Hill; 2018.

Kang S, Amagai M, Bruckner AL, et al, eds. *Fitzpatrick's Dermatology*. 9th ed. New York, NY: McGraw Hill; 2019.

Knoop KJ, Stack LB, Storrow AB, Thurman R, eds. *The Atlas of Emergency Medicine*. 4th ed. New York, NY: McGraw Hill; 2016.

Papadakis MA, McPhee SJ, Rabow MW, eds. *Current Medical Diagnosis & Treatment 2019*. New York, NY: McGraw Hill; 2019.

Soutor C, Hordinsky MK, eds. *Clinical Dermatology*. New York, NY: McGraw Hill; 2017.

**Dermatomyositis**
Gaulding J, Owen CE, Callen JP. Internal malignancy. In: Kelly A, Taylor SC, Lim HW, Serrano A, eds. *Taylor and Kelly's Dermatology for Skin of Color*. 2nd ed. New York, NY: McGraw Hill; 2016. http://accessmedicine mhmedical.com/content.aspx?bookid=2585&sectionid=211768534. Accessed April 20, 2019.

Lewis M, Fiorentino D. Dermatomyositis. In: Kang S, Amagai M, Bruckner AL, et al, eds. *Fitzpatrick's Dermatology*. 9th ed. New York, NY: McGraw Hill; 2019. http://accessmedicine.mhmedical.com/content.aspx?bookid=2570&sectionid=210426360. Accessed April 03, 2019.

Usatine RP, Smith MA, Chumley HS, Mayeaux EJ Jr, eds. Dermatomyositis. *The Color Atlas of Family Medicine*. 2nd ed. New York, NY: McGraw Hill; 2013:chap 181. http://accessmedicine.mhmedical.com/content.aspx?bookid=685&sectionid=45361250. Accessed April 20, 2019.

**Discoid Lupus Erythematosus (DLE)**
Denyk J. Skin signs of systemic disease. In: Soutor C, Hordinsky MK, eds. *Clinical Dermatology*. New York, NY: McGraw Hill; 2017.

Wong V, Rashighi M, Tan B, Burgin S. Discoid lupus erythematosus. VisualDx. https://www.visualdx.com/visualdx/diagnosis/discoid+lupus+erythematosus?diagnosisId=51882&moduleId=101

**Drug Eruptions**
Wilson R, Allred A, Smith MA, Usatine RP. Cutaneous drug reactions. In: Usatine RP, Smith MA, Mayeaux EJ Jr, Chumley HS, eds. *The Color Atlas and Synopsis of Family Medicine*. 3rd ed. New York, NY: McGraw Hill; 2019. http://accessmedicine.mhmedical.com/content.aspx?bookid=2547&sectionid=206781337. Accessed June 21, 2019.

Heelan K, Sibbald C, Shear NH. Cutaneous reactions to drugs. In: Kang S, Amagai M, Bruckner AL, et al, eds. *Fitzpatrick's Dermatology*. 9th ed. New York, NY: McGraw Hill; 2019. http://accessmedicine.mhmedical.com/content.aspx?bookid=2570&sectionid=210424280. Accessed June 21, 2019.

Ogunleye TA. Drug eruptions. In: Kelly A, Taylor SC, Lim HW, Serrano A, eds. *Taylor and Kelly's Dermatology for Skin of Color*. 2nd ed. New York, NY: McGraw Hill; 2016. http://accessmedicine.mhmedical.com/content.aspx?bookid=2585&sectionid=211765415. Accessed June 21, 2019.

**Erythema Multiforme**
Roujeau J, Mockenhaupt M. Erythema multiforme. In: Kang S, Amagai M, Bruckner AL, et al, eds. *Fitzpatrick's Dermatology*. 9th ed. New York, NY: McGraw-Hill; 2019. http://accessmedicine.mhmedical.com/content.aspx?bookid=2570&sectionid=210424093. Accessed April 03, 2019.

**Erythema Nodosum**
Hammer GD, McPhee SJ, eds. *Pathophysiology of Disease: An Introduction to Clinical Medicine*. 8th ed. New York, NY: McGraw Hill; 2019.

Kang S, Amagai M, Bruckner AL, et al, eds. *Fitzpatrick's Dermatology*. 9th ed. New York, NY: McGraw-Hill; 2019.

Knoop KJ, Stack LB, Storrow AB, Thurman R, eds. *The Atlas of Emergency Medicine*. 4th ed. New York, NY: McGraw Hill; 2016.

Papadakis MA, McPhee SJ, Rabow MW, eds. *Current Medical Diagnosis & Treatment 2019*. New York, NY: McGraw Hill; 2019.

Usatine RP, Smith MA, Chumley HS, Mayeaux EJ Jr, eds. *The Color Atlas of Family Medicine*. 2nd ed. New York, NY: McGraw Hill; 2013.

**Eyelid Lesions**
Jameson JL, Fauci AS, Kasper DL, Hauser SL, Longo DL, Loscalzo J, eds. *Harrison's Principles of Internal Medicine*. 20th ed. New York, NY: McGraw Hill; 2018.

Papadakis MA, McPhee SJ, Rabow MW, eds. *Current Medical Diagnosis and Treatment 2020*. 59th ed. New York, NY: McGraw Hill; 2016.

Riordan-Eva P, Augsburger JJ, eds. *Vaughan & Asbury's General Ophthalmology*. 19th ed. New York, NY: McGraw Hill; 2017.

Usatine RP, Smith MA, Mayeaux EJ Jr, Chumley HS, eds. *The Color Atlas and Synopsis of Family Medicine*. 3rd ed. New York, NY: McGraw Hill; 2019.

**Folliculitis**
Hammer GD, McPhee SJ, eds. *Pathophysiology of Disease: An Introduction to Clinical Medicine*. 8th ed. New York, NY: McGraw Hill; 2019.

Kang S, Amagai M, Bruckner AL, et al, eds. *Fitzpatrick's Dermatology*. 9th ed. New York, NY: McGraw Hill; 2019

Kelly A, Taylor SC, Lim HW, Serrano A, eds. *Taylor and Kelly's Dermatology for Skin of Color*. 2nd ed. New York, NY: McGraw Hill; 2016.

Usatine RP, Smith MA, Mayeaux EJ Jr, Chumley HS, eds. *The Color Atlas and Synopsis of Family Medicine*. 3rd ed. New York, NY: McGraw Hill; 2019.

**Gangrene**
Hamm RL, ed. *Text and Atlas of Wound Diagnosis and Treatment*. 2nd ed. New York, NY: McGraw Hill; 2019.

Jameson JL, Fauci AS, Kasper DL, Hauser SL, Longo DL, Loscalzo J, eds. *Harrison's Principles of Internal Medicine*. 20th ed. New York, NY: McGraw Hill; 2018.

Kang S, Amagai M, Bruckner AL, et al, eds. *Fitzpatrick's Dermatology*. 9th ed. New York, NY: McGraw Hill; 2019

Knoop KJ, Stack LB, Storrow AB, Thurman R, eds. *The Atlas of Emergency Medicine*. 4th ed. New York, NY: McGraw Hill; 2016.

Usatine RP, Smith MA, Mayeaux EJ Jr, Chumley HS, eds. *The Color Atlas and Synopsis of Family Medicine*. 3rd ed. New York, NY: McGraw Hill; 2019.

## Guttate Psoriasis

Goldsmith LA, Katz SI, Gilchrest BA, Paller AS, Leffell DJ, Wolff K, eds. *Fitzpatrick's Dermatology in General Medicine*. 8th ed. New York, NY: McGraw Hill; 2012.

Jameson JL, Fauci AS, Kasper DL, Hauser SL, Longo DL, Loscalzo J, eds. *Harrison's Principles of Internal Medicine*. 20th ed. New York, NY: McGraw Hill; 2018.

Kang S, Amagai M, Bruckner AL, et al, eds. *Fitzpatrick's Dermatology*. 9th ed. New York, NY: McGraw-Hill; 2019.

Soutor C, Hordinsky MK, eds. *Clinical Dermatology*. New York, NY: McGraw Hill; 2017.

Usatine RP, Smith MA, Chumley HS, Mayeaux EJ Jr, eds. *The Color Atlas of Family Medicine*. 2nd ed. New York, NY: McGraw Hill; 2013.

## Herpes Simplex

Hay WW Jr, Levin MJ, Deterding RR, Abzug MJ, eds. *Current Diagnosis & Treatment: Pediatrics*. 24th ed. New York, NY: McGraw Hill; 2018.

Jameson JL, Fauci AS, Kasper DL, Hauser SL, Longo DL, Loscalzo J, eds. *Harrison's Principles of Internal Medicine*. 20th ed. New York, NY: McGraw Hill; 2018.

Knoop KJ, Stack LB, Storrow AB, Thurman R, eds. *The Atlas of Emergency Medicine*. 4th ed. New York, NY: McGraw Hill; 2016.

Stone C, Humphries RL, eds. *CURRENT Diagnosis & Treatment: Emergency Medicine*. 8th ed. New York, NY: McGraw Hill; 2017.

Tintinalli JE, Stapczynski J, Ma O, Yealy DM, Meckler GD, Cline DM, eds. *Tintinalli's Emergency Medicine: A Comprehensive Study Guide*. 8th ed. New York, NY: McGraw Hill; 2016.

## Impetigo

Jameson JL, Fauci AS, Kasper DL, Hauser SL, Longo DL, Loscalzo J, eds. *Harrison's Principles of Internal Medicine*. 20th ed. New York, NY: McGraw Hill; 2018.

Kang S, Amagai M, Bruckner AL, et al, eds. *Fitzpatrick's Dermatology*. 9th ed. New York, NY: McGraw Hill; 2019.

Kelly A, Taylor SC, Lim HW, Serrano A, eds. *Taylor and Kelly's Dermatology for Skin of Color*. 2nd ed. New York, NY: McGraw Hill; 2016.

Papadakis MA, McPhee SJ, Rabow MW, eds. *Current Medical Diagnosis & Treatment 2019*. New York, NY: McGraw Hill; 2019.

Usatine RP, Smith MA, Chumley HS, Mayeaux EJ Jr, eds. *The Color Atlas of Family Medicine*. 2nd ed. New York, NY: McGraw Hill; 2013.

## Kaposi's Sarcoma

Harbour P, Song DH. The skin and subcutaneous tissue. In: Brunicardi F, Andersen DK, Billiar TR, et al, eds. *Schwartz's Principles of Surgery*. 11th ed. New York, NY: McGraw Hill; 2019. http://accessmedicine.mhmedical.com/content.aspx?bookid=2576&sectionid=216206374. Accessed June 22, 2019.

Lipworth AD, Freeman EE, Saavedra AP. Cutaneous manifestations of HIV and human T-lymphotropic virus. In: Kang S, Amagai M, Bruckner AL, et al, eds. *Fitzpatrick's Dermatology*. 9th ed. New York, NY: McGraw Hill; 2019. http://accessmedicine.mhmedical.com/content.aspx?bookid=2570&sectionid=210439988. Accessed June 22, 2019.

Rios A, Hagemeister FB. The acquired immunodeficiency syndrome–related cancers. In: Kantarjian HM, Wolff RA, eds. *The MD Anderson Manual of Medical Oncology*. 3rd ed. New York, NY: McGraw Hill; 2016. http://accessmedicine.mhmedical.com/content.aspx?bookid=1772&sectionid=121902208. Accessed June 22, 2019.

Shinkai K, Fox LP. Dermatologic disorders. In: Papadakis MA, McPhee SJ, Rabow MW, eds. *Current Medical Diagnosis & Treatment 2019*. New York, NY: McGraw Hill; 2019. http://accessmedicine.mhmedical.com/content.aspx?bookid=2449&sectionid=194431938.

## Lichen Planus

Bolognia J, Schaffer J, Duncan K, Ko C, eds. *Dermatology Essentials*. Saunders/Elsevier; 2014.

Morrell DS, Brooks K. Skin disorders: trunk. In: Tintinalli JE, Stapczynski J, Ma O, Yealy DM, Meckler GD, Cline DM, eds. *Tintinalli's Emergency Medicine: A Comprehensive Study Guide*. 8th ed. New York, NY: McGraw-Hill; 2016.

## Melanoma

Hassel JC, Enk AH. Melanoma. In: Kang S, Amagai M, Bruckner AL, et al, eds. *Fitzpatrick's Dermatology*. 9th ed. New York, NY: McGraw Hill; 2019. http://accessmedicine.mhmedical.com/content.aspx?bookid=2570& sectionid=210435350._Accessed June 22, 2019.

Swanson DL. Nevi and melanoma. In: Soutor C, Hordinsky MK, eds. *Clinical Dermatology*. New York, NY: McGraw Hill; 2017. http://accessmedicine.mhmedical.com/content.aspx?bookid=2184&sectionid= 165460425. Accessed June 22, 2019.

Washington CV, Mishra V, Soon SL. Melanomas. In: Kelly A, Taylor SC, Lim HW, Serrano A, eds. *Taylor and Kelly's Dermatology for Skin of Color*. 2nd ed. New York, NY: McGraw Hill; 2016. http://accessmedicine.mhmedical .com./content.aspx?bookid=2585&sectionid=211766255. Accessed June 22, 2019.

## Molluscum Contagiosum

Isaacs SN. Molluscum contagiosum. *Uptodate*. https://www.uptodate.com/contents/molluscum-con tagiosum?search=molluscum+contagiosum&source=search_result&selectedTitle=1~61&usage_ type=default&display_rank=1. Accessed August 26, 2019.

## Mycosis Fungoides (MF)

Bolognia J, Schaffer J, Duncan K, Ko C, eds. Cutaneous T-cell lymphoma. *Dermatology Essentials*. Saunders/ Elsevier; 2014.

## Necrotizing Fasciitis

Bolognia J, Schaffer J, Duncan K, Ko C, eds. *Dermatology Essentials*. Saunders/Elsevier; 2014.

## Pediculosis

Jameson JL, Fauci AS, Kasper DL, Hauser SL, Longo DL, Loscalzo J, eds. *Harrison's Principles of Internal Medicine*. 20th ed. New York, NY: McGraw Hill; 2018.

Kang S, Amagai M, Bruckner AL, et al, eds. *Fitzpatrick's Dermatology*. 9th ed. New York, NY: McGraw Hill; 2019.

Levinson W, Chin-Hong P, Joyce EA, Nussbaum J, Schwartz B, eds. *Review of Medical Microbiology & Immunology: A Guide to Clinical Infectious Diseases*. 15th ed. New York, NY: McGraw Hill; 2018.

Soutor C, Hordinsky MK, eds. *Clinical Dermatology*. New York, NY: McGraw Hill; 2017.

Tintinalli JE, Stapczynski J, Ma O, Yealy DM, Meckler GD, Cline DM, eds. *Tintinalli's Emergency Medicine: A Comprehensive Study Guide*. 8th ed. New York, NY: McGraw Hill; 2016.

Usatine RP, Smith MA, Mayeaux EJ Jr, Chumley HS, eds. *The Color Atlas and Synopsis of Family Medicine*. 3rd ed. New York, NY: McGraw Hill; 2019.

## Pemphigus Vulgaris

Hertl M, Sitaru C. *Uptodate*. https://www.uptodate.com/contents/pathogenesis-clinical-manifestations-and-diagnosis-of-pemphigus?search=Pemphigus+Vulgaris&source=search_result&selectedTitle=2~50&usage_ type=default&display_rank=2. Accessed August 26, 2019.

## Petechiae & Purpura

Jameson JL, Fauci AS, Kasper DL, Hauser SL, Longo DL, Loscalzo J, eds. *Harrison's Principles of Internal Medicine*. 20th ed. New York, NY: McGraw Hill; 2018.

Kang S, Amagai M, Bruckner AL, et al, eds. *Fitzpatrick's Dermatology*. 9th ed. New York, NY: McGraw Hill; 2019.

LeBlond RF, Brown DD, Suneja M, Szot JF, eds. *DeGowin's Diagnostic Examination*. 10th ed. New York, NY: McGraw Hill; 2014.

Stern SC, Cifu AS, Altkorn D, eds. *Symptom to Diagnosis: An Evidence-Based Guide*. 4th ed. New York, NY: McGraw Hill; 2020.

Soutor C, Hordinsky MK, eds. *Clinical Dermatology*. New York, NY: McGraw Hill; 2017.

Usatine RP, Smith MA, Mayeaux EJ Jr, Chumley HS, eds. *The Color Atlas and Synopsis of Family Medicine*. 3rd ed. New York, NY: McGraw Hill; 2019.

## Pilonidal Disease

Brunicardi F, Andersen DK, Billiar TR, et al, eds. *Schwartz's Principles of Surgery*. 11th ed. New York, NY: McGraw Hill; 2019.

Doherty GM, ed. *CURRENT Diagnosis & Treatment: Surgery*. 14th ed. New York, NY: McGraw Hill; 2019.

Knoop KJ, Stack LB, Storrow AB, Thurman R, eds. *The Atlas of Emergency Medicine*. 4th ed. New York, NY: McGraw Hill; 2016.

Stone C, Humphries RL, eds. *CURRENT Diagnosis & Treatment: Emergency Medicine*. 8th ed. New York, NY: McGraw Hill; 2017.

Usatine RP, Smith MA, Mayeaux EJ Jr, Chumley HS, eds. *The Color Atlas and Synopsis of Family Medicine*. 3rd ed. New York, NY: McGraw Hill; 2019.

## Pityriasis Rosea

Kang S, Amagai M, Bruckner AL, et al, eds. *Fitzpatrick's Dermatology*. 9th ed. New York, NY: McGraw Hill; 2019.

Kelly A, Taylor SC, Lim HW, Serrano A, eds. *Taylor and Kelly's Dermatology for Skin of Color*. 2nd ed. New York, NY: McGraw Hill; 2016.

Papadakis MA, McPhee SJ, Rabow MW, eds. *Current Medical Diagnosis and Treatment 2020*. 59th ed. New York, NY: McGraw Hill; 2016.

Usatine RP, Smith MA, Mayeaux EJ Jr, Chumley HS, eds. *The Color Atlas and Synopsis of Family Medicine*. 3rd ed. New York, NY: McGraw Hill; 2019.

Wolff K, Johnson R, Saavedra AP, Roh EK, eds. *Fitzpatrick's Color Atlas and Synopsis of Clinical Dermatology*. 8th ed. New York, NY: McGraw Hill; 2017.

## Plaque Psoriasis

Kang S, Amagai M, Bruckner AL, et al, eds. *Fitzpatrick's Dermatology*. 9th ed. New York, NY: McGraw Hill; 2019.

McKean SC, Ross JJ, Dressler DD, Scheurer DB, eds. *Principles and Practice of Hospital Medicine*. 2nd ed. New York, NY: McGraw Hill; 2017.

Soutor C, Hordinsky MK, eds. *Clinical Dermatology*. New York, NY: McGraw Hill; 2017.

Usatine RP, Smith MA, Mayeaux EJ Jr, Chumley HS, eds. *The Color Atlas and Synopsis of Family Medicine*. 3rd ed. New York, NY: McGraw Hill; 2019.

## Pressure Ulcers

Goldsmith LA, Katz SI, Gilchrest BA, Paller AS, Leffell DJ, Wolff K, eds. *Fitzpatrick's Dermatology in General Medicine*. 8th ed. New York, NY: McGraw Hill; 2012.

Halter JB, Ouslander JG, Studenski S, et al, eds. *Hazzard's Geriatric Medicine and Gerontology*. 7th ed. New York, NY: McGraw Hill; 2017.

Knoop KJ, Stack LB, Storrow AB, Thurman R, eds. *The Atlas of Emergency Medicine*. 4th ed. New York, NY: McGraw Hill; 2016.

Maitin IB, Cruz E, eds. *CURRENT Diagnosis & Treatment: Physical Medicine & Rehabilitation*. New York, NY: McGraw Hill; 2014.

Mitra R, ed. *Principles of Rehabilitation Medicine*. New York, NY: McGraw Hill; 2019.

## Rosacea

Jameson JL, Fauci AS, Kasper DL, Hauser SL, Longo DL, Loscalzo J, eds. *Harrison's Principles of Internal Medicine*. 20th ed. New York, NY: McGraw Hill; 2018.

Kang S, Amagai M, Bruckner AL, et al, eds. *Fitzpatrick's Dermatology*. 9th ed. New York, NY: McGraw Hill; 2019.

Kelly A, Taylor SC, Lim HW, Serrano A, eds. *Taylor and Kelly's Dermatology for Skin of Color*. 2nd ed. New York, NY: McGraw Hill; 2016.

Soutor C, Hordinsky MK, eds. *Clinical Dermatology*. New York, NY: McGraw Hill; 2017.

Usatine RP, Smith MA, Mayeaux EJ Jr, Chumley HS, eds. *The Color Atlas and Synopsis of Family Medicine*. 3rd ed. New York, NY: McGraw Hill; 2019.

**Scabies**

Kang S, Amagai M, Bruckner AL, et al, eds. *Fitzpatrick's Dermatology*. 9th ed. New York, NY: McGraw Hill; 2019.

Knoop KJ, Stack LB, Storrow AB, Thurman R, eds. *The Atlas of Emergency Medicine*. 4th ed. New York, NY: McGraw Hill; 2016.

Usatine RP, Smith MA, Mayeaux EJ Jr, Chumley HS, eds. *The Color Atlas and Synopsis of Family Medicine*. 3rd ed. New York, NY: McGraw Hill; 2019.

**Seborrheic Keratosis**

Cuda JD, Rangwala S, Taube JM. Benign epithelial tumors, hamartomas, and hyperplasias. In: Kang S, Amagai M, Bruckner AL, et al, eds. *Fitzpatrick's Dermatology*. 9th ed. New York, NY: McGraw Hill; 2019. http://accessmedicine.mhmedical.com/content.aspx?bookid=2570&sectionid=210433401. Accessed June 22, 2019.

Smith MA, Usatine RP. Seborrheic keratosis. In: Usatine RP, Smith MA, Mayeaux EJ Jr, Chumley HS, eds. *The Color Atlas and Synopsis of Family Medicine*. 3rd ed. New York, NY: McGraw Hill; 2019. http://accessmedicine.mhmedical.com/content.aspx?bookid=2547&sectionid=206798820. Accessed June 23, 2019.

**Stevens–Johnson Syndrome (SJS)**

Mockenhaupt M, Roujeau J. Epidermal necrolysis (Stevens-Johnson syndrome and toxic epidermal necrolysis). In: Kang S, Amagai M, Bruckner AL, et al, eds. *Fitzpatrick's Dermatology*. 9th ed. New York, NY: McGraw Hill; 2019.

Walls A, Burgin S. Stevens-Johnson syndrome. VisualDx. https://www.visualdx.com/visualdx/diagnosis/stevens-johnson+syndrome?diagnosisId=52342&moduleId=101

**Tinea Capitis**

Craddock LN, Schieke SM. Superficial fungal infection. In: Kang S, Amagai M, Bruckner AL, et al, eds. *Fitzpatrick's Dermatology*. 9th ed. New York, NY: McGraw-Hill; 2019. http://accessmedicine.mhmedical.com.ezp-prod1.hul.harvard.edu/content.aspx?bookid=2570&sectionid=210432218. Accessed October 07, 2019.

Heath CR, Mazza JM, Silverberg NB. Pediatrics. In: Kelly A, Taylor SC, Lim HW, Serrano A, eds. *Taylor and Kelly's Dermatology for Skin of Color*. 2nd ed. New York, NY: McGraw-Hill; 2016. http://accessmedicine.mhmedical.com.ezp-prod1.hul.harvard.edu/content.aspx?bookid=2585&sectionid=211769575. Accessed October 07, 2019.

Prawer S, Prawer S, Bershow A. Superficial fungal infections. In: Soutor C, Hordinsky MK, eds. *Clinical Dermatology*. New York, NY: McGraw-Hill; 2017. http://accessmedicine.mhmedical.com.ezp-prod1.hul.harvard.edu/content.aspx?bookid=2184&sectionid=165459177. Accessed October 07, 2019.

Usatine RP, Smith MA. Tinea cruris. In: Usatine RP, Smith MA, Mayeaux EJ Jr., Chumley HS, eds. *The Color Atlas and Synopsis of Family Medicine*. 3rd ed. New York, NY: McGraw-Hill; 2019. http://accessmedicine.mhmedical.com.ezp-prod1.hul.harvard.edu/content.aspx?bookid=2547&sectionid=206793178. Accessed October 17, 2019.

**Tinea Corporis**

Craddock LN, Schieke SM. Superficial fungal infection. In: Kang S, Amagai M, Bruckner AL, et al, eds. *Fitzpatrick's Dermatology*. 9th ed. New York, NY: McGraw-Hill; 2019. http://accessmedicine.mhmedical.com.ezp-prod1.hul.harvard.edu/content.aspx?bookid=2570&sectionid=210432218. Accessed October 07, 2019.

Prawer S, Prawer S, Bershow A. Superficial fungal infections. In: Soutor C, Hordinsky MK, eds. *Clinical Dermatology*. New York, NY: McGraw-Hill; 2017. http://accessmedicine.mhmedical.com.ezp-prod1.hul.harvard.edu/content.aspx?bookid=2184&sectionid=165459177. Accessed October 07, 2019.

Stein S. Rash. In: Stern SC, Cifu AS, Altkorn D, eds. *Symptom to Diagnosis: An Evidence-Based Guide*. 4th ed. New York, NY: McGraw-Hill; 2020. http://accessmedicine.mhmedical.com.ezp-prod1.hul.harvard.edu/content.aspx?bookid=2715&sectionid=228250466. Accessed October 07, 2019.

Usatine RP, Smith MA. Tinea cruris. In: Usatine RP, Smith MA, Mayeaux EJ Jr., Chumley HS, eds. *The Color Atlas and Synopsis of Family Medicine*. 3rd ed. New York, NY: McGraw-Hill; 2019. http://accessmedicine.mhmedical.com.ezp-prod1.hul.harvard.edu/content.aspx?bookid=2547&sectionid=206793178. Accessed October 17, 2019.

## Tinea Cruris

Craddock LN, Schieke SM. Superficial fungal infection. In: Kang S, Amagai M, Bruckner AL, et al, eds. *Fitzpatrick's Dermatology*. 9th ed. New York, NY: McGraw-Hill; 2019. http://accessmedicine.mhmedical.com.ezp-prod1.hul.harvard.edu/content.aspx?bookid=2570&sectionid=210432218. Accessed October 07, 2019.

Shinkai K, Fox LP. Fungal infections of the skin. In: Papadakis MA, McPhee SJ, Rabow MW, eds. *Current Medical Diagnosis and Treatment 2020*. New York, NY: McGraw-Hill; 2016. http://accessmedicine.mhmedical.com.ezp-prod1.hul.harvard.edu/content.aspx?bookid=2683&sectionid=225034522. Accessed October 17, 2019.

Usatine RP, Smith MA. Tinea cruris. In: Usatine RP, Smith MA, Mayeaux EJ Jr., Chumley HS, eds. *The Color Atlas and Synopsis of Family Medicine*. 3rd ed. New York, NY: McGraw-Hill; 2019. http://accessmedicine.mhmedical.com.ezp-prod1.hul.harvard.edu/content.aspx?bookid=2547&sectionid=206793178. Accessed October 17, 2019.

## Tinea Pedis/Manuum

Bhandari RA, Morrell DS. Skin disorders: extremities. In: Tintinalli JE, Stapczynski J, Ma O, Yealy DM, Meckler GD, Cline DM, eds. *Tintinalli's Emergency Medicine: A Comprehensive Study Guide*. 8th ed. New York, NY: McGraw-Hill; 2016. http://accessmedicine.mhmedical.com.ezp-prod1.hul.harvard.edu/content.aspx?bookid=1658&sectionid=109445168. Accessed October 17, 2019.

Craddock LN, Schieke SM. Superficial fungal infection. In: Kang S, Amagai M, Bruckner AL, et al, eds. *Fitzpatrick's Dermatology*. 9th ed. New York, NY: McGraw-Hill; 2019. http://accessmedicine.mhmedical.com.ezp-prod1.hul.harvard.edu/content.aspx?bookid=2570&sectionid=210432218. Accessed October 17, 2019.

Shinkai K, Fox LP. Fungal infections of the skin. In: Papadakis MA, McPhee SJ, Rabow MW, eds. *Current Medical Diagnosis and Treatment 2020*. New York, NY: McGraw-Hill; 2016. http://accessmedicine.mhmedical.com.ezp-prod1.hul.harvard.edu/content.aspx?bookid=2683&sectionid=225034522. Accessed October 17, 2019.

Usatine RP, Smith MA. Tinea cruris. In: Usatine RP, Smith MA, Mayeaux EJ Jr., Chumley HS, eds. *The Color Atlas and Synopsis of Family Medicine*. 3rd ed. New York, NY: McGraw-Hill; 2019. http://accessmedicine.mhmedical.com.ezp-prod1.hul.harvard.edu/content.aspx?bookid=2547&sectionid=206793178. Accessed October 17, 2019.

## Tinea Versicolor

Ledet JJ, Elewski BE, Gupta AK. Fungal and yeast infections. In: Kelly A, Taylor SC, Lim HW, Serrano A, eds. *Taylor and Kelly's Dermatology for Skin of Color*. 2nd ed. New York, NY: McGraw-Hill; 2016. http://accessmedicine.mhmedical.com.ezp-prod1.hul.harvard.edu/content.aspx?bookid=2585&sectionid=211768042. Accessed October 06, 2019.

Prawer S, Prawer S, Bershow A. Superficial fungal infections. In: Soutor C, Hordinsky MK, eds. *Clinical Dermatology*. New York, NY: McGraw-Hill; 2017. http://accessmedicine.mhmedical.com.ezp-prod1.hul.harvard.edu/content.aspx?bookid=2184&sectionid=165459177. Accessed October 06, 2019.

Usatine RP, MacGilvray PD. Tinea versicolor. In: Usatine RP, Smith MA, Mayeaux EJ Jr., Chumley HS, eds. *The Color Atlas and Synopsis of Family Medicine*. 3rd ed. New York, NY: McGraw-Hill; 2019. http://accessmedicine.mhmedical.com.ezp-prod1.hul.harvard.edu/content.aspx?bookid=2547&sectionid=206793753. Accessed October 06, 2019.

## Toxic Epidermal Necrolysis (TEN)

Mockenhaupt M, Roujeau J. Epidermal necrolysis (Stevens-Johnson syndrome and toxic epidermal necrolysis). In: Kang S, Amagai M, Bruckner AL, et al, eds. *Fitzpatrick's Dermatology*. 9th ed. New York, NY: McGraw Hill; 2019.

Walls A, Burgin S. Toxic epidermal necrolysis. VisualDx: https://www.visualdx.com/visualdx/diagnosis/toxic+epidermal+necrolysis?diagnosisId=52413&moduleId=101

## Type 1 Hypersensitivity Reaction

Le Tao, Bhushan Vikas, Sochat Matthew, C et al. *First Aid for the USMLE Step 1 2019*. 29th ed. New York, NY: McGraw Hill; 2019.

Kang S, Amagai M, Bruckner AL, et al, eds. *Fitzpatrick's Dermatology*. 9th ed. New York, NY: McGraw-Hill; 2019.

Jameson JL, Fauci AS, Kasper DL, Hauser SL, Longo DL, Loscalzo J, eds. *Harrison's Principles of Internal Medicine*. 20th ed. New York, NY: McGraw Hill; 2018.

**Type 2 Hypersensitivity Reaction**

Le Tao, Bhushan Vikas, Sochat Matthew, C et al. *First Aid for the USMLE Step 1 2019*. 29th ed. New York, NY: McGraw Hill; 2019.

Kang S, Amagai M, Bruckner AL, et al, eds. *Fitzpatrick's Dermatology*. 9th ed. New York, NY: McGraw-Hill; 2019.

Jameson JL, Fauci AS, Kasper DL, Hauser SL, Longo DL, Loscalzo J, eds. *Harrison's Principles of Internal Medicine*. 20th ed. New York, NY: McGraw Hill; 2018.

**Type 3 Hypersensitivity Reaction**

Le Tao, Bhushan Vikas, Sochat Matthew, C et al. *First Aid for the USMLE Step 1 2019*. 29th ed. New York, NY: McGraw Hill; 2019.

Kang S, Amagai M, Bruckner AL, et al, eds. *Fitzpatrick's Dermatology*. 9th ed. New York, NY: McGraw-Hill; 2019.

Jameson JL, Fauci AS, Kasper DL, Hauser SL, Longo DL, Loscalzo J, eds. *Harrison's Principles of Internal Medicine*. 20th ed. New York, NY: McGraw Hill; 2018.

**Type 4 Hypersensitivity Reaction**

Le Tao, Bhushan Vikas, Sochat Matthew, C et al. *First Aid for the USMLE Step 1 2019*. 29th ed. New York, NY: McGraw Hill; 2019.

Kang S, Amagai M, Bruckner AL, et al, eds. *Fitzpatrick's Dermatology*. 9th ed. New York, NY: McGraw-Hill; 2019.

Jameson JL, Fauci AS, Kasper DL, Hauser SL, Longo DL, Loscalzo J, eds. *Harrison's Principles of Internal Medicine*. 20th ed. New York, NY: McGraw Hill; 2018.

**Urticaria (Hives)**

Soutor C, Hordinsky MK, eds. *Clinical Dermatology*. New York, NY: McGraw Hill; 2017.

Kang S, Amagai M, Bruckner AL, et al, eds. *Fitzpatrick's Dermatology*. 9th ed. New York, NY: McGraw Hill; 2019.

Usatine RP, Smith MA, Mayeaux EJ Jr, Chumley HS, eds. *The Color Atlas and Synopsis of Family Medicine*. 3rd ed. New York, NY: McGraw Hill; 2019.

**Varicella-Zoster Virus (VZV)**

Burgin S, High WA, Goldsmith LA. Herpes zoster. VisualDx. https://www.visualdx.com/visualdx/diagnosis/herpes+zoster?diagnosisId=52552&moduleId=101

McDonald J. Vaccines for postexposure prophylaxis against varicella (chickenpox) in children and adults. *Paediatr Child Health*. 2016;21(2):91-92. doi:10.1093/pch/21.2.91

Plovanich M, Burgin S. Varicella. VisualDx. https://www.visualdx.com/visualdx/diagnosis/varicella?diagnosisId=52483&moduleId=101#top

Shinkai K, Fox LP. Dermatologic disorders In: Papadakis MA, McPhee SJ, Rabow MW, eds. *Current Medical Diagnosis & Treatment 2019*. New York, NY: McGraw Hill; 2019:chap. 6.

**Verrucae (Warts)**

Kang S, Amagai M, Bruckner AL, et al, eds. *Fitzpatrick's Dermatology*. 9th ed. New York, NY: McGraw Hill; 2019.

Soutor C, Hordinsky MK, eds. *Clinical Dermatology*. New York, NY: McGraw Hill; 2017.

Usatine RP, Smith MA, Mayeaux EJ Jr, Chumley HS, eds. *The Color Atlas and Synopsis of Family Medicine*. 3rd ed. New York, NY: McGraw Hill; 2019.

**Vitiligo**

Grimes PE. Vitiligo: Pathogenesis, clinical features, and diagnosis. *Uptodate*. https://www.uptodate.com/contents/vitiligo-pathogenesis-clinical-features-and-diagnosis?search=vitiligo&source=search_result&selectedTitle=2~143&usage_type=default&display_rank=2. Accessed August 26, 2019.

# Emergency Medicine

*Alicia Lydecker, MD and Kathryn Mutter, MD, MPH*

# Acid and Alkali Ingestion

 Most injuries occur at a pH under 3 or over 11

## Clinical Presentation

- Eschar
- Drooling
- Odynophagia/dysphagia
- Stridor
- Vocal hoarseness
- Chest pain

Children:
- Vomiting
- Refusing oral intake

> ! 
> - Respiratory distress may be caused by edema of the upper airway, aspiration of the caustic substance into the tracheobronchial tree, or inhalation of fumes
> - Absence of oral burns does NOT exclude esophageal injury

## Diagnosis and Workup

### Acid or Alkali?

- Detailed history to determine substance pH, concentration, volume, and patient intent
- Acids = superficial coagulation necrosis
- Alkaline = deeper liquefactive necrosis
- Check for coingestants in suicidal patients

Early endoscopy (within 12-24 hours of ingestion) for severe ingestions or persistent symptoms

Ingestion of lye in pediatric patient

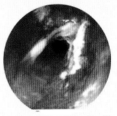

### Complications

- Early: perforations leading to hemodynamic instability/mediastinitis/subcutaneous emphysema
- Late: scarring of pylorus and esophageal strictures

Increased risk of squamous cell esophageal cancer

 Reproduced with permission from Knoop KJ, Stack LB, Storrow AB, et al: The Atlas of Emergency Medicine, 4th ed. New York, NY: McGraw Hill 2016. Photo contributor: Philip E. Stack, MD.

## Management

- Establish large-bore IV access and resuscitate with crystalloids
- Manage airway and monitor for hemodynamic instability

Oral intubation with direct visualization **OR** Cricothyrotomy due to oropharyngeal edema, tissue friability, and bleeding

 ### Contraindicated:
- Activated charcoal/induced emesis (if caustic agent is only known ingestant)
- Blind nasotracheal intubation
- Dilution/neutralization therapy

# Acute Abdomen

New-Onset, Severe Abdominal Pain & Tenderness Often Requiring Surgical Intervention

## Inflammation

Appendicitis      Cholecystitis

↓           ↓

Periumbilical to RLQ Pain    RUQ Pain
Rebound Tenderness        "Four Fs"

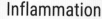

## Perforation

Bowel Perforation → PUD, Diverticulitis, IBD

Ruptured AAA → age >55

Ruptured Ectopic → Young Female with + β-hCG

## Obstruction

Bowel Obstruction      Volvulus

↓           ↓

Vomiting, Constipated
Secondary to Adhesions,
Hernia, or Malignancy    Extremes of Age

## Ischemic

Mesenteric Ischemia → Elderly Atrial Fibrillation

Strangulated Hernia → Bulging Abdominal Mass

Ovarian Torsion → Intermittent Pelvic Pain; Young Female

## Intra-abdominal

PID
Pancreatitis
Nephrolithiasis
UTI/Pyelonephritis

## Nonsurgical MIMICS

## Extra-abdominal

Myocardial Infarction
Pulmonary Embolism
Pneumonia

Cholecystitis,
Screens for
Free Fluid
(Ectopic,
Trauma)

Reproduced with permssion from Papadakis MA, McPhee SJ, Rabow MW: Current Medical Diagnosis & Treatment 2019. New York, NY: McGraw Hill; 2019.

Screens for
Perforation
(Free Air),
SBO (Air
Fluid Levels)

Appendicitis,
Obstruction,
Ruptured AAA,
and Ischemic
Bowel

## Management

- Stabilize Patient
- Obtain Diagnostic Imaging
- Consider Antibiotics to Cover Intra-abdominal Pathogens
- Consult with Surgical Subspecialty as Appropriate for Definitive Therapy
- Pain Management

# #1
Cause of acute liver failure in the United States

# Acute Acetaminophen
## Toxicity

## Clinical Presentation

Most patients are...

asymptomatic

But some may present with...

anorexia,
nausea, vomiting,
right upper quadrant pain,
liver failure,
hepatic encephalopathy,
renal failure,
metabolic acidosis,
death

## Workup

Serum acetaminophen level

Liver function tests, coagulation tests

The above labs may initially be normal

Helpful adjuncts:
complete metabolic panel, drug screen, electrocardiogram

## Management

Consider activated charcoal if presentation <1 hour status post-ingestion

If single, acute ingestion, use...

### Rumack–Matthew Nomogram

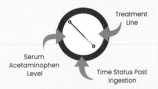

Treatment Line

Serum Acetaminophen Level

Time Status Post Ingestion

Nomogram cannot be used for levels <4 hours status post ingestion

Acetaminophen level >150 mcg/mL at 4 hours status post ingestion = Possibly toxic

If acetaminophen level = Possibly toxic per Rumack–Matthew nomogram...

### N-Acetylcysteine (NAC)

Repletes antioxidant glutathione

If chronic ingestion, consider...

NAC if serum acetaminophen level or liver function tests elevated

Liver transplant may be needed for severe cases (ie, fulminant liver failure)

Survivors of acetaminophen toxicity rarely have sequelae

# Acute Appendicitis

Obstruction and subsequent inflammation and bacterial overgrowth of the vermis appendix

## Etiology

- Fecalith (most common)
- Lymphoid tissue
- Tumors
- Helminthic infection

## Clinical Presentation

- Generalized abdominal pain that moves to RLQ (McBurney's point)
- May be associated with nausea, vomiting, fever, anorexia

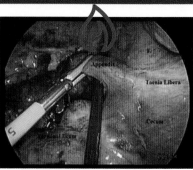

Reproduced with permission from Brunicardi FC, Andersen DK, Billiar TR, et al: Schwartz's Principles of Surgery, 11th ed. New York, NY: McGraw Hill; 2019.

## McBurney's Point

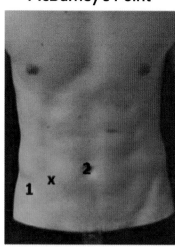

## Diagnosis

- Clinical diagnosis: Imaging for surgical planning
- CT for most. US or MRI for pregnant or pediatric patients
- Labs are frequently nonspecific but may aid in excluding other diagnosis

## Treatment

- Most patients require urgent appendectomy to prevent perforation
- Pre-op patients should be given antibiotics: cefoxitin, piperacillin/tazobactam, or ceftriaxone and metronidazole

# Acute Isoniazid Toxicity

Active and latent tuberculosis treatment

Decreases mycolic acid synthesis

One of World Health Organization's essential medicines

May also decrease γ-aminobutyric acid (GABA) synthesis

Clinical diagnosis based on history of tuberculosis treatment and seizure

Helpful adjuncts: fingerstick glucose, complete metabolic panel, toxicology screen, electrocardiogram

## Clinical Presentation

## Management

## Clinical Use

## Workup

Altered mental status, seizure, metabolic acidosis, coma, death

Vitamin B6 (ie, pyridoxine) facilitates GABA synthesis

Benzodiazepines may also be given to potentiate GABA activity

Supportive (ie, airway management by assisting oxygenation, ventilation, etc.)

Recurrent, refractory seizures are pathognomonic

# *Alcohol Intoxication*

## Ethanol ($CH_3CH_2OH$)

### *Epidemiology*

- Significant global impact
- **30-40% of all medical or surgical patients** have an alcohol-related health problem
- Alcohol use disorder estimated to affect 3-5% of the population

### *Metabolism*

- Ethanol absorbed in the stomach within 30-45 minutes
- Oxidation through **alcohol dehydrogenase to acetaldehyde**
- Reduction of NAD to NADH

### *Mechanism*

- **Increased GABA** activity and **decreased NMDA** activity
- Dopamine release contributes to its addictive potential
- Euphoria and disinhibition at lower doses
- At higher doses, respiratory depression and coma can occur

### *Elimination*

- Oxidation follows **zero-order kinetics**
- Concentration of alcohol in tissues has negligible effects on the rate of oxidation
- In healthy individuals, metabolized at a rate of approximately 150 mg of alcohol per kilo of body weight per hour or **one drink per hour**

# Alcohol Withdrawal

## A life-threatening condition

## Mild Withdrawal

- Initial **tremor**
- **High blood pressure**
- **Tachycardia**
- **Anxiety/agitation**

### 3-36 hours (after last drink)

## Alcoholic Hallucinations

- **Visual hallucinations** without delirium present after more prolonged abstinence
- **Withdrawal seizures** also possible

### 12-48 hours

## Delirium Tremens

- Most severe form of withdrawal
- **Visual hallucinations**
- Severe **autonomic hyperactivity** with vital sign abnormalities
- **Seizures**
- **Can lead to death**

### 2-7 days

## Management

- **First line: Benzodiazepines**
- Consider **thiamine** and **folate** replacement for nutritional deficiencies

### EtOH & benzos activate GABA receptors

# Anaphylactic Shock

## Causes
- **Hymenoptera** (eg, bee) stings
- **Food** (eg, nuts)
- **Drug** (eg, penicillin)
- Plasma proteins in **transfusion** (patients with IgA deficiency)
- *Echinococcus granulosus* cyst rupture

## Cascade
- **IgE** degranulates **mast** cells
- **Histamine** and tryptase released
- Sudden drop in **SVR** & **PCWP**
- Compensatory increase in cardiac output
- **Distributive** shock (warm and dry)
- Chemokines and cytokines cause tissue damage

## Care
- Airway management
- IM epinephrine (1:1000)
- Anti-H1 and anti-H2
- Steroids

**MIMIC**
Scombroid poisoning

# Antiarrhythmic Toxicity and Overdose

## Class Ia
### Sodium Channel Blockers

Disopyramide, Procainamide, Quinidine

 **Clinical presentation:**
Dysrhythmia, hypotension, anticholinergic effects, SLE-like reaction (procainamide, chronic), cinchonism (quinidine, chronic)

**EKG:** Wide QRS and prolonged QTc

**Treatment \*:**
Lidocaine
Sodium bicarbonate for hypotension

## Class Ib
### Sodium Channel Blockers

Lidocaine

**Clinical presentation:**
 Neuro: Circumoral numbness, tongue paresthesia -> anxiety -> seizure -> coma
Cardio: Hypotension, bradycardia, dysrhythmia
Heme: Methemoglobinemia

**EKG:** Normal QRS and short QTc

**Treatment \*:**
Seizure precautions
Lipid emulsion therapy

## Class Ic
### Sodium Channel Blockers

Flecainide

**Clinical presentation:**
 Dysrhythmia, hypotension
Labs: Hyponatremia

**EKG:**  Prolongation of PR, QRS, and QTc. Ventricular tachyarrhythmia and bradycardia

**Treatment \*:**
Mainly supportive care
Consider lipid emulsion therapy for refractory toxicity

## Class II
### β-Blockers

**Clinical presentation:**
Bradycardia, hypotension, AMS
Labs: HYPOglycemia

**EKG:**  QRS widening (propranolol), heart block

**Treatment \*:**
Calcium
Glucagon
High-dose insulin
Consider lipid emulsion therapy for refractory toxicity

General presentation:
Antiarrhythmic toxicity may cause hypotension, dysrhythmias, and AMS

## Class III
### Potassium Channel Blockers

Amiodarone

**Clinical presentation:**
Acute toxicity: Hypotension, ventricular dysrhythmia, bradycardia
Chronic toxicity: Pulmonary fibrosis, thyroid dysfunction, corneal, hepatic, and cutaneous toxicity (blue-gray discoloration)

 **EKG:** Prolonged QTc

**Treatment \*:**
Magnesium to treat torsades

Treatments:
QRS widening: Sodium bicarbonate
QTc prolongation: Magnesium

## Class IV
### Calcium Channel Blockers

**Clinical presentation:**
Bradycardia, hypotension, AMS
Labs: HYPERglycemia

**EKG:** 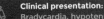 Heart block

**Treatment \*:**
Calcium
Glucagon
High-dose insulin
Consider lipid emulsion therapy for refractory toxicity

\*Supportive care (required by all):
Airway management
Breathing assistance
Circulation support

# Anticholinergic Toxicity

**Causes of Toxicity:**

Medications (ie, antihistamines, atropine); Mushrooms; Plants
(ie, Jimsonweed)

## Clinical Presentation

### Tachycardia
- Earliest & most reliable sign!!!!

### "Red as a beet"
- Cutaneous vasodilation to compensate for loss of sweat production

### "Dry as a bone"
- Sweat glands are innervated by muscarinic receptors, and thus anticholinergics produce dry skin

### "Hot as a hare"
- Interference with normal heat dissipation (sweating) leading to hyperthermia

### "Blind as a bat"
- Dilation and ineffective accommodation that manifests as blurry vision

### "Mad as a hatter"
- Delirium; hallucinations

### "Full as a flask"
- Reduced detrusor muscle contraction and inhibited sphincter relaxation leads to urinary retention

## Evaluation & Management

**1** Understand the clinical features of overdose

- ✓ Tachycardia
- ✓ Flushing, anhidrosis, hyperthermia, blurry vision (mydriasis), agitated delirium, and diminished bowel sounds

**2** Perform basic screening tests    *Diagnosis is based on clinical findings*

- ✓ Fingerstick glucose—to rule out hypoglycemia
- ✓ Acetaminophen and salicylate levels—to rule out common coingestions
- ✓ ECG—to rule out conduction system poisoning
- ✓ Pregnancy test of all women of childbearing age

**3** Manage anticholinergic toxicity

- ✓ Stabilization of airway, breathing, and circulation
- ✓ IV access, supplemental $O_2$, cardiac monitoring, and continuous pulse oximetry
- ✓ Antidotal therapy with physostigmine in the case of both peripheral and moderate central toxicity
- ✓ Symptomatic treatment as needed including sodium bicarbonate (prolonged QRS or arrhythmias), benzodiazepines (agitation and seizures), and possibly activated charcoal

# Anticoagulant Toxicity and Overdose

**Classes: Vitamin K antagonists (warfarins), direct thrombin inhibitors, factor Xa inhibitors, and heparins**

## Clinical Presentation

| | |
|---|---|
| Hemoptysis | Widespread bruising |
| Bloody stools | Fatigue  |
| Lightheadedness | Intracranial hemorrhage |
| Gross hematuria | |

## Diagnosis and Workup

 For **warfarins:** Increased PT within 24-72 hours is diagnostic

For **heparins:** Increased activated PTT (aPTT) is diagnostic

Warfarins are also found in rodenticides!

For **Xa inhibitors and direct thrombin inhibitors:** Specific labs are not available
Increased PT or PTT is suggestive but nonspecific

 **Other useful labs:**
BUN, creatinine, CBC, blood type, and cross-match

## Management

For **warfarins,** use PO/IV vitamin K (delayed effect) or FFP (immediate effect)

Protamine reverses **heparins**

Idarucizumab reverses **dabigatran (direct thrombin inhibitor)**

Andexanet reverses **factor Xa inhibitors**

Vitamin K not indicated!

 Support for serious bleeding:
FFP, prothrombin complex concentrate, blood product replacement, or activated factor VII as needed

# Anticonvulsant Overdose

## Mechanism of Action

| Enhanced GABA Transmission | Calcium Channel Inhibition | Sodium Channel Inhibition | NMDA Inhibition | SV2A Stimulation |
|---|---|---|---|---|
| Benzodiazepines | Lamotrigine | Lamotrigine | Lamotrigine | Levetiracetam |
| Barbiturates | Topiramate | Topiramate | Topiramate | |
| Tiagabine | Carbamazepine | Carbamazepine | Carbamazepine | |
| Vigabatrin | Valproic acid | Valproic acid | | |
| | Ethosuximide | Phenytoin | | |
| | Gabapentin | Oxcarbazepine | | |

## Clinical Presentation

**Confusion**  **Ataxia**  **Nystagmus**  **Seizure**  **Cardiac Arrhythmias**  **Hypotension**

## Workup and Management

Obtain drug history

Electrocardiogram

Basic metabolic panel

Serum anticonvulsant concentrations

Ammonia level for suspected valproic acid toxicity

Activated charcoal

Benzodiazepines for seizures

Sodium bicarbonate for QRS prolongation

L-carnitine or hemodialysis for valproic acid overdose

# Antipsychotic Overdose

## Clinical Presentation

| Lethargy and sedation | Hypotension and tachycardia | Agitated delirium and confusion | Extrapyramidal symptoms | Neuroleptic malignant syndrome |
|---|---|---|---|---|

**! Presentation depends on the specific antipsychotic ingested as well as the patient's age, tolerance, and co-intoxicants.**

 **! QTc Prolongation and Torsades des Pointes**

## Diagnosis and Workup

Fingerstick glucose to rule out hypoglycemia

EKG to rule out conduction system abnormality

Acetaminophen and salicylate levels

**! Serum concentrations of the ingested antipsychotic can be obtained, but these tests are not readily available or useful in the acute setting.**

Evaluation mainly consists of excluding other more harmful agents as the cause of the patient's presentation.

## Management

Activated charcoal if no contraindications

Treatment is primarily supportive

**! Antipsychotic overdose generally has a good prognosis. The mainstay of treatment is supportive care.**

# Barbiturate Overdose

 ⬆ Duration Cl⁻ channel open = ⬆GABA = ⬇ CNS Activity

## Clinical Presentation

 Lethargy

 Slurred speech

 Nystagmus

 Ataxia

 Bradycardia

 Hypotension

 Hypothermia

 Diminished pupillary reflex/pinpoint pupils

 Respiratory arrest

 Coma

Mild - - - - - - Moderate - - - - - - Severe

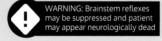 WARNING: Brainstem reflexes may be suppressed and patient may appear neurologically dead

## Diagnosis

 ### Specific Findings:

- Patient history of barbiturate ingestion
- Urine drug screen

 ### Nonspecific Findings:

- Skin bullae
- Altered electrolytes, glucose, BUN, creatinine, arterial blood gas
- Abnormal pulse oximetry, chest radiograph

## Management

 ### Supportive:

- Protect airway and assist ventilation
- Increase blood pressure
- Treat hypothermia

 ### Decontamination & Elimination:

- Activated charcoal *(if mental status allows)*
- Hemodialysis in severe cases
- Urine alkalinization *(phenobarbital only!)*

# Bee and Wasp Stings

## Uncomplicated Local Reactions

 **Clinical Presentation**

- 1-5 cm area of painful redness/swelling
- Develops within minutes, resolves within a few hours/days

 **Management**

- Remove stinger from wound if present
- Cold compresses
- Oral antihistamine and topical corticosteroids for pruritus

## Large Local Reactions

 **Clinical Presentation**

- Exaggerated redness and swelling at sting site that ENLARGES over 1-2 days
- Peaks at 48 hours, resolves in 5-10 days

 **Management**

- Cold compresses
- Oral prednisone for swelling
- NSAIDs
- Oral antihistamines and topical corticosteroids for pruritus

 IgE-mediated

## Anaphylaxis

Acute, life-threatening IgE-mediated type I hypersensitivity reaction affecting 2 or more organ systems, or sudden hypotension after allergen exposure

 **Clinical Presentation**

- Tachycardia
- Vasodilation ⟶ hypotension, edema

- Upper airway edema ⟶ stridor, hoarseness
- Bronchospasm ⟶ wheezing

- Urticaria, pruritus, flushing

- Abdominal pain, nausea, vomiting

 **Management**

- **IM epinephrine 1:1000**
  - ⟶ Vasoconstriction
  - ⟶ Bronchodilation
- Airway management
- Volume resuscitation
- Adjunctive therapy (antihistamines, H2-blockers, glucocorticoids)

 IgE-mediated

# Benzodiazepine and Barbiturate Withdrawal

Shorter half-life drugs = quicker onset of withdrawal symptoms

## Mechanism of Action

Decreased GABA receptor activation

Unchecked excitatory neurotransmitter activity

## Clinical Presentation

Sleep disturbances

Delirium

Depression

Seizures

Tremors

Cardiovascular collapse

## Management

 Support airway, breathing, and circulation

Restore GABA tone with long-acting benzodiazepine/barbiturate, followed by slow dose taper

**122**

# Benzodiazepine Toxicity and Overdose

**Examples**:
Alprazolam
Diazepam
Lorazepam
Clonazepam
Clorazepate
Chlordiazepoxide

## Clinical Presentation: Sedative-Hypnotic Toxidrome

- 🚶 Ataxia
- 📢 Slurred speech
- 🫁 Minor respiratory depression
- 🧠 AMS (usually depressed)
- 📋 Normal vital signs
- ❗ Severe toxicity: stuporous or comatose

## Diagnosis

- **Clinical diagnosis**
- ❗ "coma with normal vital signs"
- **Rule out** other causes of poisoning

### Urine

- May **NOT** be detected in standard urine screening tests
- Urine screening test designed to identify **oxazepam & derivatives**
- Positive test indicates **recent** exposure, but **does NOT** confirm toxicity or overdose

## Management

- Ensure airway is protected: intubation may be required
- Oxygen as needed
- **Flumazenil**: rarely used as it can precipitate withdrawal seizures if patient is benzodiazepine tolerant
- **Naloxone**: if concomitant use of opioids
- ❗ Avoid activated charcoal if mental status is depressed as it increases risk of **aspiration**

# Beta-Blocker
# Toxicity & Overdose

Examples: Ateno**lol**, Carvedi**lol**, Labeta**lol**, Metopro**lol**, Nado**lol**, Proprano**lol**

## Clinical Presentation

 **Bradycardia & hypotension**

 Heart block     **Cardiogenic shock**

 Altered mental status, seizure, hypoglycemia

Other chronic/adverse effects: bronchospasm, erectile dysfunction, depression

## Diagnosis

β-Blocker toxicity and overdose is a **clinical diagnosis**.
**Rule out** other causes of poisoning
**ECG** = bradycardia, PR prolongation, heart block
**Labs** = fingerstick glucose, serum chemistry (Ca, BUN, Cr)

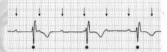

Reproduced with permission from Hammer GD, McPhee SJ: Pathophysiology of Disease:
An Introduction to Clinical Medicine, 8th ed. New York, NY: McGraw Hill; 2019.
Complete Heart Block

## Management

- ABCs
- Atropine & IV fluids
- If severe—IV glucagon, calcium salts, and hyperinsulinemia euglycemia therapy. Consider pressors and lipid emulsion therapy for refractory hypotension/bradycardia. Cardiac pacing may be trialed but may not be effective
- Supportive treatment—Sodium bicarbonate and magnesium, IV dextrose (D50W), benzodiazepines

# Blunt Abdominopelvic Trauma

## Common Injuries

Spleen
Liver
Hollow organs
Kidneys
Urethra
Pelvic fracture

## Symptoms

Hypotension
Tachycardia
Tenderness
Guarding
Rigidity

## Trauma Workup

1.  **A**irway
2.  **B**reathing
3.  **C**irculation
4.  **D**isability (GCS)
5.  **E**xposure

Stable ⟶ FAST  ⟶ CT

Unstable ⟶ FAST  ⟶ OR

 X-ray pelvis
X-ray spine

## Treatment

### Ex Lap if:
- Peritonitis
- Free air under diaphragm
- Hemorrhage/shock

### Observe with serial exams if:
- Negative FAST
- Stable
- Low-risk mechanism of injury

### Pelvic Fracture

 Pelvic binder | Early resuscitation

#### Surgery if:
- Open/unstable fracture
- Urologic injury
- Hemorrhage

## Complications

High risk of thrombosis for pelvic injuries

Shock

Abdominal compartment syndrome

Post-op infection

# Blunt Chest Trauma

## Injuries

Rib fractures/flail chest
Hemothorax
Pneumothorax
Pulmonary contusions
Blunt cardiac injury
Aortic disruption
Splenic/liver laceration
Tracheobronchial injury

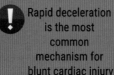 Rapid deceleration is the most common mechanism for blunt cardiac injury

## Signs & Symptoms

Hypotension
Tachycardia
Chest pain/SOB
Dysrhythmia
JVD
Murmurs
↓ Breath sounds

## Workup

ECG    CXR    FAST ultrasound    Troponin

 Consider ABG and lactate

 CK-MB has no predictive value

Troponin elevation → Serial troponin, cardiac monitor for dysrhythmias

Unstable, signs of severe injury, or abnormal ECG → Echo CTA

Concern for esophageal injury → Water-soluble contrast esophagogram

## Treatment

### Stable

Normal ECG & no major injuries → Cardiac monitoring with reassessment for 4-6 hours & repeat ECGs

Discharge home if no change    Abnormal ECG, then admit with telemetry

### Unstable

- ACLS algorithms
- Rib fractures → analgesia & $O_2$
- Chest tube if PTX/HTX suspected
- Aortic disruption → permissive hypotension (sys <120) and permissive bradycardia
- Intrabronchial bleed → bronchoscopy
- Inotropic support
- Surgery if: tracheobronchial, aortic, valvular, myocardial, diaphragmatic, papillary muscle, chordae tendineae, or coronary vessel injuries

## Complications

Formation of aneurysms or fistulas    Shock & dysrhythmias    Acute HF, valvular dysfunction, or cardiac free wall rupture    Dressler's syndrome

# Blunt Head Trauma

## Common Injuries

Brain contusion
Bleeding (subdural, epidural, intraparenchymal, intraventricular, subarachnoid)
Diffuse axonal injury
Edema
Skull fracture

Consider C-spine injury → spinal precautions

## Signs & Symptoms

Altered mentation
Focal neurologic deficit
Hypertension
Bradycardia
Irregular respirations
Headache

## Workup

 Neurologic exam

 Determine pupillary response:

- Fixed, dilated → uncal herniation
- Bilateral pinpoint → opiates, central pontine lesion, cerebellotonsillar herniation

 CSF leak increases risk for meningitis → PPx antibiotics

### CT rules

1. New Orleans and Canadian head rules
2. NEXUS and Canadian C-spine rules

## Treatment

 MAP goal >80

Intubation & sedation (etomidate or propofol) if patient uncooperative or combative

| Primary Goals | Secondary Goals |
| --- | --- |
| Maintain cerebral perfusion | Prevent secondary injury by correcting: |
| Optimize intravascular volume | Hypoglycemia |
| Optimize ventilation | Hyperglycemia |
| Prevent and control seizures | Hypoxia (SpO$_2$ >90%) |
| Treat elevated ICP (HOB 30°, mannitol, hypertonic saline, etc.) | Hypercapnia |
| | Hyperthermia |
| | Hypoperfusion |

 **Neurosurgical consult for**: intracranial mass lesion, ICP monitoring, ventriculostomy

## Complications

Irreversible neurologic deficits | Infection (eg, meningitis) | Amnesia, cognitive, and/or behavioral changes | Chronic traumatic encephalopathy

# Carbon Monoxide Poisoning

## History

- Automobile or boat exhaust
- Smoke inhalation
- Gas, propane, or kerosene heaters, generators, stoves, etc.
- Poorly functioning furnaces
- Camp stoves or other appliances used in poorly ventilated spaces

**!** Others living in the same house presenting with the same symptoms at the same time

##  Pathophysiology

- Colorless, odorless gas
- Carbon monoxide competitively binds to hemoglobin with 200× the affinity of $O_2$
- Causes a left shift in the oxyhemoglobin dissociation curve
- Does not affect dissolved $O_2$ ($PaO_2$)

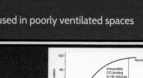

Reproduced with permission from Kibble JD, Halsey CR: Medical Physiology: The Big Picture. New York, NY: McGraw Hill; 2009.

## Clinical Presentation

- Nonspecific
- Headache
- Confusion
- Nausea
- Dizziness
- Ataxia
- Myalgias
- Seizure
- Coma
- Death

**!** Red skin is a very late sign and is rarely seen in living patients

##  Diagnosis

- Arterial blood gas with serum carboxyhemoglobin (COHb) level

**!** SpO$_2$ will be falsely elevated

| Normal COHb | May also have | COHb levels may not correlate with symptom severity or prognosis |
|---|---|---|
| • <5% in nonsmokers <br> • <10% in smokers | • Anion gap metabolic acidosis <br> • ↑ Lactate <br> • ↑ Creatinine phosphokinase <br> • ↑ Troponin <br> • Ischemic EKG changes | |

##  Management

- 100% oxygen until symptoms resolve
- Supportive care

Consider hyperbaric oxygen therapy for:
- COHb >25%
- Pregnant patients with COHb >15%
- Severe symptoms including syncope, altered mental status, focal neurologic deficit, myocardial ischemia, seizure, or coma

# Cardiogenic Shock

## Causes

- Acute myocardial infarction
- Heart failure
- Valvular dysfunction
- Cardiomyopathy
- Myocarditis
- Arrhythmia

## Clinical Presentation

- Hypotension (SBP <90 mm Hg)
- Not always with chest pain
- Cold, clammy, tachypnea, JVD
- Heart rate
  - Tachycardia (compensatory)
  - Bradycardia (infarcted AV node)

## Physiology

 Preload  CO  Afterload

- Narrow pulse pressure
- Insufficient pumping ability to support the oxygenation of the tissues

## Diagnosis & Treatment

- EKG and ECHO
- Chest radiograph
- Labs: troponin, lactate, CMP, BNP
- Treatment targeted at cause:
  - Inotropes: dobutamine, dopamine
  - Diuresis: furosemide
  - Mechanical: aortic balloon pump

# Cocaine and Amphetamine Toxicity

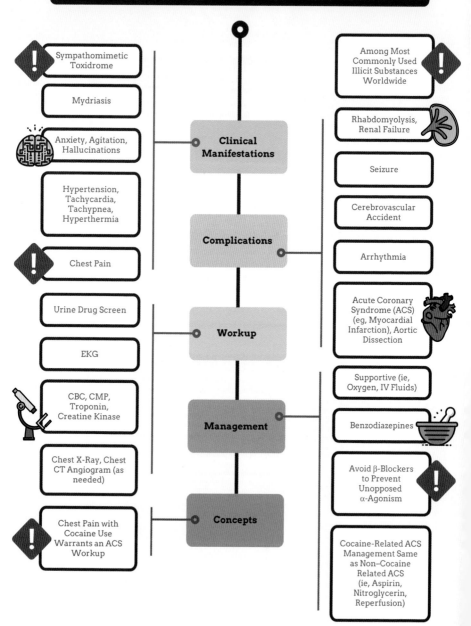

**Clinical Manifestations**
- Sympathomimetic Toxidrome
- Mydriasis
- Anxiety, Agitation, Hallucinations
- Hypertension, Tachycardia, Tachypnea, Hyperthermia
- Chest Pain

Among Most Commonly Used Illicit Substances Worldwide

**Complications**
- Rhabdomyolysis, Renal Failure
- Seizure
- Cerebrovascular Accident
- Arrhythmia
- Acute Coronary Syndrome (ACS) (eg, Myocardial Infarction), Aortic Dissection

**Workup**
- Urine Drug Screen
- EKG
- CBC, CMP, Troponin, Creatine Kinase
- Chest X-Ray, Chest CT Angiogram (as needed)

**Management**
- Supportive (ie, Oxygen, IV Fluids)
- Benzodiazepines
- Avoid β-Blockers to Prevent Unopposed α-Agonism

**Concepts**
- Chest Pain with Cocaine Use Warrants an ACS Workup
- Cocaine-Related ACS Management Same as Non–Cocaine Related ACS (ie, Aspirin, Nitroglycerin, Reperfusion)

# Cocaine and Amphetamine Withdrawal

## Clinical Presentation:

- Depression/anhedonia 😞
- Lethargy 🛋️
- Drug craving
- Increased appetite 🍽️
- Sleep disturbances (insomnia or increased sleep) 🛏️
- Vivid nightmares (increased REM)

## Diagnosis

- Clinical diagnosis
  - ⚠️ "Postuse crash"
- Urine drug screen
- Blood screen
- Rule out other causes of poisoning

## Drug Screen Times:

- Blood and urine screens may help identify recent drug **exposure**, but **cannot** diagnose withdrawal without clinical picture
- Urine screen may be positive up to 4 days after exposure
- Blood screen may be positive up to 1 day after exposure

## Management

- Symptoms typically begin within hours of drug cessation, peak in 1-2 days, and decrease by 2 weeks
- Supportive care
- Consider referral to drug rehab

Consider Using:
- Benzodiazepines
- Antidepressants
- Antipsychotics
- Naltrexone
- Behavioral therapy

# Cyanide Toxicity

## 1 Exposure

 **Smoke inhalation** from burning synthetic products

 Industrial products: metallurgy, photographic development

 Natural sources: cassava processing, bitter almonds, peach pits

## Clinical Presentation 2

Shortness of breath, agitation, and tachycardia

Progresses to seizures, coma, hypotension, and death

Symptoms occur within minutes of exposure

Patient may smell like **bitter almond** odor (not reliable)

Patients are not cyanotic appearing!

## 3 Mechanism of Action

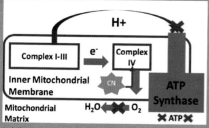

Inhibits oxygen utilization in electron transport chain leading to lactic acidosis and hypoxia

## Diagnosis and Workup 4

 Severe metabolic **LACTIC** acidosis

 Normal $O_2$ saturation; elevated venous $pO_2$

Cyanide level not clinically useful

If cyanide toxicity is from a fire, test carboxyhemoglobin level for carbon monoxide poisoning

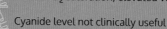

 Assume patients in house fires have cyanide poisoning

## 5 Management

 Treatment:
**A**irway, **B**reathing, **C**irculation
**Hydroxocobalamin (preferred)**
Amyl nitrite or sodium nitrite followed by sodium thiosulfate

 Complications:
Parkinsonism symptoms

# Digoxin Toxicity

## Etiology

Acute and chronic overdose
NARROW therapeutic index !

Ingestion of the foxglove plant
& other digoxin-like toxins

Failure to adjust dose
to renal function

## Physiology & Mechanism

Paralyzes the
**Na+-K+-ATPase** pump

Increases intracellular calcium
Increases *inotropy*/contractility

Shortens repolarization
Lengthens SA/AV conduction

## Clinical Presentation & Diagnosis

Nausea, vomiting,
diarrhea

Hypotension, AV block,
bradycardia, VFib
Bidirectional VTach !

Acute: HYPERkalemia
Chronic: hypo/hyperkalemia
Elevated digoxin level

BLURRED vision
Yellowing of vision !
(chronic)

## Management

Correct electrolyte imbalances
! Caution: theoretical risk of "stone heart"
with IV calcium

Tachyarrhythmias = Antidysrhythmics
Bradycardia/AV block = Atropine, pacing

Digoxin immune Fab
Directly binds drug !

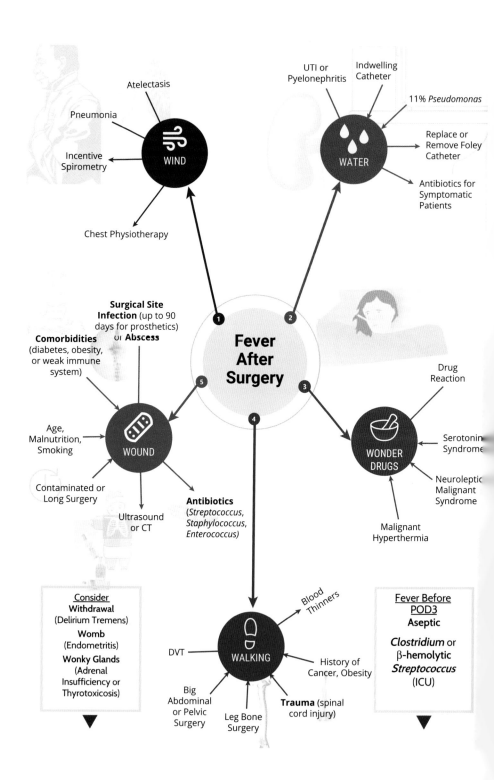

**WIND**
- Atelectasis
- Pneumonia
- Incentive Spirometry
- Chest Physiotherapy

**WATER**
- UTI or Pyelonephritis
- Indwelling Catheter
- 11% *Pseudomonas*
- Replace or Remove Foley Catheter
- Antibiotics for Symptomatic Patients

**Fever After Surgery**

1. WIND
2. WATER
3. WONDER DRUGS
4. WALKING
5. WOUND

**WOUND**
- **Surgical Site Infection** (up to 90 days for prosthetics) or **Abscess**
- **Comorbidities** (diabetes, obesity, or weak immune system)
- Age, Malnutrition, Smoking
- Contaminated or Long Surgery
- Ultrasound or CT
- **Antibiotics** (*Streptococcus, Staphylococcus, Enterococcus*)

**WONDER DRUGS**
- Drug Reaction
- Serotonin Syndrome
- Neuroleptic Malignant Syndrome
- Malignant Hyperthermia

**WALKING**
- Blood Thinners
- DVT
- History of Cancer, Obesity
- Big Abdominal or Pelvic Surgery
- Leg Bone Surgery
- **Trauma** (spinal cord injury)

Consider
**Withdrawal** (Delirium Tremens)
**Womb** (Endometritis)
**Wonky Glands** (Adrenal Insufficiency or Thyrotoxicosis)

Fever Before POD3
**Aseptic**

*Clostridium* or β-hemolytic *Streptococcus* (ICU)

# Fibrinolytic Overdose

## Pharmacology and Indications

### Tissue Plasminogen Activator Analogs (tPA)

Alteplase, Reteplase, Tenecteplase

Used for clot-related conditions such as ischemic stroke, acute myocardial infarction, pulmonary embolism

### Streptokinases

Natural Streptokinase, Anistreplase

Alternative to tPA Lower cost, but worse side effect profile

 Antigenic

### Urokinase

Used only for pulmonary embolism

## Clinical Presentation

| Intracranial Hemorrhage | Catheterization Site Bleeding | Gastrointestinal Bleeding | Wound Bleeding | Epistaxis |

## Management

| Fibrinogen Concentrate and/or Fresh Frozen Plasma | Aminocaproic Acid | Tranexamic Acid | Packed Red Blood Cells (as needed) |

# Heavy Metal Toxicity

## Mercury

**Exposure:**
Elemental: Thermometers, dental amalgam
Inorganic: Chemistry sets/antiseptics
Organic: Seafood

**Presentation:**
Elemental (inhaled): Respiratory distress
Inorganic: GI symptoms, renal failure, tremor, neurasthenia, erethism
Organic: Delayed neurotoxicity

**Diagnosis:**
Urine, blood, hair, fecal

**Treatment:**
Dimercaprol, succimer

## Arsenic

**Exposure:**
Contaminated soil, water, food, industrial applications (metal alloy plating), medicinal, and suicide/homicide attempts

**Presentation:**
Acute: Rice water diarrhea, garlic odor, QT prolongation. Cardiogenic shock. Multiorgan failure
Chronic: Cancers, hyperpigmentation

**Diagnosis:**
Urine, hair, nails

**Treatment:**
Dimercaprol, succimer

## MOST IMPORTANTLY REMOVE EXPOSURE!

## Copper

**Exposure:** Fungicide, algicide, industrial uses, chemistry sets

**Presentation:**
Acute: GI distress and perforation. Blue vomit. Jaundice
Chronic: Common in children from copper-contaminated water. Similar to Wilson's disease. Childhood cirrhosis. "Vineyard sprayer's lung" leads to adenocarcinoma

**Diagnosis:**
Primary: Clinical diagnosis
Secondary: Copper levels in blood, urine, elevated serum ceruloplasmin

**Treatment:**
D-penicillamine, dimercaprol

## Gold

**Exposure:**
Treatment for rheumatoid arthritis. Electroplating

**Presentation:**
Acute: Mucocutaneous (dermatitis, pruritus, urticaria, stomatitis); metallic taste, enterocolitis; Renal: Glomerulonephritis; eosinophilia; GI: Hepatotoxicity, pancreatitis encephalopathy, interstitial pneumonitis
Chronic: Dermal chrysiasis, ocular chrysiasis, cytopenias

**Diagnosis:** Clinical diagnosis, tissue biopsy, hair, nails

**Treatment:**
Consider D-penicillamine

# HYPERTHERMIA

>40°C
(>104°F)

## Narrow Diagnosis with Focused History & Physical

### Environmental

#### Exertional

- Rapid onset
- Athletes
- Military

#### Nonexertional

- Prolonged exposure
- Elderly
- Infants

### Infectious & Drug Induced

Overdoses →
- NMS (antipsychotics)
- Serotonin syndrome

Malignant Hyperthermia →
- Inhaled anesthetics
- Succinylcholine

### Neuroendocrine

Evaluate mental status
- Stroke
- Intracranial hemorrhage
- Seizure

Thyroid

DKA

## Treatment

Treat underlying etiology of hyperthermia

- Antipyretics
- Cooling blankets
- Cold IV fluids
- Submersion ice bath

Gold standard

- Benzodiazepines ——— NMS/SS
- Dantrolene ——— MH
- Thyroid storm ——— β-Blocker, PTU

# Hypomagnesemia

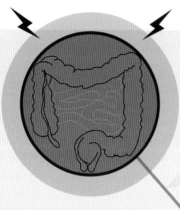

## CAUSES

- **Less intake:** malnutrition, small bowel dysfunction, TPN, PPIs, EtOH
- **More excretion (outpatient):** loop/thiazide diuretics, vomiting/diarrhea, hypercalcemia, EtOH, hyperaldosteronism, Gitelman, Bartter, familial HHNC, aminoglycosides, tacrolimus, cyclosporine
- **More excretion (inpatient):** NG suction, amphotericin
- **Serum shifts:** DKA treatment, acute pancreatitis, refeeding syndrome, postparathyroidectomy

## SIGNS

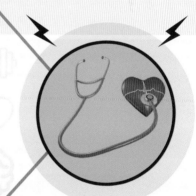

- **Exam:** tetany, Chvostek sign, Trousseau sign, hyperactive reflexes, tremor, fasciculations, weakness, hypertension (preeclampsia), seizures
- **ECG:** flat T waves, U waves, long QT (hypokalemia), arrhythmia, torsades de pointes
- **Labs:** hypokalemia, hypocalcemia, dysglycemia

## TREATMENT

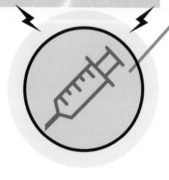

- IV (over 12-24 hours except in renal insufficiency)
- PO (magnesium gluconate)
- Replete potassium and calcium
- Consider potassium-sparing diuretic if hypervolemic
- Discontinue PPI
- **Diet:** green leafy vegetables, nuts, legumes, seeds, whole grains

# Hyp❄thermia

## ❄ Causes ❄

- Environmental exposure
- Hypoglycemia
- Hypothyroidism
- Adrenal insufficiency
- Sepsis
- Trauma

## Signs & Symptoms

- Shivering (stops below 32°C)
- Frostbite (soak in warm water bath to thaw)
- Confusion
- Lethargy -> coma
- Cardiac arrhythmias

## Management

**32-35°C:** Passive external rewarming with removal of wet clothing and application of blankets

**28-32°C:** Active external rewarming with warm water immersion or forced warm air heating blankets

**<28°C:** Active internal rewarming with warm IV fluids and consideration of thoracic/peritoneal lavage or ECMO

# <35°C (95°F)

**CORE Body Temperature**

## J (Osborn) Waves

**Classic ECG Finding**

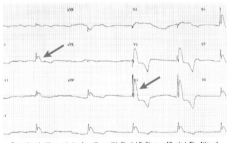

Reproduced with permission from Knoop KJ, Stack LB, Storrow AB, et al: The Atlas of Emergency Medicine, 5th ed. New York, NY: McGraw Hill 2021. Photo contributor: Michael L. Juliano, MD.

No patient is dead until they are **warm and dead**. Do not stop resuscitation efforts until patient has been warmed!

# \* Iron Salts Toxicity

## Causes
- Majority are unintentional
- Prenatal vitamins and ferrous sulfate tablets can often be bright and attractive to children
- Containers left open or improperly closed not in a child-safe location
- Intentional ingestion

## Range of Toxicity

### <20 mg/kg
Asymptomatic

### 20-60 mg/kg
May be symptomatic

### >60 mg/kg
Potential for serious toxicity
- Death can occur

## Mechanism of Toxicity

- Mucosal cell necrosis
- Impairment of capillary permeability
- Alteration of lipid membrane of mitochondria
- Inhibition of Krebs cycle
- Uncoupling of oxidative phosphorylation
- Direct vasodilation
- Inhibition of proteases (eg, thrombin)

## Clinical Presentation

**Abdominal Pain**

**Vomiting**

**Diarrhea**

**GI Bleeding**

## Serious Toxicity Can Cause:        Renal and Neurologic Dysfunction

Metabolic Acidosis

Liver Failure

Multisystem Organ Failure

Shock

Bowel Obstruction (delayed)

## Management

- Prevention
- Supportive care—ABCs

- GI decontamination if there are multiple radiopaque pill fragments
- IV deferoxamine for serious ingestion (iron level >500 µg/dL)

# Mammalian Bites

## Common Bugs

- *Staphylococcus* and *Streptococcus*
- *Pasteurella multocida*
- *Capnocytophaga canimorsus*
- Anaerobes
- Often polymicrobial
- Rabies most common with raccoons, skunks, & bats

**!** Wounds >6 hours old with increasing pain and redness are likely infected

## Workup

- Assess for proximity to underlying structures
- Distal pulse, motor, and sensation
- Exam or 2D imaging for foreign bodies
- XR indicated for all infected puncture wounds
- CT or MRI for persistent pain or failure to respond to therapy

## Special Cases

 Osteomyelitis    Septic arthritis

- Immediate surgical referral
- Withhold antibiotics until operative debridement cultures obtained
- Antibiotics should cover *Staphylococcus* and *Pseudomonas*

### Herpetic whitlow

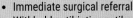

Reproduced with permission from Wolff K, Johnson RA, Saavedra AP, et al: Fitzpatrick's Color Atlas and Synopsis of Clinical Dermatology, 8th ed. New York, NY: McGraw Hill; 2017.

- Hand bite from human with HSV
- Acyclovir × 7-10 days

### Rodent bite

- Rat-bite fever rare
- 3-10 day incubation period
- Rigors and fevers
- Migratory polyarthralgia + petechial or purpuric rash
- 10-15% mortality without IV PCN 5-7 days

## Risk Factors for Puncture Wound Complications

Elderly
Diabetes
Immunocompromised
Peripheral vascular disease
Contamination (soil, debris)
Hand or foot wounds
Deep or crushing dog bites
Puncture wounds from cats
Human bites
Early infection
Treatment delay >12 hours

## Treatment

 Meticulous wound care → ↓ infection rate

 Antibiotics if high risk of complication: Amoxicillin-clavulanate

 Tetanus prophylaxis

 High-risk rabies exposure  PEP: Ig + vaccine

 Observe healthy domestic animals for 10 days

 Leave deep puncture wounds open

# Methanol and Ethylene Glycol Toxicity

## Pathophysiology

**Toxic Metabolite:**
**Formate/Formic Acid**

- Toxic to the optic nerve

## Clinical

- Inebriation, ataxia, coma
- Cloudy, blurred vision, **snowstorm in visual field**
- Retinal edema
- Headache, nausea, vomiting, abdominal pain

## Methanol

## Diagnosis

- Clinical suspicion
- Elevated **osmolar gap**
- Severe **anion gap metabolic acidosis**

### Ingestion of antifreeze, paint solvent, windshield washer fluid

## Treatment

- **Fomepizole**—inhibits alcohol dehydrogenase
- **Ethanol**—competes for alcohol dehydrogenase binding
- **Hemodialysis**

## Ethylene Glycol

## Pathophysiology

**Toxic Metabolite:**
**Glycolate/Glycolic Acid**
**Oxalate/Oxalic Acid**

- **Nephrotoxic**
- Acute tubular necrosis
- **Oxalate crystalluria** & calcium oxalate stones

## Clinical

- Inebriation, ataxia, coma **(CNS stage)**
- Tachycardia, tachypnea, hypertension **(Cardiopulmonary stage)**
- Flank pain, CVA tenderness, renal failure **(Renal stage)**

# Methemoglobin Toxicity

## Physiology ☼

1. Oxidation of heme group(s) $Fe^{2+} \rightarrow Fe^{3+}$, ❗ which cannot carry oxygen
2. Remaining heme groups have **higher affinity** for oxygen
3. Oxygen–hemoglobin dissociation curve shifts **Left** (**Low** oxygen release)
4. Tissue hypoxia

## Etiology ⚛

Accelerated oxidation due to medications:
- **Benzocaine** ❗
- **Lidocaine**
- **Nitroglycerin**
- **Sulfamethoxazole**
- Nitrate-based preservatives
- Dapsone

Genetic predisposition:
- Cytochrome b5 reductase deficiency
- G6PD deficiency

## Clinical Presentation

Similar to acute anemia:
- Dizziness
- Shortness of breath
- Headache
- Palpitations
- Seizures
- Coma
- Vascular collapse

Severe **metabolic acidosis**

Elevated methemoglobin level

Pulse oximetry is unreliable

**Chocolate-brown arterial** blood ❗

## Treatment

Intravenous **Methylene Blue** ❗ reduces $Fe^{3+} \rightarrow Fe^{2+}$
(*note: give **Meth**ylene blue for **Meth**emoglobinemia)

Exchange transfusion for resistant cases

# Neurogenic Shock

High-Impact Trauma

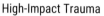

Spinal Anesthesia

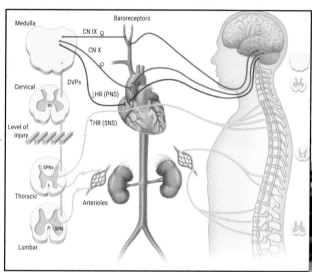

Spinal cord injury (typically T1-L3)
Loss of sympathetic tone

Bradycardia

Decreased vascular resistance leading to hypotension and bradycardia. Peripheral vascular pooling will lead to warm extremities but systemic hypothermia

Decreased Urinary Output

---

**Secure Airway**

**Fluid Resuscitate**
30 cc/kg

**Hemodynamic Support**

- Vasopressors (NE, dopamine, phenylephrine)
- Atropine
- Rule out other causes of shock

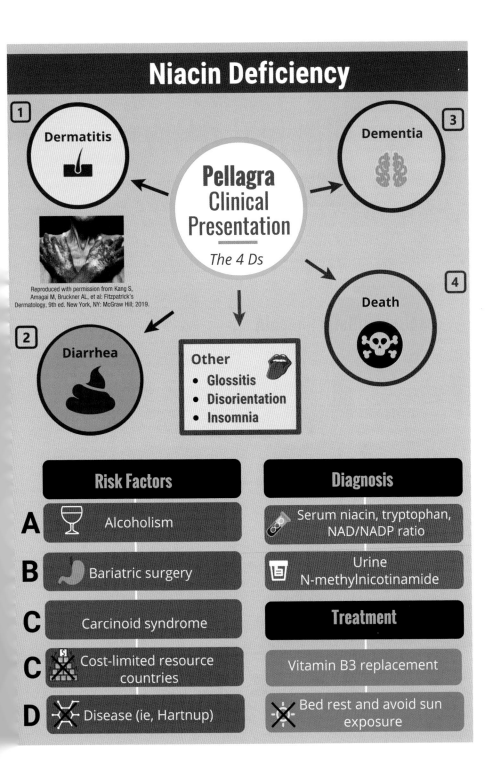

# Niacin Deficiency

**1** Dermatitis

Reproduced with permission from Kang S, Amagai M, Bruckner AL, et al: Fitzpatrick's Dermatology, 9th ed. New York, NY: McGraw Hill; 2019.

**2** Diarrhea

**Pellagra Clinical Presentation**

*The 4 Ds*

**3** Dementia

**4** Death

**Other**
- Glossitis
- Disorientation
- Insomnia

| Risk Factors | | Diagnosis |
|---|---|---|
| A | Alcoholism | Serum niacin, tryptophan, NAD/NADP ratio |
| B | Bariatric surgery | Urine N-methylnicotinamide |
| C | Carcinoid syndrome | **Treatment** |
| C | Cost-limited resource countries | Vitamin B3 replacement |
| D | Disease (ie, Hartnup) | Bed rest and avoid sun exposure |

Ibuprofen is most common!

# NSAID Toxicity

## Clinical Presentation

### Early-Onset Symptoms

 Abdominal pain, nausea, vomiting

 Most have minimal or no symptoms!

### Cardiovascular

 Hypotension, shock, bradyarrhythmia (in severe cases)

### Metabolic

### Central Nervous System

 Headache, nystagmus, diplopia, altered mental status, coma, muscle twitching, and seizures

 Hyperkalemia, hypocalcemia, hypomagnesemia, metabolic acidosis

### Gastrointestinal and Renal

 Continued abdominal pain, nausea, vomiting, hepatic injury, pancreatitis (rare), acute kidney injury, upper GI bleeding

## Diagnosis and Workup

Diagnosis is mostly clinical—a thorough history is needed

- For ibuprofen, is the amount ingested...

  <100 mg/kg?
    Unlikely to result in toxicity

  >400 mg/kg?
    Toxicity is likely

- Consider screening for potentially dangerous coingestants
  - Acetaminophen level
  - Salicylate level
  - Obtain an ECG

- Obtain a CBC and comprehensive metabolic profile

 Serum NSAID levels do not correlate with toxicity or outcomes!

## Management

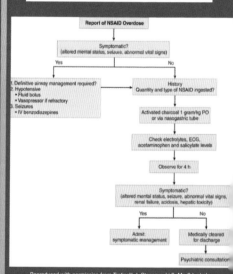

Reproduced with permission from Tintinalli J, Stapczynski S, Ma OJ, et al: Tintinalli's Emergency Medicine: A Comprehensive Study Guide, 8th ed. New York, NY: McGraw Hill; 2016.

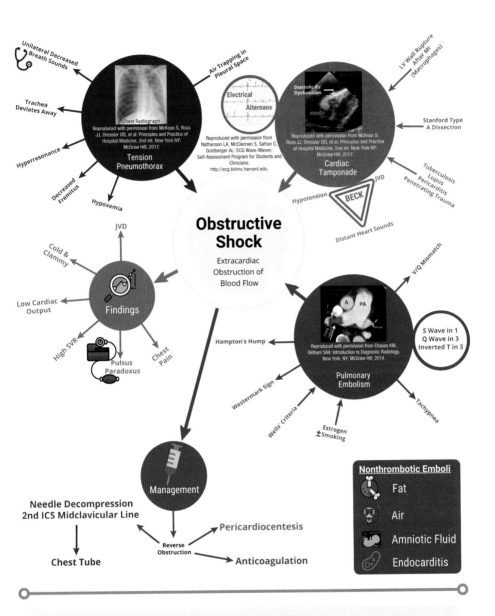

**Obstructive Shock**

Extracardiac Obstruction of Blood Flow

**Tension Pneumothorax**
- Unilateral Decreased Breath Sounds
- Trachea Deviates Away
- Hyperresonance
- Decreased Fremitus
- Hypoxemia
- Air Trapping in Pleural Space

Chest Radiograph
Reproduced with permission from McKean S, Ross JJ, Dressler DD, et al: Principles and Practice of Hospital Medicine, 2nd ed. New York NY: McGraw Hill; 2017.

Electrical Alternans
Reproduced with permission from Nathanson LA, McClennen S, Safran C, Goldberger AL: ECG Wave-Maven: Self-Assessment Program for Students and Clinicians. http://ecg.bidmc.harvard.edu.

**Cardiac Tamponade**
- LV Wall Rupture After MI (Macrophages)
- Stanford Type A Dissection
- Tuberculosis
- Lupus
- Pericarditis
- Penetrating Trauma
- Diastolic RV Dysfunction
- JVD
- Hypotension
- Distant Heart Sounds

BECK

Reproduced with permission from McKean S, Ross JJ, Dressler DD, et al: Principles and Practice of Hospital Medicine, 2nd ed. New York NY: McGraw Hill; 2017.

**Findings**
- JVD
- Cold & Clammy
- Low Cardiac Output
- High SVR
- Pulsus Paradoxus
- Chest Pain

**Pulmonary Embolism**
- V/Q Mismatch
- S Wave in 1, Q Wave in 3, Inverted T in 3
- Tachypnea
- Estrogen ± Smoking
- Wells' Criteria
- Westermark Sign
- Hampton's Hump

Reproduced with permission from Elsayes KM, Oldham SAA: Introduction to Diagnostic Radiology. New York, NY: McGraw Hill; 2014.

**Management**

Needle Decompression 2nd ICS Midclavicular Line

**Chest Tube**

Reverse Obstruction
- Pericardiocentesis
- Anticoagulation

**Nonthrombotic Emboli**
- Fat
- Air
- Amniotic Fluid
- Endocarditis

## Reversible Causes of PEA Arrest

- **Thrombosis of Pulmonary Artery**
- **Tamponade**
- **Tension Pneumothorax**
- Toxic Ingestion
- Thrombosis of Coronary Artery

- Hypovolemia
- Hypoxia
- Hydrogen Ion Excess (Acidosis)
- Hyperkalemia or Hypokalemia
- Hypothermia

# Opioids
# Overdose and Withdrawal

 **Most common cause of drug overdose death**

| Acute Opioid Overdose | Opioid Withdrawal |
|---|---|

 ## Clinical Presentation

### Physical Exam

 Respiratory depression/apnea

 Miosis

 Altered or depressed mental status

 **Beware of polysubstance use!**

### Physical Exam

 Piloerection

 Mydriasis

 Sweating, lacrimation, rhinorrhea

 Yawning

 Nausea, vomiting, diarrhea

### Vital Signs

 Bradypnea

 Hypoxia

 Hypothermia may be present

### Vital Signs

 Tachycardia if patient is distressed

 Hypertension if patient is distressed; hypotension if patient is volume depleted

## Management

 Assist with ventilation if apneic (eg, rescue breaths, bag-valve mask, etc)

 Naloxone

 Opioid replacement therapy (methadone or buprenorphine)

 Treat symptomatically with antiemetics, antidiarrheals, and anxiolytics

 Clonidine for sympathetic excess

# Organophosphate and Carbamate Toxicity

 **Remember:** Acetylcholine (ACh) is a neurotransmitter degraded by acetylcholinesterase (AChE)

 Organophosphates and carbamates are potent AChE inhibitors, thereby increasing ACh and parasympathetic activity

## Exposures

Inhalation, Ingestion, Topical

## Clinical Manifestations

 **Muscarinic:** DUMBBELLS

 **Nicotinic:** MTWtHF

## Management

 Insecticides

 Herbicides

 Industrial

 Nerve Gas

 Medicinal (ie, glaucoma, myasthenia gravis, dementia)

Suicide attempts

 Defecation, urination

 Miosis

 Bradycardia

 Bronchorrhea, bronchospasm

 Emesis

Lacrimation, salivation

 Mydriasis

 Tachycardia

 Weakness

 Hypertension

 Fasciculations

 External decontamination

 Supportive management (ie, assisting oxygenation, ventilation, etc.)

 **Atropine** (competitive muscarinic receptor antagonist): titrate to resolution of bradycardia and secretions

 **Pralidoxime** (reactivates AChE): treats muscle weakness

 Fatalities are typically secondary to acute respiratory failure

# PEA
## Pulseless Electrical Activity

A rhythm that should have a pulse in a patient who does not

Look for reversible causes of PEA...the Hs and Ts

# Hs AND Ts

| Hs | Ts |
|---|---|
| Hypovolemia | Toxins |
| Hyper- or hypokalemia | Tamponade |
| Hypothermia | Tension pneumothorax |
| Hydrogen ions (Acidosis) | Thrombosis (Cardiac) |
| Hypoxia | Thrombosis (Pulmonary) |

Reproduced with permission from Tintinalli J, Stapczynski S, Ma OJ, et al: Tintinalli's Emergency Medicine: A Comprehensive Study Guide, 8th ed. New York, NY: McGraw Hill; 2016.

**Tx: CPR, epinephrine, +/– Vasopressin, review Hs and Ts**

**Same strategy for asystole**

# Penetrating Trauma–Abdomen

## Common Injuries

Diaphragm
Liver
Spleen
Kidneys
Intestines

## Abdomen

- Nipples to groin crease anteriorly
- Tips of the scapulae to the gluteal skin crease posteriorly

⚠ Assume penetrating injury to lower chest, pelvis, flank, or back has penetrated abdominal cavity until proven otherwise

## Primary Survey

 Airway

 Breathing

 Circulation

 Disability (GCS)

 Exposure

## Physical Exam

### Inspection
- Abrasions
- Lacerations
- Contusions
- Seat belt marks
- Cullen's sign: periumbilical ecchymosis
- Grey Turner's sign: flank ecchymosis

⚠ Normal-appearing abdomen does not exclude serious intra-abdominal injury

### Palpation
- Tenderness
- Rigidity
- Tympany

 If organ evisceration, cover wound with moist, sterile dressing before surgery

Serial exams for stable patients being observed in the ED

## Imaging

 FAST exam

 Chest X-ray
Pelvis X-ray

 CT if stable

 ⚠ A negative FAST does not exclude significant abdominal injury

## Exploratory Laparotomy Indications

- Injury to abdomen, flank, or back with hypotension
- Free air under the diaphragm
- GI evisceration
- High suspicion for transabdominal trajectory after gunshot wound
- CT-diagnosed injury requiring surgery (eg, ureter or pancreas)

## Management

Unstable    FAST    OR

Stable    FAST    CT

# Penetrating Trauma—Chest

## Primary Survey

 Airway

 Breathing

 Circulation

 Disability (GCS)

 Exposure

## Cardiac Box

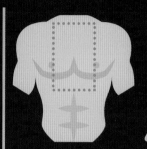

Borders:
- Sternal notch (superior)
- Nipples (lateral)
- Xiphoid process (inferior)

⚠ Increased risk of cardiac injury inside cardiac box

## Imaging

 FAST

 Chest X-ray

## Common Injuries

Heart
Lungs
Diaphragm
Chest wall
Mediastinum
Great vessels: Aorta and SVC

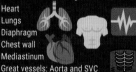

### Tension Pneumothorax

- Decreased breath sounds
- Hyperresonant to percussion
- Tracheal deviation away from affected lung
- Distended neck veins
- Hypotension

### Hemothorax

- Decreased breath sounds
- Dull to percussion

### Beck's Triad for Cardiac Tamponade

- Muffled heart sounds
- Distended neck veins
- Hypotension

## Complications

### Tension Pneumothorax

1 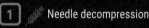 Needle decompression

2 Chest tube

### Open Pneumothorax

1 Sterile occlusive dressing on three sides

2 Chest tube

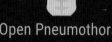
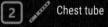

### Hemothorax

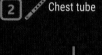

Chest tube

### Cardiac Tamponade

1 Pericardiocentesis

2 Surgery

# Penetrating Trauma—Musculoskeletal

## Hard Signs of Major Injury

Diminished distal pulses
Obvious arterial bleeding
Expanding or pulsatile hematoma
Audible bruit
Palpable thrill
Distal ischemia (**p**ain, **p**allor,
**p**aralysis, **p**ulselessness,
**p**aresthesias, **p**oikilothermia)

## Soft Signs of Major Injury

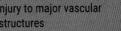

Small hematoma
Injury to anatomically related nerve
Unexplained hypotension
History of hemorrhage
Proximity of injury to major vascular
structures
Complex fracture

## Workup

Primary Survey → Secondary Survey

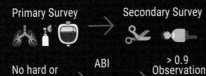

No hard or → ABI → > 0.9 Observation
soft signs

< 0.9 CTA

AP/lateral
X-ray to look
for fractures
& foreign
bodies
(glass, metal,
bone, gravel)

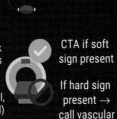

CTA if soft
sign present

If hard sign
present →
call vascular

## Management

Control bleeding  → Direct pressure
Pressure dressing
Tourniquet

Bone fractures from
penetrating trauma = open fx → Admit, IV Abx

Wound management → Copiously irrigate and
scrub

| Wound | Management |
| --- | --- |
| Well irrigated, clean | Immediate closure |
| Contaminated | Delayed closure at 72-96 hours |
| Foreign body | Delayed closure at 72-96 hours |
| Major tissue destruction | Delayed closure at 72-96 hours |

Hard signs of major
injury → Consult vascular
surgery

## Complications

Vascular or
nerve injury

Limb ischemia or
loss

Degenerative
arthritis

Compartment
syndrome

Infections

# Penetrating Trauma—Neck

## Hard Signs of Major Injury

Neurologic deficit
Airway compromise
Diffuse SQ emphysema
Expanding hematoma
Brisk bleeding
Hemorrhagic shock
Hematemesis

## Soft Signs of Major Injury

Hemoptysis
Oropharyngeal blood
Dysphagia
Dyspnea
Dysphonia

## Trauma Workup

| 1 | | Airway |
| 2 | | Breathing |
| 3 | | Circulation |
| 4 | | Disability (GCS) |
| 5 | | Exposure |

X-ray to look for PTX or hemothorax

CTA, MRI, or MRA if no hard sign present if hard sign present

## Management

Stable

↓

Platysma violation

↓ ❌        ↓ ✓

Observe    Hard signs

Unstable

↓

OR/IR for exploration and repair

Hard signs ✓

❌

Soft signs

↓ ✓

Observe + CTA

Pharyngoesophageal injury → esophagram or esophagoscopy

Laryngotracheal injury → endoscopy

Vascular injury → OR/IR for repair

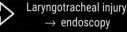

## Complications

Cerebral infarction

Hemorrhagic shock

Airway obstruction

Pneumothorax Hemothorax

# Rabies

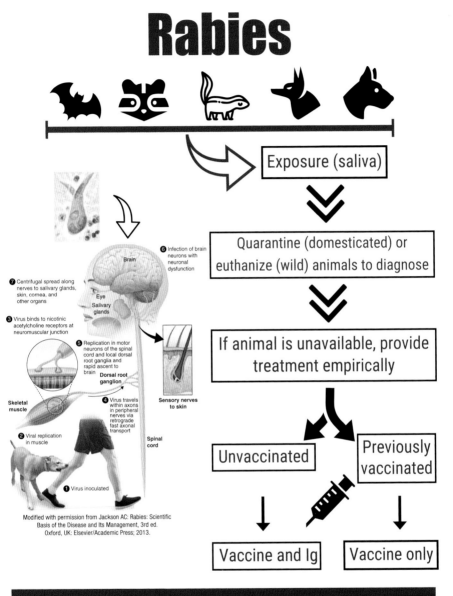

Exposure (saliva)

Quarantine (domesticated) or euthanize (wild) animals to diagnose

If animal is unavailable, provide treatment empirically

Unvaccinated

Previously vaccinated

Vaccine and Ig

Vaccine only

**6** Infection of brain neurons with neuronal dysfunction

Brain

**7** Centrifugal spread along nerves to salivary glands, skin, cornea, and other organs

Eye
Salivary glands

**3** Virus binds to nicotinic acetylcholine receptors at neuromuscular junction

**5** Replication in motor neurons of the spinal cord and local dorsal root ganglia and rapid ascent to brain

Dorsal root ganglion

Skeletal muscle

**4** Virus travels within axons in peripheral nerves via retrograde fast axonal transport

Sensory nerves to skin

**2** Viral replication in muscle

Spinal cord

**1** Virus inoculated

Modified with permission from Jackson AC: Rabies: Scientific Basis of the Disease and Its Management, 3rd ed. Oxford, UK: Elsevier/Academic Press; 2013.

- Fatal once patient presents with symptoms
- Symptoms delayed due to incubation period: fever, fatigue, insomnia, anxiety, hydrophobia, respiratory depression, itching at wound site, changes in mental status
- Bites from bats may not be noticed, so exposures of unknown timing are treated
- Treatment requires vaccine series on days 0, 3, 7, and 14; rabies Ig only on initial visit

# Salicylate Toxicity and Overdose

Aspirin, oil of wintergreen (methyl salicylate), Pepto-Bismol
(bismuth subsalicylate), salicylic acid, some herbal medications

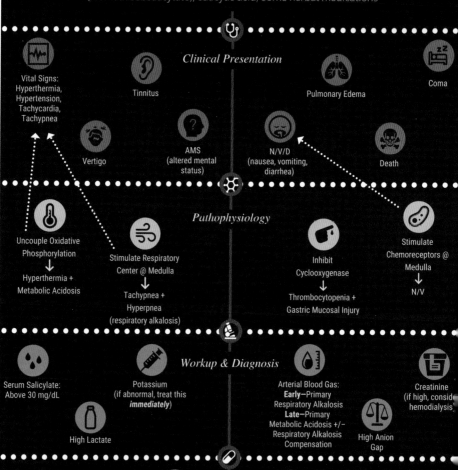

## Clinical Presentation

**Vital Signs:**
Hyperthermia,
Hypertension,
Tachycardia,
Tachypnea

Tinnitus

Pulmonary Edema

Coma

Vertigo

AMS
(altered mental
status)

N/V/D
(nausea, vomiting,
diarrhea)

Death

## Pathophysiology

Uncouple Oxidative
Phosphorylation
↓
Hyperthermia +
Metabolic Acidosis

Stimulate Respiratory
Center @ Medulla
↓
Tachypnea +
Hyperpnea
(respiratory alkalosis)

Inhibit
Cyclooxygenase
↓
Thrombocytopenia +
Gastric Mucosal Injury

Stimulate
Chemoreceptors @
Medulla
↓
N/V

## Workup & Diagnosis

Serum Salicylate:
Above 30 mg/dL

Potassium
(if abnormal, treat this
*immediately*)

Arterial Blood Gas:
**Early**–Primary
Respiratory Alkalosis
**Late**–Primary
Metabolic Acidosis +/–
Respiratory Alkalosis
Compensation

Creatinine
(if high, consider
hemodialysis)

High Lactate

High Anion
Gap

## Management

***Avoid Intubation!!***
(if you must due to
severe respiratory
distress, maintain
alkalemia with high
minute ventilation)

Decontamination:
Multidose
Activated
Charcoal

Volume
Resuscitation with
IV Saline
(caution if
pulmonary or
cerebral edema)

Urine Alkalinization:
IV Sodium
Bicarbonate

Supplemental Glucose
for AMS
(low cerebral glucose
can occur despite
normal serum glucose)

Hemodialysis
(salicylate level
>100 mg/dL, AKI,
severe signs/
symptoms,
ARDS, pulmonary
edema)

# Sedative-Hypnotic Agent Overdose

## Pathophysiology

Depression of the CNS reticular activating system, cerebral cortex, and cerebellum

## Clinical Manifestations

### Mild Intoxication

- Euphoria
- Slurred speech
- Ataxia
- Altered mental status

### Severe Intoxication

Coma
Hypotension
Hypothermia
Respiratory arrest

## Diagnosis

Primarily a clinical diagnosis
Serum drug levels may be available
(ie, ethanol, phenobarbital, etc.)
Consider coingestants

## Management

### Supportive Care

- ABCs
- IV fluids for hypotension or dehydration
- Control of paradoxical agitation

### Decontamination

- Consider activated charcoal if patient is alert, has bowel sounds, and presents within 1 hour of ingestion

### Specific Therapy

- Consider naloxone if concurrent opioid use
- Flumazenil: Benzodiazepine antagonist

 Supportive care is the mainstay of management

 Flumazenil contraindicated if patient is benzodiazepine-tolerant

# Selenium Deficiency

 ## Background

- Component of glutathione peroxidase and deiodinase enzymes
- Occurs in areas with low selenium soil content and low dietary intake (<20 μg/d) including Keshan China and parts of New Zealand and Scandinavia
- Also occurs in strict vegetarians or those on total parenteral nutrition without supplementation

## Diagnosis and Workup

- _Serum selenium of 7 μg/L or less_

 ## Clinical Presentation

### Keshan Disease

- Primarily in young women and children
- Multifocal myocarditis
- Muscle pain/weakness
- White nailbeds and hypopigmentation of skin/hair

### Kashin–Beck Disease

- Osteoarthropathy of epiphyseal and articular cartilage and epiphyseal growth plates
- Enlarged joints and shortened digits

⚠ **May lead to arrhythmia and fatal cardiomyopathy**

## Management

Tuna 94 μg    Beef 33 μg

**55 μg** Recommended Daily Value

Eggs 15 μg    Bread 13 μg

- Supplementation to correct deficiency
- Addition of selenium to total parenteral nutrition to prevent deficiency

# Snake Bites

| Crotalids | | Elapids |
|---|---|---|

**Crotalids**

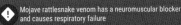
Elliptical pupil — Nostril — Heat sensing pit

Reproduced with permission from Tintinalli J, Stapczynski S. Ma OJ, et al: Tintinalli's Emergency Medicine: A Comprehensive Study Guide, 8th ed. New York, NY: McGraw Hill; 2016.

**"Pit Vipers"**
Rattlesnakes, copperheads, water moccasins, massasauga

**Elapids**

Reproduced with permission from Knoop KJ, Stack LB, Storrow AB, et al: The Atlas of Emergency Medicine, 4th ed. New York, NY: McGraw Hill; 2016. Photo contributor: Mike Cardwell, MS.

**Coral Snakes**
*"red on yellow, kill a fellow; red on black, venom lack"*

| Crotalids | | Elapids |
|---|---|---|
| • Found in all states except ME, AK, and HI<br>• Most common in young, intoxicated males<br>• Bites more common in warmer months |  **Epidemiology** | • Small, nocturnal snakes that **primarily** bite when handled<br>• Deep southeast, TX, and AZ<br>• Snake often holds on to or chews victim |
| • Digestive enzymes causing coagulopathy and local tissue necrosis<br><br>**(!)** Mojave rattlesnake venom has a neuromuscular blocker and causes respiratory failure |  **Venom** | • Neurotoxin causing paralysis<br><br>**(!)** Potent venom is primarily in the eastern coral snake (*M. fulvus*) |
| **Localized**<br>• Puncture wound<br>• Severe pain and swelling at bite site<br>• Bullae, necrosis, compartment syndrome<br><br>**(!)** 5% of bites are dry. Observe for 8-12 hours to confirm<br><br>**Systemic**<br>• Nausea, vomiting, diarrhea, perioral paresthesias, salivation, weakness<br>• Respiratory failure, seizures, coma, GI and pulmonary hemorrhage, cardiovascular collapse |  **Clinical Presentation** | **Localized**<br>• Minimal local damage, may not see bite<br>• Burning, numbness, or weakness of extremity<br><br>**(!)** Systemic symptoms may be delayed by hours<br><br>**Systemic**<br>• Weakness, drowsiness, nausea, vomiting, fasciculations, tremors, bulbar paralysis, seizures, respiratory depression<br>• Cranial nerve palsies and rapidly progressing paralysis |
| • Coagulopathy, hemolysis, thrombocytopenia<br>• Pulmonary edema<br>• Arrhythmias or ischemic changes on EKG<br>• Blood, protein, or glucose in urine |  **Laboratory and Imaging Findings** | • Primarily diagnosed by history and physical<br>• Creatinine kinase may be elevated<br>• Other tests as clinically indicated |
| • Wound care and tetanus prophylaxis<br><br>**Antivenom**<br>• Indicted for worsening localized injury, systemic symptoms, or lab abnormalities<br><br>**(!)** 8% have immediate hypersensitivity to antivenom. 13% develop serum sickness |  **Management** | • Splint extremity<br>• Wound care and tetanus prophylaxis<br>• Supportive care<br>• Patients recover over days to weeks with or without antivenom<br><br>**(!)** Antivenom no longer available in the USA<br><br>**Antivenom**<br>• If available, give antivenom; redose if symptoms progress |

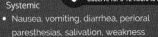

# Spider and Scorpion Envenomation

These US endemic species generally only bite or sting humans when provoked

Children are at greatest risk of severe envenomation due to their small size

## Black Widow
### *Latrodectus mactans*

Reproduced with permission from Knoop KJ, Stack LB, Storrow AB, et al: The Atlas of Emergency Medicine, 4th ed. New York, NY: McGraw Hill; 2016. Photo contributor: Lawrence B. Stack, MD.

Females have red hourglass on ventral surface

- Throughout the United States
- Woodpiles, sheds, and privies

 • Neurotoxin

- Pain and erythema of the site
- Hypertension, tachycardia, headache, fasciculations, salivation, paralysis, nausea, and vomiting

- Myalgias and muscle spasm can mimic acute abdomen

- Supportive care and local wound care, tetanus ppx
- Analgesics, muscle relaxants, Ca⁺, and benzos
- Antivenom for severe cases, high risk of anaphylaxis

## Arizona Bark Scorpion
### *Centruroides exilicauda*

Reproduced with permission from Knoop KJ, Stack LB, Storrow AB, et al: The Atlas of Emergency Medicine, 4th ed. New York, NY: McGraw Hill; 2016. Photo contributor: Sean P. Bush, MD.

Small spine at base of stinger

 • AZ, NM, CA, and TX

 • Neurotoxin

- Immediate pain and paresthesias around sting
- CN deficits, spastic muscle contractions, nausea, vomiting, tachycardia, and agitation
- Symptoms typically last 24-48 hours without treatment

- Supportive care: analgesics, ice, and benzos
- Atropine for excessive salivation
- Scorpion antivenom reduces length of symptoms

## Brown Recluse
### *Loxosceles reclusa*

Reproduced with permission from Knoop KJ, Stack LB, Storrow AB, et al: The Atlas of Emergency Medicine, 4th ed. New York, NY: McGraw Hill; 2016. Photo contributor: R. Jason Thurman, MD.

Fiddle shape on cephalothorax

 • Southcentral and southeast US

- Closets, attics, clothes, bedding
- Hemolytic and tissue-destroying proteins

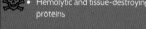
- Initially painless bite that usually heals in days to weeks
- Occasional severe reaction: severe pain and hemorrhagic blister can lead to tissue necrosis
- Nausea, vomiting, chills

Loxoscelism: rare systemic reaction
- Arthralgias, myalgias, hemolysis, seizures, renal failure, DIC, and death

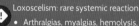
- Supportive care: pain control, tetanus, antibiotics for infection
- Antivenom not available in the United States
- Surgery 2-3 weeks post bite for lesions >2 cm

---

## Hobo Spider (*Eratigena agrestis*)

- Pacific northwest (AK to UT)
- Woodpiles, basements, and crawlspaces
- Similar to brown recluse bites: Initially painless bite that can develop erythema, blistering, and necrosis
- Headache, nausea, fatigue, and rarely aplastic anemia
- No antivenom available

Antivenoms are animal derived and have a high risk of anaphylaxis

## Tarantula (*Theraphosidae*)

- Hairy spiders that are frequently kept as pets and flick their urticating hairs in self-defense
- Reactions range from contact dermatitis to granulomatous reactions
- Eyes: Barbed hairs are highly irritating if they become imbedded in the eye, requiring surgical removal of hairs and topical steroids

### C. tetani

- Spore-forming Gram-positive bacteria that secretes the tetanus toxin
- Ubiquitous in soil and dirt

### Immunizations

- DTaP: kids under 7
- Tdap: people over 7
- Three doses are given in initial series
- After 10 years: patients should be given Tdap booster

### Exposures

- Often from wounds
- Tdap series and booster in past 10 years
- Tetanus Ig given to patients without primary series
- Update if last booster unknown

# Tetanus

*Clostridium tetani*

### Mechanism

- Toxin prevents release of the inhibitory glycine and GABA in the presynaptic neuron
- Lack of inhibition leads to excitation in peripheral nervous system

### Symptoms

- Muscle contractions
- Autonomic instability
- Including: risus sardonicus (sardonic smile), "lockjaw," opisthotonos, and laryngospasm

### Treatment

- Tetanus Ig
- Ig before wound debridement
- Antibiotic of choice: metronidazole
- Benzodiazepines may be needed for spasm

# Theophylline Toxicity

## Clinical Presentation:

- Vomiting
- Seizures
- Hallucinations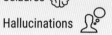
- Cardiac Arrhythmias

- Hypokalemia
- Hyperglycemia
- Coarse Tremor
- Hypotension

## Diagnosis:

- **Clinical** diagnosis
- **Rule out** other toxicities that manifest similarly:
  - β₂-agonists
  - Caffeine
  - Cocaine
  - Iron
  - Salicylates

Obtain the following:

- Serum theophylline level
- Serum glucose
- Potassium
- Calcium
- Bicarbonate
- ECG

## Management:

- GI decontamination: Multiple-dose activated charcoal
- Supportive care: Including potassium repletion, symptomatic management, etc.
- Hemodialysis for the following circumstances:
  - Severe toxicity (life-threatening arrythmia, seizure, clinical instability)
  - Rising theophylline level despite optimal care
  - Serum theophylline >100 mg/L for acute or 50-60 mg/L for chronic

# THER▲AL BURNS

## Airway & Breathing

- Perioral full-thickness or circumferential neck burns; progressing hoarseness ➡️ **intubate**
- Smoke inhalation ➡️ CO poisoning ➡️ 100% oxygen
- Furniture ➡️ CN poisoning ➡️ antidote
- Singed nasal hairs or soot ➡️ minimize fluids
- Circumferential chest ➡️ escharotomy

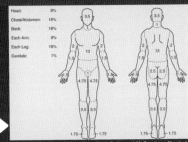

Reproduced with permission from Kang S, Amagai M, Bruckner AL, et al: Fitzpatrick's Dermatology, 9th ed. New York. NY: McGraw Hill; 2019.

## Circulation

- Capillary permeability ➡️ hypovolemia
- <u>Adults:</u> 2 × (kg) × % mL of LR within first 8 hours
- Superficial partial-thickness: painful and blanching (usually from hot water)
- Deep partial-thickness: painless and nonblanching ➡️ scar formation over weeks
- Superficial burns excluded in calculations
- Indwelling Foley to monitor urine output

## Management

- VBG, lactate, urine myoglobin, creatine kinase
- Update tetanus
- Opiates ± anxiolytics ➡️ irrigation
- <u>Debride blisters:</u> big intact; open; mobile joints
- 1% silver sulfadiazine on nonfacial burns
- Antibiotic ointment on face

## Disposition

- Breadth; age; involvement of sensitive areas (genitalia); comorbidities ➡️ admission to burn center vs admission to nonburn center
- Discharge minor burns (prompt follow-up)

## Complications

- Hypovolemic shock
- *Pseudomonas* infection

# Thiamine Deficiency

## Clinical Presentation

### Infantile Beriberi

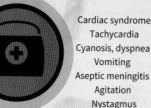

Cardiac syndrome
Tachycardia
Cyanosis, dyspnea
Vomiting
Aseptic meningitis
Agitation
Nystagmus
Purposeless movements
Altered consciousness
Seizure

### Adult Beriberi

**Dry**
Symmetrical peripheral neuropathy
(sensory + motor)

**Wet**
Cardiomegaly, cardiomyopathy, heart failure, peripheral edema, tachycardia, in addition to neuropathy

❗ Complication of weight loss surgery or TPN

### Wernicke–Korsakoff

**C**onfusion
**A**taxia
**N**ystagmus
Ophthalmoplegia
Memory loss
Confabulation
Personality changes

## Diagnosis

Primarily a **clinical diagnosis**
Consider in all patients presenting with acute delirium or acute ataxia

*Tests not readily available, especially in emergency setting

*Thiamine level alone may be unreliable

Labs:
- Erythrocyte transketolase activity (ETKA) before and after addition of thiamine pyrophosphate (TPP). Low ETKA = thiamine deficiency
- Serum thiamine or TPP level

## Management

Treat presumptively

**Vitamin B1 (thiamine) supplementation**

 Higher doses are typically required for Wernicke–Korsakoff

 **Delay administration of dextrose** to patients with <u>prolonged starvation or alcoholism</u> until thiamine supplementation to avoid precipitating Wernicke's encephalopathy

# Trauma Management

## Primary Survey

### Airway
- Assess airway patency
- Clear foreign bodies
- Insert oral or nasal airway when necessary: obtunded/unconscious patients should be intubated
- If unable to intubate --> cricothyrotomy

 If patient can talk, airway is patent

### Breathing
- Breath sounds
- Inspect chest and neck for wounds, crepitus, deviated trachea, abnormal chest wall motion, etc.

### Circulation
- Control hemorrhage
- Assess circulatory status

### Disability
- Pupil size, symmetry, and reactivity
- Glasgow Coma Scale

### Exposure
- Completely disrobe patient
- Logroll patient to check back
- Rectal exam

## Secondary Survey

Head-to-toe survey once primary survey is complete

## Glasgow Coma Scale

Eye
- 4 Open spontaneously
- 3 Open to verbal command
- 2 Open to pain
- 1 None

Verbal
- 5 Oriented and converses
- 4 Confused
- 3 Inappropriate words
- 2 Incomprehensible sounds
- 1 None

Motor
- 6 Obeys commands
- 5 Localizes pain to painful stimuli
- 4 Flexion withdrawal to pain
- 3 Abnormal flexion, decorticate posture
- 2 Extensor response, decerebrate posture
- 1 None

 Use best motor response if sides unequal

GCS ≤ 8 = Intubate!

## Imaging

### During Primary Survey:

 FAST exam

 Chest X-ray
Pelvis X-ray

### During Secondary Survey:

 Other imaging as needed, including C-spine films

 Pregnancy test for women of childbearing age

# Tricyclic Antidepressant Overdose

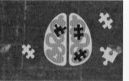

## Clinical Presentation

### Cardiovascular

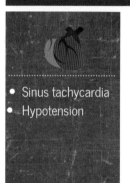

- Sinus tachycardia
- Hypotension

### Neurologic

- Sedation/coma
- Confusion, delirium, hallucinations
- Seizures

### Anticholinergic

Hyperthermia

Flushing

Dilated pupils

Absent bowel sounds

Urinary retention

## Diagnostic Testing

**Clinical Diagnosis!**
- Can confirm with serum TCA levels
- Not reliable or fast
- Fingerstick glucose to rule out hypoglycemia

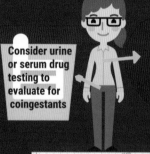

**Consider urine or serum drug testing to evaluate for coingestants**

**ECG**
- Sinus tachycardia
- Ventricular dysrhythmia
- QRS widening (>100 ms) due to Na channel blockade
- Tall R wave in aVR
- Deep S wave in 1 & aVL

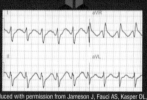

## Management

- ABCs
- Ventricular dysrhythmias: Sodium bicarbonate, defibrillation/cardioversion
- Hypotension: IV fluids +/− vasopressors (eg, norepinephrine)
- Seizures: Sodium bicarbonate, benzodiazepines
- Consider IV lipid emulsion for life-threatening toxicity not responsive to other therapies

**! Sodium bicarbonate is the mainstay treatment for TCA toxicity**

# Vitamin A Deficiency

## Clinical Presentation

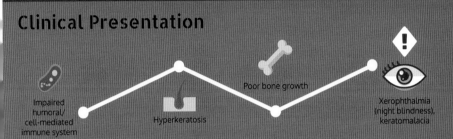

Impaired humoral/ cell-mediated immune system

Hyperkeratosis

Poor bone growth

Xerophthalmia (night blindness), keratomalacia

Vitamin A deficiency occurs in approximately 30% of children age <5 worldwide and nearly 50% in young children in South Asia and sub-Saharan Africa

## Diagnosis

**Clinical Findings**
Diagnosis is primarily made based on history and physical exam

**Serum Retinol**
<20 µg/dL
(0.7 µmol/L)
suggests deficiency

**Serum Carotene**
Low levels may indicate malabsorption and nutritional status

## Management

### Targeted Supplementation: Disease
(repeated on days 2 and 14)

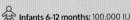

 **Infants <6 months:** 50,000 IU

**Infants 6-12 months:** 100,000 IU

**Children/adults >12 months:** 200,000 IU

### Periodic Supplementation: Endemic Populations

 **Infants 6-12 months:** 100,000 IU
(30 mg retinol equivalent)—one dose

 **Children 12-59 months:** 200,000 IU
(60 mg retinol equivalent)— repeated every 4-6 months

 **Pregnant:** 10,000 IU daily or 25,000 IU weekly—minimum of 12 weeks until delivery

# Vitamin B2 (Riboflavin) Deficiency

## About Riboflavin

Riboflavin (B₂)

Ribityl

Reproduced with permission from Jameson J, Fauci AS, Kasper DL, et al: Harrison's Principles of Internal Medicine, 20th ed. New York, NY: McGraw Hill; 2018.

- Acts as an electron donor and cofactor in reduction-oxidation reactions, cellular respiration
- Precursor for FMN & FAD (required for flavoenzymes)
- Involved in drug, steroid, carbohydrate, fat, and protein metabolism, and in detoxification reactions

## Causes of Deficiency

- Malnutrition, drug interactions, alcoholism
- Riboflavin is photosensitive and can be degraded during phototherapy

- Usually associated with other vitamin deficiencies

## Clinical Manifestations

- **Magenta cobblestone tongue**
- **Cheilosis, angular stomatitis**
- **Corneal vascularization**
- Ocular canthi lesions
- Nasolabial fold lesions
- Superficial keratitis
- Conjunctival injection
- Personality changes
- Mild burning of the tongue
- Hyperplastic sebaceous glands

## Diagnosis

- Erythrocyte glutathione reductase requires riboflavin in the form of FAD. Deficiency is indicated if erythrocyte glutathione reductase activity coefficients are >1.2-1.4
- Can also measure concentration of riboflavin in red blood cells or urine

## Management

- Nutrition with diet consisting of **milk/dairy products, enriched cereals or breads**, fish, eggs, lean meat, legumes, broccoli
- Vitamin B2 oral preparations (treat until symptoms resolve)

## Toxicity and Other Notes

- Vitamin B2 toxicity not documented
- Vitamin B2 deficiency is reversible, with the exception of anatomic changes (eg, cataracts)

# Vitamin B5 (Pantothenate) Deficiency

## About Pantothenate

$$O=C-OH$$
$$|$$
$$CH_2$$
$$|$$
$$CH_2$$
$$|$$
$$NH$$
$$|$$
$$C=O$$
$$|$$
$$CHOH$$
$$H_3C-C-CH_3$$
$$|$$
$$CH_2OH$$

Pantothenic acid

Reproduced with permission from Rodwell VW, Bender DA, Botham KM, et al: Harper's Illustrated Biochemistry, 31st ed. New York, NY: McGraw Hill; 2018.

- Precursor for phosphopantetheine and thus coenzyme A
- Also needed by acyl carrier protein (ACP)
- Involved in fatty acid, acyl group, and carbohydrate metabolism
- Also has role in cholesterol and steroid hormone synthesis, and protein acetylation

## Causes of Deficiency

- Rare due to vitamin ubiquity— deficiency rarely observed outside of experiments

- Patients with vitamin B5 deficiency most likely have deficiencies in other nutrients as well

## Clinical Manifestations

- **Dermatitis**
- **Enteritis**
- **Alopecia**
- **Adrenal insufficiency**
- Mood changes
- Hypoglycemia
- Muscle cramps
- Paresthesias
- Ataxia
- Fatigue, insomnia, restlessness
- Upper respiratory infections
- Headache

## Diagnosis

- Check vitamin B5 levels in urine

  - 2.6 mg/day is the normal excretion rate

  - Deficiency indicated if levels are <1 mg/day

## Management

- Nutrition with diet consisting of vegetables, whole grains, legumes, lentils, milk, yeast, egg yolks, liver, meat

- Vitamin B5 supplements

## Toxicity and Other Notes

- Vitamin B5 toxicity not documented

- PANK2 gene mutations ➡ less activity or lower levels of pantothenate kinase ➡ poor vitamin B5 metabolism into CoA ➡ pantothenate kinase-associated neurodegeneration (PKAN)

  - Vitamin B5 supplementation may help in some cases of PKAN

# Vitamin B6 Deficiency

## Etiology:

### Medications:

**Isoniazid** | B6 given with INH |
**Oral contraceptives**

 **Alcoholism**

 **Associated with other B vitamin deficiencies**

## Clinical Presentation:

 **Convulsions**

 **Sideroblastic anemias**

Reproduced with permission from Lichtman MA, Shafer MS, Felgar RE, et al: Lichtman's Atlas of Hematology 2016. New York, NY: McGraw Hill; 2017.

 **Peripheral neuropathy**

 **Mouth sores**

## Diagnosis:

 Mean plasma pyridoxal-5-phosphate **(PLP)** concentration

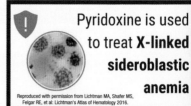
Pyridoxine is used to treat **X-linked sideroblastic anemia**

Reproduced with permission from Lichtman MA, Shafer MS, Felgar RE, et al: Lichtman's Atlas of Hematology 2016. New York, NY: McGraw Hill; 2017.

# Vitamin B7 Deficiency

## Role of Vitamin B7 (Biotin)

An important cofactor in **carboxylation** reactions
Most notably:

**Fatty acid synthesis:** acetyl-CoA (2C) $\xrightarrow{\text{Acetyl-CoA carboxylase}}$ malonyl-CoA (3C)

**Gluconeogenesis:** pyruvate (3C) $\xrightarrow{\text{Pyruvate carboxylase}}$ oxaloacetate (4C)

**Odd-chain fatty acid metabolism:** propionyl-CoA (3C) $\xrightarrow{\text{Propionyl-CoA carboxylase}}$ methylmalonyl-CoA (4C)

## Etiology
### (Rare)

May be caused by

- **Antibiotics (destruction of GI flora)**
- Excessive **raw egg white** consumption
  - **Avidin** in eggs binds & sequesters biotin in the GI tract ➔ biotin is eliminated in feces instead of being absorbed
  - Heating egg whites denatures avidin, preventing it from binding biotin

## Clinical Presentation

- **Dermatitis**
- **Alopecia**
- **Enteritis**

## Treatment

- Biotin supplementation
- Biotin-rich foods (avocado, nuts, yeast, spinach, liver, sweet potatoes, etc.)

# Vitamin B9 (Folate) Deficiency

## Role of Folate

- Converts to tetrahydrofolate (THF), a C-carrier critical to the **methylation reactions** in the synthesis of nitrogenous bases in **nucleic acids**

- Therefore, there is increased folate demand in states of ***rapid cell division***

### Etiology

- **Malnutrition**
- **Alcohol abuse**
- **Malabsorption** (eg, celiac disease, IBD)
- **Increased replication demand** (eg, pregnancy, hemolytic anemia)
- **Drugs** (eg, methotrexate, phenytoin, bactrim, anticonvulsants)

> THE LIVER ONLY STORES 3-4 MONTHS, SUPPLY SO IT ONLY TAKES A FEW **MONTHS** TO BECOME B9 DEFICIENT

## Physiologic Effects

- **Neural tube defects** in pregnancy
- **Macrocytic megaloblastic anemia**

> IMPORTANT CLINICAL DISTINCTIONS between similar B12 deficiency anemia
> - NO neurologic Sxs
> - B12 stores take **years** to deplete, **B9 months**
> - ↑Homocysteine, nml methylmalonic acid

Reproduced with permission from McKean S, Ross JJ, Dressler DD, et al: Principles and Practice of Hospital Medicine, 2nd ed. New York NY: McGraw Hill; 2017.

**Hypersegmented neutrophil** often seen in megaloblastic anemia

## Clinical Presentation

- Signs/Sxs of **anemia**
- **Glossitis**

Reproduced with permission from Aster JC, Bunn H: Pathophysiology of Blood Disorders, 2nd ed. New York, NY: McGraw Hill; 2017.

## Treatment

- **Oral supplementation**

> ***Women should begin folate supplementation at least 1 month prior to conception****

- **Dietary sources** (leafy green vegetables, fortified foods, animal liver)

# Vitamin B12 Deficiency

## Etiologies

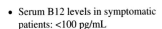

1. Inadequate dietary intake

Food cobalamin (Cbl)

Cbl transferred to intrinsic factor produced by gastric parietal cells

2. Absence of gastric acid

Gastric acid

3. Absence of intrinsic factor

4. Dysfunction of terminal ileum

Liver

IF-Cbl complex binds to receptor in terminal ileum (cubulin)

Reproduced with permission from Aster JC, Bunn H: Pathophysiology of Blood Disorders, 2nd ed. New York, NY: McGraw Hill; 2017.

## Clinical Presentation

- Moderate to severe megaloblastic anemia (fatigue, SOB, muscle weakness, etc.)

- Vague GI disturbances (diarrhea, anorexia)

- Peripheral neuropathy

- Diminished proprioception, vibration, and balance

- Dementia and neuropsychiatric symptoms (advanced cases)

## Diagnosis

- Serum B12 levels in symptomatic patients: <100 pg/mL

- Confirm with elevated serum methylmalonic acid (>1000 nmol/L) or homocysteine (>16.2 mmol/L)

- Macrocytic anemia typically moderate to severe with elevated MCV (110–140 fL)

- Peripheral blood smear is megaloblastic, defined as red blood cells that appear as macro-ovalocytes, and hypersegmented neutrophils

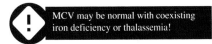

> ⚠ MCV may be normal with coexisting iron deficiency or thalassemia!

## Management

- Intramuscular or subcutaneous injections of 100 mcg of vitamin B12

- Replacement is usually given daily for the first week, weekly for the next month, and then monthly for life

- Serum B12 levels must be monitored frequently to ensure adequate replacement

- Simultaneous folic acid replacement (1 mg daily) is recommended for the first several months of vitamin B12 replacement

# Vitamin C Deficiency

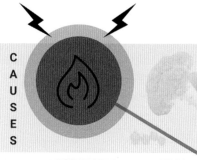

**CAUSES**

- **Malnutrition:** grapefruits, oranges, lemons, limes, breast milk, and fortified formula
- **Heating:** potatoes, spinach, broccoli, red peppers, tomatoes

- **Lab:** leukocyte level <7 mg/dL
- **Early:** irritability, anorexia
- **Abnormal collagen synthesis (cannot hydroxylate proline and lysine):** swollen gums, bleeding mucosa, petechiae, poor wound healing
- **Ophthalmology:** flame hemorrhages, cotton-wool spots, retrobulbar hematomas
- **Orthopedics:** hemarthrosis, subperiosteal hemorrhage
- **Hematology:** hemolysis (anemia and jaundice)

**SIGNS**

**TREATMENT**

- **Replete:** 1 month 300 mg daily (children) or 1000 mg daily (adults)
- **Dermatology:** dermoscopy and biopsy (corkscrew and swan-neck hairs and perifollicular hemorrhages)
- **Screen:** B12, folate, calcium, zinc, iron

# Vitamin D Deficiency

## Etiology:

 **Lack of sun exposure**

 **Renal failure**
Defective 1-α 25-hydroxylation

 **Poor diet**
**Malabsorption**

 **Cirrhosis**
Defective 25-hydroxylation

## Clinical Presentation:

**Rickets (children):**

Bone pain

Deformity

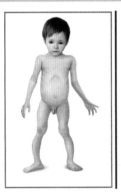

**Osteomalacia (adults):**

 **Bone pain**

 **Muscle weakness**

## Diagnosis:

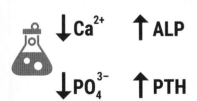 $\downarrow Ca^{2+}$    $\uparrow ALP$

$\downarrow PO_4^{3-}$    $\uparrow PTH$

 **Biochem review:**

$D_2$ = Ergocalciferol (obtained from plants)
$D_3$ = Cholecalciferol (from sun exposure, milk)
25-OH $D_3$ (storage, made in liver)
1,25-$(OH)_2 D_3$ (active form, made in kidney)

# Vitamin E Deficiency

## Etiology (Rare):

### Fat malabsorption:

 **Pancreatic insufficiency**

 **Cholestatic liver disease**

 **Extensive bowel resection**

 **Premature infants**

 **Familial isolated vitamin E deficiency**

## Clinical Presentation:

 **Ataxia**

 **Hyporeflexia**

 **Loss of proprioception and vibration sensation**

 **Hemolytic anemia**

 **Acanthocytosis**

Reproduced with permission from Jameson J, Fauci AS, Kasper DL, et al: Harrison's Principles of Internal Medicine, 20th ed. New York, NY: McGraw Hill; 2018.

## Diagnosis:

 **Serum $\alpha$-tocopherol**

 Vitamin E enhances the anticoagulant effects of warfarin

# Vitamin K Deficiency

## Sources

- Dietary: green vegetables (eg, spinach, kale, and broccoli)
- Small amount produced by the gut microflora
- Easily recycled in cells

## Functions

- Activation of coagulation factors VII, IX, X, and prothrombin
- Activation of protein C and S
- Involved in bone mineralization

## Causes

- Any cause of fat malabsorption
- High risk: infants, cystic fibrosis, biliary disease, inflammatory bowel
- High-dose vitamin E
- Antibiotic : β-lactams

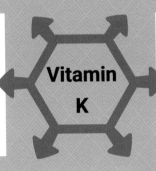

**Vitamin K**

## Symptoms

- Easy bruisability
- Mucosal bleeding
- Splinter hemorrhages
- Melena
- Hematuria
- Newborns: intracranial hemorrhage

## Diagnosis

- Prolonged INR and PT
- Mild: only PT prolonged due to predominate effect on factor VII
- Severe: PT and PTT prolonged

## Newborns

- Most commonly affected
- Immature liver does not efficiently utilize vitamin K
- Low vitamin K stores
- Prophylactic vitamin K given at birth

 Treatment: IV or IM Vitamin K

# References _____

**Acid and Alkali Ingestion**
Bouchard NC, Carter WA. Caustic ingestions. In: Tintinalli JE, Stapczynski J, Ma O, Yealy DM, Meckler GD, Cline DM, eds. *Tintinalli's Emergency Medicine: A Comprehensive Study Guide*. 8th ed. New York, NY: McGraw Hill; 2016. http://accessmedicine.mhmedical.com.elibrary.amc.edu/content.aspx?bookid= 1658&sectionid=109438171. Accessed July 15, 2019.

**Acute Abdomen**
Le T, Bhushan V, Deol M, et al. *First Aid for the USMLE Step 2 CK*. New York, NY: McGraw Hill Education; 2019.
McQuaid KR. Gastrointestinal disorders. In: Papadakis MA, McPhee SJ, Rabow MW, eds. *Current Medical Diagnosis & Treatment 2019*. New York, NY: McGraw Hill; 2019. http://accessmedicine.mhmedical.com .proxy01.its.virginia.edu/content.aspx?bookid=2449&sectionid=194439115. Accessed April 1, 2019.

**Acute Acetaminophen Toxicity**
Heard K, Dart R. Acetaminophen (paracetamol) poisoning in adults: treatment. In: Traub SJ, Grayzel J, eds. *UpToDate*. Waltham, MA: UpToDate Inc. https://www.uptodate.com
Olson KR. Acetaminophen. In: Olson KR, ed. *Poisoning & Drug Overdose*. 6th ed. New York, NY: McGraw Hill; 2012.

**Acute Appendicitis**
Le T, Bhushan V, Sochat M, et al. *First Aid for the USMLE Step 1 2018*. New York, NY: McGraw Hill; 2017.
Liang MK, Andersson RE, Jaffe BM, Berger DH. The appendix. In: Brunicardi F, Andersen DK, Billiar TR, et al, eds. *Schwartz's Principles of Surgery*. 10th ed. New York, NY: McGraw Hill; 2014. https://accessmedicine .mhmedical.com/content.aspx?sectionid=59610872&bookid=980&Resultclick=2. Accessed March 21, 2019.

**Acute Isoniazid Toxicity**
Minns AB. Isoniazid (INH). In: Olson KR, ed. *Poisoning & Drug Overdose*. 6th ed. New York, NY: McGraw Hill; 2012.
Rao RB. Isoniazid (INH) poisoning. In: Traub SJ, Burns MM, Grayzel J, eds. *UpToDate*. Waltham, MA: UpToDate Inc. https://www.uptodate.com
World Health Organization. WHO model list of essential medicines, 20th list (March 2017, amended August 2017). World Health Organization; 2017. https://apps.who.int/iris/handle/10665/273826

**Alcohol Intoxication**
Ropper AH, Samuels MA, Klein JP, eds. Alcohol and alcoholism. *Adams & Victor's Principles of Neurology*. 10th ed. New York, NY: McGraw Hill; 2014:chap 42. http://accessmedicine.mhmedical.com/content.aspx? bookid=690&sectionid=50910893. Accessed April 2, 2019.

**Alcohol Withdrawal**
Bernstein E, Bernstein JA, Weiner SG, D'Onofrio G. Substance use disorders. In: Tintinalli JE, Stapczynski J, Ma O, Yealy DM, Meckler GD, Cline DM, eds. *Tintinalli's Emergency Medicine: A Comprehensive Study Guide*. 8th ed. New York, NY: McGraw Hill; 2016. http://accessmedicine.mhmedical.com/content.aspx?bookid= 1658&sectionid=109448503. Accessed April 18, 2019.
Le T, Bhushan V, Deol M, et al. *First Aid for the USMLE Step 2 CK*. New York, NY: McGraw Hill; 2019.

## Anaphylactic Shock
Le T, Bhushan V, Deol M, et al. *First Aid for the USMLE Step 2 CK*. New York, NY: McGraw Hill; 2019.

Le T, Bhushan V, Sochat M, et al. *First Aid for the USMLE Step 1 2019*. New York, NY: McGraw Hill; 2019.

## Antiarrhythmic Toxicity and Overdose
Giardina E. 2019. Major side effects of class I antiarrythmic drugs. In: Downey B, ed. *UpToDate*. Retrieved June 25, 2019. Retrieved from https://www-uptodate-com.elibrary.amc.edu/contents/major-side-effects-of-class-i-antiarrhythmic-drugs?search=antiarrhythmic%20drug%20classes&source=search_result&selectedTitle=3~150&usage_type=default&display_rank=3

Hoffman R, Nelson L, Howland M, Lewin N, Flomenbaum N, Goldfrank L. *Goldfrank's Toxicologic Emergencies*. 8th ed. New York, NY: McGraw Hill; 2006.

Olson KR, Anderson IB, Benowitz NL, et al, eds. *Poisoning & Drug Overdose*. 7th ed. New York, NY: McGraw Hill; 2018.

## Anticholinergic Toxicity
Su M, Goldman M. Anticholinergic poisoning. In: Traub SJ, Burns MM, eds. *UpToDate*. Waltham, MA: UpToDate Inc. https://www.uptodate.com

## Anticoagulant Toxicity and Overdose
Dillon BE, Morrissey RP. Poisoning. In: Stone C, Humphries RL, eds. *CURRENT Diagnosis & Treatment: Emergency Medicine*. 8th ed. New York, NY: McGraw Hill; 2017. http://accessmedicine.mhmedical.com/content.aspx?bookid=2172&sectionid=165070133.

Olson KR, Anderson IB, Benowitz NL, et al. Specific poisons and drugs: diagnosis and treatment. *Poisoning & Drug Overdose*. 7th ed. New York, NY: McGraw Hill; 2018. http://accessmedicine.mhmedical.com/content.aspx?bookid=2284&sectionid=177337924.

Papadakis MA, McPhee SJ, Bernstein J, eds. Anticoagulant overdose. *Quick Medical Diagnosis & Treatment 2019*. New York, NY: McGraw Hill; 2019. http://accessmedicine.mhmedical.com/content.aspx?bookid=2566&sectionid=206878196.

## Anticonvulsant Overdose
LoVecchio F. Anticonvulsants. In: Tintinalli JE, Ma O, Yealy DM, et al, eds. *Tintinalli's Emergency Medicine: A Comprehensive Study Guide*. 9th ed. New York, NY: McGraw Hill; 2020. http://accessmedicine.mhmedical.com/content.aspx?bookid=2353&sectionid=220745528. Accessed December 1, 2019.

Schachter SC. Antiseizure drugs: mechanism of action, pharmacology, and adverse effects. In: Dashe JF, ed. *UpToDate*. Retrieved December 1, 2019 from uand-adverse-effects?search=antiseizure%20drugs&source=search_result&selectedTitle=1~150&usage_type=default&display_rank=1.

Springer C, Nappe TM. Anticonvulsants toxicity. [Updated August 22, 2019]. In: StatPearls [Internet]. Treasure Island (FL): StatPearls Publishing; 2019 Jan. https://www.ncbi.nlm.nih.gov/books/NBK537206/.

## Antipsychotic Overdose
Kapitanyan R, Su M. Second-generation (atypical) antipsychotic medication poisoning. In: Grayzel J, ed. *UpToDate*. 2018. Retrieved November 26, 2019 from https://www.uptodate.com/contents/second-generation-atypical-antipsychotic-medication-poisoning?search=second%20generaltion%20antipsychotic%20poisoning&source=search_result&selectedTitle=2~150&usage_type=default&display_rank=2.

Lavonas EJ. First-generation (typical) antipsychotic medication poisoning. In: Grayzel J, ed. *UpToDate*. 2018. Retrieved November 26, 2019 from https://www.uptodate.com/contents/first-generation-typical-antipsychotic-medication-poisoning?search=second%20generaltion%20antipsychotic%20poisoning&source=search_result&selectedTitle=1~150&usage_type=default&display_rank=1.

## Barbiturate Overdose
Le T, Bhushan V. *First Aid for the USMLE Step 1 2019*. 29th ed. New York, NY: McGraw Hill; 2018.

Olson KR, Anderson IB, Benowitz NL, et al, eds. Specific poisons and drugs: diagnosis and treatment. In: *Poisoning & Drug Overdose*. 7th ed. New York, NY: McGraw Hill; 2018. http://accessmedicine.mhmedical.com/content.aspx?bookid=2284§ionid=177337924. Accessed June 6, 2019.

## Bee and Wasp Stings

Freeman T. Bee, yellow jacket, wasp, and other hymenoptera stings: reaction types and acute management. In: Golden DBK, Feldweg AM. *UpToDate*. Waltham, MA: UpToDate Inc. https://www.uptodate.com/contents/bee-yellow-jacket-wasp-and-other-hymenoptera-stings-reaction-types-and-acute-management?search=bee wasp sting&source=search_result&selectedTitle=1~137&usage_type=default&display_rank=1. Wolters Kluwer, 2019. Accessed November 2019.

Schneir A, Clark RF. Bites and stings. In: Tintinalli JE, Ma O, Yealy DM, et al, eds. *Tintinalli's Emergency Medicine: A Comprehensive Study Guide*. 9th ed. New York, NY: McGraw Hill; 2020. http://accessmedicine.mhmedical.com/content.aspx?bookid=2353&sectionid=220746649. Accessed December 2, 2019.

## Benzodiazepine and Barbiturate Withdrawal

https://www-uptodate-com.elibrary.amc.edu/contents/phenobarbital-drug-information?search=barbiturates&source=search_result&selectedTitle=2~150&usage_type=default&display_rank=2#F208914

https://www-uptodate-com.elibrary.amc.edu/contents/benzodiazepine-poisoning-and-withdrawal?search=benzodiazepine%20withdrawal&source=search_result&selectedTitle=1~65&usage_type=default&display_rank=1#H16

## Benzodiazepine Toxicity and Overdose

Greller H, Gupta A. Benzodiazepine poisoning and withdrawal. In: Traub SJ, Grayzel J, eds. *UpToDate*. Waltham, MA: UpToDate Inc. https://www.uptodate.com

https://www-uptodate-com.elibrary.amc.edu/contents/benzodiazepine-poisoning-and-withdrawal?search=benzodiazepine%20overdose&source=search_result&selectedTitle=1~29&usage_type=default&display_rank=1#H9

Le T, Bhushan V, eds. Psychiatry. *First Aid for the USMLE Step 1 2019*. 29th ed. New York, NY: McGraw Hill; 2018:558.

## β-Blocker Toxicity & Overdose

Barrueto F Jr. Beta blocker poisoning. In: Traub SJ, Grayzel J, eds. *UpToDate*. Waltham, MA: UpToDate Inc. https://www.uptodate.com

Le T, Bhushan V. *First Aid for the USMLE Step 1 2019*. 29th ed. New York, NY: McGraw Hill; 2018.

## Blunt Abdominopelvic Trauma

French L, Gordy S, Ma O. Abdominal trauma. In: Tintinalli JE, Stapczynski J, Ma O, Yealy DM, Meckler GD, Cline DM, eds. *Tintinalli's Emergency Medicine: A Comprehensive Study Guide*. 8th ed. New York, NY: McGraw Hill; 2016. http://accessmedicine.mhmedical.com/content.aspx?bookid=1658&sectionid=109445917. Accessed July 26, 2019.

## Blunt Chest Trauma

Jones D, Nelson A, Ma O. Pulmonary trauma. In: Tintinalli JE, Stapczynski J, Ma O, Yealy DM, Meckler GD, Cline DM, eds. *Tintinalli's Emergency Medicine: A Comprehensive Study Guide*. 8th ed. New York, NY: McGraw Hill; 2016. http://accessmedicine.mhmedical.com/content.aspx?bookid=1658&sectionid=109445746. Accessed July 26, 2019.

Ross C, Schwab T. Cardiac trauma. In: Tintinalli JE, Stapczynski J, Ma O, Yealy DM, Meckler GD, Cline DM, eds. *Tintinalli's Emergency Medicine: A Comprehensive Study Guide*. 8th ed. New York, NY: McGraw Hill; 2016. https://accessmedicine.mhmedical.com/content.aspx?bookid=1658&sectionid=109387651. Accessed July 26, 2019.

## Blunt Head Trauma

Wright DW, Merck LH. Head trauma. In: Tintinalli JE, Stapczynski J, Ma O, Yealy DM, Meckler GD, Cline DM, eds. *Tintinalli's Emergency Medicine: A Comprehensive Study Guide*. 8th ed. New York, NY: McGraw Hill; 2016. http://accessmedicine.mhmedical.com/content.aspx?bookid=1658&sectionid=109445450. Accessed July 26, 2019.

## Carbon Monoxide Poisoning

Le T, Bhushan V. *First Aid for the USMLE Step 1 2019*. 29th ed. New York, NY: McGraw Hill; 2018.

Le T, Bhushan V. *First Aid for the USMLE Step 2 CK*. 10th ed. New York, NY: McGraw Hill; 2018.

Cydulka RK, Fitch MT, Joing SA, Wang VJ, Cline DM, Ma O, eds. *Tintinalli's Emergency Medicine*. 8th ed. New York, NY: McGraw Hill; 2017.

## Cardiogenic Shock

Casey G, David M. Cardiogenic shock. In: Tintinalli JE, Stapczynski J, Ma O, Yealy DM, Meckler GD, Cline DM, eds. *Tintinalli's Emergency Medicine: A Comprehensive Study Guide*. 8th ed. New York, NY: McGraw Hill; 2016. http://accessmedicine.mhmedical.com/content.aspx?bookid=1658&sectionid=109449831. Accessed April 1, 2019.

Le T, Bhushan V, Sochat M, et al. *First Aid for the USMLE Step 1 2018*. New York, NY: McGraw Hill; 2017.

## Cocaine and Amphetamine Toxicity

Morgan JP. Clinical manifestations, diagnosis, and management of the cardiovascular complications of cocaine abuse. In: Downey BC, ed. *UpToDate*. Waltham, MA: UpToDate Inc. Retrieved December 1, 2019 from https://www.uptodate.com/contents/cocaine-acute-intoxication?search=cocaine%20acute%20intoxication&source=search_result&selectedTitle=1~150&usage_type=default&display_rank=1

Nelson L, Odujebe O. Cocaine: acute intoxication. In: Grayzel J, ed. *UpToDate*. Waltham, MA: UpToDate Inc. Retrieved December 1, 2019 from https://www.uptodate.com/contents/cocaine-acute-intoxication?search=cocaine%20acute%20intoxication&source=search_result&selectedTitle=1~150&usage_type=default&display_rank=1

## Cocaine and Amphetamine Withdrawal

Boyer EW, Seifert SA, Hernon C. Methamphetamine: acute intoxication. In: Traub SJ, Burns MM, Grayzel J, eds. *UpToDate*. Waltham, MA: UpToDate Inc. https://www-uptodate-com.elibrary.amc.edu/contents/methamphetamine-acute-intoxication?search=amphetamine%20withdrawal&source=search_result&selectedTitle=1~150&usage_type=default&display_rank=1#H24

Gorelick DA. Cocaine use disorders in adults: epidemiology, pharmacology, clinical manifestations, medical consequences, and diagnosis. In: Saxon AJ, Friedman M, eds. *UpToDate*. Waltham, MA: UpToDate Inc. https://www-uptodate-com/contents/cocaine-use-disorder-in-adults-epidemiology-pharmacology-clinical-manifestations-medical-consequences-and-diagnosis?search=cocaine%20withdrawal&source=search_result&selectedTitle=1~26&usage_type=default&display_rank=1

Le T, Bhushan V. *First Aid for the USMLE Step 1 2016*. New York, NY: McGraw Hill; 2016:522.

## Cyanide Toxicity

Kirk MA, Holstege CP, Isom GE. Cyanide and hydrogen sulfide. In: Nelson LS, Lewin NA, Howland M, Hoffman RS, Goldfrank LR, Flomenbaum NE, eds. *Goldfrank's Toxicologic Emergencies*. 9th ed. New York, NY: McGraw Hill; 2011. https://accesspharmacy.mhmedical.com/content.aspx?bookid=454&sectionid=4019955

## Digoxin Toxicity

Katzung BG, Kruidering-Hall M, Trevor AJ, eds. Drugs used in heart failure. *Katzung & Trevor's Pharmacology: Examination & Board Review*. 12th ed. New York, NY: McGraw Hill; 2019.

Papadakis MA, McPhee SJ, Bernstein J, eds. Digitalis toxicity. *Quick Medical Diagnosis & Treatment 2019*. New York, NY: McGraw Hill; 2019.

**Fever After Surgery**

Le T, Bhushan V, Skelley N, et al. *First Aid for the USMLE Step 2 CK*. New York, NY: McGraw Hill; 2014.

Maday KR, Hurt JB, Harrelson P, Porterfield J. Evaluating postoperative fever. *JAAPA*. 2016;29(10):23-28.

**Fibrinolytic Overdose**

French KF, White J, Hoesch RE. Treatment of intracerebral hemorrhage with tranexamic acid after thrombolysis with tissue plasminogen activator. *Neurocrit Care*. 2012;17(1):107-111. doi: 10.1007/s12028-012-9681-5. https://www.ncbi.nlm.nih.gov/pubmed/22311234. Accessed November 21, 2019.

Gibson CM, Levin T. Characteristics of fibrinolytic (thrombolytic) agents and clinical trials in acute ST elevation myocardial infarction. In: Saperia GM, ed. *UpToDate*. Waltham, MA: UpToDate Inc. Retrieved November 29, 2019 from https://www.uptodate.com/contents/characteristics-of-fibrinolytic-thrombolytic-agents-and-clinical-trials-in-acute-st-elevation-myocardial-infarction?search=characteristics%20thrombolytic%20agents%20clinical%20trials%20acute%20ST&source=search_result&selectedTitle=1~150&usage_type=default&display_rank=1.

Slattery DE, Pollack CV Jr. Thrombotics and antithrombotics. In: Tintinalli JE, Ma O, Yealy DM, et al, eds. *Tintinalli's Emergency Medicine: A Comprehensive Study Guide*. 9th ed. New York, NY: McGraw Hill; 2020. http://accessmedicine.mhmedical.com/content.aspx?bookid=2353&sectionid=221179142. Accessed November 27, 2019.

Tapson VF, Weinberg AS. Thrombolytic (fibrinolytic) therapy in acute pulmonary embolism and lower extremity deep vein thrombosis. In: Finlay G, ed. *UpToDate*. Waltham, MA: UpToDate Inc. Retrieved November 29, 2019 from https://www.uptodate.com/contents/thrombolytic-fibrinolytic-therapy-in-acute-pulmonary-embolism-and-lower-extremity-deep-vein-thrombosis?search=thrombolytic%20therapy%20acute%20pulmonary%20embolism&source=search_result&selectedTitle=1~150&usage_type=default&display_rank=1.

**Heavy Metal Toxicity**

Hoffman R, Nelson L, Howland M, Lewin N, Flomenbaum N, Goldfrank L. *Goldfrank's Toxicologic Emergencies*. New York, NY: McGraw Hill; 2006.

Klinkhoff A. Major side effects of gold therapy. In: Romain P, ed. *UpToDate*. Waltham, MA: UpToDate Inc. 2017. Retrieved July 1, 2019 from https://www-uptodate-com.elibrary.amc.edu/contents/major-side-effects-of-gold-therapy#H5

Olson K. *Poisoning & Drug Overdose*. New York, NY: McGraw Hill; 2018.

**Hyperthermia**

Le T, Bhushan V, Deol M, et al. *First Aid for the USMLE Step 2 CK*. New York, NY: McGraw Hill; 2019.

DoVecchio F. Heat emergencies. In: Tintinalli JE, Stapczynski J, Ma O, Yealy DM, Meckler GD, Cline DM, eds. *Tintinalli's Emergency Medicine: A Comprehensive Study Guide*. 8th ed. New York, NY: McGraw Hill; 2016. http://accessmedicine.mhmedical.com/content.aspx?bookid=1658&sectionid=109438541. Accessed April 1, 2019.

**Hypomagnesemia**

Ahmed F, Mohammed A. Magnesium: the forgotten electrolyte-a review on hypomagnesemia. *Med Sci (Basel)*. 2019;7(4):56.

Le T, Bhushan V, Skelley N, et al. *First Aid for the USMLE Step 2 CK*. New York, NY: McGraw Hill; 2014.

Le T, Bhushan V, Sochat M, Kallianos K, Chavda Y, Kalani M. *First Aid for the USMLE Step 1 2019: A Student-to-Student Guide*. New York, NY: McGraw Hill; 2019.

**Hypothermia**

Brown D. Hypothermia. In: Tintinalli JE, Stapczynski J, Ma O, Yealy DM, Meckler GD, Cline DM, eds. *Tintinalli's Emergency Medicine: A Comprehensive Study Guide*. 8th ed. New York, NY: McGraw Hill; 2016. http://accessmedicine.mhmedical.com/content.aspx?bookid=1658&sectionid=109385768. Accessed April 18, 2019.

Le T, Bhushan V, Deol M, et al. *First Aid for the USMLE Step 2 CK*. New York, NY: McGraw Hill; 2019.

### Iron Salts Toxicity
Liebelt EL. Acute iron poisoning. In: Burns MM, Wiley JF, eds. *UpToDate*. Waltham, MA: UpToDate Inc. https://www.uptodate.com

Mycyk MB. Poisoning and drug overdose. In: Jameson J, Fauci AS, Kasper DL, Hauser SL, Longo DL, Loscalzo J, eds. *Harrison's Principles of Internal Medicine*. 20th ed. New York, NY: McGraw Hill; 2018.

### Mammalian Bites
James Q. Puncture wounds and bites. In: Tintinalli JE, Stapczynski J, Ma O, Yealy DM, Meckler GD, Cline DM, eds. *Tintinalli's Emergency Medicine: A Comprehensive Study Guide*. 8th ed. New York, NY: McGraw Hill; 2016. http://accessmedicine.mhmedical.com/content.aspx?bookid=1658&sectionid=109449392. Accessed July 26, 2019.

### Methanol and Ethylene Glycol Toxicity
Mossop E, DiBlasio F. Overdose, poisoning, and withdrawal. In: Oropello JM, Pastores SM, Kvetan V, eds. *Critical Care*. New York, NY: McGraw Hill; 2017.

### Methemoglobin Toxicity
Agarwal AM, Prchal JT. Methemoglobinemia and other dyshemoglobinemias. In: Kaushansky K, Lichtman MA, Prchal JT, et al, eds. *Williams Hematology*. 9th ed. New York, NY: McGraw Hill; 2015.

In: Papadakis MA, McPhee SJ, Bernstein J, eds. Methemoglobinemia. *Quick Medical Diagnosis & Treatment 2019*. New York, NY: McGraw Hill; 2019.

### Neurogenic Shock
Le T, Bhushan V, Deol M, et al. *First Aid for the USMLE Step 2 CK*. New York, NY: McGraw Hill; 2019.

Le T, Bhushan V, Sochat M, et al. *First Aid for the USMLE Step 1 2019*. New York, NY: McGraw Hill; 2019.

Oropello JM, Mistry N, Ullman JS. Spinal injuries. In: Hall JB, Schmidt GA, Kress JP, eds. *Principles of Critical Care*. 4th ed. New York, NY: McGraw Hill; 2014. http://accessmedicine.mhmedical.com/content.aspx?bookid=1340&sectionid=80027179. Accessed April 1, 2019.

### Niacin Deficiency
Amato AA, Barohn RJ. Peripheral neuropathy. In: Jameson J, Fauci AS, Kasper DL, Hauser SL, Longo DL, Loscalzo J, eds. *Harrison's Principles of Internal Medicine*. 20th ed. New York, NY: McGraw Hill; 2018.

Pazirandeh S, Burns DL. Overview of water-soluble vitamins. In: Seres D, Kunins L. *UpToDate*. Waltham, MA: UpToDate Inc. https://www.uptodate.com/contents/overview-of-water-soluble-vitamins

### NSAID Toxicity
Rella JG, Wallace A. Carter. Nonsteroidal anti-inflammatory drugs. *Tintinalli's Emergency Medicine: A Comprehensive Study Guide*. 8th ed. New York, NY: McGraw Hill; 2016. http://accessmedicine.mhmedical.com/content.aspx?bookid=1658&sectionid=109414780.

### Obstructive Shock
Le T, Bhushan V, Deol M, et al. *First Aid for the USMLE Step 2 CK*. New York, NY: McGraw Hill; 2019.

Le T, Bhushan V, Sochat M, et al. *First Aid for the USMLE Step 1 2019*. New York, NY: McGraw Hill; 2019.

### Opioids Overdose and Withdrawal
Stolbach A, Hoffman RS. Opioid withdrawal in the emergency setting. *UpToDate*. Waltham, MA: UpToDate Inc. https://www.uptodate.com/contents/opioid-withdrawal-in-the-emergency-setting. Accessed April 5, 2019.

### Organophosphate and Carbamate Toxicity
Bird, S. 2019. Organophosphate and carbamate poisoning. In: Grayzel J, ed. *UpToDate*. https://www.uptodate.com/contents/organophosphate-and-carbamate-poisoning?search=organophosphate%20carbamate&source=search_result&selectedTitle=1~52&usage_type=default&display_rank=1. Accessed December 1, 2019.

**Pulseless Electric Activity (PEA)**
Long B, Koyfman A, Venkataraman A, Han S, Ong MH, Tan KK. Cardiac resuscitation. In: Tintinalli JE, Stapczynski J, Ma O, Yealy DM, Meckler GD, Cline DM. *Tintinalli's Emergency Medicine: A Comprehensive Study Guide*. 8th ed. New York, NY: McGraw Hill; 2016. https://accessmedicine.mhmedical.com/content.aspx?sectionid=109427215&bookid=1658&jumpsectionid=109427280&Resultclick=2. Accessed March 22, 2019.

**Penetrating Trauma—Abdomen**
French L, Gordy S, Ma OJ. Abdominal trauma. In: Tintinalli JE, Stapczynski JS, Ma OJ, Yealy DM, Meckler GD, Cline D, eds. *Tintinalli's Emergency Medicine: A Comprehensive Study Guide*. 8th ed. New York, NY: McGraw Hill; 2016:1761-1764.

Ma O. Abdominal injuries. In: Cydulka RK, Fitch MT, Joing SA, Wang VJ, Cline DM, Ma OJ. *Tintinalli's Emergency Medicine Manual*. 8th ed. New York, NY: McGraw Hill; 2017:909-913.

**Penetrating Trauma—Chest**
Nystrom P. Cardiothoracic injuries. In: Cydulka RK, Fitch MT, Joing SA, Wang VJ, Cline DM, Ma OJ, eds. *Tintinalli's Emergency Medicine Manual*. 8th ed. New York, NY: McGraw Hill; 2017:903-908.

Ross C, Schwab T. Cardiac trauma. In: Tintinalli JE, Stapczynski JS, Ma OJ, Yealy DM, Meckler GD, Cline D. *Tintinalli's Emergency Medicine: A Comprehensive Study Guide*. 8th ed. New York, NY: McGraw Hill; 2016:1752-1761.

**Penetrating Trauma—Musculoskeletal**
Heilman J. Trauma to the extremities. In: Tintinalli JE, Stapczynski J, Ma O, Yealy DM, Meckler GD, Cline DM, eds. *Tintinalli's Emergency Medicine: A Comprehensive Study Guide*. 8th ed. New York, NY: McGraw Hill; 2016. http://accessmedicine.mhmedical.com/content.aspx?bookid=1658&sectionid=109387808. Accessed July 26, 2019.

**Penetrating Trauma—Neck**
Bean AS. Trauma to the neck. In: Tintinalli JE, Stapczynski J, Ma O, Yealy DM, Meckler GD, Cline DM, eds. *Tintinalli's Emergency Medicine: A Comprehensive Study Guide*. 8th ed. New York, NY: McGraw Hill; 2016. http://accessmedicine.mhmedical.com/content.aspx?bookid=1658&sectionid=109445628. Accessed July 26, 2019.

**Rabies**
Jackson AC. Rabies and other rhabdovirus infections. In: Jameson J, Fauci AS, Kasper DL, Hauser SL, Longo DL, Loscalzo J, eds. *Harrison's Principles of Internal Medicine*. 20th ed. New York, NY: McGraw Hill; 2018. http://accessmedicine.mhmedical.com/content.aspx?bookid=2129&sectionid=192026000. Accessed April 6, 2019.

**Salicylate Toxicity and Overdose**
Boyer EW, Weibrecht KW. Salicylate (aspirin) poisoning in adults. In: Traub SJ, Grayzel J, eds. *UpToDate*. Waltham, MA: UpToDate Inc. https://www.uptodate.com/contents/salicylate-aspirin-poisoning-in-adults?search=Salicylate%20(aspirin)%20Poisoning%20in%20Adults&source=search_result&selectedTitle=1~150&usage_type=default&display_rank=1

**Sedative-Hypnotic Agent Overdose**
Mossop E, DiBlasio F. Overdose, poisoning, and withdrawal. In: Oropello JM, Pastores SM, Kvetan V, eds. *Critical Care*. New York, NY: McGraw Hill; 2017. http://accessmedicine.mhmedical.com/content.aspx?bookid=1944&sectionid=143520164.

Papadakis MA, McPhee SJ, Bernstein J, eds. Sedative-hypnotic agent overdose. *Quick Medical Diagnosis & Treatment 2019*. New York, NY: McGraw Hill; 2019. http://accessmedicine.mhmedical.com/content.aspx?bookid=2566&sectionid=206894641.

## Selenium Deficiency

Arbustini E, Serio A, Favalli V, Dec G, Narula J. Dilated cardiomyopathy. In: Fuster V, Harrington RA, Narula J, Eapen ZJ, eds. *Hurst's The Heart*. 14th ed. New York, NY: McGraw Hill; 2017. http://accessmedicine.mhmedical.com/content.aspx?bookid=2046&sectionid=176571642. Accessed November 28, 2019.

Suter PM, Russell RM. Vitamin and trace mineral deficiency and excess. In: Jameson J, Fauci AS, Kasper DL, Hauser SL, Longo DL, Loscalzo J, eds. *Harrison's Principles of Internal Medicine*. 20th ed. New York, NY: McGraw Hill; 2018. http://accessmedicine.mhmedical.com/content.aspx?bookid=2129&sectionid=192283003. Accessed November 28, 2019.

Yan AC. Cutaneous changes in nutritional disease. In: Kang S, Amagai M, Bruckner AL, et al, eds. *Fitzpatrick's Dermatology*. 9th ed. New York, NY: McGraw Hill; 2019. http://accessmedicine.mhmedical.com/content.aspx?bookid=2570&sectionid=210437119. Accessed November 28, 2019.

## Snake Bite

Dart RC, White J. Reptile bites. In: Tintinalli JE, Stapczynski J, Ma O, Yealy DM, Meckler GD, Cline DM, eds. *Tintinalli's Emergency Medicine: A Comprehensive Study Guide*. 8th ed. New York, NY: McGraw Hill; 2016. http://accessmedicine.mhmedical.com/content.aspx?bookid=1658&sectionid=109385974. Accessed November 20, 2019.

Wolfson AB, Cloutier R, Hendey GW, Ling LJ, Rosen CL, Schaider JJ. *Harwood-Nuss' Clinical Practice of Emergency Medicine*. Philadelphia, PA: Wolters Kluwer Health; 2012.

Zafren K, Thurman R, Jones ID. Environmental conditions. In: Knoop KJ, Stack LB, Storrow AB, Thurman R, eds. *The Atlas of Emergency Medicine*. 4th ed. New York, NY: McGraw Hill; 2016. http://accessmedicine.mhmedical.com/content.aspx?bookid=1763&sectionid=125436840. Accessed November 20, 2019.

## Spider and Scorpion Envenomation

Schneir A, Clark RF. Bites and stings. In: Tintinalli JE, Ma O, Yealy DM, et al, eds. *Tintinalli's Emergency Medicine: A Comprehensive Study Guide*. 9th ed. New York, NY: McGraw Hill; 2020. http://accessmedicine.mhmedical.com/content.aspx?bookid=2353&sectionid=220746649. Accessed November 20, 2019.

Schwartz RA, Steen CJ. Arthropod bites and stings. In: Kang S, Amagai M, Bruckner AL, Enk AH, Margolis DJ, McMichael AJ, Orringer JS, eds. *Fitzpatrick's Dermatology*. 9th ed. New York, NY: McGraw Hill; 2020. http://accessmedicine.mhmedical.com/content.aspx?bookid=2570&sectionid=210441917. Accessed November 20, 2019.

Wolfson AB, Cloutier R, Hendey GW, Ling LJ, Rosen CL, Schaider JJ. *Harwood-Nuss' Clinical Practice of Emergency Medicine*. Philadelphia, PA: Wolters Kluwer Health; 2012.

## Tetanus

Moll JL, Carden DL. Tetanus. In: Tintinalli JE, Stapczynski J, Ma O, Yealy DM, Meckler GD, Cline DM, eds. *Tintinalli's Emergency Medicine: A Comprehensive Study Guide*. 8th ed. New York, NY: McGraw Hill; 2016. http://accessmedicine.mhmedical.com/content.aspx?bookid=1658&sectionid=109435736. Accessed March 28, 2019.

## Theophylline Toxicity

Ghannoum M, Wiegand TJ, Liu KD, et al. Extracorporeal treatment for theophylline poisoning: systematic review and recommendations from the EXTRIP workgroup. *Clin Toxicol (Phila)*. 2015;53(4):215-229.

Perry H. Theophylline poisoning. In: Wiley JF, ed. *UpToDate*. Waltham, MA: UpToDate Inc. https://www.uptodate.com/contents/theophylline-poisoning. Accessed November 22, 2019.

## Thermal Burns

DeKoning E. Thermal burns. In: Tintinalli JE, Stapczynski J, Ma O, Yealy DM, Meckler GD, Cline DM, eds. *Tintinalli's Emergency Medicine: A Comprehensive Study Guide*. 8th ed. New York, NY: McGraw Hill; 2016. http://accessmedicine.mhmedical.com/content.aspx?bookid=1658&sectionid=109438787. Accessed June 16, 2019.

Le T, Bhushan V, Sochat M, Kallianos K, Chavda Y, Kalani M. *First Aid for the USMLE Step 1 2019: A Student-to-Student Guide*. New York, NY: McGraw Hill; 2019.

Levi B, Wang S. Burns. In: Kang S, Amagai M, Bruckner AL, et al, eds. *Fitzpatrick's Dermatology*. 9th ed. New York, NY: McGraw Hill; 2019. http://accessmedicine.mhmedical.com/content.aspx?bookid=2570&sectionid=210422321. Accessed June 15, 2019.

## Thiamine Deficiency

Le T, Bhushan V, Sochat M, et al. *First Aid for the USMLE Step 1 2018*. New York, NY: McGraw Hill; 2017.

Pazirandeh S, Burns DL. Overview of water-soluble vitamins. In: Seres D, Kunins L. *UpToDate*. Waltham, MA: UpToDate Inc. https://www.uptodate.com/contents/overview-of-water-soluble-vitamins?search=thiamine:%20Drug%20information&source=search_result&selectedTitle=1~150&usage_type=default&display_rank=1

So YT. Wernicke encephalopathy. *UpToDate*. https://www.uptodate.com/contents/wernicke-encephalopathy. Accessed April 11, 2019.

## Trauma Management

Cameron P, Knapp BJ. Trauma in adults. In: Tintinalli JE, Stapczynski JS, Ma OJ, Yealy DM, Meckler GD, Cline D. *Tintinalli's Emergency Medicine: A Comprehensive Study Guide*. 8th ed. New York, NY: McGraw Hill; 2016:1681-1688.

Cydulka RK. Trauma in adults. In: Cydulka RK, Fitch MT, Joing SA, Wang, VJ, Cline DM, Ma OJ. *Tintinalli's Emergency Medicine Manual*. 8th ed. New York, NY: McGraw Hill Education; 2017:865-868.

## Tricyclic Antidepressant Overdose

Murray E, Walthall L, Wise KR. Drug overdose and withdrawal. In: McKean SC, Ross JJ, Dressler DD, Scheurer DB, eds. *Principles and Practice of Hospital Medicine*. 2nd ed. New York, NY: McGraw Hill; 2017.

Raj KS, Williams N, DeBattista C. Psychiatric disorders. In: Papadakis MA, McPhee SJ, Rabow MW, eds. *Current Medical Diagnosis and Treatment 2020*. New York, NY: McGraw Hill; 2020.

Salhanick SD. Tricyclic antidepressant poisoning. In: Traub SJ, Grayzel J, eds. *UpToDate*. Waltham, MA: UpToDate Inc. https://www.uptodate.com/contents/tricyclic-antidepressant-poisoning?search=Tricyclic%20Antidepressant%20Poisoning&source=search_result&selectedTitle=1~51&usage_type=default&display_rank=1

## Vitamin A Deficiency

Pazirandeh S, Burns DL. Overview of vitamin A. *UpToDate*. Waltham, MA: UpToDate Inc. https://www.uptodate.com/contents/overview-of-water-soluble-vitamins?search=thiamine:%20Drug%20information&source=search_result&selectedTitle=1~150&usage_type=default&display_rank=1. Accessed November 22, 2019.

## Vitamin B2 (Riboflavin) Deficiency

Baron RB. Nutritional disorders. In: Papadakis MA, McPhee SJ, Rabow MW, eds. *Current Medical Diagnosis & Treatment 2019*. New York, NY: McGraw-Hill. http://accessmedicine.mhmedical.com.elibrary.amc.edu/content.aspx?bookid=2449&sectionid=194580060. Accessed November 15, 2019.

Bender DA. Micronutrients: vitamins & minerals. In: Rodwell VW, Bender DA, Botham KM, Kennelly PJ, Weil P, eds. *Harper's Illustrated Biochemistry*. 31st ed. New York, NY: McGraw-Hill. http://accessmedicine.mhmedical.com.elibrary.amc.edu/content.aspx?bookid=2386&sectionid=187836268. Accessed November 15, 2019.

Green R. Anemia resulting from other nutritional deficiencies. In: Kaushansky K, Lichtman MA, Prchal JT, et al, eds. *Williams Hematology*. 9th ed. New York, NY: McGraw-Hill. http://accessmedicine.mhmedical.com.elibrary.amc.edu/content.aspx?bookid=1581&sectionid=94304463. Accessed November 15, 2019.

Riboflavin deficiency. In: Papadakis MA, McPhee SJ, Bernstein J, eds. *Quick Medical Diagnosis & Treatment 2020*. New York, NY: McGraw-Hill. http://accessmedicine.mhmedical.com.elibrary.amc.edu/content.aspx?bookid=2750&sectionid=231379826. Accessed November 15, 2019.

Saunders KH, Igel LI, Baron RB. Riboflavin (B2) deficiency. In: Papadakis MA, McPhee SJ, Rabow MW, eds. *Current Medical Diagnosis and Treatment 2020*. New York, NY: McGraw-Hill. http://accessmedicine.mhmedical.com.elibrary.amc.edu/content.aspx?bookid=2683&sectionid=225136226. Accessed November 15, 2019.

Suter PM, Russell RM. Vitamin and trace mineral deficiency and excess. In: Jameson J, Fauci AS, Kasper DL, Hauser SL, Longo DL, Loscalzo J, eds. *Harrison's Principles of Internal Medicine*, 20th ed. New York, NY: McGraw-Hill. http://accessmedicine.mhmedical.com.elibrary.amc.edu/content.aspx?bookid=2129&sectionid=192283003. Accessed November 15, 2019.

The Head and Neck. In: LeBlond RF, Brown DD, Suneja M, Szot JF, eds. *DeGowin's Diagnostic Examination*, 10th ed. New York, NY: McGraw-Hill; 2014. http://accessmedicine.mhmedical.com.elibrary.amc.edu/content.aspx?bookid=1192&sectionid=68666272. Accessed November 15, 2019.

### Vitamin B5 (Pantothenate) Deficiency

Bender DA. Micronutrients: vitamins & minerals. In: Rodwell VW, Bender DA, Botham KM, Kennelly PJ, Weil P, eds. *Harper's Illustrated Biochemistry*. 31st ed. New York, NY: McGraw Hill; 2018. http://accessmedicine.mhmedical.com/content.aspx?bookid=2386&sectionid=187836268. Accessed November 16, 2019.

Linus Pauling Institute or Oregon State University. Pantothenic acid. https://lpi.oregonstate.edu/mic/vitamins/pantothenic-acid

Mount Sinai Today Blog. Vitamin B5 (pantothenic acid). https://www.mountsinai.org/health-library/supplement/vitamin-b5-pantothenic-acid

National Organization for Rare Disorders (NORD). Pantothenate kinase-associated neurodegeneration. https://rarediseases.org/rare-diseases/pantothenate-kinase-associated-neurodegeneration/.

NIH Office of Dietary Supplements (ODS). Pantothenic acid. https://ods.od.nih.gov/factsheets/PantothenicAcid-HealthProfessional/. Updated June 3, 2020.

NIH Office of Dietary Supplements (ODS). Pantothenic acid. https://ods.od.nih.gov/factsheets/PantothenicAcid-Consumer/. Updated July 11, 2019.

Suter PM, Russell RM. Vitamin and trace mineral deficiency and excess. In: Jameson J, Fauci AS, Kasper DL, Hauser SL, Longo DL, Loscalzo J, eds. *Harrison's Principles of Internal Medicine*. 20th ed. New York, NY: McGraw Hill; 2018. http://accessmedicine.mhmedical.com/content.aspx?bookid=2129&sectionid=192283003. Accessed November 16, 2019.

### Vitamin B6 Deficiency

Le T, Bhushan V. *First Aid for the USMLE Step 1 2016*. New York, NY: McGraw Hill; 2016:180.

Le T, Bhushan V. *First Aid for the USMLE Step 1 2016*. New York, NY: McGraw Hill; 2016:389.

Papadakis MA, McPhee SJ, Bernstein J, eds. Vitamin B6 deficiency. *Quick Medical Diagnosis & Treatment 2019*. New York, NY: McGraw Hill; 2019. http://accessmedicine.mhmedical.com/content.aspx?bookid=2566&sectionid=206898086.

### Vitamin B7 Deficiency

Bender DA. Micronutrients: vitamins & minerals. In: Rodwell VW, Bender DA, Botham KM, Kennelly PJ, Weil P, eds. *Harper's Illustrated Biochemistry*. 31st ed. New York, NY: McGraw Hill; 2018. https://accessmedicine.mhmedical.com/content.aspx?bookid=2386&sectionid=187836268. Accessed December 2, 2019.

Suter PM, Russell RM. Vitamin and trace mineral deficiency and excess. In: Jameson J, Fauci AS, Kasper DL, Hauser SL, Longo DL, Loscalzo J, eds. *Harrison's Principles of Internal Medicine*. 20th ed. New York, NY: McGraw Hill; 2018. http://accessmedicine.mhmedical.com/content.aspx?bookid=2129&sectionid=192283003. Accessed December 2, 2019.

### Vitamin B9 (Folate) Deficiency

Bender DA. Micronutrients: vitamins & minerals. In: Rodwell VW, Bender DA, Botham KM, Kennelly PJ, Weil P, eds. *Harper's Illustrated Biochemistry*. 31st ed. New York, NY: McGraw Hill; 2018. http://accessmedicine.mhmedical.com/content.aspx?bookid=2386&sectionid=187836268. Accessed December 2, 2019.

Bunn H, Heeney M. Megaloblastic anemias. In: Aster JC, Bunn H, eds. *Pathophysiology of Blood Disorders*. 2nd ed. New York, NY: McGraw Hill; 2016. http://accessmedicine.mhmedical.com/content.aspx?bookid=1900&sectionid=137394859. Accessed November 17, 2019.

Leonard BN, Leber B. Disorders of the white cell. In: McKean SC, Ross JJ, Dressler DD, Scheurer DB, eds. *Principles and Practice of Hospital Medicine.* 2nd ed. New York, NY: McGraw Hill; 2017. http://accessmedicine .mhmedical.com/content.aspx?bookid=1872&sectionid=146983474. Accessed November 17, 2019.

Suter PM, Russell RM. Vitamin and trace mineral deficiency and excess. In: Jameson J, Fauci AS, Kasper DL, Hauser SL, Longo DL, Loscalzo J, eds. *Harrison's Principles of Internal Medicine.* 20th ed. New York, NY: McGraw Hill; 2018. http://accessmedicine.mhmedical.com/content.aspx?bookid=2129&sectionid=192283003. Accessed December 2, 2019.

**Vitamin B12 Deficiency**

Damon LE, Andreadis C. Vitamin B12 deficiency. In: Papadakis MA, McPhee SJ, Rabow MW, eds. *Current Medical Diagnosis and Treatment 2020.* New York, NY: McGraw Hill; 2020. http://accessmedicine.mhmedical .com/content.aspx?bookid=2683&sectionid=225044108.

Kumar N, Law A, Choudhry NK, eds. B12 deficiency. *Teaching Rounds: A Visual Aid to Teaching Internal Medicine Pearls on the Wards.* New York, NY: McGraw Hill; 2016. http://accessmedicine.mhmedical.com/content.aspx? bookid=1856&sectionid=130944573.

Papadakis MA, McPhee SJ, Bernstein J, eds. Vitamin B12 deficiency. *Quick Medical Diagnosis & Treatment 2019.* New York, NY: McGraw Hill; 2019. http://accessmedicine.mhmedical.com/content.aspx?bookid=2566& sectionid=206898095.

**Vitamin C Deficiency**

Le T, Bhushan V, Sochat M, Kallianos K, Chavda Y, Kalani M. *First Aid for the USMLE Step 1 2019: A Student-to-Student Guide.* New York, NY: McGraw Hill; 2019.

Maxfield L, Crane JS. Vitamin C deficiency (scurvy) In: StatPearls [Internet]. Treasure Island (FL): StatPearls Publishing; 2019 Jan. https://www.ncbi.nlm.nih.gov/books/NBK493187/. Updated June 14, 2019.

**Vitamin D Deficiency**

Bringhurst F, Demay MB, Kronenberg HM. Bone and mineral metabolism in health and disease. In: Jameson J, Fauci AS, Kasper DL, Hauser SL, Longo DL, Loscalzo J, eds. *Harrison's Principles of Internal Medicine.* 20th ed. New York, NY: McGraw Hill; 2018. http://accessmedicine.mhmedical.com/content.aspx?bookid=2129& sectionid=192530305.

Fitzgerald PA. Endocrine disorders. In: Papadakis MA, McPhee SJ, Rabow MW, eds. *Current Medical Diagnosis & Treatment 2019.* New York, NY: McGraw Hill; 2019. http://accessmedicine.mhmedical.com.proxy01.its.virginia .edu/content.aspx?bookid=2449&sectionid=194577758.

Le T, Bhushan V. *First Aid for the USMLE Step 1 2016.* New York, NY: McGraw Hill; 2016:81.

Le T, Bhushan V. *First Aid for the USMLE Step 1 2016.* New York, NY: McGraw Hill; 2016:313.

**Vitamin E Deficiency**

Aaron RB. Nutritional disorders. In: Papadakis MA, McPhee SJ, Rabow MW, eds. *Current Medical Diagnosis & Treatment 2019.* New York, NY: McGraw Hill; 2019. http://accessmedicine.mhmedical.com.proxy01.its.virginia .edu/content.aspx?bookid=2449&sectionid=194580060.

Le T, Bhushan V. *First Aid for the USMLE Step 1 2016.* New York, NY: McGraw Hill; 2016:76.

Le T, Bhushan V. *First Aid for the USMLE Step 1 2016.* New York, NY: McGraw Hill; 2016:81.

Papadakis MA, McPhee SJ, Bernstein J, eds. Vitamin E deficiency. *Quick Medical Diagnosis & Treatment 2019.* New York, NY: McGraw Hill; 2019. http://accessmedicine.mhmedical.com/content.aspx?bookid=2566& sectionid=206898132.

**Vitamin K Deficiency**

Le T, Bhushan V. *First Aid for the USMLE Step 1 2015.* 25th anniversary edition. New York, NY: McGraw Hill; 2015.

Nazirandeh MD, Burns MD. Overview of vitamin K. In: Post TW, ed. *UpToDate.* Waltham, MA: UpToDate Inc. https://www.uptodate.com. Accessed November 10, 2019.

# Endocrinology

*Gregory Hong, MD*

# Acromegaly

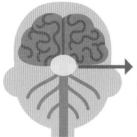

Growth hormone-secreting pituitary adenoma

## Diagnosis
- ↑Serum IGF-1
- Failure to suppress GH during oral glucose tolerance test
- Pituitary tumor seen on brain MRI

## Skeletal Changes

- Macrognathia
- Enlarged, swollen hands and feet
- Osteoarthritis
- Coarse facial features

 *Gigantism results if acromegaly occurs in children prior to fusion of epiphysis in long bones*

## Skin and Soft Tissue Changes

- Macroglossia
- Deepening of voice
- Carpel tunnel syndrome
- Obstructive sleep apnea

## Visceral Enlargement

- Thyroid enlargement
- Heart, liver, lung, and kidney enlargement
- ↑Colonic polyps

## Treatment

 Pituitary adenoma resection
(first-line)

 Medical management
(second-line)

*most effective*
- Pegvisomant (growth hormone receptor antagonist)
- Somatostatin analogs
*least effective*
- Cabergoline (dopamine agonist)

 Radiation therapy
(for refractory disease)

## Cardiovascular Disease

- Hypertension
- Left ventricular hypertrophy
- Cardiomyopathy

## Metabolic Changes

- Insulin resistance
- Hyperphosphatemia

# Acute Hyperglycemic

# Diabetic Complications

## Diabetic Ketoacidosis (DKA)

**Etiology:**
FA can't break down into TAGs without insulin, so are made into ketone bodies

**Presentation:**
- Kussmaul respirations to expel $CO_2$
- Fruity breath
- N/V/abd pain, AMS

**Labs at presentation:**
- Glucose 200-300
- ↑AG acidosis
- Ketonuria
- ↓Na (↑gluc shifts $H_2O$ out)
- ↑Serum $K^+$, ↓total $K^+$

*(K+ shifts extracellularly from acidosis, total body K lost from polyuria)*

**type 1**

**type 2**

## Hyperosmolar Hyperglycemic Syndrome (HHS)

**Etiology:**
Hyperglycemia → increased osmolarity → osmotic diuresis, dehydration

**Presentation:**
- Polyuria, thirst
- Visual changes
- Lethargy, AMS

**Labs at presentation:**
- Glucose usually 600+
- Serum osm >320

## ⚠ Complications
- Arrhythmia
- Cerebral edema in peds
- Respiratory failure (resp. acidosis)
- Treatment-related hypoglycemia, ↓phos, ↓$K^+$
- Seizure
- **Coma**

## 💊 Treatment of both
- Treat underlying stressor (infection, etc.)
- Volume resuscitation
- IV insulin infusion until AG normalizes
- Frequent electrolyte monitoring with PRN repletion can add 5% dextrose or KCl to IVF to avoid ↓glucose or ↓$K^+$ from insulin Rx

# Adrenal Insufficiency

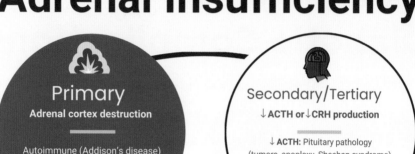

## Primary
**Adrenal cortex destruction**

---

Autoimmune (Addison's disease)
Hemorrhage (Waterhouse–Friderichsen)
Infection (TB, HIV, fungal)
Metastatic disease

## Secondary/Tertiary
↓ ACTH or ↓ CRH production

---

↓ **ACTH:** Pituitary pathology
(tumors, apoplexy, Sheehan syndrome)
↓ **CRH:** Hypothalamic pathology
(tumors, iatrogenic suppression from
long-standing glucocorticoids)

---

**1**

**Autoimmune is
most common
cause of AI**

### History & Physical

- Weakness, fatigue, malaise
- ↓ wt / appetite
- Abdominal pain
- ↑ Pigmentation (primary disease only)

### Diagnostic Evaluation

- 8A cortisol
- ACTH (↑ in primary, ↓ in secondary)
- Cosyntropin stimulation test (gold standard)

**TB is common
cause of AI in
endemic areas**

### Lab Findings

| | Primary | | Secondary/Tertiary |
|---|---|---|---|
| ↓ | | Cortisol | ↓ |
| ↓ | | Aldosterone | preserved |
| ↑ | | ACTH | ↓ |
| ↓ | | Na⁺ | ↓ |
| ↑ | | K⁺ | preserved |

### Treatment

- Glucocorticoids (hydrocortisone, prednisone, dexamethasone) for *all* forms
- Mineralocorticoid (fludrocortisone) for primary
- Higher doses of steroids needed for significant operative procedures or physiologic stressors (eg, febrile illness)

### Acute Adrenal Crisis

#### Presentation
- Usually precipitated by a stressor
- N/V/severe malaise
- Significant ↓ BP

#### Management:
- **IV hydrocortisone** (has mineralocorticoid & glucocorticoid effects at high doses)
- IVF resuscitation with 0.9% NS
- Dextrose PRN hypoglycemia

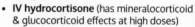

# Adrenal Neoplasms

## Adrenal Adenomas

- Arise from the adrenal cortex
- Can secrete aldosterone, cortisol, or rarely; sex hormones
- Most are unilateral and nonfunctioning
- Rarely develop into carcinomas

### Aldosterone Secreting (Conn Syndrome)

**Clinical Features**

- Hypertension
- Headache
- Hypokalemia and muscle weakness
- Metabolic alkalosis and polyuria

**Dx**

- ↑ Aldosterone and aldosterone-to-plasma renin activity ratio
- CT/MRI reveals mass

**Tx**

- Medical therapy with aldosterone antagonists (spironolactone, eplerenone)
- Surgical resection (preferred)

### Adrenal Carcinoma

- Usually diagnosed by histology based on findings of metastasis
- Typically >4 cm
- Can be nonfunctioning or functioning (usually Cushing's)

### Sex Hormone Secreting

- Very rare
- Androgen secreting: Causes virilization in females
- Estrogen secreting: Causes feminization/gynecomastia in males

### Cortisol Secreting

- Can be a cause of Cushing's syndrome
- Presentation and diagnosis similar to Cushing's disease from pituitary tumor, except ↓ACTH
- Atrophy of uninvolved gland
- Surgical resection for definitive tx

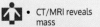

## Pheochromocytoma

- Tumor of chromaffin tissue, most commonly in the adrenal medulla
- Associated with MEN2, VHL, NF-1 (all autosomal dominant)

### Clinical Features

- Hypertension
- Paroxysmal tachycardia and palpitations
- Headache and anxiety
- Diaphoresis
- Chest pain
- Tremor

### Diagnosis and Treatment

- ↑ Plasma free metanephrines or 24-hour urine metanephrines
- CT/MRI reveal mass; nuclear scan can reveal extra-adrenal lesions
- Treatment: Surgical resection (adrenalectomy)
- Avoid β-blocker monotherapy in the absence of an α-blocker—Unopposed α-stim will worsen HTN

---

**α Preoperative management β**

- Risk of tumor releasing metanephrines during resection and causing life-threatening HTN
- Must pretreat with α-blockade for HTN followed by β-blockade for tachycardia
- IV antihypertensives as needed to control BP perioperatively

# Chronic ⚠ Diabetic Complications

**Retinopathy—**Can appear after 3-5 years of diabetes

**Nephropathy—**Can occur after 10 years of diabetes

## Macrovascular
### CAD, PVD

Diabetes often associated with HTN & atherosclerosis → ↑ risk for MI, stroke, amputation

CV disease = Most common cause of death in diabetic patients

Reproduced with permission from Riordan-Eva P, Augsburger JJ: Vaughan & Asbury's General Ophthalmology, 19th ed. New York, NY: McGraw Hill; 2018.

## Eyes

### 1 Retinopathy

Chronic hyperglycemia → retinal damage

**Nonproliferative (top):** Damaged capillaries leak blood → lipids & fluid seep into retina, which results in hemorrhages (solid arrow), cotton wool spots (hollow arrow).

**Therapy:** Blood sugar control, annual exam

**Proliferative (bottom):** Chronic hypoxia → new Blood vessel formation with resultant traction of the retina

**Therapy:** Laser photocoagulation (arrow indicates sites of laser rx), anti-VEGF, annual exam

### 2 Cataracts

**Therapy—**Surgery

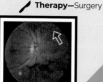

Reproduced with permission from Jameson J, Fauci AS, Kasper DL, et al: Harrison's Principles of Internal Medicine, 20th ed. New York, NY: McGraw Hill; 2018.

## Kidneys
### Nephropathy

Mesangial expansion, GBM thickening, Kimmelstiel–Wilson lesions (arrow)

**Etiology:** Nonenzymatic glycosylation of GBM → hyaline arteriosclerosis → ↑ GFR → ↑ permeability and thickness

**Diagnostics:** Yearly spot urine microalbumin/creatinine. Dipstick will not detect microalbuminuria

**Therapy:** BP control with ACE inhibitors & ARBs: ↓GFR by preventing constriction of efferent arterioles, ↓intraglomerular pressure, which slows GBM thickening

## Extremities, Bladder, Gut

### 1 Peripheral Neuropathy

Stocking-glove pattern: Affects longest nerves

**Symptoms:** Numbness, paresthesias, pain

**Complications:** Ulcers, infections leading to amputation, masking of PVD

**Pain management and symptom control:** Gabapentin, tricyclic antidepressants, serotonin norepinephrine reuptake inhibitors, regular foot care

### 2 Gastroparesis

Delayed gastric emptying → nausea/vomiting

**Therapy:** Dietary modifications; if symptoms persist add prokinetic (metoclopramide or macrolides)

### 3 Neurogenic Bladder

↓ Voiding sensation results in overflow incontinence

**Therapy:** α-Adrenergic blocker (↑ ureteral sphincter tone)

# Congenital Adrenal Hyperplasia

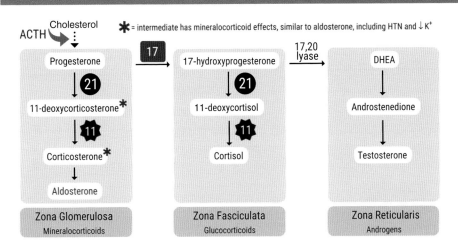

ACTH → Cholesterol

✱ = intermediate has mineralocorticoid effects, similar to aldosterone, including HTN and ↓K⁺

**Zona Glomerulosa** — Mineralocorticoids
- Progesterone → (21) → 11-deoxycorticosterone ✱ → (11) → Corticosterone ✱ → Aldosterone

**Zona Fasciculata** — Glucocorticoids
- 17-hydroxyprogesterone → (21) → 11-deoxycortisol → (11) → Cortisol

**Zona Reticularis** — Androgens
- DHEA → Androstenedione → Testosterone

17 / 17,20 lyase

## Deficiencies

⚠ All deficiencies have ↑adrenal size due to ↑ACTH from ↓cortisol

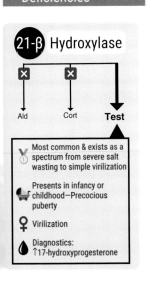

### 21-β Hydroxylase

Ald ✗  Cort ✗  **Test** ▲

- Most common & exists as a spectrum from severe salt wasting to simple virilization
- Presents in infancy or childhood—Precocious puberty
- ♀ Virilization
- Diagnostics: ↑17-hydroxyprogesterone

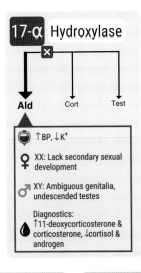

### 17-α Hydroxylase

✗  **Ald** ▲  Cort  Test

- ↑BP, ↓K⁺
- ♀ XX: Lack secondary sexual development
- ♂ XY: Ambiguous genitalia, undescended testes
- Diagnostics: ↑11-deoxycorticosterone & corticosterone, ↓cortisol & androgen

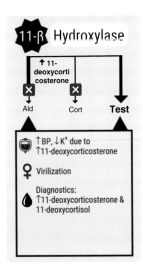

### 11-β Hydroxylase

↑11-deoxycorticosterone

Ald ✗  Cort ✗  **Test** ▲

- ↑BP, ↓K⁺ due to ↑11-deoxycorticosterone
- ♀ Virilization
- Diagnostics: ↑11-deoxycorticosterone & 11-deoxycortisol

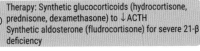

Therapy: Synthetic glucocorticoids (hydrocortisone, prednisone, dexamethasone) to ↓ACTH
Synthetic aldosterone (fludrocortisone) for severe 21-β deficiency

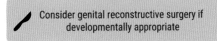

Consider genital reconstructive surgery if developmentally appropriate

# Cushing's Syndrome
## ↑ Cortisol

😣 **Clinical Presentation**  ⚠ Patients may exhibit a spectrum of symptoms from few to many

 ↑ Weight (centripetal obesity)

🐂 Buffalo Hump

⚫ Moon Facies

Abdominal Striae

<small>Reproduced with permission from Knoop KJ, Stack LB, Storrow AB, et al. The Atlas of Emergency Medicine, 4th ed. New York, NY: McGraw Hill, 2016.</small>

🔌 Hypertension

🍳 Hyperglycemia (insulin resistance)

🙂 Mood Lability

💪 Proximal Muscle Weakness

📖 Insomnia

Hypothalamus

Exogenous Steroids

↓ CRH

Pituitary

↓ ACTH

Adrenal

Cortisol (diurnal secretion)

🔬 **Testing**

1. **Overnight dexamethasone suppression test (1 mg):**
Failure to suppress = Cushing's

2. **24-hour urinary free cortisol:**
Elevated = Cushing's

3. **Late-night salivary cortisol:**
Elevated = Cushing

 **Causes**   Measure plasma ACTH to determine cause

| ACTH Independent | | ACTH Dependent | |
|---|---|---|---|
| **Ectopic Steroids** 💊 | **Adrenal Tumor** | **Pituitary Adenoma** ❤ | **Ectopic ACTH Syndrome** 🫁 |
| • ↓ Plasma ACTH<br>• Adrenal atrophy | • ↓ Plasma ACTH<br>• Atrophy of uninvolved adrenal<br>• Adrenal CT scan for diagnosis | **Cushing's Disease**<br>• ↑ Plasma ACTH<br>• Bilateral adrenal hyperplasia<br>• Skin hyperpigmentation<br>• Pituitary adenoma on MRI (50% of time adenoma is too small to be detected) | • ↑ Plasma ACTH<br>• Bilateral adrenal hyperplasia<br>• Skin hyperpigmentation<br>• Chest CT (often caused by lung cancer) |

**Inferior petrosal sinus sampling** can be used to differentiate whether ACTH is from pituitary or periphery

# Diabetes Treatment

**Action Site**  Insulin sulfonylurea DPP-IVi GLP-1A   DPP-IVi GLP-1A acarbose   SGLT2i   Insulin metformin TZD   TZD insulin

## Insulin

- ↑Glucose uptake into skeletal muscle & inhibits hepatic glucose production
- Potent lowering of BG, very precise control possible in motivated pts with technology (insulin pump: Typically only used in DM1)
- ☹ ↑Wt, edema, $$$ (some insulins)
- ⚠ Highest risk of hypoglycemia

**Long-acting/basal** (NPH, detemir, glargine)
Suppress hepatic glucose production when not eating (eg, overnight)

**Short-acting/prandial** (aspart, lispro, glulisine, reg)
Use with meals to prevent postprandial ↑BG

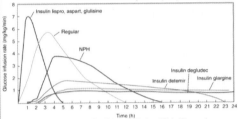

Reproduced with permission from Katzung BG: Basic and Clinical Pharmacology, 14th ed. New York, NY: McGraw Hill; 2018.

## Metformin

- ↑Insulin sensitivity & ↓hepatic glucose production
- Wt neutral, cheap, no hypoglycemia risk **Avoid use in renal failure**
- ☹ GI upset, ↓B12 (chronic use), lactic acidosis risk in severe volume depletion

## Sulfonylureas

- Targets ATP-dependent K+ channel on β-cell → insulin release (independent of eating)
- Cheap, easy dosing (PO daily)
- ☹ ↑Wt, hypoglycemia, theoretical cross reactivity if sulfa allergy

## DPP-IV Inhibitors, GLP-1 Agonists

- Eating → ↑ GLP1 → ↑ insulin/↓ glucagon/↓gastric emptying (↑ satiety); DPP-IV normally degrades GLP1
- Wt loss, less risk of ↓ BG compared to sulfonylureas (insulin only rises after eating)
- ☹ GI upset, $$$, subcutaneous injection (GLP-1A)

**Improved CV outcomes with GLP-1A & SGLT2i**

## SGLT2 Inhibitors

- Block uptake of glucose & Na in PCT → glucosuria
- Wt loss, ↓BP, low risk of ↓BG, convenient (PO daily)
- ☹ UTI/yeast, euglycemic DKA, amputation risk, $$$

## 👎 Rarely Used Therapies

- **TZDs:** Insulin sensitizer, use limited by side-effects (↑ wt, edema/CHF, ↑vascular risk, ↑fx risk)
- **Acarbose:** Block digestion of carbohydrate, limited efficacy & significant side effects (severe GI upset)
- **Amylin analogs:** Similar to GLP-1A except without insulin effects, use limited by high burden of injection (TID-AC), $$$, minimal evidence re: long-term outcomes

## General Strategies for DM Management

### DM1

- Intensive insulin Rx (basal + prandial) is cornerstone of management
- Limited data on benefit of adding adjunctive Rx (eg, GLP-1A, SGLT2i, etc.) to intensive insulin therapy: Currently not recommended

### DM2

- *First-line Rx: Metformin + lifestyle intervention*
- Additional Rx dictated by weighing pros/cons of various treatments for each individual patient (wt, cost, presence of comorbid conditions: CKD, CAD)

## PTH Physiology

*(PTH maintains Ca & PO4 homeostasis)*

### PTH Secretion
- Triggered by ↓Ca
- Inhibited by calcitriol & FGF23

### PTH Targets / Actions

1. **Bone:** Ca & PO4 efflux
2. **Kidney**
   ↑1∝OHase → ↑1,25-vitD*
   ↑ Ca resorption & ↓PO4 resorption
3. **Gut:** ↑ Ca, PO4 absorption (via calcitriol)

*\*Aka calcitriol (activated vitamin D)*

**often asx**

## Clinical Presentation

<u>Hyper Ca</u>
- **Stones:** Nephrolithiasis & hypercalciuria (→ osmotic diuresis / polyuria)

- **Groans / moans:** Constipation, malaise, anorexia, neuropsych sx
- **Severe (Ca >14):** Dehydration, n/v, AMS ↓QT interval

<u>Hyper PTH-Specific</u>
- ↓ **Bone density** @ hip, radius → ↑fx risk

## Hypercalcemia Rx

- **IV 0.9% NS** w/prn loop diuretics

- Short term: Calcitonin

- Long term: IV bisphosphonates

---

# Hypercalcemia & Hyperparathyroidism

**DDx of ↑Ca**

**↑PTH**
**Malignancy** *(mets, PTHrP)*
MM
Milk-alkali syndrome
VitD intoxication
Granulomatous dz

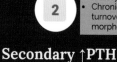

**Renal Osteodystrophy**
- Seen in secondary & tertiary ↑PTH
- Chronic ↑PTH → ↑bone turnover → altered bone morphology (↑fx risk)

---

**1**  **2**   **3**

## Primary ↑PTH

- **Common:** Parathyroid adenoma
- **Rare:** Parathyroid hyperplasia (MEN1,2), carcinoma

**Ca:** Usually ↑

**PO₄:** Usually ↓ (can be nml)

**VitD:** nml

**Surgery** if +sx, Ca >1 mg/dl above nml osteoporosis, CKD, nephrolithiasis (or UCa >400 mg/24 h)

## Secondary ↑PTH

**↓Calcitriol → ↑PTH**
- CKD: ↓Production of calcitriol
- ↓VitD: Malnutrition, celiac, GBypass

**Ca:** nml

**PO₄:** ↑

**VitD:** ↓

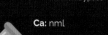
- CKD: Calcitriol supplementation
- ↓VitD: Replete vitamin D

## Tertiary ↑PTH

Chronic PTH stimulation leads to **severe parathyroid hyperlasia & autonomy** (only seen in ESRD)

**Ca:** ↑↑ (also ↑↑↑PTH)

**PO₄:** ↑

**VitD:** ↓

**Cinacalcet** w/prn **parathyroidectomy**

---

# Hyperthyroidism

## Clinical Features

-  ↓ Weight
- Heat intolerance
-  Menstrual irregularity
-  Tremor
-  Insomnia
-  Hyperdefecation
-  Hyperreflexia
-  Warm, moist skin
-  Mood disturbances
-  Palpitations, tachycardia, afib
- Myopathy

## Causes

### Graves' Disease

Reproduced with permission from Longnecker DE, Mackey SC, Newman MF, et al: Anesthesiology, 3rd ed. New York, NY: McGraw Hill; 2018.

- ↑Thyroid hormone (TH) synthesis
- Caused by stimulating antibodies to the TSH receptor
- Nontender diffusely enlarged thyroid
- Can present w/eye disease, pretibial myxedema
- Most common cause of thyrotoxicosis

### Toxic Adenoma/ Toxic Multinodular Goiter (TMNG)

- Autonomous hyperactive thyroid tissue
- Production from one or multiple nodules
- Nontender nodule(s) on physical exam

### Subacute Thyroiditis

- Granulomatous inflammation of thyroid
- Hyperthyroid state followed by hypothyroidism
- Usually post viral infection or post-partum
- Tender thyroid gland may be present

### Fetal Thyrotoxicosis

- Infants born to mothers with Graves' disease
- TSH-R stimulating antibodies cross placenta
- May present a few days after birth
- Intrauterine growth restriction, premature birth, irritability

### Other Causes

- TSH-producing pituitary adenoma (very rare)
- Amiodarone (can also cause ↓ TH)
- Exogenous TH use: Only type of hyperTH that leads to low thyroglobulin

## Management

### Diagnosis

- **Serum TSH level (1st-line test):** Low (except for TSH-producing adenoma)
- Serum free T4 levels: Can help in the setting of hypothalamus/pituitary damage (can have low TSH in the absence of hyperthyroidism)
- RAI uptake scan can help distinguish between overproductive (Graves', TMNG) and destructive (thyroiditis) causes

### Treatment

- All patients: Symptom control w/β-blockers as needed
- Overproductive causes: Antithyroid drugs (PTU, methimazole), RAI therapy, surgery
- Destructive causes: Corticosteroids if severe hyperTH (usually self-limited)

### Complications

**Thyroid Storm**

- Severe hyperTH induced by stress (infxn, trauma, surgery)
- Agitation, delirium, fever, diarrhea, coma
- Life-threatening tachyarrhythmia
- Treat urgently with β-blockers, PTU, corticosteroids, and KI

**Bone Loss**—In the setting of untreated disease

**Cardiovascular**—AFib high output cardiomyopathy

# Hypogonadism

## Hypergonadotrophic Hypogonadism

**Clinical Consequences of Hypogonadism**
- Impaired development of 2° sex characteristics
- ↓Bone density, hot flashes
- ↓Reproductive function (infertility)
  - Oligo/amenorrhea in women
  - ↓Libido, erectile dysfunction, Gynecomastia in men

- Genetic: Turner's (XO), Fragile X premutation carrier
- Autoimmune ovarian destruction
- Ovarian toxicity: Chemo, radiation

- Congenital: Klinefelter (XXY), cryptorchidism
- Infection: Mumps orchitis
- Autoimmune
- Testicular toxicity: Chemo, radiation
- Trauma: Testicular torsion

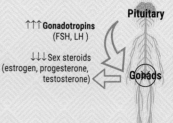

↑↑↑Gonadotropins (FSH, LH )

↓↓↓Sex steroids (estrogen, progesterone, testosterone)

**Pituitary**

**Gonads**

## Hypogonadotrophic Hypogonadism

↓↓↓Gonadotropins (FSH, LH )

↓↓↓Sex steroids (estrogen, progesterone, testosterone)

**Pituitary**

**Gonads**

**Pituitary Pathology**
- Tumors (mass effect)
- Apoplexy
- Hyperprolactinemia
- Cushing's syndrome
- Infiltrative disease (eg, sarcoid)

**Iatrogenic**
- Pituitary surgery
- Radiation
- Medication induced (glucocorticoids, opioids, meds that elevate prolactin)

**Significant Extremes in Weight**
- Anorexia
- Morbid obesity

**Critical Illness/ Severe Systemic Disease**

**Traumatic Brain Injury**

**Congenital**
- GnRH mutation
- Kallmann's syndrome
- FSH/LH subunit mutations
- Prader–Willi syndrome

# Hypopituitarism

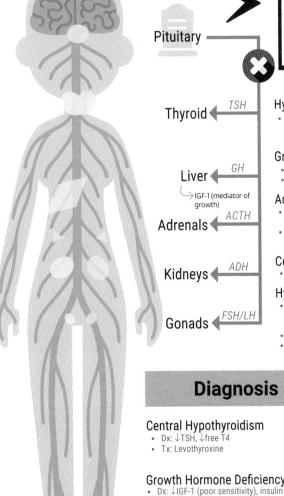

**Neoplasm**
**Iatrogenic (pituitary surgery, radiation)**
**Hypophysitis (inflammatory disease)**
**Genetic and congenital causes**
**Apoplexy (ischemic necrosis)**
**Trauma**

Pituitary

*TSH* → Thyroid

## Hypothyroidism
- Cold intolerance, constipation, dry skin, ↓HR

*GH* → Liver

↳ IGF-1 (mediator of growth)

## Growth Hormone Deficiency
- Children: ↓linear growth
- Adults: ↑fat mass, ↓lean body mass, fatigue

*ACTH* → Adrenals

## Adrenal Insufficiency (secondary)
- Fatigue, weakness, nausea, weight loss, irritability
- No hyperkalemia or ↑pigmentation (only seen in primary)

*ADH* → Kidneys

## Central Diabetes Insipidus
- Polyuria (>3 L/d), ↑thirst

*FSH/LH* → Gonads

## Hypogonadism
- Premenopausal women: Irregular periods/amenorrhea, infertility, hot flashes, vaginal atrophy
- Postmenopausal women: Largely asymptomatic
- Men: Infertility, ↓libido, erectile dysfunction, ↓energy/muscle

# Diagnosis & Treatment

## Central Hypothyroidism
- Dx: ↓TSH, ↓free T4
- Tx: Levothyroxine

## Growth Hormone Deficiency
- Dx: ↓IGF-1 (poor sensitivity), insulin tolerance test (gold standard)
- Tx: Growth hormone (SC injection)

## Adrenal Insufficiency (secondary)
- Dx: ↓ACTH, ↓cortisol
- Tx: Glucocorticoid

## Central Diabetes Insipidus
- Dx: ↓urine osm, $H_2O$ deprivation test (gold standard)
- Tx: Desmopressin (synthetic ADH)

## Central Hypogonadism
- Dx (female): ↓FSH, ↓LH, ↓estradiol
- Tx (female): Estrogen/progesterone (premenopausal)
- Dx (male): ↓FSH, ↓LH, ↓testosterone
- Tx (male): Testosterone (topical or IM)

# Hypothyroidism

## Clinical Features

 • ↑Weight

 • Cold intolerance

• Constipation

• Mood disturbances

 **31** • Menstrual irregularity

• Hyporeflexia

• Bradycardia

 • Myxedema

Reproduced with permission from Jameson J, Fauci AS, Kasper DL, et al: Harrison's Principles of Internal Medicine, 20th ed. New York, NY: McGraw Hill; 2018.

• Hair loss

• Myopathy

 • Fatigue & weakness

## Causes

 **Autoimmune Hypothyroidism (Hashimoto Thyroiditis)**
- Antithyroid peroxidase and/or antithyroglobulin Ab present
- Can have transient ↑TH state early in dz
- Enlarged nontender thyroid

 **Subacute Thyroiditis**
- Granulomatous inflammation of thyroid
- May have initial ↑TH followed by ↓TH
- Presents post-viral infection or postpartum
- Thyroid tenderness may be present

 **Secondary Hypothyroidism**
- Deficient TSH production → ↓TH
- Common etiologies: Pituitary tumors, surgery, radiation

 **Riedel's Thyroiditis**
- Fibrosis of the thyroid gland and/or surrounding structures (parathyroid, recurrent laryngeal nerve, trachea)
- Rock-like, immobile, painless gland

 **Congenital Hypothyroidism**
- Usually due to thyroid dysgenesis
- FTT, hypotonia, jaundice, long-term intellectual disability if untreated

 **Substance Related**
- Iodine deficiency
- Amiodarone use (also causes ↑TH)
- Lithium
- Checkpoint inhibitor chemotherapy (leads to destructive thyroiditis)

## Management

### Diagnosis
- **Serum TSH level**
- PRN serum free T4 levels if secondary dz suspected
- May also present with increased LDL, triglycerides, CK

 **Treatment**
- Primary treatment: Levothyroxine (synthetic T4)
- Rx if TSH >10 or if +sx

 **Complications**

**Myxedema coma**
- Severe life-threatening↓TH
- MS changes, ↓↓BP, ↓↓HR, ↓↓RR
- Immediate Rx with IV levothyroxine (T4) & liothyronine (T3)

**Increased incidence of cancer**
- Thyroid lymphoma seen w/Hashimoto's thyroiditis (chronic lymphocytic stimulation)
- Presents as rapidly enlarging goiter

# Multiple Endocrine Neoplasia

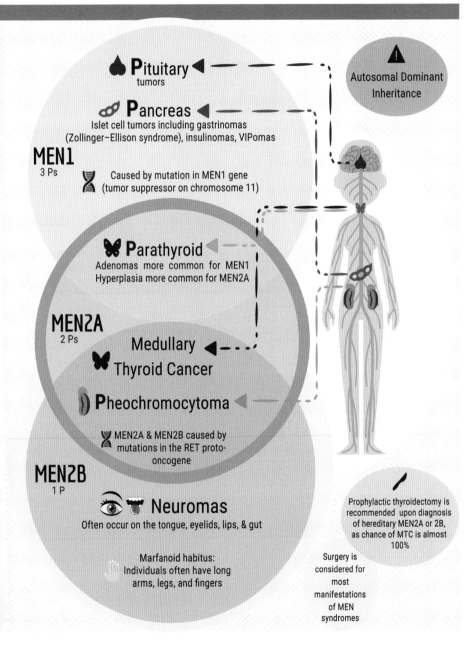

**Pituitary** tumors

**Pancreas**
Islet cell tumors including gastrinomas (Zollinger–Ellison syndrome), insulinomas, VIPomas

**MEN1**
3 Ps

Caused by mutation in MEN1 gene (tumor suppressor on chromosome 11)

Autosomal Dominant Inheritance

**Parathyroid**
Adenomas more common for MEN1
Hyperplasia more common for MEN2A

**MEN2A**
2 Ps

Medullary Thyroid Cancer

Pheochromocytoma

MEN2A & MEN2B caused by mutations in the RET proto-oncogene

**MEN2B**
1 P

**Neuromas**
Often occur on the tongue, eyelids, lips, & gut

Marfanoid habitus: Individuals often have long arms, legs, and fingers

Prophylactic thyroidectomy is recommended upon diagnosis of hereditary MEN2A or 2B, as chance of MTC is almost 100%

Surgery is considered for most manifestations of MEN syndromes

# Osteoporosis

## Characteristics

- ↓ Bone strength
- Deterioration in skeletal microarchitecture
- ↑ Risk of fracture (fx)

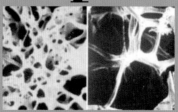

Reproduced with permission from Barrett KE, Barman SM, Brooks HL, et al: Ganong's Review of Medical Physiology, 26th ed. New York, NY: McGraw Hill; 2019.

## Definition

Bone mineral density (BMD) 2.5 SD or more below the young adult mean (T-score of ≤−2.5)

---

### Risk Factors

| | | |
|---|---|---|
| Female (esp. postmenopausal) | Inadequate nutrition | Smoking |
| Age (>50) | ↓ Peak bone mass | EtOH |
| Prior fx | ↓ Body weight | Long-term |
| Parental hip fx | | glucocorticoid Rx |

---

### Clinical Presentation

**Most common in _postmenopausal Caucasian female_**

**_Fragility fx_** from minor trauma (fall from < standing height)
- No clinical manifestations until fx

Common fx sites: L-spine, femoral neck, Colles (wrist)
- Vertebral fx = most common (2/3 asymptomatic, incidentally found on XR)

---

### Dx & Workup

**Whom to Screen**
_All F >65_
F <65 if menopausal + RFs
M >50 if RFs present

**Diagnosis**
Measure BMD:
**_DEXA T-score_ ≤−2.5**

**Prognosis**
Calculate 10y fx risk
(FRAX score )

**PRN eval for Secondary Causes of Bone Loss**
↓Vit D
Malabsorption
↑PTH
Multiple myeloma
Cushing's

---

### Treatment

1. **RF modification: All patients**
   ↑exercise, ↓glucocorticoids, ↓smoking/EtOH
   adequate Ca (1200 mg/d) & vitD (800 IU/d)

2. **Pharmacologic Rx: If 10 years fx risk ≥20% (any fx) or ≥3% (hip fx)** **_Bisphosphonates_** (1st line)
   Denosumab (if CKD)
   PTH analogs (for severe or refractory dz)
   SERM (if ↑BrCA risk)

# Pituitary Neoplasms

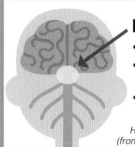

## Presentation of Sellar Mass

- Often incidental imaging finding
- Symptoms from pituitary mass effect
- Hormonal abnormalities

*Bitemporal hemianopsia headache*

↙ ↘

*Hormone excess (from secreting tumors)*    *Hypopituitarism (compression of pituitary by mass)*

## DDx of Sellar Mass

**1. Pituitary adenoma**
Most common, see below

**2. Rathke's cleft cyst**
Congenital lesion
symptoms / hypopit if very large

**3. Craniopharyngioma**
Often present with hypopit & DI

**4. Hypophysitis**
Typically seen postpartum or with
checkpoint inhibitor chemotherapy

**5. Metastatic disease**
Most common: Breast or
lung CA

## Classification of Pituitary Adenomas   *Secretory Adenomas*

Size ⟨
  **<1 cm:** Microadenoma
  **>1 cm:** Macroadenoma

Activity ⟨
  Nonfunctioning /Nonsecretory
  Functioning/secretory

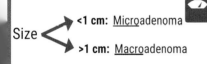 **Cushing's disease** (↑ACTH)
Wt gain, striae, bruising
Proximal muscle weakness
Hypogonadism (men/women)
Hyperandrogenism (women)
HTN, DM2

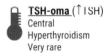 **TSH-oma** (↑ ↓SH)
Central
Hyperthyroidism
Very rare

 **Prolactinoma** (↑PRL)
Galactorrhea
Hypogonadism
Osteopenia/osteoporosis

 **Acromegaly** (↑GH)
↑Ring/shoe size
Coarse facies
HTN, DM2

## Treatment of Pituitary Adenomas

 **Medical Management**

 **Transsphenoidal Resection (TSR)**

 **Radiation**

Prolactinoma: Initially treated
with dopamine agonists, TSR
if tumor growth on medication
or medication side-effects

Other functional tumors: Medical Rx
often used as adjunct Rx after TSR

First-line treatment for all types
of pituitary adenomas other than
prolactinomas

Typically used as adjunct for
refractory or residual disease
after medical Rx and/or TSR

# Thyroid Neoplasms

## __Benign__ (90-95%) thyroid nodules

- Can be functional (secrete thyroid hormone)
- **Adenomas**, nodules, cysts
- US-guided FNA performed
- if US appearance suspicious for malignancy (gold standard)

Check TSH

High, normal

Thyroid US

US-guided FNA if suspicious for malignancy

Low

Radioactive iodine uptake scan

⇩

Autonomous/hyperfunctioning = very low risk

⇩

Treat hyperthyroidism (antithyroid drugs, radioactive iodine ablation, surgery)

---

## __Malignant__

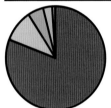

- Papillary
- Follicular
- Medullary
- Anaplastic
- Misc. (inc. Thyroid Lymphoma)

"Psammoma bodies" circular calcifications

Reproduced with permission from Reisner H. Pathology: A Modern Case Study, 2nd ed. New York, NY: McGraw Hill; 2020.

**DIFFERENTIATED** Good prognosis

### Papillary

Thyroglobulin

**TUMOR MARKER**

Clear, glassy intranuclear inclusion bodies

**MOST COMMON**

Reproduced with permission from Kantarjian HM, Wolff RA: The MD Anderson Manual of Medical Oncology, 3rd ed. New York, NY: McGraw Hill Education; 2016.

### Follicular

Thyroglobulin

**TUMOR MARKER**

Hematogenous spread is common distinguished from benign follicular adenoma by presence of __capsular/vascular invasion__

### Medullary

**TUMOR MARKERS**
CEA
Calcitonin

Neuroendocrine neoplasm
Parafollicular "C" cells secrete calcitonin and CEA
Sheets of cells separated by Congo red staining substance
20% familial (RET mutations—MEN2A and 2B)—*so screen*

Reproduced with permission from Reisner H. Pathology: A Modern Case Study, 2nd ed. New York, NY: McGraw Hill; 2020.

### Anaplastic

__Poorly__ Differentiated
__Poor__ Prognosis
RARE
Older patients present with invasion of local structures ➡ dysphagia, hoarseness, dyspnea

### Lymphoma

RARE

# Type 1 Diabetes

*Incidence in the United States: 0.4%*
*Mean age of onset <30 years*
*Severe glucose intolerance*

✓ **Goals:**

**A1C ≤7% in adults**
(avg bld glc
154 mg/dL)

*Consider goal A1C*
*≤6 in pregnancy*
*≤7.5 in children*
*≤8 in older adults with comorbidities*

## Etiology

-Autoimmune destruction of pancreatic β-cells mediated by
several autoantigens (GAD65, IA-2, ZnT8, insulin itself)
-Weak genetic association (polygenic)
-Associated with HLA DR3,4

**HLA associations**
Graves': DR3
Hashimoto's: DR3,5
Pernicious anemia: DRS
Addison's: B8, DR3,4

## Pathophysiology

-Gradually progressive defect in insulin secretion (leukocytes
infiltrate islets resulting in β-cell destruction) → ↑hyperglycemia
over time
-Occasional insulin resistance also seen if patients have
concurrent obesity

## Clinical Presentation

-Classically: Nonobese patient <30 years
-Polyuria, polydipsia, polyphagia, ↓weight over days-weeks
-Can present in DKA: Severe dehydration, AMS,
Kussmaul respirations, n/v/abd pain

*A1C reflects*
*3 months of*
*glucose control*
*(RBC lifespan)*
**test q3-6**
**months**

## Diagnosis

*Diabetes mellitus (both Types 1 & 2):*
Fasting plasma glucose level ≥126 mg/dL on 2 occasions
**OR** random plasma glucose level ≥200 mg/dL with symptoms
**OR** 2-hour OGTT glucose level ≥200 mg/dL
**OR** A1C ≥6.5%

Y **Type 1 classification made clinically** (can confirm w/anti-GAD65, anti-islet Abs)

## DM1-Specific Complications

-DKA → **mucormycosis**, cerebral edema, arrhythmia, heart failure, death
-↓Glucagon from pancreatic destruction → more predisposed to
hypoglycemia from insulin therapy ("brittle" diabetic)

*CAD is*
*MCC death*
*in DM*

## Treatment

Insulin always required

# Type 2 Diabetes

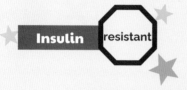

**Insulin resistant**

*90% of adult diabetics are type 2*
*Prevalence in the United States: 9%*
*Mean age of onset <40 years*
*Moderate glucose intolerance*

## Etiology

-Differing degrees of insulin resistance/relative insulin deficiency from *complex interaction* between:
   -<u>Environmental factors:</u> Physical inactivity, obesity → systemic inflammation
   -<u>Genetic susceptibility:</u> Genes involved in pancreatic development, β-cell function/insulin release, & insulin receptor signaling
-Strong polygenic inheritance—90% monozygotic twin concordance

## Pathophysiology

**-Insulin resistance in tissues**
-Initially hyperinsulinemic to respond to hyperglycemia
-A relative insulin deficiency can develop over time
(pancreas increases secretion but **even high insulin levels cannot overcome insulin resistance**)

## Clinical presentation

-Classically: Obese adult patient, ↑ incidence in AAs and native Americans
-Often clinically silent but can have polyuria, polydipsia, vision Δ
-Can present in HHS: Severe dehydration, lethargy/AMS, seizure, vision Δ, coma
-*Very rarely can present in DKA ("ketosis prone" diabetes)*

*A1C reflects 3 months of glucose control (RBC lifespan) test q3-6 months*

## Diagnosis

Fasting plasma glucose level ≥126 mg/dL on 2 occasions
**OR** random plasma glucose level ≥200 mg/dL with symptoms
**OR** 2-hour glucose level ≥200 after OGTT
**OR** A1C ≥ 6.5%

*CAD is MCC death in DM*

## Treatment

**-1st Line: Lifestyle Δ (↓wt, ↑exercise) & metformin**
-Additional rx tailored to individual pt: Consider risks/benefits (oral hypoglycemics, SGL T2i, GLP-1A, insulin)
-Insulin often required (can cause ↑↑ wt)
-Frequent complication monitoring: Foot & eye exams
-Manage other comorbidities: BP <130/80, statin Rx

**✅ Goals:**
A1C ≤7% in adults
(avg bld glc 154 mg/dL)

*Consider goal A1C ≤6 in pregnancy ≤8 for older adults with comorbidities*

# References

**Acromegaly**

Le T, Bhushan V, Sochat M, et al. *First Aid for the USMLE Step 1 2018*. New York, NY: McGraw Hill; 2017.

Melmed S, Katznelson L. Causes and clinical manifestations of acromegaly. In: Snyder PJ, Martin KA. *UpToDate*. Waltham, MA: UpToDate Inc. https://www.uptodate.com/contents/causes-and-clinical-manifestations-of-acromegaly?search=acromegaly&source=search_result&selectedTitle=2~89&usage_type=default&display_rank=2#H9

**Acute Hyperglycemic Diabetic Complications**

Le T, Bhushan V. *First Aid for the USMLE Step 1 2016*. New York, NY: McGraw Hill; 2016.

Le T, Skelley NW, Bhushan V. *First Aid for the USMLE Step 2 CK*. 8th ed. New York, NY: McGraw Hill; 2012.

**Adrenal Insufficiency**

Le T, Bhushan V, Chen V, King M. *First Aid for the USMLE Step 2 CK*. 9th ed. New York: McGraw Hill; 2015.

Le T, Bhushan V, Sochat M, et al. *First Aid for the USMLE Step 1 2018*. New York, NY: McGraw Hill; 2017.

**Adrenal Neoplasms**

Le T, Bhushan V, Chen V, King M. *First Aid for the USMLE Step 2 CK*. 9th ed. New York: McGraw Hill; 2015.

Le T, Bhushan V, Sochat M, et al. *First Aid for the USMLE Step 1 2018*. New York, NY: McGraw Hill; 2017.

Molina PE, ed. Adrenal Gland. *Endocrine Physiology*. 5th ed. New York, NY: McGraw Hill; 2018. http://accessmedicine.mhmedical.com/content.aspx?bookid=2343&sectionid=183488502.

**Chronic Diabetic Complications**

Le T, Bhushan V. *First Aid for the USMLE Step 1 2016*. New York, NY: McGraw Hill; 2016.

Le T, Skelley NW, Bhushan V. *First Aid for the USMLE Step 2 CK*. 8th ed. New York, NY: McGraw Hill; 2012.

**Congenital Adrenal Hyperplasia**

Le T, Bhushan V, Chen V, King M. *First Aid for the USMLE Step 2 CK*. 9th ed. New York: McGraw Hill; 2015.

Le T, Bhushan V, Sochat M, et al. *First Aid for the USMLE Step 1 2018*. New York, NY: McGraw Hill; 2017.

**Cushing's Syndrome**

Le T, Bhushan V, Chen V, King M. *First Aid for the USMLE Step 2 CK*. 9th ed. New York: McGraw Hill; 2015.

Le T, Bhushan V, Sochat M, et al. *First Aid for the USMLE Step 1 2018*. New York, NY: McGraw Hill; 2017.

Hardin J. Cutaneous conditions. In: Knoop KJ, Stack LB, Storrow AB, Thurman R, eds. *The Atlas of Emergency Medicine*. 4th ed. New York, NY: McGraw Hill; 2016.

**Diabetes Treatment**

Le T, Bhushan V. *First Aid for the USMLE Step 1 2016*. New York, NY: McGraw Hill; 2016.

Le T, Skelley NW, Bhushan V. *First Aid for the USMLE Step 2 CK*. 8th ed. New York, NY: McGraw Hill; 2012.

Molina PE, ed. *Endocrine Physiology*. 5th ed. New York, NY: McGraw Hill; 2018.

**Hypercalcemia & Hyperparathyroidism**

Jameson JL, Fauci AS, Kasper DL, Hauser SL, Longo DL, Loscalzo J, eds. *Harrison's Principles of Internal Medicine*. 20th ed. New York, NY: McGraw Hill; 2018.

Le T, Bhushan V. *First Aid for the USMLE Step 1 2016*. New York, NY: McGraw Hill; 2016.

Le T, Skelley NW, Bhushan V. *First Aid for the USMLE Step 2 CK*. 8th ed. New York, NY: McGraw Hill; 2012.

Molina PE, ed. *Endocrine Physiology*. 5th ed. New York, NY: McGraw Hill; 2018.

**Hyperthyroidism**

Le T, Bhushan V. *First Aid for the USMLE Step 1 2016*. New York, NY: McGraw Hill; 2016.

Le T, Skelley NW, Bhushan V. *First Aid for the USMLE Step 2 CK*. 8th ed. New York, NY: McGraw Hill; 2012.

**Hypogonadism**

Law D. Adhesion and its role in the virulence of enteropathogenic Escherichia coli. *Clin Microbiol Rev*. 1994;7(2):152-173. doi:10.1128/cmr.7.2.152. https://www.ncbi.nlm.nih.gov/pmc/articles/PMC3583156/

Snyder PJ. Causes of primary hypogonadism in males. In: Matsumoto AM, Martin KA, eds. *UpToDate*. Waltham, MA: UpToDate Inc. https://www.uptodate.com/contents/causes-of-primary-hypogonadism-in-males?search=hypogonadism&source=search_result&selectedTitle=4~150&usage_type=default&display_rank=4

Snyder PJ. Causes of secondary hypogonadism in males. In: Matsumoto AM, Geffner ME, Martin KA, eds. UpToDate. Waltham, MA: UpToDate Inc. https://www.uptodate.com/contents/causes-of-secondary-hypogonadism-in-males?search=hypogonadism&source=search_result&selectedTitle=3~150&usage_type=default&display_rank=3

Snyder PJ. Clinical features and diagnosis of male hypogonadism. In: Matsumoto AM, Martin KA, eds. *UpToDate*. Waltham, MA: UpToDate Inc. https://www.uptodate.com/contents/clinical-features-and-diagnosis-of-male-hypogonadism?search=hypogonadism&source=search_result&selectedTitle=1~150&usage_type=default&display_rank=1

Welt CK. Pathogenesis and causes of spontaneous primary ovarian insufficiency (premature ovarian failure). In: Barbieri RL, Crowley WF Jr, Martin KA, eds. *UpToDate*. Waltham, MA: UpToDate Inc. https://www.uptodate.com/contents/pathogenesis-and-causes-of-spontaneous-primary-ovarian-insufficiency-premature-ovarian-failure?search=hypogonadism&source=search_result&selectedTitle=7~150&usage_type=default&display_rank=7

**Hypopituitarism**

Snyder PJ. Clinical manifestations of hypopituitarism. In: Cooper DS, Martin KA, eds. *UpToDate*. Waltham, MA: UpToDate Inc. https://www.uptodate.com/contents/clinical-manifestations-of-hypopituitarism?search=hypopituitarism&source=search_result&selectedTitle=1~150&usage_type=default&display_rank=1#H4

Snyder PJ. Diagnostic testing for hypopituitarism. In: Cooper DS, Martin KA, eds. *UpToDate*. Waltham, MA: UpToDate Inc. https://www.uptodate.com/contents/diagnostic-testing-for-hypopituitarism?search=hypopituitarism&source=search_result&selectedTitle=2~150&usage_type=default&display_rank=2

Snyder PJ. Treatment of hypopituitarism. In: Cooper DS, Martin KA, eds. *UpToDate*. Waltham, MA: UpToDate Inc. https://www.uptodate.com/contents/treatment-of-hypopituitarism?search=hypopituitarism&source=search_result&selectedTitle=3~150&usage_type=default&display_rank=3

**Hypothyroidism**

Le T, Bhushan V. *First Aid for the USMLE Step 1 2016*. New York, NY: McGraw Hill; 2016.

Le T, Skelley NW, Bhushan V. *First Aid for the USMLE Step 2 CK*. 8th ed. New York, NY: McGraw Hill; 2012.

**Multiple Endocrine Neoplasia**

Le T, Bhushan V. *First Aid for the USMLE Step 1 2016*. New York, NY: McGraw Hill; 2016.

Le T, Skelley NW, Bhushan V. *First Aid for the USMLE Step 2 CK*. 8th ed. New York, NY: McGraw Hill; 2012.

**Osteoporosis**

Lindsay R, Cosman F. Osteoporosis. In: Jameson J, Fauci AS, Kasper DL, Hauser SL, Longo DL, Loscalzo J, eds. *Harrison's Principles of Internal Medicine*. 20th ed. New York, NY: McGraw Hill; 2018.

South-Paul JE. Osteoporosis. In: South-Paul JE, Matheny SC, Lewis EL, eds. *CURRENT Diagnosis & Treatment: Family Medicine*. 4th ed. New York, NY: McGraw Hill; 2015.

**Pituitary Neoplasm**

Loeffler JS, Shih HA. Radiation therapy of pituitary adenomas. In: Snyder PJ, Martin KA, eds. *UpToDate*. Waltham, MA: UpToDate Inc. https://www.uptodate.com/contents/radiation-therapy-of-pituitary-adenomas?search=pituitary%20adenoma%20treatment&source=search_result&selectedTitle=3~150&usage_type=default&display_rank=3

Snyder PJ. Causes, presentation, and evaluation of sellar masses. In: Cooper DS, Martin KA, eds. *UpToDate*. Waltham, MA: UpToDate Inc. https://www.uptodate.com/contents/causes-presentation-and-evaluation-of-sellar-masses

Snyder PJ. Management of hyperprolactinemia. In: Cooper DS, Martin KA, eds. *UpToDate*. Waltham, MA: UpToDate Inc. https://www.uptodate.com/contents/management-of-hyperprolactinemia?search=pituitary%20adenoma%20treatment&source=search_result&selectedTitle=1~150&usage_type=default&display_rank=1

Swearingen B. Transsphenoidal surgery for pituitary adenomas and other sellar masses. In: Snyder PJ, Martin KA, eds. *UpToDate*. Waltham, MA: UpToDate Inc. https://www.uptodate.com/contents/transsphenoidal-surgery-for-pituitary-adenomas-and-other-sellar-masses?search=pituitary%20adenoma%20treatment&source=search_result&selectedTitle=2~150&usage_type=default&display_rank=2

**Thyroid Neoplasms**

Allweiss P, Hueston WJ, Carek PJ. Endocrine disorders. In: South-Paul JE, Matheny SC, Lewis EL, eds. *CURRENT Diagnosis & Treatment: Family Medicine*. 4th ed. New York, NY: McGraw Hill; 2015.

Cooper DS, Ladenson PW. The thyroid gland. In: Gardner DG, Shoback D, eds. *Greenspan's Basic & Clinical Endocrinology*. 9th ed. New York, NY: McGraw Hill; 2011.

Esfandiari NH, McPhee SJ. Thyroid disease. In: Hammer GD, McPhee SJ, eds. *Pathophysiology of Disease: An Introduction to Clinical Medicine*. 8th ed. New York, NY: McGraw Hill; 2019.

**Type 1 Diabetes**

Introduction: *Standards of Medical Care in Diabetes-2019. Diabetes Care*. 2019;42(Suppl 1):S1-S2. doi:10.2337/dc19-Sint01.

Le T, Bhushan V. *First Aid for the USMLE Step 1 2016*. New York, NY: McGraw Hill; 2016.

Le T, Skelley NW, Bhushan V. *First Aid for the USMLE Step 2 CK*. 8th ed. New York, NY: McGraw Hill; 2012.

**Type 2 Diabetes**

Le T, Bhushan V. *First Aid for the USMLE Step 1 2016*. New York, NY: McGraw Hill; 2016.

Le T, Skelley NW, Bhushan, V. *First Aid for the USMLE Step 2 CK*. 8th ed. New York, NY: McGraw Hill; 2012.

# Gastroenterology/Hepatology

*Neeral Shah, MD*

# Ascites

## Physical Exam Findings

Abdominal distention

Fluid wave & shifting dullness

**!** Most common complication of cirrhosis

## DDx

Cirrhosis, portal HTN
CHF
Chronic renal disease
Fluid overload
TB peritonitis
Malignancy
Hypoalbuminemia
Pancreatitis

## Manifestations of Cirrhosis

Ascites
Hepatic encephalopathy
Asterixis
Jaundice
Spider angioma
Caput medusae
Varices
Peripheral edema
Gynecomastia
Hepatorenal syndrome
Thrombocytopenia
Anemia

## Diagnostic Paracentesis

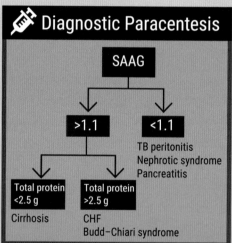

SAAG

>1.1     <1.1

<1.1:
TB peritonitis
Nephrotic syndrome
Pancreatitis

>1.1:
Total protein <2.5 g → Cirrhosis
Total protein >2.5 g → CHF, Budd–Chiari syndrome

## Therapy

 Na restriction

 Furosemide

 Spironolactone

 Therapeutic paracentesis
Albumin 6-8 g/L
Removed if LVP >5 L

 Transjugular intrahepatic portosystemic shunt (TIPS)

## Cirrhosis Etiology

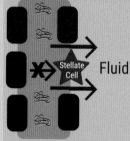

Stellate Cell → Fluid

Stellate cells cause fibrosis
Protein can't exude

## CHF Etiology

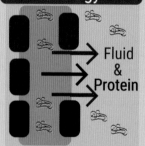

Fluid & Protein

Protein exudes in the absence of fibrosis

## ⚠ Complications

 Spontaneous bacterial peritonitis (SBP)

 Hepatorenal syndrome

# ASH & NASH

## Alcoholic Steatohepatitis

🍷 Caused by long-term consumption of alcohol

### Clinical Presentation

- 🫀 Hepatosplenomegaly
- ❓ Jaundice
- 🧍 Ascites
- Hepatic encephalopathy
- 🌡️ Fever

✳️ Elevated LFTs: AST > ALT (ratio > 2:1)
Mitochondrial injury from alcohol metabolites

## Nonalcoholic Steatohepatitis

Metabolic syndrome etiology:
- 🍟 Obesity, HTN, dyslipidemia
- 💉 Diabetes mellitus

### Clinical Presentation

- 🏃 Vague RUQ pain
- 🛌 Fatigue, malaise
- 🫀 Hepatomegaly

In the absence of significant alcohol consumption
Elevated LFTs: ALT > AST

**❗ Both often present asymptomatically**

---

 ## Liver Biopsy

Histology of the liver is identical in ASH & NASH—requires clinical history to differentiate

Cellular ballooning & necrosis of hepatocytes

Mallory bodies

Reproduced with permission from Jameson J, Fauci AS, Kasper DL, et al: Harrison's Principles of Internal Medicine, 20th ed. New York, NY: McGraw Hill; 2018.

Steatosis (fatty change)

Neutrophilic infiltration

Sclerosis around central vein

---

## Disease Progression

ASH

**Alcoholic hepatitis**
Profound bilirubin rise

Reversible with alcohol abstinence

**Alcoholic cirrhosis**

Alcoholic hepatitis + alcoholic cirrhosis

☠️

## Disease Progression

Associated disorders:
- 🫀 Vitamin D deficiency
- Cardiovascular disease
- 🛌 Obstructive sleep apnea
- 🦋 Hypothyroidism
- Polycystic ovarian syndrome

Disease reversible:
- ⚖️ Weight loss
- 💉 Control of diabetes

NASH

⬇️

Cirrhosis

⬇️

Better long-term survival than ASH patients

# Autoimmune Hepatitis

## Clinical Features

 Female predominance (4:1)

 PMH: Autoimmune disorders
Celiac disease, diabetes, lupus, thyroid disease, UC, etc.

 ANA+ lab findings

## Presentation

 Acute liver failure
Or asymptomatic

 Elevated LFTs

 Liver biopsy
Interface hepatitis
Inflammation in portal tracts

**A scoring system is available in the AASLD Practice Guidelines to predict likely autoimmune hepatitis.

## Type I

 Antismooth muscle antibody

 Usually adult onset

## Type II

 Anti-liver-kidney microsomal antibody

 Usually childhood onset

## Treatment

Immunosuppression
18-24 months at minimum
(if normal LFTs)

Usually indefinite because of high relapse rate

**Prednisone**
**Azathioprine**

Liver biopsy essential prior to discontinuing therapy: ensure no inflammation

## Etiology

Acute illness
Initiating medication
Hormonal changes

Inflammation of hepatocytes

# Biliary Tract Conditions

## 1. Cholelithiasis

**Cholesterol Stones:**
80% of stones
Risk factors:
4 Fs: Female, Fat, Fertile, Forty
Crohn disease, Pima Native
American ancestry, cirrhosis

**Pigmented Stones:**
Chronic hemolysis, alcoholic
cirrhosis, biliary infections

**Most cases are asymptomatic**

## 2. Biliary Colic

**Clinical Presentation:**
Intermittent RUQ pain after
eating & at night

**Etiology:**
Temporary obstruction of
cystic duct by gallstone

**Treatment:**
Cholecystectomy

## 3. Acute Cholecystitis

**Clinical Presentation:**
RUQ pain with rebound tenderness
Murphy's sign
Nausea & vomiting

**Etiology:**
Gallstone obstruction of cystic duct
Inflammation of gallbladder wall

**Diagnosis:**
RUQ ultrasound
HIDA scan

**Treatment:**
IV fluids, NPO, IV antibiotics
Cholecystectomy

## 5. Cholangitis

**Clinical Presentation:**
Charcot triad (RUQ pain, jaundice, &
fever)
Reynolds pentad (Charcot triad,
septic shock, & altered mental status)

**Etiology:**
Infection within biliary tree due to
obstruction

**Diagnosis:**
RUQ ultrasound
Elevated bilirubin & WBCs/leukocytes
ERCP or percutaneous transhepatic
cholangiography (PTC)

**Treatment:**
IV antibiotics & IV fluids
Decompress common bile duct with
ERCP or PTC

## 4. Choledocholithiasis

**Clinical Presentation:**
RUQ pain & jaundice
May be asymptomatic

**Etiology:**
Gallstone in the common bile duct

**Diagnosis:**
RUQ ultrasound then ERCP
Elevated alk phos & bilirubin

**Treatment:**
ERCP with sphincterotomy, stone
extraction, & stent placement

# Celiac Disease

## Clinical Presentation

- Steatorrhea
- Weight loss & delayed growth
- Bloating
- Dermatitis herpetiformis
- Decreased bone density

⚠ Increased risk of T-cell lymphoma

## Treatment

🚫 Gluten-free diet

## Diagnosis

### Serology

IgA antitissue transglutaminase (IgA tTG)

Anti-endomysial antibody

Anti-deamidated gliadin peptide antibodies

### Endoscopy

Scalloped mucosa in duodenum

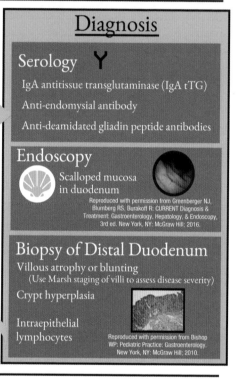

Reproduced with permission from Greenberger NJ, Blumberg RS, Burakoff R: CURRENT Diagnosis & Treatment: Gastroenterology, Hepatology, & Endoscopy, 3rd ed. New York, NY: McGraw Hill; 2016.

### Biopsy of Distal Duodenum

Villous atrophy or blunting
(Use Marsh staging of villi to assess disease severity)

Crypt hyperplasia

Intraepithelial lymphocytes

Reproduced with permission from Bishop WP: Pediatric Practice: Gastroenterology. New York, NY: McGraw Hill; 2010.

## Etiology

### Associations

HLA-DQ2 & HLA-DQ8

Northern European descent

Primary biliary cholangitis

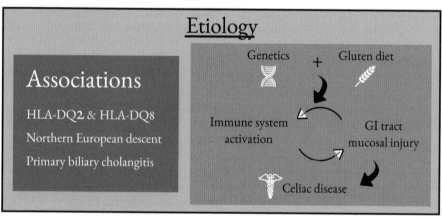

Genetics + Gluten diet

Immune system activation

GI tract mucosal injury

Celiac disease

# *Clostridioides difficile* Colitis

 *Pseudomembranous Colitis*

## Clinical Presentation

 **Profuse, watery diarrhea**
Usually no blood or mucus

 **Recent antibiotic use**
Clindamycin, ampicillin, cephalosporins
Symptoms present 1-6 weeks following therapy

 **Leukocytosis**

 **Crampy abdominal pain**

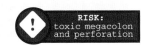
**RISK:** toxic megacolon and perforation

## Diagnosis & Workup

 **Toxins in stool**
By PCR or antigen detection

 **Abdominal radiograph**
Rule out toxic megacolon and perforation

## Therapy

**Initial**
**Oral vancomycin**
**Oral fidaxomicin**

**Recurrent**
**Repeat prior regimen**
Or switch to **oral** vancomycin/long-term vancomycin **taper**
**Fecal microbiota transplant**

**Contagious:** ensure proper hand hygiene in health care facilities

## Pathology

 **Toxin A** (enterotoxin): binds to brush border of the gut and alters fluid secretion

**Toxin B** (cytotoxin): disrupts cytoskeleton via **actin** depolymerization

# ✚ Colorectal Cancer

## Clinical Presentation

Iron deficiency anemia in males & postmenopausal females

"Apple-core" lesion on barium enema

## Common Locations

Right side bleeds
Left side obstructs

## Colonoscopy Screening

Start at age 50

First-degree relative with CRC, start screening at 40 or 10 years before relative's presentation

Special screening protocol for patients with IBD

## 🚬 Risk Factors

Familial cancer syndromes & IBD

Tobacco, processed meats, low fiber

## Malignant Potential

### Adenomatous polyps

May have occult bleeding
**Mutations:**
APC & K-Ras
**Malignant potential:**
Villous > tubulovillous > tubular

### Serrated polyps

**Mutations:**
Microsatellite instability
*B-Raf* mutation
**Biopsy:**
"Saw-tooth" appearance

---

# Polyposis Syndromes

## ✚ Familial Adenomatous Polyposis (FAP)

Thousands of colon polyps starting after puberty

**APC**
Two-Hit
Hypothesis

**Location:**
Pancolonic
Always involves the rectum

**Treatment:**
Prophylactic pancolectomy

⚠ 100% progress to CRC

### Gardner

FAP
+
Osseous & soft tissue tumors

Impacted teeth

Retinal pigment epithelium hypertrophy

### Turcot

FAP or
Lynch syndrome
+
Malignant CNS tumors

Medulloblastoma, glioma, etc.

---

## ✚ Peutz–Jeghers

Autosomal dominant

Numerous hamartomas throughout GI tract

Hyperpigmented lips, hands, genitalia

Increased risk of breast & GI cancers

## ✚ Juvenile Polyposis

Autosomal dominant

Typically in children (<5 years old)

Numerous hamartomas in colon, stomach, small bowel

Increased risk of CRC

## ✚ Lynch (HNPCC)

Autosomal dominant

Microsatellite instability

Mismatch repair genes

Proximal colon is always involved

**Associations:**
Endometrial cancer
Ovarian cancer
Skin cancers

⚠ 80% progress to CRC

# Crohn Disease

## Clinical Features

**Diarrhea**
Usually nonbloody

**Abdominal pain**

**Weight loss**
Malabsorption of B12 and bile acids

## Extraintestinal Manifestations

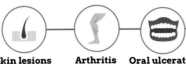

**Skin lesions**
Erythema nodosum*

**Arthritis**

**Oral ulceration**
Aphthous stomatitis
Peripheral sacroilitis

**Eye inflammation**
Uveitis
Episcleritis

*Distinction from UC

## Diagnosis

**"String sign" on barium swallow**

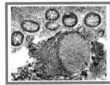

Reproduced with permission from Reisner H. Pathology: A Modern Case Study, 2nd ed. New York, NY: McGraw Hill; 2020.

### Pathology

Noncaseating granuloma
Lymphoid aggregates
Transmural inflammation

Reproduced with permission from Reisner H. Pathology: A Modern Case Study, 2nd ed. New York, NY: McGraw Hill; 2020.

### Gross Pathology

Skip lesions
Cobblestone mucosa
Creeping fat
Bowel wall thickening
Linear ulcers and fissures

### Distribution

Mostly terminal ileum and colon (but any portion of the GI tract)
Rectal sparing

## Treatment

**Avoid antidiarrheals**

**1** **5 Aminosalicylates**
(mesalamine, sulfasalazine)

**2** **Antibiotics**
(metronidazole, ciprofloxacin)

**3** **Corticosteroids**
(prednisone, budesonide)

**4** **Immunomodualtors**
(azathioprine, 6-mercaptopurine, methotrexate)

**5** **Biologics**
(certolizumab pegol, vedolizumab, ustekinumab, inflixamab, adalimumab, etc.)

## Complications

**Colorectal cancer**          **Growth retardation**

**Fistulas**                   **Nephrolithiasis**

**Strictures & SBO**           **Cholelithiasis**

**Perianal diseases:**
fissures, abscesses

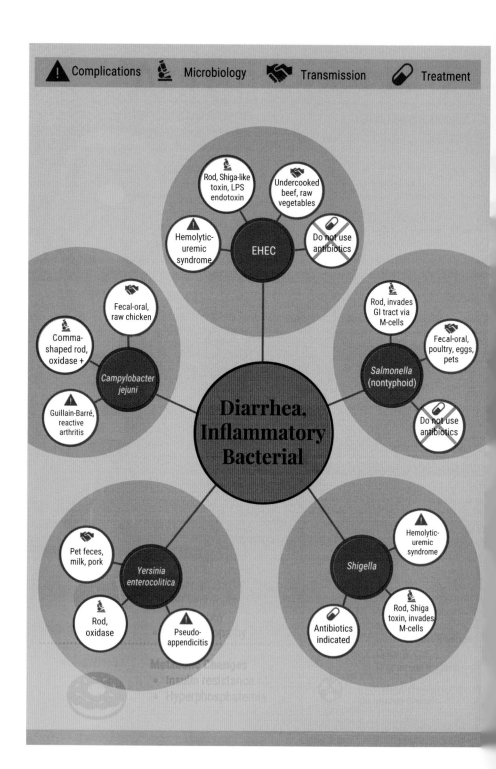

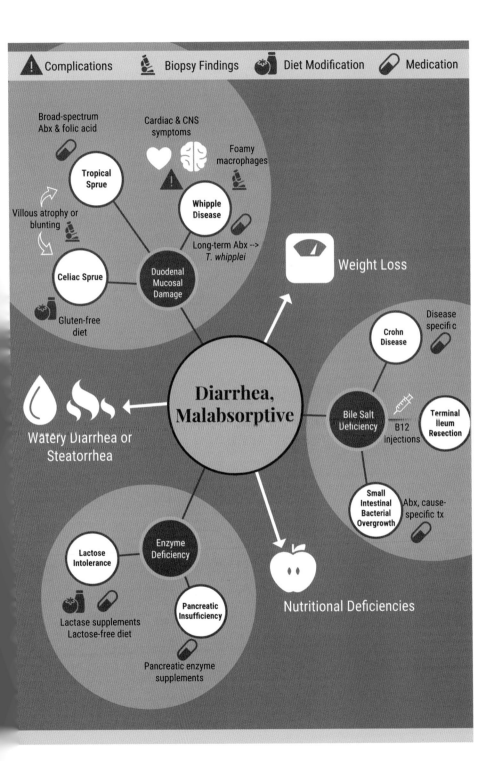

Complications • Biopsy Findings • Diet Modification • Medication

**Diarrhea, Malabsorptive**

Watery Diarrhea or Steatorrhea

Weight Loss

Nutritional Deficiencies

**Duodenal Mucosal Damage**
- Tropical Sprue — Broad-spectrum Abx & folic acid
- Villous atrophy or blunting
- Celiac Sprue — Gluten-free diet
- Whipple Disease — Cardiac & CNS symptoms — Foamy macrophages — Long-term Abx --> T. whipplei

**Bile Salt Deficiency**
- Crohn Disease — Disease specific
- Terminal Ileum Resection — B12 injections
- Small Intestinal Bacterial Overgrowth — Abx, cause-specific tx

**Enzyme Deficiency**
- Lactose Intolerance — Lactase supplements, Lactose-free diet
- Pancreatic Insufficiency — Pancreatic enzyme supplements

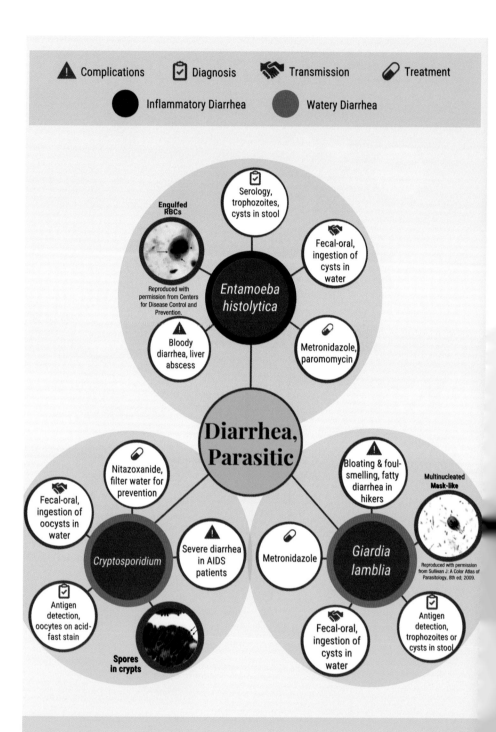

**Complications**    **Diagnosis**    **Transmission**    **Treatment**

**Inflammatory Diarrhea**    **Watery Diarrhea**

**Entamoeba histolytica**

Serology, trophozoites, cysts in stool

Engulfed RBCs

Reproduced with permission from Centers for Disease Control and Prevention.

Fecal-oral, ingestion of cysts in water

Bloody diarrhea, liver abscess

Metronidazole, paromomycin

**Diarrhea, Parasitic**

**Cryptosporidium**

Nitazoxanide, filter water for prevention

Fecal-oral, ingestion of oocysts in water

Severe diarrhea in AIDS patients

Antigen detection, oocytes on acid-fast stain

Spores in crypts

**Giardia lamblia**

Bloating & foul-smelling, fatty diarrhea in hikers

Multinucleated Mask-like

Reproduced with permission from Sullivan J: A Color Atlas of Parasitology, 8th ed; 2009.

Metronidazole

Fecal-oral, ingestion of cysts in water

Antigen detection, trophozoites or cysts in stool

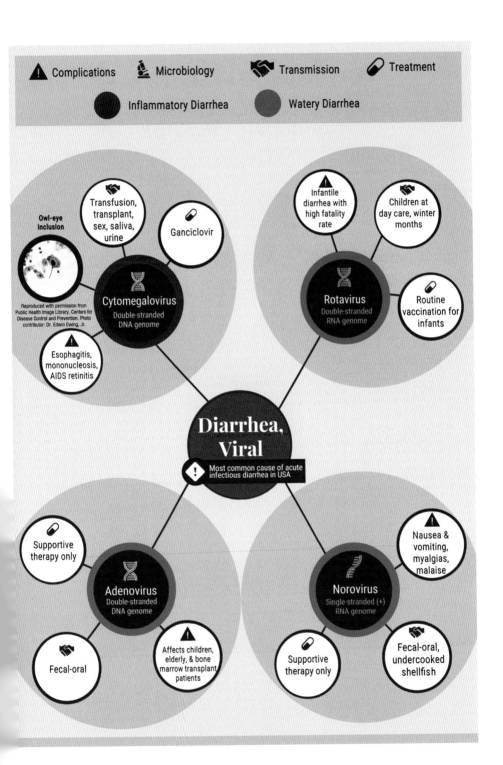

**Complications** **Microbiology** **Transmission** **Treatment**

**Inflammatory Diarrhea** **Watery Diarrhea**

Owl-eye inclusion

Reproduced with permission from Public Health Image Library, Centers for Disease Control and Prevention. Photo contributor: Dr. Edwin Ewing, Jr.

Transfusion, transplant, sex, saliva, urine

Ganciclovir

**Cytomegalovirus**
Double-stranded DNA genome

Esophagitis, mononucleosis, AIDS retinitis

Infantile diarrhea with high fatality rate

Children at day care, winter months

**Rotavirus**
Double-stranded RNA genome

Routine vaccination for infants

**Diarrhea, Viral**

Most common cause of acute infectious diarrhea in USA

Supportive therapy only

**Adenovirus**
Double-stranded DNA genome

Fecal-oral

Affects children, elderly, & bone marrow transplant patients

Nausea & vomiting, myalgias, malaise

**Norovirus**
Single-stranded (+) RNA genome

Supportive therapy only

Fecal-oral, undercooked shellfish

 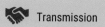
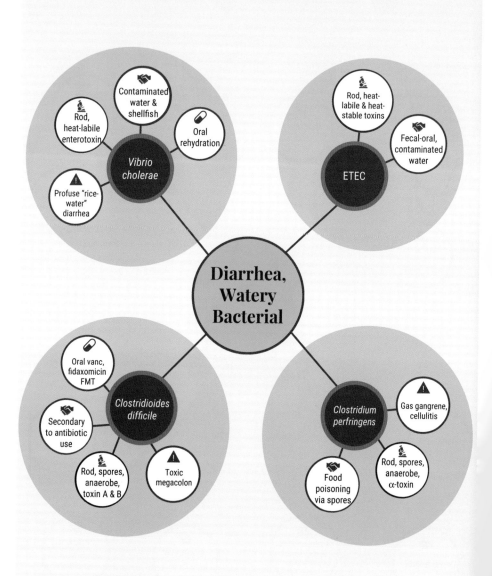

# Diverticular Disease

Blind Pouch That Communicates with Lumen

## Colonic Diverticulum

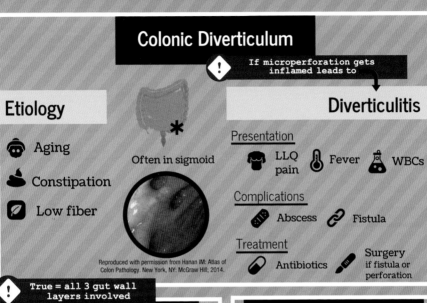

**If microperforation gets inflamed leads to**

## Etiology

- 🦠 Aging
- 💩 Constipation
- 🌿 Low fiber

Often in sigmoid *

Reproduced with permission from Hanan iM: Atlas of Colon Pathology. New York, NY: McGraw Hill; 2014.

## Diverticulitis

### Presentation
- LLQ pain
- Fever
- WBCs

### Complications
- Abscess
- Fistula

### Treatment
- Antibiotics
- Surgery if fistula or perforation

**True = all 3 gut wall layers involved**

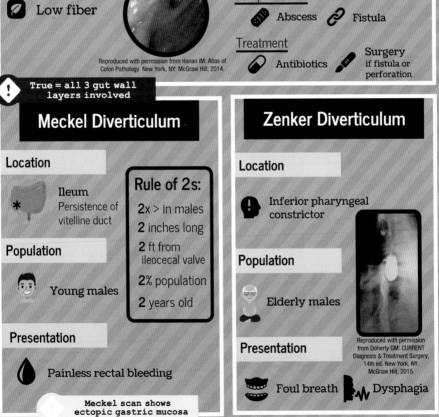

## Meckel Diverticulum

### Location
* Ileum
Persistence of vitelline duct

**Rule of 2s:**
- 2x > in males
- 2 inches long
- 2 ft from ileocecal valve
- 2% population
- 2 years old

### Population
- Young males

### Presentation
- Painless rectal bleeding

Meckel scan shows ectopic gastric mucosa

## Zenker Diverticulum

### Location
- Inferior pharyngeal constrictor

### Population
- Elderly males

Reproduced with permission from Doherty GM: CURRENT Diagnosis & Treatment Surgery, 14th ed. New York, NY: McGraw Hill; 2015.

### Presentation
- Foul breath
- Dysphagia

# Drug- & Toxin-Induced Liver Injury

## Acute Liver Failure

**<8 weeks**
### Fulminant
Hepatic encephalopathy **within 8 weeks of** acute liver disease Coagulopathy (INR ≥1.5)

**8 weeks to 6 months**
### Subfulminant
Hepatic encephalopathy and coagulopathy between **8 weeks and 6 months** of acute liver disease

**\*\*INR: surrogate marker to follow liver synthetic function**

> ❗ Don't use blood products to correct INR

## Causative Agents

**Drugs    Alcohol    Herbals    Other toxins**

| Drugs | Other toxins |
|---|---|
| Halothane | *Amanita phalloides* |
| Valproic acid | (death cap mushroom) |
| Acetaminophen | OCPs |
| Niacin | Herbals |
| Statins | Dietary supplements |
| Tetracyclines | Alcohol |

*Other drugs may cause idiosyncratic reactions or damage due to a genetic deficiency in an individual

## Histology

**Zone 1 (periportal)**

Particularly susceptible to toxin-induced damage

## Treatment

Discontinue toxin

Supportive care

Transplant

 ❗ Sibilinin: mushroom antidote

---

## Reye Syndrome

 **Rare, often fatal childhood hepatic encephalopathy**

 **Clinical Presentation**

| | |
|---|---|
| Mitochondrial abnormalities | Hypoglycemia Vomiting |
| Fatty liver | Hepatomegaly Coma |

**Etiology**
After viral infection (VZV & influenza B), aspirin metabolites decrease β-oxidation by reversible inhibition of mito enzymes

> ❗ Avoid aspirin in children

---

# Acetaminophen Toxicity

 ❗ LFTs can rise into the tens of thousands

## Etiology
**Acetaminophen (overdose)**

### Histology
**Zone 3**
Centrilobular necrosis

*High concentration of CYP450

### Treatment
**N-Acetylcysteine**
**Transplant**

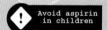

Small amount

p450 ➡ ☠ Toxic metabolites

+

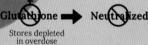 Glutathione ➡ 🚫 Neutralized

Stores depleted in overdose

# Eosinophilic Esophagitis

## Clinical Presentation

**Young Children**
Food refusal
Texture aversion
Vomiting with meals

**Older Children**
Abdominal pain
Vomiting

**Young Adults**
Dysphagia
Food impaction

## Diagnosis

**Clinical Symptoms**

+

Reproduced with permission from Brunicardi FC, Andersen DK, Billiar TR, et al: Schwartz's Principles of Surgery, 11th ed. New York, NY: McGraw Hill; 2019.

**Endoscopy**
Linear furrows
Esophageal rings
Possible strictures

+

Reproduced with permission from Jameson J, Fauci AS, Kasper DL, et al: Harrison's Principles of Internal Medicine, 20th ed. New York, NY: McGraw Hill; 2018.

**Biopsy**
15 eosinophils per high-power field in proximal and distal esophagus
Absent in stomach

## Management

**Proton-Pump Inhibitor**
Twice daily
For diagnosis & management of PPI-responsive EoE

**Topical Steroids**
Swallowed, not inhaled ie, fluticasone

**Dietary Modifications**
Milk, wheat, soy, eggs, nuts, fish

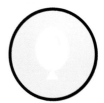

**Dilation**
If strictures are present

# Esophageal Swallowing Disorders

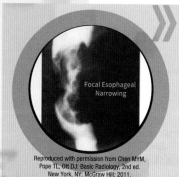

Focal Esophageal Narrowing

Reproduced with permission from Chen MYM, Pope TL, Ott DJ: Basic Radiology, 2nd ed. New York, NY: McGraw Hill; 2011.

##  Dysphagia: "Difficulty swallowing"

| Oropharyngeal | Esophageal |
|---|---|
| Issue initiating swallow | Secs after swallow |
| Neuro causes (MS, Parkinson's) | Structural causes (stricture, ring) |

**!** Can be progressive or intermittent

## Achalasia

### Clinical Presentation

- High lower esophageal sphincter pressure *(loss of myenteric plexus)*
- Loss of peristalsis
- Dysphagia to solids and liquids

**!** Sphincter fails to relax

### Treatment

- Balloon dilation
- Botulin injection
- Pharmacologic *(nitrates, Ca channel blockers)*

"Bird's Beak" Sign

Reproduced with permission from Lalwani AK: CURRENT Diagnosis & Treatment in Otolaryngology—Head & Neck Surgery, 4th ed. New York, NY: McGraw Hill; 2020.

## Structural Issues

Esophageal Ring

Reproduced with permission from Jameson J, Fauci AS, Kasper DL, et al: Harrison's Principles of Internal Medicine, 20th ed. New York, NY: McGraw Hill; 2018.

**Stricture:** *narrowing*
From reflux, caustic injection, drugs

**Web:** *thin membrane*
With Plummer-Vinson or Zenker diverticulum

**Ring:** *diaphragm of tissue*
From reflux and esophagitis

### Treatment

- Balloon dilation
- Incision
- Acid suppression

# Esophageal Varices

## Clinical Features

 Hematemesis

 Melena

Occurs in patients with cirrhosis

## Diagnosis

Upper GI endoscopy

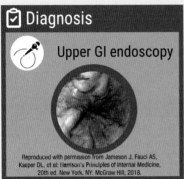

Reproduced with permission from Jameson J, Fauci AS, Kasper DL, et al: Harrison's Principles of Internal Medicine, 20th ed. New York, NY: McGraw Hill; 2018.

## Etiology

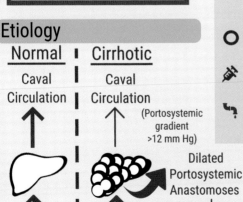

| Normal | Cirrhotic |
|---|---|
| Caval Circulation | Caval Circulation |

(Portosystemic gradient >12 mm Hg)

Dilated Portosystemic Anastomoses
↓
Esophageal, gastric, & rectal varices

Gut | Gut

## Manifestations of Cirrhosis

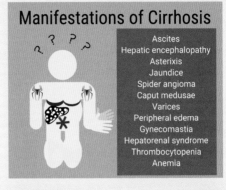

Ascites
Hepatic encephalopathy
Asterixis
Jaundice
Spider angioma
Caput medusae
Varices
Peripheral edema
Gynecomastia
Hepatorenal syndrome
Thrombocytopenia
Anemia

## Therapy

Hemodynamic stabilization

IV octreotide
Shunt splanchnic circulation

Blakemore tube balloon tamponade
Prolong time until definitive treatment

Endoscopic variceal banding
May need repeated sessions

Endoscopic sclerotherapy
Less favored due to strictures

TIPS procedure
May result in hepatic encephalopathy

## ⚠ Complications

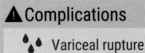 Variceal rupture

Variceal hemorrhage has high mortality rate

# Gastroesophageal Reflux Disease
### Transient Decrease in LES Tone

## Clinical Presentation

- **Heartburn, dysphagia, & regurgitation**

- **Pain**
  - Dyspepsia
  - Postprandial retrosternal pain
    - Exacerbated by lying down
    - May mimic cardiac chest pain

- **Laryngopharyngeal reflux**
  - Chronic cough, hoarseness
  - associated with asthma

## Treatment

Behavior modification
- Diet & smoking
- Elevated sleeping

Antacid
Proton-pump inhibitors
$H_2$ inhibitors

## Complications

Erosive esophagitis
Peptic stricture
Esophageal ulcer
Barrett's esophagus
Recurrent pneumonia
Laryngitis
Dental erosions

# Barrett's Esophagus
### Specialized Intestinal Metaplasia

Nonkeratinized stratified squamous epithelium is replaced by intestinal epithelium

Nonciliated columnar with goblet cells in distal esophagus

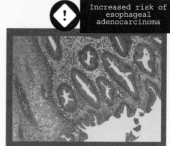

**! Increased risk of esophageal adenocarcinoma**

Reproduced with permission from Kemp WL, Burns DK, Brow TG: Pathology: The Big Picture. New York, NY: McGraw Hill; 2008.

# Esophageal Adenocarcinoma

## Incidence
Caucasians and men
More common in
the United States

## Location
Lower 1/3
of esophagus

## Risk Factors
Chronic GERD
Barrett's esophagus
Smoking & alcohol**
*not as important as in SCC*

## Clinical Presentation
Progressive dysphagia
First solids, then liquids
Weight loss & anorexia
Odynophagia

### Differentiating from
## Squamous Cell Carcinoma

**Incidence**
More common worldwide
Higher in African
American men

**Risk factors**
Alcohol & smoking
Hot liquids & diet
Achalasia & HPV

**Location**
Upper 2/3 of esophagus

**! BOTH: poor prognosis**

# Gastroparesis
### Delayed Gastric Emptying

## Clinical Presentation

 **Chronic nausea & vomitting**
With bloating

 **Early satiety**
Prolonged postprandial fullness

 **Malnutrition & weight loss**

 **Hypoglycemia**
In diabetics, taking insulin before meals

## Diagnosis

 **Gastric emptying study (scintigraphic)**
- Patient consumes radiolabeled eggs
- Timed X-rays to quantify:
  Half-life of gastric emptying
  Percent of meal remaining

## Treatment

 **Promotility agent**
Metoclopramide
Erythromycin

 **Variable & Severe Side Effects:**

**Metoclopramide:**
Tardive dyskinesia
Parkinson-like tremors

**Erythromycin:**
Prolonged QT interval

 **Diet & exercise**
Low-fat diet
Smaller, more frequent meals

 **Avoid narcotics & anticholinergics**
Further delay gastric emptying

 **Advanced options**
Jejunal feeding tube
Gastric electrical stimulators (severe refractory cases)

 **Diabetes Mellitus**
Autonomic neuropathy

 **Postsurgical**

 **Idiopathic**
Possibly postviral, drug induced, or degenerative

 **Obstructive & Ischemic**
Reversible

# GI Neuroendocrine Tumors

## Carcinoid Tumors

### Serotonin-Secreting Tumors of Neuroendocrine Origin

**Frequency of carcinoid tumors by location**

| Appendiceal | Small Intestine | Gastric | Pancreatic |
| Respiratory tract | Rectal | Colonic | |

■ Commonly present with carcinoid syndrome

Carcinoid metastases to the liver bypass hepatic detoxification of serotonin resulting in **carcinoid syndrome**

### Diagnosis & Localization
- 24-hour urinary 5-HIAA excretion
- Somatostatin receptor scintigraphy

### Carcinoid Syndrome
- Flushing of the face & neck
- Watery diarrhea
- Right heart abnormalities
- Wheezing
- Pellagra-like skin rash

### Treatment
- Somatostatin analogs (octreotide)
- Surgical resection of metastases

## Gastrinoma

### (Zollinger–Ellison Syndrome)
Gastrin-secreting tumor of neuroendocrine origin

Pancreatic & duodenal tumors causing gastric acid hypersecretion

### Diagnosis
Measure fasting serum gastrin

Secretin stimulation test

Somatostatin receptor scan

### Clinical Features
- Abdominal pain
- Peptic ulcer disease
- GERD
- Diarrhea

25% of patients with ZES have MEN-1

### Treatment
- PPI
- Gastrinoma resection

## VIPoma
VIP-secreting tumor of neuroendocrine origin

### Clinical Features
- Watery diarrhea
- ↓K Hypokalemia
- ↓Cl Hypochlorhydria

High plasma VIP levels

### Treatment
- Fluid & electrolyte replenishment
- Octreotide
- Surgical resection

# Hemochromatosis

## Autosomal Recessive Iron Absorption Disease

Presents **after** 40

## Clinical Features

### Classic Triad

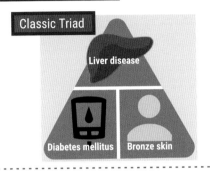

Liver disease

Diabetes mellitus | Bronze skin

### ⚠ Complications

**Cirrhosis & HCC**
**Cardiomyopathy**: *CHF, arrhythmia*
**Arthritis**
**Hypogonadism**: *impotence, amenorrhea*
**Hypothyroidism**

### ☑ Diagnosis

⬆ Serum iron & ferritin

⬆ Iron saturation

⬇ Total iron-binding capacity

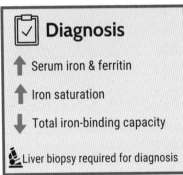 Liver biopsy required for diagnosis

### ⬭ Treatment

**Repeated phlebotomy**

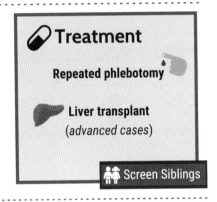

**Liver transplant**
(*advanced cases*)

👫 Screen Siblings

### Etiology

A mutation in *HFE* gene on chromosome 6 (C282Y > H63D) leads to low regulator protein, **hepcidin**. Abnormal iron sensing causes excess iron absorption in the intestine & deposition in various organs.

Increased accumulation of iron (as ferritin and hemosiderin) generates hydroxyl free radicals that cause fibrosis of organs.

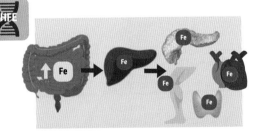

# Hepatic Encephalopathy

## Clinical Features—West Haven Grade

**1** Mild confusion

**2** Personality changes & asterixis

**3** Somnolence

**4** Coma

Occurs in patients with cirrhosis

## Manifestations of Cirrhosis

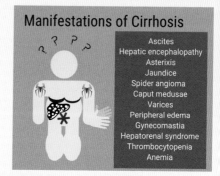

Ascites
Hepatic encephalopathy
Asterixis
Jaundice
Spider angioma
Caput medusae
Varices
Peripheral edema
Gynecomastia
Hepatorenal syndrome
Thrombocytopenia
Anemia

! **Diagnosis of Exclusion**
Ammonia level rarely useful for diagnosis

## Therapy

 Lactulose

Rifaximin

## Precipitating Factors

↳ TIPS procedure

⬭ Diuretics (altered electrolytes)

⬭ Sedating drugs

💧 GI bleed, hypovolemia

⚗ Alkalosis

🦠 Systemic infection (SBP)

🚫 Renal failure

## Etiology

Ammonia and other toxins from the gut cannot
be detoxified by the liver. They accumulate &
travel to the brain causing encephalopathy.

# Hepatitis A & E

ssRNA (+)
Nonenveloped

## General Characteristics

**Acute Infection**

- Jaundice, RUQ pain, & hepatomegaly
- Nausea, vomiting, & anorexia
- Fever & malaise
- Elevated AST & ALT

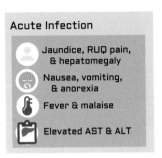

! No chronic carrier state

**Transmission**

Fecal-oral

**Therapy**

Supportive

---

# Hepatitis A

! Vaccination for travelers ✻

🦠 *Picornavirus*

**Serologies**

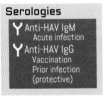

Y Anti-HAV IgM
Acute infection

Y Anti-HAV IgG
Vaccination
Prior infection
(protective)

**Associations**

- Travel
- Day care
- Shellfish

**Differential Presentation**

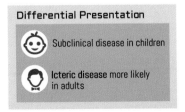

- Subclinical disease in children
- Icteric disease more likely in adults

# Hepatitis E

🦠 *Hepevirus*

**Prevalent in**
India
Pakistan
SE Asia
Parts of Africa

Fulminant liver failure in pregnant women

**Transmission**
Especially waterborne

! High mortality in expectant mothers

# Hepatitis B

**Hepadnavirus**

**Transmission**
- Parenteral
- Sexual
- Perinatal

dsDNA enveloped

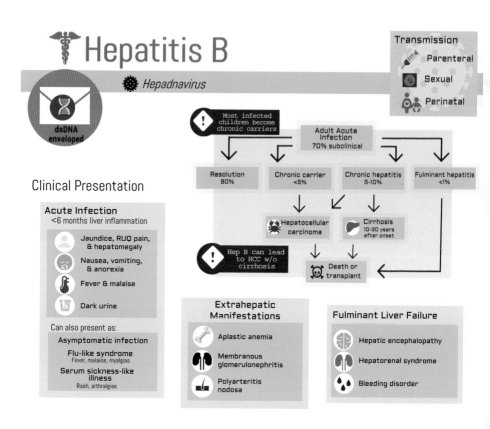

**Most infected children become chronic carriers**

**Adult Acute Infection 70% subclinical**

| Resolution 90% | Chronic carrier <5% | Chronic hepatitis 5-10% | Fulminant hepatitis <1% |

Hepatocellular carcinoma

Cirrhosis 10-30 years after onset

**Hep B can lead to HCC w/o cirrhosis**

Death or transplant

## Clinical Presentation

### Acute Infection
<6 months liver inflammation

- Jaundice, RUQ pain, & hepatomegaly
- Nausea, vomiting, & anorexia
- Fever & malaise
- Dark urine

Can also present as:

**Asymptomatic infection**

**Flu-like syndrome**
Fever, malaise, myalgias

**Serum sickness-like illness**
Rash, arthralgias

### Extrahepatic Manifestations
- Aplastic anemia
- Membranous glomerulonephritis
- Polyarteritis nodosa

### Fulminant Liver Failure
- Hepatic encephalopathy
- Hepatorenal syndrome
- Bleeding disorder

## Diagnosis

**Vaccine: Anti-HBs**

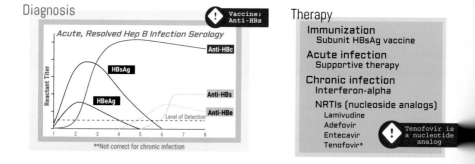

Acute, Resolved Hep B Infection Serology

- Anti-HBc
- HBsAg
- Anti-HBs
- HBeAg
- Anti-HBe

Level of Detection

Reactant Titer

**Not correct for chronic infection

## Therapy

### Immunization
Subunit HBsAg vaccine

### Acute infection
Supportive therapy

### Chronic infection
Interferon-alpha

**NRTIs (nucleoside analogs)**
- Lamivudine
- Adefovir
- Entecavir
- Tenofovir*

**Tenofovir is a nucleotide analog**

# Hepatitis D

**Deltavirus**

ssRNA (-) enveloped

**Requires HBsAg for replication**

**Coinfection** (simultaneous Hep B & D infection)
Long, milder clinical course
Similar course to HBV infection

**Superinfection** (infection in chronic Hep B)
Short, severe clinical course (fulminant hepatitis)
Increased severity of disease

# Hepatitis C

 *Flavivirus*

ssRNA (+)
enveloped

## Clinical Presentation

### Transmission

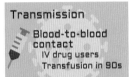

**Blood-to-blood contact**
IV drug users
Transfusion in 90s

### Extrahepatic Manifestations

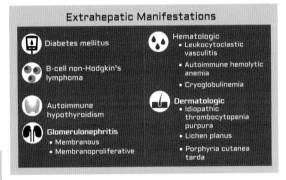

Diabetes mellitus

B-cell non-Hodgkin's lymphoma

Autoimmune hypothyroidism

Glomerulonephritis
- Membranous
- Membranoproliferative

**Hematologic**
- Leukocytoclastic vasculitis
- Autoimmune hemolytic anemia
- Cryoglobulinemia

**Dermatologic**
- Idiopathic thrombocytopenia purpura
- Lichen planus
- Porphyria cutanea tarda

### Acute Infection
Usually subclinical, but 25% develop

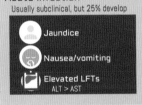

Jaundice

Nausea/vomiting

Elevated LFTs
ALT > AST

### Complications

Cirrhosis and liver failure

Hepatocellular carcinoma

High rate of chronicity (80%)

Treatment regimens all oral

### Diagnosis

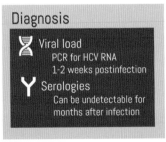

Viral load
PCR for HCV RNA
1-2 weeks postinfection

Serologies
Can be undetectable for months after infection

### Therapy

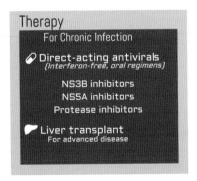

For Chronic Infection

**Direct-acting antivirals**
*(Interferon-free, oral regimens)*

NS3B inhibitors
NS5A inhibitors
Protease inhibitors

**Liver transplant**
For advanced disease

# Hepatocellular Carcinoma

## Clinical Presentation

- Abdominal pain
- Weight loss & anorexia
- Fatigue
- Portal HTN
- Ascites
- Jaundice
- Splenomegaly
- Paraneoplastic syndromes

Accounts for >80% of primary liver cancers

High-risk areas are Africa & Asia

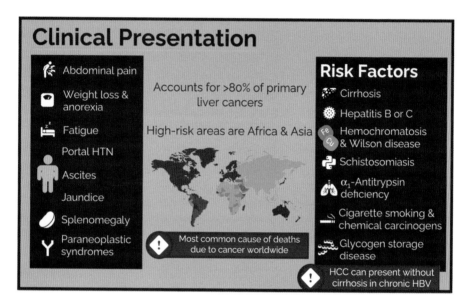

⚠ Most common cause of deaths due to cancer worldwide

### Risk Factors

- Cirrhosis
- Hepatitis B or C
- Hemochromatosis & Wilson disease
- Schistosomiasis
- $\alpha_1$-Antitrypsin deficiency
- Cigarette smoking & chemical carcinogens
- Glycogen storage disease

⚠ HCC can present without cirrhosis in chronic HBV

## Diagnosis

- Liver biopsy
  Gold standard of HCC diagnosis
- Imaging studies
  Ultrasound, triple-phase CT, or MRI
- Lab tests (underlying condition)
  Hepatitis B & C serologies
  Liver function tests (LFTs)

HCC screening in high-risk patients:
Ultrasound +/- alpha fetoprotein (AFP) every 6 months

## Treatment

- Liver resection
  Only 10% are resectable tumors
- Liver transplantation
  Milan criteria
- Locoregional therapy options
  Transcatheter arterial chemoembolization (TACE)
  Radiofrequency ablation (RFA)

AFP can be used to monitor disease progression & response to therapy

# Infectious Esophagitis

### Suspect with Odynophagia/Dysphagia in the Immunocompromised

---

## Candida

### Endoscopic Appearance

Reproduced with permission from McKean SC, Ross JJ, Dressler DD, et al: Principles and Practice of Hospital Medicine, 2nd ed. New York, NY: McGraw Hill; 2017.

Gray-white
pseudomembranes

### Biopsy Appearance

Reproduced with permission from Reisner H. Pathology: A Modern Case Study, 2nd ed. New York, NY: McGraw Hill; 2020.

Yeast forms and pseudo-
hyphae

---

## Herpes

### Endoscopic Appearance

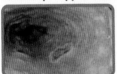

Reproduced with permission from Jameson J, Fauci AS, Kasper DL, et al: Harrison's Principles of Internal Medicine, 20th ed. New York, NY: McGraw Hill; 2018.

"Punched out" ulcers

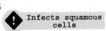 Infects squamous cells

### Biopsy Appearance

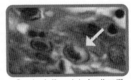

Reproduced with permission from Kemp WL, Burns DK, Brow TG: Pathology: The Big Picture. New York, NY: McGraw Hill; 2008.

Intranuclear inclusions
with clear halo

---

## CMV

### Endoscopic Appearance

Reproduced with permission from Jameson J, Fauci AS, Kasper DL, et al: Harrison's Principles of Internal Medicine, 20th ed. New York, NY: McGraw Hill; 2018.

Linear ulcers

### Biopsy Appearance

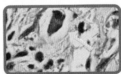

Reproduced with permission from Kemp WL, Burns DK, Brow TG: Pathology: The Big Picture. New York, NY: McGraw Hill; 2008.

Enlarged cells with halo
("owl eye")

---

# Inguinal and Femoral Hernias

### Protrusion of Abdominal/Pelvic Contents Through Defect

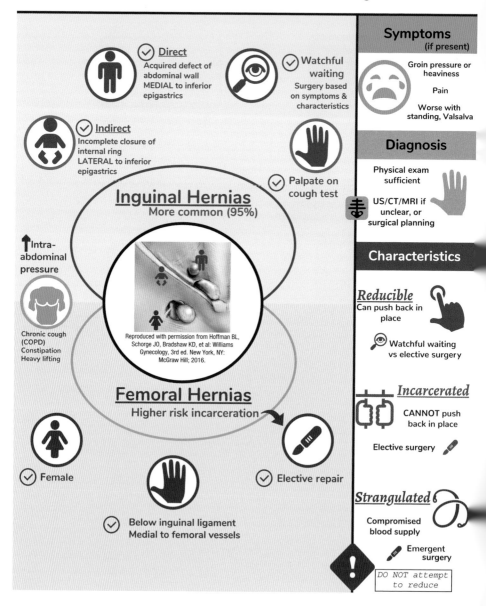

**Direct**
Acquired defect of abdominal wall MEDIAL to inferior epigastrics

**Indirect**
Incomplete closure of internal ring LATERAL to inferior epigastrics

## Inguinal Hernias
### More common (95%)

↑ Intra-abdominal pressure

Chronic cough (COPD)
Constipation
Heavy lifting

Reproduced with permission from Hoffman BL, Schorge JO, Bradshaw KD, et al: Williams Gynecology, 3rd ed. New York, NY: McGraw Hill; 2016.

## Femoral Hernias
### Higher risk incarceration

Female

Below inguinal ligament
Medial to femoral vessels

Elective repair

**Watchful waiting**
Surgery based on symptoms & characteristics

Palpate on cough test

## Symptoms
(if present)

Groin pressure or heaviness

Pain

Worse with standing, Valsalva

## Diagnosis

Physical exam sufficient

US/CT/MRI if unclear, or surgical planning

## Characteristics

*Reducible*
Can push back in place

Watchful waiting vs elective surgery

*Incarcerated*
CANNOT push back in place

Elective surgery

*Strangulated*
Compromised blood supply

Emergent surgery

DO NOT attempt to reduce

# Irritable Bowel Syndrome
## Functional Abdominal Pain with Altered Bowel Patterns

## Clinical Presentation

**Young female with anxiety and...**

(really all ages/genders affected)

**Intermittent abdominal pain**
Relieved with defecation

**Alternating frequency and caliber of bowel movements**
Diarrhea (IBS-D), constipation (IBS-C), mixed

**NO red flag symptoms**

## Diagnosis

**History alone sufficient**
labs/colonoscopy normal

**Rome IV Criteria**
Recurrent abdominal pain 1x/week for >3 months with at least two of the following:
- related to defecation
- associated with change in frequency of stool
- associated with change in form/appearance of stool

## Pharmacologic Treatment

###  Constipation

**Osmotic laxatives**
Polyethylene glycol

**Chloride-channel activator**
Lubiprostone

**Guanylate cyclase agonists**
Linaclotide

###  Abdominal Pain & Bloating

**Antispasmodics**
Dicyclomine

**Antidepressants**
TCAs

**Antibiotics**
Rifaximin

### Diarrhea

**Opioid agonists**
Loperamide

**Bile acid binders**
Cholestyramine

**5-HT$_3$ antagonists**
Alosetron

!
Danger: Alosetron may cause ischemic colitis.

## Nonpharmacologic Treatment

### Psychosocial
Frequent follow-up visits
Counseling & reassurance

### Dietary Changes
Trigger avoidance
Low FODMAP diet

### Fiber Supplements
Bran, psyllium

### Physical Activity

# Pancreatitis, Acute

Autodigestion of the Pancreas by Pancreatic Enzymes

## Diagnosis

Must meet two of three diagnostic criteria

### 1 Clinical Presentation

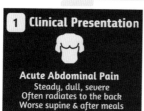

**Acute Abdominal Pain**
Steady, dull, severe
Often radiates to the back
Worse supine & after meals

### 2 Lab Findings

**Elevated (to 3x normal)**
Serum lipase (*most specific*)
Serum amylase

### 3 Imaging

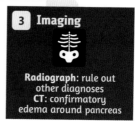

**Radiograph:** rule out other diagnoses
**CT:** confirmatory edema around pancreas

### Other presentations:

**Fever & Tachycardia**
With hypotension & leukocytosis (in severe acute pancreatitis)

**Elevated LFTS**
In gallstone pancreatitis

**Hemorrhagic Pancreatitis**
Gray Turner sign: flank ecchymosis
Cullen sign: periumbilical ecchymoses

## Causes & Complications

**I** Idiopathic

**G** Gallstones (*at the ampulla of vater*)

**E** Ethanol

**T** Trauma (*including surgery*)

**S** Steroids

**M** Mumps (*& Coxsackievirus B*)

**A** Autoimmune disease

**S** Scorpions

**H** Hypercalcemia & hypertriglyceridemia

**E** ERCP

**D** Drugs: Sulfonamides, thiazide diuretics, furosemide, estrogens, HIV meds

⚠ **Pseudocyst**
Lacks epithelial lining
Rupture, infection, obstruction

⚠ **ARDS**
Acute respiratory distress syndrome

⚠ **Pancreatic abscess**
Lacks epithelial lining

⚠ **Organ failure**
Shock & renal failure

⚠ **Pancreatic necrosis**
Sterile or infected
Tx with antibiotics

⚠ **Ascending cholangitis**
Gallstone pancreatitis

⚠ **Hemorrhagic pancreatitis**
Cullen & Gray Turner signs

⚠ **Hypocalcemia**
Saponification of calcium salts

## Treatment

**Mild**
Supportive (bowel rest, fluids, pain control)
NG tube with severe N/V

**Severe**
Admission to ICU
Enteral nutrition (NJ tube)
Prophylactic antibiotics (if 30% necrosis)

! **Avoid morphine**
Increases pressure at sphincter of Oddi

# Pancreatitis, Chronic
Persistent Inflammation Leading to Permanent Pancreatic Damage

## Diagnosis

### 1 Clinical Presentation

**Abdominal pain:** may be absent unlike acute
**Pancreatic insufficiency:** steatorrhea and later DM

### 2 Lab Findings

**Often normal**
Fibrotic pancreas with minimal enzyme increase

### 3 Imaging

**CT/MRI:** calcifications +/- pseudocysts
**MRCP:** calcifications and ductal dilation
**EUS:** stones

Other useful lab tests:

**Fecal Fat Quantification**
>7 g in 72 hours is diagnostic for malabsorption

**Fecal Elastase**
Sensitive and specific

**Liver Function Tests**
Typically normal
Elevated bilirubin & alk phos indicate duct compression ⚠

## Causes & Complications

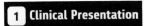

- **Ethanol** (most frequent cause in adults) ⚠
- **Genetics** (*CFTR, SPINK-1, PRSS-1*)
- **Ductal obstruction** (trauma, mass, stones)
- **Systemic disease** (SLE, hypertriglyceridemia)
- **Tropical disease**
- **Autoimmune pancreatitis**
- **Smoking**
- **Idiopathic**

⚠ **Pseudocyst**
Lacks epithelial lining
Rupture, infection, obstruction

⚠ **Obstruction**
Of bile duct or duodenum
From inflammation & compression

⚠ **Splenic vein thrombosis**
Results in gastric varices

⚠ **Pseudoaneurysms**
Bleeding into pseudocyst

⚠ **Pancreatic fistula**
Chronic inflammation

⚠ **Cancer**
Increased risk of adenocarcinoma

⚠ **Pancreatic ascites**
From duct disruption or pseudocyst rupture

⚠ **Pleural effusion**
Related to ascites

## Treatment

**Lifestyle modifications**
Quit drinking alcohol & smoking
Small low-fat meals & hydration

**Intervention**
Targeted analgesia
Pancreatic enzyme supplementation
Lithotripsy or surgery (esp. if concerned about cancer)

# Peptic Ulcer Disease

 **Clinical Presentation**
Dyspepsia
Aching or gnawing pain

 **Treatment**
Acid suppression
  PPIs (omeprazole)
  $H_2$-receptor blockers
  Bismuth subsalicylate
Cytoprotection
  Sucralfate

**Complications**

💧 Hemorrhage
  Lesser curvature of
  stomach
    (left gastric artery)
  Posterior wall of
  duodenum
    (gastroduodenal artery)

🚧 Obstruction

✂ Perforation
  Free air under
  diaphragm
  Referred pain to
  shoulder
    (phrenic nerve)

☑ **Diagnosis & Workup**
Upper endoscopy
Biopsy ulcers
  If refectory or no clear etiology

❗ **Stop NSAID use**

 ***H. pylori***
Curved, Gram-negative rod
in antrum of stomach

🔬 **Catalase, oxidase, urease positive**
Urease produces *ammonia* creating
alkaline environment for bacteria to
survive in acidic mucosa

⚠ **Complications**
Gastritis (type B)
Peptic ulcer disease
Gastric adenoma
MALT lymphoma

💊 **Triple therapy:**
Amoxicillin
  (metronidazole if allergic)
Clarithromycin
PPI

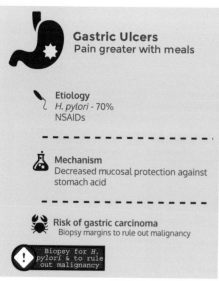

**Gastric Ulcers**
Pain greater with meals

**Etiology**
*H. pylori* - 70%
NSAIDs

**Mechanism**
Decreased mucosal protection against
stomach acid

🦀 **Risk of gastric carcinoma**
Biopsy margins to rule out malignancy

❗ **Biopsy for *H. pylori* & to rule out malignancy**

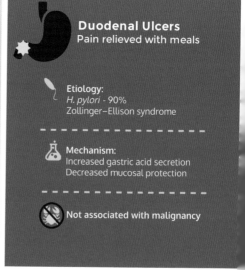

**Duodenal Ulcers**
Pain relieved with meals

**Etiology:**
*H. pylori* - 90%
Zollinger–Ellison syndrome

**Mechanism:**
Increased gastric acid secretion
Decreased mucosal protection

🚫 Not associated with malignancy

# Primary Sclerosing Cholangitis & Primary Biliary Cholangitis

## PSC

### Clinical Presentation

- Jaundice & pruritus
- Fatigue & malaise
- Weight loss

Chronic progressive disease

**Associations**
- Ulcerative colitis
- Crohn disease

♂ > ♀

### Diagnosis

 ERCP or MRCP

Bead-like stricturing & dilatations of intrahepatic & extrahepatic bile ducts

### Management

- Cholestyramine
- ERCP
  Stent placement & duct dilation
- **!** Only curative treatment is liver transplantation

## PBC

### Clinical Presentation

- Jaundice & pruritus
- Fatigue
- Hepatomegaly
- Xanthomata & xanthelasmata

Chronic progressive disease

**Associations**
- Other autoimmune disorders

♀ > ♂

### Diagnosis

- AMA (antimitochondrial antibodies)
- Livery biopsy—florid duct lesion
  Lymphocytic infiltration into epithelium of small intrahepatic bile ducts

### Management

- Cholestyramine
- Ursodeoxycholic acid
  Slows disease progression
- **!** Only curative treatment is liver transplantation

## Complications of Disease Progression

 Cirrhosis & end-stage liver disease

# Spontaneous Bacterial Peritonitis

## Clinical Features

 Abdominal pain & tenderness

 Fever, chills

 Occasional vomiting

 In patients with ascites & cirrhosis

## Diagnostic Paracentesis

 Ascitic fluid

 PMNs >250

Culture & Gram stain

## Therapy

 Ceftriaxone

 Albumin
Day 1: 1.5 g/kg
Day 3: 1 g/kg

Prophylaxis:

 Ciprofloxacin

 TMP/SMX (Bactrim)

## Manifestations of Cirrhosis

Ascites
Hepatic encephalopathy
Asterixis
Jaundice
Spider angioma
Caput medusae
Varices
Peripheral edema
Gynecomastia
Hepatorenal syndrome
Thrombocytopenia
Anemia

## Common SBP Bacteria

**E. coli** is the most common

 *Escherichia coli*

Reproduced with permission from Riedel S, Hobden JA, Miller S, et al: Jawetz, Melnick, & Adelberg's Medical Microbiology, 28th ed. New York, NY: McGraw Hill; 2019.

 *Klebsiella*

Reproduced with permission from Papadakis MA, McPhee SJ, Rabow MW: Current Medical Diagnosis & Treatment 2020. New York, NY: McGraw Hill; 2020.

 *Streptococcus pneumoniae*

Reproduced with permission from Knoop KJ, Stack LB, Storrow AB, et al: The Atlas of Emergency Medicine, 4th ed. New York, NY: McGraw Hill; 2016. Photo contributor: Roche Laboratories, Division of Hoffman-LaRoche Inc. Nutley, NJ.

## Complications

 Hepatorenal syndrome

 Hepatic encephalopathy

 Sepsis

 Death

# Ulcerative Colitis

## Clinical Features

**Diarrhea**
Bloody (**hematochezia**)
Frequent, small BMs
Tenesmus

**Abdominal pain**

**Weight loss,
fever, anorexia**
(severe cases)

## Extraintestinal Manifestations

**Skin Lesions**
Pyoderma gangrenosum*

**Arthritis**
Peripheral
sacroilitis
Ankylosing spondylitis*

**Oral Ulceration**
Aphthous stomatitis

**Eye Inflammation**
Uveitis
Episcleritis

*Distinction from Crohn disease

## Diagnosis

Stool cultures
(rule out
infection)

Reproduced with permission from Reisner H.
Pathology: A Modern Case Study, 2nd ed.
New York, NY: McGraw Hill; 2020.

**Histology**

Mucosal and submucosal inflammation
Crypt abscesses (PMNs accumulate)

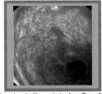

Reproduced with permission from Zinner MJ,
Ashley SW, Hines OJ: Maingot's Abdominal Operations,
13th ed. New York, NY: McGraw Hill; 2019.

**Colonoscopy**

Friable mucosa with superficial
and/or deep ulcerations
Loss of haustra ("lead pipe"
appearance on imaging)

**Distribution**

Uninterrupted involvement of
rectum and/or colon

## Treatment

### Acute
**Corticosteroids** (prednisone)

### Maintenance
**5-Aminosalicylates** (mesalamine,
sulfasalazine)
**Immunomodulators** (6-mercaptopurine,
cyclosporine)
**Biologics** (vedolizumab, infliximab,
adalimumab, etc)

### Surgical
**Total colectomy**
for severe, unresponsive disease or to
manage complications

## ⚠ Complications

**Colorectal cancer:**   **Sclerosing cholangitis**
Strictures          **Cholangiocarcinoma**
**Hemorrhage:**
Iron deficiency anemia
**Toxic megacolon**

CRC is more
common in UC

# Upper GI Cancers

## Esophageal

Weight loss and dysphagia to first solids then liquids

 **Often poor prognosis**

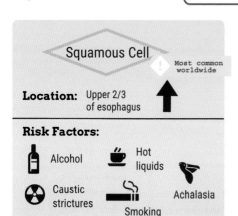

### Squamous Cell

**Most common worldwide**

**Location:** Upper 2/3 of esophagus

**Risk Factors:**
- Alcohol
- Hot liquids
- Achalasia
- Caustic strictures
- Smoking

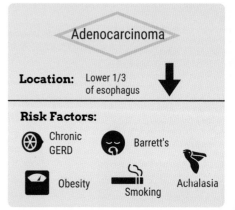

### Adenocarcinoma

**Location:** Lower 1/3 of esophagus

**Risk Factors:**
- Chronic GERD
- Barrett's
- Obesity
- Smoking
- Achalasia

## Gastric

Weight loss, abdominal pain, and early satiety

**Most commonly adenocarcinoma**

### Paraneoplastic Syndromes

**Acanthosis nigricans**

Reproduced with permission from Jameson J, Fauci AS, Kasper DL, et al: Harrison's Principles of Internal Medicine, 20th ed. New York, NY: McGraw Hill; 2018.

**Leser-Trelat sign**
*Sudden diffuse seborrheic keratoses*

Reproduced with permission from Jameson J, Fauci AS, Kasper DL, et al: Harrison's Principles of Internal Medicine, 20th ed. New York, NY: McGraw Hill; 2018.

### Intestinal Type

**Associated with:**
- H. pylori
- Smoked foods
- Smoking
- Chronic gastritis

### Diffuse Type

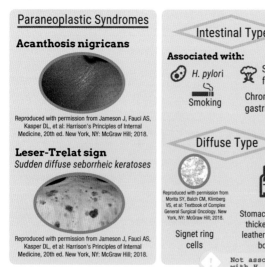

Reproduced with permission from Morita SY, Balch CM, Klimberg VS, et al: Textbook of Complex General Surgical Oncology. New York, NY: McGraw Hill; 2018.

Signet ring cells

Stomach appears thickened and leathery: "Leather bottle"

**Not associated with H. pylori**

### Notable Metastases

**Virchow node**
*Left supraclavicular node*

**Krukenberg tumor**
*Bilateral ovarian mets*

**Sister Mary Joseph nodule**
*Periumbilical mets*

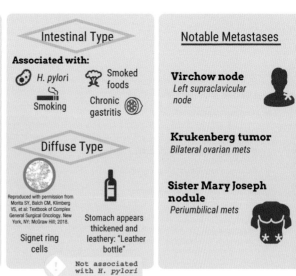

# Vascular

*GI Disorders*

## Mesenteric Angina
*"Mesenteric Artery Disease"*

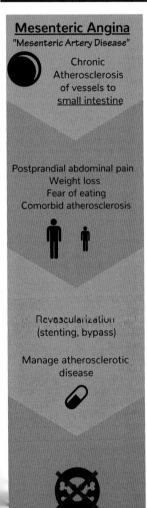

Chronic Atherosclerosis of vessels to <u>small intestine</u>

Postprandial abdominal pain
Weight loss
Fear of eating
Comorbid atherosclerosis

Revascularization (stenting, bypass)

Manage atherosclerotic disease

(but can progress to full occlusion)

## Mesenteric Ischemia
*"Gut Attack"*

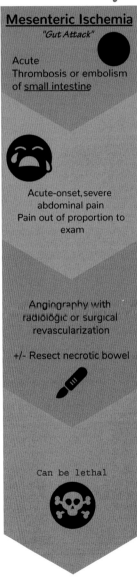

Acute Thrombosis or embolism of <u>small intestine</u>

Acute-onset, severe abdominal pain
Pain out of proportion to exam

Angiography with radiologic or surgical revascularization

+/- Resect necrotic bowel

Can be lethal

## Ischemic Colitis

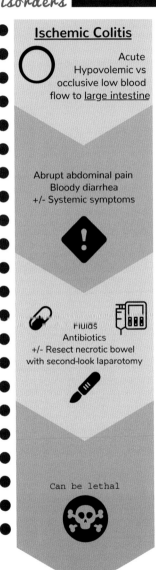

Acute Hypovolemic vs occlusive low blood flow to <u>large intestine</u>

Abrupt abdominal pain
Bloody diarrhea
+/- Systemic symptoms

Fluids
Antibiotics
+/- Resect necrotic bowel with second-look laparotomy

Can be lethal

# Wilson's Disease

Autosomal Recessive Disease of Copper Metabolism

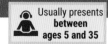 Usually presents **between ages 5 and 35**

## Copper accumulates in organ systems

## Clinical symptoms

**Kayser–Fleischer rings**
Cu deposits in cornea

**Liver disease**
Acute hepatitis, cirrhosis, fulminant failure

**Renal involvement**
Aminoaciduria, nephrocalcinosis

**Neurological & psychological deficits**
Dysarthria, dystonia, tremor, parkinsonism

## ✓ Diagnosis

↑ Urine copper

↑ LFTs

↓ Ceruloplasmin

↓ Alkaline phosphatase ✴

 Liver biopsy shows elevated Cu levels

## ⊘ Therapy

⊘ Chelation
**D-penicillamine or trientine**
Removes and detoxifies the excess Cu deposits in symptomatic patients

⊘ Oral **zinc**
Prevents uptake of dietary Cu
Given to presymptomatic & symptomatic patients

## Etiology

Autosomal recessive mutations in hepatocyte copper transporting ATPase (*ATP7B* gene on chromosome 13)

Leads to decreased copper excretion into bile and incorporation into apoceruloplasmin→ decreased serum ceruloplasmin and Cu accumulation

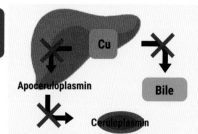

ATP7B

Apoceruloplasmin · Cu · Bile · Ceruloplasmin

# References _____

**Ascites**
Greenberger NJ. Ascites and spontaneous bacterial peritonitis. In: Greenberger NJ, Blumberg RS, Burakoff R, eds. *Current Diagnosis & Treatment: Gastroenterology, Hepatology, & Endoscopy*. 3rd ed. New York, NY: McGraw Hill; 2016.

**ASH & NASH**
Dienstag JL, Bhan AK. Atlas of liver biopsies. In: Jameson J, Fauci AS, Kasper DL, Hauser SL, Longo DL, Loscalzo J, eds. *Harrison's Principles of Internal Medicine*. 20th ed. New York, NY: McGraw Hill; 2018.

**Autoimmune Hepatitis**
Friedman L. Liver, biliary tract and pancreas disorders. In: Papadakis MA, McPhee SJ, Rabow MW, eds. *Current Medical Diagnosis & Treatment 2019*. New York, NY: McGraw Hill, 2019.
Le T, Bhushan V. *First Aid for the USMLE Step 1 2019*. 29th ed. New York, NY: McGraw Hill; 2018.

**Biliary Tract Conditions**
Le T, Bhushan V. *First Aid for the USMLE Step 1 2019*. 29th ed. New York, NY: McGraw Hill; 2018.
McQuaid KR. Gastrointestinal disorders. In: Papadakis MA, McPhee SJ, Rabow MW, eds. *Current Medical Diagnosis & Treatment 2019*. New York, NY: McGraw Hill; 2019.

**Celiac Disease**
McQuaid KR. Gastrointestinal disorders. In: Papadakis MA, McPhee SJ, Rabow MW, eds. *Current Medical Diagnosis & Treatment 2019*. New York, NY: McGraw Hill; 2019.

**Clostridioides difficile Colitis**
Gerding DN, Johnson S. *Clostridium difficile* infection, including pseudomembranous colitis. In: Jameson J, Fauci AS, Kasper DL, Hauser SL, Longo DL, Loscalzo J, eds. *Harrison's Principles of Internal Medicine*. 20th ed. New York, NY: McGraw Hill; 2018.

**Colorectal Cancer**
Greene KG, Trembath D. Pathology of the gastrointestinal tract. In: Reisner HM, ed. *Pathology: A Modern Case Study*. New York, NY: McGraw Hill; 2015.

**Crohn Disease**
Friedman S, Blumberg RS. Inflammatory bowel disease. In: Jameson J, Fauci AS, Kasper DL, Hauser SL, Longo DL, Loscalzo J, eds. *Harrison's Principles of Internal Medicine*. 20th ed. New York, NY: McGraw Hill; 2018.

**Diarrhea, Inflammatory Bacterial**
Le T, Bhushan V. *First Aid for the USMLE Step 1 2019*. 29th ed. New York, NY: McGraw Hill; 2018.
Frier JS. Acute diarrheal disorders. In: Greenberger NJ, Blumberg RS, Burakoff R, eds. *Current Diagnosis & Treatment: Gastroenterology, Hepatology, & Endoscopy*. 3rd ed. New York, NY: McGraw Hill; 2016.

**Diarrhea, Malabsorption**
McQuaid KR. Gastrointestinal disorders. In: Papadakis MA, McPhee SJ, Rabow MW, eds. *Current Medical Diagnosis & Treatment 2019*. New York, NY: McGraw Hill; 2019.

**Diarrhea, Parasitic**
Le T, Bhushan V. *First Aid for the USMLE Step 1 2019*. 29th ed. New York, NY: McGraw Hill; 2018.

Trier JS. Acute diarrheal disorders. *Current Diagnosis & Treatment: Gastroenterology, Hepatology, & Endoscopy.* 3rd ed. New York, NY: McGraw Hill; 2016.

### Diarrhea, Viral
Levinson W, Chin-Hong P, Joyce EA, Nussbaum J, Schwartz B, eds. Herpesviruses, poxviruses, & human papilloma virus. In: *Review of Medical Microbiology & Immunology: A Guide to Clinical Infectious Diseases.* 16th ed. New York, NY: McGraw Hill; 2020.

### Diarrhea, Watery Bacterial
Charles RC, Calderwood SB, LaRocque RC. Acute infectious diarrheal diseases and bacterial food poisoning. In: Jameson J, Fauci AS, Kasper DL, Hauser SL, Longo DL, Loscalzo J, eds. *Harrison's Principles of Internal Medicine.* 20th ed. New York, NY: McGraw Hill; 2018.

### Diverticular Disease
Doherty GM, eds. *Current Medical Diagnosis & Treatment Surgery.* 14th ed. New York, NY: McGraw Hill; 2014.

Le T, Bhushan V. *First Aid for the USMLE Step 1 2019.* 29th ed. New York, NY: McGraw Hill; 2018.

McQuaid KR. Gastrointestinal disorders. In: Papadakis MA, McPhee SJ, Rabow MW, eds. *Current Medical Diagnosis & Treatment 2019.* New York, NY: McGraw Hill; 2019.

### Drug- and Toxin-Induced Liver Injury
Maddrey WC. Drug induced liver disease. In: Greenberger NJ, Blumberg RS, Burakoff R, eds. *Current Diagnosis & Treatment: Gastroenterology, Hepatology, & Endoscopy.* 3rd ed. New York, NY: McGraw Hill; 2016.

### Eosinophilic Esophagitis
Jobe BA, Hunter JG, Watson DI. Esophagus and diaphragmatic hernia. In: Brunicardi F, Andersen DK, Billiar TR, et al, eds. *Schwartz's Principles of Surgery.* 10th ed. New York, NY: McGraw Hill; 2015.

Kahrilas PJ, Hirano I. Diseases of the esophagus. In: Jameson J, Fauci AS, Kasper DL, Hauser SL, Longo DL, Loscalzo J, eds. *Harrison's Principles of Internal Medicine.* 20th ed. New York, NY: McGraw Hill; 2018.

### Esophageal Swallowing Disorders
Jameson J, Fauci AS, Kasper DL, Hauser SL, Longo DL, Loscalzo J, eds. *Harrison's Principles of Internal Medicine.* 20th ed. New York, NY: McGraw Hill; 2018.

Le T, Bhushan V. *First Aid for the USMLE Step 1 2019.* 29th ed. New York, NY: McGraw Hill; 2018.

McQuaid KR. Gastrointestinal disorders. In: Papadakis MA, McPhee SJ, Rabow MW, eds. *Current Medical Diagnosis & Treatment 2019.* New York, NY: McGraw Hill; 2019.

### Esophageal Varices
Song L, Topazian M. Gastrointestinal endoscopy. In: Jameson J, Fauci AS, Kasper DL, Hauser SL, Longo DL, Loscalzo J, eds. *Harrison's Principles of Internal Medicine.* 20th ed. New York, NY: McGraw Hill; 2018.

### Gastroesophageal Reflux Disease
Kemp WL, Burns DK, Brown TG, eds. Gastrointestinal pathology. In: *Pathology: The Big Picture.* New York, NY: McGraw Hill; 2008.

McQuaid KR. Gastrointestinal disorders. In: Papadakis MA, McPhee SJ, Rabow MW, eds. *Current Medical Diagnosis & Treatment 2019.* New York, NY: McGraw Hill; 2019.

### Gastroparesis
McQuaid KR. Gastrointestinal disorders. In: Papadakis MA, McPhee SJ, Rabow MW, eds. *Current Medical Diagnosis & Treatment 2019.* New York, NY: McGraw Hill; 2019.

**GI Neuroendocrine Tumors**
Jensen RT. Neuroendocrine tumors of the gastrointestinal tract and pancreas. In: Jameson J, Fauci AS, Kasper DL, Hauser SL, Longo DL, Loscalzo J, eds. *Harrison's Principles of Internal Medicine*. 20th ed. New York, NY: McGraw Hill; 2018.

**Hemochromatosis**
Powell LW. Hemochromatosis In: Jameson J, Fauci AS, Kasper DL, Hauser SL, Longo DL, Loscalzo J, eds. *Harrison's Principles of Internal Medicine*. 20th ed. New York, NY: McGraw Hill, 2018.

**Hepatic Encephalopathy**
Greenberger NJ. Portal systemic encephalopathy and hepatic encephalopathy. In: Greenberger NJ, Blumberg RS, Burakoff R, eds. *Current Diagnosis & Treatment: Gastroenterology, Hepatology, & Endoscopy*. 3rd ed. New York, NY: McGraw Hill; 2016.

**Hepatitis A & E**
Friedman L. Liver, biliary tract and pancreas disorders. In: Papadakis MA, McPhee SJ, Rabow MW, eds. *Current Medical Diagnosis & Treatment 2019*. New York, NY: McGraw Hill; 2019.
Le T, Bhushan V. *First Aid for the USMLE Step 1 2019*. 29th ed. New York, NY: McGraw Hill; 2018.

**Hepatitis B and D**
Friedman L. Liver, biliary tract and pancreas disorders. In: Papadakis MA, McPhee SJ, Rabow MW, eds. *Current Medical Diagnosis & Treatment 2019*. New York, NY: McGraw Hill; 2019.
Le T, Bhushan V. *First Aid for the USMLE Step 1 2019*. 29th ed. New York, NY: McGraw Hill; 2018.

**Hepatitis C**
Friedman L. Liver, biliary tract and pancreas disorders. In: Papadakis MA, McPhee SJ, Rabow MW, eds. *Current Medical Diagnosis & Treatment 2019*. New York, NY: McGraw Hill; 2019.
Le T, Bhushan V. *First Aid for the USMLE Step 1 2019*. 29th ed. New York, NY: McGraw Hill; 2018.

**Hepatocellular Carcinoma**
Cornett PA, Wang S, Friedman LS, et al. Cancer. In: Papadakis MA, McPhee SJ, Rabow MW, eds. *Current Medical Diagnosis & Treatment 2019*. New York, NY: McGraw Hill; 2019.
Le T, Bhushan V. *First Aid for the USMLE Step 1 2019*. 29th ed. New York, NY: McGraw Hill; 2018.

**Infectious Esophagitis**
McQuaid KR. Gastrointestinal disorders. In: Papadakis MA, McPhee SJ, Rabow MW, eds. *Current Medical Diagnosis & Treatment 2019*. New York, NY: McGraw Hill; 2019.

**Inguinal and Femoral Hernias**
Hoffman BL, Owens DM, Rogers DE. Pelvic pain. In: Hoffman BL, Schorge JO, Bradshaw KD, Halvorson LM, Schaffer JI, Corton MM, eds. *Williams Gynecology*. 3rd ed. New York, NY: McGraw Hill; 2016.
McQuaid KR. Gastrointestinal disorders. In: Papadakis MA, McPhee SJ, Rabow MW, eds. *Current Medical Diagnosis & Treatment 2019*. New York, NY: McGraw Hill; 2019.

**Irritable Bowel Syndrome**
Friedman S. Irritable bowel syndrome. In: Greenberger NJ, Blumberg RS, Burakoff R, eds. *Current Diagnosis & Treatment: Gastroenterology, Hepatology, & Endoscopy*. 3rd ed. New York, NY: McGraw Hill; 2016.

**Pancreatitis, Acute**
Conwell DL, Banks PA. Acute pancreatitis. In: Greenberger NJ, Blumberg RS, Burakoff R, eds. *Current Diagnosis & Treatment: Gastroenterology, Hepatology, & Endoscopy*. 3rd ed. New York, NY: McGraw Hill; 2016.
Le T, Bhushan V. *First Aid for the USMLE Step 1 2019*. 29th ed. New York, NY: McGraw Hill; 2018.

## Pancreatitis, Chronic
McQuaid KR. Gastrointestinal disorders. In: Papadakis MA, McPhee SJ, Rabow MW, eds. *Current Medical Diagnosis & Treatment 2019*. New York, NY: McGraw Hill; 2019.

## Peptic Ulcer Disease
McQuaid KR. Gastrointestinal disorders. In: Papadakis MA, McPhee SJ, Rabow MW, eds. *Current Medical Diagnosis & Treatment 2019*. New York, NY: McGraw Hill; 2019.

Valle J. Peptic ulcer disease and related disorders. In: Jameson J, Fauci AS, Kasper DL, Hauser SL, Longo DL, Loscalzo J, eds. *Harrison's Principles of Internal Medicine*. 20th ed. New York, NY: McGraw Hill; 2018.

## Primary Sclerosing Cholangitis & Primary Biliary Cholangitis
Greenberger NJ, Saltzman JR. Primary sclerosing cholangitis. In: Greenberger NJ, Blumberg RS, Burakoff R, eds. *Current Diagnosis & Treatment: Gastroenterology, Hepatology, & Endoscopy*. 3rd ed. New York, NY: McGraw Hill; 2016.

Le T, Bhushan V. *First Aid for the USMLE Step 1 2019*. 29th ed. New York, NY: McGraw Hill; 2018.

Pratt DS. Primary biliary cirrhosis. In: Greenberger NJ, Blumberg RS, Burakoff R, eds. *Current Diagnosis & Treatment: Gastroenterology, Hepatology, & Endoscopy*. 3rd ed. New York, NY: McGraw Hill; 2016.

## Spontaneous Bacterial Peritonitis
Bechtel B. Microscopic findings. In: Knoop KJ, Stack LB, Storrow AB, Thurman R, eds. *The Atlas of Emergency Medicine*. 4th ed. New York, NY: McGraw Hill; 2016.

Carroll KC, Hobden JA, Miller S, et al, eds. Enteric gram-negative rods (Enterobacteriaceae). In: *Jawetz, Melnick, & Adelberg's Medical Microbiology*. 27th ed. New York, NY: McGraw Hill; 2019.

## Ulcerative Colitis
Greene KG, Trembath D. Pathology of the gastrointestinal tract. In: Reisner HM, eds. *Pathology: A Modern Case Study*. New York, NY: McGraw Hill; 2015.

McQuaid KR. Gastrointestinal disorders. In: Papadakis MA, McPhee SJ, Rabow MW, eds. *Current Medical Diagnosis & Treatment 2019*. New York, NY: McGraw Hill; 2019.

## Upper GI Cancers
Jameson J, Fauci AS, Kasper DL, Hauser SL, Longo DL, Loscalzo J, eds. *Harrison's Principles of Internal Medicine*. 20th ed. New York, NY: McGraw Hill; 2018.

Le T, Bhushan V. *First Aid for the USMLE Step 1 2019*. 29th ed. New York, NY: McGraw Hill; 2018.

McQuaid KR. Gastrointestinal disorders. In: Papadakis MA, McPhee SJ, Rabow MW, eds. *Current Medical Diagnosis & Treatment 2019*. New York, NY: McGraw Hill; 2019.

## Vascular GI Disporders
Stoffel EM, Jajoo K, Greenberger NJ. Mesenteric vascular disease. In: Greenberger NJ, Blumberg RS, Burakoff R, eds. *Current Diagnosis & Treatment: Gastroenterology, Hepatology, & Endoscopy*. 3rd ed. New York, NY: McGraw Hill; 2016.

## Wilson's Disease
Friedman L. Liver, biliary tract and pancreas disorders. In: Papadakis MA, McPhee SJ, Rabow MW, eds. *Current Medical Diagnosis & Treatment 2019*. New York, NY: McGraw Hill; 2019.

# Hematology/Oncology

*Michael E. Devitt, MD*

# Amyloidosis

Group of Protein Misfolding Disorders Characterized by Extracellular Deposition of Proteins

**Proteins aggregate into β-pleated linear sheets** → **Cause insoluble polymeric protein fibrils** → **Leads to cellular damage and apoptosis**

 Disease of the elderly

## Diagnosis

Tissue biopsy          Congo-red stain

Reproduced with permission from Lichtman MA, Shafer MS, Felgar RE, et al: Lichtman's Atlas of Hematology 2016. New York, NY: McGraw Hill; 2017.

*Apple-green birefringence under polarized light*

---

# Systemic Amyloidoses

## AL Amyloidosis

**Ig light chain** deposition

Caused by plasma cell disorders:
- Multiple myeloma
- Waldenstrom macroglobulinemia
- B-cell lymphomas

Affects multiple organ systems

## AA Amyloidosis

**Serum amyloid A** deposition

Caused by chronic inflammation:
- Rheumatoid arthritis
- Inflammatory bowel disease
- Spondyloarthropathies
- Chronic infection

Affects multiple organ systems

Nephrotic syndrome          Restrictive cardiomyopathy

## Dialysis-Related

**β2-microglobulin** deposition

Occurs in patients with ESRD on long-term dialysis

Often presents with carpal tunnel syndrome

Peripheral & autonomic neuropathy          Splenomegaly, Hepatomegaly, easy bruising

## ATTR Amyloidosis

**Transthyretin protein (TTR)** deposition

Familial (mutated TTR) and age-related subtypes

Typically affects the heart and peripheral nerves

---

# Organ-Specific/Localized Amyloidoses

## Alzheimer's Disease

Deposition of **β-amyloid protein**

Cleavage product of **amyloid precursor protein (APP)**

## Islet Amyloid Polypeptide (IAPP)

Deposition of **amylin** in pancreatic islets

Seen in patients with type 2 diabetes mellitus

## Thyroid Medullary Carcinoma

**Calcitonin** deposition by parafollicular cells

Associated with MEN2A and MEN2B

## Isolated Atrial Amyloidosis

**Atrial natriuretic peptide** deposition

Common in normal aging

Increased risk of atrial fibrillation

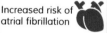

# Anemia, Aplastic

## Diagnostic Criteria

Pancytopenia, usually requiring **ALL** of the below

    HgB <10

    Platelets <50,000

    Neutrophils <1500

    Absolute reticulocyte count <40,000

Hypocellular bone marrow WITHOUT abnormal or malignant cells or fibrosis (often exhibiting **fatty replacement**)

Lack of hematopoietic cell precursors

## Clinical Features

Symptoms usually develop **gradually**

Symptoms of **anemia**: Pallor, weakness, dyspnea, fatigue

Symptoms of **thrombocytopenia**: Petechiae, bruising, gingival bleeding

Lymphadenopathy and splenomegaly suggest an alternative diagnosis

Reproduced with permission from Kaushansky K, Lichtman MA, Prhal JT, et al: Williams Hematology, 9th ed. New York, NY: McGraw Hill; 2016.

Normal bone marrow biopsy from young adult

Severe aplastic anemia with fatty replacement

## Acquired Aplastic Anemia

Most common form

Highest frequency 15-25 years old, second peak 65-69 years old

Causes can include:

    Autoimmune

    Drugs (antineoplastic drugs, etc.)

    Toxins (benzenes, organophosphates)

    Viruses (EBV, hepatitis, HIV)

    Iatrogenic (radiation, chemo)

    Autoimmune diseases (RA, SLE)

    Pregnancy

## Hereditary Aplastic Anemia

**Fanconi anemia** most common cause:

    Autosomal recessive

    Genetic mutations cause DNA instability

    Growth retardation and skeletal abnormalities

    Thumb abnormalities (agenesis or supernumerary digits) common

Other rare genetic disease such as dyskeratosis congenita, Shwachman-Diamond syndrome, and WT syndrome also associated with aplastic anemia

# Anemia, Autoimmune Hemolytic

## Type II Hypersensitivity Reaction

- Autoantibody binds to antigen (component of Rh system) on red blood cell surface
- Macrophages in spleen recognize Fc portion of antibody and remove the RBC from circulation

## Causes

- Idiopathic (~50%)
- Autoimmune diseases (ie, SLE)
- CLL or lymphomas
- Infections (mycoplasma pneumonia and mononucleosis)
- Certain drugs (ie, penicillins, cephalosporins)

## Signs and Symptoms

### Clinical Findings

Jaundice
Splenomegaly
Dyspnea
Fatigue
Painful, blue fingers in the cold (**COLD** type only)

Anemia (often very severe)

↑ Reticulocytes ↓ Bilirubin ↑ Haptoglobin

Spherocytes on peripheral smear (most common in **WARM** type)

RBC agglutinates in **COLD** type

## Warm vs Cold Autoimmune Hemolytic Anemia

**Antibody**
**WARM:** IgG
**COLD:** IgM and complement

**Diagnosis**
**WARM:** Direct Coombs + for IgG
**COLD:** RBCs agglutinate only at cold temps, direct Coombs + for complement only

**Treatment**
**WARM:** Prednisone, consider splenectomy
**COLD:** Avoid cold temps, rituximab

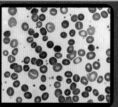

WARM hemolytic anemia: Spherocytosis and reticulocytosis

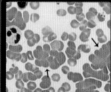

COLD hemolytic anemia: RBC agglutination at cold temperatures

# Anemia, Chronic Inflammation

## Risk Factors

**Autoimmune diseases**
- Rheumatoid arthritis
- Systemic lupus

**Cancer**

**Chronic kidney disease (CKD)**

**Infection**

## Mechanism of Disease

Inflammation
↓
↑Hepcidin
↓
↓Iron release from macrophages
+
↓Iron absorption

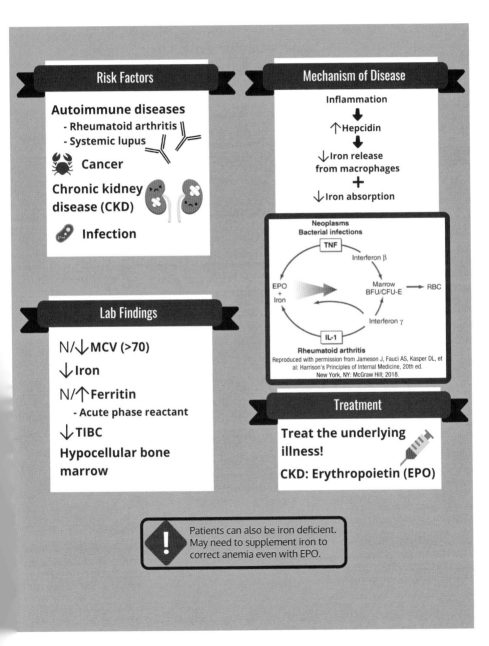

Reproduced with permission from Jameson J, Fauci AS, Kasper DL, et al: Harrison's Principles of Internal Medicine, 20th ed. New York, NY: McGraw Hill; 2018.

## Lab Findings

N/↓MCV (>70)

↓Iron

N/↑Ferritin
- Acute phase reactant

↓TIBC

Hypocellular bone marrow

## Treatment

**Treat the underlying illness!**

**CKD: Erythropoietin (EPO)**

! Patients can also be iron deficient. May need to supplement iron to correct anemia even with EPO.

# Anemia, Iron Deficiency

## Risk Factors

**Blood Loss**
 - Heavy periods
 - GI bleed (ulcers, cancer, hookworms)

↓ Iron intake

↓ Absorption
 - Gastrectomy
 - Crohn's, Celiac

Pregnancy

## Symptoms

**Fatigue**          **Pallor**

**Koilonychia**

Reproduced with permission from Knoop KJ, Stack LB, Storrow AB, et al: The Atlas of Emergency Medicine, 4th ed. New York, NY: McGraw Hill; 2016. Photo contributor: Andreas Fischer, RN.

          **Pica**

Reproduced with permission from Lichtman MA, Shafer MS, Felgar RE, et al: Lichtman's Atlas of Hematology 2016. New York, NY: McGraw Hill; 2017.

## Lab Findings

**Microcytic hypochromic RBCs**

↓ MCV
↑ RDW
↓ Iron
↓ Ferritin
↑ TIBC
↓ % Iron saturation

Reproduced with permission from Lichtman MA, Shafer MS, Felgar RE, et al: Lichtman's Atlas of Hematology 2016. New York, NY: McGraw Hill; 2017.

## Treatment

**Oral iron**          **IV iron**

*Absorbs better with OJ!*

**Blood transfusion:**
 - CV instability
 - Severe symptoms
Temporarily fixes the anemia and gives patient some iron

**Treat the underlying cause!**

 Iron deficiency in an older person is GI bleeding until proven otherwise. Do a colonoscopy!

# Anemia, Megaloblastic

## Causes & Mechanism of Disease

**Folate Deficiency**
- Malnutrition (alcoholism)
- Malabsorption
- Drugs (methotrexate)
- Pregnancy

**Orotic Aciduria**
- Autosomal recessive
- Orotic acid ⊘ UMP

Recall folate & Vitamin $B_{12}$ metabolism!

**Cobalamin ($B_{12}$) Deficiency**
- Veganism
- Malabsorption (Crohn's)
- Pernicious anemia
- Gastrectomy
- Fish tapeworm

**Impaired purine/pyrimidine formation**

⬇

**Defective DNA synthesis in bone marrow**

⬇

**Delayed nuclear maturation**

⬇

**Megaloblastic anemia**

## Clinical & Laboratory Findings

**Hypersegmented neutrophils**
**RBC: Macro-ovalocytes**
↑ **MCV**
**Glossitis**

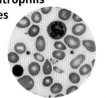

**Orotic Aciduria**
↑ Urine orotic acid
Developmental delay
Failure to thrive
Unresponsive to
$B_{12}$ or folate
Treatment: Uridine!

Reproduced with permission from Lichtman MA, Shafer MS, Felgar RE, et al: Lichtman's Atlas of Hematology 2016. New York, NY: McGraw Hill; 2017.

**Folate Deficiency**
↑ Homocysteine
Normal methylmalonic acid
No neurological symptoms

**Cobalamin ($B_{12}$) Deficiency**
↑ Homocysteine
↑ Methylmalonic acid
Neurological symptoms
- Dementia
- Loss of vibration/proprioception

**!** Folate supplementation may correct anemia due to $B_{12}$ deficiency, but neurological symptoms will persist.

# Anemia, Sickle Cell

## Genetics and Pathophysiology

Sickle cell trait: Single amino acid substitution in β-globulin gene (**Glu -> Val**)

Sickle cell disease is autosomal recessive (**HbSS**), but the trait (**HbAS**) provides some **malarial resistance,** so it has persisted. **Patients with trait are generally asymptomatic.**

## Clinical Manifestations and Complications

**Pain crisis:** Often precipitated by dehydration, cold weather, or infection → increased vasoocclusion → tissue hypoxia → severe pain (common in chest, back, and extremities)

## Many Organ Systems are Affected by Sickle Cell Disease!

 **Acute chest syndrome:** Alveolar consolidation on CXR, represents intrapulmonary sickling. High mortality

 **Stroke:** Increased risk, especially in children. **Transcranial Doppler U/S** with increased blood flow = greater stroke risk

 **Sequestration crisis:** Acute drop in Hb due to pooling of blood in spleen or liver. Can lead to **autosplenectomy**

 **Aplastic crisis:** Low retics with hemolysis, often precipitated by parvovirus

 **Sickle cell nephropathy:** Often leads to renal failure requiring dialysis

## Evidence of Hemolysis

↑ LDH, reticulocytes, indirect bilirubin

↓ Serum haptoglobin

### Anemia
Normochromic, normocytic, normal MCHC

## Evidence of Chronic Inflammation

↑ Platelets, neutrophils

### Blood Smear Demonstrates Sickling

Reproduced with permission from Aster JC, Bunn H: Pathophysiology of Blood Disorders, 2nd ed. New York, NY: McGraw Hill; 2017.

## Treatment and Management

**Hydroxyurea** is the only FDA therapy approved for SCD → it helps increase the proportion of HbF and thus decrease sickling

**Stem cell transplant** is a potentially curative therapy, but not often used due to possibility of severe complications and difficulty finding donor

Indication for **blood transfusion**:
- Acute chest syndrome
- Aplastic or sequestration crisis
- Stroke

**DO NOT NEED TRANSFUSION FOR CHRONIC, STEADY ANEMIA**

**Exchange transfusion** can be useful for reducing stroke risk and limiting risk of iron overload

# Anemia, Sideroblastic

## Common Features

1. "Ringed sideroblasts" in bone marrow (shape is due to abnormal iron accumulation in mitochondria)

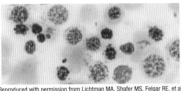

**Prussian blue stain necessary to see granules**

Reproduced with permission from Lichtman MA, Shafer MS, Felgar RE, et al: Lichtman's Atlas of Hematology 2016. New York, NY: McGraw Hill; 2017.

2. Elevated iron levels in tissue
3. Ineffective erythropoiesis
4. Hypochromic erythrocytes (in varying proportions)

## Different Types

Acquired
- Idiopathic (may be precursor for MDS)
- **Toxins** (lead, ethanol, zinc)
- **Drugs** (isoniazid, cycloserine, pyrazinamide, chloramphenicol)

Hereditary
- X-linked, autosomal, or mitochondrial

## Laboratory and Clinical Findings

### Primary Acquired
Anemia
Increased iron and ferritin

### Secondary to Drugs or Toxins
Anemia that improves with **pyridoxine administration** or stopping drug

### Hereditary
Some variants also present with **neurologic symptoms** (ie, ataxia)
Splenomegaly often present
Microcytic, hypochromic anemia common in X-linked variant
Anemia can be **macrocytic in mitochondrial variant**

## Treatment

Often responsive to **daily pyridoxine and folic acid**

Iron overload is a common cause of death → **phlebotomy or iron chelation** is usually necessary

Bone marrow transplant has been used occasionally in severe cases

# Antiphospholipid Syndrome
## A Hypercoagulable State

##  Etiology & Definitions

- **Acquired autoimmune disease**: Antibody-mediated thrombophilia
- <u>Primary:</u> Alone
- <u>Secondary:</u> With other autoimmune diseases, ie, Lupus
- Females primarily affected
- Incidence 5 per 100,000 persons per year

##  Clinical Presentation

- **Venous thrombosis**

| PE | DVT | Retinal Vein Thrombosis |

- **Arterial thrombosis**

| Brain | Extremity | Heart | Bone |

- **Pregnancy morbidity**

| Recurrent Miscarriages | Preterm Delivery | Preeclampsia |

- Livedo reticularis
- Glomerular disease
- MSK: Arthralgias, arthritis, osteoporosis, fracture

## Diagnosis & Workup

- Suspect if:
  - Thrombosis or CVA in patients <55
  - Recurrent pregnancy loss with thrombocytopenia
- Common laboratory findings:
  - Thrombocytopenia
  - Coombs-positive hemolytic anemia
  - False-positive VDRL (antibodies cross-react with *T. pallidum*-cholesterol complexes)
- Diagnostic criteria: Presence of at least one clinical and one laboratory criterion in the absence of other thrombophilia causes

| Clinical | Laboratory |
|---|---|
| Vascular thrombosis | Lupus anticoagulant antibody |
| Pregnancy morbidity | Anticardiolipin antibody |
| | Anti-β2 glycoprotein I antibody |

##  Treatment

- After initial thrombotic event: Warfarin for life (INR goal 2.5-3.5) +/− 80 mg aspirin daily. IVIG daily for 5 days if still symptomatic
- Abortion prevention: IVIG daily for 5 days
- Steroids are ineffective

##  Pathogenesis

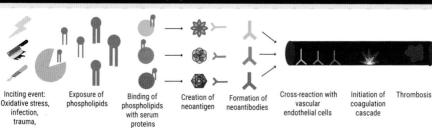

| Inciting event: Oxidative stress, infection, trauma, surgery | Exposure of phospholipids | Binding of phospholipids with serum proteins | Creation of neoantigen | Formation of neoantibodies | Cross-reaction with vascular endothelial cells | Initiation of coagulation cascade | Thrombosis |

# AT III Deficiency *A Hypercoagulable State*

## Etiology

- Inherited gene mutation of AT III
- Asparaginase therapy (ALL)
- Nephrotic syndrome: Loss of AT III in urine

## Presentation

- Venous thromboembolism

DVT    PE

- Heparin resistance (diminished rise in PTT following heparin administration)

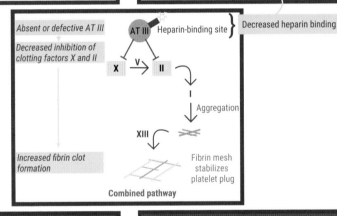

*Absent or defective AT III*

*Decreased inhibition of clotting factors X and II*

AT III  Heparin-binding site } Decreased heparin binding

X  V → II

Aggregation

XIII

*Increased fibrin clot formation*

Fibrin mesh stabilizes platelet plug

**Combined pathway**

## Diagnosis

- Functional assay for AT III activity
- Test when patient is off of anticoagulation
- Do NOT order aPTT, PT, TT
- Do NOT routinely test patients with VTE

AT III Activity

## Treatment

- Anticoagulation
- AT III replacement
- Only treat if symptomatic

# Blood Transfusion Reactions

## Anaphylactic Reaction

**Within minutes**

**Why?**
IgA-deficient patients make IgA antibodies that react with donor blood

**Signs**
Angioedema
Hypotension
Respiratory distress

**Treatment**
Fluids
Epinephrine
Vasopressors if needed

## Allergic Reaction

**Within 1 hour**

**Why?**
Donor plasma interacts with recipient IgE, leads to mast cell activation and histamine release

**Signs**
Urticaria
Less severe than anaphylaxis

**Treatment**
Antihistamines
Consider restarting transfusion if symptoms resolve

## Acute Hemolytic Transfusion Reaction

**Within 1 hour**

**Why?**
ABO incompatibility leads to lysis of donor blood by preformed antibodies

**Signs**
Fever and chills
Flank pain
Hemoglobinuria
DIC

**Treatment**
Aggressive fluids
Vasopressors and/or diuretics, if needed

## Febrile Nonhemolytic Transfusion Reaction

**Within 6 hours**

**Why?**
Release of cytokines from leukocytes in donor blood

**Signs**
Fever (↑ temperature 1-2°C from baseline)
No vascular collapse

**Treatment**
Antipyretics
Supportive care

## Transfusion-Related Acute Lung Injury (TRALI)

**Within 6 hours**

**Why?**
Donor blood activates recipient neutrophils, causing them to aggregate in pulmonary capillaries

**Signs**
Respiratory distress
Pulmonary infiltrates on CXR

**Treatment**
Oxygenation
Mechanical ventilation, if needed

# Disseminated Intravascular Coagulation

## Acute Symptoms

Sudden bleeding from multiple venipuncture sites

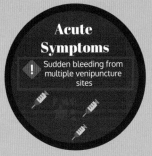

## Chronic Symptoms

Bruising, mucosal bleeding, thrombophlebitis, renal and neurologic dysfunction

## Labs

Decreased clotting factors
Thrombocytopenia
Increased PT, PTT, bleeding time
Increased D-Dimer
Schistocytes on smear

## Fibrin Deposition in Blood Vessels

### Thrombosis Hemorrhage End-Organ Damage

## Associated with Severe Illness

Obstetric Complications
Sepsis
Neoplasm
APML
ARDS
Massive Trauma

## Differences from TTP

PT, PTT are INCREASED
FACTORS ARE CONSUMED

### Pathologic Activation of **full** Clotting Cascade

## Treatment

Underlying Cause
Transfuse: RBCs, Platelets, Fresh Frozen Plasma

**WATCH OUT!**

Need to distinguish from TTP, in which PLT transfusion is CONTRAINDICATED

# Dysfibrinogenemia

## Definitions

**Dysfibrinogenemia (DF)**: Normal levels, dysfunctional fibrinogen

**Hypodysfibrinogenemia (HDF)**: Low levels, dysfunctional fibrinogen

## Etiologies

Hereditary:

  **Autosomal dominant**, many mutations

Acquired:
  **Liver disease**, DIC, autoimmune disease

## Clinical Presentation

- Mostly **asymptomatic**
- Post-op **bleeding**
- Spontaneous **abortion**
- Puerperium **hemorrhage**
- Some mutations: Paradoxical **thrombosis**

## Diagnosis

- Screen with fibrinogen levels (functional + immunological)
  - DF dx if **clottable < immunoreactive** fibrinogen
- Gold standard: **Genotype** analysis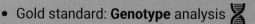
- **Prolonged** PT, aPTT, thrombin time (TT)

**↑ PT, aPTT, TT**

## Treatment

- If **bleeding**: Supplement **fibrinogen >1 g/L** until hemostatic
- If **thrombophilic** subtype: **Anticoagulate**

## Complications

Some forms cause **hereditary amyloidosis** → Renal failure → Needs combined kidney and liver **transplant**

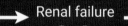

# Eosinophilia

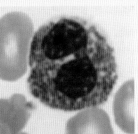

## Parasites

- Eosinophils target parasitic infections
- More severe in Löffler's syndrome–Eosinophils accumulate in the lung after parasitic infection

## Vasculitis

- Churg–Strauss syndrome
- **Mepolizumab** targets eosinophil growth factor IL-5
  - More effect in these diseases more than asthma

## Hypersensitivity

- Drug reactions
- Asthma
- Eosinophilic esophagitis
- Allergies

## Eosinophils

- Stain **red**–Major basic protein
- **Eosinophil peroxidase** kills organisms, triggers mast cell secretion

## Eosinophilia

- **>500 eosinophils**/μL of blood
- Up to 50,000–100,000/μL in Löffler's syndrome

## Idiopathic Hypereosinophilic syndrome

- Multiorgan dysfunction due to deposition of toxic eosinophil proteins
- Heart, CNS, kidneys, lungs, GI tract, and skin

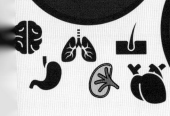

## Malignancy

- Hematologic (eg, Hodgkins, CML)
- Solid tumors (eg, lung, stomach, pancreas, ovary)

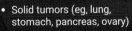

## Eosinophilia-myalgia syndrome

- Eosinophil count >1000/μL
- Caused by ingesting contaminants in **L-tryptophan**
- Disabling myalgia, pneumonitis, myocarditis
  - **Steroids** to treat

# Erythrocytosis

**Primary**  **Secondary**

## Etiology

Erythropoietin (EPO) **hypersensitivity**

Polycythemia vera (**PV**)

  *JAK2* V617F mutation

Primary familial and congenital
polycythemia (**PFCP**)

  *EPOR* mutation

Increased EPO **production**

  **Appropriate**: Normal hypoxia response
  Lung disease, Eisenmenger, altitude

  **Inappropriate**: Aberrant EPO production
  Tumors, postrenal transplant

**Relative**: Due to low plasma volume—
NOT true erythrocytosis

## Clinical Presentation

**PV**
Splenomegaly, <u>aquagenic</u>
<u>pruritus</u> hyperviscosity (eg, TIAs, tinnitus)
**PFCP**
Isolated erythrocytosis (unlike PV)

Most etiologies are **asymptomatic**

Altitude
Ruddy cyanosis, palpitations,
headache, sleeplessness

## Diagnosis

**PV**
Clinical findings plus *JAK2* V617F mutation
**PFCP**
<u>Low serum EPO</u>, normal *JAK2* allele

**Appropriate** ↓O₂
Arterial hypoxia. Etiology usually clear
**Inappropriate**
Findings related to underlying defect

## Treatment

**PV**
- **Phlebotomy** for hyperviscosity
- **Anticoagulation,** if thrombosis present
- JAK1/2 inhibitor **ruxolitinib,**
  **hydroxyurea** for pruritis

⚠ Chemo can increase uric acid,
prevent with allopurinol

Postrenal transplant
- <u>ACEs or ARBs</u>
Neoplasm
- Surgical removal
Other causes: **Phlebotomy,** if
symptomatic

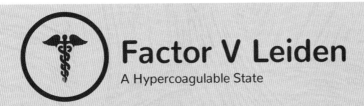

# Factor V Leiden
## A Hypercoagulable State

## Etiology

- Autosomal dominant mutation in Factor V gene
- Mutated factor V protein (procoagulant) is resistant to inactivation by activated protein C (anticoagulant)
- Hypercoagulable state
- Most common hereditary thrombophilia in Caucasians

## Clinical Presentation

- Asymptomatic (majority of patients)
- Venous thromboembolism (VTE) in a small portion of heterozygotes (estimated at 5%)

DVT

PE

Miscarriages

## Diagnosis & Workup

- Use genetic testing or functional APC resistance assay
- Do not routinely test patients
- Consider test if:
  - Thrombophilic family
  - VTE and age <50 years
  - VTE in unusual location (brain)
  - Recurrent VTE

## Treatment

- Avoid oral contraceptives
- Anticoagulation, if symptomatic
  - Choice of oral anticoagulant
  - Indefinite anticoagulation NOT necessary for first VTE, especially if provoked
  - IVC filter, if anticoagulation contraindicated

## Pathogenesis

Activated Protein C + Protein S

$\downarrow\!\!\dashv$

Xa + Va $\longrightarrow$ Thrombin (IIa) $\longrightarrow$ Fibrin Clot

*Va resistance to cleavage* - - - - - - - - - - - - - -> *Increased clot formation*

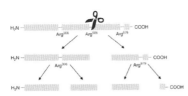

Wild-type factor V is inactivated by protein C cleavage at $Arg^{506}$

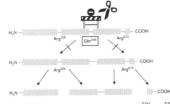

G→A DNA point mutation → $Arg^{506}$→$Gln^{506}$ amino acid substitution at protein C cleavage site

# G6PD Deficiency

## Genetics

X-linked recessive trait

Most common human enzyme deficiency

More prevalent among African Americans (potentially due to conferring malarial resistance)

## Biochemistry

G6PD Deficiency = ↓ NADPH

↓ NADPH = Poor defense against **oxidizing agents**

Poor defense against oxidizing = agents

Free radical production and damage to RBCs

## What Happens to Red Blood Cells?

Exposure to infection or oxidative agent

↓

Free radicals diffuse into RBCs, forming **Heinz bodies** (denatured hemoglobin)

↓

Phagocytes remove Heinz bodies, forming **bite cells**

↓

Overall result: **Hemolysis**

## Oxidizing Agents to Watch Out For

Sulfonamides (ie, Bactrim)

Primaquine

Anti-TB drugs

Dapsone

Nitrofurantoin

Fava Beans

## Clinical Manifestations

Hours to days following ingestion of oxidizing agent or illness, patient develops:
- Pallor
- Jaundice
- Dark Urine

Also need to consider this diagnosis in neonates with persistent jaundice

Reproduced with permission from Lichtman MA, Shafer MS, Felgar RE, et al: Lichtman's Atlas of Hematology 2016. New York, NY: McGraw Hill; 2017.

Reproduced with permission from Hillman RS, Ault KA, Leporrier M, et al: Hematology in Clinical Practice, 5th ed. New York, NY: McGraw Hill; 2011.

**Created By:** Ryan Sutyla, MS4 **Sources:** First Aid for USMLE Step 1 (2017); Up to Date
**Images:** Harrison's Principles of Internal Medicine, 20e, Figure 58-22; Lichtman's Atlas of Hematology 2016, Figure 1.A.007

**Top:** Bite cells. **Bottom:** Heinz bodies (need crystal violet stain to visualize)

# Graft vs Host Disease (GVHD)

## Etiology

 After hematopoietic cell transplant (**HCT**), transplanted immune (mainly T) cells recognize host as foreign

## Acute GVHD | Chronic GVHD

### Clinical Presentation

**Acute GVHD**

 Erythematous maculopapular rash

 Anorexia/diarrhea

 Liver dysfunction

**Chronic GVHD**

**THINK AUTOIMMUNE DISEASE!**

Malar rash
Sicca syndrome
Arthritis and myositis
Obliterative bronchiolitis
Cholestasis

## Diagnosis ☑

**Acute GVHD**

🕐 Usually within 3 months of HCT

 **Clinical** diagnosis

⬆ Bilirubin
AST, ALT, alkaline phosphatase

🌡 +/− Biopsy for confirmation
Lymphocytic infiltrate + endothelial damage

**Chronic GVHD**

🕐 3 months to 2 years after HCT

❗Timing can **overlap**—focus on **symptoms**

🩺 **Clinical** diagnosis

🌡 +/− Biopsy for confirmation
Lymphocytic infiltrate + endothelial damage

## Prevention & Treatment 💊

**Acute GVHD**

Prevention—Immunosuppression
Calcineurin inhibitor + antimetabolite

Treatment
Glucocorticoids (eg, prednisone)
If failing, other immunosuppressants

**Chronic GVHD**

Prevention—Immunosuppression
Calcineurin inhibitor + antimetabolite

Treatment
Like acute, but can be local or systemic

❗Infection **prophylaxis** with TMP-SMX

# Hemophilia A and B

## Etiology

Hemophilia **A**: X-linked deficiency of Factor **VIII** **A8**

Hemophilia **B**: X-linked deficiency of Factor **IX** **B9**

→ Decreased Factor X activation ⬇**Xa** → **Coagulopathy**

## Clinical Presentation

<u>Keep in mind...</u>
- A and B are clinically the same
- Mostly males, usually with family history
- Less clotting factor
  ↳ More severe symptoms

<u>Symptoms</u>
- **Hemarthroses** → Debilitating hemarthropathy
  - Iron deposition and inflammation
- Hematuria
- Post-op hemorrhage
- Hematomas, blood pseudotumors

(!) Rare but serious: Intracranial and retropharyngeal bleeding

## Diagnosis

- Prolonged aPTT—Corrects when mixed with normal plasma
- Normal PT
- Need specific enzymes assays to distinguish A and B

## Treatment

- Avoid COX-1 inhibitors (aspirin)
- Factor **replacement** (esp. pre-op)

(!) If intracranial/retropharyngeal bleed, give factors until at normal levels

## Complications

- Replacement therapy → **Inhibitor antibodies** against coag factors
- Patients transfused pre-1985 are high-risk for **HIV, HBV, HCV**

### Heparin Exposure Timing

**If no prior heparin exposure:**
Platelet drop 5-10 days after first heparin dose
**Heparin exposure in prior 30 days:**
Platelet drop with 24 hours of first heparin dose
**Other scenarios decrease likelihood of HIT**

### Thrombocytopenia

Antibodies to complex of heparin and
**PF4** *activate platelets,* causing thrombosis
and drop in platelet count
**Decrease of >50%, not less than 20,000**
*and* **no surgery in prior 3 days**
Other scenarios decrease likelihood of HIT

### Clinical Diagnosis

Lab tests such as **PF4 antibody test** and
**serotonin release assay** are less helpful
than timing, symptoms, and ruling out
other causes (4Ts Score)

## Diagnosis

# Heparin-Induced Thrombocytopenia (HIT)

A patient exposed to heparin develops
thrombocytopenia AND clots due to an
*immunologic reaction*

## Treatment

### Discontinue Heparin

Should immediately stop the
offending agent

### Start Argatroban or Lepirudin

Direct thrombin inhibitors

### Identify and Treat Thrombosis

Consider lower extremity ultrasound
and other tests. Treat accordingly

# Hereditary Spherocytosis

## Genetics and Biochemistry

Mainly autosomal dominant inheritance

There are defects in proteins that normally help with interactions between RBC cytoskeleton and plasma membrane—this leads to a decreased amount of membrane **(and a smaller surface area: volume ratio)** (!)

Defects in **ankyrin and spectrin** (!) proteins are two major causes

RBCs are small, round, and have no central pallor

Increased membrane fragility = increased hemolysis

## Laboratory Findings and Diagnosis

**Suspect Hereditary Spherocytosis When...**

⬆ MCHC

Coomb's negative hemolysis

Spherocytes on blood smear

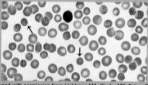

Reproduced with permission from Lichtman MA, Shafer MS, Felgar RE, et al: Lichtman's Atlas of Hematology 2016. New York, NY: McGraw Hill; 2017.

**Confirmatory Tests**

**EMA Binding Test:** Uses eosin-based dye that binds to RBC membrane proteins. **Flow cytometry fluorescence** in patients with HS will be decreased.

**Osmotic Fragility Test:** Measures hemolysis in buffered salt solutions. **Hemolysis** will be increased in patients with HS.

## Clinical Presentation and Treatment

**Hereditary Spherocytosis Can Present As...**

Splenomegaly

Neonatal jaundice

Pigmented gallstones

Aplastic crisis (ie, after a parvovirus B19 infection)

Reproduced with permission from Brunicardi FC, Andersen DK, Billiar TR, et al: Schwartz's Principles of Surgery, 11th ed. New York, NY: McGraw Hill; 2019.

**Management**

Initial treatment is focused on limiting effects of chronic hemolysis and anemia (ie, with transfusions and infection precautions)

(!) For those with severe hemolysis, consider **splenectomy** (want to wait until child is older than 6-7 though)

# Hyperhomocysteinemia (HHcy)

## Etiology and Definitions

**Severe HHcy:** Homocysteine (Hcy) >100 mmol/L

Most common: Cystathione β-synthase **(CBS) deficiency**
**Classic homocystinuria: Autosomal recessive**
Less common: MTHFR deficiency if severe
(see MTHFR Infographic)

**Mild-to-Moderate HHcy:** Hcy 12-100 mmol/L

More common than severe form in general population
Especially males, elderly, and those with more muscle mass

(!) This infographic covers severe HHcy. See MTHFR Card for mild/moderate

## Clinical Presentation

Infants are normal, symptoms develop if untreated

**Vascular**
<u>Thromboembolism</u>
Frequent cause of death

 **Bone**
Osteoporosis
<u>Marfanoid habitus</u>

**Neurodevelopmental**
Developmental delay, intellectual disability
Seizures

 **Ocular**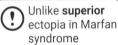
Glaucoma, myopia
<u>Inferior ectopia lentis</u>

(!) Unlike **superior** ectopia in Marfan syndrome

## Screening and Diagnosis

Newborn screening for CBS deficiency

Can also screen prenatally

Definitive diagnosis requires tissue confirmation for enzyme activity

## Treatment

Goal: Reduce Hcy levels
**Pyridoxine (B6) and folate** supplementation
Low methionine, high cysteine diet
Refractory: **Betaine** supplements to remethylate Hcy

# Idiopathic Thrombocytopenic Purpura

Diagnosis of Exclusion!
Rule out other causes
of thrombocytopenia

-Minor mucocutaneous
bleeding

-Easy bruising and
petechiae

Abrupt: Children 2-6
after viral illness

-Chronic: women of
childbearing age

↑ older age

Associations:
HIV, HCV,
lymphoma,
leukemia, SLE

## Symptoms

## Patients

-Thrombocytopenia
-Blood Smear: Look for
*normal RBCs, large
immature platelets, and
abnormal leukocytes*

IgG attacks platelets
and they are consumed
in the spleen

IgG

First Line:
Corticosteroids
IVIG

Second Line: Splenectomy,
rituximab, or
TPO agonists

## Tests

## Etiology

## Treatment

 WATCH OUT!

In older patients order a
**bone marrow biopsy** to fully
assess for *alternative
causes*

## TREAT IF....

CLINICALLY
SIGNIFICANT
SYMPTOMS
PLT >30

or  **PLT <30**

# Leukemia, Acute

Rapid, Unregulated Growth of Progenitor White Blood Cells in the Bone Marrow

## Acute Myeloid Leukemia

Clonal proliferation of **myeloblasts**

**!** Findings pathognomonic for AML: Auer rods, t(8;12), inv(16), t(15;16)

 Older patients, median age 67

## Acute Lymphoblastic Leukemia

Clonal proliferation of **lymphoblasts** B-cell ALL & T-cell ALL

**!** Most common pediatric malignancy

Incidence Peaks:
- Children
- Young adults
- Elderly

## Presentation

Leukemic cell marrow infiltration decreases other cell lines

 Anorexia

Weight loss

Weakness

Headache

Hepatosplenomegaly

Bone Pain
- Especially in kids with ALL

Anemia
- Fatigue
- Pallor
- Dyspnea

Thrombocytopenia
- Bleeding
- Petechiae
- Purpura

Dysfunctional leukocytes (WBC: Elevated, normal, or decreased)
- Infection
- Fever

## Diagnosis

 CBC

Blood Smear

Bone Marrow Biopsy
- >20% blasts in the marrow

Flow Cytometry:
- AML: Myeloperoxidase
- B-ALL: TdT, CD10, CD20
- T-ALL: TdT, CD3

## Cytogenetics

### AML

**Favorable**
- t(8;12)
- inv(16)

**Unfavorable**
- t(6;9)
- t(9;22)
- del(5q) & del(7q)
- FLT3 mutation

### ALL

**Favorable**
- t(12;21)
- Hyperdiploidy
- Age 1-10

**Unfavorable**
- t(9;22)
- Hypodiploidy
- CNS or testicular involvement

## Acute Promyelocytic Leukemia

AML subtype—Promyelocyte proliferation
- Caused by t(15;17), produces PML-RARA

**!** PML-RARA fusion protein blocks promyelocyte differentiation

High rates of DIC

Diagnosis:
- Auer rods are common

Treatment:
- All-trans-retinoic acid (ATRA)
- Arsenic trioxide
- Watch out for <u>differentiation syndrome</u>

Prognosis:
- 85% treatment response rate

## Treatment

 Chemotherapy
- Induction
- Consolidation
- Maintenance

**!** ALL may require intrathecal chemo

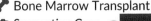 Bone Marrow Transplant

Supportive Care
- Transfusions
- Antibiotics

**!** High ALL remission rates in children

## ⚠ Complications

Disseminated Intravascular Coagulation

Tumor Lysis Syndrome

Febrile Neutropenia

Leukostasis

# Leukemia, Chronic Lymphocytic

Unregulated growth of mature lymphoid cells in the bone marrow

Clonal proliferation of functionally incompetent, well-differentiated **B lymphocytes**

Lymphocytes accumulate in:
- Bone marrow
- Peripheral blood
- Lymph nodes
- Spleen & Liver

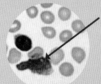

**Smudge cells**
- Found on blood smear in CLL
- Fragile leukemia cells that have been crushed by the slide

! CLL is the most common type of leukemia

CLL is a slowly progressive disease

Reproduced with permission from Lichtman MA, Shafer MS, Felgar RE, et al: Lichtman's Atlas of Hematology 2016. New York, NY: McGraw Hill; 2017.

 **Affects older adults**
- Median age 71
- Male-to-female ratio is 2:1

## Presentation

 Fatigue & Malaise

! Most patients are asymptomatic at diagnosis

 Lymphadenopathy

 Granulocytopenia
- Infection

 Splenomegaly
- Early satiety
- LUQ pain

## Diagnosis

 CBC
- Lymphocytosis
- Granulocytopenia
- Anemia
- Thrombocytopenia

Flow Cytometry:
- B-cell clonality
- CD19, CD20, CD23
- CD5 (T-cell marker)

Blood Smear

Hypogammaglobulinemia
- Abnormal lymphocyte function

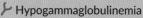

### Small Lymphocytic Lymphoma

B-cell lymphoma with **lymphadenopathy** & **splenomegaly** (+/–circulating CLL component)

- Tissue-based disease rather than blood or marrow
- Genetic and molecular features are identical to CLL

### Monoclonal B-cell Lymphocytosis

Asymptomatic clonal B-cell proliferation not meeting criteria for CLL

- Higher counts → higher risk for progression to CLL
- Not all MBL will progress to CLL, but all CLL is preceded by MBL

## Treatment

 Chemotherapy

Anti-CD20 Antibodies
- Rituximab
- Obinutuzumab

Indications for treatment:
- Recurrent infections
- Anemia
- Thrombocytopenia
- Severe lymphadenopathy
- Splenomegaly

 ! Do not treat if patients are asymptomatic

## Prognosis

CLL is not a curable disease
- Treatment controls symptoms and prevents disease progression.
- Many patients live for a long time with the disease.
- 5-year overall survival is ~90%.

## Complications

Infection
- Abnormal lymphocytes do not produce immunoglobulins
- Give IVIG to reduce infection risk

Autoimmune Complications
- Autoimmune hemolytic anemia
  - Warm IgG antibodies (DAT +
  - Elevated bilirubin & LDH
  - Decreased haptoglobin
- Immune thrombocytopenic purpura (ITP)

Richter Transformation
- CLL transformation into aggressive lymphoma (DLBCL)

# Leukemia, Chronic Myelogenous

Unregulated Growth of Myeloid Precursor Cells in the Bone Marrow

## Clonal proliferation of **granulocytes** at multiple stages of maturation

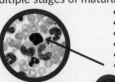

- Myelocytes
- Metamyelocytes
- Band forms
- Neutrophils
- Eosinophils
- Basophils

Reproduced with permission from Lichtman MA, Shafer MS, Felgar RE, et al: Lichtman's Atlas of Hematology 2016. New York, NY: McGraw Hill; 2017.

! **Basophilia is a key feature of CML**

**Affects middle-aged patients**
- Median age 64

## Philadelphia chromosome: t(9;22)
- BCR-ABL fusion product (RTK that is always "on")

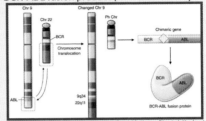

Reproduced with permission from Jameson J, Fauci AS, Kasper DL, et al: Harrison's Principles of Internal Medicine, 20th ed. New York, NY: McGraw Hill; 2018.

## Presentation

- Weight loss
- Anorexia
- Fever & chills
- Splenomegaly
  - Early satiety
  - LUQ pain

! **Most patients are asymptomatic at diagnosis**

**Anemia**
- Fatigue
- Pallor
- Dyspnea

## Diagnosis

- CBC
  - Extreme leukocytosis
  - WBC >100,000
  - Granulocytosis
  - Absolute basophilia
- Blood smear
- PCR or FISH for t(9;22)

! **t(9;22) required for diagnosis of CML**

## Leukocyte alkaline phosphatase (LAP)

Differentiate leukemia from leukemoid reaction

| Leukemia | Leukemoid reaction |
|---|---|
| ↓ LAP | ↑ LAP |

## 3 Phases of CML

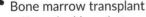

**Chronic Phase**
- Detection of t(9;22)
- Complications are rare
- Lasts for years
- Can be prolonged by treatment

**Accelerated Phase**
- Increase in peripheral & bone marrow WBC count
- Increased basophilia (>20%)
- Thrombocytosis or thrombocytopenia
- Resistance to tyrosine kinase inhibitors

**Blast Crisis**
- Transformation to acute leukemia (AML or ALL)
- 20% or more blasts in the blood or bone marrow
- Survival of 3-6 months

Diagnosis — Years — Death

## Treatment

- BCR-ABL tyrosine kinase inhibitor
  - Imatinib (Gleevec)
  - Dasatinib
- Bone marrow transplant
  - Young, healthy patients

! **Blast crisis management is the same as for acute leukemia**

## Complications

**Blast crisis**

**Leukostasis**
- Blasts occlude the microcirculation
- Occurs in blast crisis (rare in chronic phase)
- Presentation:
  - Pulmonary edema
  - CNS symptoms
  - Ischemic injury
- Treatment:
  - Leukophoresis
  - Hydroxyurea

# Leukemia, Hairy Cell

## General

Malignant neoplasm of well-differentiated B-lymphocytes
- Cells have distinct membrane projections

Rare disease
- Only 2% of adult leukemias

Most commonly affects older men

Associated with *BRAF V600E* mutation

## Presentation

Pancytopenia

Weakness, fatigue

Petechiae, bruising

Infection
- Especially atypical mycobacteria

Splenomegaly

Abdominal pain

Early satiety

Weight loss

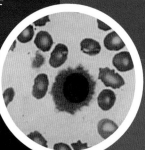

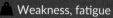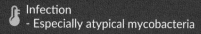
Reproduced with permission from Lichtman MA, Shafer MS, Felgar RE, et al: Lichtman's Atlas of Hematology 2016. New York, NY: McGraw Hill; 2017.

## Diagnosis

CBC

Pancytopenia

Blood smear

**Hairy cells:** Mononuclear cells with filamentous membrane projections

Positive staining with tartrate-resistant acid phosphatase (TRAP)

Flow cytometry

Most accurate diagnostic test

Identifies TRAP staining hairy cells

 **!** Dry tap with bone marrow aspiration

## Treatment

Splenectomy

Nucleoside analogs
Cladribine
Pentostatin

 Other agents
Interferon-α
Vemurafenib (BRAF inhibitor)
Rituximab

If untreated:
Progressive pancytopenia
Median survival of 5 years

# Lymphoma, Cutaneous B-Cell

Extranodal B-cell lymphoma originating in the skin without disease elsewhere

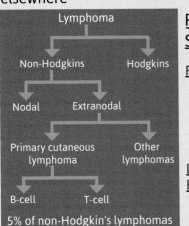

Lymphoma

Non-Hodgkins | Hodgkins

Nodal | Extranodal

Primary cutaneous lymphoma | Other lymphomas

B-cell | T-cell

5% of non-Hodgkin's lymphomas
18% of extranodal lymphomas

## Primary Cutaneous Lymphoma Subtypes

### Follicular Center
Most common CBCL
Slower growing
Head, neck, torso

### Diffuse Large B-Cell (Leg-Type)
Less common
Aggressive & faster growing
Legs & arms

### Marginal Zone
2nd most common
Slower growing
Torso & arms

### Diffuse Large B-Cell (Other)
Group of very rare lymphomas
Affect entire body

## Management

### Staging
Ensure disease is limited to the skin
Labs & imaging
Bone marrow biopsy is NOT recommended

### Indolent Types
Local radiation therapy
Intralesional steroids
Topical therapies

### Aggressive Types
(DLBC Leg-Type)
Systemic chemotherapy
Rituximab

### Regular Skin Exams
High recurrence rate after response to treatment
Prognosis remains good

## Skin Findings
Can present as:
Erythematous rash
Lump or Nodule

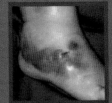

Raised & smooth in appearance

# Lymphoma, Hodgkin's
Malignant Transformation of Lymphoid Cells Residing in Lymphoid Tissues (B-cell)

## General

B-cell malignancy

Associated with EBV

Men > Women

**Bimodal age distribution**
- Peaks at ages 30 & 60

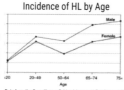
Incidence of HL by Age

Reed–Sternberg cells are a hallmark of HL

## Presentation

Cervical lymphadenopathy
- Single group of localized nodes, contiguous spread
- Usually above the diaphragm
- Alcohol-induced pain at nodal sites (highly specific)

B-symptoms: Fever, night sweats, weight loss, pruritus

Hepatosplenomegaly

Pel-Ebstein fever:
- High fever & afebrile intervals alternating weekly

## Diagnosis

Excisional lymph node biopsy with Reed–Sternberg cells

Chest X-ray, CT, or PET scan
- Evaluate for hilar lymphadenopathy & disease dissemination

Ann Arbor classification system is used for staging
- Number of nodal groups
- Presence/absence of B-symptoms
- Disease involving both sides of diaphragm

### Reed–Sternberg Cells

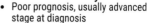

CD15+ & CD30+

Large abnormal B-cells

Bipolar nuclei & huge, eosinophilic nucleoli

"Owl's Eye" appearance

## Treatment

Chemotherapy: ABVD regimen
Adriamycin, bleomycin, vinblastine, dacarbazine

Radiation therapy

Monoclonal Antibodies
Brentuximab—mAb against CD30 with MT inhibitor
Pembrolizumab & Nivolumab—mAb against PD-L1

## Prognosis

HL has a very high cure rate with treatment

Good prognosis

5-Year survival rate: 86%

Long-term complications of treatment:
- Secondary malignancies (acute leukemia)
- Coronary artery disease
- Hypothyroidism

## Subtypes of Hodgkin's Lymphoma

### Nodular Sclerosing
- Most common type (60-70% of HL)
- Women > men
- Adolescents & young adults
- Histology: Bands of fibrosis divide the lymphoid tissue into nodules

### Mixed Cellularity
- Poor prognosis, usually advanced stage at diagnosis
- Older adults
- Histology: Cellular background contains eosinophils, plasma cells, histiocytes, and granulocytes

### Nodular Lymphocyte Predominant
- Best prognosis
- Men > women
- Older adults
- Histology: Benign B-lymphocytes make up most of the cellular background
- Treatment: Rituximab alone (different from other HL)

### Lymphocyte Depleted
- Least common type (1% of HL)
- Poorest prognosis
- Elderly patients
- Associated with HIV
- Histology: Few lymphocytes compared to other types

# Lymphoma, Non-Hodgkin's

Malignant Transformation of Lymphoid Cells Residing in Lymphoid Tissues (B- and T-cell)

## Presentation

Features vary considerably with the type of NHL

NHL is 5x more common than Hodgkin's lymphoma

Median age of onset is >50

**Childhood forms are more aggressive**

Common themes:
- Peripheral Lymphadenopathy
- Presence of a mass on exam

B-symptoms:
- Fevers
- Night sweats
- Weight loss

## Diagnosis

 CSF examination for:

- Excisional lymph node biopsy

- HIV infection
- Neurologic symptoms
- Primary CNS lymphoma

Ann Arbor classification system is used for staging

## Treatment

Radiation, chemotherapy, or combination
Depends on histologic classification

Low-grade, indolent NHL ⟶ palliative intent

High-grade, aggressive NHL ⟶ curative intent

---

# B-Cell Lymphomas

## Burkitt's Lymphoma

- Children and adolescents
- High grade
- Jaw (African) or abdominal mass
- t(8;14): c-Myc overexpression
- Treatment: Aggressive chemotherapy

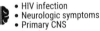

Reproduced with permission from Jameson J, Fauci AS, Kasper DL, et al: Harrison's Principles of Internal Medicine, 20th ed. New York, NY: McGraw Hill; 2018.

*Starry sky appearance:*
*Medium-sized cells with pale tingible-body macrophages*

## Diffuse Large B-Cell Lymphoma (DLBCL)

- Most common NHL in adults
- Many patients present with advanced disease
- Nonnodal involvement is a poor prognostic feature
- Treatment: R-CHOP chemotherapy

Reproduced with permission from Aster JC, Bunn H: Pathophysiology of Blood Disorders, 2nd ed. New York, NY: McGraw Hill; 2017.

*Large cells with prominent nucleoli*

## Follicular Lymphoma

- Adults (mean age 55)
- Low grade with indolent course
- Waxing and waning adenopathy
- t(14;18): Abnormal BCL-2 expression

Reproduced with permission from Press OW, Lichtman MA, Leonard JP: Williams Hematology Malignant Lymphoid Diseases. New York, NY: McGraw Hill; 2018.

*Expansion of lymph node follicle with small cleaved cells*

## Primary CNS Lymphoma

- Affects HIV-positive patients
- Often a DLBCL
- Presentation: Confusion, memory loss, and seizures
- Associated with EBV infection
- Brain imaging shows periventricular mass lesion

Reproduced with permission from Jameson J, Fauci AS, Kasper DL, et al: Harrison's Principles of Internal Medicine, 20th ed. New York, NY: McGraw Hill; 2018.

## Marginal Zone Lymphoma (MZL)

- Indolent lymphoma
- MALT lymphoma: Caused by chronic inflammation
  - Autoimmune diseases (Hashimoto thyroiditis)
  - Chronic infections (*Helicobacter pylori*)
  - Treatment of underlying infection may be curative

## Mantle Cell Lymphoma

- Rare lymphoma affecting elderly men
- Intermediate grade but often presents at late stage
- t(11;14): Cyclin D1 overexpression
- Tumor cells express B-cell markers (CD19, CD20) & CD5

---

# T-Cell Lymphomas

## Mycosis Fungoides

- Indolent cutaneous lymphoma
- Eczematous lesions and pruritis
- Diagnose with skin biopsy
- Can progress to **Sezary syndrome**
  - T-cell leukemia
  - Cerebriform Sezary cells present on blood smear

Reproduced with permission from Hillman RS, Ault KA, Leporrier M, et al: Hematology in Clinical Practice, 5th ed. New York, NY: McGraw Hill; 2011.

*Cerebriform cells with irregular, cleaved nuclei*

## Adult T-Cell Lymphoma

- Elderly adults (mean age 60)
- Common in Japan and Caribbean
- Etiology: Infection with HTLV-1
- Associated with IV drug use
- Presents with cutaneous and lytic bone lesions

Reproduced with permission from Matutes E, Bain BJ, Wotherspoon A: Lymphoid Malignancies: An Atlas of Investigation and Diagnosis. New York, NY: McGraw Hill; 2007.

*Cancer cell with "flower-shaped" nucleus*

# MTHFR Mutations

## Etiology and Definitions

**Results in hyperhomocysteinemia (HHcy)**

**Severe HHcy:** Homocysteine (Hcy) > 100 mmol/L

Less commonly due to MTHFR mutations, but possible

 See main HHcy card for details on severe HHcy

**Mild-to-Moderate HHcy:** Hcy 12-100 mmol/L

More common than severe form in general population

**MTHFR is the most common genetic cause**

Often multifactorial:
Dietary (folate deficiency)
Medications (eg, metformin)
Caffeine, alcohol

 **AR**

## Clinical Presentation

Lack of extensive data for mild MTHFR mutation symptoms

**Vascular**
<u>Atherosclerosis</u> (exact assoc. unclear)
MTHFR mutation alone is **NOT**
considered a VTE risk factor

**Obstetrics**
Preeclampsia and
miscarriages
Neural tube defects

**Neurodevelopmental**
Cognitive impairment in dementia
Possible assoc. with MS and Parkinson's

 Risks compounded when paired with other factors (eg, Factor V Leiden)

## Screening and Diagnosis

Currently no recommended screen for mild HHcy in older adults

Newborn screen does not account for MTHFR mutations

May be useful in patients with CV disease without known risk factors

## Treatment

Lack of clear benefit for treating mild HHcy from MTHFR mutation

**Pyridoxine (B6), folate, and betaine** supplementation do not improve CV outcomes

These approaches are more useful in severe or multifactorial HHcy

# Multiple Myeloma

## Clinical Features

HyperCalcemia
Renal involvement (**Bence Jones** proteins in urine)
Anemia
Bone lytic lesions

## Imaging

**"Punched out"** osteolytic lesions with little to no osteoblastic activity

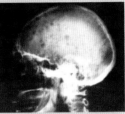

Used with permission from Dr. Geraldine Schechter.

## Characteristic Findings

**Plasma cells with "clock face" chromatin**

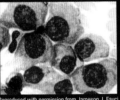

Reproduced with permission from Jameson J, Fauci AS, Kasper DL, et al: Harrison's Principles of Internal Medicine, 20th ed. New York, NY: McGraw Hill; 2018.

**M**

**"M-spike" on serum protein electrophoresis (usually IgG)**

### ! Diagnostic Criteria !

CRAB symptoms <u>OR</u> bone marrow clonal plasmacytosis of ≥60% <u>OR</u> kappa : lambda light chain ratio of ≥100:1
**PLUS**
≥10% plasma cells on bone marrow biopsy <u>OR</u> biopsy proven plasmacytoma

## Treatment

Induction chemotherapy

↓

Autologous hematopoietic cell transplant

↓

Maintenance chemotherapy

## ! Differentiate From... !

**Monoclonal Gammopathy of Unknown Significance (MGUS):** Asymptomatic on presentation, no CRAB symptoms. Develop MM at a rate of 1-2% per year.

**Waldenström Macroglobulinemia:** M-spike is IgM. Patients present with hyperviscoscity symptoms. No CRAB findings.

# Neutropenia

## Clinical Presentation

**Asymptomatic** at first
Recurrent bacterial **infection**

## Diagnosis

**ANC <1500 cells/μL, severe <500 cells/μL**

At <1000 cells/μL, infection risk increases sharply
At <500 cells/μL, impaired control of endogenous flora
At <200 cells/μL, inflammation is absent

## Etiologies

**Decreased Production**
Chemotherapy, aplastic anemia
**Peripheral Destruction**
Autoimmune, drug haptens
**Peripheral Pooling**
Usually transient (eg, hemodialysis)
**Hereditary**
Wiskott–Aldrich, Felty syndrome

## Neutropenic Fever

### Diagnosis
**Neutropenia** (ANC <1500 cells/μL)
+ any fever **>38.4°C (101°F)**
or **>38°C (100.4°F)**
for **>1 hour**

### Low-risk
Expected neutropenia <7 days, no comorbidities
### High-risk
Expected neutropenia >7 days, symptomatic, disease progression, neurologic changes, unstable hemodynamics

### Management
No DRE as it can cause peritoneal infection via microtears

Low-risk: Oral antibiotics (eg, fluoroquinolones, β-lactams)

High-risk:
**Culture** blood, urine, sputum. Include fungal cultures
**Broad spectrum** ABX with *Pseudomonas* coverage (eg, cefepime)
+/− vancomycin
Add **antifungals** if suspicious or if no improvement after 4-7 days

# Paroxysmal Nocturnal Hemoglobinuria

## Pathology

Deficiency in RBC's GPI anchor molecules (most commonly caused by mutation in the PIGA enzyme) →

Loss of CD55 and CD59 complement regulators → Complement attack of RBCs → Intravascular hemolysis

GPI

CD 55     CD 59

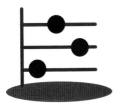

## Symptoms

Episodic dark urine
Anemia
Thrombosis
Abdominal Pain

## Diagnosis

Flow cytometry showing decreased or absent CD55/CD59 expression on surface of subset of RBCs

## Treatment

Mild: No intervention
Moderate: RBC transfusion, **eculizumab** (antibody to complement C5)
Severe: Stem cell transplant

# Plasminogen Deficiency
## A Hypercoagulable State

## Etiology & Background

- Genetic mutation in the gene for plasminogen
- Very rare
- Type I deficiency (hypoplasminogenemia)
  - ↓ Levels
  - Normal functional activity
  - Presents with ligneous conjunctivitis
- Type II deficiency (dysplasminogenemia)
  - ↓ Functional activity
  - Normal levels
- Acquired deficiency
  - ↓ Synthesis and/or increased catabolism
  - Eg: Liver disease, sepsis
- Plasminogen deficiency alone is unlikely to represent a true risk for thrombosis
- *Mutations promote thrombosis in the presence of other genetic defects such as Factor V Leiden mutation*
- Most data comes from mice in implicating plasminogen deficiency as a thrombotic risk factor

## Diagnosis & Workup

- Immunoassay to assess plasminogen levels

## Clinical Presentation

- Asymptomatic: Affected individuals do not routinely develop thrombosis
- Ligneous conjunctivitis

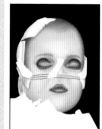

- *Deposition of fibrin in conjunctiva and mucous membranes*
- *Fibrin-rich pseudomembranes on the upper tarsal conjunctiva*
- *Pseudomembranes are white, yellow-white, or red with wood-like consistency*

- Venous thrombosis in presence of other thrombophilias such as Factor V Leiden

DVT      PE      Miscarriages

## Treatment

- No established guidelines for treatment
- Ligneous conjunctivitis: Lys-plasminogen, surgical excision

## Pathogenesis

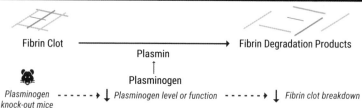

Fibrin Clot  ——————————→  Fibrin Degradation Products

Plasmin

↑

Plasminogen

*Plasminogen knock-out mice* ------→ ↓ *Plasminogen level or function* ------→ ↓ *Fibrin clot breakdown*

# Porphyria

**Etiology:** Porphyrias are metabolic disorders that are the result of deficiency or overactivity of enzymes in the **heme biosynthetic pathway** leading to accumulation of precursors. Symptoms can be triggered by **certain drugs, steroids, or alcohol,** among other things.

**Types:** Classified as **hepatic or erythropoietic,** depending on the primary site of heme synthesis dysregulation.

**Diagnosis:** Clinical suspicion based on symptoms (abdominal pain, sunlight sensitivity, blistering rash). Porphyrin precursors **(ALA or PBG)** in urine or porphyrins in urine, plasma, or feces. **Confirm with genetic testing.**

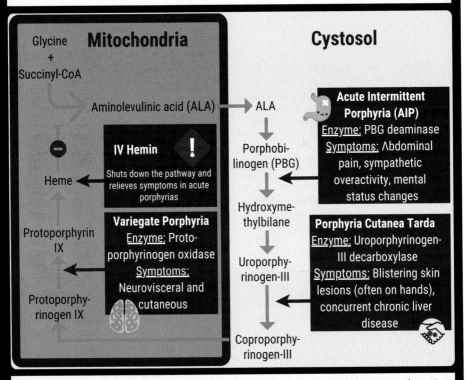

Treatment of cases of acute porphyrias refractory to hemin can include liver transplantation (for hepatic porphyrias) or stem cell transplantation (for erythropoietic porphyrias)

Most porphyrias are inherited disorders, but porphyria cutanea tarda is typically acquired and associated with iron overload, chronic hepatitis C, and HIV

# Protein C Deficiency
## A Hypercoagulable State

## Etiology

- **Inherited** deficiency of Protein C levels or activity
- **Acquired**
  - Acute liver injury
  - DIC
  - Meningococcal infections
  - Uremia
  - Cancer
  - Asparaginase
  - Autoantibodies
  - Vitamin-K antagonists

## Diagnosis & Workup

- Test when off of anticoagulants
- Protein C level and functional assay
- Do not routinely test patients
- Only test if:
  - Thrombophilic family
  - VTE and age <50 years
  - VTE in unusual location (brain)
  - Recurrent VTE

## Clinical Presentation

- Asymptomatic
- Venous thromboembolism (VTE)

DVT          PE          Miscarriages

- Neonatal purpura fulminans (homozygotes only)

Reproduced with permission from Mishkin DR, Rosh AJ: Female infant with Fever and rash, Ann Emerg Med. 2009 Aug;54(2):155.

- Warfarin-induced skin necrosis

Reproduced with permission from Kang S, Amagai M, Bruckner AL, et al: Fitzpatrick's Dermatology, 9th ed. New York, NY: McGraw Hill; 2019.

## Pathogenesis

IXa + VIIIa → Xa + Va → Thrombin → Fibrin Clot
(IIa)

Activated Protein C + Protein S

↓ Protein C activity          Increased
↓ Protein C levels  --------→ clot formation

## Treatment

- Avoid oral contraceptives
- VTE: Anticoagulation, if symptomatic
  - Heparin followed by Warfarin
  - NOAC
  - IVC filter if anticoagulation contraindicated
- Warfarin-induced skin necrosis:
  1. Stop Warfarin
  2. IV vitamin K
  3. Protein C source (FFP, PCC)
  4. Unfractionated heparin

# Protein S Deficiency
## A Hypercoagulable State

## Etiology

- **Inherited** deficiency of Protein S levels or activity
- Autosomal dominant
- Most patients heterozygous
- Protein S acts as a natural anticoagulant
- Defects in Protein S level or activity leads to a hypercoagulable state.
- Difficult to diagnose, as Protein S levels vary widely within the population.

## Diagnosis & Workup

- Use genetic testing or functional APC resistance assay
- Do not routinely test patients
- Only test if:
  - Thrombophilic family
  - VTE and age <50 years
  - VTE in unusual location (brain)
  - Recurrent VTE

## Pathogenesis

IXa + VIIIa → Xa + Va → Thrombin → Fibrin Clot
(IIa)

Activated Protein C + Protein S

↓ Protein S activity          Increased
↓ Protein S levels    --------→  clot
                              formation

## Clinical Presentation

- Asymptomatic
- Venous thromboembolism (VTE)

DVT         PE          Miscarriages

- Neonatal purpura fulminans
  (homozygotes only)

Reproduced with permission from Mishkin DR, Rosh AJ: Female infant with Fever and rash, Ann Emerg Med. 2009 Aug;54(2):155.

- Warfarin-induced skin necrosis

Reproduced with permission from Kang S, Amagai M, Bruckner AL, et al: Fitzpatrick's Dermatology, 9th ed. New York, NY: McGraw Hill; 2019.

## Treatment

- Avoid oral contraceptives
- Anticoagulation if symptomatic
  - Heparin followed by Warfarin (3-6 months for first event, 6-12 months for second event, lifelong for subsequent events)
- IVC filter if anticoagulation contraindicated

# Prothrombin G20210A Mutation

### A Hypercoagulable State

## 🍃 Etiology

- Prothrombin gene intron **point mutation**
- Gain-of-function mutation ⟶ increased prothrombin levels ⟶ hypercoagulable state
- Second-most common hereditary thrombophilia in Caucasians after Factor V Leiden

## 👤 Clinical Presentation

- Asymptomatic
- Venous thromboembolism (VTE)

DVT          PE

## ✅ Diagnosis & Workup

- Use genetic testing (PCR, ELISA)
- Do not use prothrombin levels to diagnose
- Do not routinely test patients
- Only consider testing if:
  - Thrombophilic family
  - VTE and age <50 years
  - VTE in unusual location (brain)
  - Recurrent VTE

## 💊 Treatment

- Avoid oral contraceptives
- Anticoagulation only if symptomatic

  - Heparin followed by Warfarin or NOAC (3-6 months for first event, 6-12 months for second event, lifelong for subsequent events)
- IVC filter if anticoagulation contraindicated

## 🧬 Pathogenesis

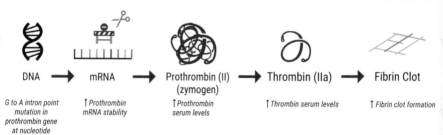

DNA ⟶ mRNA ⟶ Prothrombin (II) (zymogen) ⟶ Thrombin (IIa) ⟶ Fibrin Clot

*G to A intron point mutation in prothrombin gene at nucleotide 20210*

*↑Prothrombin mRNA stability*

*↑Prothrombin serum levels*

*↑Thrombin serum levels*

*↑Fibrin clot formation*

# Thalassemia

## α-Thalassemia

**2 α-globulin genes located on chromosome 16**

**Silent Carrier and Trait:** Asymptomatic
**Hb H:** Signs of significant hemolytic anemia
**Hydrops Fetalis:** Severely edematous at birth, **often stillborn or die within a day**

**Silent Carrier:**
CBC: Slight microcytosis
Electrophoresis: Normal
Smear: Normal

**Trait:**
CBC: MCV 65-78
Electrophoresis: **Increased beta: alpha ratio**
Smear: Occasional target cell

**Hb H:**
CBC: MCV 60-75
Electrophoresis: Increased beta:alpha ratio; **Hb H tetramer (10%)**
Smear: Many target cells and **Heinz bodies**

**Hydrops Fetalis:**
CBC: MCV 60-75
Electrophoresis: **90% Hb Barts**
Smear: Small, misshapen cells

## β-Thalassemia

**1 β-globulin gene located on chromosome 11**
Heterozygous for mutation = **β-thalassemia minor (trait)**
Homozygous = **β-thalassemia major (Cooley Anemia)**

### Genetics

### Signs and Symptoms

**Minor:**
Asymptomatic, normal life expectancy
**Major:**
**Significant anemia, iron overload** (bronze skin) **erythropoiesis** (hepatosplenomegaly, facial bone expansion with "chipmunk facies")

### Lab Findings and Diagnosis

**Minor:**
CBC: Mild microcytosis
Electrophoresis: Hemoglobin A2 increased
Smear: Target cells

**Major:**
CBC: Severe microcytosis
Electrophoresis: **Hemoglobin A2 and F increased**
Smear: Target cells; **variation in size and shape of RBCs**

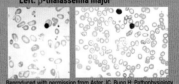

Left: β-thalassemia major

**Right:** β-thalassemia minor

 WATCH OUT!

Hemolytic-Uremic Syndrome (HUS) presents with only the 3 top symptoms and is usually associated with *E. coli* diarrhea

**Microangiopathic Hemolysis**

Deficiency OR autoantibody to
<u>ADAMTS13</u>

↓

Abnormally large VWF multimers

"Sticky" VWF multimers cause platelet aggregation, consuming platelets

Platelet microthrombi cause damage to red blood cells and stick in blood vessels causing end-organ damage

**Thrombocytopenia**

**Renal Impairment**

**Neurologic Impairment**

**Fever**

 Treat suspected cases with plasma exchange therapy +/- steroids ASAP

 Platelet transfusion is CONTRAINDICATED (they will just be consumed)

# Thymomas
## Thymic Tumors

## Clinical Presentation

 Broad peak from 35 to 70

 Equal incidence in women and men

 1/3 have no symptoms

 1/3 have local compressive symptoms: Cough, dyspnea, chest pain

1/3 have paraneoplastic syndromes: Myasthenia gravis (40-45%), other autoimmune (pure red cell aplasia, agammaglobulinemia)

## Workup

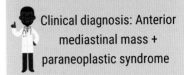 Clinical diagnosis: Anterior mediastinal mass + paraneoplastic syndrome

- CT: Solid anterior mass
- Assess for myasthenia gravis: AchR autoantibody screening, EMG, Tensilon test

## Treatment

Surgical: Complete resection

Medical: Treat paraneoplastic syndrome *prior* to surgery

## Outcomes

If early stage, 70-90% 10-year survival with resection

Indolent: Tends to recur locally

# Tumor Lysis Syndrome

## Diagnosis

**Laboratory TLS**
Changes in 2 or more of the **"PUCK"** lab values →

**Clinical TLS**
**Laboratory TLS**
+
1 or more clinical **symptoms** (see below)

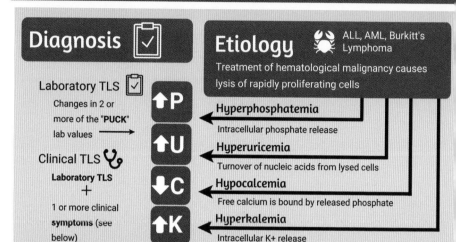

**↑P**
**↑U**
**↓C**
**↑K**

## Etiology
ALL, AML, Burkitt's Lymphoma
Treatment of hematological malignancy causes lysis of rapidly proliferating cells

**Hyperphosphatemia**
Intracellular phosphate release

**Hyperuricemia**
Turnover of nucleic acids from lysed cells

**Hypocalcemia**
Free calcium is bound by released phosphate

**Hyperkalemia**
Intracellular K+ release

## Clinical Presentation

 **Acute Renal Failure**
**Uric acid** crystals precipitate in renal tubules
**Calcium phosphate** buildup and hyperphosphatemia contribute
Elevated serum **creatinine**

 **Seizure**
Due to electrolyte disturbances in the CNS

 **Neuromuscular Irritability**
**Hypocalcemia** causes painful muscle spasms

 **Ventricular Arrhythmias**
Due to **hyperkalemia**, particularly in the case of acute renal failure
Can cause sudden **death**

## Prevention and Treatment

Prior to chemotherapy
 Reduce serum uric acid
**Allopurinol**
If resistant, **rasburicase**
- unless G6PD deficient
 **Aggressive hydration**

 If acute renal failure occurs, initiate **dialysis**
K >6.0 mEq/L
Uric acid >10 mg/dL
Creatinine >10 mg/dL
Phosphate >10 mg/dL

 **Calcium gluconate** reduces risk of arrhythmia due to hyperkalemia. Oral potassium-lowering drugs can also be used.

# von Willebrand Disease (vWD)

## Etiology

**von Willebrand Factor (vWF)**
- Connects platelets to damaged vessel wall
- Stabilizes **Factor VIII**

20 forms of vWD based on *vWF* gene mutation

Most commonly, inherited AD

vWF is cleaved by ADAMTS13 (see TTP card)

## Clinical Presentation

**Most commonly...**
- Symptoms vary depending on mutation/penetrance
- **Mucocutaneous** bleeding/epistaxis
- Menorrhagia
- **Hematomas**/bruising

**Rarely...**
- Hemarthroses are very rare (UNLIKE in hemophilia)
- ONLY Type 2B has thrombocytopenia

## Diagnosis

- PT and PTT not useful (but ⬆ PTT due to low Factor VIII)
- Quantitative vWF antigen levels
- **Ristocetin cofactor** assay to assess vWF activity

**Normal PT**
**⬆ PTT**

## Treatment

- **Desmopressin**
  - Increases secretion of vWF and Factor VIII
- More **severe** cases may need vWF supplementation

**DDAVP**
**⬆ vWF,**
**FVIII**

# Waldenström Macroglobulinemia

## Symptoms of Hyperviscosity

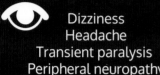

Dizziness
Headache
Transient paralysis
Peripheral neuropathy
Tinnitus
Vision changes
Epistaxis

## Other Symptoms

Constitutional "B" symptoms
Recurrent infections
Hepatosplenomegaly
Lymphadenopathy

## Distinct from

## Multiple Myeloma

No CRAB symptoms
M-spike is IgM rather than IgG

**Lymphoplasmacytic lymphoma (≥10% in bone marrow required for dignosis)**

## Treatment

<u>Asymptomatic</u> = follow and reevaluate every 4-6 months
<u>Hyperviscosity symptoms</u> = consider emergency plasmapheresis
<u>Symptomatic without hyperviscosity</u> = chemo

## Lab Findings

Anemia
Rouleaux formation
Monoclonal IgM on SPEP
Elevated serum viscosity

# IgM

# References _____

**Amyloidosis**
Berk JL, Sanchorawala V. Amyloidosis. In: Jameson J, Fauci AS, Kasper DL, Hauser SL, Longo DL, Loscalzo J, eds. *Harrison's Principles of Internal Medicine*. 20th ed. New York, NY: McGraw Hill; 2018.

Le T, Bhushan V, Chen V, King M. *First Aid for the USMLE Step 2 CK*. 9th ed. New York: McGraw Hill; 2015.

Le T, Bhushan V, Sochat M, et al. *First Aid for the USMLE Step 1 2017*. New York, NY: McGraw Hill; 2017.

**Anemia, Aplastic**
Kaushansky K, Lichtman MA, Prchal JT, et al, eds. *Williams Hematology*. 9th ed. New York, NY: McGraw Hill; 2015.

**Anemia, Autoimmune Hemolytic**
Le T, Bhushan V, Sochat M, et al. *Pediatrics. First Aid for the USMLE Step 1 2017: A Student-to-Student Guide*. New York, NY: McGraw Hill; 2017.

Papadakis MA, McPhee SJ, Rabow MW, eds. *Current Medical Diagnosis & Treatment 2019*. New York, NY: McGraw Hill; 2019.

**Anemia, Chronic Inflammation**
Jameson J, Fauci AS, Kasper DL, Hauser SL, Longo DL, Loscalzo J, eds. *Harrison's Principles of Internal Medicine*. 20th ed. New York, NY: McGraw Hill; 2018.

Le T, Bhushan V, Sochat M, et al. *First Aid for the USMLE Step 1 2017*. New York, NY: McGraw Hill; 2017.

**Anemia, Iron Deficiency**
Jameson J, Fauci AS, Kasper DL, Hauser SL, Longo DL, Loscalzo J, eds. *Harrison's Principles of Internal Medicine*. 20th ed. New York, NY: McGraw Hill; 2018.

Le T, Bhushan V, Sochat M, et al. *First Aid for the USMLE Step 1 2017*. New York, NY: McGraw Hill; 2017.

**Anemia, Megaloblastic**
Jameson J, Fauci AS, Kasper DL, Hauser SL, Longo DL, Loscalzo J, eds. *Harrison's Principles of Internal Medicine*. 20th ed. New York, NY: McGraw Hill; 2018.

Le T, Bhushan V, Sochat M, et al. *First Aid for the USMLE Step 1 2017*. New York, NY: McGraw Hill; 2017.

**Anemia, Sickle Cell**
Kaushansky K, Lichtman MA, Prchal JT, et al, eds. *Williams Hematology,* 9th ed. New York, NY: McGraw-Hill; 2015.

**Anemia, Sideroblastic**
Ponka P, Prchal JT. Polyclonal and hereditary sideroblastic anemias. In: Kaushansky K, Lichtman MA, Prchal JT, et al, eds. *Williams Hematology,* 9th ed. New York, NY: McGraw Hill; 2015.

**Antiphospholipid Syndrome**
Bauer KA. Screening for inherited thrombophilia in asymptomatic adults. *UpToDate*. Waltham, MA: UpToDate Inc. https://www.uptodate.com

Le T, Bhushan V, Chen V, King M. *First Aid for the USMLE Step 2 CK*. 9th ed. New York, NY: McGraw Hill; 2016.

Le T, Bhushan V, Sochat M, Chavda Y. *First Aid for the USMLE Step 1 2017*. New York, NY: McGraw Hill; 2017.

Erkan D, Zuily S. Clinical manifestations of antiphospholipid syndrome. *UpToDate*. Waltham, MA: UpToDate Inc. https://www.uptodate.com

Moutsopoulos HM. Antiphospholipid syndrome. In: Jameson J, Fauci AS, Kasper DL, Hauser SL, Longo DL, Loscalzo J, eds. *Harrison's Principles of Internal Medicine*. 20th ed. New York, NY: McGraw-Hill; 2018. http://accessmedicine.mhmedical.com/content.aspx?bookid=2129&sectionid=192284956. Accessed August 24, 2021.

Rand JH, Wolgast L. The antiphospholipid syndrome. In: Kaushansky K, Lichtman MA, Prchal JT, et al, eds. *Williams Hematology*. 9th ed. New York, NY: McGraw-Hill; 2015. http://accessmedicine.mhmedical.com/content.aspx?bookid=1581&sectionid=108084775. Accessed August 24, 2021.

## AT III Deficiency
Bauer KA. Screening for inherited thrombophilia in asymptomatic adults. *UpToDate*. Waltham, MA: UpToDate Inc. https://www.uptodate.com

Le T, Bhushan V, Chen V, King M. *First Aid for the USMLE Step 2 CK*. 9th ed. New York, NY: McGraw Hill; 2016.

Le T, Bhushan V, Sochat M, Chavda Y. *First Aid for the USMLE Step 1 2017*. New York, NY: McGraw Hill; 2017.

Middeldorp S, Coppens M. Hereditary thrombophilia. In: Kaushansky K, Lichtman MA, Prchal JT, et al, eds. *Williams Hematology*. 9th ed. New York, NY: McGraw-Hill; 2015. http://accessmedicine.mhmedical.com/content.aspx?bookid=1581&sectionid=108084622. Accessed August 24, 2021.

## Blood Transfusion Reactions
Kumar N, Law A, Choudhry NK, eds. *Teaching Rounds: A Visual Aid to Teaching Internal Medicine Pearls on the Wards*. New York, NY: McGraw-Hill; 2016.

Silvergleid AJ. Immunologic transfusion reactions. In: Kleinman S, Tirnauer JS, eds. *UpToDate*. Waltham, MA: UpToDate Inc. https://www.uptodate.com

## Disseminated Intravascular Coagulation
Arruda VR, Katherine AH. Coagulation disorders. In: Jameson J, Fauci AS, Kasper DL, Hauser SL, Longo DL, Loscalzo J, eds. *Harrison's Principles of Internal Medicine*. 20th ed. New York, NY: McGraw Hill; 2018. http://accessmedicine.mhmedical.com/content.aspx?bookid=2129§ionid=192018684.

Jameson J, Fauci AS, Kasper DL, Hauser SL, Longo DL, Loscalzo J, eds. *Harrison's Principles of Internal Medicine*. 20th ed. New York, NY: McGraw Hill; 2018.

Le T, Bhushan V, Chen V, King M. *First Aid for the USMLE Step 2 CK*. 9th ed. New York: McGraw Hill; 2015.

Le T, Bhushan V, Sochat M, et al. *First Aid for the USMLE Step 1 2017*. New York, NY: McGraw Hill; 2017.

## Dysfibrinogenemia
Neerman-Arbez M, de Moerloose P. Hereditary fibrinogen abnormalities. In: Kaushansky K, Lichtman MA, Prchal JT, et al, eds. *Williams Hematology*. 9th ed. New York, NY: McGraw Hill; 2015.

## Eosinophilia
Abonia JP, Putnam PE. Mepolizumab in eosinophilic disorders. *Expert Rev Clin Immunol*. 2011;7(4):411-417.

Holland SM, Gallin JI. Disorders of granulocytes and monocytes. In: Jameson J, Fauci AS, Kasper DL, Hauser SL, Longo DL, Loscalzo J, eds. *Harrison's Principles of Internal Medicine*. 20th ed. New York, NY: McGraw Hill; 2018.

## Erythrocytosis
Prchal JT. Primary and secondary erythrocytoses. In: Kaushansky K, Lichtman MA, Prchal JT, et al, eds. *Williams Hematology*. 9th ed. New York, NY: McGraw Hill; 2015.

Spivak JL. Polycythemia vera and other myeloproliferative neoplasms. In: Jameson J, Fauci AS, Kasper DL, Hauser SL, Longo DL, Loscalzo J, eds. *Harrison's Principles of Internal Medicine*. 20th ed. New York, NY: McGraw Hill; 2018.

## Factor V Leiden
Bauer KA. Screening for inherited thrombophilia in asymptomatic adults. *UpToDate*. Waltham, MA: UpToDate Inc. https://www.uptodate.com

Le T, Bhushan V, Chen V, King M. *First Aid for the USMLE Step 2 CK*. 9th ed. New York, NY: McGraw Hill; 2016.

Le T, Bhushan V, Sochat M, Chavda Y. *First Aid for the USMLE Step 1 2017*. New York, NY: McGraw Hill; 2017.

Middeldorp S, Coppens M. Hereditary thrombophilia. In: Kaushansky K, Lichtman MA, Prchal JT, et al, eds. *Williams Hematology*. 9th ed. New York, NY: McGraw-Hill; 2015. http://accessmedicine.mhmedical.com/content.aspx?bookid=1581&sectionid=108084622. Accessed August 24, 2021.

## G6PD Deficiency
Le T, Bhushan V, Sochat M, et al. Pediatrics. *First Aid for the USMLE Step 1 2017: A Student-to-Student Guide*. New York, NY: McGraw Hill; 2017.

## Graft vs Host Disease (GVHD)
Appelbaum FR. Hematopoietic cell transplantation. In: Jameson J, Fauci AS, Kasper DL, Hauser SL, Longo DL, Loscalzo J, eds. *Harrison's Principles of Internal Medicine*. 20th ed. New York, NY: McGraw Hill; 2018.

## Hemophilia A and B
Escobar MA, Key NS. Hemophilia A and hemophilia B. In: Kaushansky K, Lichtman MA, Prchal JT, et al, eds. *Williams Hematology*. 9th ed. New York, NY: McGraw Hill; 2015.

## Heparin-Induced Thrombocytopenia (HIT)
Konkle BA. Disorders of platelets and vessel wall. In: Jameson J, Fauci AS, Kasper DL, Hauser SL, Longo DL, Loscalzo J, eds. *Harrison's Principles of Internal Medicine*. 20th ed. New York, NY: McGraw Hill; 2018.

Le T, Bhushan V. *First Aid for the USMLE Step 2 CK*. 10th ed. New York: McGraw Hill; 2018.

## Hereditary Spherocytosis
Le T, Bhushan V, Sochat M, et al. Pediatrics. *First Aid for the USMLE Step 1 2017: A Student-to-Student Guide*. New York, NY: McGraw Hill; 2017.

## Hyperhomocysteinemia (HHcy)
Weisfeld-Adams J, Kirmse B. Hyperhomocysteinemia. In: Murray MF, Babyatsky MW, Giovanni MA, Alkuraya FS, Stewart DR, eds. *Clinical Genomics: Practical Applications in Adult Patient Care*. New York, NY: McGraw Hill; 2014.

## Idiopathic Thrombocytopenic Purpura
Le T, Bhushan V, Chen V, King M. *First Aid for the USMLE Step 2 CK*. 9th ed. New York: McGraw Hill; 2015.

Le T, Bhushan V, Sochat M, et al. *First Aid for the USMLE Step 1 2017*. New York, NY: McGraw Hill; 2017.

## Leukemia, Acute
Blum W, Bloomfield CD. Acute myeloid leukemia. In: Jameson J, Fauci AS, Kasper DL, Hauser SL, Longo DL, Loscalzo J, eds. *Harrison's Principles of Internal Medicine*. 20th ed. New York, NY: McGraw Hill; 2018.

Hoelzer D. Acute lymphoid leukemia. In: Jameson J, Fauci AS, Kasper DL, Hauser SL, Longo DL, Loscalzo J, eds. *Harrison's Principles of Internal Medicine*. 20th ed. New York, NY: McGraw Hill; 2018.

Le T, Bhushan V, Chen V, King M. *First Aid for the USMLE Step 2 CK*. 9th ed. New York: McGraw Hill; 2015.

Le T, Bhushan V, Sochat M, et al. *First Aid for the USMLE Step 1 2017*. New York, NY: McGraw Hill; 2017.

## Leukemia, Chronic Lymphocytic
Le T, Bhushan V, Chen V, King M. *First Aid for the USMLE Step 2 CK*. 9th ed. New York: McGraw Hill; 2015.

Le T, Bhushan V, Sochat M, et al. *First Aid for the USMLE Step 1 2017*. New York, NY: McGraw Hill; 2017.

Woyach JA, Byrd JC. Chronic lymphocytic leukemia. In: Jameson J, Fauci AS, Kasper DL, Hauser SL, Longo DL, Loscalzo J, eds. *Harrison's Principles of Internal Medicine*. 20th ed. New York, NY: McGraw Hill; 2018.

## Leukemia, Chronic Myelogenous
Kantarjian H, Cortes J. Chronic myeloid leukemia. In: Jameson J, Fauci AS, Kasper DL, Hauser SL, Longo DL, Loscalzo J, eds. *Harrison's Principles of Internal Medicine*. 20th ed. New York, NY: McGraw Hill; 2018.

Le T, Bhushan V, Chen V, King M. *First Aid for the USMLE Step 2 CK*. 9th ed. New York: McGraw Hill; 2015.
Le T, Bhushan V, Sochat M, et al. *First Aid for the USMLE Step 1 2017*. New York, NY: McGraw Hill; 2017.

**Leukemia, Hairy Cell**
Le T, Bhushan V, Chen V, King M. *First Aid for the USMLE Step 2 CK*. 9th ed. New York: McGraw Hill; 2015.
Le T, Bhushan V, Sochat M, et al. *First Aid for the USMLE Step 1 2017*. New York, NY: McGraw Hill; 2017.
Tefferi A, Longo DL. Less common hematologic malignancies. In: Jameson J, Fauci AS, Kasper DL, Hauser SL, Longo DL, Loscalzo J, eds. *Harrison's Principles of Internal Medicine*. 20th ed. New York, NY: McGraw Hill; 2018.

**Lymphoma, Cutaneous B-Cell**
Bagot M, Stadler R. Cutaneous lymphoma. In: Kang S, Amagai M, Bruckner AL, et al, eds. *Fitzpatrick's Dermatology*. 9th ed. New York, NY: McGraw Hill; 2019.
Lymphoma Research Foundation. Cutaneous B-Cell Lymphoma. https://www.lymphoma.org/aboutlymphoma/nhl/cbcl/. Accessed November 21, 2019.

**Lymphoma, Hodgkin's**
Jacobson CA, Longo DL. Hodgkin's lymphoma. In: Jameson J, Fauci AS, Kasper DL, Hauser SL, Longo DL, Loscalzo J, eds. *Harrison's Principles of Internal Medicine*. 20th ed. New York, NY: McGraw Hill; 2018.
Le T, Bhushan V, Chen V, King M. *First Aid for the USMLE Step 2 CK*. 9th ed. New York: McGraw Hill; 2015.
Le T, Bhushan V, Sochat M, et al. *First Aid for the USMLE Step 1 2017*. New York, NY: McGraw Hill; 2017.

**Lymphoma Non-Hodgkin's**
Jacobson CA, Longo DL. Non-Hodgkin's lymphoma. In: Jameson J, Fauci AS, Kasper DL, Hauser SL, Longo DL, Loscalzo J, eds. *Harrison's Principles of Internal Medicine*. 20th ed. New York, NY: McGraw Hill; 2018.
Le T, Bhushan V, Chen V, King M. *First Aid for the USMLE Step 2 CK*. 9th ed. New York: McGraw Hill; 2015.
Le T, Bhushan V, Sochat M, et al. *First Aid for the USMLE Step 1 2017*. New York, NY: McGraw Hill; 2017.

**MTHFR Mutation**
Weisfeld-Adams J, Kirmse B. Hyperhomocysteinemia. In: Murray MF, Babyatsky MW, Giovanni MA, Alkuraya FS, Stewart DR, eds. *Clinical Genomics: Practical Applications in Adult Patient Care*. New York, NY: McGraw Hill; 2014.

**Multiple Myeloma**
Jameson J, Fauci AS, Kasper DL, Hauser SL, Longo DL, Loscalzo J, eds. *Harrison's Principles of Internal Medicine*. 20th ed. New York, NY: McGraw Hill; 2018.
Kantarjian HM, Wolff RA, eds. *The MD Anderson Manual of Medical Oncology*. 3rd ed. New York, NY: McGraw-Hill; 2016.
Le T, Bhushan V, Sochat M, et al. Pediatrics. *First Aid for the USMLE Step 1 2017: A Student-to-Student Guide*. New York, NY: McGraw Hill; 2017.

**Neutropenia**
Holland SM, Gallin JI. Disorders of granulocytes and monocytes. In: Jameson J, Fauci AS, Kasper DL, Hauser SL, Longo DL, Loscalzo J, eds. *Harrison's Principles of Internal Medicine*. 20th ed. New York, NY: McGraw Hill; 2018.
Orellana VM, Winer ES. Hematologic malignancies. In: McKean SC, Ross JJ, Dressler DD, Scheurer DB, eds. *Principles and Practice of Hospital Medicine*. 2nd ed. New York, NY: McGraw Hill; 2017.

**Paroxysmal Nocturnal Hemoglobinuria**
Damon LE, Babis Andreadis C. Blood disorders. In: Papadakis MA, McPhee SJ, Rabow MW, eds. *Current Medical Diagnosis & Treatment 2019*. New York, NY: McGraw Hill; 2019. http://accessmedicine.mhmedical.com/content.aspx?bookid=2449&sectionid=194437986
Le T, Bhushan V. *First Aid for the USMLE Step 2 CK*. 10th ed. New York, NY: McGraw Hill; 2018.

Luzzatto L. Hemolytic anemias. In: Jameson J, Fauci AS, Kasper DL, Hauser SL, Longo DL, Loscalzo J, eds. *Harrison's Principles of Internal Medicine*. 20th ed. New York, NY: McGraw Hill; 2018. http://accessmedicine.mhmedical.com/content.aspx?bookid=2129&sectionid=192017418

## Plasminogen Deficiency

Bauer KA. Screening for inherited thrombophilia in asymptomatic adults. *UpToDate*. Waltham, MA: UpToDate Inc. https://www.uptodate.com

Bauer KA, Lip GYH. Overview of the causes of venous thrombosis. *UpToDate*. Waltham, MA: UpToDate Inc. https://www.uptodate.com

Fay WP. Thrombotic and hemorrhagic disorders due to abnormal fibrinolysis. *UpToDate*. Waltham, MA: UpToDate Inc. https://www.uptodate.com

Garcia-Ferrer FJ, Augsburger JJ, Corrêa ZM. Conjunctiva & tears. In: Riordan-Eva P, Augsburger JJ, eds. *Vaughan & Asbury's General Ophthalmology*. 19th ed. New York, NY: McGraw-Hill; 2017. http://accessmedicine.mhmedical.com/content.aspx?bookid=2186&sectionid=165516586. Accessed August 24, 2021.

Le T, Bhushan V, Chen V, King M. *First Aid for the USMLE Step 2 CK*. 9th ed. New York, NY: McGraw Hill; 2016.

Le T, Bhushan V, Sochat M, Chavda Y. *First Aid for the USMLE Step 1 2017*. New York, NY: McGraw Hill; 2017.

Rollins-Raval M. Hemostasis and thrombosis. In: Reisner HM, ed. *Pathology: A Modern Case Study*. 2nd ed. New York, NY: McGraw-Hill; 2015. http://accessmedicine.mhmedical.com/content.aspx?bookid=2748&sectionid=230840092. Accessed August 24, 2021.

Schott D, Dempfle CE, Beck P, et al. Therapy with a purified plasminogen concentrate in an infant with ligneous conjunctivitis and homozygous plasminogen deficiency. *N Eng J Med*. 1998;339:1679-1686.

## Porphyria

Le T, Bhushan V. *First Aid for the USMLE Step 2 CK*. 10th ed. New York: McGraw Hill; 2018.

## Protein C Deficiency

Bauer KA. Protein C deficiency. *UpToDate*. Waltham, MA: UpToDate Inc. https://www.uptodate.com

Bauer KA. Screening for inherited thrombophilia in asymptomatic adults. *UpToDate*. Waltham, MA: UpToDate Inc. https://www.uptodate.com

Heelan K, Sibbald C, Shear NH. Cutaneous reactions to drugs. In: Kang S, Amagai M, Bruckner AL, et al, eds. *Fitzpatrick's Dermatology*. 9th ed. New York, NY: McGraw-Hill; 2019. http://accessmedicine.mhmedical.com/content.aspx?bookid=2570&sectionid=210424280. Accessed August 24, 2021.

Le T, Bhishan V, Chen V, King M. *First Aid for the USMLE Step 2 CK*. 9th ed. New York, NY: McGraw Hill; 2016.

Le T, Bhushan V, Sochat M, Chavda Y. *First Aid for the USMLE Step 1 2017*. New York, NY: McGraw Hill; 2017.

Middeldorp S, Coppens M. Hereditary thrombophilia. In: Kaushansky K, Lichtman MA, Prchal JT, et al, eds. *Williams Hematology*. 9th ed. New York, NY: McGraw-Hill; 2015. http://accessmedicine.mhmedical.com/content.aspx?bookid=1581&sectionid=108084622. Accessed August 24, 2021.

## Protein S Deficiency

Bauer KA. Protein C deficiency. *UpToDate*. Waltham, MA: UpToDate Inc. https://www.uptodate.com

Bauer KA. Screening for inherited thrombophilia in asymptomatic adults. *UpToDate*. Waltham, MA: UpToDate Inc. https://www.uptodate.com

Heelan K, Sibbald C, Shear NH. Cutaneous reactions to drugs. In: Kang S, Amagai M, Bruckner AL, et al, eds. *Fitzpatrick's Dermatology*. 9th ed. New York, NY: McGraw-Hill; 2019. http://accessmedicine.mhmedical.com/content.aspx?bookid=2570&sectionid=210424280. Accessed August 24, 2021.

Le T, Bhishan V, Chen V, King M. *First Aid for the USMLE Step 2 CK*. 9th ed. New York, NY: McGraw Hill; 2016.

Le T, Bhushan V, Sochat M, Chavda Y. *First Aid for the USMLE Step 1 2017*. New York, NY: McGraw Hill; 2017.

Middeldorp S, Coppens M. Hereditary thrombophilia. In: Kaushansky K, Lichtman MA, Prchal JT, et al, eds. *Williams Hematology*. 9th ed. New York, NY: McGraw-Hill; 2015. http://accessmedicine.mhmedical.com/content.aspx?bookid=1581&sectionid=108084622. Accessed August 24, 2021.

## Prothrombin G20210A Mutation
Bauer KA. Prothrombin G2021A. *UpToDate*. Waltham, MA: UpToDate Inc. https://www.uptodate.com

Bauer KA. Screening for inherited thrombophilia in asymptomatic adults. *UpToDate*. Waltham, MA: UpToDate Inc. https://www.uptodate.com

Le T, Bhushan V, Chen V, King M. *First Aid for the USMLE Step 2 CK*. 9th ed. New York, NY: McGraw Hill; 2016.

Le T, Bhushan V, Sochat M, Chavda Y. *First Aid for the USMLE Step 1 2017*. New York, NY: McGraw Hill; 2017.

Middeldorp S, Coppens M. Hereditary thrombophilia. In: Kaushansky K, Lichtman MA, Prchal JT, et al, eds. *Williams Hematology*. 9th ed. New York, NY: McGraw-Hill; 2015. http://accessmedicine.mhmedical.com/content.aspx?bookid=1581&sectionid=108084622. Accessed August 24, 2021.

## Thalassemia
Bunn H, Sankaran VG. Thalassemia. In: Aster JC, Bunn H, eds. *Pathophysiology of Blood Disorders*. 2nd ed. New York, NY: McGraw Hill; 2016.

## Thrombotic Thrombocytopenic Purpura
Konkle BA. Disorders of platelets and vessel wall. In: Jameson J, Fauci AS, Kasper DL, Hauser SL, Longo DL, Loscalzo J, eds. *Harrison's Principles of Internal Medicine*. 20th ed. New York, NY: McGraw Hill; 2018. http://accessmedicine.mhmedical.com/content.aspx?bookid=2129&ionid=192018598.

Le T, Bhushan V, Chen V, King M. *First Aid for the USMLE Step 2 CK*. 9th ed. New York: McGraw Hill; 2015.

Le T, Bhushan V, Sochat M, et al. *First Aid for the USMLE Step 1 2017*. New York, NY: McGraw Hill; 2017.

## Thymoma
Burt BM, Shrager JB. Benign and malignant neoplasms of the mediastinum. In: Grippi MA, Elias JA, Fishman JA, et al. *Fishman's Pulmonary Diseases and Disorders*. 5th ed. New York, NY: McGraw Hill; 2015.

Dunphy CH, Fedoriw Y, Mathews SP, Perjar I. Hematopathology. In: Reisner HM, ed. *Pathology: A Modern Case Study*. 2nd ed. New York, NY: McGraw Hill; 2020.

Le T, Bhushan V, Chen V, King M. *First Aid for the USMLE Step 2 CK*. 9th ed. New York: McGraw Hill; 2015.

Le T, Bhushan V, Sochat M, et al. *First Aid for the USMLE Step 1 2017*. New York, NY: McGraw Hill; 2017.

## Tumor Lysis Syndrome
Bishop KD, Rizack T. Oncologic emergencies. In: McKean SC, Ross JJ, Dressler DD, Scheurer DB, eds. *Principles and Practice of Hospital Medicine*. 2nd ed. New York, NY: McGraw Hill; 2017.

Gucalp R, Dutcher JP. Oncologic emergencies. In: Jameson J, Fauci AS, Kasper DL, Hauser SL, Longo DL, Loscalzo J, eds. *Harrison's Principles of Internal Medicine*. 20th ed. New York, NY: McGraw Hill; 2018.

## von Willebrand Disease (vWD)
Johnsen J, Ginsburg D. von Willebrand disease. In: Kaushansky K, Lichtman MA, Prchal JT, et al, eds. *Williams Hematology*. 9th ed. New York, NY: McGraw Hill; 2015.

## Waldenström Macroglobulinemia
Munshi NC, Longo DL, Anderson KC. Plasma cell disorders. In: Jameson J, Fauci AS, Kasper DL, Hauser SL, Longo DL, Loscalzo J, eds. *Harrison's Principles of Internal Medicine*. 20th ed. McGraw Hill; 2018.

# Infectious Diseases

*Onyema Ogbuagu, MBBCh, FACP, FIDSA*

# Acute Pharyngitis

## Epidemiology

**Acute pharyngitis is extremely common and ~30% cases have unknown etiology**

**Viral is most common etiology**
- Rhinovirus/enterovirus, coronavirus
- EBV, CMV, HIV, adenovirus

**Bacterial**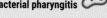

- *S. pyogenes* (β-hemolytic *Streptococci*)
- *C. diphtheriae, N. gonorrhoeae*
- *Fusobacterium necrophorum* causative agent in Lemierre's disease

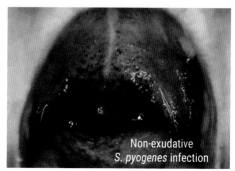

Non-exudative
*S. pyogenes* infection

Reproduced with permission from Public Health Image Library, Centers for Disease Control and Prevention. Photo contributor: Dr. Heinz F. Eichenwald.

## Clinical Presentation

**\*\*Symptoms are not reliably diagnostic\*\***

**Viral pharyngitis**
- Typically less severe, resembles URI
- Splenomegaly, malaise, and exudates suggest EBV or CMV
- Significant constitutional symptoms suggest acute HIV infection
- Concurrent conjunctivitis and fever suggest adenovirus

**Bacterial pharyngitis**
- Fever and tender cervical LAD
- Exudative pharyngitis suggests *S. pyogenes*
- Centor score for strep throat: Age, exudates, cervical LAD, fever, and cough
- Cough is uncommon
- Sexual history may suggest *N. gonorrhoeae*
- Pseudomembrane formation seen in *C. diphtheriae* infections
- Lemierre's disease is rapidly progressive

## Diagnosis & Management

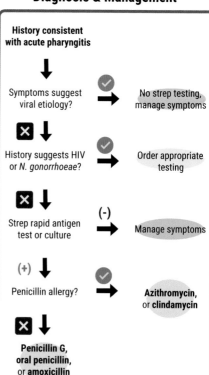

History consistent with acute pharyngitis

Symptoms suggest viral etiology? → No strep testing, manage symptoms

History suggests HIV or *N. gonorrhoeae*? → Order appropriate testing

Strep rapid antigen test or culture → (-) Manage symptoms

(+) Penicillin allergy? → **Azithromycin, or clindamycin**

**Penicillin G, oral penicillin, or amoxicillin**

# Anaplasmosis

*Anaplasma phagocytophilum* is a member of the Rickettsiaceae family that causes human granulocytic anaplasmosis (HGA).

*A. phagocytophilum* is an **obligate intracellular bacteria**, which survives and propagates within the host cell and can evade neutrophil antimicrobial functions.

## Pathogenesis

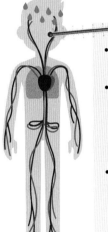

- Caused by *Anaplasma phagocytophilum*
- Carried by the black-legged tick (*Ixodes scapularis*) in the Northeast/Midwestern and the western black-legged tick (*Ixodes pacificus*) along the West Coast
- Causes a disease similar to but more severe than human monocytic ehrlichiosis (HME), caused by *Ehrlichia chaffeensis*

## Clinical Manifestation

- High fever, severe headache, and myalgias are prominent symptoms.
- Lymphopenia, elevated liver enzyme values, and thrombocytopenia are seen.

## Epidemiology

- Disease is endemic in northeastern and north central states (eg, Connecticut and Wisconsin).
- Distribution is similar to that of Lyme disease.

**Most cases of ehrlichiosis and anaplasmosis are clinically similar to Rocky Mountain spotted fever** and are characterized by fever, headache, and often severe multisystem involvement but with a lower incidence of rash.

## Diagnosis

- Antibody assays and PCR are diagnostically useful.
- **Morulae** can be seen in **PMN cells** on peripheral blood smears during acute illness.
- Serial antibody assays and PCR are diagnostically useful.

## Treatment

- Doxycycline, chloramphenicol

# Anthrax (*Bacillus anthracis*)

## Etiology

- *Bacillus anthracis*—Gram (+) rod
- Spores found in animal products and soil
- Spore-forming, nonmotile
- **Unique capsule of D-glutamate**
- Facultative anaerobe

**Exotoxins**
- Edema factor—Raises cAMP, causes edema
- Lethal factor—Inactivates MAPK, cell death

**Transmission**
- Spores enter skin abrasion or ingested/inhaled
- No human-to-human transmission
- Classically **"wool-sorter's disease"**

Reproduced with permission from Public Health Image Library, Centers for Disease Control and Prevention. Photo contributor: Dr. James H. Steele.

**Necrotic eschar**

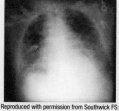

Reproduced with permission from Southwick FS: Infectious Diseases: A Clinical Short Course, 4th ed. New York, NY: McGraw Hill; 2020.

Reproduced with permission from Public Health Image Library, Centers for Disease Control and Prevention.

Reproduced with permission from Tintinalli J, Ma O, Yealy DM, et al: Tintinalli's Emergency Medicine: A Comprehensive Study Guide. 9th ed. New York, NY: McGraw Hill; 2020.

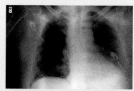

Reproduced with permission from Tintinalli J, Ma O, Yealy DM, et al: Tintinalli's Emergency Medicine: A Comprehensive Study Guide. 9th ed. New York, NY: McGraw Hill; 2020.

## Diagnosis

- Generates "box-car" like chains
- Spores not seen on smears
- Nonhemolytic colonies on blood agar
- **"Comet's tail"** seen with colonies
- PCR available for suspected bioterrorism

## Clinical Manifestations

**Cutaneous**
- Painless **black eschar**
- Cellular necrosis due to lethal factor
- Progresses to bacteremia in untreated

**Gastrointestinal**
- Abdominal pain, vomiting, bloody diarrhea

**Pulmonary**
- High case fatality
- Begins as dry cough, substernal pressure
- Hemorrhagic mediastinitis can occur
- **Mediastinal widening seen on chest X-ray**
- Rapidly progresses to hemorrhagic pleural effusions, shock, and death
- Hemorrhagic meningitis possible

## Treatment

- **Ciprofloxacin or doxycycline**
- Raxibacumab or obiltoxaximab for pulmonary anthrax
- Drug resistance not documented

## Prevention

- Prophylactic antibodies if potentially exposed to spores
- Six-dose **BioThrax vaccine available** for at-risk populations (ie, military personnel)
- Incinerate animals that die from suspected anthrax infections

# Aspergillus

*Aspergillus* species, especially *Aspergillus fumigatus*, cause infections of the skin, ears, and other organs; "fungus ball" in the lungs; and allergic bronchopulmonary aspergillosis (ABPA).

## Pathogenesis

**1** Colonization

| Paranasal sinuses | Cornea | Wounds, burns | External ear |

**2** Invasion

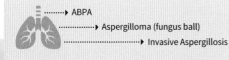

........▶ ABPA
...............▶ Aspergilloma (fungus ball)
.......................▶ Invasive Aspergillosis

| Condition | Risk Factor |
|---|---|
| Lung invasion, with hemoptysis and granulomas | Immunocompromised (especially neutropenia) |
| Aspergilloma (fungus ball) | Existing cavities within the lungs, especially produced by TB |
| Allergic bronchopulmonary aspergillosis (ABPA) | Hypersensitivity reaction to *Aspergillus* in the bronchi |

## Properties and Transmission

*Aspergillus* species exist **only as molds.** They have **septate hyphae** (long arrow, A) that form V-shaped (dichotomous) branches (short arrow, A).

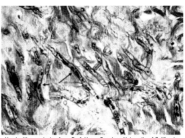

Used with permission from Prof. Henry Sanchez, University of California, San Francisco School of Medicine.

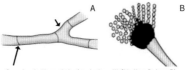

Reproduced with permission from Levinson W, Chin-Hong P, Joyce EA, et al: Review of Medical Microbiology & Immunology: A Guide to Clinical Infectious Diseases, 15th ed. New York, NY: McGraw Hill; 2018.

These molds are widely distributed in nature. They grow on decaying vegetation, producing chains of condida (B). **Transmission is by airborne conidia.**

## Laboratory Diagnosis

- Biopsy specimens show septate, branching hyphae invading tissue (as in figure above).
- Cultures show colonies with characteristic radiating chains of conidia (B).
- Positive culture does not prove disease; colonization is common.
- Invasive aspergillosis may cause high titers of galactomannan antigen in serum.
- Patients with ABPA have high levels of IgE specific for *Aspergillus* antigens and prominent eosinophilia.

## Treatment

- Invasive aspergillosis is treated with voriconazole or amphotericin B.
- Liposomal amphotericin B should be used in patients with preexisting kidney damage.
- A fungus ball growing in a sinus or in a pulmonary cavity can be surgically removed.
- ABPA can be treated with corticosteroids and antifungal agents, such as itraconazole.

### Epidemiology and prevention

- Most cases of *aspergillosis* are sporadic, not outbreaks.
- Hospital construction/renovation has been associated with outbreaks of *invasive aspergillosis*.

# Babesiosis
## *Babesia microti*

**Source:** Ixodes tick (endemic Northeast United States)

**Pathogenesis:** Infects red blood cells and lyse

**More likely to be severe in hyposplenic/asplenic, immunocompromised, malignancy, children and elderly**

**Ixodes tick coinfections:**
Lyme (incubation = 3-32 days)
Anaplasma (incubation = 4-8 days)
Babesia (incubation = 7-28 days)
Powassan virus (incubation = 7-30 days, leads to severe encephalitis)

## Clinical Presentation and Sequelae

**Non-severe**
Fever
Hemolytic anemia
Thrombocytopenia
Parasitemia
Coinfection with Lyme disease and anaplasma (look for erythema migrans to confirm)

**Severe**
ARDS
DIC
Acute CHF
Renal failure
Splenic infarcts/rupture

## Diagnosis

**Blood smear:** Giemsa stain
- Maltese cross (pathognomonic)
- Ring form
- May require repeated blood smears over several days if levels are too low

**Real-time PCR**

**Serology:**
- Tests must be repeated to differentiate current infection vs recent or past infections.
- IgM > 1:64 2 weeks after onset
- IgG > 1:1024

- 4x rise in Babesia IgG titers in acute and convalescent serum confirms infection.

**Ring form**

**Maltese cross**

Reproduced with permission from Centers for Disease Control and Prevention. U.S. Department of Health & Human Services https://www.cdc.gov/parasites/babesiosis/diagnosis.html

Reproduced with permission from Public Health Image Library, Centers for Disease Control and Prevention. Photo contributor: Dr. S. Glenn.

## Treatment

**Mild\***
Atovaquone + Azithromycin

**Severe\***
Quinine + Clindamycin
(Quinine may lead to adverse effects collectively called "Cinchonism")

\*Add doxycycline if suspect Lyme/anaplasma coinfection

# Brain Abscess

A brain abscess is a localized, walled-off collection of pus surrounded by a fibrous capsule. **Bacteria** are the most common cause, but **fungi** and **protozoa** may be causative agents. Viruses do not cause brain abscesses. A brain abscess is a recognized complication of head/neck pyogenic infections.

## Pathophysiology

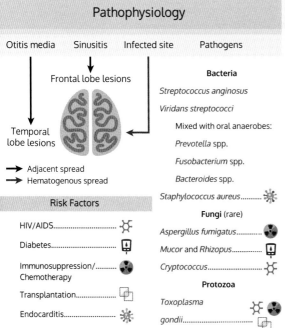

Otitis media    Sinusitis    Infected site    Pathogens

Frontal lobe lesions

Temporal lobe lesions

→ Adjacent spread
→ Hematogenous spread

**Bacteria**

*Streptococcus anginosus*

*Viridans streptococci*

Mixed with oral anaerobes:

*Prevotella* spp.

*Fusobacterium* spp.

*Bacteroides* spp.

*Staphylococcus aureus*...........

**Fungi** (rare)

*Aspergillus fumigatus*.............

*Mucor* and *Rhizopus*...............

*Cryptococcus*...........................

**Protozoa**

*Toxoplasma gondii*...................................

### Risk Factors

HIV/AIDS................................
Diabetes.................................
Immunosuppression/...........
Chemotherapy
Transplantation....................
Endocarditis..........................

## Clinical Manifestation

**Headache** alone is the most common symptom of brain abscess, and thus can often be easy to miss early in presentation.

As the lesion expands, patients may develop **focal neurologic deficits** and **seizures**.

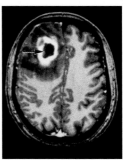

Brain abscess. Red arrow points to a characteristic ring-enhancing lesion.

## Diagnosis

- **Imaging**: CT or MRI with contrast (preferred); can reveal a "ring-enhancing" lesion (see image)
- **Microbiologic Diagnosis**: Pus obtained from the abscess by biopsy is cultured for bacteria and fungi
- **Diagnosis of Toxoplasma**: Usually made by identifying specific radiographic findings in an at-risk host (eg, HIV/AIDS) with a positive toxoplasma IgG and a response to specific antimicrobial therapy
- **Notes**: (1) Bacterial brain abscesses, the Gram stain frequently reveals a mixed infection, (2) aspiration of pus from the lesion is both diagnostic and therapeutic, draining the abscess

## Treatment

- Empiric antimicrobial therapy for **bacterial brain abscesses** consists of a third-generation cephalosporin, such as ceftriaxone or cefotaxime, plus metronidazole (for anaerobic bacteria).
- Treatment of **toxoplasma brain abscess** includes a combination of pyrimethamine and sulfadiazine.
- Surgical therapy may be required for bacterial and fungal brain abscesses in addition to drug administration.

**Prevention** **(1)** Treatment of AIDS with antiretroviral therapy, **(2)** primary prophylaxis with trimethoprim-sulfamethoxazole when the CD4 count is <100 cells/μL, **(3)** early treatment of head/neck infections, and **(4)** tight control of blood glucose.

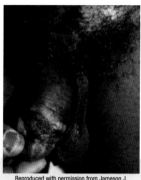

Reproduced with permission from Jameson J, Fauci AS, Kasper DL, et al: Harrison's Principles of Internal Medicine, 20th ed. New York, NY: McGraw Hill; 2018.

## Epidemiology & Etiology

- *Haemophilus ducreyi*
- **Sexually transmitted infection**
- Fastidious, **Gram (−)** *coccobacillus*
- Most common in developing world
- Increases risk of HIV transmission
- **M:F ratio 3:1 to 25:1 in outbreaks**

## Clinical Presentation

- Incubation period of 4-7 days
- Non-indurated, painful **genital ulcer(s)**
- Ulcer begins as papule then pustule
- **Inguinal lymphadenopathy**

 **Clinical Pearl**

Syphilitic chancre is painless, not painful like chancroid or HSV

# Chancroid
*Haemophilus ducreyi*

## Diagnosis

- *H. ducreyi* is fastidious and culture often not obtained

- **Culture from chancroid lesion**

- Aspiration of suppurative lymph node possible

- **Rule out syphilis and HSV**

## Prevention
- Avoid high-risk behavior

- Prior infection doesn't confer immunity to chancroid

## Management
**Multiple Options**
- Single dose of azithromycin
- Single shot of ceftriaxone
- 3 days ciprofloxacin

**Treatment failure may indicate incorrect diagnosis (ie, HSV)**

Contact tracing needs performed

# Chlamydiae

- Obligate intracellular bacteria
- Cell wall lacks muramic acid
- Cause **conjunctivitis, GU infections, pneumonia**
- Life cycle involves infectious elementary bodies

## *Chlamydia trachomatis*

**Epidemiology**
- Most common bacterial STI in the United States
- Transmitted by sexual contact or perinatal
- A-B strains (trachoma), D-K strains (STI), L1-L3 (lymphogranuloma venereum [LGV])

**Clinical Presentation**
- Asymptomatic infections are common
- Acute dysuria, non-purulent urethral discharge in men
- Proctitis in men who practice anoreceptive sex
- Cervicitis, vaginal discharge in women
- Trachoma—chronic conjunctivitis
- LGV—genital ulcer, inguinal LAD

**Sequelae**
- Pelvic inflammatory disease
- Reiter's snydrome—Autoimmune mediated arthritis, uveitis, conjunctivitis
- Trachoma—Blindness

**Diagnosis**
- NAAT on urine sample

**Management**
- Azithromycin for D K strains
- Oral erythromycin for neonatal conjunctivitis
- Treat possible coinfection of *N. gonorrhoeae* with ceftriaxone
- Doxycycline for L1-L3 strains

**Prevention**
- Contact tracing, routine screening
- Safe sex practices

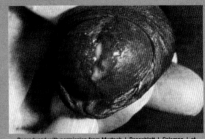

Reproduced with permission from Murtagh J, Rosenblatt J, Coleman J, et al: Murtagh's General Practice, 7th ed. New York, NY: McGraw Hill; 2018.

## *Chlamydia pneumoniae*

**Epidemiology**
- Transmitted human-to-human by respiratory droplets

**Clinical Presentation**
- Atypical "walking" pneumonia
- Asymptomatic presentation possible
- Diffuse infiltrates on chest X-ray

**Diagnosis**
- Serology

**Management**
- Doxycycline is first-line

## *Chlamydia psittaci*

**Epidemiology**
- No human-to-human transmission
- Spread by inhalation of droppings from infected bird (ie, parrot)

**Clinical Presentation**
- High fever and pneumonia
- Hepatomegaly, myocarditis possible if severe symptomatology

**Diagnosis**
- Serology
- History consistent with bird exposure

**Management**
- Doxycycline is first-line

**Prevention**
- Treat infected birds with doxycycline in bird feed

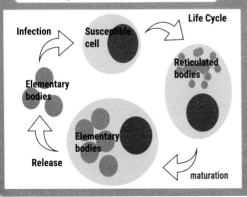

Life Cycle

Infection — Susceptible cell — Reticulated bodies — Elementary bodies — Release — maturation — Elementary bodies

# Coccidioidomycosis

## Etiology and Epidemiology

- *Coccidioides immitis* and *C. posadasi*
- Endemic to Southwestern United States and Latin America
- Arthrospores in soil, **spherules in lungs**
- Transmitted by inhalation of arthrospores, no human-to-human transmission
- **Risk factors** for disseminated disease: HIV, pregnancy, immunosuppressed, African American, Filipino

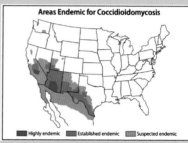

Areas Endemic for Coccidioidomycosis

Highly endemic    Established endemic    Suspected endemic

Reproduced with permission from Centers for Disease Control
https://www.cdc.gov/fungal/diseases/coccidioidomycosis/index.html

## Management

- **No treatment required for self-limited Valley Fever**
- Persistent lung lesions require fluconazole
- Disseminated disease requires **amphotericin B**
- Fluconazole +/− amphotericin B for meningitis

## Clinical Presentation

- Fever, malaise, cough resembling CAP
- **"Valley Fever" is self-limited**
- 10% patients have erythema nodosum or athralgias
- **Disseminated disease** in bone, meninges, skin, etc. if cell-mediated immunity impaired

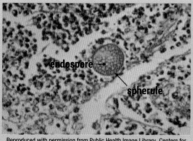

Reproduced with permission from Public Health Image Library, Centers for Disease Control and Prevention. Photo contributor: Dr. L. Georg.

**Erythema nodosum** (seen at right) is immune mediated and carries a favorable prognosis

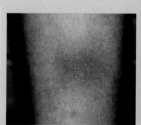

Reproduced with permission from Soutor C, Hordinsky MK: Clinical Dermatology. New York, NY: McGraw Hill; 2013.

## Diagnosis

- Demonstration of **spherules** in lung tissue biopsy is diagnostic
- Culture (+) Sabouraud's agar
- IgM and IgG titers, PCR available

## Prevention

- Avoid travel to endemic areas
- Prophylaxis with fluconazole may benefit immunocompromised patients

# Conjunctivitis

Conjunctivitis ("pink eye") is an inflammation of the conjunctiva that results in dilation of the blood vessels in the membrane causing the white sclera to become red.

## Pathogenesis

**Adenovirus**
**Enterovirus**

## Otitis media

*Haemophilus influenzae*
*Streptococcus pneumoniae*

## Pharyngitis

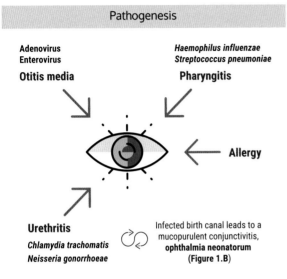

← **Allergy**

## Urethritis

*Chlamydia trachomatis*
*Neisseria gonorrhoeae*

Infected birth canal leads to a mucopurulent conjunctivitis, **ophthalmia neonatorum** (Figure 1.B)

## Clinical Manifestation

Inflammation in conjunctivitis causes the blood vessels in the conjunctiva to dilate and the underlying white sclera to appear red **(Figure 1.A)**. See Diagnosis for more details.

Conjunctivitis
Reproduced with permission from Prentice WE: Essentials of Athletic Injury Management, 10th ed. New York, NY: McGraw Hill; 2016.

Reproduced with permission from Public Health Image Library, Centers for Disease Control and Prevention.
Photo contributor: Dr Pledger J.

**1.A** Woman with conjunctivitis in the left eye
**1.B** Mucopurulent neonatal conjunctivitis

| Key: | | Neonates | Infants and Children | Adolescents and Adults |
|---|---|---|---|---|
| ↑ | If coexistent with this **syndrome**, these **organisms** are often **etiology** | *Chlamydia trachomatis* *Neisseria gonorrhoeae* | *Haemophilus influenzae* *Streptococcus pneumoniae* Adenovirus Enterovirus | Adenovirus *Chlamydia trachomatis* *Neisseria gonorrhoeae* |

## Diagnosis

- Diagnosis is based on clinical assessment
- Characteristic of exudate informative to differentiate between bacterial and viral
- **Purulent discharge common in bacterial causes of conjunctivitis**
- Examine the exudates by Gram stain and culture if patients do not improve within 48-72 hours despite treatment

## Treatment

### Viral conjunctivitis
- Supportive care: Artificial tears, cold compress, antibiotic drops to prevent bacterial infection
- Topical corticosteroids may also be used, but herpes virus infection must be excluded

### Bacterial conjunctivitis
- Treat with appropriate antimicrobial
- Topicals: Sulfacetamide, macrolides, ciprofloxacin
- Gonococcal: Ceftriaxone; Chlamydia: Tetracycline
- Prevention: Post birth topical erythromycin or tetracycline

# Cytomegalovirus

Double-stranded DNA virus (HHV-5)
Carriage in 40-100% of an adult population, yet asymptomatic in immunocompetent adults

## Transmission:

**Congenital**

**Primary** infection of mother during pregnancy

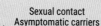
**Immunocompetent**

Sexual contact
Asymptomatic carriers

**Transplant**

Blood transfusions
CMV reactivation
Infection from donor tissue

**HIV**

Symptomatic if <50 CD4+
T-cells/microliter, CMV
seropositivity

## Clinical Manifestation:

Cytomegalic inclusion disease
Intracranial calcifications
Encephalitis
Microcephaly
Hearing loss

Mononucleosis
syndrome similar to
Epstein–Barr virus

Febrile leukopenia,
gastrointestinal disease,
pneumonia

CMV retinitis,
gastrointestinal disease,
neurologic disease

Reproduced with permission from Jameson J,
Fauci AS, Kasper DL, et al: Harrison's
Principles of Internal Medicine, 20th ed.
New York, NY: McGraw Hill; 2018.

**CMV Retinitis**

## Diagnosis:

**PCR** (most common method)

**Histology:**
"Owl's-eye" inclusions (similar to EBV mononucleosis)

**Serology:**
CMV antigenemia testing with immunofluorescence
assays

IgG anti-CMV antibodies are useful to predict CMV
infection risk in **transplant recipients**

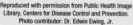

Reproduced with permission from Public Health Image
Library, Centers for Disease Control and Prevention.
Photo contributor: Dr. Edwin Ewing, Jr.

**Owl's-eye inclusion bodies in nucleus**

## Treatment:

**First-line:**

**Ganciclovir** or **Valganciclovir**
(adverse effects include bone marrow suppression)

**If resistant to Ganciclovir/Valganciclovir (ie, UL97 or
UL54 mutations):**

**Foscarnet**
(adverse effects include nephrotoxicity, electrolyte
disturbances, nausea, paresthesia)

**Cidofovir**
(adverse effects include nephrotoxicity)

# Ehrlichiosis

## Etiology & Epidemiology

- *Ehrlichia chaffeensis*, a rickettsial species
- Transmitted by **Ixodes** spp. ticks, **Lone Star** ticks (*Amblyomma* spp.), and **Dermacentor** spp. ticks

- South central and southeastern states
- Suspect in patients with recent tick exposure (ie, camping)

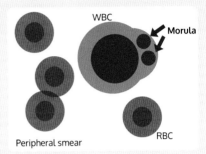

Peripheral smear

## Clinical Presentation

- One-week incubation period
- **High fever, severe headache, myalgias**
- Petechial rash often absent
- **Morula formation** in mononuclear leukocytes can be seen on blood smear

## Diagnosis

- Physical exam findings
- Serology with rise in antibody titer
- **Labs show elevated AST/ALT, thrombocytopenia, leukopenia**

**Clinical Pearl**

- Coinfection with *Rickettsia* spp. or *B. burgdorferi* possible

## Management

- **Treat with doxycycline**
- Empiric treatment often used
- **Uncommonly, untreated cases may require ICU**
- Complications include septicemic shock and disseminated intravascular coagulation (DIC)

# Encephalitis

Encephalitis is an infection of the brain parenchyma predominantly caused by viruses. Sometimes both the brain and the meninges are involved, a condition called meningoencephalitis (see Meningitis).

## Pathophysiology

### Route of Virus Introduction

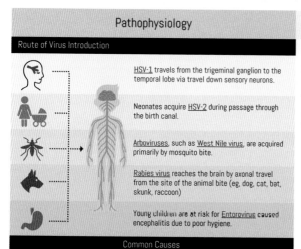

HSV-1 travels from the trigeminal ganglion to the temporal lobe via travel down sensory neurons.

Neonates acquire HSV-2 during passage through the birth canal.

Arboviruses, such as West Nile virus, are acquired primarily by mosquito bite.

Rabies virus reaches the brain by axonal travel from the site of the animal bite (eg, dog, cat, bat, skunk, raccoon)

Young children are at risk for Enterovirus caused encephalitis due to poor hygiene.

### Common Causes

HSV-1

HSV-2

West Nile Virus
Eastern Equine Encephalitis Virus
Western Equine Encephalitis Virus
St. Louis Encephalitis Virus

Enteroviruses

Rabies Virus

## Clinical Manifestation

Symptoms include fever, headache, and altered mental status, as well as seizures and focal neurologic deficits.

Rabies can present with hyperactivity, agitation, delirium, hydrophobia, and seizures (4/5 of cases) OR ascending paralysis without hyperactivity (1/5 of cases).

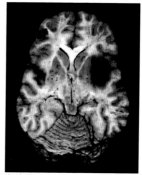

Reproduced with permission from Reisner H. Pathology a Modern Case Study, 2nd ed. New York, NY: McGraw Hill; 2020.

Encephalitis caused by herpes simplex virus-1. Note destruction of temporal lobe on left side of image.

## Diagnosis

- CSF analysis: Increased protein and normal to low glucose (can be variable)
- PCR-based testing of CSF: Used to determine etiology
- Radiographic imaging: Can be useful as in HSV encephalitis with temporal lobe abnormalities
- West Nile virus encephalitis is often diagnosed by finding WNV-specific IgM in the spinal fluid
- Rabies can be diagnosed by direct fluorescent antibody staining of a biopsy of skin from the nape of the neck; a PCR assay using CSF, saliva, or tissue can also be done

## Treatment

- Intravenous acyclovir is the treatment of choice for HSV-1, HSV-2, and VZV encephalitis.
- There is no antiviral therapy for Arboviral or Rabies encephalitis.

## Prevention

- Rabies: Pre-exposure prophylaxis: Killed vaccine should be given to veterinarians and at-risk people. Postexposure prophylaxis: Killed vaccine and hyperimmune globulins that contain a high titer of anti-rabies virus antibodies.
- There is no vaccine for HSV-1, HSV-2, WNV, and Enteroviruses.

# Endocarditis

Infection of the inside lining of the heart (endocardium), usually involving the cardiac valves. It can lead to extensive tissue damage and is often fatal.

## Pathogenesis

Endocardial surface injury

⬇

Platelet–fibrin–thrombus formation at the site of injury

⬇

Bacterial entry into the circulation

⬇

Bacterial adherence to the injured endocardial surface

## Host Risk Factors

- Acquired valvular heart lesions
- Hypertrophic cardiomyopathy
- Congenital heart diseases
- Prosthetic heart valve 🦷
- Intravenous drug use ✒
- Poor dentition 🦷

### Bacterial Virulence

- *S. aureus*.............. ❗ ✒ ~30%
- *Viridans strep*........ ❗ 🦷 ~18%
- *S. epidermidis*....... ❗ 🦷 ~10%
- *Enterococcus species*... ❗ ~10%
- *Coxiella burnetii*........... ❗ Rare

Native valve endocarditis accounts for 60-80% of patients, especially in intravenous drug use

## Clinical Course

### ❗ Acute ❗

- Rapidly progressive illness with high fever and shaking chills
- Highly virulent organism, such as *Staphylococcus aureus*, is causal
- Can affect healthy valves

### 🛡 Subacute 🛡

- Insidious clinical course
- Caused by less virulent organisms such as *Viridans streptococci*
- Tends to affect damaged valves

### Peripheral Stigmata

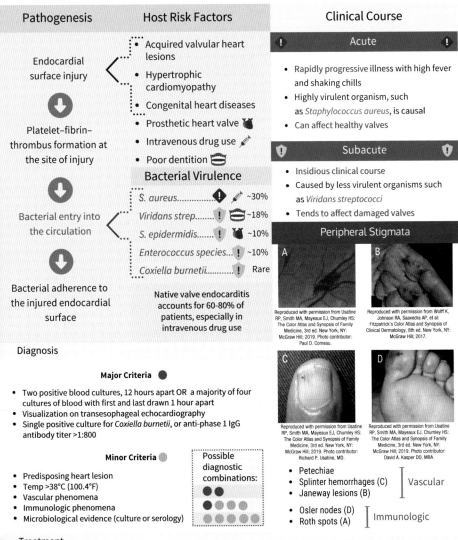

Reproduced with permission from Usatine RP, Smith MA, Mayeaux EJ, Chumley HS: The Color Atlas and Synopsis of Family Medicine, 3rd ed. New York, NY: McGraw Hill; 2019. Photo contributor: Paul D. Comeau.

Reproduced with permission from Wolff K, Johnson RA, Saavedra AP, et al: Fitzpatrick's Color Atlas and Synopsis of Clinical Dermatology, 8th ed. New York, NY: McGraw Hill; 2017.

Reproduced with permission from Usatine RP, Smith MA, Mayeaux EJ, Chumley HS: The Color Atlas and Synopsis of Family Medicine, 3rd ed. New York, NY: McGraw Hill; 2019. Photo contributor: Richard P. Usatine, MD.

Reproduced with permission from Usatine RP, Smith MA, Mayeaux EJ, Chumley HS: The Color Atlas and Synopsis of Family Medicine, 3rd ed. New York, NY: McGraw Hill; 2019. Photo contributor: David A. Kasper DO, MBA.

## Diagnosis

### Major Criteria ⬤

- Two positive blood cultures, 12 hours apart OR a majority of four cultures of blood with first and last drawn 1 hour apart
- Visualization on transesophageal echocardiography
- Single positive culture for *Coxiella burnetii*, or anti-phase 1 IgG antibody titer >1:800

### Minor Criteria ◐

- Predisposing heart lesion
- Temp >38°C (100.4°F)
- Vascular phenomena
- Immunologic phenomena
- Microbiological evidence (culture or serology)

Possible diagnostic combinations:

- Petechiae
- Splinter hemorrhages (C) ⎤ Vascular
- Janeway lesions (B) ⎦
- Osler nodes (D) ⎤ Immunologic
- Roth spots (A) ⎦

## Treatment

**Bactericidal drugs should be used.** Empiric antimicrobial coverage should be active against methicillin-resistant *S. aureus*, viridans group streptococci, enterococci, and HACEK organisms (eg, vancomycin plus either ceftriaxone or gentamicin).

# Enteroviruses

Enteroviruses are transmitted by fecal-oral route. The enteric tract is an important site of viral replication, and viruses are commonly isolated from feces. They are undeveloped ("naked") and stable in the gut. Clinically relevant viruses listed below.

## Pathogenesis

Ingestion

▼

Infection of GI-tract mucosal epithelial cells

▼

Spread and replication in regional lymph nodes

▼

CNS invasion may lead to meningoencephalitis, **paralytic poliomyelitis in polio**

▼

Virus shedding: Oropharynx up to 3 weeks & GI tract for up to 12 weeks after infection

▼

Infection controlled by humoral immunity in GI tract

## Clinical Manifestations

**Poliovirus**

- 3-6 day incubation --> greater than **90%** have asymptomatic infection; ~**5%** of pts with minor illness; ~**1%** with aseptic meningitis (proximal, asymmetric, legs > arms) with decreased reflexes on physical exam. May affect bulbar or cardiopulmonary regions of brain stem.
- Postpolio syndrome: New weakness 20-40 years after poliomyelitis.
- Paralytic disease: Severe back, neck, and muscle pain + gradually developing motor weakness

**Coxsackie virus**

- Aseptic meningitis, herpangina, pleurodynia, myocarditis, pericarditis, and hand, foot, and mouth disease are the most important diseases.

**Enteroviruses 70 and 71**

- Associated with severe CNS disease; particularly, a form of acute and extremely contagious hemorrhagic conjunctivitis (70)

**Echovirus**

- Aseptic meningitis, upper respiratory tract infection, febrile illness with and without rash, infantile hepatitis, and hemorrhagic conjunctivitis

**Norovirus**

- Sudden onset of vomiting and non-bloody diarrhea with low-grade fever and abdominal cramping

+ssRNA
Icosahedral
Naked

"Non-polio" enteroviruses

## Diagnosis

Enterovirus can be isolated from throat or rectal swabs, stool, and/or normally sterile body fluids.

- (+) results for CSF and serum reflect disease.
- (+) stool and throat cultures may simply reflect colonization.

In general, serotyping is not clinically useful

- PCR detects all serotypes that infect humans, with high sensitivity (70-100%) and specificity (>80%).
- PCR of CSF is less likely to be positive ≥3 days after meningitis onset or with enterovirus 71 infection.

## Treatment

- No specific antiviral treatment is available.
- Most enteroviral illness resolves spontaneously.
- Exogenous immunoglobulin treatment may be helpful.
- Glucocorticoids are contraindicated.

## Prevention

Hand hygiene, use of gowns and gloves, and enteric precautions prevent nosocomial transmission.

The availability of poliovirus vaccines has largely eliminated disease due to wild-types poliovirus.

- Both oral poliovirus vaccine (OPV) and inactivated poliovirus vaccine (IPV) induce IgG and IgA antibodies that persist for at least 5 years.

# Fever of Unknown Origin (FUO)

**FUO:** Fever of >101°F and illness for >3 weeks and no known immunocompromised state that remains unexplained after history-taking, physical exam, and recommended investigations suggested by current guidelines

## Recommended Investigations

**Laboratory Studies**
- ESR
- CRP
- WBC w/differential
- Platelet count
- Hemoglobin
- LDH
- AST/ALT
- ANA/RF serology
- Total protein
- SPEP
- HIV testing
- Ferritin
- BMP
- Creatinine
- Alkaline phosphatase
- PPD or IGRA
- Creatine kinase
- Urinalysis
- Blood/urine cultures

**Imaging Studies**
- Abdominal ultrasound
- Chest X-ray

## Etiology

Varies by host factors and geography
- ~40% unknown causes
- **~25% noninfectious inflammatory diseases**
- ~20% infectious diseases
- ~10% neoplasms
- In LMICs, ~40% infectious diseases

## Differential Diagnosis

**More often an atypical presentation of a common disease**

**Infectious diseases**
- Endocarditis
- Diverticulitis
- Vertebral osteomyelitis
- Tuberculosis

**Noninfectious inflammatory diseases**
- Large-vessel vasculitis
- Familial Mediterranean fever
- Polymyalgia rheumatica
- Sarcoidosis
- Adult-onset Still's disease

**Neoplasms**
- Lymphoma, leukemia, hepatoma
- Metastatic malignancy

**Miscellaneous**
- Factitious fever
- Drug-induced fever
- Exercise-induced hyperthermia

## Diagnostic Approach

Rule out manipulation of thermometer
↓
History, PE, recommended investigations
*Questions include: Travel, animal exposure, recent procedures, medications, vaccine history, etc.*

 Diagnostic clues / 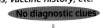 No diagnostic clues

Diagnostic clues → Guided testing

No diagnostic clues → Stop meds to exclude drug fever

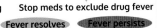 Fever resolves / Fever persists

Fever persists → CT of abdomen/pelvis with contrast
↓
Assign to most likely category

**Infection** | **Malignancy** | **Autoimmune** | **Misc.**

**Infection**
- Blood/urine cultures
- CMV, EBV serology
- HIV test
- Guided tests

**Autoimmune**
- Temporal artery biopsy
- Lymph node biopsy

**Misc.**
- Continue testing based on history, PE findings

No diagnosis → 
- Lumbar puncture
- Gallium 67 scan
- CT scan-sinuses

**Hematologic**
- Blood smear
- SPEP

No diagnosis →
- Bone marrow biopsy

**Nonhematologic**
- Mammogram
- Chest CT with contrast
- Endoscopy
- Gallium 67 scan

 No diagnosis →
- MRI of brain
- Biopsy skin, lymph nodes, or liver
- Laparoscopy

## Treatment

- **Avoid empiric antimicrobial therapy or steroids unless patient unstable**
- Supportive care
- Treat syndromes or infections if diagnosed

# Flaviviruses: Zika, Dengue, and Yellow Fever

Flaviviruses are **(+) sense ssRNA** viruses distributed worldwide and transmitted by **mosquito** and **ixodid tick** vectors. The genus includes West Nile virus, Japanese Encephalitis virus, and many others.

**Worldwide distribution in tropical and subtropical latitudes**

## Zika Virus

**Epidemiology**
- *Aedes* spp. mosquito vectors
- Transmitted by blood and bodily fluids
- First isolated in Uganda, now found in New World
- 440,000 to 1.3 million cases in Brazil by 2015

**Clinical Presentation**
- Often asymptomatic
- Fever, malaise, headache
- Maculopapular rash, arthralgia
- Vomiting, hearing impairment possible

**Diagnosis**
- Serology assays available

**Management**
- Supportive care and monitoring

**Feared Sequelae and Complications**
- Guillain–Barré syndrome
- Microcephaly if congenital transmission

## Dengue Serotypes 1-4

**Epidemiology**
- *Aedes* spp. mosquito vectors
- Tropical latitudes worldwide
- 390 million infections globally per year, 96 million symptomatic

**Clinical Presentation**
- Week-long incubation period
- Rapid onset headache, intense myalgias, fever
- "Break-bone fever"
- Rash, scleral injection, epistaxis, petechiae all possible findings

**Diagnosis**
- Leukopenia, thrombocytopenia
- Elevated AST/ALT
- IgM ELISA, paired serology, or RT-PCR available

**Management**
- Supportive care
- Close monitoring for signs of viral hemorrhagic fever (VHF)

**Fear Complications**
- Progression to severe dengue
- Serotype 1 infection followed by serotype 2 has high risk of VHF

## Yellow Fever

**Epidemiology**
- *Aedes* spp. mosquito vectors
- Africa and South America
- 29,000-60,000 deaths in Africa in 2013

**Clinical Presentation**
- Rapid onset fever/myalgia
- Increasing prostration, headache, abdominal pain
- Jaundice, delirium, hematemesis ("black vomit")
- Hepatic necrosis and shock in terminal stages

**Diagnosis**
- Hemoconcentration, elevated AST/ALT
- Raising BUN, albuminuria

**Management**
- ICU supportive care
- Fluid resuscitation that accounts for high vascular permeability

**Fear Complications**
Shock, DIC, seizures, death

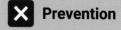 **Prevention**
- Avoidance of endemic regions, vector control, mosquito nets, DEET
- Yellow Fever 17D live-attenuated vaccine available
- Dengue and Zika vaccines under development

# Gonorrhea

- Gram (–), oxidase (+) diplococci
- Urethritis, cervicitis, conjunctivitis, and pharyngitis
- Virulence factor: **IgA protease**

## Epidemiology

- **Causative agent:** *Neisseria gonorrhoeae*
- 80 million cases worldwide in recent years
- Sexually transmitted or neonatal
- Common cause of septic arthritis in sexually active adults
- WHO reports **antibiotic resistance** increasing in recent years

## Diagnosis

- **NAAT (+)** on urine, pharyngeal, rectal, etc. specimen
- Intracellular Gram (–) cocci within PMNs of urethral discharge
- Growth on **Thayer-Martin** medium
- DGI difficult to diagnose since blood cultures frequently (–)

## Clinical Presentation

- Men more often symptomatic
- **Men:** Acute dysuria, purulent urethral discharge, urethritis
- **Women:** Purulent cervicitis, risk of developing PID if untreated
- **Disseminated gonococcal infection (DGI):** Arthritis, skin pustules, tenosynovitis following untreated GU infection
- **Ophthalmia neonatorum:** Purulent conjunctivitis in neonate

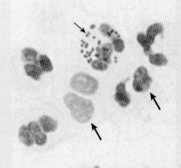

Reproduced with permission from Riedel S, Hobden JA, Miller S, et al: Jawetz, Melnick, & Adelberg's Medical Microbiology, 28th ed. New York, NY: McGraw Hill; 2019.

## Management

- **Ceftriaxone & doxycycline (or azithromycin) is first-line** for uncomplicated infections
- Screen for other STIs
- Topical erythromycin or silver nitrate for neonatal conjunctivitis
- **DGI or PID management requires hospitalization**

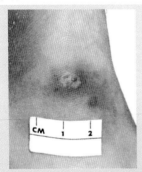

Reproduced with permission from Public Health Image Library, Centers for Disease Control and Prevention.

**Figures A-F:** Pustules in patient with DGI
**Figure G:** Neonatal conjunctivitis

Reproduced with permission from Levinson W, Chin-Hong P, Joyce EA, et al: Review of Medical Microbiology & Immunology: A Guide to Clinical Infectious Diseases, 15th ed. New York, NY: McGraw Hill; 2018.

## Prevention

- Safe sex practices and contact tracing
- No vaccine available, unlike *N. meningitidis*
- Routine screening in high-risk individuals
- Prophylactic erythromycin ointment for newborns delivered vaginally

# Granuloma Inguinale

*Klebsiella granulomatis*, a Gram-negative intracellular bacteria, causes donovanosis, a sexually transmitted genital ulcer disease, also known as granuloma inguinale.

## Pathophysiology

Sexually transmitted infection classically associated with genital ulcers that demonstrate **Donovan bodies** on tissue smear samples.

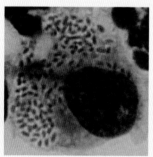

Reproduced with permission from Kasper DL, Fauci AS: Harrison's Infectious Diseases, 3rd ed. New York, NY: McGraw Hill; 2017.

Donovan bodies can be seen in large, mononuclear (**Pund**) cells as *gram-negative intracytoplasmic cysts* filled with deeply staining bodies that may have a safety-pin appearance.

## Epidemiology

The disease is rare in the United States but is endemic in India, the Caribbean, southern Africa, and central Australia. *Important to gather relevant travel and immigration history.*

Endemic in **Paupua, New Guinea**

## Clinical Manifestations

Four types of lesions have been described (**1 & 2 most common, see image**):

1. **Ulcerogranulomatous lesion that bleeds readily when touched**
2. **Hypertrophic or verrucous ulcer with a raised irregular edge**
3. Necrotic, offensive-smelling ulcer causing tissue destruction
4. Sclerotic or cicatricial lesion with fibrous and scar tissue

The genitals are affected in 90% of patients and the inguinal region in 10%.

~50 day incubation (uncertain) > painless papule/ subcutaneous nodule > Classic "beefy-red" appearance

## Diagnosis

- Painless, ulcerative vulvitis, chronic, or recurrent
- Donovan bodies revealed by Giemsa stain
- PCR is also available

## Treatment

- Azithromycin for at least 3 weeks and until all lesions have healed
- Doxycycline, ciprofloxacin, erythromycin base, and trimethoprim-sulfamethoxazole are alternatives for at least 3 weeks and until the lesions heal
- Consult guide for pregnancy

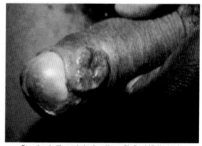

Reproduced with permission from Kasper DL, Fauci AS: Harrison's Infectious Diseases, 3rd ed. New York, NY: McGraw Hill; 2017.

Ulcerogranulomatous penile lesion of donovanosis, with some hypertrophic features

# Human Immunodeficiency Virus (HIV)

HIV is the etiologic agent of acquired human immunodeficiency syndrome or AIDS; it belongs to the family of human retroviruses (*Retroviridae*) and the subfamily of *lentiviruses*.

## Pathophysiology

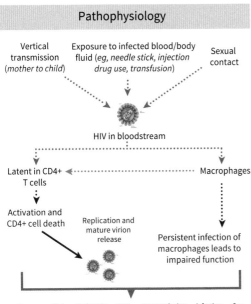

Vertical transmission (*mother to child*) — Exposure to infected blood/body fluid (*eg, needle stick, injection drug use, transfusion*) — Sexual contact

HIV in bloodstream

Latent in CD4+ T cells ← Macrophages

Activation and CD4+ cell death — Replication and mature virion release

Persistent infection of macrophages leads to impaired function

**Can**, candidal esophagitis; **CMV**, cytomegalovirus infection; **Crp**, cryptosporidiosis; **Cry**, cryptococcal meningitis; **DEM**, AIDS dementia complex; **HSV**, herpes simplex virus infection; **HZos**, herpes zoster; **KS**, Kaposi's sarcoma; **MAC**, *Mycobacterium avium* complex bacteremia; **NHL**, non-Hodgkin's lymphoma; **PCP**, primary Pneumocystis jirovecii pneumonia; **PCP2**, secondary P. jirovecii pneumonia; **PML**, progressive multifocal leukoencephalopathy; **Tox**, *Toxoplasma gondii* encephalitis; **WS**, wasting syndrome.

## Structure of HIV

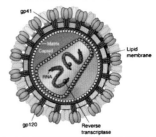

Reproduced with permission from Jameson J, Fauci AS, Kasper DL, et al: Harrison's Principles of Internal Medicine, 20th ed. New York, NY: McGraw Hill; 2018.

## Opportunistic Infections (**OIs**)

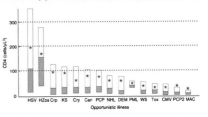

**Relationship between CD4+ T-cell counts and the development of opportunistic diseases**

Median (line inside the box), first quartile (bottom of the box), third quartile (top of the box), and mean (asterisk)

## Diagnosis

- Antibody detection test or antibody/antigen detection test, *3rd- and 4th-generation tests*, respectively
- Confirm with HIV-1/HIV-2 antibody differentiation assay
- Nucleic acid detection test should be used to acquire HIV viral load level for acute infection and disease tracking

## Treatment: Combined Antiretroviral Therapy (cART)

**Commonest**:

Integrase strand transfer inhibitor (INSTI)
Dolutegravir
Bictegravir
**+**
2 Nucleo(side/tide) reverse transcriptase inhibitors (NRTIs)
Tenofovir disoproxil fumarate (TDF) **or** Tenofovir alafenamide (TAF) with Emtricitabine (FTC) **or** Lamivudine (3TC)

**Others**:

Protease inhibitor **+** 2 NRTIs

Non-nucleoside reverse transcriptase inhibitors (NNRTIs) **+** 2 NRTIs

## OI Prophylaxis

| Name of durg | Infection prevented |
|---|---|
| Trimethoprim/ sulfamethoxazole | Pneumocystis pneumonia, Toxoplasmosis |
| Azithromycin | Mycobacterium avian complex (MAC) |
| Immunizations | Influenza, *Streptococcus pneumonia*, HPV, HBV, HAV |

## Prevention

**Behavioral**: Decreasing number of sexual partners, avoidance of sharing needles or other paraphernalia

**Biomedical**: Condom use (male or female), male circumcision, pre-exposure prophylaxis (PrEP) with oral antiretroviral drugs such as Truvada (tenofovir + emtricitabine), prompt treatment of sexually transmitted infections (STIs)

# Human Papillomavirus (HPV)

Human papillomavirus causes *papillomas*, benign tumors of squamous cells (eg, warts on the skin). There are at least 60 types (determined by DNA sequence), and some HPV types cause **carcinoma of the cervix, penis, and anus.**

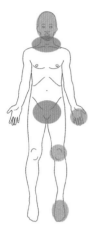

| Nonenveloped | Icosahedral nucleocapsid | Circular double-stranded DNA |

## Cutaneous Warts

- Most common warts benign/resolve
- Warts can lead to epidermodysplasia and squamous cell carcinoma in genetically predisposed

## Mucosal Infections

- Benign laryngeal papillomas
- Anogenital warts usually benign
- Certain types can lead to cervical carcinoma

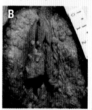

Reproduced with permission from Prentice WE: Essentials of Athletic Injury Management, 10th ed. New York, NY: McGraw Hill; 2016.

A. Papilloma (wart) on finger. Note dry, raised verrucous lesion

B. Warts on the vulva of the vagina caused by HPV.

Reproduced with permission from Wolff K, Johnson RA, Saavedra AP, et al: Fitzpatrick's Color Atlas and Synopsis of Clinical Dermatology, 8th ed. New York, NY: McGraw Hill; 2017.

## Cutaneous warts are primarily caused by **types 1-4**

- Classified as **common** (fingers and hands), **plantar** (sole of foot), or **flat** (arms, face, and knee)
- **Epidermodysplasia verruciformis** appear in certain patients with genetic predisposition and may progress to squamous cell carcinoma in several years

## Oral infections are caused by **types 13 and 32**

- Most of these infections result in benign papillomas.

## Genital tract infection (**types 6, 11, 16, 18**)

- Acquired via sexual contact
- **Types 6 and 11 cause 90% of genital papillomas**
- Can also produce anogenital warts (**condyloma acuminata**); larger in immunocompromised patients
- **Types 16 and 18 are associated with up to 70% of all cervical cancers**
- Along with 13 other rarer types, HPV causes more than 95% of all cervical cancers are caused by these high-risk types of HPV
- Malignant transformation more common in HIV

## Diagnosis

*Diagnosis can often be made by visual inspection*, but laboratory identification serves to:

- Determine HPV presence in cervical sample or abnormal tissue (**Pap smear**)
- Determine **type** to assess risk for malignancy

PCR assays that detect HPV DNA are available. Virus isolation and serologic tests are not done.

## Treatment and Prevention

The following treatments are available, and their use may vary according to the site of lesions:

- Liquid nitrogen
- Podophyllin
- Salicylic acid

Preventative vaccines:

- The current vaccine contains capsid proteins of nine HPV types (**6, 11, 16, and 18 + five others**)

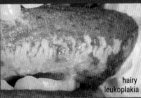

hairy leukoplakia

Reproduced with permission from Jameson J, Fauci AS, Kasper DL, et al: Harrison's Principles of Internal Medicine, 20th ed. New York, NY: McGraw Hill; 2018.

## Etiology & Epidemiology

- 90% US adults have antibody
- EBV is a gamma herpesvirus
- dsDNA, enveloped
- Infects pharyngeal epithelial cells and B lymphocytes
- Life-long infection of B cells
- Transmitted by saliva and respiratory secretions
- The "kissing disease"

## Associated Malignancies

- Burkitt's lymphoma in Africa or patient with AIDS
- Nasopharyngeal carcinoma in southern China
- Gastric carcinoma
- Posttransplant lymphoproliferative disease (PTLD)

### Clinical Pearl

- Treat PTLD by reducing immunosuppression

## Clinical Presentation

- Acute infection lasts 2-3 weeks
- Fever, pharyngitis
- Pronounced fatigue
- Lymphadenopathy of posterior cervical chain
- Splenomegaly
- Immunocompromised hosts may present with hairy leukoplakia

# Infectious Mononucleosis
## Epstein–Barr Virus (EBV)

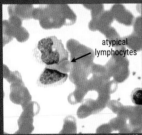

atypical lymphocytes

Reproduced with permission from Jameson J, Fauci AS, Kasper DL, et al: Harrison's Principles of Internal Medicine, 20th ed. New York, NY: McGraw Hill; 2018.

## Diagnosis

- Monospot test (+) during acute infection
- IgM serology for viral capsid antigen (VCA) in acute infection
- Elevated liver function tests
- IgG for VCA indicates prior infection
- Atypical lymphocytes (T cells) on peripheral blood smear

## Prevention

- No vaccine available
- IgG serology for transplant patients to assess for latent infection

## Treatment

- Supportive care
- No antiviral therapy needed
- Prednisone if severe pharyngitis compromises airway
- Avoid abdominal trauma if splenomegaly

# Influenza

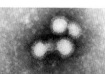

## Etiology & Epidemiology

**Influenza virus**

- Negative-sense ssRNA, segmented genome
- **Surface proteins:** Hemagglutinin, neuraminidase
- *Antigenic shift:* Novel segment acquired (HA)
- *Antigenic drift:* Accumulated mutations
- **Transmitted by respiratory droplets**
- Influenza A (**H1N1, H3N2**) most common

**Epidemiology**

- 12,000-79,000 yearly deaths in the United States
- **Elderly patients at highest risk**
- Seasonal spike from December to February

- Avian flu (H5N1) from antigenic shift
- Pandemics/epidemics from antigenic shift

| Avian genome segments | Swine surface proteins | Transmittable to humans |

## Clinical Presentation

- Incubation period of 1-2 days

- Sudden onset headache, fever, and cough

- **Prostration and severe myalgias**

- Chest X-ray reveals interstitial pneumonia

⭐ **Clinical Pearl** ⭐

- Closely monitor for secondary bacterial pneumonia caused by *S. aureus* or *S. pneumoniae*

## Diagnosis

- **Influenza season and classic symptoms**

- PCR for respiratory secretions or nasopharyngeal swab

- Rapid ELISA assays for neuraminidase or flu-specific antibodies (low sensitivity)

- Direct immunofluorescence assays

- Blood cultures not informative, **viremia is rare**

## Yearly Vaccination

- Trivalent and quadrivalent vaccines made annually
- **Covers influenza A and influenza B strains**
- High-dose killed vaccine for patients >65 y.o.
- Recombinant vaccine now available
- Live attenuated vaccine no longer recommended

- **Watch for anaphylaxis if severe egg allergy**

## Management

- Supportive care guided by severity of infection

- **Oseltamivir** or **zanamivir** (neuraminidase inhibitors) within 48 hours of symptom onset

- Rimantadine and amantadine (M2 blockers) no longer recommended

- **Aspirin is contraindicated for children** due to feared complication of Reye's syndrome

# Liver Abscess

## Pyogenic Liver Abscess     80%

| Example | Pathogenesis |
|---|---|
| Infective endocarditis | Bacteremia |
| Cholecystitis, perforated ulcer | Extension from RUQ infection |
| Cholangitis, surgical procedures | Biliary disease |
| Appendicitis, diverticulitis | Portal venous seeding from intra-abdominal infections |

## Amebic Liver Abscess    20%

Extraintestinal complication of *Entamoeba histolytica* dysentery

Intestinal focus

⌄⌄

Portal vein route to liver

⌄⌄

Liver abscess

~10% of the world's population (50 mil/yr) is infected with *E. histolytica*, mostly in developing countries.

Computed tomographic scan of pyogenic liver abscesses. Multiple hepatic abscesses are seen in this patient after an episode of diverticulitis.

Reproduced with permission from Brunicardi FC, Andersen DK, Billiar TR, et al: Schwartz's Principles of Surgery, 11th ed. New York, NY: McGraw Hill; 2019.

## Clinical Manifestation

- Fever
- Abdominal pain
- Anorexia
- Lethargy
- Jaundice
- Weight loss

Common organisms causing pyogenic liver abscess include *E. coli*, *Klebsiella*, *Enterococcus*, anaerobic *Streptococcus*, and *Bacteroides*.

## Diagnosis

- CBC with differential (leukocytosis) and liver enzymes (alkaline phosphatase are elevated in ~70% of pts)
- CXR may show right pleural effusion
- **Ultrasound** or **CT**

Ask about:

- History of biliary disease
- Intra-abdominal infection
- Trauma
- Endocarditis
- Travel to an endemic region with *E. histolytica*

## Treatment

- **Drainage is the mainstay of treatment**
- Multiple, sizable abscesses may require surgery
- Antibiotics aimed at causative microbe—eg, penicillin + β-lactamase inhibitor or a combination of a fluoroquinolone or third-generation cephalosporin + metronidazole

# Lung Abscess

Necrosis or cavitation of lung parenchyma following microbial infection

## Epidemiology & Etiology

**Primary Abscess**

- Accounts for ~80% lung abscesses
- Most often in **aspiration** in right lung
- Aspiration of anaerobic bacteria or Viridans group *Streptococcus* spp.
- Mycobacteria or fungi possible
- **Risk factors:** Altered mental status, alcohol/drug use, poor dental hygiene, motility disorder

**Secondary Abscess**

- Causative pathogen depends on the host and prior disease
- Causes: Bronchial obstruction, septic embolus, systemic infection, tuberculosis
- **Risk factors:** Disseminated disease, organ transplant, HIV, cancer

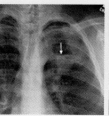 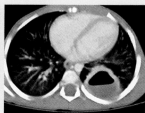

Reproduced with permission from Chen MYM, Pope TL, Ott DJ: Basic Radiology, 2nd ed. New York, NY: McGraw Hill; 2011.

Reproduced with permission from Wells RG: Diagnostic Imaging of Infants and Children. New York, NY: McGraw Hill; 2013.

## Diagnosis

- Leukocytosis on CBC
- Chest CT shows air–fluid level in area of cavitation
- Sputum culture may yield oral flora
- **Rule out tuberculosis**
- Bronchoalveolar lavage or bronchoscopy for **secondary abscess**
- Isolation of microbe not always necessary for **primary abscess**

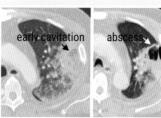

Used with permission from Dr. Ritu Gill, Division of Chest Radiology, Brigham and Women's Hospital, Boston.

## Clinical Presentation

- Pneumonia-like symptoms
- Fatigue, fever, cough, night sweats, and sputum
- Chest pain

⭐ **Clinical Pearl** ⭐

- Gingival disease, poor dentition on exam suggests primary abscess

## Management

**Primary Abscess**

- Antibiotics with anaerobic coverage; cover fungi if indicated
- Assess response with imaging

**Secondary Abscess**

- Treat causative pathogen
- Resolve bronchial obstruction if present
- Address immunocompromised status if relevant (ie, reduce steroids)

**Abscess >6-8 cm**

- Percutaneous drainage or surgical resection

# Lyme Disease

## Etiology

- *Borrelia burgdorferi*, a spirochete
- *Ixodes* tick vector

Reproduced with permission from Centers for Disease Control and Prevention. Photo contributors: Drs. Amanda Loftis, Will Reeves, and Chris Paddock.

- Tick must be attached **>24 hours** to transmit
- 20,000 cases per year in the United States

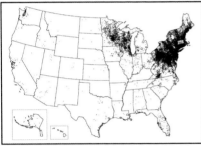

Reproduced with permission from Centers for Disease Control and Prevention, National Center for Emerging and Zoonotic Infectious Diseases (NCEZID), Division of Vector-Borne Diseases (DVBD). https://www.cdc.gov/lyme/datasurveillance/maps-recent.html

Reproduced with permission from Southwick FS: Infectious Diseases: A Clinical Short Course, 4th ed. New York, NY: McGraw Hill; 2020.

## Clinical Presentation

- **Stage 1**: *Erythema migrans*, flu-like symptoms, incubation period of days to weeks
- *Erythema migrans* only found in 75% of cases
- **Stage 2**: Heart block, Bell's palsy, incubation period of several weeks to months
- **Stage 3**: Autoimmune polyarthritis, encephalopathy, incubation period of months

## Diagnosis

- Physical exam findings
- Serology for **IgM** and/or **IgG**
- **PCR** for *B. burgdorferi* available
- Confirm serology with Western blot

**Clinical Pearl**

- Rule out coinfection with *Babesia*, *Ehrlichia*, or *Anaplasma* (all carried by same tick vector)

## Management

- Treat stage 1 with 200 mg/day **doxycycline** for 10-21 days
- Prophylaxis treatment same as stage 1
- Severe disease requires **ceftriaxone**
- Treat children and pregnant women with **amoxicillin**
- Prevent reinfection with protective clothing and 30% DEET bug spray

# Malaria

## Epidemiology

- Intraerythrocytic parasite
- 5 *Plasmodium* spp.: *P. falciparum*, *P. ovale*, *P. vivax*, *P. malariae*, *P. knowlesi*
- Transmitted by **Anopheles spp.** mosquito vectors
- **Synchronized release** of merozoites from RBCs
- **Susceptible hosts:** Asplenic, children, pregnant women, patients with sickle cell disease

Country phase
- Control
- Elimination
- Pre-elimination
- Prevention of re-introduction

## Diagnosis

- *P. falciparum*—**Banana-shaped gametocyte**
- If blood smear (−) but suspect malaria, RDT (ELISA) available
- PfHRP2 dipstick or card test for rapid ID of *P. falciparum*

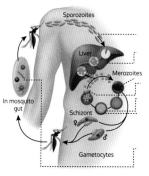

Sporozoites

Liver

Merozoites

In mosquito gut

Schizont

Gametocytes

## Treatment

*Treatment complex, consult ID*

Chloroquine-sensitive *P. falciparum* or *P. malariae*

- Chloroquine

Chloroquine-sensitive *P. vivax* or *P. ovale*
- Chloroquine and primaquine
- **Primaquine required to clear hypnozoites from liver**

Chloroquine-resistant *P. falciparum*
- Artemisinin combo regimen

Severe *P. falciparum* infection
- IV artesunate or quinidine

⭐ **Clinical Pearl** ⭐
- Test for G6PD deficiency before administering primaquine

## Clinical Presentation

- High fever, chills, headache, malaise 2 weeks after inoculation
- Nausea, vomiting, diarrhea, arthralgia, myalgia common
- Splenomegaly, anemia, thrombocytopenia
- Dark-colored urine—**"Blackwater fever"**
- *P. vivax*/*P. ovale* can manifest years after inoculation

⭐ **Clinical Pearl** ⭐

Severe *P. falciparum* infection
- Nonimmune hosts at risk
- Coma, DIC, renal failure, pulmonary edema, shock

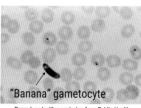

**"Banana" gametocyte**

Schizont

## Prevention

Chemoprophylaxis
- Mefloquine, chloroquine, atovaquone/proguanil, tetracyclines
- **Tetracyclines contraindicated if pregnant**

Recombinant protein **malaria vaccine in trials** (Mosquirix)

**Mosquito-bite prevention**
Drainage of stagnant water
Insecticide-infused bed nets, protective clothing

# Meningitis

Meningitis is an infection of the meninges, the membranes that line the brain and spinal cord, and can be categorized as acute ( ◆ ), subacute ( ! ), or chronic ( 🕐 ) depending on speed of the initial presentation and rate of progression of the illness. Different pathogens can present with different rates.

## Pathophysiology

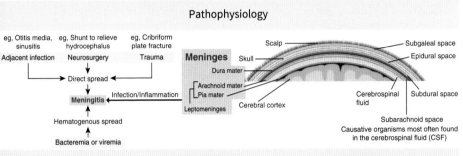

eg, Otitis media, sinusitis — Adjacent infection

eg, Shunt to relieve hydrocephalus — Neurosurgery

eg, Cribriform plate fracture — Trauma

→ Direct spread ←

Meningitis ← Infection/Inflammation

↑ Hematogenous spread

↑ Bacteremia or viremia

Meninges
- Dura mater
- Arachnoid mater — Leptomeninges
- Pia mater

Cerebral cortex

Scalp
Skull
Subgaleal space
Epidural space
Cerebrospinal fluid
Subdural space
Subarachnoid space

Causative organisms most often found in the cerebrospinal fluid (CSF)

## Pathogens

 **Acute meningitis**
(hours to days)

Caused by pyogenic bacteria, such as *Streptococcus pneumoniae or Neisseria meningitidis* or viruses, such as Enteroviruses and herpes simplex virus type 2.

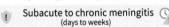 **Subacute to chronic meningitis** 🕐
(days to weeks)

Caused by *Mycobacterium tuberculosis* and fungi, such as *Cryptococcus*.

| Predisposing Factor | Common Organisms |
|---|---|
| Neonates | *Streptococcus agalactiae* (group B *Streptococcus*), *Escherichia coli, Listeria monocytogenes* |
| Teenagers and young adults | *Streptococcus pneumoniae, Neisseria meningitidis*; also herpes simplex virus type 2 |
| Older adults | *S. pneumoniae, N. meningitidis, L. monocytogenes* |
| Immunocompromised; HIV/AIDS | *L. monocytogenes*, aerobic gram-negative rods (*Pseudomonas* and *Klebsiella*); *Cryptococcus neoformans* |

## Clinical Manifestations

Early symptoms include fever, headache, photophobia, and stiff neck (nunchal rigidity; Kernig and Brudzinski signs may be seen in patients with severe disease)

*untreated progression*

⌄

Elevated intracranial pressure (ICP), vomiting, seizures, focal neurological deficits, and altered mental status

## Treatment

Empiric therapy for acute bacterial meningitis must penetrate CSF and be bactericidal with activity against common pathogens:

- **Older children and adults:** Ceftriaxone or cefotaxime + vancomycin, ampicillin added if Listeria is likely
- **Neonates:** Ampicillin + ceftriaxone or cefotaxime

*Acyclovir* is used for treatment of HSV and VZV infection.

**Prevention:** Vaccines against *S. pneumoniae*, *N. meningitidis*, and *H. influenzae*

## Diagnosis

Microbiological diagnosis method for meningitis depends on the causative pathogen:

**Bacterial meningitis:** Gram stain and culture of CSF
**Viral meningitis:** PCR assay for viral DNA/RNA in CSF
**Fungal meningitis:** Culture or serologic tests (India ink for *Cryptococcus*)

Analysis of spinal fluid can also help to distinguish between acute bacterial and viral meningitis (see table below). Although CSF analysis is important, *lumbar puncture (LP) should not be performed with signs of increased ICP, such as focal neurological deficits, seizures, or papilledema; if elevated ICP, head CT should be performed prior to LP.*

| Etiology | Pressure (mm H₂O) | Cells (microL) | Proteins (mg/100cc) | Glucose (CSF/blood) |
|---|---|---|---|---|
| Normal | <200 | 0-5 Lymphs, 0 Polys | <45 | >0.6 |
| Acute bacterial | Increased | 200-5000; mostly (>90%) Polys | >100 | <0.6 |
| Acute viral | Slight increase | 100-700 Lymphs | Slight increase | Normal |
| Subacute/chronic (TB, fungus) | Increased | 25-500 Lymphs | >100 | <0.6 |

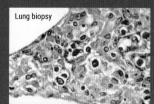

Lung biopsy

Reproduced with permission from Public Health Image Library, Centers for Disease Control and Prevention. Photo contributor: Dr. Edwin P. Ewing, Jr.

## Etiology & Epidemiology

- *Cryptococcus neoformans* and *C. gattii* species
- **Monomorphic yeast with large polysaccharide capsule**
- *C. neoformans* found in soil contaminated with avian feces
- *C. gattii* associated with eucalyptus trees, tropical climates
- No human-to-human spread

## Susceptible Hosts

- People living with HIV (PLWH) with CD4 counts <100
- Organ transplant patients
- Patients receiving chemotherapy
- Patients on corticosteroids
- *C. gattii* can infect **immunocompetent hosts**

## Clinical Presentation

- Chronic meningitis, several weeks of symptoms unlike bacterial
- Headache, fever, neural findings
- **Meningismus often absent**
- Disseminated disease with skin lesions (ie, subcutaneous nodules), pulmonary symptoms are possible

# Meningitis, Cryptococcal

## Secondary Prophylaxis Required if CD4 Count <100

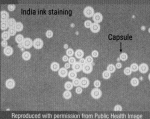

India ink staining

Capsule

Reproduced with permission from Public Health Image Library, Centers for Disease Control and Prevention. Photo contributor: Dr. L. Haley.

## Diagnosis

- **India ink staining for CSF**
- CSF often shows high protein and high mononuclear cells
- **Latex particle agglutination test for capsular antigen in CSF or blood**

## Prophylaxis

- Ensure PLWH have appropriate HAART regimen
- Fluconazole (200 mg/day) if CD4 count <100

## Treatment

- Amphotericin B and flucytosine
- Use liposomal amphotericin if kidney disease coexisting
- Fluconazole for consolidation therapy if immunocompromised

**\*\*Caution starting HAART due to immune reconstitution inflammatory syndrome (IRIS)\*\***

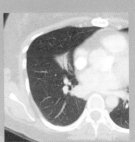

## Etiology & Epidemiology

- *M. avium* and *M. intracellulare*
- *M. avium* is most common
- Type III atypical mycobacteria
- **Ubiquitous in soil and water**
- Found in showers and hot tubs
- No human-to-human transmission
- Highly drug resistant

## Susceptible Hosts

- People living with HIV (PLWH) with **CD4 count <50**
- Organ transplant patients
- Preexisting lung disease
- Immunosuppressed patients
- People with cystic fibrosis
- The elderly

## Clinical Presentation

- **Fever, night sweats, weight loss mimicking TB**
- Abdominal pain, diarrhea
- Diffuse lymphadenopathy
- Hepatomegaly
- **"Tree-in-bud"** bronchiolar inflammation on chest CT
- **Presents as disseminated disease in PLWH**

# *Mycobacterium avium-Intracellulare* Complex (MAC)
## Prophylaxis required if CD4 count <50

## Diagnosis

- 85% MAC infections will have mycobacteremia
- **Acid-fast (+) bacilli smear**
- Labs show anemia and elevated alkaline phosphatase
- 25% have abnormal chest X-ray
- **Gold standard** is (+) culture of blood or involved tissue
- Noncaseating granulomas on histology

## Treatment

- **Macrolide with ethambutol**
- May add on rifabutin, ciprofloxacin, or amikacin for immunocompromised host or complicated case
- Continue treatment for months

## Prophylaxis

- PLWH with CD4 counts <50 require prophylaxis

Choose between:
- Azithromycin 1200 mg/week
- Clarithromycin 500 mg/bid

# Orbital Cellulitis

Orbital cellulitis is a <u>postseptal</u> bacterial infection characterized by fever, proptosis, restriction of extraocular movements, and swelling with redness of the lids (see Figure 1.A).

## Pathogenesis and Clinical Manifestation

### Pathogenesis:

- Most common cause of **proptosis in children**; elderly and immunocompromised patients may also be affected

- Majority of childhood orbital cellulitis arises from extension of acute sinusitis through the ethmoid bone

- Organisms usually responsible are *Staphylococcus aureus* including MRSA, *Streptococcus pneumonia*, and *Streptococcus pyogenes*

- *S. aureus*, Including MRSA, and *S. pyogenes* commonly responsible in penetrating trauma

### Clinical Manifestations:

- Characterized by fever, pain, eyelid edema and erythema, proptosis, chemosis, and limitation of extraocular movements

- <u>Extension to the cavernous sinus</u> can lead to contralateral orbital involvement, trigeminal dysfunction, and marked systemic illness

- <u>Intracranial extension</u> can result in subdural empyema and meningitis

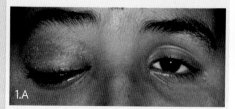

1.A

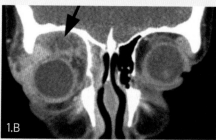

1.B

Reproduced with permission from Riordan-Eva P, Augsburger JJ: Vaughan & Asbury's General Ophthalmology, 19th ed. New York, NY: McGraw Hill; 2018.

1.A Orbital cellulitis secondary to frontal sinusitis
1.B Coronal computed tomography scan of the right orbital abscess (arrow)

## Diagnosis

- Diagnosis is usually <u>made on clinical grounds</u>
- Leukocytosis and increased ESR are almost always present, but not specific
- Blood cultures may be positive
- <u>CT scan or MRI</u> provides crucial information on source and extent of infection
- <u>MRI > CT</u> to detect cavernous sinus thrombosis

## Treatment

- <u>Prompt treatment is essential</u>
- Immediate treatment with <u>IV antibiotics</u> before causative organism is known
- Penicillinase-resistant penicillin (eg, nafcillin) recommended, with metronidazole or clindamycin to cover anaerobic infection
- Cefazolin or ceftriaxone added if trauma; Vancomycin or clindamycin if MRSA a concern
- Surgery may be required to drain the paranasal sinuses or orbital abscess (not common)

# Osteomyelitis

Osteomyelitis is an infection of the bone. The term *osteo* refers to bone and *myelo* refers to the bone marrow. Osteomyelitis is classified as either acute ( ⬤ ) or chronic ( 🕙 ).

| Pathogenesis | Predisposing Factors | Common Organisms |
|---|---|---|
| | Neonates | *Streptococcus agalactiae* (group B *Streptococcus*) |
| **Bacterial entry into the circulation** | Children and adults | *Staphylococcus aureus* |
| | Adults with vertebral osteomyelitis | *S. aureus*, *Mycobacterium tuberculosis* |
| | Intravenous drug users | *S. aureus, Pseudomonas aeruginosa, Serratia marcescens, Candida albicans* |
| | Puncture wound of foot | *P. aeruginosa* |
| | Cat bite | *Pasteurella multocida* |
| | Sickle cell anemia | *Salmonella* species |
| | Exposure in endemic areas | *Coccidioides immitis, Histoplasma capsulatum* |

Mycobacteria
Fungi

Pyogenic skin infection
Puncture wound
IV drug use
Animal bite

⌄

**Contiguous extension or hematogenous spread to bone**

**Children:** Hematogenous spread tends to result in osteomyelitis located at the end of **long bones** (metaphyses) that are rich with blood vessels.

**Adults:** Hematogenous spread results most commonly in **vertebral osteomyelitis** and **discitis**, not osteomyelitis of the long bones.

**Note:** Osteomyelitis can also occur following trauma that results in an open fracture and direct contamination of the bone. Consider prophylaxis in such a case.

## Diagnosis

- A specimen of the bone lesion should be obtained by biopsy and cultured to diagnose acute osteomyelitis most consistently; blood cultures are positive in approximately 1/2 of cases

- X-rays and even CT scans may be negative early in the disease; MRI is the most sensitive test for diagnosis of osteomyelitis

- Finding in acute osteomyelitis is a defect in the bone accompanied by periosteal elevation

## Clinical Manifestation

- Bone pain and localized tenderness at site of infection
- Constitutional symptoms (most patients)
- Limited range of motion of affected extremity
- In vertebral osteomyelitis, lumbar is more affected than thoracic or cervical

Acute osteomyelitis symptoms occur abruptly and progress rapidly.

Chronic osteomyelitis follows an indolent course with necrosis of the bone; a sequestrum (an avascular piece of infected bone) can form at the site of the lesion.

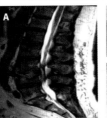

Chronic osteomyelitis tends to occur in the lower extremity, especially in diabetics who often have vascular insufficiency.

**A.** Vertebral osteomyelitis; arrow indicates site of lesion. **B.** Chronic osteomyelitis; Above: draining fistula at site of infection, below: necrotic bone caused by chronic osteomyelitis

## Treatment

- Empiric therapy should include bactericidal drugs that penetrate well into bone and include coverage for *S. aureus*. Vancomycin, nafcillin, or cephalexin administered parenterally can be used.
- The duration of therapy ranges from 3 to 6 weeks or longer.
- Surgical debridement of chronic osteomyelitis lesions is often necessary.
- Proper foot care in diabetics can prevent osteomyelitis.

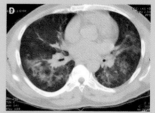

Reproduced with permission from Elsayes KM, Oldham SA: Introduction to Diagnostic Radiology. New York, NY: McGraw Hill; 2014.

## Susceptible Hosts

- People living with HIV (PLWH) with CD4 counts <200
- Malnourished children
- Organ transplant patients

## Clinical Presentation

- Sudden onset fever and nonproductive cough
- Dyspnea worse on exertion
- May present with pneumothorax
- "Ground glass" appearance on chest CT scan

# *Pneumocystis jiroveci* Pneumonia
## Prophylaxis required if CD4 count <200

Reproduced with permission from Southwick FS: Infectious Diseases: A Clinical Short Course, 4th ed. New York, NY: McGraw Hill; 2020.

## Diagnosis

- Bronchoalveolar lavage or lung biopsy is gold standard
- Lung biopsy carries risk of pneumothorax
- Methenamine silver stain to visualize cysts
- Labs often show elevated LDH

## Prophylaxis

- PLWH with CD4 counts <200
- Patients on high dose steroids
- Organ transplant patients
- Chemotherapy patients

## Management

- Trimethoprim/sulfamethoxazole is standard
- Pentamidine/atovaquone if sulfa drug allergy

# Pneumonia
### Infection of Lung Parenchyma

## Pathophysiology

- **Source:** Aspiration, hematogenous spread, nosocomial, altered microbiota, immunocompromised
- Inflammation leads to capillary leak
- **V/Q mismatch**, hypoxemia

## Pathology

- Intra-alveolar or interstitial edema
- **Red hepatization** (RBCs/neutrophils in alveoli)
- **Grey hepatization** (neutrophils/macrophages)
- Resolution (Masson bodies)

## Community-Acquired

### Clinical Presentation

- Fever, chills/rigors
- Tachycardia, tachypnea
- Purulent/mucoid/blood-tinged sputum
- **Elderly may present with delirium**

| Typical Pattern | Atypical Pattern |
|---|---|
| • *S. pneumoniae* | • Influenza |
| • *H. influenzae* | • Respiratory virus (ie, RSV) |
| • *Klebsiella* spp. | • *Mycoplasma* spp. |
| • *P. aeruginosa* | • *Legionella* spp. |
| • *S. aureus* | • *C. pneumoniae* |

### Risk Factors and Pathogens

- Alcohol-use disorder—Oral anaerobes, *Klebsiella* spp.
- COPD/smoking—*Legionella* spp. *Moraxella* spp.
- Cystic fibrosis—*P. aeruginosa, Burkholderia* spp.
- Aspiration risks—Oral anaerobes, **Gram (–) rods**
- Ohio River Valley—*Histoplasma* spp.
- Southwest USA—*Coccidioides* spp.
- Exposure to birds—*C. psittaci*

### Diagnosis

- **CAP often diagnosed by clinical presentation**
- (+) sputum culture or PCR
- Urinary antigen test for *Legionella* spp. or *S. pneumoniae*

### Management & Treatment

- **CURB-65 scale** to choose whether to admit
- Uncomplicated CAP treat with **macrolide** or **doxycycline**
- Cover MRSA or *Pseudomonas* spp. if indicated

### Prevention

- Pneumococcal polysaccharide vaccine
- *H. influenzae* type B conjugated vaccine
- Yearly influenza vaccination

## Nosocomial or Ventilator-Associated

### Etiology

- Normal defense barrier compromised
- Contaminated endotracheal tube (ETT)

### Clinical Presentation

- Fever, tachycardia
- Increased ETT secretions
- **New infiltrate on repeat chest X-ray**

### Suspected Pathogens

- *P. aeruginosa*, MRSA, etc.
- *Acinetobacter* spp.
- MDR **Enterobacteriaceae**
- Consult specific hospital's trends

### Diagnosis

- Clinical picture
- Culture of endotracheal aspirates

### Treatment

- **Consult local antibiogram**
- If uncomplicated, use antipseudomonal β-lactam
- If MDR suspected, add 2 antipseudomonal drugs and 1 for MRSA

### Prevention

- Hand washing
- Avoid intubation if possible

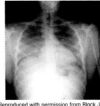

Reproduced with permission from Block J. Jordanov MI, Stack LB, et al: The Atlas of Emergency Radiology. New York, NY: McGraw Hill; 2013.

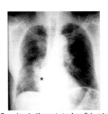

Reproduced with permission from Schwartz DT: Emergency Radiology: Case Studies. New York, NY: McGraw Hill; 2008.

# Pyelonephritis

Pyelonephritis is an infection of the kidney(s). "Pyelo" refers to the renal pelvis and "nephritis" means inflammation of the kidney.

## Pathophysiology

Bacteria spread hematogenously (minor pathway)
> Seen most commonly with *Staphylococcus aureus*
> Also occurs with *Mycobacterium tuberculosis* and can been seen in disseminated *fungal infection*

### Risk factors

- Obstructive uropathy and catheters
- Vesicoureteral reflux (esp. in children)
- Postmenopausal women
- Kidney stones

> *E. coli* is the most common pathogen causing pyelonephritis
>
> Enteric GNRs, such as *Klebsiella* and *Proteus*, are also involved.
>
> *P. aeruginosa* can cause nosocomial urinary tract infection.
>
> *Candida albicans* is a common cause of nosocomial fungal urinary tract infections.

(major pathway)
Bacteria ascend from the urethra

## Clinical Manifestation

- Fever, flank pain, nausea, and vomiting
- May or may not have signs and symptoms of lower tract infection (dysuria, frequency, hematuria, suprapubic tenderness)

- **Uncomplicated:** Pyelonephritis in an otherwise healthy woman
- **Complicated:** Pyelonephritis in immunocompromised patients and pregnant patients with urinary tract abnormality

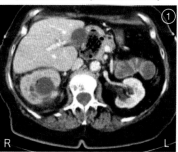

R     L

Reproduced with permission from McKean SC, Ross JJ, Dressler DD, et al: Principles and Practice of Hospital Medicine. New York, NY: McGraw Hill; 2012.

Pyelonephritis. Note enlarged right kidney caused by a stone at the ureteropelvic junction.

## Diagnosis

- Pyuria—WBC on microscopy or (+) leukocyte esterase on urine dipstick—often with (+) nitrite
- WBC count elevated with urinary WBC casts (Figure 2)
- Positive urine cultures + consistent symptoms (+ or −) RBCs
- Obstruction perinephric abscess on ultrasound and CT (Figure 1)
- Patients with renal *M. tuberculosis* may have sterile pyuria
- Patients with recurrent *Proteus* pyelonephritis should be evaluated for struvite stones

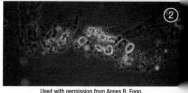

Used with permission from Agnes B. Fogo.

WBC casts. Note cylindrical-shaped casts containing round, refractile white blood cells (arrow).

## Treatment

- Empiric regimens for community-onset infection include a fluoroquinolone (ciprofloxacin or levofloxacin) or a third-generation cephalosporin, such as ceftriaxone
- Patients with heavy exposure to prior antibiotics, to the hospital setting, or to other risk factors  be treated with antibiotics with reliable activity against *Pseudomonas*, such as cefepime, piperacillin/tazobactam, or meropenem

# Retinitis

An inflammation of the retina, the sensory portion of the eye. Retinitis can endanger vision, and is an important cause of blindness in immunocompromised patients.

## Etiology

### In immunocompromised patients

- Cytomegalovirus (CMV) in patients with compromised cell-mediated immunity, as in HIV. **\*Most common\***
- *Toxoplasma gondii* likewise causes retinitis in immunocompromised patients.
- Varicella-zoster virus (VZV) and herpes simplex virus (HSV) types 1 and 2 are implicated in progressive outer retinal necrosis (PORN) syndrome.

### In immunocompetent patients

- Infectious etiologies are rare.
- Neurosyphilis work-up may be indicated based on sexual history.
- Autoimmune or drug-related causes should be considered.

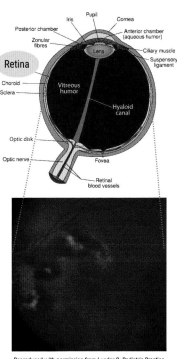

| Fungi | Parasite | Bacteria |
|---|---|---|
| Candida chorioretinitis | Toxocara canis | Tuberculosis |
| Aspergillus fumigatus | | Syphilis |
| Cryptococcus neoformans | | |

## Clinical Manifestation

- Painless loss of night vision, peripheral and/or central vision; floaters, blurry vision
- Seen in immune reconstitution after HAART induction
- **Perivascular hemorrhages and white fluffy exudates**

Reproduced with permission from Lueder G: Pediatric Practice Ophthalmology. New York, NY: McGraw Hill; 2011.

CMV infection in a patient with AIDS appears as an arcuate zone of retinitis with hemorrhages and optic disk swelling.

## Diagnosis

- Clinical diagnosis is made based on altered vision and funduscopic exam for CMV, fungal retinitis, ARN/PORN.
- Syphilis, *Toxoplasma gondii*, and *Toxocara canis* are diagnosed serologically.
- Ocular tuberculosis is suspected on clinical grounds and confirmed with appropriate workup.
- High risk in HIV when CD+ T-cell count <50/μL.

## Treatment

- Treat underlying condition (eg, Ganciclovir for CMV, "triple therapy" for tuberculosis, penicillin for syphilis, antifungals and anthelminthics for candidiasis and toxoplasmosis, respectively, etc.)
- Consult trusted resources on updated treatments

## Prophylaxis

- Routine funduscopic exam for patients with CD+ T-cell count <100/μL

# Rocky Mountain Spotted Fever
## *Rickettsia rickettsii*

 # Clinical Presentation

**Early:** Nonspecific symptoms
**Later:** Headache, fever, myalgia, rash

**Time of year and region:**
Northern Hemisphere, April-September (Tick Season)

**Activities**
History of tick exposure, outdoors, pets,

**Most prevalent** in southeastern and south central states

 # Treatment

**DO NOT DELAY TREATMENT:** Immediate empirical administration of doxycycline on high index of suspicion. Serologic tests usually negative at time of presentation.

**First-line:** Doxycycline

**Pregnancy or allergy:** Chloramphenicol

# Disease Progression

Incubation (2-14 days)

**Early: Nonspecific illness**
Symptoms include fever, headache, malaise, myalgia, nausea, vomiting, anorexia
Macular rash on wrists and ankles

**Late: Appearance of classic signs**
Maculopapular or petechial rash first appearing in hands and feet, then spreading to trunk

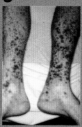

Used with permission from Dr. Lindsey Baden.

 # Diagnosis

**Early and late**
3-mm punch biopsy of rash lesion
(70% sensitive, 100% specific)

Reproduced with permission from Kang S, Amagai M, Bruckner AL, et al: Fitzpatrick's Dermatology, 9th ed. New York, NY: McGraw Hill; 2019.

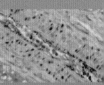

Reproduced with permission from Biggs HM, Behravesh CB, Bradley KK, et al: Diagnosis and Management of Tickborne Rickettsial Diseases: Rocky Mountain Spotted Fever and Other Spotted Fever Group Rickettsioses, Ehrlichioses, and Anaplasmosis - United States, MMWR Recomm Rep. 2016 May 13;65(2):1-44.

**Histology of skin lesion biopsies.**
**Left:** Vascular lesion in skin arteriole. **Right:** Immunohistochemistry of endothelial cells.

**Late**
Indirect immunofluorescence assay IgG
(only detectable 7-10 days after onset)
89-100% sensitive, 99-100% specific

# Differential Diagnosis

**Early: Fever, headache, myalgia without rash.** Influenza, enterovirus, infectious mononucleosis, viral hepatitis, leptospirosis, typhoid fever, bacterial sepsis, HME, HGA, typhus, rickettsialpox.

**Later: Fever, headache, myalgia with rash.** Rubeola, rubella, meningococcemia, gonococcus, syphilis, toxic shock syndrome, drug hypersensitivity, idiopathic thrombocytopenic purpura, thrombotic thrombocytopenic purpura, Kawasaki syndrome, immune complex vasculitis.

# >> Sepsis <<

**Definition:** Life-threatening organ dysfunction caused by dysregulated immune response to infection

## Epidemiology

- 1 million cases per year in the United States
- **30-50% mortality rate**
- 50% cases due to Gram (−) bacteria

**Common sources of infection**
- Lungs, abdomen, urinary tract, SSTI

**Risk factors**
- Neonate, >65 y.o., CKD, diabetes, cirrhosis, cancer, HIV, transplant patient

## Evidence of Organ Dysfunction

- **Pulmonary:** Hypoxemia on ABG labs
- **Renal:** Oliguria, elevated Cr
- **Hepatic:** Elevated AST/ALT and bilirubin
- **Cardiac:** Hypokinesis seen on echo
- **Coagulopathy:** DIC, thrombocytopenia
- **Lactic acidosis** due to widespread hypoperfusion of organs

Purpuric lesions

Reproduced with permission from Wolff K, Johnson RA, Saavedra AP, et al: Fitzpatrick's Color Atlas and Synopsis of Clinical Dermatology, 8th ed. New York, NY: McGraw Hill; 2017.

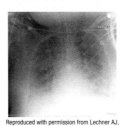

Reproduced with permission from Lechner AJ, Matuschak GM, Brink DS: Respiratory: An Integrated Approach to Disease. New York, NY: McGraw Hill; 2012.

### Sepsis

SOFA score assesses severity
qSOFA score (>2 = worse prognosis)
- RR >22/min
- Altered mentation
- Systolic BP <100 mm Hg

### Septic Shock

- SOFA score >2
- Vasopressor requirement to have MAP >65 mm Hg
- Lactate >2 mmol/L

### Multiple Organ Dysfunction Syndrome

## Clinical Manifestations

**\*\*Requires prompt diagnosis\*\***

- Fever, chills, or hypothermia
- Altered mental status
- Tachycardia, tachypnea, hypotension
- Petechiae or purpuric lesions
- **Ecthyma gangrenosum** seen in *Pseudomonas* spp. infections
- **May progress to multi-organ failure (ie, ARDS, AKI, adrenal insufficiency)**

## Diagnosis & Management

**Diagnosis**
- 2016 SCCM/ESICM task force criteria (eg, SOFA scoring system)
- Blood, sputum, and urine cultures
- Culture of abscess drainage, if applicable

**Treatment**
- Admission to the ICU; source control
- **Prompt initiation of broad-spectrum antimicrobial therapy**
- Fluid resuscitation and vasopressors
- Ventilation or dialysis as needed

# Sinusitis

Inflammation of one or more sinuses caused by built up mucus and/or infectious process involving virus, bacterium, or fungus

## Pathophysiology

- Mucus accumulates due to obstruction, structural abnormality, or impaired flow
- Obstruction causes inflammation and allows for pathogen growth
- **Maxillary sinus most commonly involved**, sphenoid least common
- **Concern for spread to cranium!** (ie, cerebral abscess, meningitis)

## Acute Sinusitis (<4 weeks)

### Epidemiology

- Noninfectious: Nasal polyp, CF, vasculitis
- Viral: Rhinovirus, parainfluenza
- Bacterial: *S. pneumoniae, H. influenzae*
- Fungal: *Mucor* spp., *Rhizopus* spp. (if DM II)
- **Nosocomial sinusitis from NG tube may have MDR GNRs or *Pseudomonas* spp.**

### Clinical Presentation

- Often follows or accompanies viral URI
- Congestion, nasal drainage, headache
- **Facial pain may localize to affected sinus**
- Mucormycosis has severe symptoms with retro-orbital pain, CN palsy, cellulitis

### Diagnosis

- Difficult to distinguish causative pathogen from colonizing commensal
- **>10 days purulent mucus suggests bacteria**
- Sinus aspirate culture
- **CT scan not indicated unless severe**
- Mucormycosis requires visualization of hyphae in biopsy specimen

### Management

- Oral decongestant if uncomplicated sinusitis
- **Amoxicillin/clavulanate** if >10 days symptoms
- Emergent ENT surgery and IV amphotericin B if mucormycosis

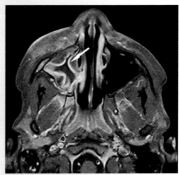

## Chronic Sinusitis (>12 weeks)

### Epidemiology

- Often suspected to be bacterial or fungal

### Clinical Presentation

- Long-standing congestion and sinus pressure
- **Persistent symptoms despite repeated rounds of antimicrobial therapy**

### Diagnosis

- CT scan may help localize lesion or abnormality
- Endoscopy may be informative

### Management

- Chronic use of antibiotics or antifungals
- **ENT surgery** (ie, removal of mycetoma)

# Syphilis

## Transmission and Stages

### Inoculation

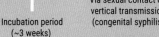

Via sexual contact or vertical transmission (congenital syphilis)

**No symptoms:** Average incubation period is 3 weeks. Organism spread via lymph or blood.

Incubation period (~3 weeks)

↓

### Primary Syphilis

**Chancre:** Likely found on site of inoculation, like penis, labia, or vagina.

Reproduced with permission from Wolff K, Johnson RA, Saavedra AP, et al: Fitzpatrick's Color Atlas and Synopsis of Clinical Dermatology, 8th ed. New York, NY: McGraw Hill; 2017.

Asymptomatic period (2-24 weeks)

↓

### Secondary Syphilis

**Rash:** May be accompanied by hepatitis, meningitis, or glomerulonephritis. Flat papules seen primarily in the anogenital region (*condylomata lata*).

Reproduced with permission from Centers for Disease Control Public Health Image Library.

### Early Latent Syphilis

(<1 year infected)

**No symptoms:** *T. pallidum* presents in latent state. Seen here on dark-field illumination.

Reproduced with permission from Centers for Disease Control and Prevention. Photo contributor: Dr. Schwartz.

Asymptomatic period (3-30 years)

↓

### Late Latent Syphilis

(>1 year infected)

**Gumma:** Granulomatous lesions (gummas) in the liver, skin, and bones. Nervous system degeneration including **dementia**; cardiovascular lesions, such as **aortic regurgitation** and **ascending aortic aneurysm.**

## Etiology

*Treponema pallidum* causes syphilis
- Obligate intracellular spirochete

## Diagnosis

**Nonspecific serologic tests:** Non-treponemal antigens (eg, cardiolipin from beef heart) react with antibodies in serum samples from patients with syphilis ("reagin antibodies").

- Venereal Disease Reference Laboratory (VDRL) test
- Rapid Plasma Reagin (RPR)
- Fourfold decline after treatment is adequate

**Specific serologic tests:** Treponemal antigens react with specific antibodies in the patient's serum.

- FTA-ABS (immunofluorescence)
- TPHA, MHA-TP (hemagglutination)
- Tests remain positive for life

## Treatment

- Treat with **penicillin**
- For allergic patients, treat with doxycycline or ceftriaxone
- For pregnant patients allergic to penicillin, desensitize and treat

## Congenital Syphilis

*T. pallidum* can be transmitted through the placenta to a fetus after the first 10-15 weeks of pregnancy

- Infection can cause fetal or infant death or abortion
- Infants who live develop condition similar to secondary syphilis with CNS and structural abnormalities
- Late congenital syphilis can occur after age 2: Clutton joints, deafness, Hutchinson's teeth (notched incisors), mulberry-shaped molars, saddle nose, saber shins, and rhagades

# Toxoplasmosis

*Toxoplasma gondii* is an intracellular sporozoan, distributed worldwide, that infects all vertebrate species, although the definitive host is the cat.

## Pathogenesis

**Humans can become infected by:**

1. Accidental ingestion of oocysts present in cat feces
2. Eating raw or undercooked meat
3. Congenitally from an infected mother
4. Blood transfusion

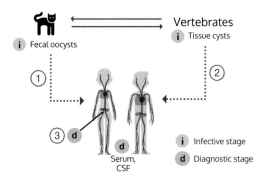

## Clinical Manifestation

Asymptomatic in **immunocompetent host**, but can resemble mononucleosis

Life-threatening disseminated diseases, primarily encephalitis, in **immune compromised hosts** (eg, AIDS)

**Congenital infection**: Stillbirth, encephalitis, chorioretinitis hepatosplenomegaly, mental retardation, blindness

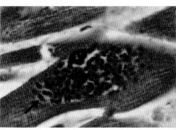

Reproduced with permission from Public Health Image Library, Centers for Disease Control and Prevention. Photo contributor: Dr. E. Ewing, Jr.

*Toxoplasma gondii*—**Tachyzoite**. Arrow points to a tachyzoite of *T. gondii* in cardiac muscle.

**Tachyzoites** ("tachy-" = rapid)
Seen in body fluids in early, acute infections. Tachyzoites directly destroy cells, particularly parenchymal and reticuloendothelial cells (see image).

**Bradyzoites** ("brady-" = slow)
Contained in cysts in muscle and brain tissue and in the eye. Ruptured cysts cause local inflammation with vessel blockage and necrosis. The reaction can be very severe in **immunocompromised individuals**.

## Diagnosis

- Giemsa-stained preparations show crescent-shaped trophozoites during acute infection.
- **IgG** antibody can be used to diagnose acute infection.
- Immunofluorescence assay for **IgM** antibody is used to diagnose congenital infection.

## Treatment

- Congenital and immunocompromised toxoplasmosis: Combination of sulfadiazine and pyrimethamine
- Acute toxoplasmosis in an immunocompetent individual is usually self-limited

**Prevention** — Cook meat thoroughly to kill the cysts. Pregnant women should avoid undercooked meat and contact with cat feces. Trimethoprim-sulfamethoxazole used to prevent toxoplasma encephalitis in patients infected with human immunodeficiency virus (HIV).

# Transverse Myelitis

Transverse myelitis is a rare inflammatory process affecting a focal area of the spinal cord that may lead to rapid onset of irreversible paraplegia.

## Pathogenesis

### Primary

- Usually preceded by GI, respiratory, or systemic illness; can be bacterial, viral, fungal, or parasitic

- Viral causes include herpesviruses (HSV, VZV, CMV, EBV, WNV), Zika, hep B, measles, mumps, and rubella

- Bacterial causes include syphilis, tuberculosis, Actinomyces, and Lyme

### Secondary

#### Multiple Sclerosis (MS)

Can be first complaint of a new MS diagnosis

#### Guillain-Barré syndrome

#### Systemic lupus erythematosus (SLE)

#### Neuromyelitis optica (NMO)

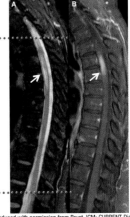

Reproduced with permission from Brust JCM: CURRENT Diagnosis & Treatment: Neurology, 3rd ed. New York, NY: McGraw Hill; 2019.

Sagittal T2 MRI with abnormal cord signal in acute transverse myelitis.

## Clinical Manifestations

- The present symptoms include motor weakness, sensory loss or paresthesia, and back and radicular pain.

- Vertebral tenderness to percussion is noted in about half of cases. The onset is rapid (hours to days).

## Diagnosis

**Exclude Compressive Cord Lesion**

**Lumbar Puncture**
Elevated CSF WBC of >10 cells/mm³
Get oligoclonal bands, DRL, IgG index, cytology, and routine spinal studies

**MRI** with and without gadolinium of the entire spine and brain

**Serum:** Elevated IgG

**Other Workup**
TSH, autoimmune labs such as ANA/RF, ESR, CRP, rule out vascular myelopathies, metabolic and nutritional myelopathies, neoplasm, NMO-IgG, and radiation myelitis

## Treatment

**Acute Medical Management**

Give high-dose burst steroids for 3-5 days
Methylprednisolone
Dexamethasone

Longer steroid treatment may be needed
If motor impairment is present, consider plasma exchange
If severe TM, consider cyclophosphamide

**Chronic Medical Management**

Consider chronic immunomodulatory therapy for patients with recurrent disease
Azathioprine
Methotrexate
Mycophenolate

# Tuberculosis

## Etiology & Epidemiology

- *Mycobacterium tuberculosis*
- **Acid-fast bacilli**, aerobic
- Transmitted as aerosol
- **1/3 world population is infected**

## Screening

- Purified protein derivative (PPD) test
- **BCG vaccine can cause false positive**
- Interferon-gamma release assay (IGRA)
- Need to have chest X-ray and sputum culture if (+) PPD or IGRA
- **Risk factors for infection:** From endemic country, jail, homelessness, IVDU, contact with active case, HIV, healthcare worker

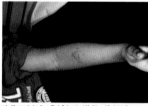

## Clinical Presentation

- **Any organ system, variable manifestations**
- Fever, fatigue, night sweats, weight loss
- Primary pulmonary TB can be asymptomatic or mild

⭐ **Clinical Pearl** ⭐

- **Reactivation TB:** Upper lobe cavitation, meningitis, osteomyelitis, **Pott's disease**, etc.

## Pathogenesis

- Primary TB often creates Ghon complex

⭐ **Clinical Pearl** ⭐

- **Risk factors for reactivation:** HIV/AIDS, malnutrition, age, TNF-α inhibition, corticosteroids, diabetes

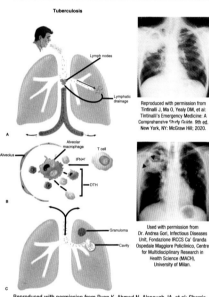

Tuberculosis

## Diagnosis

- **Acid-fast stain** for sputum
- Genexpert for diagnosis, early info on resistance
- Lowenstein—Jensen medium, yield in 6-8 weeks

## Treatment/Prevention

- BCG vaccine in endemic areas
- Latent infection: Isoniazid regimen
- Reactivation TB: 2 months **rifampin, isoniazid, ethambutol, and pyrazinamide (RIPE)**; 4 months of isoniazid and rifampin
- **MDR/XDR TB: Consult with ID**

# Viral Hemorrhagic Fever

Rapidly progressive viral syndrome characterized by vascular leak and instability with wide range of systemic symptoms

## Epidemiology and Etiology

**Examples of Causative Viruses**
**Arenavirus:** Lassa virus, Junin virus
**Filovirus:** Ebola virus, Marburg virus
**Nairovirus:** Crimean-Congo hemorrhagic fever
**Flavivirus:** Dengue types 1-4, Yellow Fever virus
**Hantavirus:** Seoul virus, Hantaan virus

**Variable Transmission**
Mosquitoes and **Ixodid ticks** (all arboviruses)
Contact with **excreta of rodents** (eg, Hantavirus)
Contact with **bodily fluids** or skin (eg, Filovirus)

Reproduced with permission from Centers for Disease Control and Prevention.

Ebolavirus, a Filovirus

## Diagnosis

**Prompt diagnosis is needed to identify virus-specific therapy options**

- Diagnosis requires thorough travel history and history of animal exposures, arthropod bites
- Multiplex PCR assays or RT-PCR
- **ELISA for IgM-capture or viral antigens**
- Paired serum samples allow for diagnosis when infection resolves

### Clinical Pearl

Dengue virus types 1-4 induce cross-reactive antibodies to other flaviviruses

## Clinical Presentation

 Symptom Onset

- Abrupt onset fever and myalgia
- Anorexia, headache, nausea common
- **Arenaviruses have gradual onset**

 Progressive Deterioration

- **1-2 days after initial symptoms**
- Prostration, vomiting, abdominal pain
- Petechiae and conjunctival suffusion
- **Hemoconcentration** due to fluid loss
  - Black vomit with **Yellow Fever**
- AKI with oliguria if **Hantavirus** infection

 Terminal Stage

- Refractory hypotension
- Visceral effusions ("**third spacing**")
- Multi-organ failure or DIC

## Management and Prevention

### Management

- **Cautious fluid resuscitation**
- Vasopressors to maintain systemic BP
- Monitor and treat secondary infections
- Clotting factor and platelet infusion as needed

### Prevention

- Judicious use of DEET/mosquito nets
- Avoid contact with animal vectors
- Contact precautions for all suspected human cases
- **Yellow Fever virus vaccination**
- Junin virus vaccine available in Argentina

# References _____

**Acute Pharyngitis**
Levinson W, Chin-Hong P, Joyce EA, Nussbaum J, Schwartz B. Upper respiratory tract infections. *Review of Medical Microbiology & Immunology: A Guide to Clinical Infectious Diseases*. 15th ed. New York, NY: McGraw Hill; 2018:624-627.

**Anaplasmosis**
Jameson J, Fauci AS, Kasper DL, Hauser SL, Longo DL, Loscalzo J. Rickettsial diseases. *Harrison's Principles of Internal Medicine*. 20th ed. New York, NY: McGraw-Hill; 2018. https://accessmedicine.mhmedical.com/content.aspx?bookid=2129&sectionid=192024087. Accessed December 13, 2019.

**Anthrax (*Bacillus anthracis*)**
Jameson J, Fauci AS, Kasper DL, Hauser SL, Longo DL, Loscalzo J. Microbial bioterrorism. *Harrison's Principles of Internal Medicine*. 20th ed. New York, NY: McGraw Hill; 2018.

Levinson W, Chin-Hong P, Joyce EA, Nussbaum J, Schwartz B. Gram-positive rods. *Review of Medical Microbiology & Immunology: A Guide to Clinical Infectious Diseases*. 15th ed. New York, NY: McGraw Hill; 2018:131-142.

**Aspergillus**
Levinson W, Chin-Hong P, Joyce EA, Nussbaum J, Schwartz B. *Review of Medical Microbiology & Immunology: A Guide to Clinical Infectious Diseases*. New York, NY: McGraw-Hill Education; 2018.

**Babesiosis**
Jameson J, Fauci AS, Kasper DL, Hauser SL, Longo DL, Loscalzo J. Babesiosis. *Harrison's Principles of Internal Medicine*. 20th ed. New York, NY: McGraw Hill; 2018:1590-1594.

**Brain Abscess**
Levinson W, Chin-Hong P, Joyce EA, Nussbaum J, Schwartz B. *Review of Medical Microbiology & Immunology: A Guide to Clinical Infectious Diseases*. New York, NY: McGraw-Hill Education; 2018.

**Chancroid**
Jameson J, Fauci AS, Kasper DL, Hauser SL, Longo DL, Loscalzo J. Haemophilus and Moraxella infections. *Harrison's Principles of Internal Medicine*. 20th ed. New York, NY: McGraw Hill; 2018:1129-1133.

**Chlamydiae**
Levinson W, Chin-Hong P, Joyce EA, Nussbaum J, Schwartz B. Chlamydiae. *Review of Medical Microbiology & Immunology: A Guide to Clinical Infectious Diseases*. 15th ed. New York, NY: McGraw Hill; 2018:201-204.

**Coccidioidomycosis**
Centers for Disease Control and Prevention. Sources of valley fever (coccidioidomycosis). cdc.gov. https://www.cdc.gov/fungal/diseases/coc cidioidomycosis/causes.html. Updated January 2, 2019. Accessed November 24, 2019.

Jameson J, Fauci AS, Kasper DL, Hauser SL, Longo DL, Loscalzo J. Atlas of skin manifestations of internal disease. *Harrison's Principles of Internal Medicine*. 20th ed. New York, NY: McGraw Hill; 2018.

Levinson W, Chin-Hong P, Joyce EA, Nussbaum J, Schwartz B. Systemic mycoses. *Review of Medical Microbiology & Immunology: A Guide to Clinical Infectious Diseases*. 15th ed. New York, NY: McGraw Hill; 2018:394-399.

## Conjunctivitis
Chamberlain NR. *The Big Picture: Medical Microbiology*. New York, NY: McGraw-Hill Medical; 2009.

## Cytomegalovirus
Jameson J, Fauci AS, Kasper DL, Hauser SL, Longo DL, Loscalzo J. Cytomegalovirus and human herpesvirus types 6, 7, and 8. *Harrison's Principles of Internal Medicine*. 20th ed. New York, NY: McGraw Hill; 2018:1361-1364.

Levinson W, Chin-Hong P, Joyce EA, Nussbaum J, Schwartz B. Herpesviruses, poxviruses, & human papilloma virus. *Review of Medical Microbiology & Immunology: A Guide to Clinical Infectious Diseases*. 15th ed. New York, NY: McGraw Hill; 2018:648-651.

## Ehrlichiosis
Centers for Disease Control and Prevention. Ehrlichiosis. cdc.gov. https://www.cdc.gov/ehrlichiosis/index.html. Updated January 17, 2019. Accessed October 19, 2019.

## Encephalitis
Levinson W, Chin-Hong P, Joyce EA, Nussbaum J, Schwartz B. *Review of Medical Microbiology & Immunology: A Guide to Clinical Infectious Diseases*. New York, NY: McGraw-Hill Education; 2018.

## Endocarditis
Levinson W, Chin-Hong P, Joyce EA, Nussbaum J, Schwartz B. *Review of Medical Microbiology & Immunology: A Guide to Clinical Infectious Diseases*. New York, NY: McGraw-Hill Education; 2018.

## Enteroviruses
Levinson W, Chin-Hong P, Joyce EA, Nussbaum J, Schwartz B. *Review of Medical Microbiology & Immunology: A Guide to Clinical Infectious Diseases*. New York, NY: McGraw-Hill Education; 2018.

## Fever of Unknown Origin (FUO)
Jameson J, Fauci AS, Kasper DL, Hauser SL, Longo DL, Loscalzo J. Fever of unknown origin. *Harrison's Principles of Internal Medicine*. 19th ed. New York, NY: McGraw-Hill; 2014.

## Flaviviruses
Jameson J, Fauci AS, Kasper DL, Hauser SL, Longo DL, Loscalzo J. Ebolavirus and Marburgvirus infections. *Harrison's Principles of Internal Medicine*. 20th ed. New York, NY: McGraw-Hill; 2018. https://accessmedicine.mhmedical.com/content.aspx?sectionid=192026062&bookid=2129#196911944. Accessed December 13, 2019.

## Gonorrhea
Jameson J, Fauci AS, Kasper DL, Hauser SL, Longo DL, Loscalzo J. Gonococcal infections. *Harrison's Principles of Internal Medicine*. 20th ed. New York, NY: McGraw Hill; 2018:1127.

Levinson W, Chin-Hong P, Joyce EA, Nussbaum J, Schwartz B. Gram-negative cocci. *Review of Medical Microbiology & Immunology: A Guide to Clinical Infectious Diseases*. 15th ed. New York, NY: McGraw Hill; 2018:124-129.

## Granuloma Inguinale
Jameson JL, Fauci AS, Kasper DL, Hauser SL, Longo DL, Loscalzo J. *Harrison's Principles of Internal Medicine*. New York, NY: McGraw Hill Education; 2018.

## Human Immunodeficiency Virus (HIV)
Jameson JL, Fauci AS, Kasper DL, Hauser SL, Longo DL, Loscalzo J. *Harrison's Principles of Internal Medicine*. New York, NY: McGraw Hill Education; 2018.

## Human Papillomavirus (HPV)
Levinson W, Chin-Hong P, Joyce EA, Nussbaum J, Schwartz B. *Review of Medical Microbiology & Immunology: A Guide to Clinical Infectious Diseases*. New York, NY: McGraw-Hill Education; 2018.

## Infectious Mononucleosis
Jameson J, Fauci AS, Kasper DL, Hauser SL, Longo DL, Loscalzo J. Epstein-Barr virus infections, including infectious mononucleosis. *Harrison's Principles of Internal Medicine.* 20th ed. New York, NY: McGraw Hill; 2018:1358-1361.

## Influenza
Jameson J, Fauci AS, Kasper DL, Hauser SL, Longo DL, Loscalzo J. Influenza. *Harrison's Principles of Internal Medicine.* 20th ed. New York, NY: McGraw Hill; 2018:1382-1387.

## Liver Abscess
Brunicardi FC, Anderson DK, Billar TR. *Schwartz's Principles of Surgery.* New York, NY: McGraw-Hill; 2016.

## Lung Abscess
Jameson J, Fauci AS, Kasper DL, Hauser SL, Longo DL, Loscalzo J. Infections due to mixed anaerobic organisms. *Harrison's Principles of Internal Medicine,* 20th ed. New York, NY: McGraw Hill; 2018:1227-1236.

Jameson J, Fauci AS, Kasper DL, Hauser SL, Longo DL, Loscalzo J. Lung abscess. *Harrison's Principles of Internal Medicine.* 20th ed. New York, NY: McGraw Hill; 2018:919-921.

## Lyme Disease
Centers for Disease Control and Prevention. Lyme Disease Maps: Most Recent Year. cdc.gov. https://www.cdc.gov/lyme/datasurveillance/maps-recent.html. Updated December 21, 2018. Accessed October 19, 2019.

Levinson W, Chin-Hong P, Joyce EA, Nussbaum J, Schwartz B. Spirochetes. *Review of Medical Microbiology & Immunology: A Guide to Clinical Infectious Diseases.* 15th ed. New York, NY: McGraw Hill; 2018:192-201.

## Malaria
Jameson J, Fauci AS, Kasper DL, Hauser SL, Longo DL, Loscalzo J. Atlas of blood smears of malaria and babesiosis. *Harrison's Principles of Internal Medicine.* 20th ed. New York, NY: McGraw Hill; 2018.

Jameson J, Fauci AS, Kasper DL, Hauser SL, Longo DL, Loscalzo J. Malaria. *Harrison's Principles of Internal Medicine.* 20th ed. New York, NY: McGraw Hill; 2018:1575-1590.

Levinson W, Chin-Hong P, Joyce EA, Nussbaum J, Schwartz B. Blood & tissue protozoa. *Review of Medical Microbiology & Immunology: A Guide to Clinical Infectious Diseases.* 15th ed. New York, NY: McGraw Hill; 2018:421-436.

## Meningitis
Chamberlain NR. *The Big Picture: Medical Microbiology.* New York, NY: McGraw-Hill Medical; 2009.

## Meningitis, Cryptococcal
Levinson W, Chin-Hong P, Joyce EA, Nussbaum J, Schwartz B. Opportunistic mycoses. *Review of Medical Microbiology & Immunology: A Guide to Clinical Infectious Diseases.* 15th ed. New York, NY: McGraw Hill; 2018:401-410.

## *Mycobacterium avium-Intracellulare* Complex (MAC)
Jameson J, Fauci AS, Kasper DL, Hauser SL, Longo DL, Loscalzo J. Nontuberculous mycobacterial infections. *Harrison's Principles of Internal Medicine.* 20th ed. New York, NY: McGraw Hill; 2018:1266-1270.

## Orbital Cellulitis
Riordan-Eva P, Augsburger J. *Vaughan & Asbury's General Ophthalmology.* New York, NY: Lange Medical Books/McGraw-Hill; 2004.

## Osteomyelitis
Levinson W, Chin-Hong P, Joyce EA, Nussbaum J, Schwartz B. *Review of Medical Microbiology & Immunology: A Guide to Clinical Infectious Diseases.* New York, NY: McGraw-Hill Education; 2018.

### *Pneumocystis jiroveci* Pneumonia

Jameson J, Fauci AS, Kasper DL, Hauser SL, Longo DL, Loscalzo J. Pneumocystis infections. *Harrison's Principles of Internal Medicine.* 20th ed. New York, NY: McGraw Hill; 2018:1547-1551.

### Pneumonia

Jameson J, Fauci AS, Kasper DL, Hauser SL, Longo DL, Loscalzo J. Pneumococcal infections. *Harrison's Principles of Internal Medicine.* 20th ed. New York, NY: McGraw Hill; 2018:1062-1071.

Jameson J, Fauci AS, Kasper DL, Hauser SL, Longo DL, Loscalzo J. Pneumocystis infections. *Harrison's Principles of Internal Medicine.* 20th ed. New York, NY: McGraw Hill; 2018:1547-1551.

### Pyelonephritis

Levinson W, Chin-Hong P, Joyce EA, Nussbaum J, Schwartz B. *Review of Medical Microbiology & Immunology: A Guide to Clinical Infectious Diseases.* New York, NY: McGraw-Hill Education; 2018.

### Retinitis

Kasper DL, Fauci AS, Hauser SL, Longo DL, Jameson JL, Loscalzo J. *Harrison's Principles of Internal Medicine.* New York, NY: McGraw Hill Professional; 2018.

### *Rickettsia rickettsii*

Centers for Disease Control and Prevention. Diagnosis and management of tickborne rickettsial diseases: Rocky mountain spotted fever and other spotted fever group rickettsioses, ehrlichioses, and anaplasmosis – United States. cdc.gov. https://www.cdc.gov/mmwr/volumes/65/rr/pdfs/rr6502.pdf. Updated May 13, 2016. Accessed December 13, 2019.

Jameson J, Fauci AS, Kasper DL, Hauser SL, Longo DL, Loscalzo J. Rickettsial diseases. *Harrison's Principles of Internal Medicine.* 20th ed. New York, NY: McGraw Hill; 2018:1305.

Liaqat M, Halpern AV, Green JJ, Heymann WR. The rickettsioses, ehrlichioses, and anaplasmoses. In: Kang S, Amagai M, Bruckner AL, et al, eds. *Fitzpatrick's Dermatology.* 9th ed. New York, NY: McGraw Hill; 2018. http://accessmedicine.mhmedical.com/content.aspx?bookid=2570&sectionid=210441791. Accessed December 13, 2019.

### Sepsis

Jameson J, Fauci AS, Kasper DL, Hauser SL, Longo DL, Loscalzo J. Acute respiratory distress syndrome. *Harrison's Principles of Internal Medicine.* 20th ed. New York, NY: McGraw Hill; 2018: 2032.

Levinson W, Chin-Hong P, Joyce EA, Nussbaum J. Schwartz B. Sepsis & septic shock. In: *Review of Medical Microbiology & Immunology: A Guide to Clinical Infectious Diseases.* 15th ed. New York, NY: McGraw Hill; 2018:648-651.

### Sinusitis

Levinson W, Chin-Hong P, Joyce EA, Nussbaum J, Schwartz B. Upper respiratory tract infections. *Review of Medical Microbiology & Immunology: A Guide to Clinical Infectious Diseases.* 15th ed. New York, NY: McGraw Hill; 2018:625-626.

Nasal Cavity. In: Morton DA, Foreman K, Albertine KH, eds. *The Big Picture: Gross Anatomy. 2nd ed.* New York, NY: McGraw Hill; 2019. http://accessmedicine.mhmedical.com/content.aspx?bookid=2478&sectionid=202021185. Accessed November 24, 2019.

### Syphilis

Levinson W, Chin-Hong P, Joyce EA, Nussbaum J, Schwartz B. *Review of Medical Microbiology & Immunology: A Guide to Clinical Infectious Diseases.* New York, NY: McGraw-Hill Education; 2018.

### Toxoplasmosis

Levinson W, Chin-Hong P, Joyce EA, Nussbaum J, Schwartz B. *Review of Medical Microbiology & Immunology: A Guide to Clinical Infectious Diseases.* New York, NY: McGraw-Hill Education; 2018.

**Transverse Myelitis**

Mitra R. *Principles of Rehabilitation Medicine*. New York, NY: McGraw-Hill Education; 2019.

**Tuberculosis**

Jameson J, Fauci AS, Kasper DL, Hauser SL, Longo DL, Loscalzo J. Tuberculosis. *Harrison's Principles of Internal Medicine*. 20th ed. New York, NY: McGraw Hill; 2018:1236-1259.

Levinson W, Chin-Hong P, Joyce EA, Nussbaum J, Schwartz B. Mycobacteria. *Review of Medical Microbiology & Immunology: A Guide to Clinical Infectious Diseases*. 15th ed. New York, NY: McGraw Hill; 2018:176-183.

**Viral Hemorrhagic Fever**

Jameson J, Fauci AS, Kasper DL, Hauser SL, Longo DL, Loscalzo J. Ebolavirus and Marburgvirus infections. *Harrison's Principles of Internal Medicine*. 20th ed. New York, NY: McGraw Hill; 2018:1509-1514.

Levinson W, Chin-Hong P, Joyce EA, Nussbaum J, Schwartz B. Arboviruses. *Review of Medical Microbiology & Immunology: A Guide to Clinical Infectious Diseases*. 15th ed. New York, NY: McGraw Hill; 2018:343.

# Musculoskeletal

*Brett R. Levine, MD, MS*

# Achilles Tendon Rupture

### Risk Factors

Episodic athletes
Decreased physical condition
Fluoroquinolone use
Steroid injections
Diabetes

### Clinical Presentation

Males > females; 30-40 years of age
Audible pop during exercise
"Stabbing pain" in calf
Decreased resting plantar flexion tone
Weak plantar flexion
Palpable gap in tendon 3-5 cm proximal to calcaneal insertion
- *Thompson Test*—Lack of plantar flexion when calf is squeezed

### Diagnosis & Workup

<u>Clinical diagnosis based on physical exam</u>
  X-rays to rule out fracture, may show heel spur (Haglund's deformity)
Ultrasound—Can distinguish partial vs full tear
MRI—Helpful if exam is equivocal, especially in chronic tears

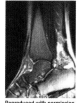

Reproduced with permission from Skinner HB, McMahon PJ: Current Diagnosis & Treatment in Orthopedics, 5th ed. New York, NY: McGraw Hill; 2014.

### Treatment

Nonoperative
Short-term cast/brace in plantar flexion
Early functional rehabilitation

Operative
Direct, end-to-end repair
Percutaneous vs open
Faster return to activity

*Overall outcomes similar at 1 year*

### Complications

**Rerupture** ~3% regardless of treatment type
**Wound complications** ~2% after surgery
 - Higher in smokers, diabetics, steroid users
**Sural nerve injury** associated with percutaneous repair technique

# Ankylosing Spondylitis

## Pathology

- Chronic autoimmune spondyloarthropathy affecting axial spine of unclear etiology
- More common in males under the age of 45
- Thought to be related to autoimmune attack following *Klebsiella pneumoniae* infection
- Heavily associated with HLA-B27 histocompatibility complex on chromosome 6
- Results in inflammation and destruction at tendon insertion sites and surrounding tissue

## Orthopedic Manifestations

- Insidious buttock pain
- Morning stiffness lasting longer than 30 minutes
- SI joint tenderness
- Progressive kyphotic deformity leading to loss of horizontal gaze
- Shortness of breath secondary to reduced chest expansion
- Hip flexion contractures

## Systemic Manifestations

- Acute uveitis and iritis
- Conduction abnormalities–Right bundle branch & AV node blockade
- Pulmonary fibrosis
- Renal amyloidosis
- Ascending aorta inflammation, stenosis, and regurgitation
- Secondary psoriasis
- Inflammatory bowel disease

## Radiographic Features

- Squaring of vertebrae
- Syndesmophytes
- Vertebral scalloping "Bamboo spine"
- Sacroiliitis grading scale: 1 (normal), 2 (blurring joint margins), 3 (partial ankylosing), and 4 (complete ankylosing)
- CT scan indicated if suspicious of occult spinal fracture

## Treatment

- 1st line: NSAIDs and physical therapy
- 2nd line: TNF-α antagonists
- Operative indications: Unstable fractures, end-stage degenerative joint disease, and severe kyphotic deformity
- Local intra-articular corticosteroid injections may offer relief
- Lack of evidence to support use of methotrexate or systemic corticosteroids

# Anterior Cruciate Ligament Injuries

## 1 Etiology

**Noncontact, twisting injuries**
**Females > Males (4:1)**
- Females have smaller notch, generalized ligamentous laxity, and quadriceps dominant landing biomechanics

**ACL = Primary restraint to anterior translation of the tibia on the femur**
- Secondary role in rotational stability

## 2 Clinical Presentation

**"Pop"** sensation during twisting/noncontact injury; posterior knee pain
Immediate effusion: Hemarthrosis

**Lachman Test:** Examiner anteriorly translates tibia of the femur
Grade 1: 3-5 mm translation
Grade 2: 5-10 mm
Grade 3: >10 mm

**A:** Firm endpoint
**B:** Soft endpoint

**Pivot Shift Test:** IT band reduces tibia at 20-30 degrees of flexion
May be difficult to perform due to guarding

## 3 Diagnosis & Workup

**X-rays** are usually normal—Can show **Segond fracture**—Bony avulsion of the ACL
**MRI** to confirm diagnosis, show additional injuries

- "Kissing lesion" bone bruise pattern
- MCL injury
- Lateral meniscus tear
- Lateral femoral condyle articular cartilage lesion

## 4 Treatment

**Nonsurgical Management:** Low demand patients who can modify activity
Increased risk of meniscal and chondral injuries with ACL-deficient knee

**ACL Reconstruction:** Young and/or active patients
Address concomitant injuries
Approx 6 months rehab before return to sport
Multiple graft choices (allograft vs autograft)
Physeal-sparing techniques in skeletally immature patients

**Graft choices:**
Bone-patellar tendon-bone
Hamstring
Quadriceps

## 5 Complications

Failure of reconstruction
Contralateral ACL tear
Stiffness, arthrofibrosis
Cyclops lesion
Infection

**Reasons for reconstruction failure:**
Tunnel malposition
Inadequate graft fixation
Overaggressive rehab

# Back Pain

## Initial Evaluation and Treatment

The majority of acute low back pain cases require little diagnostic workup and are responsive to conservative management. A thorough clinical history and physical is however necessary to evaluate for red flags that would indicate further evaluation.

## Etiologies of Low Back Pain

- Mechanical (85%): Paraspinal muscle strain, degenerative disk or joint disease, spinal deformity, vertebral fracture, spondylolisthesis (gymnasts & offensive lineman)
- Neurological (10%): Herniated disk, spinal stenosis
- Nonmechanical (1%): Neoplastic, infection, inflammatory
- Referred visceral (1%): GI disease, AAA, renal disease
- Other (3%): Fibromyalgia, psychosomatic, malingering

## Red Flags

- Major trauma (minor in elderly)
- Age <15 or >50 years old
- History of signs of malignancy (ie, night pain, weight loss)
- Recent fevers or chills
- History of IV drug use
- Immunocompromised
- Saddle anesthesia
- Urinary or bowel incontinence
- Progressive neurological deficits
- Unrelenting pain

**The presence of red flags necessitates additional diagnostic studies otherwise a trial of conservative management may be started without additional workup**

## Treatment

- Acetaminophen vs NSAIDs for pain control with avoidance of narcotics
- Physical therapy and low-stress exercise
- Avoid immobilization and bed rest
- Patient education regarding prognosis and observation for red flags
- Traction, transcutaneous electrical nerve stimulation, acupuncture, orthosis, prolotherapy, and trigger point injections remain controversial
- Surgery indicated for cases with acute neurological deficits and pain secondary to mechanical disease recalcitrant to conservative management

# Boxer's Fracture

## Presentation

Boxer's fractures are classically metacarpal neck fractures of the 5th metacarpal resulting in an apex dorsal deformity

Metacarpal fractures make up 30% of all hand fractures

Most common patient: 20-30's punching injury

Inspect for any lacerations over the MCP joint Fight bite injuries require broad spectrum antibiotics with anaerobic coverage

## Conservative Treatment

Immobilize the hand in intrinsic plus position with AROM exercises to follow

Reproduced with permission from Knoop KJ, Stack LB, Storrow AB, et al: The Atlas of Emergency Medicine, 4th ed. New York, NY: McGraw Hill; 2016. Photo contributor: Alexander T. Trott, MD.

Reproduced with permission from Knoop KJ, Stack LB, Storrow AB, et al: The Atlas of Emergency Medicine, 4th ed. New York, NY: McGraw Hill; 2016. Photo contributor: Alexander T. Trott, MD.

Can accept up to 40 degrees of flexion before patients encounter issues with grip strength

Rotational deformity is assessed by flexion of fingers. Evaluate for overlap. Normally, fingers point toward the scaphoid

Complications with closed treatment include: Pseudoclawing, malunion, grip weakness, sunken knuckle

## Surgical Fixation

Indications for surgery: Rotational deformity, >25% of intra-articular MCP involvement, postreduction shortening >5 mm

Used with permission of Justin Montgomery, MD. University of Kentucky Radiology.

Reproduced with permission from Diaz-Garcia R, Waljee JF: Current management of metacarpal fractures. Hand Clin. 2013 Nov;29(4):507-518.

When comparing K-wire vs non-op, K-wire patients had higher satisfaction but no differences in ROM or grip strength at 1 year

### K-wire Fixation

K-wires can be placed in a crossed pin or transverse pin fashion. Complications include pin site infection.

### Intramedullary Fixation

More rigid construct than K-wires. Complications include intra-articular penetration and loss of reduction.

### Plate Fixation

More common in metacarpal shaft fractures. Complications include increased dissection and soft tissue adhesions.

# Carpal Tunnel Syndrome

##  Background

Entrapment of **median nerve** in carpal tunnel at wrist

**Predisposing Factors:**
- Wrist overuse
- Obesity
- Pregnancy
- Arthritis

Endocrinopathy (hypothyroidism, acromegaly, diabetes)

##  Clinical Features

Hand **pain and paresthesias** worse at night

↓ Pinprick sensation in **median nerve distribution**

Weakness of thumb abduction and thumb opposition

Thenar atrophy if long-standing disease

Positive **Tinel sign** and **Phalen sign** (modest sensitivity and specificity)

**Tinel**        **Phalen**

Reproduced with permission from Sherman SC: Emergency Orthopedics: The Extremities, 8th ed. New York, NY: McGraw Hill; 2019.

Pain/paresthesias in median nerve distribution upon:
- ❖ Percussion over median nerve (Tinel sign)
- ❖ 1-minute sustained wrist flexion (Phalen sign)

## 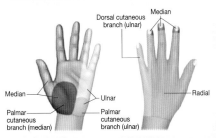 Median Nerve

**Sensory Distribution**

Dorsal cutaneous branch (ulnar)

Median

Median — Ulnar — Radial

Palmar cutaneous branch (median)    Palmar cutaneous branch (ulnar)

 Sensation over palmar surface of thenar eminence is spared in CTS as palmar cutaneous branch does not pass through carpal tunnel!

**Motor Deficit:**
Abductor pollicis brevis and opponens pollicis ⇨ impaired **thumb abduction and opposition**

##  Diagnosis

**Clinical Diagnosis**

Can confirm with EMG/NCS (slow median nerve conduction across wrist)

##  Treatment

Splint wrist in neutral position

NSAIDs for pain

Corticosteroid injections into carpal tunnel (for severe pain)

Surgical release of carpal tunnel (for severe or refractory cases)

# Colles' Fracture

## Definition

Classically described as an extra-articular distal radius fracture with dorsal angulation

Reproduced with permission from Knoop KJ, Stack LB, Storrow AB, et al: The Atlas of Emergency Medicine, 4th ed. New York, NY: McGraw Hill; 2016. Photo contributor: Kristin L. Stevens, MD.

**Elderly Patients**

**Younger Patients**

"Dinner fork" deformity: Dorsal angulation, dorsal displacement, radial shortening

Mechanism: Low energy, fall from standing height, fall onto outstretched hand

Mechanism: High energy, vehicle collision, athletics

## Associated Complications

Used with permission of Justin Montgomery, MD: University of Kentucky Radiology.

**Median Nerve Neuropathy**

**Rupture of the Extensor Pollicis Longus Tendon**

**Chronic Regional Pain Syndrome**

**Scapholunate and lunotriquetral ligament injury**

**DRUJ instability and incongruity with dorsal angulation**

## Treatment

Prereduction and post-reduction radiographs of the wrist will help decide nonoperative vs operative treatment

### Non-Op

**Reduction and Rigid Immobilization**

Elderly age is the most predictive factor of loss of reduction

Other factors include: Dorsal angulation >20, dorsal cortex comminution, involvement of the distal radioulnar joint

**Surgical Fixation**

Indications for surgery: Postreduction radial shortening >3 mm, dorsal tilt >10 degrees, intra-articular step-off 2 mm

Long-term data suggest that there is no difference in wrist range of motion or patient-reported outcomes between ORIF vs closed reduction in patients >70 years old

Complications of volar plate fixation include flexor tendon rupture, extensor tendon irritation, carpal tunnel syndrome.

When comparing ORIF vs external fixation, patient-reported outcomes are not statistically different at 2-year follow-up.

# Compartment Syndrome

## Anatomy

- The extremities are composed of relatively nonyielding fascial compartments and compartment syndrome can occur anywhere that skeletal muscle is surrounded by fascia.
- **Leg** (most common) has 4 compartments: Anterior, lateral, posterior, and deep posterior.
- **Forearm** has 3 compartments: Volar, dorsal, and mobile wad (lateral).
- **Hand** has 10 compartments: Hypothenar, thenar, adductor pollicis, dorsal interosseous (x4), volar interosseous (x3).
- **Arm** has 2 compartments: Flexor and extensor.
- **Foot** has 9 compartments (controversial): Medial, lateral, interosseous (x4), and central (x3)
- **Thigh** has 3 compartments: Anterior, posterior, and medial.

## Pathophysiology

- Occurs when pressure within an osseofascial compartment rises to a level that decreases the perfusion gradient across tissue capillary beds leading to muscle ischemia and death.
- Critical tissue pressure differentials are **≤20 mm Hg** from **diastolic pressure** or **≤30 mm Hg** from **mean arterial blood pressure.**
- Cascade of events: Local trauma and soft tissue injury lead to edema, intracellular swelling and bleeding causing increased interstitial pressure and eventual vascular occlusion and myoneural ischemia.
- Irreversible changes to nerves and muscle occur following **8 hours** of complete ischemia.

## Risk Factors

- Trauma, fracture, crush injury, contusion, gunshot wounds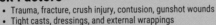
- Tight casts, dressings, and external wrappings
- Thermal injury, burn eschar
- Extravasation of IV infusion
- Reperfusion injury following prolonged ischemia

## Clinical Manifestations

- **The 5 P's:** Pain, pulselessness, paralysis, paresthesia, and pallor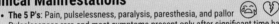
- Pulselessness rare and most symptoms present only after significant time has elapsed following onset of compartment syndrome
- **Pain out of proportion** to injury and **pain with passive stretching** of muscles in the corresponding compartment are the earliest and most sensitive indicators of compartment syndrome
- In pediatrics, **increased analgesia requirement** is often the first sign of compartment syndrome

## Diagnostic Evaluation

- Based primarily on physical exam in patients with intact mental status
- **Patient history** is important to determine mechanism of injury and associated risk factors for developing compartment syndrome
- Compartment pressure measurement is indicated when diagnosis is uncertain in an at risk patient
- Two most common measurement techniques involve the use of a **slit catheter** and a **side port needle**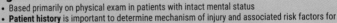
- Serum **creatine phosphokinase** has been used as an indicator of compartment syndrome and can be trended to monitor compartment decompression

## Treatment

- Casts or occlusive dressings should be removed completely and affected limb should be elevated no higher than level of patient heart.
- If clinical diagnosis of compartment syndrome remains unclear, **emergent fasciotomy** of compartments is necessary.

**Indications for emergent fasciotomy in setting of unclear clinical diagnosis:**
- Absolute compartment pressure >30 mm Hg
- Difference between diastolic pressure and compartment pressure of ≤20 mm Hg
- Compartment pressure ≤30 mm Hg from mean arterial blood pressure
- Fasciotomy is also performed in setting of concerning physical exam and elevated pressures with a pressure differential of >20 mm Hg

# Distal Humerus Fracture

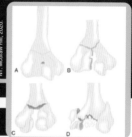

## 1 Etiology

**Trauma to the lower extremity**
- High-energy (MVC, peds vs auto) in younger patients
- Lower-energy falls in older patients

**Pathological fractures** associated with tumors

## 2 Clinical Presentation

Elbow pain and swelling
Gross elbow instability
**Neurovascular injury**
    Brachial artery
    Ulnar > Median > Radial nerve palsy

**Associated Injuries:**
Olecranon fracture
Coronoid fracture
Ligamentous injury
Elbow dislocation
Compartment syndrome

## 3 Diagnosis & Workup

<u>X-ray</u>: **AP, lateral, and oblique views of elbow**
    Image adjacent joints (shoulder and wrist) to rule out
    concomitant injuries

 <u>Traction view</u> of elbow helps delineate specific fragments

<u>CT Scan:</u> Surgical planning

## 4 Treatment

Long arm cast in extra-articular fractures, high-risk surgical candidates

<u>**Surgical Management:**</u>

- **Closed reduction, percutaneous pinning**—Minimally displaced fractures in pediatric patients
- **ORIF**—Intracolumnar, bicolumnar fractres
- **Total elbow arthroplasty**—Severely comminuted articular fractures in low demand patients

## 5 Complications

**Elbow stiffness occurs in almost all cases**
Heteroptic ossification
Post-traumatic arthritis
Nonunion, malunion
Compartment syndrome
Volkmann's contracture

# Elbow Dislocation

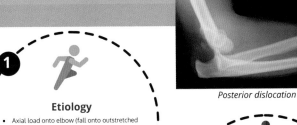

*Posterior dislocation*

**1**

## Etiology

- Axial load onto elbow (fall onto outstretched hand)
- Common in ages 10-20 years (M > F)
- 2nd most common major joint dislocation after shoulder
- **Risk Factors:**
    Shallow olecranon fossa
    Prominent olecranon tip

**2**

## Clinical Presentation

- Elbow pain and swelling
- Elbow held in flexion, resist ROM
- Associated neurovascular injury (ulnar n. most common)
- Posterolateral > posteromedial > anterior dislocation

  *Direction depends on location of the ulna*

**3**

## Diagnosis and Workup

- AP, lateral and oblique X-ray views of the elbow
- Assess ipsilateral wrist and shoulder for associated injuries
    - Distal radioulnar joint injury
    - Distal radius fracture
- **Simple** Dislocation—No associated fracture
- **Complex** Dislocation—Fracture of radial head, coronoid, medial epicondyle in peds

**4**

## Treatment

- Closed reduction and short-term immobilization for simple, stable dislocations

  Immobilize in position of maximum stability

- Open reduction internal fixation for elbows that are unstable after reduction, or for associated fractures

**5**

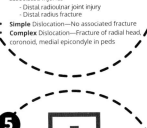

## Complications

- Compartment syndrome
- Elbow stiffness, contracture
- Chronic instability
- Heterotopic ossification
- Nerve injury (ulnar > median)

# Femoral Neck Fracture

## 1

### Etiology

- Young: High-energy trauma (MVC)
  - Associated with ipsilateral femoral shaft fracture (9%)
- Elderly: Low-energy fall, osteoporosis

## 2

### Clinical Presentation

Impacted, stress fracture
- Able to walk
- Groin pain
- No obvious deformity

Displaced fracture
- Unable to walk
- Pain in entire hip
- Leg externally rotated, abducted with shortening

## 4

### Classification (Garden)

**Type 1**
Incomplete
valgus
impacted

**Type 2**
Complete
Nondisplaced

**Type 3**
Complete
Partially
displaced

**Type 4**
Complete
Fully displaced

Reproduced with permission from Parks E: Practical Office Orthopedics. New York, NY: McGraw Hill; 2018.

## 3

### Diagnosis & Workup

- X-ray: AP pelvis, AP/lateral hip
- Internal rotation-traction: Helps define fracture type
- If groin pain and pain with walking/weight bearing, need further workup
  - MRI if suspect occult fracture
  - Bone scan if MRI not possible

Reproduced with permission from Ahern G, Brygel M: Exploring Essential Radiology. New York, NY: McGraw Hill; 2014.

## 5

### Treatment

| Type 1 | → | Non-op |
| Type 2 | → | Internal Fixation — Fix within 48 hours to prevent AVN |
| Type 3 / Type 4 | → | Arthroplasty — Hemi: Less dislocations THA: Less revisions |

CRPF: 3 screws oriented in inverted triangle

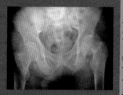

Reproduced with permission from Parks E: Practical Office Orthopedics. New York, NY: McGraw Hill; 2018.

Type 2-4 are treated nonoperatively if the patient is too old or too sick to undergo surgery

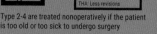

Reproduced with permission from Butterworth JF, Mackey DC, Wasnick JD: Morgan & Mikhail's Clinical Anesthesiology, 6th ed. New York, NY: McGraw Hill; 2018.

## 6

### Complications

- High mortality rate: 20-35%
- Avascular necrosis (femoral head infarct)
- Nonunion/malunion: Shortened neck & decreased offset leads to limp/decreased walking capacity over time
- Trochanteric bursitis/hardware pain
- Post-traumatic arthritis

# Femoral Shaft Fracture

## 1 Etiology

**Trauma to the lower extremity**
- High-energy trauma (MVC, peds vs auto) in younger patients
- Lower-energy fall or twisting mechanism in older patients

**Bisphosphonate** use associated with atypical subtrochanteric and femoral shaft fractures

**Pathological fractures** associated with tumors

## 2 Clinical Presentation

Extreme pain and deformity of lower extremity

Pain secondary to muscle spasm

**Tense, swollen thigh**
- **Close monitoring for compartment syndrome**

Shortening of affected limb

Look for additional injuries with high-energy trauma
- Ipsilateral femoral neck fractures with high energy mechanism

## 3 Diagnosis & Workup

AP and lateral X-rays of femur

X-rays of adjacent joints (hip and knee) to rule out concomitant injuries

Monitor for blood loss, even in closed injuries
- Can lose up to 5 liters of blood into the thigh

Consider CT scan if concerned for tumor

**Fracture Patterns**
- Transverse
- Oblique
- Spiral
- Segmental
- Comminuted

## 4 Treatment

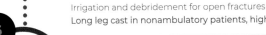

Surgical Management
- **Traction pin**—temporary management if fixation is delayed
- **Antegrade nail**—gold standard
- **Retrograde nail**—concomitant femoral neck or tibial fracture
- **ORIF**—fracture at diaphyseal-metaphyseal junction
- **Flexible nail**—pediatric femoral shaft fractures (pts <100 lbs)

Irrigation and debridement for open fractures

Long leg cast in nonambulatory patients, high-risk surgical candidates

## 5 Complications

Fat embolism syndrome (fever, altered mental status, petechiae, hypoxia)

Nonunion, malunion—Rotational malalignment

Missed femoral neck fracture

Infection

# Galeazzi's Fracture

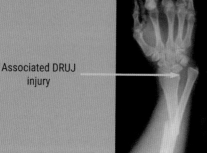
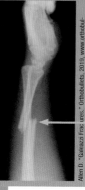

Associated DRUJ injury →

← Distal 1/3 radial shaft fracture

Allen D. "Galeazzi Fractures." Orthobullets, 2019, www.orthobullets.com/trauma/1029/galeazzi-fractures.

## Presentation

Reproduced with permission from OrthoInfo © American Academy of Orthopaedic Surgeons. http://orthoinfo.aaos.org

Fall on outstretched hand         Direct wrist trauma

**Pain**
**Swelling**
**Deformity**

## Treatment

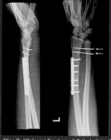

ORIF of radius with reduction and stabilization of DRUJ

Anatomic reduction of DRUJ is required

Allen D. "Galeazzi Fractures." Orthobullets, 2019, www.orthobullets.com/trauma/1029/galeazzi-fractures.

 Acute operative treatment superior to late reconstruction

## Evaluation

Allen D. "Distal Radial Ulnar Joint (DRUJ) Injuries." Orthobullets, 2018, www.orthobullets.com/trauma/1028/distal-radial-ulnar-joint-druj-injuries.

DRUJ stress causes wrist or midline forearm pain

Test forearm pronation/ supination for stability

Point tenderness over fracture site

## Complications

**1**                **2**                **3**

Compartment syndrome

- High energy crush injury
- Open fractures
- Diagnosis: Pain with passive stretch

Open fractures

- Neurovascular injuries

DRUJ subluxation

- Displaced by: Gravity, pronator quadratus, or brachioradialis

**MUGR**          **Don't get confused!**
**Monteggia**
**Ulna (with proximal radial dislocation)**
**Galeazzi**
**Radius (with DRUJ dislocation)**

# Humeral Shaft Fracture

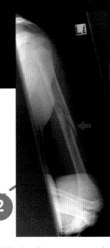

### 1  Etiology

- Direct trauma to upper arm

**Young patients:** High-energy injuries
**Older patients:** Low-energy falls

*Rule out underlying tumor*

### 2 Clinical Presentation

- Pain and weakness in arm
- **Radial nerve palsy:** Wrist drop, loss of thumb extension

### 3  Diagnosis and Workup

- AP and lateral X-rays of humerus
- Assess ipsilateral shoulder and elbow
- **CT scan**—Evaluate complex fractures

### 4 Treatment

- **Acute:** Coaptation splint
- **Nonoperative:** Sarmiento brace
- **External fixator**-associated soft tissue defects
- **Open reduction internal fixation**

*Absolute Indications for Surgery:*
- Severe soft tissue defect
- Vascular injury
- Open fracture
- Ipsilateral forearm fracture (floating elbow)
- Compartment syndrome
- Pathological fractures

### 5  Complications

- Radial nerve palsy
- Malunion
- Nonunion

# Intertrochanteric Hip Fracture

**1**

## Etiology

- Young: High-energy trauma (motor vehicle collision)
- Elderly: Low-energy fall, osteoporosis
- Direct blow to side of hip

**2**

## Clinical Presentation

Physical Exam
- Pain
- Shortened leg
- Externally rotated lower extremity
- Beware: Morel-Lavallée lesion—A closed degloving injury over the greater trochanter

**4**

## Classification (AO/OTA)

**Stable**

Standard obliquity: Greater trochanter to lesser trochanter (as illustrated)

Greater trochanter

Posteromedial Cortex Comminution

Lesser trochanter

Subtrochanteric Extension

**Unstable Features**

Reproduced with permission from Parks E: Practical Office Orthopedics. New York, NY: McGraw Hill; 2018.

Reverse obliquity (fracture originates on lesser trochanter and extends inferolateral)

**3**

## Diagnosis & Workup

- X-ray: AP pelvis, AP/lateral hip, traction/IR view
- MRI: Consider if persistent pain with negative X-rays
- Labs: CK for rhabdomyolysis (prolonged immobilization)
- Preoperative clearance
  - Cardiac workup doesn't need to be performed on every patient: Leads to delay in treatment, unnecessary costs

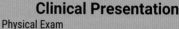

Reproduced with permission from Knoop KJ, Stack LB, Storrow AB, et al: The Atlas of Emergency Medicine, 4th ed. New York, NY: McGraw Hill; 2016. Photo contributor: Cathleen M. Vossler, MD.

**5**

## Treatment

| Nonoperative | Operative |
|---|---|
| | Urgent (fix ASAP, typically within 48 hours) |

**Not a surgical candidate (too sick)**

Stable: Dynamic Hip Screw

Reproduced with permission from Doherty GM: CURRENT Diagnosis & Treatment Surgery, 14th ed. New York, NY: McGraw Hill; 2015.

Unstable: Intramedullary nail

Tip-apex distance: Tip of the screw to the apex of the femoral head on AP and lateral views (<25 mm to prevent failure)

**Long nail:** Unstable fx
**Short nail:** Stable fx

**6**

## Complications

- Implant failure/cutout
  - Increased risk when tip-apex distance >25 mm
- Nonunion
- Malunion
- Abductor lurch
- Limb shortening
- Heterotopic ossification
- Decreased function

# Knee Dislocation

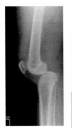

**"Dashboard injury"**

## Etiology

✳ **RARE** *High-Energy Injury*

**Anterior dislocation**—Hyperextension injury
**Posterior dislocation**—Posterior force on tibia with knee flexed

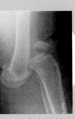

Anterior Dislocation

## Clinical Presentation

**Thorough Vascular Exam**

- Pain and deformity of lower extremity
- 50% self reduce prior to arrival at the hospital
- Distal pulses may be absent

## Diagnosis & Workup

- Ensure reduction
- Evaluate for associated fractures
- Vascular injury
- Ligamentous injury
- Neurologic exam

**X-rays of affected knee**
X-ray: Femur, tibia
ABIs, CT angiogram
MRI
Neurologic exam

## Treatment

- **Emergent closed reduction** (open reduction if needed)
- Surgical stabilization—External fixation
- Vascular exploration/repair if needed
- Timing of ligamentous repair is controversial

## Complications

- **Overall prognosis is poor**
  - ⊘ Patients rarely return to previous level of function
- Stiffness
- Laxity
- Recurrent instability

# Meniscal Tear

Major functions of the meniscus:

1. Joint stability and proprioception. 2. Shock absorption. 3. Joint lubrication.

## Anatomy:

Three zones:
- *Red:* 3 mm from capsular junction (good healing)
- *Red/White:* 3-5 mm
- *White:* >5 mm (poor healing)

**Lateral meniscus:**
- More mobile and circular in shape

**Medial meniscus:**
- Less mobile and "C" shaped

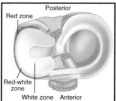

Posterior
Red zone
Red-white zone
White zone    Anterior

## Presentation:

1. Joint line tenderness and pain
2. Effusion or swelling
3. Sensation of "catching," "locking," or "slipping"
4. Decreased ROM and stiffness

  More common in older individuals/ athletes because the meniscus becomes more brittle with age (seen in ~40% of people >65 y.o.)

## Provocative Tests:

 Apley Test: Prone with knee at 90 degrees, compress and rotate knee

 Thessaly Test: Standing on isolated leg with knee slightly flexed to 20 degrees, internally and externally rotate

 McMurray Test: Supine, flex knee with valgus force and internal rotation or varus force and external rotation, then extend

## Imaging:

**MRI**
most sensitive (~94%)

 X-ray will not help identify meniscal tears, but may show concomitant DJD/OA

## Mechanism of Injury:

- Twisting motion of a flexed knee on a fixed or planted foot
- Rapid deceleration with a concurrent change in direction

 Associated injuries include ligamentous injuries such as ACL or MCL tears.

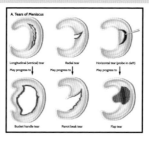

A. Tears of Meniscus

Longitudinal (vertical) tear
May progress to

Radial tear
May progress to

Horizontal tear (probe in cleft)
May progress to

Bucket handle tear

Parrot beak tear

Flap tear

## Types of Tears:

Longitudinal tears

Radial tears

Horizontal tears

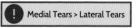 Medial Tears > Lateral Tears

## Treatment:

**Small** ➝ Physical therapy and rest, NSAIDs, Tylenol

**Central tear** ➝ Arthroscopic partial meniscectomy

**Peripheral tear** ➝ Arthroscopic meniscal repair

 Inside-Out Technique: For posterior horn, middle third, peripheral capsule, and bucket-handle tears

 Outside-In Technique: For anterior, middle and radial tears

 All-Inside Technique: For vertical longitudinal tears in the red-white zone and posterior horn

  Overall highly successful and effective procedure with best age predictor of success or those <40 y.o. (~90% good outcomes)

 Do not perform surgical treatment for degenerative/osteoarthritic meniscal tears.
Surgery is equal to physical therapy in degenerative tears.

# Monteggia Tear

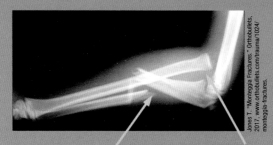

Jones T. "Monteggia Fractures." Orthobullets, 2017, www.orthobullets.com/trauma/1024/monteggia-fractures.

Proximal 1/3 ulnar shaft fracture

Associated radial head dislocation/instability

## Presentation and Evaluation

"Gymnastics Injuries." Beginning Exercises for the Wrist. https://gymnasticsinjuries.wordpress.com/tag/wrist-pain/

"Gymnastics Injuries." Beginning Exercises for the Wrist. https://gymnasticsinjuries.wordpress.com/tag/wrist-pain/

PIN neuropathy: Radial deviation of hand with wrist extension

Peak incidence 4-10 years old

Pain and swelling at elbow, +/– obvious dislocation of radioulnar joint

## Treatment

Closed reduction and casting in children (ensure anatomic alignment and stability)

ORIF of ulnar shaft fracture +/- open reduction of radial head

IM nailing of ulna for transverse or short oblique fractures

Reproduced with permission from Tenenbein M, Macias CG, Sharieff GQ, et al: Strange and Schafermeyer's Pediatric Emergency Medicine, 5th ed. New York, NY: McGraw Hill; 2019.

## Complications

1

PIN neuropathy
• Up to 10% in acute injuries

2

Malunion with radial head dislocation

## Don't get confused!

**MUGR**
**Monteggia**
**Ulna (with proximal radial dislocation)**
**Galeazzi**
**Radius (with DRUJ dislocation)**

# Native Hip Dislocation

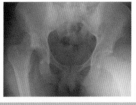

## Etiology

**High energy mechanism** in young patients

| **Simple Dislocation** | No associated fracture |

| **Complex Dislocation** | Dislocation with acetabular and/or femur fracture |

Posterior Dislocation

## Clinical Presentation

| **Posterior Dislocation** | **Axial load to flexed hip**<br>Associated with: Posterior acetabular fractures<br>Femoral head fractures<br>Sciatic nerve injury |

| **Anterior Dislocation** | **Axial load to hip in abduction and external rotation**<br>Associated with: Femoral head chondral injuries |

Anterior Dislocation

## Diagnosis & Workup

- **X-rays**: Pelvis series (AP, cross-table lateral, Judet views, inlet, outlet)

    Evaluate closely for ipsilateral femoral neck fracture

- **CT scan**: After reduction, helps operative planning
- Detailed neurovascular exam

## Treatment

- **Emergent closed reduction with 6 hours of dislocation**
    Delayed reduction increases risk of femoral head osteonecrosis

- **Traction pin indications:**
    1. To maintain reduction if hip grossly unstable
    2. Intra-articular fragments

- **ORIF**: Remove intra-articular fragments
    Fix associated acetabular, femoral head fractures

## Complications

- Post-traumatic arthritis
- Femoral head osteonecrosis
- Sciatic nerve injury (8-20%)—From initial injury or surgery

# Olecranon Bursitis

## Anatomy

- Bursae are closed synovial lined sacs found throughout the body that facilitate the movement of musculoskeletal structures.
- The olecranon bursa forms after age 6 in response to shear forces and pressure.
- The floor of the olecranon bursa lies on the distal triceps tendon and olecranon, while the roof lies directly beneath the subcutaneous tissue of the dorsal elbow.

## Pathophysiology

- Olecranon bursitis is the most common cause of superficial bursitis.
- Bursitis is typically classified as acute, chronic, or septic, but these are not exclusive diagnoses and often have overlapping symptoms.
- Chronic bursitis is typically associated with a concomitant medical disorder (ie, crystalline deposition disorders, psoriasis, or rheumatoid arthritis).
- Elbow pain has many etiologies so it is important to keep a broad differential.

## Risk Factors

- Previous history of bursitis
- Elbow trauma or soft tissue wounds
- History of repetitive elbow movement or direct pressure (miner, gardeners, athletes, mechanics, and desk jobs)
- Ipsilateral dialysis vascular access site or retained hardware

## Clinical Manifestations

- Bursal edema, erythema, and tenderness are present in the majority of cases
- Elbow range of motion remains largely unchanged and is generally painless
- Mild pain at maximum elbow flexion secondary to increased bursal pressure
- Soft tissue lesions: Lacerations, abrasions, tophi, rash, and skin discoloration
- Skin temperature >2° Celsius warmer than contralateral elbow
- Systemic symptoms (septic bursitis): Fevers, chills, weight loss, and nausea

## Diagnostic Evaluation

- Peripheral blood: ESR, CRP, glucose, CBC with differential
- Bursal aspiration: Culture, Gram stain, cell count, crystals, and glucose
- Aspiration consistent with septic bursitis: + cultures/Gram stain, >10K WBC, >50% PMN, <50% serum glucose
- *Staphylococcus aureus* is the most common organism identified
- Radiographs to rule out foreign bodies, underlying fracture, or bone spur
- Consider arthrocentesis to rule out septic joint if significant pain with elbow ROM

## Treatment

- NSAIDs, rest, compression, ice, and padded extension splint mainstay of treatment
- Oral vs parenteral antibiotics based on culture sensitivities for septic bursitis
- Partial or complete bursectomy indicated in severe medically refractory disease
- Great care and planning of surgical approach needed to avoid wound complications
- Treatment of any underlying medical conditions in secondary bursitis
- Corticosteroid injections associated with infection, persistent pain, and skin atrophy

# Osteoarthritis

## Risk Factors

| Increasing age | Joint trauma | Obesity | Female gender | Genetic |
|---|---|---|---|---|
|  |  |  |  |  |

## Pathology: Degeneration of the Whole Joint

A) Cartilage degeneration

B) Osteophyte formation (bone spur)

C) Subchondral bone sclerosis

D) Subchondral cyst formation

E) Synovitis and synovial hyperplasia

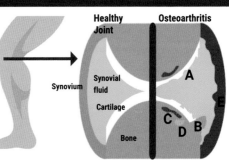

## History/Physical Exam

Pain

Impaired mobility

Decreased range of motion

Swelling

## Most Common Joints Affected

Knee

Hip

Spine

Finger

Toe

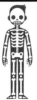
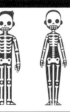

## Imaging: X-Ray Gold Standard

Joint space narrowing (loss of cartilage)

Osteophyte formation (bone spur)

Subchondral bone sclerosis

Subchondral bone cyst

## Treatment

Weight loss/activity modification

Physical therapy/bracing

Acetaminophen/NSAIDs

Intra-articular (IA) injections: Corticosteroid, hyaluronic acid

Joint replacement (arthroplasty)

## Presentation

- ☑ Soft tissue extension or mass
- ☑ Localized **pain** that is worse with **activity** and at **night**
- ☑ Swelling
- ☑ Pathological fracture (15-20%)

## Distribution

**Bimodal Distribution**
Teenagers (10-20 y.o.) >> Elderly (>65 y.o.)
↳ *primary origin*  ↳ *secondary origin*

Males > Females (1.22:1)

## Location

Located in **metaphysis** of bone
1. Distal femur (30%)
2. Proximal tibia (20%)
3. Proximal humerus (10%)
4. Pelvis = Jaw/skull (8%)

### CLASSIFICATIONS

| Intramedullary | vs | Surface Lesions |
|---|---|---|
| ☑ Conventional | | ☑ Parosteal |
| ☑ Telangiectatic | | ☑ Periosteal |
| ☑ Small Cell | | ☑ High-Grade |
| ☑ Low-Grade | | *(worse prognosis)* |

⚠ Long-term survival is >70% for patients who receive combination surgical resection and neoadjuvant chemotherapy.

⚠ 80% of osteosarcoma patients have metastatic or micro-metastatic disease at diagnosis.

# Osteosarcoma
## Malignant proliferation of osteoblasts

## Diagnosis

**X-ray** -> First-line imaging
↳ *"Codman's Triangle"*
↳ *"Sunburst Pattern"*

**Biopsy** -> Diagnostic

**Histological Appearance**
- ☑ Pleomorphic spindle cells
- ☑ Cellular atypia
- ☑ Osteoid producing

**MRI/CT-chest/whole body**
**Technetium scan** -> Staging and metastasis

## Treatment/Therapy

 - Surgical "en bloc" excision and reconstruction

 - Chemotherapy (Neo/adjuvant)
↳ *Methotrexate, doxorubicin, cisplatin, ifosfamide*

### AJCC STAGING
Stage I: Low grade
Stage IIA: High grade <8 cm
Stage IIB: High grade >8 cm
Stage III: High grade with skip metastasis
Stage IVA: Pulmonary metastasis
Stage IVB: Other metastasis

## Risk Factors

 Paget's disease (adults > 40 y.o.)

 Radiation exposure

 Familial retinoblastoma (↑500x)

 Bone infarcts

 *p*53 mutations
↳ *"Li-Fraumeni syndrome"*

**385**

# Prepatellar Bursitis
## Housemaid's Knee

### Anatomy
- The prepatellar bursa is actually composed of 2 anatomically distinct bursae (subcutaneous prepatellar bursa and the superficial intrapatellar bursa).
- The subcutaneous prepatellar bursa lies between the skin and patella, while the superficial intrapatellar bursa is between the skin and the tibial tubercle.
- These structures **do not** communicate with the knee joint.
- Their function is to **enhance gliding** of tissue over the patella.

### Pathophysiology
- Prepatellar bursitis may be caused by many inflammatory phenomena, however, **infection** is the primary concern.
- 20% of prepatellar bursitis cases are septic in etiology.
- Most common causative organism is *Staphylococcus aureus* (80%).
- Mechanism of infection is usually by direct inoculation from a cut or break in the skin and perpetuated by the poor vascular supply to the bursa.

### Risk Factors
- Prior history of bursal inflammation
- Knee trauma especially repetitive microtrauma or open wounds
- **History of excessive kneeling** (plumbers, roofers, carpet layers, gardeners)
- Immunocompromised status, alcoholism, chronic obstructive pulmonary disease, amyloid deposition secondary to chronic renal failure, rheumatoid arthritis, history of local corticosteroid therapy
- Athletes who participate in wrestling, basketball, football

### Clinical Manifestations
- Swelling, pain, erythema, and warmth (if septic) about the anterior knee
- Local tenderness to palpation
- **Pain with joint range of motion is atypical**
- Discomfort at extreme knee flexion can be seen due to compression of the inflamed bursa
- Activity medication such as avoiding stair climbing or athletics

### Diagnostic Evaluation
- Basic labs: CBC with differential, erythrocyte sedimentation rate (ESR), C-reactive protein (CRP)
- Aspiration of bursa is often necessary to exclude infectious etiology. Bursa aspiration should include culture, Gram stain, cell count, crystals, and glucose
- **Lateral approach** for aspiration recommended as entering bursa anteriorly increases risk of iatrogenic sinus tract formation
- Diagnosis threshold for septic prepatellar bursitis: + cultures/Gram stain, >1000 WBC, >50% PMN, <50% serum glucose

### Treatment
- Aseptic prepatellar bursitis consists of **rest, compression, and nonsteroidal anti-inflammatory drugs (NSAIDs).**
- Some patients may opt to have local corticosteroid injection.
- Corticosteroid injection may lead to faster symptom relief but has been associated with risk such as infection, skin atrophy, and chronic pain.
- Patients with suspected septic prepatellar bursitis should be treated with a course of antibiotics (IV vs PO antibiotics is controversial).
- First-generation cephalosporins and penicillinase-resistant penicillins are first-line agents for *Staphylococcus* and *Streptococcus* species.
- In refractory cases, surgical treatment with either open or arthroscopic bursectomy have shown good outcomes.
- Complications include wound healing issues, atrophic skin changes, subcutaneous hematoma, and severe tenderness.

# Prosthetic Hip Dislocation

## Etiology

- Occurs in 1-3% of primary total hip arthroplasties
- Risk of dislocation higher after revision THA
- Most dislocations occur within 1 year of surgery

*Dislocation risk is related to larger preoperative range of motion*

**Risk Factors**

Previous hip surgery
Prior dislocation
Malpositioned components
Neuromuscular disease (ie, Parkinson's)
Females > males
Rhematoid arthritis
Avascular necrosis
Previous hip fracture
Abductor deficiency

## Clinical Presentation

- 90% of dislocations are posterior
- **Posterior dislocations:** Hip in flexion, adduction, and internal rotation
- **Anterior dislocations:** Hip in extension, abduction, external rotation
- Acute onset pain
- Inability to bear weight on limb

## Diagnosis & Workup

- **X-rays:** AP and cross-table lateral of affected hip

Evaluate for aseptic loosening
Determine direction of dislocation
Evaluate components for improper positioning
Eccentric polyethylene liner wear
Periprosthetic fracture
Obtain CT scan for definitive version of the cup

## Treatment

- Closed reduction under conscious sedation

**Recurrent dislocation (>2 dislocations)**

**Revision THA:** Maximize head-neck offset: Larger femoral head, abductor advancement, constrained acetabular component, dual mobility implant

## Complications

- **Beware of a difficult closed reduction**
  Periprosthetic fracture
  Skin tear from pressure during reduction maneuver
- **Recurrent dislocation:** Sciatic nerve stretch injury, loss of soft tissue envelope (capsular compromise), acetabular or femoral bone loss

# Proximal Humerus Fracture

## 1 Etiology

- Young: High-energy trauma (motor vehicle collision)
- Elderly: Direct blow to sholder, fall in osteoporotic patient

## 2 Clinical Presentation

- Pain, swelling, decreased motion
- Ecchymosis of chest, arm, forearm
- Axillary nerve injury: Shoulder paralysis (deltoid muscle) and paresthesias
- Delayed: Hand & finger swelling

## 4 Classification (Neer)

1
2 Anatomical neck
3

Surgical neck

### 4 Parts:

1. Greater tuberosity
2. Lesser tuberosity
3. Humeral head
4. Humeral shaft

45° Angulation

4 Translation

Reproduced with permission from Tintinalli J, Ma OJ, Yealy DM, et al: Tintinalli's Emergency Medicine: A Comprehensive Study Guide, 9th ed. New York, NY: McGraw Hill; 2020.

## 3 Diagnosis & Workup

- X-ray: True AP (Grashey), scapular Y, axillary
- CT: Preoprative planning
- MRI: Rarely used

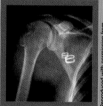

Reproduced with permission from Ahern G, Brygel M: Exploring Essential Radiology. New York, NY: McGraw Hill; 2013.

## 5 Treatment

(Based on position of individual parts)

| | Minimally displaced | Displaced |
|---|---|---|
| Translation | <1 cm | >1 cm |
| Angulaion | <45° | >45° |
| Treatment | Nonoperative/too sick – sling | Operative –2 part CRPP/IMN/ORI –3 or 4 parts: –Young: Hemiarthroplasty –Rotator cuff pathology or tuberosity comminution: Reverse shoulder arthroplasty |

## 6 Complications

- Shoulder stiffness
- Avascular necrosis of the humeral head (disruption of arcuate branch off anterior circumflex humeral artery leading to infarct)

# Radial Nerve Palsy

## Causes

**Saturday Night Palsy**

Draping of arm while asleep compresses nerve in the spiral groove of humerus

**Fractures**

Associated with 12% of proximal to mid-shaft humerus fractures

**Open Reduction Internal Fixation**

Radial nerve damaged during repair of humerus, distal humerus, and proximal forearm fractures

**Crutches**

Causes axillary compression of radial nerve

## Diagnosis

Motor deficits associated with level of radial nerve injury: Axilla to mid-forearm

Inability to extend the fingers, wrist, and occasionally the elbow

Decreased sensation over the dorsum of digits 1-4

EMG/NCS used to evaluate nerve continuity 3-4 months after nonoperative treatment

## Treatment

Non-Op

**Bracing and Observation**

70% return of sensation and motor function at 7 weeks for humeral shaft fractures

Atraumatic etiologies are appropriately treated with extension bracing to protect passive ROM

**Nerve Repair**

Nerve injuries classified by which layers of the nerve are damaged: Endoneurium, perineurium, epineurium

Higher rates of motor recovery if repaired <5 months of injury: 80%+ of patients recover wrist extension

## Etiology

## Clinical Presentation

### Tear Classification

Mechanism — Acute traumatic tears
Chronic/degenerative tear

Thickness — Partial thickness
Full thickness

Location — Articular side
Bursal side

Shoulder pain
Worse with overhead activity
Night pain
Loss of active ROM
Maintain passive ROM

Not all tears are symptomatic!

# Rotator Cuff Tear

**Rotator Cuff Function:**
- 4 muscles
  Supraspinatus
  Infraspinatus
  Teres minor
  Subscapularis
- Dynamic stabilizers of the glenohumeral joint
- Maintain a stable fulcrum for shoulder motion

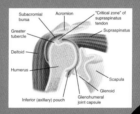

## Diagnosis

## Treatment

**X-ray** Usually normal
Rotator cuff arthropathy in chronic tears
· Proximal migration of the humerus

**MRI** Gold standard
Shows tear size, characteristics
Fatty atrophy of muscles
*Supraspinatus* = most commonly involved tendon

## Complications

*Nonoperative*

**Therapy, NSAIDs, injections**
- Partial tears
- Chronic tears
- Preserved shoulder function

*Operative*

**Arthroscopic rotator cuff repair**
- >50% partial thickness tears
- Acute full thickness tears
- Tear without significant retractio
- No fatty atrophy of muscles

Recurrence, repair failure
Axillary or subscapular nerve injury
Stiffness
Infection

# Scaphoid Fracture

## Anatomy

① Articulates with the distal radius, lunate, trapezium, capitate, and trapezoid
② 65-75% of fractures occur at the waist

③ Blood Supply:
- _Dorsal scaphoid branches_ of the radial artery account for blood supply to the proximal 70-80% of the scaphoid.
    -> In a **retrograde** fashion
- _Volar scaphoid branches_ of the radial artery account for blood supply to the distal 20-30% of scaphoid.
- _Anterior interosseous artery_ provides collateral circulation.

 Blood supply to waist and proximal pole is highly tenuous. -> High risk for nonunion and avascular necrosis if fracture occurs here

## Presentation

☑ Edema and Echymosis
☑ Usually no visible deformity
☑ Decreased ROM and grip strength
☑ Pain with palpation of **anatomical snuffbox**
☑ Pain with axial loading of thumb
☑ Usual mechanism is **fall on outstretched hand**

All patients with snuffbox/scaphoid tubercle tenderness should be treated as having a scaphoid fracture until proved otherwise

## Diagnosis & Imaging

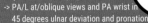

① X-ray is 1st-line imaging
   -> PA/L at/oblique views and PA wrist in 45 degrees ulnar deviation and pronation
   -> **Most common carpal fracture**

Negative radiographs with symptoms
   -> **Repeat radiographs in 10-14 days**
Advanced imaging (CT/MRI)
   -> _CT:_ Degree of displacement and surgical planning
   -> _MRI:_ Vascular compromise +/– avascular necrosis
      MRI sensitivity/specificity >97% for fracture
Radiographs tend to underestimate true displacement

Approximately 20% of patients with negative radiographs have an occult fracture.

## Treatment/Management

**Nondisplaced (stable) fractures:**
- Cast for 8-12 weeks, with above elbow thumb spica first 4-6 weeks then below elbow thumb spica for remainder.

**Displaced (unstable) fractures:**
- ORIF with possible cancellous bone autograft

Proximal pole fractures always managed with screw fixation even if nondisplaced due to high risk for avascular necrosis or nonunion

Controversy surrounds management of truly nondisplaced scaphoid waist fractures. Similar union rates and functional results have been demonstrated with cast immobilization compared to screw fixation.

## Fracture Classifications

| Herbert Classification (most common) | Russe Classification |
|---|---|
| **A**: Stable (tubercle or incomplete waist) | **Horizontal Oblique:** |
| **B**: Unstable (distal oblique, proximal pole, complete waist, trans-scaphoid- | -> Most stable |
| perilunate fracture/dislocation) | **Transverse:** |
| | -> Intermediate |
| **C**: Delayed union | **Vertical Oblique:** |
| **D**: Established nonunion | -> Least stable |

## Complications

- SLAC (scapholunate advanced collapse)
   -> If concurrent scapholunate ligament disruption or nonunion not identified
- Avascular necrosis (30% of proximal fractures)
- Nonunion/malunion
- Wrist arthritis
- Significantly increased rate of complications with surgical vs nonsurgical intervention

## Etiology

**Common Pathogens:**
- *Staph aureus*: >50% of cases
- *Strep pyogenes*
- *Neisseria gonorrhoeae*: sexually active patients

**Risk Factors:**
- Bacteremic spread
- Direct inoculation from open injury
- Spread from adjacent osteomyelitis
- Endocarditis/IV drug use

## Clinical Presentation

Joint effusion, erythema
**Significant pain with any range of motion**

**Location:** Knee > hip > shoulder
Sternoclavicular joint involved in IV drug users

# Septic Arthritis

## Diagnosis

✓ **Gold Standard**
Joint aspiration >50,000 WBC
Positive synovial Gram stain and culture

### Differential Diagnosis
- Gout
- Pseudogout
- Cellulitis
- Bursitis
- Hemarthrosis

Reproduced with permission from Murtagh J, Rosenblatt J, Coleman J, et al: Murtagh's General Practice, 7th ed. New York, NY: McGraw Hill; 2018.

## Treatment

**URGENT** surgical irrigation and debridement

↓

Followed by empirical antibiotic coverage, narrowed with culture results

## Complications

Cartilage damage within hours ➡ Arthritis
Sepsis
Osteomyelitis
Recurrent infection

# Shoulder Dislocation

## Etiology

### High-Energy Trauma

Younger age = higher risk of recurrent dislocation, chronic instability

 **ANTERIOR** Force to shoulder while arm in abduction, external rotation

**POSTERIOR** Force to shoulder while arm in adduction, flexion, internal rotation
**seizures, electrocution injuries*

## Clinical Presentation

Lack of shoulder ROM
- Palpable defect over lateral deltoid
- Fullness of humeral head in axilla
- Axillary nerve palsy (5%)

## Diagnosis & Workup

**X-Ray** ⇒ Views: AP, lateral, scapular Y, axillary
- Show dislocation direction
- Greater tuberosity fracture
**Hill-Sachs lesion**—Impaction of humeral head on glenoid

**CT Scan** ⇒ Glenoid bone loss in cases of chronic instability

**MRI** ⇒ Evaluate for rotator cuff injury in older patients

## Treatment

First-Time Dislocation:
Acute reduction + immobilization
Delayed physical therapy

Operative Repair/Reconstruction:
Recurrent dislocations with soft tissue injury
In cases of large glenoid bone loss

## Complications

**Risk factors for chronic instability**
Age <20 at first dislocation
Contact sports
Hyperlaxity
>25% glenoid bone loss

# Spinal Stenosis

Narrowing of the spinal canal ⟶ root or cord compression

 Lumbar Stenosis > Cervical Stenosis >> Thoracic Stenosis

## Presentation

 Pain exacerbated with walking or extension
of the back and improves when hunched over
-> **neurogenic claudication**

Paresthesias in posterolateral aspects of
legs and buttocks

Tingling and numbness

Weakness

+/− bowel or bladder dysfunction

 Most commonly seen in the 6th
and 7th decade of life

Most common
reason for lumbar
spine surgery in
patients >65 y.o.

## Classification Systems

### Etiology (Congenital vs Acquired)
* **Acquired Stenosis >> Congenital Stenosis**
* Congenital: Due to short pedicles and thick lamina
* Congenital stenosis measured by sagittal diameter
  Absolute Stenosis: <10 mm; relative stenosis: 10-12 mm

### Location of Stenosis
* *Central*: Disc osteophyte & ligamentum flavum hypertrophy
* *Lateral recess*: Facet hypertrophy & facet osteophytes
* *Foraminal*: Loss of disc height & foraminal disc protrusion
* *Extraforaminal*: Lateral disc herniation

### Radiographic Severity
* *Central*: Absolute if sagittal <10 mm, relative if 10-13 mm;
  cross-section area: Moderate <100 mm$^2$, severe <75 mm$^2$
* *Foraminal*: Diameter <3 mm or height <15 mm
* *Lateral*: Height <2 mm, depth <3 mm, or angle <30 degrees

Most commonly
occurs at L4-L5,
then L3-L4 & L5-S1

## Etiology

**Degenerative/Spondylotic**
Congenital (ie, achondroplasia)
Traumatic
Hypertrophy of facet capsule
Hypertrophy of ligamentum flavum
Osteophyte formation
Herniated disc
Space occupying lesions
-> Synovial cyst, neoplasm
Secondary disease process
-> Endocrinopathies, calcium
metabolism disorders,
inflammatory diseases

 80% of patients report good or
excellent outcomes after surgery,
but patient-reported satisfaction
tends to decrease over time.

## Treatment

 Nonoperative:
-> Oral meds: NSAIDs
-> Physical therapy
-> Bracing, weight loss
-> Steroid injections
-> Nerve block

2 Operative:
-> Indications: 3-6 months
persistent pain or progressive
neurological deficit
-> Surgical decompression and
fusion (ie, laminectomy,
foraminotomy, discectomy)

## Diagnostic Tools

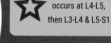 Radiographs (AP/Lat, Flex/Ext)
-> Osteophytes, disc space
narrowing, spondylolisthesis

MRI
-> Cord/root compression

CT/CT-myelogram
-> Canal narrowing

EMG/NCV
-> Nerve root damage, but NOT
REQUIRED

Not all patients with a narrowed
spinal canal have spinal stenosis.
The diagnosis requires symptoms!

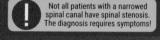  Complications of surgery include
thromboembolic events, dural tears,
infection, nerve root injury, epidural
hematoma, nonunion, and
spondylolisthesis.

# Spondylolisthesis

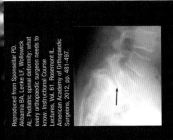

**Definition:** Forward slippage of one vertebral body relative to the one below it

## Isthmic

Spondylolisthesis with defect in pars interarticularis (spondylolysis)

- Axial back pain
- Neurogenic claudication
- Repetitive hyperflexion

>80% at L5-S1
- L5 radiculopathy: (EHL weakness)

Younger patients, gymnasts, football linemen, weight lifters

## Degenerative

Spondylolisthesis without a pars defect

- Axial back pain
- Neurogenic claudication
- L4 radiculopathy

L4-L5 (Quad/tib ant weakness)

Older patients

## Diagnosis

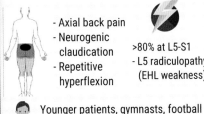
X-ray (AP, lateral, flexion/extension)     MRI

## Meyerding Classification

Grade 1: <25%
Grade 2: 25-50%
Grade 3: 50-75%
Grade 4: >75%

## Treatment

PT/NSAIDs     Epidural injections     Posterior spinal fusion

- Most patients can be treated nonoperatively
- Injections are second line to PT/NSAIDs
- Surgery indicated if fail 6 months of treatment

# Tibial Shaft Fracture

## Presentation

24% of long bone fractures are open fractures

60% of open fractures are Gustilo III severity

Risk for infection by Gustilo Class:
Type 1: 0-2%
Type 2: 2-10%
Type 3: 10-50%

HIV, diabetes, Smokers: Increased nonunion

## Initial Care

Assess neurovascular status
Angiography for ABI <0.9
Assess tetanus status for open fracture

Compartment syndrome pressures <30 mm Hg different from diastolic BP necessitates fasciotomy

Type 1-3A: Cephalosporin antibiotics within 3 hours of injury for 24-72 hours
Type 3B, 3C: +Gentamicin farm injuries: +Penicillin

Urgent irrigation and debridement for open Fx's

## Treatment

Early surgical stabilization allows for pain control, soft tissue management, and early mobility

### Plate Fixation

As definitive fixation for open fx's, there is a risk of osteomyelitis and hardware failure

### External Fixation

Malunion rate of 20%
Complication: Infection rate 16%, pin loosening, pin site infection

### Intramedullary Nailing

Preferred fixation method for closed fractures
Improved alignment, earlier bone union, earlier mobility

SPRINT Trial: Reaming vs Nonreamed open fracture nailing did not show a statistically significant difference in revision rates or further dynamization procedures at 1 year

Amputation is a complex issue. Limb salvage scores are not consistent in guiding clinical decision-making

LEAP Trial: Regardless of salvage vs amputation, patient outcomes tied to socioeconomic status
Poor prognosis for smokers, low self-efficacy

# Trochanteric Bursitis

Trochanteric Pain Syndrome

## Anatomy

- The trochanteric bursae lies **deep to the iliotibial band** just superficial to the gluteus medius at the lateral aspect of the thigh.
- The gluteus medius and minimus attach to the greater trochanter superiorly and anteriorly and act to abduct and internally rotate the hip.
- The gluteus medius and minimus have additional bursae deep to their respective tendons in the peritrochanteric area.
- Identification of multiple bursae about the trochanteric region has led many to refer to inflammatory bursa pathology about the hip as **trochanteric pain syndrome.**

## Pathophysiology

- Due to repetitive trauma caused by the iliotibial band tracking over the trochanteric bursa causing irritation and inflammation
- **Tendinosis** of the **gluteus medius and/or minimus tendons** is primarily responsible for the symptoms associated with trochanteric bursitis
- External snapping hip (external extra-articular coxa saltans), which involves thickened portions of the posterior iliotibial band or the anterior aspect of the gluteus maximus snapping over the greater trochanter during hip movement, may also lead to inflammation of the trochanteric bursa

## Risk Factors

- Trochanteric hip bursitis is more common in **females** (secondary to high hip offset) and middle aged or elderly people
- It is often seen in long distance **runners** and athletes that train on banked surfaces
- History of hip injury, spine disease, leg-length discrepancy, and rheumatoid arthritis also predispose patients to trochanteric bursitis
- Previous surgical treatment of hip (total hip arthroplasty or open reduction internal fixation of hip)

## Clinical Manifestations

- **Lateral hip pain** may radiate to the buttock, groin, low back, or down the iliotibial band
- Symptoms exacerbated by ambulation, uphill walking, stair climbing, and rising from a seated position
- Physical exam usually reveals **normal hip range of motion** with tenderness over the lateral aspect of the greater trochanter
- Pain reproduced with resisted abduction and internal rotation and FABER test

## Diagnostic Evaluation

- The diagnosis of trochanteric bursitis is based on **clinical** findings made after lumbar and intrinsic hip pathology have been excluded.
- Standard hip radiographs are obtained to assess for coexistent arthritic disease of the hip joint, trauma, or other confounding diagnoses.
- Diagnosis requires **lateral hip pain and tenderness over the greater trochanter,** as well as one of the following criteria: Pain at the extremes of rotation, abduction, or adduction; pain on forceful contraction of the hip abductors; and pseudoradiculopathy, with pain primarily radiating down the lateral aspect of the thigh.
- Though not a first-line test, **MRI** is often a reliable modality to diagnose trochanteric bursitis and will show increased signal in bursae on T2 sequence; can also aid in ruling out labral and other impingement processes (ultrasound can be used in patients unable to have a MRI).

## Treatment

- First-line therapy is always conservative with **nonsteroidal anti-inflammatory drugs (NSAIDs), stretching, and/or physical therapy.**
- Persistent symptoms can be treated with local corticosteroid injection.
- Refractory cases can be treated with surgical intervention based on the etiology of the pain. Techniques include bursectomy (open vs arthroscopic), abductor tendon debridement and reattachment, iliotibial band release or trochanteric reduction osteotomy.
- Published results consist of small cases series; however, outcomes for both open and arthroscopic surgical treatment have illustrated satisfactory results.
- Complications of trochanteric reduction osteotomy include nonunion and impaired abductor function.
- Patients post-total hip arthroplasty (THA), may require revision THA, while those with history of open reduction internal fixation of the hip can require removal of hardware for symptom control.

# References _____

**Achilles Tendon Rupture**
Mann JA, Chou LB, Ross SK. Foot and ankle surgery. In: Skinner HB, McMahon PJ, eds. *Current Diagnosis & Treatment in Orthopedics*. 5th ed. New York, NY: McGraw Hill; 2014.

**Ankylosing Spondylitis**
Kubiak EN, Moskovich R, Errico TJ, Di Cesare PE. Orthopaedic management of ankylosing spondylitis. *J Am Acad Orthop Surg* 2005;13:267e78.

**Anterior Cruciate Ligament Injuries**
Maitin IB, Cruz E, Hodde M. Rehabilitation of lower extremity injuries. In: Mitra R, ed. *Principles of Rehabilitation Medicine*. New York, NY: McGraw Hill; 2019.

**Back Pain**
Biyani A, Andersson GB. Low back pain: pathophysiology and management. *J Am Acad Orthop Surg.* 2004;12(2):106-115.

Karppinen J, Shen FH, Luk KDK, Andersson GBJ, Cheung KMC, Samartzis D. Management of degenerative disk disease and chronic low back pain. *Orthop Clin N Am.* 2011;42(4):513-528.

Shen FH, Samartzis D, Andersson GBJ. Nonsurgical management of acute and chronic low back pain. *J Am Acad Orthop Surg.* 2006;14(8):477-487.

U.S. Department of Health and Human Services, National Institutes of Health, National Institute of Neurologic Disorders and Stroke. *Low Back Pain*. NIH Publication; 2014.

**Boxer's Fracture**
Bednar MS, Light TR, Bindra R. Hand surgery. In: Skinner HB, McMahon PJ, eds. *Current Diagnosis & Treatment in Orthopedics*. 5th ed. New York, NY: McGraw-Hill; 2014. http://accessmedicine.mhmedical.com/content.aspx?bookid=675&sectionid=45451715. Accessed November 27, 2019.

Black W, Hosey RG, Johnson JR, Evans-Rankin K, Rankin WM. Common upper & lower extremity fractures. In: South-Paul JE, Matheny SC, Lewis EL, eds. *CURRENT Diagnosis & Treatment: Family Medicine*. 4th ed. New York, NY: McGraw-Hill; 2015. http://accessmedicine.mhmedical.com/content.aspx?bookid=1415&sectionid=77059155. Accessed November 28, 2019.

Diaz-Garcia R, Waljee JF. Current management of metacarpal fractures. *Hand Clin.* 2013. doi:10.1016/j.hcl.2013.09.004

Collitz KM, Hammert WC, Vedder NB, Huang JI. Metacarpal fractures: treatment and complications. *Hand.* 2014. doi:10.1007/s11552-013-9562-1

Raukar NP, Raukar GJ, Savitt DL. Extremity trauma. In: Knoop KJ, Stack LB, Storrow AB, Thurman R, eds. *The Atlas of Emergency Medicine*. 4th ed. New York, NY: McGraw Hill; 2016. http://accessmedicine.mhmedical.com/content.aspx?bookid=1763&sectionid=125434935. Accessed November 27, 2019.

Strub B, Schindele S, Sonderegger J, Sproedt J, Von Campe A, Gruenert JG. Intramedullary splinting or conservative treatment for displaced fractures of the little finger metacarpal neck? A prospective study. *J Hand Surg Eur Vol.* 2010. doi:10.1177/1753193410377845

**Bursitis, Olecranon**
Aaron DL, Patel A, Kayiaros S, Calfee R. Four common types of bursitis: diagnosis and management. *J Am Acad Orthop Surg.* 2011; 19(6):359-367.

Reilly D, Kamineni S. Olecranon bursitis. *J Shoulder Elb Surg.* 2016; 25(1):158-167.

Sayegh ET, Strauch RJ. Treatment of olecranon bursitis: a systematic review. *Arch Orthop Trauma Surg.* 2014; 134 (11):1517-1536.

## Carpal Tunnel Syndrome

Berkowitz AL. *Clinical Neurology and Neuroanatomy: A Localization-Based Approach.* New York, NY: McGraw Hill; 2017.

Le T, Bhushan V. *First Aid for the USMLE Step 1 2019.* 29th ed. New York, NY: McGraw Hill; 2018.

Le T, Bhushan V. *First Aid for the USMLE Step 2 CK.* 10th ed. New York, NY: McGraw Hill; 2018.

## Colles' Fracture

Arora R, Gabl M, Gschwentner M, Deml C, Krappinger D, Lutz M. A comparative study of clinical and radiologic outcomes of unstable Colles type distal radius fractures in patients older than 70 years: nonoperative treatment versus volar locking plating. *J Orthop Trauma.* 2009. doi:10.1097/BOT.0b013e31819b24e9.

Black W, Hosey RG, Johnson JR, Evans-Rankin K, Rankin WM. Common upper & lower extremity fractures. In: South-Paul JE, Matheny SC, Lewis EL, eds. *CURRENT Diagnosis & Treatment: Family Medicine.* 4th ed. New York, NY: McGraw-Hill. http://accessmedicine.mhmedical.com/content.aspx?bookid=1415&sectionid=77059155. Accessed November 28, 2019.

Chen NC, Jupiter JB. Management of distal radial fractures. *J Bone Jt Surg – Ser A.* 2007. doi:10.2106/JBJS.G.00020.

Koval K, Haidukewych GJ, Service B, Zirgibel BJ. Controversies in the management of distal radius fractures. *J Am Acad Orthop Surg.* 2014. doi:10.5435/JAAOS-22-09-566.

Lichtman DM, Bindra RR, Boyer MI, et al. Treatment of distal radius fractures. *J Am Acad Orthop Surg.* 2010. doi:10.5435/00124635-201003000-00007.

Raukar NP, Raukar GJ, Savitt DL. Extremity trauma. Figure 11.21. In: Knoop KJ, Stack LB, Storrow AB, Thurman R, eds. *The Atlas of Emergency Medicine.* 4th ed. New York, NY: McGraw-Hill. http://accessmedicine.mhmedical.com/content.aspx?bookid=1763&sectionid=125434935. Accessed November 25, 2019.

## Compartment Syndrome

Olson SA, Glasgow RR. Acute compartment syndrome in lower extremity musculoskeletal trauma. *J Am Acad Orthop Surg.* 2005;13:436-444.

Prasarn ML, Ouellette EA. Acute compartment syndrome of the upper extremity. *J Am Acad Orthop Surg.* 2011;19:49-58.

Whitesides TE, Heckman MM. Acute compartment syndrome: update on diagnosis and treatment. *J Am Acad Orthop Surg.* 1996;4:209-218.

## Distal Humerus Fractures

Vanderhave K. Orthopedic surgery. In: Doherty GM, ed. *CURRENT Diagnosis & Treatment: Surgery.* 14th ed. New York, NY: McGraw-Hill; 2015.

## Elbow Dislocation

Raukar NP, Raukar GJ, Savitt DL. Extremity trauma. In: Knoop KJ, Stack LB, Storrow AB, Thurman R, eds. *The Atlas of Emergency Medicine.* 4th ed. New York, NY: McGraw Hill; 2016.

## Femoral Neck Fractures

Ahern G, Brygel M. *Exploring Essential Radiology*; 2014. https://accessmedicine.mhmedical.com/content.aspx?bookid=870&sectionid=52144067. Accessed March 23, 2019.

Butterworth JF, Mackey DC, Wasnick JD. *Morgan & Mikhail's Clinical Anesthesiology.* 6th ed. 2018. https://accessmedicine.mhmedical.com/content.aspx?bookid=2444&sectionid=193562468. Accessed March 23, 2019.

Parks E. *Practical Office Orthopedics*; 2017. https://accessmedicine.mhmedical.com/content.aspx?bookid=220&sectionid=172778454. Accessed March 23, 2019.

**Femoral Shaft Fracture**

Courtney C. Hip and femur injuries. In: Tintinalli JE, Ma O, Yealy DM, et al, eds. *Tintinalli's Emergency Medicine: Comprehensive Study Guide*. 9th ed. New York, NY: McGraw-Hill; 2016.

**Galeazzi's Fracture**

Allen D. Distal radial ulnar joint (DRUJ) injuries. Orthobullets. www.orthobullets.com/trauma/1028/distal-radial-ulnar-joint-druj-injuries. Updated October 8, 2020.

Allen D. Galeazzi fractures. Orthobullets. www.orthobullets.com/trauma/1029/galeazzi-fractures. Updated January 19, 2019.

American Academy of Orthopaedic Surgeons. OrthoInfo. Wrist Sprains. https://orthoinfo.aaos.org/en/diseases--conditions/wrist-sprains

Egol KA, Koval KJ, Zuckerman JD. Radius and ulna shaft. *Handbook of Fractures*. Philadelphia, PA: Wolters Kluwer Health; 2010.

**Hip Dislocation – Native**

Courtney C. Hip and femur injuries. In: Tintinalli JE, Ma O, Yealy DM, et al, eds. *Tintinalli's Emergency Medicine: Comprehensive Study Guide*. 9th ed. New York, NY: McGraw-Hill; 2016.

**Humeral Shaft Fracture**

Courtney C. Hip and femur injuries. In: Tintinalli JE, Ma O, Yealy DM, et al, eds. *Tintinalli's Emergency Medicine: Comprehensive Study Guide*. 9th ed. New York, NY: McGraw-Hill; 2016.

**Intertrochanteric Hip Fracture**

Asante A, Greenberg S, Atanelov L. Rehabilitation medicine of hip fractures and falls. In: Mitra R, ed. *Principles of Rehabilitation Medicine*; 2019. https://accessmedicine.mhmedical.com/content.aspx?bookid=2550&sectionid=206767350. Accessed March 23, 2019.

Doherty GM. *CURRENT Diagnosis & Treatment: Surgery*. 14th ed. 2015. https://accessmedicine.mhmedical.com/content.aspx?bookid=1202&sectionid=71527086. Accessed March 23, 2019.

Edward (Ted) P. *Practical Office Orthopedics*. Parks E. eds. *Practical Office Orthopedics*. New York, NY: McGraw Hill; 2018.

Knoop KJ, Stack LB, Storrow AB, Thurman, RJ, eds. *The Atlas of Emergency Medicine*. 4th ed. New York, NY: McGraw Hill; 2016.

**Knee Dislocation**

Raukar NP, Raukar GJ, Savitt DL. Extremity trauma. In: Knoop KJ, Stack LB, Storrow AB, Thurman R, eds. *The Atlas of Emergency Medicine*. 4th ed. New York, NY: McGraw-Hill; 2016.

**Meniscal Tears**

Azar FM. Arthroscopic meniscectomy. In: Wiesel SW, ed. *Operative Techniques in Orthopaedic Surgery*. Philadelphia, PA: Lippincott Williams & Wilkins; 2011:263-273.

Kise NJ, Risberg MA, Stensrud S, et al. Exercise therapy versus arthroscopic partial meniscectomy for degenerative meniscal tear in middle aged patients: randomized controlled trial with two year follow-up. *BMJ*, 2016;354:1-9.

Malanga GA, Andrus S, Nadler SF, McLean J. Physical examination of the knee: a review of the original test description and scientific validity of common orthopedic tests. *Arch Phys Med Rehabil*. 2003;84(4):592-603.

McCarty EC, Walsh WM, Madden CC. Knee injuries. In: Madden CC, Putukian M, McCarty EC, Young CC, eds. *Netter's Sports Medicine*. 2nd ed. Philadelphia, PA: Elsevier; 2018:434-445.

Sgaglione NA, Angel MJ. Meniscal repair. In: Wiesel SW, ed. *Operative Techniques in Orthopaedic Surgery*. Philadelphia, PA: Lippincott Williams & Wilkins; 2011:274-283.

Thompson JC. *Netter's Concise Orthopaedic Anatomy*. 2nd ed. Philadelphia, PA: Saunders Elsevier; 2016.

## Monteggia Tear

Egol, KA. Koval KJ, Zuckerman JD. Radius and ulna shaft. *Handbook of Fractures*. Philadelphia, PA: Wolters Kluwer Health; 2010.

Gymnastics Injuries. https://gymnasticsinjuries.wordpress.com/tag/wrist-pain/. Updated November 12, 2013.

Jones T. Monteggia fractures. Orthobullets. https://www.orthobullets.com/trauma/1024/monteggia-fractures. Updated November 22, 2020.

## Osteoarthritis

Altman R, Asch E, Bloch D, et al. Development of criteria for the classification and reporting of osteoarthritis. Classification of osteoarthritis of the knee. Diagnostic and Therapeutic Criteria Committee of the American Rheumatism Association. *Arthritis Rheum*. 1986;29(8):1039-1049. Epub 1986/08/01. PubMed PMID: 3741515.

Chen D, Shen J, Zhao W, et al. Osteoarthritis: toward a comprehensive understanding of pathological mechanism. *Bone Res*. 2017;5:16044. doi: 10.1038/boneres.2016.44. PubMed PMID: 28149655; PMCID: PMC5240031.

Goldring MB. Articular cartilage degradation in osteoarthritis. *HSS J*. 2012;8(1):7-9. Epub 2013/02/02. doi: 10.1007/s11420-011-9250-z. PubMed PMID: 23372517; PMCID: PMC3295961.

Goldring SR. Alterations in periarticular bone and cross talk between subchondral bone and articular cartilage in osteoarthritis. *Ther Adv Musculoskelet Dis*. 2012;4(4):249-258. Epub 2012/08/04. doi: 10.1177/1759720X12437353. PubMed PMID: 22859924; PMCID: PMC3403248.

Hunter DJ, McDougall JJ, Keefe FJ. The symptoms of osteoarthritis and the genesis of pain. *Med Clin North Am*. 2009;93(1):83-100, xi. doi: 10.1016/j.mcna.2008.08.008. PubMed PMID: 19059023.

Loeser RF, Goldring SR, Scanzello CR, Goldring MB. Osteoarthritis: a disease of the joint as an organ. *Arthritis Rheum*. 2012;64(6):1697-707. doi: 10.1002/art.34453. PubMed PMID: 22392533; PMCID: PMC3366018.

Scanzello CR, Goldring SR. The role of synovitis in osteoarthritis pathogenesis. *Bone*. 2012;51(2):249-257. Epub 2012/03/06. doi: 10.1016/j.bone.2012.02.012. PubMed PMID: 22387238; PMCID: 3372675.

Setton LA, Elliott DM, Mow VC. Altered mechanics of cartilage with osteoarthritis: human osteoarthritis and an experimental model of joint degeneration. *Osteoarthr Cartil*. 1999;7(1):2-14. Epub 1999/06/15. doi: 10.1053/joca.1998.0170. PubMed PMID: 10367011.

## Osteosarcoma

Lindsey BA, Markel JE, Kleinerman ES. Osteosarcoma overview. *Rheumatol Ther*. 2017;4(1):25-43.

Moore DD, Luu HH. Osteosarcoma. In: Peabody T, Attar S, eds. *Orthopaedic Oncology: Primary and Metastatic Tumors of the Skeletal System*. New York, NY: Springer; 2014:65-92.

Ottaviani G, Jaffe N. The epidemiology of osteosarcoma. In: Jaffe N, Bruland O, Bielack S, eds. *Pediatric and Adolescent Osteosarcoma*. Boston, MA Springer; 2009:3-13.

## Prepatellar Bursitis

Aaron DL, Patel A, Kayiaros S, Calfee R. Four common types of bursitis: diagnosis and management. *J Am Acad Orthop Surg*. 2011;19(6):359-367.

Aguiar RO, Viegas FC, Fernandez RY, Trudell D, Haghighi P, Resnick D. The prepatellar bursa: cadaveric investigation of regional anatomy with MRI after sonographically guided bursography. *AJR Am J Roentgenol*. 2007;188(4):W355-358.

Cea-Pereiro JC, Garcia-Meijide J, Mera-Varela A, Gomez-Reino JJ. A comparison between septic bursitis caused by Staphylococcus aureus and those caused by other organisms. *Clin Rheumatol*. 2001;20(1):10-14.

Khodaee M. Common superficial bursitis. *Am Fam Physician*. 2017;95(4):224-231.

Meade TC, Briones MS, Fosnaugh AW, Daily JM. surgical outcomes in endoscopic versus open bursectomy of the septic prepatellar or olecranon bursa. *Orthopedics*. 2019;42(4):1-4.

## Prosthetic Hip Dislocation

Vanderhave K. Orthopedic surgery. In: Doherty GM, ed. *CURRENT Diagnosis & Treatment: Surgery*. 14th ed. New York, NY: McGraw-Hill; 2014.

Marchie A, Freiberg AA, Kwon Y. Approach to the patient with a painful prosthetic hip or knee. In: Imboden JB, Hellmann DB, Stone JH, eds. *CURRENT Diagnosis & Treatment: Rheumatology*. 3rd ed. New York, NY: McGraw Hill; 2013.

## Proximal Humerus Fracture
Ahern G, Brygel M. Upper limb. *Exploring Essential Radiology*. New York, NY: McGraw Hill; 2014. https://access-medicine.mhmedical.com/content.aspx?bookid=870&sectionid=52144069&jumpsectionid=52149736. Accessed March 23, 2019.

## Radial Nerve Palsy
Bhat L, Humphries RL. Neurologic emergencies. In: Stone C, Humphries RL, eds. *CURRENT Diagnosis & Treatment: Emergency Medicine*. 8th ed. New York, NY: McGraw Hill; 2017.

Chaudhry S, Ipaktchi KR, Ignatiuk A. Updates on and controversies related to management of radial nerve injuries. *J Am Acad Orthop Surg*. 2019;27:e280-e284.

DeFranco MJ, Lawton JN. Radial nerve injuries associated with humeral fractures. *J Hand Surg Am*. 2006;31(4):655-663.

LeBlond RF, Brown DD, Suneja M, Szot JF, eds. The nervous system. *DeGowin's Diagnostic Examination*. 10th ed. New York, NY: McGraw Hill; 2014.

Pan CH, Chuang DC, Rodríguez-Lorenzo A. Outcomes of nerve reconstruction for radial nerve injuries based on the level of injury in 244 operative cases. *J Hand Surg Eur Vol*. 2010;35(5):385-391.

Shao YC, Harwood P, Grotz MR, Limb D, Giannoudis PV. Radial nerve palsy associated with fractures of the shaft of the humerus: a systematic review. *J Bone Joint Surg Br*. 2005;87(12):1647-1652.

## Rotator Cuff Tear
Jameson J, Fauci AS, Kasper DL, Hauser SL, Longo DL, Loscalzo J. *Harrison's Principles of Internal Medicine*. 20th ed. New York, NY: McGraw Hill; 2018.

## Scaphoid Fracture
Fowler JR, Hughes TB. Scaphoid fractures. *Clin Sports Med*. 2015;34(1):37-50.

Ko JH, Pet MA, Khouri JS, Hammert WC. Management of scaphoid fractures. *Plast Reconstr Surg*. 2017;140(2):333-346.

Thompson JC. *Netter's Concise Orthopaedic Anatomy*. 2nd ed. Philadelphia, PA: Saunders Elsevier; 2016.

Watson JT, Weikert DR, van Zeeland N. Hand and wrist injuries. In: Madden CC, Putukian M, McCarty EC, Young CC, eds. *Netter's Sports Medicine*. 2nd ed. Philadelphia, PA: Elsevier; 2018: 391-401.

## Septic Arthritis
Le T, Bhushan V, et al. *First Aid for the USMLE Step 2 CK*. 10th ed. New York, NY: McGraw Hill Education; 2019.

## Shoulder Dislocation
Anand A, Park B. Acute management of shoulder dislocations. *J Am Acad Orthop Surg*. 2015 Apr 27;23(4):209.

Shin S-J, Yun Y-H, Kim DJ, Yoo JD. Treatment of traumatic anterior shoulder dislocation in patients older than 60 years. *Am J Sports Med*. 2012 Apr 27;40(4):822-827.

## Spinal Stenosis
Babb A, Carlson WO. Spinal stenosis. *S D Med*. 2006;59(3):103-105.

Schnebel BE. Thoracic and lumbosacral spine injuries. In: Madden CC, Putukian M, McCarty EC, Young CC, eds. *Netter's Sports Medicine*. 2nd ed. Philadelphia, PA: Elsevier; 2018: 415-424.

Schroeder GD, Kurd MF, Vaccaro AR. Lumbar spinal stenosis: how is it classified? *J Am Acad Orthop Surg*. 2016;24(12):843-852.

Thompson JC. *Netter's Concise Orthopaedic Anatomy*. 2nd ed. Philadelphia, PA: Saunders Elsevier; 2016.

Truumees E. Spinal stenosis: pathophysiology, clinical and radiologic classification. *Instr Course Lect*. 2005;54:287-302.

## Spondylolisthesis

Moore D. Adult Isthmic Spondylolisthesis. Orthobullets. 2019. https://www.orthobullets.com/spine/2038/adult-isthmic-spondylolisthesis

Moore, D. Degenerative Spondylolisthesis. Orthobullets. 2019. https://www.orthobullets.com/spine/2039/degenerative-spondylolisthesis

Spondylolysis and Spondylolisthesis. AAOS OrthoInfo, 2019. https://orthoinfo.aaos.org/en/diseases--conditions/spondylolysis-and-spondylolisthesis/

## Tibial Shaft Fracture

Bach AW, Hansen ST Jr. Plates versus external fixation in severe open tibial shaft fractures: a randomized trial. *Clin Orthop Relat Res.* 1989;(241):89-94.

Bosse MJ, MacKenzie EJ, Kellam JF, et al. An analysis of outcomes of reconstruction or amputation after leg-threatening injuries. *N Engl J Med.* 2002;347(24):1924-1931.

Cannada LK, Jones AL. Demographic, social and economic variables that affect lower extremity injury outcomes. *Injury.* 2006;37(12):1109-1116.

Court-Brown CM, McBirnie J. The epidemiology of tibial fractures. *J Bone Joint Surg Br.* 1995;77(3):417-421.

Dellinger EP, Caplan ES, Weaver LD, et al. Duration of preventive antibiotic administration for open extremity fractures. *Arch Surg.* 1988;123(3):333-339.

Giannoudis PV, Papakostidis C, Roberts C. A review of the management of open fractures of the tibia and femur. *J Bone Joint Surg Br.* 2006;88(3):281-289.

Gustilo RB, Anderson JT. Prevention of infection in the treatment of one thousand and twenty-five open fractures of long bones: retrospective and prospective analyses. *J Bone Joint Surg Am.* 1976;58(4):453-458.

Melvin SJ, Dombroski DG, Torbert JT, Kovach SJ, Esterhai JL, Mehta S. Open tibial shaft fracutres: I. Evaluation and initial wound management. *J Am Acad Orthop Surg.* 2010;18(1):10-19.

Melvin SJ, Dombroski DG, Torbert JT, Kovach SJ, Esterhai JL, Mehta S. Open tibial shaft fracutres: II. Definitive management and limb salvage. *J Am Acad Orthop Surg.* 2010;18(2):108-117.

Patzakis MJ, Wilkins J. Factors influencing infection rate in open fracture wounds. *Clin Orthop Relat Res.* 1989;(243):36-40.

Patzakis MJ, Wilkins J, Moore TM. Use of antibiotics in open tibial fractures. *Clin Orthop Relat Res.* 1983;(178):31-35.

Sanders R, Swiontkowski M, Nunley J, Spiegel P. The management of fractures with soft-tissue disruptions. *J Bone Joint Surg Am.* 1993;75(5):778-789.

Study to Prospectively Evaluate Reamed Intramedullary Nails in Patients with Tibial Fractures Investigators, Bhandari M, Guyatt G, et al. Randomized trial of reamed and unreamed intramedullary nailing of tibial shaft fractures. *J Bone Joint Surg Am.* 2008;90(12):2567-2578.

## Trochanteric Bursitis

Aaron DL, Patel A, Kayiaros S, Calfee R. Four common types of bursitis: diagnosis and management. *J Am Acad Orthop Surg.* 2011;19(6):359-367.

Lustenberger DP, Ng VY, Best TM, Ellis TJ. Efficacy of treatment of trochanteric bursitis: a systematic review. *Clin J Sport Med.* 2011;21(5):447-453.

Nurkovic J, Jovasevic L, Konicanin A, et al. Treatment of trochanteric bursitis: our experience. *J Phys Ther Sci.* 2016;28(7):2078-2081.

Redmond JM, Chen AW, Domb BG. Greater trochanteric pain syndrome. *J Am Acad Orthop Surg.* 2016;24(4):231-240.

Yen YM, Lewis CL, Kim YJ. Understanding and treating the snapping hip. *Sports Med Arthrosc Rev.* 2015;23(4):194-199.

# Nephrology

*Neeral Shah, MD and Brendan T. Bowman, MD*

# Acidosis, Metabolic (Anion Gap)

Anion Gap =
$$[Na^+] - ([Cl^-] + [HCO_3^-]) + 2.5 (4 - albumin)$$
normal: 8-12

## Notable Signs

**M**ethanol   Permanent blindness

**U**remia   Altered mental status

**D**iabetic ketoacidosis   Fruity breath

**P**ropylene glycol   CNS depression

**I**soniazid   Anticholinergic symptoms

**L**actic acidosis   **i** Most common cause

**E**thylene glycol   Renal toxicity Oxalate crystals

**S**alicylates   Tinnitus Hyperventilation

# Acidosis, Metabolic (Nongap)

$$\text{Anion Gap} = [Na^+] - ([Cl^-] + [HCO_3^-]) + 2.5 (4 - \text{albumin})$$
$$\text{normal: } 8\text{-}12$$

## Pathophysiology

**Hyperalimentation**
TPN contains $Cl^-$

**Addison's disease**
Low glucocorticoids & mineralocorticoids

**Renal tubular acidosis**
Three main types (distal, proximal, hyporeninemic)

**Diarrhea**
Loss of bicarbonate from GI tract

**Carbonic anhydrase inhibitors**
Loss of bicarbonate from kidneys

**Chloride infusion**
Chloride load from saline IV fluids

**Ureteral diversion**
Excess bicarbonate-chloride exchange

# ACIDOSIS, RESPIRATORY
## Paco₂ ≥ 45 mmHg

## Physiology

Alveolar ventilation ($V_A$) determines rate of $CO_2$ elimination
Defined by: $V_A = VE(1 - VD/VT)$

VE (Minute ventilation): Tidal volume × Respiratory rate          ↓VE leads to ↑$PaCO_2$

VT (Tidal volume): Amount of air in and out of lungs ↓ VT leads to ↑ $PaCO_2$

VD (Dead space): Amount of air not involved in gas exchange ↑VD leads to ↑$PaCO_2$

## Common Causes

Decreased respiratory drive:
Medications (benzodiazepines, opioids) and neuromuscular disorders

↓ VT and VE

COPD: Destruction of alveolar capillaries leads to poor perfusion.

↑ VD

## Renal Compensation

Acute: $HCO_3^-$ increases 1 mEq/L for each 10 mm Hg rise in $PaCO_2$.

Chronic: $HCO_3^-$ rises 3.5 mEq/L for each 10 mm Hg rise in $PaCO_2$.

## Signs and Symptoms

- Headache
- Anxiety
- Confusion
- Stupor
- Coma
- Death

Acute respiratory acidosis = more severe symptoms

Chronic is usually compensated

# Acute Kidney Injury

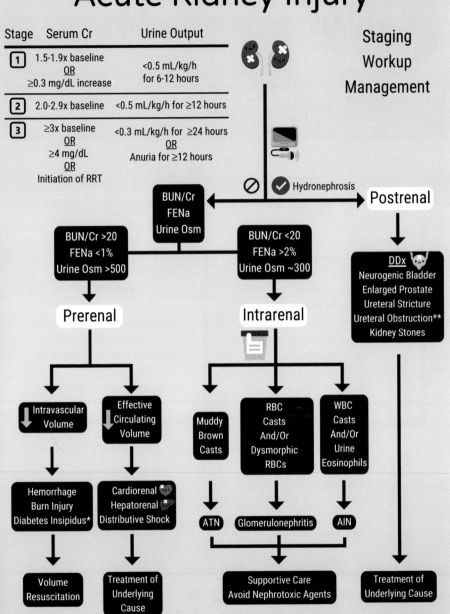

| Stage | Serum Cr | Urine Output |
|---|---|---|
| 1 | 1.5-1.9x baseline OR ≥0.3 mg/dL increase | <0.5 mL/kg/h for 6-12 hours |
| 2 | 2.0-2.9x baseline | <0.5 mL/kg/h for ≥12 hours |
| 3 | ≥3x baseline OR ≥4 mg/dL OR Initiation of RRT | <0.3 mL/kg/h for ≥24 hours OR Anuria for ≥12 hours |

**Staging**
**Workup**
**Management**

Hydronephrosis

**BUN/Cr FENa Urine Osm**

**BUN/Cr >20 FENa <1% Urine Osm >500**

**BUN/Cr <20 FENa >2% Urine Osm ~300**

**Postrenal**

**DDx**
Neurogenic Bladder
Enlarged Prostate
Ureteral Stricture
Ureteral Obstruction**
Kidney Stones

**Prerenal**

**Intrarenal**

Intravascular Volume

Effective Circulating Volume

Muddy Brown Casts

RBC Casts And/Or Dysmorphic RBCs

WBC Casts And/Or Urine Eosinophils

Hemorrhage
Burn Injury
Diabetes Insipidus*

Cardiorenal
Hepatorenal
Distributive Shock

ATN

Glomerulonephritis

AIN

Volume Resuscitation

Treatment of Underlying Cause

Supportive Care
Avoid Nephrotoxic Agents

Treatment of Underlying Cause

\* Unlike other causes of prerenal AKI, diabetes insipidus will have urine indices, demonstrating inappropriately low urine osmolality and low urine sodium due to the absence of ADH.

\*\* In healthy persons, bilateral ureteral obstruction/compression is required to cause AKI.

# Alkalosis, Metabolic

**Bicarbonate Level >28 mmol/L**
**Accompanied by Alkalemia (pH >7.45)—Not required**

## Etiology

**Can be pathologic or compensatory for acidosis**

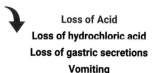

**Loss of Acid**
Loss of hydrochloric acid
Loss of gastric secretions
Vomiting
Frequent nasogastric suctioning

Increased Proton Excretion
Hyperaldosteronism
(primary or secondary/induced)

**Gain of Base**
Exogenous base administration
Bicarbonate, citrate, acetate,
oral antacids

Loop and Thiazide Diuretics
Increased chloride secretion
Increased bicarbonate reuptake

Bartter and Gitelman Syndromes

**Symptoms**

Confusion
Obtundation
Lower seizure threshold
Paresthesias
Muscle cramping/tetany

**Treatment**   Identify underlying cause
Administer hyperchloremic fluids (normal saline)
Acetazolamide to induce renal bicarbonate wasting

Expected respiratory compensation: Increase in $pCO_2$ 0.7 mm Hg for every 1 mmol/L increase in $HCO_3^-$

# Alkalosis, Respiratory
# Paco₂ <35 mm Hg

## Physiology

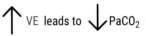

Alveolar ventilation ($V_A$) determines rate of $CO_2$ elimination
Defined by: $V_A = VE(1 - VD/VT)$

VE (Minute ventilation): Tidal volume × Respiratory rate    ↑ VE  leads to ↓ PaCO₂

VT (Tidal volume): Amount air in and out lungs    ↑ VT leads to ↓ PaCO₂

## Common Causes

Mostly caused by disorders that cause
**hyperventilation**

↑ VT and VE  =  ↓ PaCO₂

- Stress/pain/panic attack
- Acute asthma attack
- High altitude
- Pulmonary embolism
- Acute salicylate toxicity
  (increased respiratory drive in CNS)

## Renal Compensation

Acute: $HCO_3^-$ decreased
2 mEq/L for each 10 mm Hg fall
in PaCO₂

Chronic: $HCO_3^-$ decreases
5 mEq/L for each 10 mm Hg fall
in PaCO₂

## Signs and Symptoms

- Dizziness
- Lightheadedness
- Numbness
- Paresthesia
- Anxiety

Beware: Patients with
respiratory alkalosis from
severe asthma or obstructive
disease will progress to
respiratory acidosis if left
untreated.

# Chronic Kidney Disease

**Definition** — Abnormalities of kidney structure or function (GFR <60) present for >3 months

**Staging**

Albuminuria categories (mg/g)

| GFR Categories (mL/min/1.73 m²) | | A1 <30 | A2 30-300 | A3 >300 |
|---|---|---|---|---|
| G1 | >90 | | | |
| G2 | 60-89 | | | |
| G3a | 45-59 | | | |
| G3b | 30-44 | | | |
| G4 | 15-29 | | | |
| G5 | <15 | | | |

Green, low risk; Yellow, moderate risk; Orange, high risk;
Red, very high risk

**Causes**

Diabetes Mellitus

Hypertension

Glomerulonephritis

**Treatment**

- ACE inhibitors/ARBs + blood pressure control + glycemic control to slow progression
- Treat complications as below

**Complications**

**Uremia**

Due to: ↑ BUN

Presents with: Confusion, nausea, vomiting, anorexia, pericarditis, abnormal hemostasis

Treatment: Renal replacement therapy

**Anemia**

Due to: ↓ Erythropoietin production

Presents with: Fatigue

Treatment: Erythropoietin analogues

**Renal Osteodystrophy**

Due to: Secondary hyperparathyroidism, ↓ vitamin D production

Presents with: Hyperphosphatemia, hypocalcemia, bone fractures

Treatment: Phosphate binders, activated vitamin D analogues (Calcitriol)

**Fluid Retention**

Due to: ↓ Urine output, ↑ $NA^+$ retention

Presents with: HTN, edema, CHF exacerbation, pulmonary edema

Treatment: Low $Na^+$ diet, fluid restriction, diuretics, renal replacement therapy, if severe

**Hyperkalemia**

Due to: ↓ Renal excretion

Presents with: Muscle weakness, arrhythmia

Treatment: Low $K^+$ diet, renal replacement therapy, if severe

# Hydronephrosis

### "Water inside the kidney"

## Definition

**Dilation of renal pelvis and calyces**

## Imaging
**Ultrasound has 90% sensitivity and specificity**

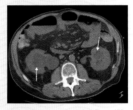

**CT can be used if ultrasound is negative**

Reproduced with permission from Elsayes KM, Oldham SA: Introduction to Diagnostic Radiology. New York, NY: McGraw Hill; 2014.

## Causes

**Urinary tract obstruction**

- Renal stones
- BPH
- Cervical cancer
- **Ureteropelvic junction**
MOST COMMON location in fetus

## Complications

**Atrophy of renal cortex and medulla**

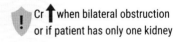

Cr ↑ when bilateral obstruction or if patient has only one kidney

**413**

# Hypercalcemia

Ca >10.5 mg/dL

## Presentation

 **Stones**
Kidney Stones

 **Bones**
Bone Pain

 **Groans**
Abdominal Pain

 **Thrones**
↑ Urinary Frequency

**Psychiatric Overtones**
Anxiety, Altered Mental Status

### Primary Hyperparathyroidism

| PTH | ↑ |
|-----|---|
| Phos | ↓ |

# PTH

- Due to parathyroid adenoma or hyperplasia

### Malignancy

| PTH | ↓ |
|-----|---|
| Phos | ↓ |

- Usually due to PTHrP, which increases resorption of calcium from bone
- Can be due to bone infiltration

### Granulomatous Disease

| PTH | ↓ |
|-----|---|
| Phos | ↑ |

- ↑ 1-α-hydroxylase activity in epithelioid histiocyes ⇒ ↑ activated vitamin D

### Milk-Alkali Syndrome

| PTH | ↓ |
|-----|---|
| Phos | ↑ |

- Excessive intake of calcium and antacid (calcium carbonate)
- Also presents with metabolic alkalosis and renal impairment

### Multiple Endocrine Neoplasia Syndrome

| PTH | ↑ |
|-----|---|
| Phos | ↓ |

- MEN 1: Parathyroid adenoma + pituitary tumor + pancreatic tumor
- MEN 2A: Parathyroid hyperplasia + medullary thyroid carcinoma + pheochromocytoma

### Familial Hypocalciuric Hypercalcemia

| PTH | ↑ |
|-----|---|
| Phos | ↓ |

- Defective calcium-sensing receptors ⇒ more calcium needed to suppress PTH
- Differentiate from primary hyperparathyroidism by hypocalciuria

### Treatment

- Increase urinary excretion with IV fluids
- If severe, consider bisphosphonates and/or calcitonin
- If granulomatous disease, add steroids

**414**

# Hyperkalemia

## Etiology

### Cellular K⁺ release
Expelling intracellular $K^+$
- Rhabdomyolysis
- Burns
- Tumor lysis

### Adrenal insufficiency
- Renal $Na^+$ wasting and $K^+$ retention

### Acidosis
Shift of intracellular $K^+$ via transporters
- $K^+$ up by 0.7 mEq/L per 0.1 pH unit decrease
- eg, Diabetic ketoacidosis

⚠ In DKA, **total body $K^+$ is down** due to urinary losses

### Iatrogenic K⁺

### Renal disease
- Renal insufficiency—decreased $K^+$ excretion
- Type IV RTA

### Drugs
- ACE inhibitors
- Potassium-sparing diuretics, trimethoprim

## Diagnosis ☑

Hyperkalemia: **K⁺ >5 mEq/L**

Obtain **ECG** ⚠ ECG does NOT correlate with $K^+$ levels
- Peaked T waves
- Very wide QRS ➡ Sine Wave
- VFib or asystole if severe

Rule out **renal** and **adrenal** etiology
- GFR, plasma renin, aldosterone

Rule out **pseudohyperkalemia**
- Artificial increase in serum $K^+$
- Hemolysis, thrombocytosis, leukocytosis
- Check CBC

## Clinical Presentation 🩺

Impaired neuromuscular transmission:
Weakness
Paresthesias
Flaccid paralysis
Hypoventilation

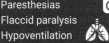 ➡

**Cardiac Toxicity**
Diagnostic ECG changes as above

 ➡

## Treatment ⚕

### Stabilize myocardium (if ECG changes present)
- First priority—Act quickly
- Central access: **Calcium chloride**
- Peripheral access: **Calcium gluconate**

### Shift K⁺ intracellularly (temporary)
- **Insulin** + dextrose
- **Albuterol** (or other $\beta_2$ agonist)
- Sodium bicarbonate

### Increase K⁺ elimination (long-term)
- Loop/thiazide diuretics
- $K^+$ binding resins
- Dialysis, if in renal failure

# Hypernatremia

## Pathophysiology

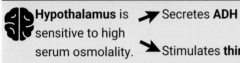

**Hypothalamus** is sensitive to high serum osmolality.
→ Secretes **ADH**
→ Stimulates **thirst**

Only 1 of these 2 is needed to maintain normal Na⁺. **Hypernatremia** occurs if both become impaired.

## Etiology—Divide by Volume Status

**Hypovolemic**
- Most common
- Renal: Diabetes insipidus
- Nonrenal: Burns, GI losses

**Euvolemic**
- Hyperaldosteronism
- Often mild and asymptomatic

**Hypervolemic**
- Saline overdose
- Seawater ingestion

## Diagnosis

Hypernatremia:
**Na⁺ >145 mEq/L**
Severe:
**Na⁺ >158 mEq/L**

<u>**Urine Osmolality**</u> to determine etiology

→ **>400 mOsm/kg**—Kidneys conserving water → **Nonrenal** (GI, skin) Osmotic diuresis

→ **<250 mOsm/kg**—Kidneys NOT conserving water → **Diabetes insipidus**

## Clinical Presentation

**Early**: Lethargy, irritability, weakness

**Severe**: Hyperthermia, delirium, seizures/coma, death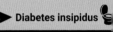

## Treatment

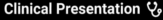

Calculate free water deficit (FWD):
$$\text{Free water deficit (in L)} = \text{Current TBW} \times \frac{[S_{Na}] - 140}{140}$$

**Hypovolemic**
- First, replete volume with isotonic crystalloid (eg, 0.9% normal saline [NS])
- Then replace remaining FWD with hypotonic crystalloid (eg, 1/2 NS or 5% dextrose)

**Euvolemic**
- Replace FWD with hypotonic crystalloid, PO free water, or free water flushes via NG tube

**Hypervolemic**
- Replace FWD with hypotonic crystalloid
- Thiazide diuretics promote natriuresis

**Isotonic → Hypotonic**    **Hypotonic**    **Hypotonic +/− diuresis**

## Complications

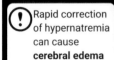Rapid correction of hypernatremia can cause **cerebral edema**

**Chronic hypernatremia** (>48 hours)
Max rate of <u>**12 mEq/L per day**</u>

**Acute hypernatremia**
<u>**Correct to near-normal in 24 hour**</u> to avoid neurologic injury from hypernatremia

# Hypocalcemia

Ca <8.5 mg/dL

## Presentation

**C**hvostek sign

**A**rrhythmia

**T**etany

**S**eizure, spasm

## Chronic Kidney Disease

| | |
|---|---|
| PTH | ↑ |
| Phos | ↑ |

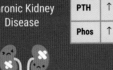

- Due to decreased production of activated vitamin D
- Can have catabolic effects on bone (osteitis fibrosa cystica)

## Hypoparathyroidism

| | |
|---|---|
| PTH | ↓ |
| Phos | ↑ |

- Most common cause
- Can be due to autoimmunity or surgical removal of the parathyroid gland (hungry bone syndrome)

## Acute Pancreatitis

| | |
|---|---|
| PTH | ↑ |
| Phos | -/↓ |

- Due to saponification as free fatty acids chelate calcium
- May have ↓ Phos if pancreatitis precipitated by alcohol

## Vitamin D Deficiency

| | |
|---|---|
| PTH | ↑ |
| Phos | ↓ |

D

- Decreased intestinal absorption of calcium and phosphorus

## Pseudo-hypoparathyroidism

| | |
|---|---|
| PTH | ↑↑ |
| Phos | ↑ |

- Autosomal recessive disease causing end-organ PTH resistance
- Usually inherited from mother

## Hypomagnesemia

| | |
|---|---|
| PTH | ↓ |
| Phos | ↓ |

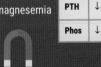

- Leads to decreased PTH secretion
- Needs to be corrected prior to treating hypocalcemia

## DiGeorge Syndrome

| | |
|---|---|
| PTH | ↓ |
| Phos | ↓ |

- Deletion of chromosome 22q11
- Absent thymus and parathyroid glands

## Treatment

- Replete magnesium
- Treat underlying disorder
- If severe, IV calcium gluconate
- For long-term treatment, give oral calcium supplements

# Hypokalemia

## Etiology

**K⁺ Intracellular Shift**
- Alkalosis
- β-agonists
- Insulin

**Renal K⁺ Loss**
- Hyperaldosteronism
- Bartter, Gitelman, Liddle
- Thiazide/Loop diuretics
- Hypomagnesemia
- RTA Type II > Type I

**Extrarenal K⁺ Loss**
- Vomiting
- Diarrhea
- Laxative abuse

## Diagnosis

Hypokalemia: **K⁺ <3.5 mEq/L**

Transtubular K Gradient **>4** → Renal K⁺ Losses

ECG changes: <2.7 mEq/L
- Large P wave
- Flat, broad T wave
- ST depressions

$$TTKG = \frac{Urine\ K^+/Plasma\ K^+}{Urine\ Osm/Plasma\ Osm}$$

- Use TTKG to distinguish renal and extrarenal etiologies
- If renal etiology suspected, get **plasma renin** and **aldosterone**

## Clinical Presentation

**Mild Hypokalemia**
- Weakness/fatigue
- Cramps
- Constipation

(!) Hypokalemia increases chance of digitalis toxicity

**Severe Hypokalemia (<2.5 mEq/L)**
- Flaccid paralysis/tetany
- Hyporeflexia
- Rhabdomyolysis

## Treatment

**Potassium Supplementation**

(!) Do not supplement K⁺ without fixing hypomagnesemia first!

**Oral**
- About 0.1 mEq/L increase per 10 mEq administered

**Intravenous**
- For severe deficiency or those who cannot take oral
- Up to 10-20 mEq/h

# 10 → 0.1

# Hyponatremia

## Serum NA⁺ <135 mEq/L

**Symptoms**
- Headache
- Nausea
- Confusion
- Seizures
- Coma

1. Determine plasma osmolarity (hypotonic vs isotonic vs hypertonic)

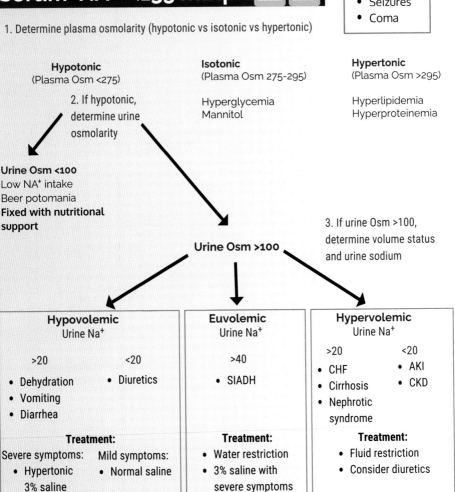

**Hypotonic**
(Plasma Osm <275)

2. If hypotonic, determine urine osmolarity

**Isotonic**
(Plasma Osm 275-295)

Hyperglycemia
Mannitol

**Hypertonic**
(Plasma Osm >295)

Hyperlipidemia
Hyperproteinemia

**Urine Osm <100**
Low NA⁺ intake
Beer potomania
**Fixed with nutritional support**

3. If urine Osm >100, determine volume status and urine sodium

**Urine Osm >100**

| **Hypovolemic**<br>Urine Na⁺ | | **Euvolemic**<br>Urine Na⁺ | **Hypervolemic**<br>Urine Na⁺ | |
|---|---|---|---|---|
| >20 | <20 | >40 | >20 | <20 |
| • Dehydration<br>• Vomiting<br>• Diarrhea | • Diuretics | • SIADH | • CHF<br>• Cirrhosis<br>• Nephrotic syndrome | • AKI<br>• CKD |
| **Treatment:** | | **Treatment:** | **Treatment:** | |
| Severe symptoms:<br>• Hypertonic 3% saline | Mild symptoms:<br>• Normal saline | • Water restriction<br>• 3% saline with severe symptoms | • Fluid restriction<br>• Consider diuretics | |

**Aim to correct serum Na⁺ no more than 10-12 mEq/L in 24 hours, any more can cause severe neurological injury and paralysis from pontine myelinolysis.**

# Nephritic Syndrome, Primary

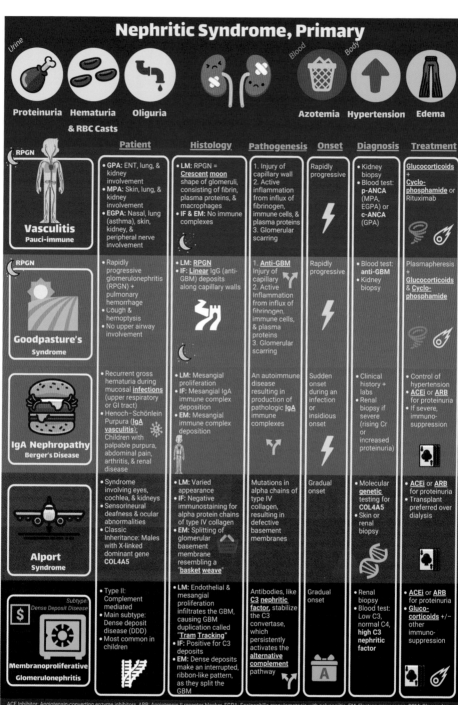

**Urine:** Proteinuria, Hematuria & RBC Casts, Oliguria

**Blood:** Azotemia, Hypertension

**Body:** Edema

| | Patient | Histology | Pathogenesis | Onset | Diagnosis | Treatment |
|---|---|---|---|---|---|---|
| **Vasculitis** Pauci-immune (RPGN) | • GPA: ENT, lung, & kidney involvement<br>• MPA: Skin, lung, & kidney involvement<br>• EGPA: Nasal, lung (asthma), skin, kidney, & peripheral nerve involvement | • LM: RPGN = **Crescent moon** shape of glomeruli, consisting of fibrin, plasma proteins, & macrophages<br>• IF & EM: No immune complexes | 1. Injury of capillary wall<br>2. Active inflammation from influx of fibrinogen, immune cells, & plasma proteins<br>3. Glomerular scarring | Rapidly progressive | • Kidney biopsy<br>• Blood test: p-ANCA (MPA, EGPA) or c-ANCA (GPA) | **Glucocorticoids** + **Cyclophosphamide** or Rituximab |
| **Goodpasture's** Syndrome (RPGN) | • Rapidly progressive glomerulonephritis (RPGN) + pulmonary hemorrhage<br>• Cough & hemoptysis<br>• No upper airway involvement | • LM: **RPGN**<br>• IF: **Linear** IgG (anti-GBM) deposits along capillary walls | 1. **Anti-GBM** Injury of capillary<br>2. Active Inflammation from influx of fibrinogen, immune cells, & plasma proteins<br>3. Glomerular scarring | Rapidly progressive | • Blood test: **anti-GBM**<br>• Kidney biopsy | Plasmapheresis + **Glucocorticoids** & **Cyclophosphamide** |
| **IgA Nephropathy** Berger's Disease | • Recurrent gross hematuria during mucosal **infections** (upper respiratory or GI tract)<br>• Henoch–Schönlein Purpura (**IgA vasculitis**): Children with palpable purpura, abdominal pain, arthritis, & renal disease | • LM: Mesangial proliferation<br>• IF: Mesangial IgA immune complex deposition<br>• EM: Mesangial immune complex deposition | An autoimmune disease resulting in production of pathologic **IgA** immune complexes | Sudden onset during an infection or insidious onset | • Clinical history + labs<br>• Renal biopsy if severe (rising Cr or increased proteinuria) | • Control of hypertension<br>• **ACEi** or **ARB** for proteinuria<br>• If severe, immunosuppression |
| **Alport** Syndrome | • Syndrome involving eyes, cochlea, & kidneys<br>• Sensorineural deafness & ocular abnormalities<br>• Classic Inheritance: Males with X-linked dominant gene COL4A5 | • LM: Varied appearance<br>• IF: Negative immunostaining for alpha protein chains of type IV collagen<br>• EM: Splitting of glomerular basement membrane resembling a "**basket weave**" | Mutations in alpha chains of type IV collagen, resulting in defective basement membranes | Gradual onset | • Molecular **genetic** testing for COL4A5<br>• Skin or renal biopsy | • **ACEi** or **ARB** for proteinuria<br>• Transplant preferred over dialysis |
| **Membranoproliferative Glomerulonephritis** Subtype: Dense Deposit Disease | • Type II: Complement mediated<br>• Main subtype: Dense deposit disease (DDD)<br>• Most common in children | • LM: Endothelial & mesangial proliferation infiltrates the GBM, causing GBM duplication called "**Tram Tracking**"<br>• IF: Positive for C3 deposits<br>• EM: Dense deposits make an interrupted, ribbon-like pattern, as they split the GBM | Antibodies, like **C3 nephritic factor**, stabilize the C3 convertase, which persistently activates the **alternative complement** pathway | Gradual onset | • Renal biopsy<br>• Blood test: Low C3, normal C4, **high C3 nephritic factor** | • **ACEi** or **ARB** for proteinuria<br>• **Glucocorticoids** +/– other immunosuppression |

ACE Inhibitor: Angiotensin-converting enzyme inhibitors, ARB: Angiotensin II receptor blocker, EGPA: Eosinophilic granulomatosis with polyangiitis, EM: Electron microscope, GBM: Glomerular basement membrane, GPA: Granulomatosis with polyangiitis, IF: Immunofluorescence, LM: Light microscope, MPA: Microscopic polyangiitis

# Nephritic Syndrome, Secondary

**Proteinuria** | **Hematuria & RBC Casts** | **Oliguria** | **Azotemia** | **Hypertension** | **Edema**

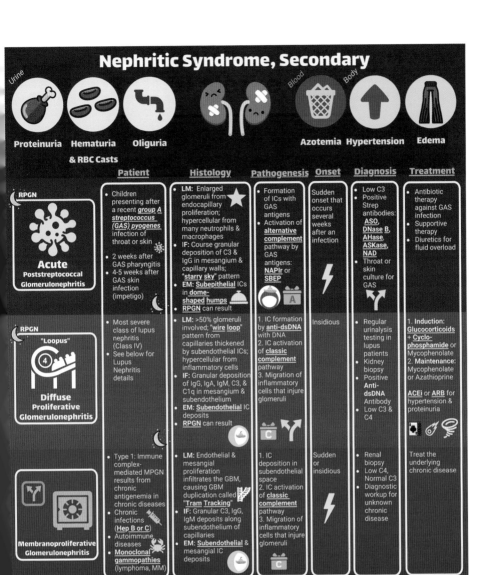

| | Patient | Histology | Pathogenesis | Onset | Diagnosis | Treatment |
|---|---|---|---|---|---|---|
| **Acute Poststreptococcal Glomerulonephritis** (RPGN) | • Children presenting after a recent _group A_ _streptococcus (GAS) pyogenes_ infection of throat or skin<br>• 2 weeks after GAS pharyngitis<br>• 4-5 weeks after GAS skin infection (impetigo) | • **LM:** Enlarged glomeruli from endocapillary proliferation; hypercellular from many neutrophils & macrophages<br>• **IF:** Course granular deposition of C3 & IgG in mesangium & capillary walls; "starry sky" pattern<br>• **EM:** Subepithelial ICs in dome-shaped humps<br>• RPGN can result | • Formation of ICs with GAS antigens<br>• Activation of alternative complement pathway by GAS antigens: NAPlr or SBEP | Sudden onset that occurs several weeks after an infection | • Low C3<br>• Positive Strep antibodies: ASO, DNase B, AHase, ASKase, NAD<br>• Throat or skin culture for GAS | • Antibiotic therapy against GAS infection<br>• Supportive therapy<br>• Diuretics for fluid overload |
| **Diffuse Proliferative Glomerulonephritis** (RPGN) "Loopus" (4) | • Most severe class of lupus nephritis (Class IV)<br>• See below for Lupus Nephritis details | • **LM:** >50% glomeruli involved; "wire loop" pattern from capillaries thickened by subendothelial ICs; hypercellular from inflammatory cells<br>• **IF:** Granular deposition of IgG, IgA, IgM, C3, & C1q in mesangium & subendothelium<br>• **EM:** Subendothelial IC deposits<br>• RPGN can result | 1. IC formation by anti-dsDNA with DNA<br>2. IC activation of classic complement pathway<br>3. Migration of inflammatory cells that injure glomeruli | Insidious | • Regular urinalysis testing in lupus patients<br>• Kidney biopsy<br>• Positive Anti-dsDNA Antibody<br>• Low C3 & C4 | 1. **Induction:** Glucocorticoids + Cyclo-phosphamide or Mycophenolate<br>2. **Maintenance:** Mycophenolate or Azathioprine<br><br>ACEi or ARB for hypertension & proteinuria |
| **Membranoproliferative Glomerulonephritis** | • Type 1: Immune complex-mediated MPGN results from chronic antigenemia in chronic diseases<br>• Chronic infections (Hep B or C)<br>• Autoimmune diseases<br>• Monoclonal gammopathies (lymphoma, MM) | • **LM:** Endothelial & mesangial proliferation infiltrates the GBM, causing GBM duplication called "Tram Tracking"<br>• **IF:** Granular C3, IgG, IgM deposits along subendothelium of capillaries<br>• **EM:** Subendothelial & mesangial IC deposits | 1. IC deposition in subendothelial space<br>2. IC activation of classic complement pathway<br>3. Migration of inflammatory cells that injure glomeruli | Sudden or insidious | • Renal biopsy<br>• Low C4, Normal C3<br>• Diagnostic workup for unknown chronic disease | Treat the underlying chronic disease |

## Lupus Nephritis (5)

| | Histology | Patient Presentation |
|---|---|---|
| • 6 classes for lupus nephritis per RPS/ISN system<br>• Classic population for lupus: Young African American women | • **Class I: Minimal mesangial.** No LM abnormalities. Only mesangial ICs on IF/EM.<br>• **Class II: Mesangial proliferative.** Mesangial expansion & hypercellularity on LM. Only mesangial ICs on IF/EM.<br>• **Class III: Focal.** <50% glomeruli with glomerulonephritis. ICs in subendothelial capillary wall & mesangium.<br>• **Class IV: Diffuse.** >50% glomeruli with glomerulonephritis. See above.<br>• **Class V: Membranous nephropathy.** Capillary wall thickening without hypercellularity. Subepithelial ICs.<br>• **Class VI: Advanced sclerosing.** >90% glomeruli are sclerosed. | • **Class I:** Normal urinalysis<br>• **Class II:** Microscopic hematuria & proteinuria<br>• **Class III:** Hematuria & proteinuria<br>• **Class IV:** Hematuria, proteinuria, nephrotic syndrome, hypertension, & reduced kidney function<br>• **Class V:** Nephrotic syndrome<br>• **Class VI:** Gradual decline in kidney function. End stage of classes III-V |

ASO: Antistreptolysin, LM: Light microscope, IF: Immunofluorescence, EM: Electron microscope, GBM: Glomerular basement membrane, ACE Inhibitor: Angiotensin-converting enzyme inhibitors, AHase: Antihyaluronidase, Anti-dsDNA: Antidouble-stranded DNA, ARB: Angiotensin II receptor blocker, ASKase: Antistreptokinase, IC: Immune complex, MM: Multiple myeloma, NAD: Nicotinamide adenine dinucleotide, NAPlr: Nephritis-associated plasmin receptor, SPE B: Streptococcal pyrogenic exotoxin B

# Nephrolithiasis

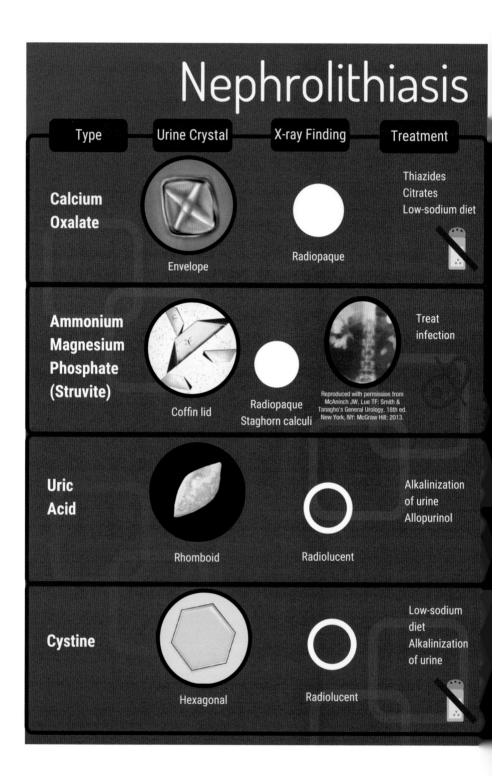

| Type | Urine Crystal | X-ray Finding | Treatment |
|------|---------------|---------------|-----------|
| **Calcium Oxalate** | Envelope | Radiopaque | Thiazides Citrates Low-sodium diet |
| **Ammonium Magnesium Phosphate (Struvite)** | Coffin lid | Radiopaque Staghorn calculi | Treat infection |
| **Uric Acid** | Rhomboid | Radiolucent | Alkalinization of urine Allopurinol |
| **Cystine** | Hexagonal | Radiolucent | Low-sodium diet Alkalinization of urine |

Reproduced with permission from McAninch JW, Lue TF: Smith & Tanagho's General Urology, 18th ed. New York, NY: McGraw Hill; 2013.

# Nephrotic Syndrome, Primary

 **Proteinuria**
Urine

 **Edema**
Body

 **Poor Immune System**

 **Hypo-albuminemia**
Blood

 **Hyper-triglyceridemia**

**Hyper-coagulability**

| | Patient | Histology | Pathogenesis | Onset | Diagnosis | Treatment |
|---|---|---|---|---|---|---|
| **Membranous Nephropathy**  | Caucasian adults | • **LM:** Diffuse capillary & GBM thickening without hypercellularity<br>• **IF:** Fine granular at GBM<br>• **EM:** Subepithelial "spike and dome" deposits; expansion of GBM | **Most common antibody:** Phospholipase A2 receptor (PLA2R)<br>**Mechanism:**<br>1. Antibodies target podocytes<br>2. ICs activate complement<br>3. Membrane attack complex (C5b-9) punctures podocytes | Gradual Onset | • Blood test for **PLA2R antibody** for primary MN<br>• Screen for secondary causes<br>• Kidney biopsy if antibody is negative or diagnosis unclear | • Supportive therapy for mild disease<br>• **Cyclo-phosphamide + Glucocorticoids**<br>• Calcineurin inhibitor +/- **Glucocorticoids** |
| **Focal Segmental Glomerulosclerosis**  | • Idiopathic: African Americans, Hispanics<br>• Genetic: Children of consanguineous parents | • **LM:** Focal & segmental sclerosis of glomeruli, hyalinosis of capillaries<br>• **IF:** Negative<br>• **EM:** Diffuse podocyte foot process effacement (>80%) | **Idiopathic:** Unknown circulating factor toxic to podocytes<br>**Genetic:** Podocyte mutation | Sudden or gradual onset | • Kidney biopsy<br>• Primary FSGS more likely if EM has diffuse podocyte effacement<br>• Consider genetic testing if genetic FSGS suspected | Supportive therapy for mild disease<br>**Idiopathic treatment:**<br>1. Glucocorticoids<br>2. Calcineurin inhibitors (Cyclosporine or tacrolimus) |
| **Minimal Change** | Children | • **LM:** Normal<br>• **IF:** Negative<br>• **EM:** Diffuse podocyte foot process effacement | 1. T-cell dysfunction<br>2. T-cell production of a circulating factor that increases glomerular permeability<br>3. Fusion of podocyte foot processes & alteration of GBM polarization | Sudden onset | Kidney biopsy in all adults, but only in the children who do not respond to steroids | Glucocorticoids |

EM: Electron microscope, GBM: Glomerular basement membrane, IC: Immune complex, IF: Immunofluorescence, LM: Light microscope

# Nephrotic Syndrome, Secondary

| Proteinuria | Edema | Poor Immune System | | | Hypo-albuminemia | Hyper-triglyceridemia | Hyper-coagulability |
|---|---|---|---|---|---|---|---|

| | Patient | Histology | Pathogenesis | Onset | Diagnosis | Treatment |
|---|---|---|---|---|---|---|
| **Diabetic** Glomerulonephropathy   | • Type 1 DM • Type 2 DM **Disease Stages:** Hyperfiltration, microalbuminuria, decreased GFR/proteinuria, ESRD | **LM:** • **Early Stage:** Mesangial expansion, GBM thickening • **Late Stage: Nodular** glomerulosclerosis from mesangial matrix expansion containing hyaline | 1. Hyperglycemia 2. Nonenzymatic protein glycation 3. Oxidative stress & inflammation leading to mesangial expansion | Gradual onset | • Clinical diagnosis • Annual screening of serum Cr & urine albumin • Kidney biopsy if diagnosis unclear | 1. Strict glycemic control 2. **ACEi/ARB** for hypertension & albuminuria management 3. For DM2, consider SGLT-2 inhibitors or GLP-1 agonists |
| **Amyloidosis** | • **AL Amyloidosis:** idiopathic **plasma cell dyscrasia** • **AA Amyloidosis:** chronic infections, chronic autoimmune diseases | **LM:** • Amorphous **"cotton-candy-like" nodules** in mesangium • **Apple-green** birefringence under polarized light after Congo red staining • **EM:** Mesangial extracellular deposits of amyloid | Extracellular deposits of β-sheet amyloid fibrils  | Gradual onset | • Fat pad biopsy • Serum & urine protein electrophoresis • Biopsy of bone marrow & other organs if diagnosis unclear | Treat the underlying cause of amyloidosis |
| **Membranous** Nephropathy | • **Infection:** HBV, HCV, syphilis • **Autoimmune:** Lupus, thyroiditis • **Malignancy:** Solid tumors • **Drugs:** NSAIDs, gold, penicillamine, captopril | **LM:** Diffuse capillary & GBM thickening without hypercellularity • **IF:** fine granular IC deposits at GBM • **EM: Subepithelial "spike and dome"** IC deposits; expansion of GBM | 1. Antibodies target podocytes 2. ICs activate complement 3. Membrane attack complex (C5b-9) punctures podocytes *No immune cell involvement; the GBM separates the ICs from blood | Gradual onset | • Blood test for **PLA2R antibody** for primary MN • Screen for secondary causes • Kidney biopsy if diagnosis unclear | Treat the underlying cause |
| **Focal Segmental** Glomerulosclerosis | • **Infection:** HIV • **Drugs:** Heroin, interferon • **Other:** Obesity, sickle cell disease, reduced renal mass (surgically or congenitally) | **LM:** Focal & segmental sclerosis of glomeruli, hyalinosis of capillaries • **IF:** Negative • **EM:** Segmental podocyte **foot process** effacement (<80%) | • Direct podocyte toxicity from drugs or infections • Complications from the kidney's adaptive response for reduced renal mass | Gradual onset | • Kidney biopsy • Screen for secondary causes • Secondary FSGS more likely if EM has segmental podocyte effacement | Treat the underlying cause |
| **Minimal Change** | • **Malignancy:** Lymphoma • **Drugs:** NSAIDs, antibiotics, lithium, bisphos-phonates • **Sequela of allergic reaction** | **LM:** Normal • **IF:** Negative • **EM:** Diffuse podocyte **foot process** effacement | Unknown circulating factor toxic to podocytes | Sudden onset | • Kidney biopsy • Screen for secondary causes | • **Glucocorticoids** • Treat the underlying cause |

| **Other Secondary Nephrotic Syndromes** | **Other HIV Condition:** HIV immune complex disease | **Multiple Myeloma:** Light or heavy chain cast nephropathy | ACEi: Angiotensin-converting enzyme inhibitor, ARB: Angiotensin II receptor blocker, BM: Bone marrow, Cr: Creatinine, DM: Diabetes mellitus, EM: Electron microscope, FSGS: Focal segmental glomerulosclerosis, GBM: Glomerular basement membrane, GLP-1: Glucagon-like peptide-1, IC: Immune complex, IF: Immunofluorescence, LM: Light microscope, MN: Membranous nephropathy, PLA2R: Phospholipase A2 receptor, SGLT-2: Sodium-glucose cotransporter-2 |
|---|---|---|---|

# Polycystic Kidney Disease (PKD)

## Autosomal Dominant | Autosomal Recessive

### Etiology

**Autosomal Dominant**

Mutations in **PKD1** and **PKD2**

Tubule cell proliferation and fluid secretion

Leads to large cysts in ~5% of tubules

Ultimately leads to **renal failure**

**Autosomal Recessive**

Mutations in **PKHD1**

Most patients are heterozygotes

Homozygotes have earlier onset of disease

**Renal failure** from fibrosis > cyst burden

### Clinical Presentation

**Autosomal Dominant**

Large, bilateral renal cysts

Age 50: 100s-1000s of cysts

Largely asymptomatic in first 4 decades

Associated **liver cysts and brain aneurysms**

Complications include:
Back pain, **pyelonephritis,
hemorrhage, nephrolithiasis**

**Most common cause of death:**
Cardiovascular complications due to
**hypertension**

**Autosomal Recessive**

Classic: Neonates born with ESRD

Death usually in first month from
**respiratory insufficiency**

Some patients diagnosed later in infancy

**Systemic hypertension**

Worsening renal function

**Liver** manifestations:
Fibrosis and biliary dilation

Kidneys become small and
**shrunken**, unlike ADPKD

### Diagnosis

**Autosomal Dominant**

Screening **ultrasound**
(# of cysts needed for dx increases with age)

Positive family history

MRI may be used to detect smaller cysts

**Genetic** testing for definitive diagnosis

**Autosomal Recessive**

Parents usually have **no** renal cysts
(distinct from ADPKD)

**Ultrasound** (even in utero) shows
**large, echogenic kidneys** with
poor corticomedullary differentiation

### Treatment

**Autosomal Dominant**

Most require **dialysis** or **renal transplant**

**Tolvaptan** for those with high-risk features

Blood pressure goal of **130/80 + ACEi/ARB**
to prevent cardiovascular complications

**Autosomal Recessive**

BP control, **dialysis**, and **renal transplant**

Liver complications may require **liver transplant**
or **portosystemic shunt**

# Renal Tubular Acidosis

| Type | Mechanism | Labs | Complications |
|---|---|---|---|
| **Distal** Type ①  |  Decreased H+ ATPase in α-intercalated cells | Urine pH >5.5  | Kidney stones  |
| **Proximal** Type ②  |  Increased excretion of $HCO_3^-$ in proximal convoluted tubule | Urine pH <5.5  | Hypophos-phatemic rickets  |
| Type ④ |  Decreased aldosterone | Urine pH <5.5 | Orthostatic hypotension |

# References _____

**Acidosis, Metabolic (Anion Gap)**
Le T, Bhushan V, Sochat M. *First Aid for the USMLE Step 1*. New York, NY: McGraw Hill Education; 2019.

**Acidosis, Metabolic (Nongap)**
Le T, Bhushan V, Sochat M, Chavda Y. *First Aid for the USMLE Step 1 2019: A Student-to-Student Guide*. New York, NY: McGraw Hill; 2018.

**Acidosis, Respiratory**
Bhagavan NV, Ha C. Water, electrolytes, and acid-base balance. In: *Essentials of Medical Biochemistry: With Clinical Cases*. Elsevier Academic Press; 2011:517-525. https://www.sciencedirect.com/science/article/pii/B9780120954612000370. Accessed August 19, 2021.

Edwards, M. Approach to arterial blood gases. *Guide to the Most Common Internal Medicine Workups and Diseases: An Evidenced Based Guide for All Healthcare Providers Regarding Common Hospital Based Workups and Diseases Seen in Internal Medicine*. Independent; 2017:275-277.

Intagliata S, Rizzo A, Gossman WG. Physiology, lung dead space. In: *StatPearls*. Treasure Island, FL: StatPearls Publishing; 2019. https://www.ncbi.nlm.nih.gov/books/NBK482501/. Updated May 15, 2019.

**Acute Kidney Injury**
Kellum JA, Lameire N, Aspelin P, et al. Kidney disease: improving global outcomes (KDIGO) acute kidney injury work group. KDIGO clinical practice guideline for acute kidney injury. *Kidney Inter Suppl*. 2012;2:1-138.

**Alkalosis, Metabolic**
DuBose TD Jr, Lipschik GY, Macrae JP. Acid–base disorders. In: Lerma EV, Rosner MH, Perazella MA, eds. *CURRENT Diagnosis & Treatment: Nephrology & Hypertension*. 2nd ed. New York, NY: McGraw Hill; 2017. http://accessmedicine.mhmedical.com/content.aspx?bookid=2287&sectionid=177426490.

**Alkalosis, Respiratory**
Bhagavan NV, Ha C. Water, electrolytes, and acid-base balance. In: *Essentials of Medical Biochemistry: With Clinical Cases*. Elsevier Academic Press; 2011:517-525. https://www.sciencedirect.com/science/article/pii/B9780120954612000370. Accessed August 19, 2021.

Brinkman JE, Sharma S. Physiology, respiratory alkalosis. In: *StatPearls*. Treasure Island (FL): StatPearls Publishing; Jan 2019. https://www.ncbi.nlm.nih.gov/books/NBK482117/. Updated June 23, 2019.

Edwards, M. Approach to arterial blood gases. *Guide to the Most Common Internal Medicine Workups and Diseases: An Evidenced Based Guide for All Healthcare Providers Regarding Common Hospital Based Workups and Diseases Seen in Internal Medicine*. Independent; 2017:275-277.

**Chronic Kidney Disease**
Kidney Disease: Improving Global Outcomes (KDIGO) Acute Kidney Injury Work Group. KDIGO clinical practice guideline for acute kidney injury. *Kidney Inter.*, Suppl. 2012;2:1-138.

Le T, Bhushan V, et al. *First Aid for the USMLE Step 2 CK*. 10th ed. New York, NY: McGraw Hill Education; 2019.

**Hydronephrosis**
Smith MA. Hydronephrosis. In: Usatine RP, Smith MA, Mayeaux EJ Jr, Chumley HS, eds. *The Color Atlas and Synopsis of Family Medicine*. 3rd ed. New York, NY: McGraw Hill; 2019.

## Hypercalcemia

Le T, Bhushan V, Sochat M, Chavda Y. *First Aid for the USMLE Step 1 2019: A Student-to-Student Guide.* New York. McGraw Hill. 2018.

Sprague SM. Disorders of calcium metabolism: hypocalcemia and hypercalcemia. In: Lerma EV, Rosner MH, Perazella MA. eds. *CURRENT Diagnosis & Treatment: Nephrology & Hypertension.* 2nd ed. New York, NY: McGraw Hill; 2017. http://accessmedicine.mhmedical.com/content.aspx?bookid=2287&sectionid=177426761. Accessed December 23, 2019.

## Hyperkalemia

Anker NB, Cho KC. Hyperkalemia. In: Papadakis MA, McPhee SJ, Rabow MW, eds. *Current Medical Diagnosis and Treatment 2020.* New York, NY: McGraw Hill; 2020.

## Hypernatremia

Anker NB, Cho KC. Hypernatremia. In: Papadakis MA, McPhee SJ, Rabow MW, eds. *Current Medical Diagnosis and Treatment 2020.* New York, NY: McGraw Hill; 2020.

## Hypocalcemia

Le T, Bhushan V, Sochat M, Chavda Y. *First Aid for the USMLE Step 1 2019: A Student-to-Student Guide.* New York: McGraw Hill; 2018.

Sprague SM. Disorders of calcium metabolism: hypocalcemia and hypercalcemia. In: Lerma EV, Rosner MH, Perazella MA, eds. *CURRENT Diagnosis & Treatment: Nephrology & Hypertension.* 2nd ed. New York, NY: McGraw Hill; 2017. http://accessmedicine.mhmedical.com/content.aspx?bookid=2287&sectionid=177426761. Accessed December 23, 2019.

## Hypokalemia

Anker NB, Cho KC. Hypokalemia. In: Papadakis MA, McPhee SJ, Rabow MW, eds. *Current Medical Diagnosis and Treatment 2020.* New York, NY: McGraw Hill; 2020.

## Hyponatremia

Edwards, M. Hyponatremia. *Guide to the Most Common Internal Medicine Workups and Diseases.* Independent; 2017:170-175.

Sterns RH. Disorders of water balance: hyponatremia and hypernatremia. In: Lerma EV, Rosner MH, Perazella MA, eds. *CURRENT Diagnosis & Treatment: Nephrology & Hypertension.* 2nd ed. New York, NY: McGraw Hill; 2017. https://accessmedicine.mhmedical.com/content.aspx?bookid=2287&sectionid=177426276. Accessed December 11, 2019.

## Nephritic Syndrome, Primary

Fogo AB, Lusco MA, Najafian B, Alpers CE. AJKD atlas of renal pathology: Alport syndrome. *Am J Kidney Dis.* 2016;68(4):e15-e16. doi:10.1053/j.ajkd.2016.08.002

Fogo AB, Lusco MA, Najafian B, Alpers CE. AJKD atlas of renal pathology: anti-glomerular basement membrane antibody-mediated glomerulonephritis. *Am J Kidney Dis.* 2016;68(5):e29-e30. doi:10.1053/j.ajkd.2016.09.003

Fogo AB, Lusco MA, Najafian B, Alpers CE. AJKD atlas of renal pathology: membranoproliferative glomerulo-nephritis. *Am J Kidney Dis.* 2015;66(3):e19-e20. doi:10.1053/j.ajkd.2015.07.007

Fogo AB, Lusco MA, Najafian B, Alpers CE. AJKD atlas of renal pathology: pauci-immune necrotizing crescentic glomerulonephritis. *Am J Kidney Dis.* 2016;68(5):e31-e32. doi:10.1053/j.ajkd.2016.09.002

Larque A. ANCA related GN. PathologyOutlines.com. http://www.pathologyoutlines.com/topic/kidneyANCArelatedgngen.html. Published November 6, 2019. Accessed December 26, 2019.

Le T, Bhushan V, Chen V, King M. Glomerular disease. In: *First Aid for the USMLE STEP2 CK.* 9th ed. New York: McGraw Hill; 2016:477-481.

Le T, Bhushan V, Sochat M, Chavda Y, Zureick A. Renal pathology. In: *First Aid for the USMLE STEP1 2018: A Student-to-Student Guide.* New York: McGraw Hill; 2018:578-588.

## Nephritic Syndrome, Secondary

Fogo AB, Lusco MA, Najafian B, Alpers CE. AJKD atlas of renal pathology: focal and diffuse lupus nephritis (ISN/RPS Class III and IV). *Am J Kidney Dis*. 2017;70(2):e9-e11. doi:10.1053/j.ajkd.2017.06.001

Fogo AB, Lusco MA, Najafian B, Alpers CE. AJKD atlas of renal pathology: IgA nephropathy. *Am J Kidney Dis*. 2015;66(5):e33-e34. doi:10.1053/j.ajkd.2015.08.001

Fogo AB, Lusco MA, Najafian B, Alpers CE. AJKD atlas of renal pathology: membranoproliferative glomerulonephritis. *Am J Kidney Dis*. 2015;66(3):e19-e20. doi:10.1053/j.ajkd.2015.07.007

Fogo AB, Lusco MA, Najafian B, Alpers CE. AJKD atlas of renal pathology: postinfectious glomerulonephritis. *Am J Kidney Dis*. 2015;66(4):e31-e32. doi:10.1053/j.ajkd.2015.08.005

Le T, Bhushan V, Chen V, King M. Glomerular disease. In: *First Aid for the USMLE STEP2 CK*. 9th ed. New York, NY: McGraw Hill; 2016:477-481.

Le T, Bhushan V, Sochat M, Chavda Y, Zureick A. Renal pathology. In: *First Aid for the USMLE STEP1 2018: A Student-to-Student Guide*. New York: McGraw Hill; 2018:578-588.

## Nephrolithiasis

Le T, Bhushan V, Sochat M. *First Aid for the USMLE Step 1*. New York, NY: McGraw Hill Education; 2019.

Le T, Bhushan V, Deol M, Reyes G. *First Aid for the USMLE Step 2 CK*. 10th ed. New York, NY: McGraw Hill Education; 2019.

## Nephrotic Syndrome, Primary

Fogo AB, Lusco MA, Najafian B, Alpers CE. AJKD atlas of renal pathology: focal segmental glomerulosclerosis. *Am J Kidney Dis*. 2015;66(2):e1-e2. doi:10.1053/j.ajkd.2015.04.007

Fogo AB, Lusco MA, Najafian B, Alpers CE. AJKD atlas of renal pathology: minimal change disease. *Am J Kidney Dis*. 2015;66(2):376-377. doi:10.1053/j.ajkd.2015.04.006

Larque A. Minimal change glomerulopathy. PathologyOutlines.com. http://www.pathologyoutlines.com/topic/kidneyminchange.html. Published April 8, 2019. Accessed December 26, 2019.

Le T, Bhushan V, Chen V, King M. Glomerular disease. In: *First Aid for the USMLE STEP2 CK*. 9th ed. New York: McGraw Hill; 2016:477-481.

Le T, Bhushan V, Sochat M, Chavda Y, Zureick A. Renal pathology. In: *First Aid for the USMLE STEP1 2018: A Student-to-Student Guide*. New York: McGraw Hill; 2018:578-588.

Safar-Boueri L, Piya A, Beck LH, Ayalon R. Membranous nephropathy: diagnosis, treatment, and monitoring in the post-PLA2R era. *Pediatr Nephrol*. December 2019:1-12. doi:10.1007/s00467-019-04425-1

Sangle N. Primary membranous glomerulonephritis. PathologyOutlines.com. http://www.pathologyoutlines.com/topic/kidneymemgn.html. Published February 26, 2019. Accessed December 26, 2019.

## Nephrotic Syndrome, Secondary

Le T, Bhushan V, Chen V, King M. Glomerular disease. In: *First Aid for the USMLE STEP2 CK*. 9th ed. New York, NY: McGraw Hill; 2016:477-481.

Le T, Bhushan V, Sochat M, Chavda Y, Zureick A. Renal pathology. In: *First Aid for the USMLE STEP1 2018: A Student-to-Student Guide*. New York, NY: McGraw Hill; 2018:578-588.

Najafian B, Fogo AB, Lusco MA, Alpers CE. AJKD atlas of renal pathology: diabetic nephropathy. *Am J Kidney Dis*. 2015;66(5):e37-e38. doi:10.1053/j.ajkd.2015.08.010

Sangle N. Diabetic renal disease: diabetic glomerulosclerosis. PathologyOutlines.com. https://www.pathologyoutlines.com/topic/kidneydiabetes.html. Published February 26, 2019. Accessed December 26, 2019.

Sangle N. Focal segmental glomerulosclerosis. PathologyOutlines.com. http://www.pathologyoutlines.com/topic/kidneyfsgs.html. Published December 27, 2018. Accessed December 26, 2019.

Sangle N. Renal amyloidosis. PathologyOutlines.com. http://www.pathologyoutlines.com/topic/kidneyamyloidosis.html. Published February 26, 2019. Accessed December 26, 2019.

**Polycystic Kidney Disease (PKD)**

Irazabal MV, Torres VE. Cystic diseases of the kidney. In: Lerma EV, Rosner MH, Perazella MA, eds. *CURRENT Diagnosis & Treatment: Nephrology & Hypertension*. 2nd ed. New York, NY: McGraw Hill; 2017.

Zhou J, Pollak MR. Polycystic kidney disease and other inherited disorders of tubule growth and development. In: Jameson J, Fauci AS, Kasper DL, Hauser SL, Longo DL, Loscalzo J, eds. *Harrison's Principles of Internal Medicine*. 20th ed. New York, NY: McGraw Hill; 2018.

**Renal Tubular Acidosis**

Le T, Bhushan V, et al. *First Aid for the USMLE Step 1*. New York, NY: McGraw Hill Education; 2019.

Le T, Bhushan V, et al. *First Aid for the USMLE Step 2 CK*. 10th ed. New York, NY: McGraw Hill Education; 2019.

# Neurology
*Aaron L. Berkowitz, MD, PhD*

# Acute Peripheral Vestibulopathy

## Vestibular Neuritis/Labyrinthitis

## Etiology 📖

**Vestibular Neuritis:** Viral/postviral inflammation of vestibular portion of vestibulocochlear nerve (CN VIII)

**Labyrinthitis**: Inflammation of inner ear ❖ may be viral, postviral, or **bacterial** spread from otitis media/meningitis

## 🩺 Clinical Features

 **Vestibular Neuritis:** Acute onset; **prolonged severe vertigo** with nausea, vomiting, gait instability, and nystagmus, often following a viral URI

 **Labyrinthitis**: Above features + unilateral tinnitus, aural fullness, hearing loss

## Diagnosis ☑️

Rule out posterior circulation stroke

Clinical diagnosis by history and exam consistent with **unilateral peripheral vestibular etiology**:

> **Acute Continuous Vertigo**
> Concern for Stroke if:
>
> Normal Head Impulse Test
> OR
> Direction-Changing Nystagmus
> OR
> Positive Test of Skew

**Abnormal vestibulo-ocular reflex** (ie. abnormal head impulse test) on affected side

**Nystagmus**: Horizontal ❖ fast phase away from affected side ❖ direction of nystagmus does not change with direction of gaze

## 💊 Management

**Corticosteroids** may hasten recovery

**Antivertigo** medications (eg, meclizine) and antiemetics

Antibiotics for bacterial labyrinthitis

! Severe symptoms resolve spontaneously within days, milder symptoms may last months

# Alzheimer's Dementia

## 1 Background

Most common **neurodegenerative dementia** in the elderly; risk increases with advancing age

Gradual onset, with early **episodic memory** and **visuospatial** impairment

Some cases may have genetic association (ApoE-4, Presenilin, APP); APP gene on Chr 21 increases risk in **Down's syndrome**

## 2 Clinical Presentation

Slow, insidious progression **inhibiting ability to perform ADLs**; mild cognitive impairment may precede AD by 10 years

**Early episodic memory loss,** followed by language, behavioral, and visuospatial (eg, getting lost) deficits

Mood symptoms including depression, agitation, psychosis

Mental status exam notable for **impaired short-term recall**; physical exam may show **frontal release signs** (grasp, snout, rooting, and palmomental reflexes)

## 3 Diagnosis

Evaluate for **reversible causes of dementia** (check TSH, B12, RPR; neuropsychological testing to rule out depression)

CT/MRI shows **medial temporal** (hippocampal) as well as **parietal atrophy** and is used to rule out other causes; may also use PET/SPECT imaging

## 4 Pathology

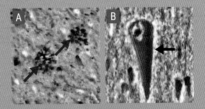

Gross pathology shows diffuse cortical atrophy, especially in temporal lobes (hippocampus)

Microscopy shows **neuritic plaques with amyloid deposition** (A), **neurofibrillary tangles** (B), and **diffuse neuronal loss**

## 5 Treatment

- No disease-modifying agents available
- Use **cholinesterase inhibitors** (donepezil, rivastigmine) in mild-mod AD and **NMDA receptor antagonist** (memantine) in mod-severe AD
- Symptomatic treatment of depression, agitation, sleep disorders, hallucinations, and delusions
- Counseling and social support for caregivers

# Amyotrophic Lateral Sclerosis

##  Background/Etiology

Neurodegenerative

Dysfunction of **upper <u>and</u> lower motor neurons**

Sporadic (90-95%) or familial (5-10%)

Familial ALS: Autosomal dominant, associated with **superoxide dismutase 1 (SOD1)** mutation

##  Clinical Features

Asymmetric, slowly progressive weakness (months-years)

→**Limb, respiratory, bulbar** (eg, tongue, oropharynx) muscles affected

→**UMN signs***: spastic weakness, hyperreflexia, + Babinski

→**LMN signs***: flaccid weakness, muscle atrophy, fasciculations (esp. of tongue), hyporeflexia

→Eye movements and bowel/bladder control usually spared

*UMN: upper motor neuron; LMN: lower motor neuron

##  Diagnosis

**Clinical diagnosis: UMN* and LMN* signs in multiple regions of body**

EMG: Muscle fiber denervation
NCS: Motor axon loss

MRI spine to rule out cervical spinal cord injury (which can cause arm LMN signs and leg UMN signs)

*UMN: upper motor neuron; LMN: lower motor neuron

##  Management

Cannot reverse or halt disease progression

Median survival 3-5 years

**Riluzole:**
→ Reduces glutamate-mediated excitotoxicity
→ Prolongs survival by several months

Symptomatic management as needed

# Benign Paroxysmal Positional Vertigo

## Etiology

Dislodged **otolith** (calcium carbonate crystal) debris from the utricle/saccule enters a semicircular canal (usually **posterior canal**) and disrupts endolymph movement with certain changes in head position

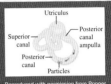

Reproduced with permission from Ropper AH, Samuels MA, Klein JP: Adams and Victor's Principles of Neurology, 11th ed. New York, NY: McGraw Hill; 2019.

## Clinical Features

Acute **transient vertigo** <1 minute with **nystagmus**
Triggered by changes in **head position** (eg, rolling over in bed)

## Diagnosis

Reproduce vertigo and nystagmus with **Dix-Hallpike** maneuver:

Turn patient's head to one side and tilt back, then move patient rapidly from seated to supine ◆ repeat on opposite side

**Nystagmus** is **torsional and upbeat** toward the affected side (ie, toward the ground when head is turned and patient supine)

Dix-Hallpike maneuver

Reproduced with permission from Ropper AH, Samuels MA, Klein JP: Adams and Victor's Principles of Neurology, 11th ed. New York, NY: McGraw Hill; 2019.

## Management

**Epley canalith repositioning maneuver:** Multistep maneuver that employs gravity and targeted head/body movements to remove otoliths from semicircular canals

Antivertigo medications are generally ineffective

Epley Maneuver

Reproduced with permission from Ropper AH, Samuels MA, Klein JP: Adams and Victor's Principles of Neurology, 11th ed. New York, NY: McGraw Hill; 2019.

# Broca's Aphasia

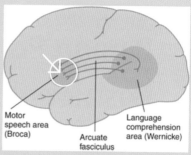

Motor speech area (Broca)

Arcuate fasciculus

Language comprehension area (Wernicke)

 **Definition**

Disorder of language production with preserved comprehension

Often secondary to stroke

| | | |
|---|---|---|
|  | **Production:** <br> (fluency, quality of speech) | Nonfluent <br> Frustrated, aware of their deficits |
|  | **Comprehension:** | Intact |
|  | **Repetition:** | Impaired |
|  | **Localization:** | Posterior inferior frontal gyrus (superior division of MCA) of dominant hemisphere (most commonly left side) |

# Cavernous Sinus Thrombosis

##  Causes

- Recent orbit, sinus, or facial infection leading to **septic thrombosis** (*S. aureus* most commonly)
- **Prothrombotic state** leading to nonseptic cerebral venous thrombosis

## Clinical Presentation

- **Headache** (most common symptom)
- Orbital pain and edema
- Diplopia, ophthalmoplegia, and/or ptosis (CN III, IV, VI)
- Red eye, proptosis (due to venous congestion)
- **Fever**

## Diagnosis

- MRI with contrast (or CTA/CTV)
- ↑WBC, +ve blood cultures
- Sinus biopsy if fungus suspected (rare)

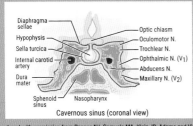

Diaphragma sellae
Hypophysis
Sella turcica
Internal carotid artery
Dura mater
Sphenoid sinus
Nasopharynx
Optic chiasm
Oculomotor N.
Trochlear N.
Ophthalmic N. (V$_1$)
Abducens N.
Maxillary N. (V$_2$)

Cavernous sinus (coronal view)

Reproduced with permission from Ropper AH, Samuels MA, Klein JP: Adams and Victor's Principles of Neurology, 11th ed. New York, NY: McGraw Hill; 2019.

##  Treatment

**Broad-spectrum IV antibiotics** for at least 3-4 weeks.
Combination of:

- Vancomycin
- + 3/4-generation cephalosporin
- + Metronidazole (anaerobes)
- +/− (antifungal for fungal infx)

**Surgical drainage** may be necessary if no response in 24 hours

Consider **anticoagulation**

## Cavernous Sinus Anatomy

Structures **passing through the cavernous sinus** include:

- CN III, CN IV, CN VI
- CN V (V$_1$ + V$_2$ divisions)
- Internal carotid artery

## ! Complications

- Confusion, drowsiness, coma (due to ↑ICP)
- Meningismus (suggests spread to CNS)
- Permanent visual damage

# Cervical & Lumbar Stenosis

## Cervical Canal Stenosis

Narrowing of the spinal canal can compress the spinal cord, causing **cervical myelopathy**

**Cervical Myelopathy:**
⇨ Hand/arm weakness and/or paresthesias
⇨ +/− hand atrophy and lower motor neuron signs
⇨ Upper motor neuron signs in arms and legs (spasticity, hyperreflexia, + Babinski)
⇨ Gait disturbance/imbalance

Imaging: MRI spine

Management: Surgery

## Cervical Foraminal Stenosis

Narrowing of intervertebral foramina can compress nerve roots, causing **cervical radiculopathy**

**Cervical Radiculopathy:**
⇨ Neck pain radiating to arm in nerve root distribution (most commonly **C6 or C7**)
⇨ +/− weakness, ↓ sensation or reflexes for affected nerve root (eg, triceps if C7)

Imaging: MRI spine if intractable pain or progressive weakness

Management:
⇨ Initially conservative (eg, NSAIDs, PT)
⇨ If refractory, epidural steroid injections +/− surgery

Common Etiologies for Cervical and Lumbar Stenosis:
⇨ **Degenerative disc disease** (eg, disc herniation)
⇨ **Spondylosis** (eg, osteoarthritis of spine causing osteophyte formation)

## Lumbar Canal Stenosis

Narrowing of the spinal canal can compress nerve roots of the cauda equina, causing **neurogenic claudication**

**Neurogenic Claudication:**
⇨ Leg pain, paresthesias, and/or weakness with standing or walking
⇨ Improves with rest and leaning forward

Imaging: MRI spine

Management:
⇨ If chronic mild symptoms: Conservative (eg, NSAIDs)
⇨ If progressive/disabling symptoms: Surgery

L4

## Lumbar Foraminal Stenosis

Narrowing of intervertebral foramina can compress nerve roots, causing **lumbosacral radiculopathy**

**Lumbosacral Radiculopathy:**
⇨ Back pain radiating to leg/foot in nerve root distribution (most commonly **L5 or S1**)
⇨ +/− weakness, ↓ sensation or reflexes for affected nerve root (eg, ankle jerk if S1)
⇨ Positive straight leg raise test

Imaging: MRI spine if intractable pain or progressive weakness

Management:
⇨ Initially conservative (eg, NSAIDs, PT)
⇨ If refractory, epidural steroid injections +/− surgery

# Cluster Headache

 ## Pain Lateralization

Unilateral

 ## Duration

15 minutes to 3 hours

 ## Pain Quality

Severe

"Stabbing," periorbital headaches

Repetitive, tends to occur in "clusters" (affecting same part of head at same time of day, commonly during sleep, during certain season of year)

 ## Other Features

**Core symptoms:**
- Trigeminal autonomic sx on ipsilateral side (eg, conjunctival erythema, conjunctival lacrimation, nasal congestion, rhinorrhea)
- Restlessness/agitation

**Associated symptoms:**
- May have Horner's syndrome

 ## Diagnosis

Based on clinical history
- Male > female
- Average age of onset 25 y/o

**If first episode:** MRI

**If Horner's syndrome present:** Consider carotid U/S to exclude associated disorders (eg, carotid artery dissection)

**If atypical features, abnormal neuro exam, new-onset in older adult, or concerning PMH:** Consider CT-head/MRI-brain

 ## Treatment

**Acute**
- 100% $O_2$
- Triptans

**Prophylaxis**
- Verapamil (1st line)
- Lithium (2nd line)

# Coma

##  Definition

A state of **unarousable unresponsiveness**

⇨ Patient is unconscious, lacks awareness, is unable to be aroused by stimuli, and is unresponsive to stimuli

##  Contrast with

**Persistent Vegetative State:**
⇨ Wakefulness without awareness
⇨ Patient lacks awareness or responsiveness, but has normal sleep-wake cycles and is arousable

**"Locked-in" Syndrome:**
⇨ Consciousness and cognition preserved but all motor function lost except blinking and vertical eye movements
⇨ Result of injury to base of pons, often due to basilar artery stroke

##  Neuroanatomy

**Ascending Reticular Activating System (ARAS):** Network of neurons that maintains arousal

⇨ Origin in upper brainstem (midbrain and upper pons), projects to thalami and cortex

⇨ ARAS dysfunction due to brainstem lesion or diffuse bilateral cerebral cortex damage can cause coma

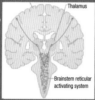

Reproduced with permission from Simon RP, Aminoff MJ, Greemberg DA: Clinical Neurology, 10th ed. New York, NY: McGraw Hill; 2018.

##  Etiologies

| | <u>Examples</u> |
|---|---|
| Structural | Brainstem infarction/hemorrhage, mass causing brainstem herniation |
| Trauma | Diffuse axonal injury from acceleration trauma |
| Metabolic | Electrolyte or endocrine disturbances |
| Toxic | Opiates, benzodiazepines |
| Infectious | Bacterial meningitis, sepsis |
| Seizure | Nonconvulsive status epilepticus |

##  Evaluation

**Collateral History and Neurologic Exam:**
⇨ Mental status, motor activity, muscle tone, noxious stimuli, brainstem reflexes

| Labs | CBC, electrolytes, ABG, tox screen, cultures |
|---|---|
| Imaging | Head CT acutely, consider brain MRI |
| Lumbar puncture | If concern for CNS infection |
| EEG | If concern for seizures |

## Management

Stabilize patient ⇨ Address ABCs

Treat potential **reversible etiologies**
⇨ eg, thiamine + dextrose, naloxone

Treatment varies by underlying etiology

# Craniopharyngioma

## Background

Most common childhood primary supratentorial brain tumor

Benign ☺

## Location

Most commonly in suprasellar region

## Symptoms

Bitemporal hemianopsia (as can be seen with pituitary adenoma)

May have hypopituitarism

## Treatment

Surgical resection

## Imaging

Calcification common

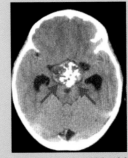

Reproduced with permission from Garnett MR, Puget S, Grill J, et al: Craniopharyngioma, Orphanet J Rare Dis. 2007 Apr 10;2:18.

## Pathology

Derived from remnants of Rathke's pouch (ectoderm)

Cholesterol crystals found in "motor oil"-like fluid within tumor

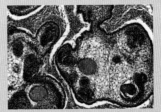

Reproduced with permission from Reisner H: Pathology: A Modern Case Study, 2nd ed. New York, NY: McGraw Hill; 2020.

# Creutzfeldt—Jakob Disease

### 1 Clinical Features

**Subacute, rapidly progressive dementia** (weeks to months)

Additional symptoms:
**Startle myoclonus**, ataxia, or other movement disorders

### 2 Pathophysiology

Accumulation of proteinaceous infectious particles (**prions**) in the brain

Normal prion protein (PrPc) --> **β-pleated form** (PrPsc) = protease-resistant and transmissible

**Usually sporadic**; rarely genetic or acquired (eg, exposure to infected beef or contaminated surgical instruments)

### 3 Differential Diagnosis

**CSF:** Elevated 14-3-3 and ⊕ RT-QuIC
**EEG:** Periodic sharp wave complexes
**Imaging:** MRI (DWI sequence) shows cortical ribboning (red arrows) and basal ganglia hyperintensity (white arrows).

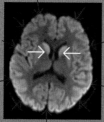

Reproduced with permission from Berkowitz AL: Clinical Neurology and Neuroanatomy: A Localization-Based Approach. New York, NY: McGraw Hill; 2017.

### 4 Pathology

Reproduced with permission from Centers for Disease Control and Prevention, Public Health Image Library. Photo contributor: Dr. Al Jenny.

**Spongiform degeneration of cortex** with accumulated protein, neuronal loss, and astrocytic proliferation

### 5 Treatment

No effective treatment at this time

Most patients die in <1 year

# Dementia with Lewy Bodies

**1** **Background**

Characterized by **dementia**
Associated with **triad of symptoms:**
- Fluctuations
- Hallucinations
- Parkinsonism

Mnemonic: ha**LEW**cinations, f**LEW**ctuations

**Clinical Presentation**
**2**

**Fluctuations** in attention and
level of arousal

**Visual hallucinations** (nonthreatening
hallucinations of people or animals)

**Parkinsonism** (tremor, rigidity,
bradykinesia, postural instability)

**Visuospatial** and **executive
dysfunction**

*Associated features:*
REM sleep behavior disorder
Autonomic dysfunction
Neuroleptic sensitivity

**3** **Differential Diagnosis**

Distinguished from **idiopathic Parkinson's
disease (PD)** by timing of onset of dementia
relative to onset of parkinsonism

**PD:** Parkinsonism <u>before onset</u> of dementia,
usually by years

**DLB:** Parkinsonism <u>at onset</u> of dementia or
<u>following onset</u> of dementia

**Pathology** **4**

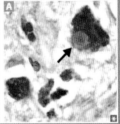

Intracellular **Lewy bodies** (eosinophilic
inclusions), primarily in the cortex

**5**

**Treatment**

- No disease modifying treatment available
- Manage with **cholinesterase inhibitors** and
**NMDA receptor blocker** (memantine)
- Usually **not responsive to levodopa**
- Symptomatic treatments for mood, REM sleep
behavior disorder, autonomic dysfunction

# Facial Palsy

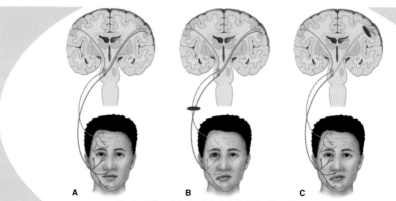

A              B              C

Reproduced with permission from Berkowitz AL: Clinical Neurology and Neuroanatomy: A Localization-Based Approach. New York, NY: McGraw Hill; 2017.

Upper face: Innervated by contralateral and ipsilateral motor cortex
Lower face: Innervated by contralateral motor cortex only

## Upper Motor Neuron Lesion

- ⊘ <u>Contralateral</u> paralysis of lower face only

- ⊘ Lesion in facial area of motor cortex or anywhere along the corticobulbar tract above the facial nucleus

- ⊘ Any cause of CNS lesion (eg, stroke, tumor, infection, demyelination)

- ⊘ Associated symptoms and treatment based on underlying etiology

## Lower Motor Neuron Lesion

- ⊘ <u>Ipsilateral</u> paralysis of lower face <u>and</u> upper face (with impaired eye closure)

- ⊘ Lesion in facial nerve (CN VII) or facial nucleus in pons

- ⊘ Causes include idiopathic (called *Bell's palsy*, increased risk with DM, pregnancy), Lyme, sarcoidosis, HIV, cerebellopontine angle tumors

- ⊘ May also cause hyperacusis, impaired taste

- ⊘ Eye care and eye patch required to prevent corneal injury

# Frontotemporal Dementia

**1** ## Background

Also referred to as **Pick's disease**

Primarily **frontal lobe and temporal lobe** degeneration

Gradual onset, with early changes in **personality and behavior**

**2** ## Clinical Presentation

Often earlier onset (age <65)

Two subtypes:

**1. Behavioral-variant FTD**
Early changes in personality and behavior may include inappropriate or impulsive behavior, obsession, inattentiveness, abulia/apathy

**2. Primary progressive aphasia**
Early language deficits

**3** ## Diagnosis

Clinical diagnosis with imaging (CT/MRI) evidence of **frontotemporal atrophy**

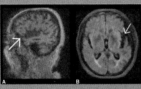

Reproduced with permission from Berkowitz AL: Clinical Neurology and Neuroanatomy: A Localization-Based Approach. New York, NY: McGraw Hill; 2017.

**4** ## Pathology

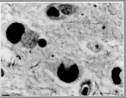

Reproduced with permission from Valle DL, Antonarakis S, Ballabio A, et al: The Online Metabolic and Molecular Bases of Inherited Disease. New York, NY: McGraw Hill; 2019.

Frontal and temporal lobe atrophy

Round, intraneuronal inclusions of hyper-phosphorylated tau (**"Pick bodies"**) or ubiquitinated TDP-43

**5** ## Management

- Symptomatic treatment: SSRIs for behavioral symptoms; **no benefit** from cholinesterase inhibitors
- Counseling and social support for patient, family, and caregivers

 # Gliomas

## Astrocytoma, Oligodendroglioma, Glioblastoma

## Background

Adult primary brain tumors arising from glial cells

Classified histologically by glial cell of origin and grade, including:
- Astrocytoma
- Oligodendroglioma
- Glioblastoma

## Location

Most commonly supratentorial

## Symptoms

Headaches

Seizures

Progressive focal neurological deficits related to location

Cranial neuropathy

## Treatment

Surgical resection, radiation, and/or chemotherapy

## Imaging

**Oligodendroglioma:** Edema with minimal/no enhancement, frontal lobe dominance

**Glioblastoma:** Ring-enhancing with necrotic center, may span corpus callosum ("butterfly pattern")

 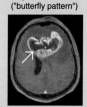

Reproduced with permission from Berkowitz AL: Clinical Neurology and Neuroanatomy: A Localization-Based Approach. New York, NY: McGraw Hill; 2017.

Reproduced with permission from Reisner H. Pathology: A Modern Case Study, 2nd ed. New York, NY: McGraw Hill; 2020.

## Pathology

**Oligodendroglioma:** Oligodendrocyte origin, "Fried egg" cells (round nuclei with clear cytoplasm)

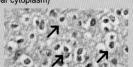

Reproduced with permission from Kantarjian HM, Wolff RA: The MD Anderson Manual of Medical Oncology, 3rd ed. New York, NY: McGraw Hill; 2016.

**Glioblastoma:** Astrocyte origin, GFAP⊕, border of "pseudopalisading" pleomorphic tumor cells (arrow) with central areas of necrosis (★), hemorrhage, and/or microvascular proliferation

Reproduced with permission from Kemp WL, Burns DK, Brow TG: Pathology: The Big Picture. New York, NY: McGraw Hill; 2008.

# Guillain–Barré Syndrome

## Background

**Acute** and **rapidly progressive post infectious** immune-mediated disorder affecting peripheral nerves

Characterized by **progressive weakness** (flaccid paralysis) and **loss of reflexes**

## Pathophysiology

Often follows recent infection (eg, viral, *Campylobacter jejuni* gastroenteritis) or vaccination

May be **demyelinating** (AIDP) or **axonal** subtype

## Presentation

Progressive (over days), ascending paralysis involving extremities +/− paresthesias; cranial nerves may be affected

**Loss of reflexes**, dysautonomia

**Diaphragmatic weakness** can lead to respiratory compromise

## Diagnosis

Clinical history

For demyelinating subtype, nerve conduction studies show ↓ **nerve conduction velocity, conduction block**

**Elevated CSF protein level** with few or no cells (ie, albuminocytologic dissociation)

## GBS Variants

- Pure motor
- Pure sensory
- Pure autonomic
- **Miller Fisher syndrome** (ophthalmoplegia, ataxia, areflexia; associated with anti-GQ1b antibodies)

## Treatment

**IVIG** or **plasmapheresis** are first line; steroids not indicated

**ICU care** for respiratory failure

**Physical therapy**

# Huntington's
## Disease

## Background/Etiology

Neurodegenerative

Autosomal dominant

↑**CAG repeats** in Huntingtin gene (chromosome 4) ⇨ abnormal huntingtin protein

**Anticipation:** Number of CAG repeats expands with each generation ⇨ earlier onset and ↑ disease severity

## Clinical Features

Onset age 20-50

**Chorea** (involuntary, irregular, dance-like movements)

**Neuropsychiatric** Symptoms:
- Personality change
- Dementia
- Depression
- Aggression/Psychosis

Other: Slowed/absent saccades, weight loss

## Diagnosis/Imaging

Genetic testing of CAG repeats in huntingtin gene (eg, PCR)

Brain Imaging: Atrophy of striatum, esp. **caudate atrophy** ⇨ enlarged lateral ventricles

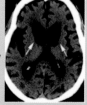

caudate atrophy + *ex vacuo* ventriculomegaly

## Management

Cannot reverse or halt disease progression

Symptomatic Treatment:

❖ Chorea: **Tetrabenazine** or **reserpine** (dopamine-depleting)

❖ Psychosis: **Atypical antipsychotics**

❖ Depression: **SSRIs**

Genetic counseling

# Intracerebral Hemorrhage

## (Intraparenchymal Hemorrhage)

## Causes

- **Hypertension (HTN) most common**
- Cerebral amyloid angiopathy (CAA)
- Trauma
- Coagulopathy (intrinsic or medication-related, eg, anticoagulant)
- Hemorrhagic conversion of ischemic stroke
- Vascular malformation
- Brain tumor
- Cocaine

## Clinical Presentation

- **Headache**

- Sudden-onset focal deficits (may be motor, sensory, visual, cerebellar, etc., depending on site of hemorrhage)

- Often have altered level of consciousness

## Diagnosis

**Noncontrast Head CT**
(acute hemorrhage appears as hyperdensity on CT)

Deep hemorrhage | Lobar hemorrhage
(common pattern in HTN) | (common pattern in CAA)

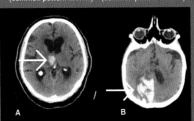

Reproduced with permission from Berkowitz AL: Clinical Neurology and Neuroanatomy: A Localization-Based Approach. New York, NY: McGraw Hill; 2017.

## Treatment

- Decrease BP

- Reverse coagulopathy if present

- Elevate head of bed

- Treatment of ICP if elevated

- May consider surgical evacuation if worsening mass effect

## Comparison to Acute Ischemic Stroke

- Although the following symptoms may be seen in acute ischemic stroke, **they are more common in ICH**: Headache, nausea/vomiting, extreme HTN, seizures, depressed level of consciousness (secondary to mass effect)

## Complications

- Mass effect from hematoma may lead to herniation, coma, and/or death
- Seizures

# Lambert–Eaton Myasthenic Syndrome

### Neuromuscular Junction Disease

## Background

**Paraneoplastic** antibody-mediated autoimmune disorder of the neuromuscular junction most commonly associated with **small-cell lung cancer**

## Pathophysiology

Autoantibodies to **presynaptic voltage-gated calcium channels (VGCCs)**

## Clinical Features

Weakness of proximal muscles; weakness is <u>**not**</u> fatigable, may **improve with increased activity**

Decreased or absent DTRs*

Extraocular, bulbar, respiratory muscles usually spared

## Diagnosis

Antibody test for **anti-VGCC antibodies**

**Chest CT:** Evaluation for underlying malignancy is essential to management, small cell lung carcinoma (SCLC) is the most commonly found tumor

Repetitive nerve stimulation shows **incremental response**

## Treatment

Treatment of underlying neoplasm if found

3,4-Diaminopyridine

Immunomodulatory treatments

*DTRs: Deep tendon reflexes; MG: Myasthenia gravis

## MG* vs LEMS

| | Myasthenia Gravis | Lambert-Eaton Syndrome |
|---|---|---|
| Antibody target | Postsynaptic ACh receptor | Presynaptic VGCC |
| Clinical presentation | Eye muscles often involved | Proximal muscles often involved |
| | Fatigable weakness; worsens with activity | Nonfatigable weakness; improves with activity |
| Associations | Thymoma | SCLC |

# Medulloblastoma

## Background

Childhood primary brain tumor 😫

Highly malignant 😈

## Location

Commonly in cerebellum

Arises from 4th ventricle

## Symptoms

Headache/papilledema due to obstructive hydrocephalus (compression of 4th ventricle) and ICP

Can send "drop metastases" to spinal cord

## Treatment

Surgical resection ✂️

Radiation ☢️

Chemotherapy 💉

## Imaging

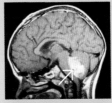
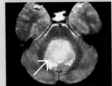

Reproduced with permission from Ropper AH, Samuels MA, Klein JP: Adams and Victor's Principles of Neurology, 11th ed. New York, NY: McGraw Hill; 2019.

## Pathology

Primitive neuroectodermal tumor (PNET)

Homer-Wright rosettes ✾

Small blue cells

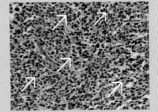

Reproduced with permission from Kemp WL, Burns DK, Brow TG: Pathology: The Big Picture. New York, NY: McGraw Hill; 2008.

#  Ménière's Disease

## Etiology 📖

Increased volume of endolymph ⟶ distention of endolymphatic system, abnormal fluid, and ion homeostasis in inner ear

## 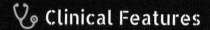 Clinical Features

 +

- Acute **episodic vertigo, hearing loss, tinnitus**, aural fullness, nausea
- Progressive low-frequency sensorineural hearing loss
- Tinnitus may occur outside of acute episodes

## Diagnosis ☑

**Clinical**: 2 episodes of vertigo ≥ 20 minutes
Tinnitus/aural fullness
**Audiometry**: **Sensorineural** hearing loss (often unilateral)

##  Management

### Acute

Vertigo:
- Antihistamines (meclizine, dimenhydrinate)
- Benzodiazepines
- Anticholinergics (scopolamine)
Nausea: Antiemetics

### Chronic

Limit salt intake
Diuretics
Intractable vertigo: Intratympanic gentamicin injection or labyrinthectomy

# Meningioma

## Background

Most common adult primary brain tumor

↑ Incidence with age

Female > Male

Usually benign ☺

## Location

Extra-axial, dural based

Usually at sites of dural reflection: Falx cerebri, skull base, tentorium

## Imaging

Dural tail

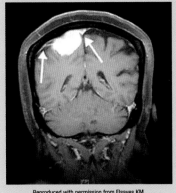

Reproduced with permission from Elsayes KM, Oldham SA: Introduction to Diagnostic Radiology. New York, NY: McGraw Hill; 2014.

## Symptoms

Headaches

Seizures

Progressive focal neurological deficits related to location

Cranial neuropathy

## Treatment

Surgical resection

Radiation

## Pathology

Arachnoid origin

Spindle cells concentrically arranged in whorled pattern

May have psammoma bodies (laminated calcifications)

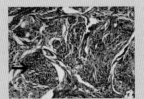

Reproduced with permission from Kemp WL, Burns DK, Brow TG: Pathology: The Big Picture. New York, NY: McGraw Hill; 2008.

# Migraine Headache

 ## Pain Lateralization

Unilateral

 ## Duration

4-72 hours (but usually <24 hours)

 ## Pain Quality

Severe

Pulsating, throbbing pain; relieved by sleep, darkness

Mnemonic: "**POUND**"
Pulsatile, one-day long, unilateral, nausea, disabling

 ## Other Features

**Core symptoms:**
- Photophobia
- Phonophobia
- Visual aura (bright, flashing lights or visual field cuts)
- Nausea/vomiting

**Nonspecific Triggers**
- Fasting, stress, poor sleep
- Menses
- OCPs
- Light

 ## Diagnosis

Based on clinical history
- Female > Male

**If atypical features, abnormal neuro exam, new-onset in older adult, or concerning PMH:** Consider CT-head/MRI-brain

 ## Treatment

**Acute:**
- Analgesics: NSAIDs, acetaminophen
- Triptans
- Antiemetics
- Dihydroergotamine

**Prophylaxis:**
- Lifestyle Δ: Diet, sleep, exercise
- Anti-HTN: β-blockers, CCBs
- TCA: Nortriptyline, amitriptyline
- Anticonvulsants: Topiramate, valproate

# Multiple Sclerosis

## Background

**Demyelinating disorder** of the **central nervous system** (brain and spinal cord)

## Epidemiology

More common in **women** and **further from the equator**; age of onset most **commonly 20-40s**

## Clinical Features

Flares of **different neurological symptoms** over time:
- Optic neuritis
- Transverse myelitis
- Internuclear ophthalmoplegia (INO)
- Bladder dysfunction
- Any other focal CNS deficits

 **+Uthoff's phenomenon**
Symptoms worse with heat

 **+Lhermitte's sign**
Electric sensation down the spine with forward neck flexion

## Diagnosis

CSF: Oligoclonal bands, ↑IgG index

MRI: Multiple **white matter lesions** in brain and spinal cord (eg, classic imaging finding is **Dawson's fingers**—periventricular lesions)

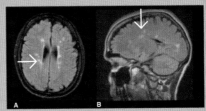

Reproduced with permission from Berkowitz AL: Clinical Neurology and Neuroanatomy: A Localization-Based Approach. New York, NY: McGraw Hill; 2017.

## MS Subtypes

There are several MS subtypes:
- Relapsing-remitting
- Primary progressive
- Secondary progressive

## Treatment

**Acute flares:** Corticosteroids

**Disease-modifying:** Interferon, glatiramer acetate, fingolomod, diethyl fumarate, natalizumab, etc.

**Symptomatic treatments**: For spasticity, fatigue, depression, etc.

# Myasthenia Gravis

Neuromuscular Junction Disease

## Background

Autoimmune antibody-mediated disorder of the neuromuscular junction (NMJ)

Epidemiology: Young females and older males

## Pathophysiology

Autoantibodies to **postsynaptic acetylcholine (ACh) receptors** at the NMJ

## Clinical Features

**Fluctuating, fatigable** weakness (worsens with muscle use or as day progresses)

May present with ptosis, diplopia, dysphagia, proximal weakness

Rarely, **myasthenic crisis** leading to acute respiratory failure

## Diagnosis

Improvement in weakness after **edrophonium test** and ptosis after **ice pack test** (hold 5 minutes)

Repetitive nerve stimulation shows **decremental response;** abnormal single-fiber EMG

Anti-AChR antibodies (80%)
Anti-MuSK antibodies (5%)

**CT chest** to look for thymoma

## Treatment

**Pyridostigmine** (AChE inhibitor)

Immunomodulators (eg, prednisone)

Thymectomy

**If acute crisis:** Plasmapheresis, IVIG

*Avoid aminoglycosides, β-blockers*

## MG vs LEMS

|  | Myasthenia Gravis | Lambert-Eaton Syndrome |
|---|---|---|
| Antibody target | Postsynaptic ACh receptor | Presynaptic VGCC |
| Clinical presentation | Eye muscles often involved | Proximal muscles often involved |
|  | Fatigable weakness; worsens with activity | Nonfatigable weakness; improves with activity |
| Associations | Thymoma | SCLC |

# Neurofibromatosis
## Types 1 and 2

## Background

### Neurofibromatosis Type 1

Mutation in **NF1** gene
⇨ Tumor suppressor **Neurofibromin**
Ras GTPase activating protein
Chromosome **17**

*Both are neurocutaneous disorders with autosomal dominant inheritance*

### Neurofibromatosis Type 2

Mutation in **NF2** gene
⇨ Tumor suppressor **Merlin**
Cytoskeletal membrane protein
Chromosome **22**

## Clinical Features

### Neurofibromatosis Type 1

**Cutaneous neurofibromas**

**Optic nerve glioma**

**Lisch nodules** (pigmented iris hamartomas)

**Café-au-lait spots** (hyperpigmented macules)

Axillary/inguinal freckling

Bone abnormalities (eg, kyphoscoliosis, long bone dysplasia)

### Neurofibromatosis Type 2

**Bilateral vestibular schwannomas**
⇨ Progressive hearing loss

**Other CNS tumors:**
❖ Meningioma
❖ Ependymoma
❖ Schwannoma

Juvenile cataracts

**Skin findings** (*less common than in NF1*):
Subcutaneous nodules, neurofibromas, café-au-lait spots

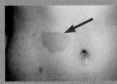

**Café-au-lait spots**

**Cutaneous neurofibromas**

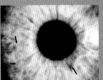

**Lisch nodules**

## Diagnosis (Types 1 and 2)

By clinical criteria in most cases
❖ Family history
❖ Physical exam
❖ MRI brain and spine

Genetic testing for NF1/NF2 mutation to confirm diagnosis or screen relatives

## Management (Types 1 and 2)

Surveillance for development of tumors and treatment of tumors, if arise

# Normal-Pressure Hydrocephalus

### 1   Definition

A potentially treatable **form of dementia** that is thought to arise from impaired reabsorption of CSF

Most commonly affects elderly

### Clinical Presentation   2

**Triad: "Wet, wobbly, and wacky"**

- Urinary incontinence
- Gait disorder (magnetic gait)
- Dementia

### Diagnosis   3

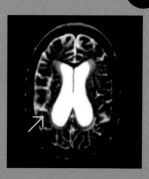

### 4

### Treatment

- LP or lumbar drainage of CSF may improve symptoms
- If so, ventriculoperitoneal (VP) shunt placement may lead to further improvement

- CT or MRI shows ventriculomegaly out of proportion to parenchymal atrophy
- LP shows normal pressure and can lead to improvement in symptoms

# Parkinson's
## Disease

## Background/Etiology

Neurodegenerative

Most cases are idiopathic
(rare genetic forms exist)

**Degeneration of dopaminergic neurons in substantia nigra**

Pathology: **Lewy bodies** (eosinophilic intracellular inclusions)

Reproduced with permission from Watts RL, Standaert DG, Obeso JA: Movement Disorders, 3rd ed. New York, NY: McGraw Hill; 2012.

## Clinical Features

**Parkinson's tetrad:**
   **Resting tremor**
   **Rigidity** ("cogwheeling")
   **Bradykinesia**
   **Postural instability**

Motor symptoms begin unilaterally, progress asymmetrically

**Gait**: Shuffling, ↓ arm swing

**Other**: Depression, dementia, REM sleep behavior disorder

## Differential Diagnosis

Secondary causes of parkinsonism:

**Drug-induced parkinsonism**
   ⇨ eg, antipsychotics, metoclopramide
**Cerebrovascular disease**
**Parkinson-plus syndromes**:
   ⇨ Progressive supranuclear palsy
   ⇨ Multiple systems atrophy
   ⇨ Corticobasal syndrome
   ⇨ Dementia with Lewy bodies
**Metabolic disorders**
   ⇨ eg, Wilson's disease
**Toxins**
   ⇨ eg, MPTP (illicit opioid contaminant)

## Management

**Levodopa + Carbidopa**

**Dopamine agonists**: Pramipexole, ropinirole

**Amantadine** (↑ release and ↓ reuptake of dopamine and other mechanisms)

**COMT inhibitors**: Entacapone, tolcapone (potentiate levodopa)

**MAO-B inhibitors**: Selegiline, rasagiline

**Anticholinergics**: Trihexyphenidyl for tremor

Deep brain stimulation

# Peripheral Neuropathy

## Mononeuropathy

Affects individual peripheral nerve

**Etiologies**
- ❖ Compression
- ❖ Entrapment
- ❖ Trauma
- ❖ Tumor or vasculitis (rare)

**Examples:** See Table

## Mononeuropathy Multiplex

Affects multiple individual peripheral nerves simultaneously or sequentially

**Etiologies**
- ❖ Vasculitis
- ❖ Infection (eg, HCV, leprosy)
- ❖ Multifocal motor neuropathy
- ❖ Malignancy rarely (neurolymphomatosis)

*Mononeuritis multiplex*: Term used if etiology is inflammatory (eg, vasculitis)

## Polyneuropathy

Affects peripheral nerves <u>diffusely</u> and <u>symmetrically</u>

May affect sensory, motor, and/or autonomic nerves

Sensory loss typically in <u>stocking-glove distribution</u> ☞

Reproduced with permission from Waxman SG: Clinical Neuroanatomy, 28th ed. New York, NY: McGraw Hill; 2017.

**Etiologies**
- ❖ Metabolic (diabetes, B12 deficiency)
- ❖ Inflammatory (CIDP, Guillain-Barré syndrome)
- ❖ Toxic (chemotherapy, EtOH)
- ❖ Infectious (HIV)
- ❖ Hereditary (Charcot-Marie-Tooth disease)

## Common Mononeuropathies

| Nerve | Common Causes | Muscles Affected (Motor Deficit) |
|---|---|---|
| Median | Carpal tunnel syndrome | Abductor pollicis brevis (thumb abduction), opponens pollicis (thumb opposition) |
| Ulnar | Compression at medial elbow or at wrist (Guyon's canal) | Adductor pollicis (thumb adduction), interossei (finger abduction and adduction) + digits 3 and 4 finger flexors if compression at elbow |
| Radial | Mid-shaft humerus fracture; compression at humerus (Saturday night palsy) or at axilla (crutches) | Brachioradialis; extensors of the wrist, fingers and thumb; supinator; + triceps if compression at axilla |
| Axillary | Anterior shoulder dislocation | Deltoid (arm abduction) |
| Peroneal | Compression at fibular head/neck | Tibialis anterior (dorsiflexion), peroneus longus + brevis (eversion) |
| Femoral | Trauma, retroperitoneal hematoma | Iliopsoas (hip flexion), quadriceps (knee extension) |

### Sensory Distributions

**Radial, Median, Ulnar**

Median — Dorsal cutaneous branch (ulnar) — Median

Median — Ulnar — Radial

Palmar cutaneous branch (median) — Palmar cutaneous branch (ulnar)

Reproduced with permission from Waxman SG: Clinical Neuroanatomy, 28th ed. New York, NY: McGraw Hill; 2017.

Axillary nerve — **Axillary**

**Peroneal**

Common peroneal

Superficial peroneal

Deep peroneal

**Femoral**

Anterior femoral cutaneous nerve
Medial femoral cutaneous nerve

Saphenous nerve

Reproduced with permission from Waxman SG: Clinical Neuroanatomy, 28th ed. New York, NY: McGraw Hill; 2017.

Reproduced with permission from Simon RP, Aminoff MJ, Greenberg DA: Clinical Neurology, 10th ed. New York, NY: McGraw Hill; 2018.

# Pilocytic Astrocytoma

## Background

Most common childhood primary brain tumor

Benign, low-grade

## Location

Commonly in posterior fossa (eg, cerebellum)

(Supratentorial also possible)

## Imaging

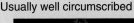
Cystic and solid components

Usually well circumscribed

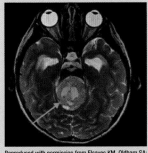

Reproduced with permission from Elsayes KM, Oldham SA: Introduction to Diagnostic Radiology. New York, NY: McGraw Hill; 2014.

## Symptoms

Drowsiness, headache, nausea, vomiting, ataxia, cranial neuropathy

Slow progression

## Treatment

Surgical resection

Radiation therapy

Good prognosis

## Pathology

Astrocyte origin

GFAP ⊕

Rosenthal fibers (eosinophilic, corkscrew fibers)

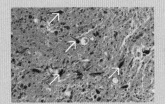

Reproduced with permission from Kemp WL, Burns DK, Brow TG: Pathology: The Big Picture. New York, NY: McGraw Hill; 2008.

# Secondary Headaches

 ## Etiologies by Location

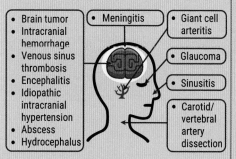

- Brain tumor
- Intracranial hemorrhage
- Venous sinus thrombosis
- Encephalitis
- Idiopathic intracranial hypertension
- Abscess
- Hydrocephalus

- Meningitis

- Giant cell arteritis
- Glaucoma
- Sinusitis
- Carotid/ vertebral artery dissection

 ## Diagnosis

- **If red flag:** CT-head/MRI-brain (see below)

- **If concern for infection/SAH with negative head CT:** Lumbar puncture (if no contraindication)

- **If concern for giant cell arteritis:** ESR/CRP

 ## Red Flags

| Red flags | Etiologies that must be considered |
|---|---|
| Thunderclap onset | Vascular (eg, SAH) |
| Worst at night, and/or with coughing/sneezing/straining | ↑ICP (eg, brain tumor) |
| New headache in older adult | Mass lesion (eg, brain tumor) |
| History of cancer | Metastasis |
| Immunosuppressed | Opportunistic infection |
| Obese younger woman, or child on tetracycline | Idiopathic intracranial hypertension |
| Headache and fever | Meningitis; encephalitis |
| Headache and focal deficits and/or seizures | Mass lesion (eg, brain tumor, abscess) |
| Headache and jaw claudication and/or scalp tenderness | Giant cell arteritis |

## Etiology

**Epilepsy** (recurrent unprovoked seizures)

**Structural brain lesions** (eg, tumor, AVM, prior stroke/ICH, prior head trauma)
**Genetic epilepsy syndromes**

**Provoked Seizures**

**Acute brain pathology** (eg, acute stroke/ICH, acute head trauma, meningitis/encephalitis)
**Metabolic** (eg, hyponatremia, hypo/hyper-glycemia)
**Systemic** (eg, infection, uremia)
**Drugs/medications** (eg, bupropion, EtOH withdrawal)

*ICH: intracranial hemorrhage
AVM: arteriovenous malformation

## Partial (Focal) Seizures

Seizure activity in discrete brain region

**Simple partial:** Consciousness preserved
**Complex partial:** Consciousness impaired

Focal motor, sensory, visual, auditory, or olfactory symptoms depending on brain region; **aura** preceding seizure

May secondarily generalize

**Todd's paralysis** (postictal weakness lasting <24 hours)

## Generalized Seizures

Diffuse seizure activity (both hemispheres)

Consciousness impaired

Postictal state (eg, confusion)

**Subtypes:**
**Tonic:** Stiffening
**Clonic:** Rhythmic movements
**Tonic-Clonic:** Mix of above
**Myoclonic:** Brief jerks
**Atonic:** Loss of postural tone
**Absence:** Brief staring episodes

 # Seizure Disorders

## Diagnostics

**Clinical:** Semiology and postictal state

**EEG**
**Partial:** Seek epileptogenic focus
**Absence 3 Hz spike-and-wave** discharges

**CT/MRI** if concern for focal brain lesion

Rule out systemic causes (CBC, serum electrolytes, glucose, etc.)

**Serum prolactin** may be ↑ briefly after generalized or complex partial seizure

## Treatment

**Antiepileptic drugs (AEDs)**

Commonly used AEDs:
| | |
|---|---|
| **Carbamazepine** | **Phenobarbital** |
| **Clobazam** | **Phenytoin** |
| **Gabapentin** | **Tiagabine** |
| **Lacosamide** | **Topiramate** |
| **Lamotrigine** | **Valproate** |
| **Levetiracetam** | **Vigabatrin** |
| **Oxcarbazepine** | **Zonisamide** |

**Absence seizures: Ethosuximide**
Second line: Valproate

Intractable temporal lobe seizures:
Anterior temporal lobectomy

## AED Adverse Effects

Many AEDs can cause: Ataxia, nystagmus/diplopia, Stevens–Johnson syndrome, hepatotoxicity, marrow suppression, teratogenicity. Notably:

**Carbamazepine:** Hyponatremia

**Lamotrigine:** Stevens–Johnson syndrome

**Phenytoin:** Gingival hyperplasia, hirsutism, fetal hydantoin syndrome

**Valproate:** Hepatotoxicity, fetal neural tube defects

**Levetiracetam:** Neuropsychiatric effect

### Definition

Seizure lasting at least 5 minutes

OR

Multiple consecutive seizures without interim return to baseline

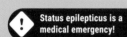

**Status epilepticus is a medical emergency!**

### Etiologies to Consider

Hypoglycemia

Alcohol/sedative withdrawal

Drug intoxication

AED withdrawal/noncompliance

Structural lesion

Infectious/inflammatory cause

Head trauma

### Diagnostic Workup

Collateral history and exam

Glucose, electrolytes, CBC
AED levels
Toxicology screen

Head CT for intracranial pathology

LP if fever or meningeal signs

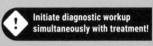

**Initiate diagnostic workup simultaneously with treatment!**

 # Status Epilepticus

### Management

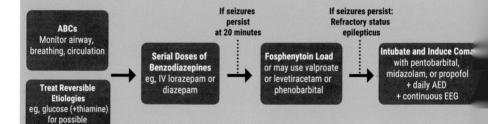

**ABCs**
Monitor airway, breathing, circulation

**Treat Reversible Etiologies**
eg, glucose (+thiamine) for possible hypoglycemia

→

**Serial Doses of Benzodiazepines**
eg, IV lorazepam or diazepam

If seizures persist at 20 minutes

**Fosphenytoin Load**
or may use valproate or levetiracetam or phenobarbital

If seizures persist: Refractory status epilepticus

**Intubate and Induce Coma**
with pentobarbital, midazolam, or propofol + daily AED + continuous EEG

# Stroke (Ischemic)

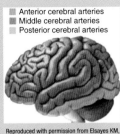

Anterior cerebral arteries
Middle cerebral arteries
Posterior cerebral arteries

Reproduced with permission from Elsayes KM, Oldham SA: Introduction to Diagnostic Radiology. New York, NY: McGraw Hill; 2014.

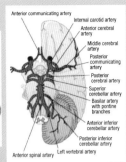

Anterior communicating artery
Internal carotid artery
Anterior cerebral artery
Middle cerebral artery
Posterior communicating artery
Posterior cerebral artery
Superior cerebellar artery
Basilar artery with pontine branches
Anterior inferior cerebellar artery
Posterior inferior cerebellar artery
Anterior spinal artery    Left vertebral artery

Reproduced with permission from Waxman SG: Clinical Neuroanatomy, 28th ed. New York, NY: McGraw Hill; 2017.

## 📖 Background

**Definition:** Brain infarction due to impaired cerebral blood flow, causing sudden-onset focal deficits localizable to affected brain region(s)

**Etiology:** Vascular, cardiac, hematologic

**Pathophysiology:** Local thrombosis, embolism (cardiac, artery-to-artery), other

## ◎ Clinical Presentation

**MCA stroke:** Contralateral face/arm > leg weakness with aphasia (left hemisphere) or neglect (right hemisphere)

**ACA stroke:** Contralateral leg > arm weakness

**PCA stroke:** Contralateral visual field deficit

**Lacunar stroke:** Contralateral pure motor or sensory deficits

## ❗ Risk Factors

**Modifiable:**
- HTN
- HL
- DM
- Afib
- CAD
- Carotid stenosis
- Hypertension
- Obesity
- Smoking
- Drug use

**Nonmodifiable:**
- Family history of MI/stroke
- Age >60 y/o
- Male gender

## 🏥 Diagnosis

CT-head              MRI-brain

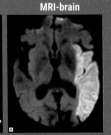

Reproduced with permission from Berkowitz AL: Clinical Neurology and Neuroanatomy: A Localization-Based Approach. New York, NY: McGraw Hill; 2017.

Hypodensity (may not be present until up to 6-12 hours after symptom onset)     Hyperintensity on DWI

## 🔗 Acute Treatment

**Antithrombotic:**
- tPA or thrombectomy if in time window
- Antiplatelet agent

**Permissive hypertension**

## 🔗 Secondary Prevention

- **Risk factor modification**: HTN, HL, DM, smoking
- **Antiplatelet agent**
- **Anticoagulation:** If Afib/hypercoagulable state
- **Carotid endarterectomy or stenting:** If moderate-severe stenosis

# Subarachnoid Hemorrhage

##  Causes

- **Saccular berry aneurysm of Circle of Willis vessels**
- Arteriovenous malformation (AVM)
- Trauma

##  Clinical Presentation

- **"Worst headache of life"**: Intensely painful, abrupt-onset thunderclap headache
- "Sentinel bleed" that occurs prior to worst headache of life and resolves

##  Diagnosis

- **Noncontrast head CT**
- LP: RBCs, xanthochromia (yellow color to CSF)
- 4-vessel catheter angiography (or CT angiography)

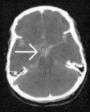

Reproduced with permission from Berkowitz AL: Clinical Neurology and Neuroanatomy: A Localization-Based Approach. New York, NY: McGraw Hill; 2017.

## Treatment

- **Secure aneurysm** (eg, surgical clipping vs endovascular coiling)
- External ventricular drain (EVD) if hydrocephalus
- Prevent rebleeding (first 48 hours) by keeping BP <150 mmHg
- Prevent vasospasm (first 5-7 days) with **nimodipine** (a CCB), IV fluids, and BP control

## ◈ Complications

- Obstructive hydrocephalus
- Vasospasm, rebleeding
- Seizures
- CN III palsy (posterior communicating artery [PCom] aneurysm)
- Increased ICP, coma, death

## Conditions Associated with Berry Aneurysm

Can **MAKE a SAH** more likely:

**M**arfan's syndrome
**A**ortic coarctation
**K**idney disease (AD, polycystic)
**E**hlers–Danlos syndrome
**S**ickle cell anemia
**A**therosclerosis
**H**istory (Familial)

# Subdural Hematoma **VS** Epidural Hematoma

| Subdural Hematoma | | Epidural Hematoma |
|---|---|---|

### Etiology

**Subdural:** Rupture of bridging veins

Head trauma; increased risk in elderly and alcoholics

**Epidural:** Tear of middle meningeal artery

Severe head trauma with skull fracture

### Presentation

**Subdural:** Acute or chronic

Headache, mental status change, hemiparesis, pseudodementia

**Epidural:** Acute

Initial LOC, +/− lucid interval, progresses to coma & uncal herniation ("blown pupil")

### Imaging

**Subdural:** CT Head — Crescent-shaped

Concave hyper-density respecting midline

**Epidural:** CT Head — Lens-shaped

Convex hyper-density, limited by sutures

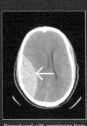

### Treatment

**Subdural:** Surgical evacuation if large, increasing, or symptomatic

**Epidural:** Immediate surgical evacuation

# Tension Headache

## Pain Lateralization

Bilateral

## Duration

30 minutes to 7 days

## Pain Quality

Mild-moderate

Squeezing/tightening ("band-like") pain

Constant, steady

Not worsened by routine physical activity (eg, walking)

## Other Features

**Core symptoms:**
- No aura, severe nausea, vomiting
- No more than one of: Photophobia, phonophobia, or mild nausea

**Nonspecific symptoms:**
- Anxiety
- Poor concentration
- Difficulty sleeping

**Nonspecific Triggers:**
- Fatigue, stress

## Diagnosis

Based on clinical history
- Most common headache diagnosed in adults

**If Age >50 y/o:** Consider ESR to rule out giant cell arteritis (GCA)
**If atypical features, abnormal neuro exam, new-onset in older adult, or concerning PMH:** Consider CT-head/MRI-brain

## Treatment

**Acute**
- Analgesics: NSAIDs, acetaminophen

**Prophylaxis:**
- Stress relief: Relaxation, massage
- TCA: eg, nortriptyline, amitriptyline

# Trigeminal Neuralgia

## Pain Lateralization

Most commonly unilateral (rarely bilateral)

Trigeminal nerve (typically V2/V3 distribution)

## Duration

Typically <1 minute, ranges seconds to 2 minutes

Brief, repetitive lightning-like episodes

## Triggers

Intense pain triggered by **innocuous stimuli** in CN V distribution, including:

- Brushing teeth; shaving, washing, or touching face
- Eating, drinking, talking
- Wind exposure to skin

Prior dental work a risk factor

## Diagnosis

Clinical history

MRI/A: Look for vascular loop compressing nerve

**Differential diagnosis:** If bilateral, consider multiple sclerosis (demyelination of trigeminal entry zone in pons)

## Treatment

**First line:** Carbamazepine

**Second line:** Other antiepileptics

**Refractory pain:** Microvascular nerve decompression or ablation/radiation of gasserian ganglion

## CN V Divisions

V1: Ophthalmic
V2: Maxillary
V3: Mandibular

Ophthalmic division

Maxillary division

Mandibular division

# Tuberous Sclerosis

## Background

Neurocutaneous disorder

**Autosomal dominant** inheritance

Mutation in tumor suppressor or **TSC1** (hamartin, chromosome 9) or **TSC2** (tuberin, chromosome 16) ⇨ small benign tumors in various organs

## Diagnosis & Imaging

Clinical diagnosis: Seizure disorder with characteristic skin lesions

**Neuroimaging:** Calcified intracranial hamartomas (tubers), subependymal nodules

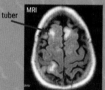
tuber

subependymal nodule

Reproduced with permission from Ropper AH, Samuels MA, Klein JP: Adams and Victor's Principles of Neurology, 11th ed. New York, NY: McGraw Hill; 2019.

Screen for cardiac rhabdomyoma (**Echo**), seizure activity (**EEG**), renal disease (**abdominal MRI**)

## Treatment

**Antiepileptics** for seizures (ACTH or vigabatrin for infantile spasms)

Screen for/treat tumors and systemic complications

## Clinical Features

Intellectual disability

**Seizures** (including infantile spasms)

### Skin Lesions
**Ash-leaf spots** (hypopigmented macules — accentuated by Wood's UV lamp)

Reproduced with permission from Tonekaboni, SH, Tousi P, Ebrahimi A. et al: Clinical and para clinical manifestations of tuberous sclerosis: a cross sectional study on 81 pediatric patients, Iran J Child Neurol. 2012 Summer; 6(3):25-31.

Reproduced with permission from Kang S, Amagai M, Bruckner AL, et al: Fitzpatrick's Dermatology, 9th ed. New York, NY: McGraw Hill; 2019.

Reproduced with permission from Bissonnette B, Luginbuehl I, Marciniak B: Syndromes: Rapid Recognition and Perioperative Implications. New York, NY: McGraw Hill; 2006.

Ash-leaf spot (left) illuminated by Wood's lamp (center); sebaceous adenoma (right).

**Sebaceous adenoma** (red facial nodules)

**Shagreen patches** (rough papule with orange-peel consistency, typically lumbosacral)

## Other Associated Tumors

❖ **Cardiac rhabdomyoma** in >50% of patients

❖ Subependymal giant cell astrocytoma

❖ Renal angiomyolipoma

❖ Retinal hamartomas

❖ Ungual fibromas

# Vascular Dementia

## ① Background

**Vascular dementia** or **multi-infarct dementia** is the result of multiple strokes and/or chronic cerebrovascular disease

## ②

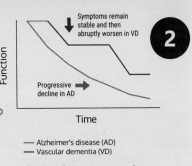

Symptoms remain stable and then abruptly worsen in VD

Function

Progressive decline in AD

Time

— Alzheimer's disease (AD)
— Vascular dementia (VD)

### Clinical Presentation

**Step-wise** or **chronic progressive** decline in cognitive function

**Executive dysfunction** and cognitive slowing

**Focal neurological deficits** (from prior strokes) may be present

## ③ Risk Factors

- Older age
- Cardiovascular risk factors: Smoking, hypertension (HTN), hyperlipidemia (HLD), diabetes mellitus (DM)
- Prior strokes

## Imaging ④

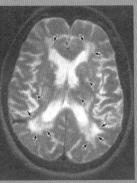

CT or MRI demonstrates **multiple cortical and/or subcortical infarcts** (eg, basal ganglia [arrowheads in image] and periventricular white matter [arrows])

## ⑤ Treatment

- There is no definitive treatment
- Management involves optimizing cardiovascular risk factors and secondary prevention of further strokes

# Vestibular Schwannoma
## (Acoustic Neuroma)

## Background

Adult primary brain tumor

Usually benign ☺

If bilateral, consider NF2

## Location

Tumor of CN VIII at cerebellopontine angle or in internal acoustic meatus

Can compress nearby CN VII, brainstem, cerebellum

## Imaging

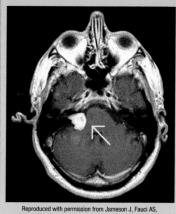

Reproduced with permission from Jameson J, Fauci AS, Kasper DL, et al: Harrison's Principles of Internal Medicine, 20th ed. New York, NY: McGraw Hill; 2018.

## Symptoms

Ipsilateral tinnitus, vertigo, hearing loss (bilateral in NF2)

Can cause facial palsy (if CN VII affected) or ataxia (if cerebellum affected)

## Treatment

Observation

Surgical resection

Radiation therapy

## Pathology

Schwann cell origin

S-100 ⊕

Biphasic: Dense, hypercellular areas containing spindle cells (yellow arrows: Antoni A) alternating with hypocellular, myxoid areas (black arrow: Antoni B)

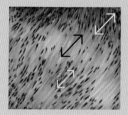

# Wernicke's Aphasia

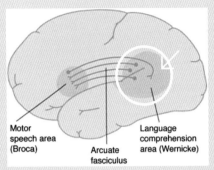

Motor speech area (Broca)

Arcuate fasciculus

Language comprehension area (Wernicke)

Reproduced with permission from Waxman SG: Clinical Neuroanatomy, 28th ed. New York, NY: McGraw Hill; 2017.

 **Definition**

Disorder of language comprehension with nonsensical speech often secondary to stroke

| | | |
|---|---|---|
|  | **Production:** (fluency, quality of speech) | Fluent "Word salad," frequent use of made-up words Unaware of deficits |
|  | **Comprehension:** | Impaired (unable to follow commands) |
|  | **Repetition:** | Impaired |
|  | **Localization:** | Posterior superior temporal gyrus (inferior division of MCA) of dominant hemisphere (most commonly left side) |

# References _____

**Acute Peripheral Vestibulopathy**
Berkowitz AL. *Clinical Neurology and Neuroanatomy: A Localization-Based Approach*. New York, NY: McGraw Hill; 2017.

Le T, Bhushan V. *First Aid for the USMLE Step 1 2019*. 29th ed. New York, NY: McGraw Hill; 2018.

**Alzheimer's Dementia**
Berkowitz AL. *Clinical Neurology and Neuroanatomy: A Localization-Based Approach*. New York, NY: McGraw Hill; 2017.

Le T, Bhushan V. *First Aid for the USMLE Step 1 2019*. 29th ed. New York, NY: McGraw Hill; 2018.

Le T, Bhushan V. *First Aid for the USMLE Step 2 CK*. 10th ed. New York, NY: McGraw Hill; 2018.

**Amyotrophic Lateral Sclerosis**
Berkowitz AL. *Clinical Neurology and Neuroanatomy: A Localization-Based Approach*. New York, NY: McGraw Hill; 2017.

Le T, Bhushan V. *First Aid for the USMLE Step 1 2019*. 29th ed. New York, NY: McGraw Hill; 2018.

Le T, Bhushan V. *First Aid for the USMLE Step 2 CK*. 10th ed. New York, NY: McGraw Hill; 2018.

Ropper AH, Samuels MA, Klein JP. *Adams and Victor's Principles of Neurology*. 10th ed. New York, NY: McGraw Hill; 2014.

**Benign Paroxysmal Positional Vertigo**
Berkowitz AL. *Clinical Neurology and Neuroanatomy: A Localization-Based Approach*. New York, NY: McGraw Hill; 2017.

Le T, Bhushan V. *First Aid for the USMLE Step 1 2019*. 29th ed. New York, NY: McGraw Hill; 2018.

Le T, Bhushan V. *First Aid for the USMLE Step 2 CK*. 10th ed. New York, NY: McGraw Hill; 2018.

**Broca's Aphasia**
Berkowitz AL. *Clinical Neurology and Neuroanatomy: A Localization-Based Approach*. New York, NY: McGraw Hill; 2017.

Le T, Bhushan V. *First Aid for the USMLE Step 1 2019*. 29th ed. New York, NY: McGraw Hill; 2018.

Le T, Bhushan V. *First Aid for the USMLE Step 2 CK*. 10th ed. New York, NY: McGraw Hill; 2018.

**Cervical & Lumbar Stenosis**
Berkowitz AL. *Clinical Neurology and Neuroanatomy: A Localization-Based Approach*. New York, NY: McGraw Hill; 2017.

Le T, Bhushan V. *First Aid for the USMLE Step 1 2019*. 29th ed. New York, NY: McGraw Hill; 2018.

Le T, Bhushan V. *First Aid for the USMLE Step 2 CK*. 10th ed. New York, NY: McGraw Hill; 2018.

**Cluster Headache**
Berkowitz AL. *Clinical Neurology and Neuroanatomy: A Localization-Based Approach*. New York, NY: McGraw Hill; 2017.

Le T, Bhushan V. *First Aid for the USMLE Step 1 2019*. 29th ed. New York, NY: McGraw Hill; 2018.

Le T, Bhushan V. *First Aid for the USMLE Step 2 CK*. 10th ed. New York, NY: McGraw Hill; 2018.

## Coma

Berkowitz AL. *Clinical Neurology and Neuroanatomy: A Localization-Based Approach*. New York, NY: McGraw Hill; 2017.

Le T, Bhushan V. *First Aid for the USMLE Step 1 2019*. 29th ed. New York, NY: McGraw Hill; 2018.

Le T, Bhushan V. *First Aid for the USMLE Step 2 CK*. 10th ed. New York, NY: McGraw Hill; 2018.

Ropper AH, Samuels MA, Klein JP. *Adams and Victor's Principles of Neurology*. 10th ed. New York, NY: McGraw Hill; 2014.

## Craniopharyngioma

Berkowitz AL. *Clinical Neurology and Neuroanatomy: A Localization-Based Approach*. New York, NY: McGraw Hill; 2017.

Le T, Bhushan V. *First Aid for the USMLE Step 1 2019*. 29th ed. New York, NY: McGraw Hill; 2018.

Le T, Bhushan V. *First Aid for the USMLE Step 2 CK*. 10th ed. New York, NY: McGraw Hill; 2018.

## Creutzfeldt–Jakob Disease

Berkowitz AL. *Clinical Neurology and Neuroanatomy: A Localization-Based Approach*. New York, NY: McGraw Hill; 2017.

Le T, Bhushan V. *First Aid for the USMLE Step 1 2019*. 29th ed. New York, NY: McGraw Hill; 2018.

Le T, Bhushan V. *First Aid for the USMLE Step 2 CK*. 10th ed. New York, NY: McGraw Hill; 2018.

## Dementia with Lewy Bodies

Berkowitz AL. *Clinical Neurology and Neuroanatomy: A Localization-Based Approach*. New York, NY: McGraw Hill; 2017.

Le T, Bhushan V. *First Aid for the USMLE Step 1 2019*. 29th ed. New York, NY: McGraw Hill; 2018.

Le T, Bhushan V. *First Aid for the USMLE Step 2 CK*. 10th ed. New York, NY: McGraw Hill; 2018.

## Facial Palsy

Berkowitz AL. *Clinical Neurology and Neuroanatomy: A Localization-Based Approach*. New York, NY: McGraw Hill; 2017.

Le T, Bhushan V. *First Aid for the USMLE Step 1 2019*. 29th ed. New York, NY: McGraw Hill; 2018.

Le T, Bhushan V. *First Aid for the USMLE Step 2 CK*. 10th ed. New York, NY: McGraw Hill; 2018.

## Frontotemporal Dementia

Berkowitz AL. *Clinical Neurology and Neuroanatomy: A Localization-Based Approach*. New York, NY: McGraw Hill; 2017.

Le T, Bhushan V. *First Aid for the USMLE Step 1 2019*. 29th ed. New York, NY: McGraw Hill; 2018.

Le T, Bhushan V. *First Aid for the USMLE Step 2 CK*. 10th ed. New York, NY: McGraw Hill; 2018.

## Gliomas

Berkowitz AL. *Clinical Neurology and Neuroanatomy: A Localization-Based Approach*. New York, NY: McGraw Hill; 2017.

Le T, Bhushan V. *First Aid for the USMLE Step 1 2019*. 29th ed. New York, NY: McGraw Hill; 2018.

Le T, Bhushan V. *First Aid for the USMLE Step 2 CK*. 10th ed. New York, NY: McGraw Hill; 2018.

## Guillain-Barre Syndrome

Berkowitz AL. *Clinical Neurology and Neuroanatomy: A Localization-Based Approach*. New York, NY: McGraw Hill; 2017.

Le T, Bhushan V. *First Aid for the USMLE Step 1 2019*. 29th ed. New York, NY: McGraw Hill; 2018.

Le T, Bhushan V. *First Aid for the USMLE Step 2 CK*. 10th ed. New York, NY: McGraw Hill; 2018.

## Huntington's Disease

Berkowitz AL. *Clinical Neurology and Neuroanatomy: A Localization-Based Approach*. New York, NY: McGraw Hill; 2017.

Le T, Bhushan V. *First Aid for the USMLE Step 1 2019*. 29th ed. New York, NY: McGraw Hill; 2018.

Le T, Bhushan V. *First Aid for the USMLE Step 2 CK*. 10th ed. New York, NY: McGraw Hill; 2018.

Ropper AH, Samuels MA, Klein JP. *Adams and Victor's Principles of Neurology*. 10th ed. New York, NY: McGraw Hill; 2014.

## Medulloblastoma

Berkowitz AL. *Clinical Neurology and Neuroanatomy: A Localization-Based Approach*. New York, NY: McGraw Hill; 2017.

Le T, Bhushan V. *First Aid for the USMLE Step 1 2019*. 29th ed. New York, NY: McGraw Hill; 2018.

Le T, Bhushan V. *First Aid for the USMLE Step 2 CK*. 10th ed. New York, NY: McGraw Hill; 2018.

## Ménière's Disease

Berkowitz AL. *Clinical Neurology and Neuroanatomy: A Localization-Based Approach*. New York, NY: McGraw Hill; 2017.

Le T, Bhushan V. *First Aid for the USMLE Step 1 2019*. 29th ed. New York, NY: McGraw Hill; 2018.

Le T, Bhushan V. *First Aid for the USMLE Step 2 CK*. 10th ed. New York, NY: McGraw Hill; 2018.

Ropper AH, Samuels MA, Klein JP. *Adams and Victor's Principles of Neurology*. 10th ed. New York, NY: McGraw Hill; 2014.

## Meningioma

Berkowitz AL. *Clinical Neurology and Neuroanatomy: A Localization-Based Approach*. New York, NY: McGraw Hill; 2017.

Le T, Bhushan V. *First Aid for the USMLE Step 1 2019*. 29th ed. New York, NY: McGraw Hill; 2018.

Le T, Bhushan V. *First Aid for the USMLE Step 2 CK*. 10th ed. New York, NY: McGraw Hill; 2018.

## Migraine Headache

Berkowitz AL. *Clinical Neurology and Neuroanatomy: A Localization-Based Approach*. New York, NY: McGraw Hill; 2017.

Le T, Bhushan V. *First Aid for the USMLE Step 1 2019*. 29th ed. New York, NY: McGraw Hill; 2018.

Le T, Bhushan V. *First Aid for the USMLE Step 2 CK*. 10th ed. New York, NY: McGraw Hill; 2018.

## Neurofibromatosis

Berkowitz AL. *Clinical Neurology and Neuroanatomy: A Localization-Based Approach*. New York, NY: McGraw Hill; 2017.

Le T, Bhushan V. *First Aid for the USMLE Step 1 2019*. 29th ed. New York, NY: McGraw Hill; 2018.

Le T, Bhushan V. *First Aid for the USMLE Step 2 CK*. 10th ed. New York, NY: McGraw Hill; 2018.

## Normal-Pressure Hydrocephalus

Berkowitz AL. *Clinical Neurology and Neuroanatomy: A Localization-Based Approach*. New York, NY: McGraw Hill; 2017.

Le T, Bhushan V. *First Aid for the USMLE Step 1 2019*. 29th ed. New York, NY: McGraw Hill; 2018.

Le T, Bhushan V. *First Aid for the USMLE Step 2 CK*. 10th ed. New York, NY: McGraw Hill; 2018.

## Parkinson's Disease

Berkowitz AL. *Clinical Neurology and Neuroanatomy: A Localization-Based Approach*. New York, NY: McGraw Hill; 2017.

Le T, Bhushan V. *First Aid for the USMLE Step 1 2019*. 29th ed. New York, NY: McGraw Hill; 2018.

Le T, Bhushan V. *First Aid for the USMLE Step 2 CK*. 10th ed. New York, NY: McGraw Hill; 2018.

Ropper AH, Samuels MA, Klein JP. *Adams and Victor's Principles of Neurology*. 10th ed. New York, NY: McGraw Hill; 2014.

## Peripheral Neuropathy
Berkowitz AL. *Clinical Neurology and Neuroanatomy: A Localization-Based Approach*. New York, NY: McGraw Hill; 2017.
Le T, Bhushan V. *First Aid for the USMLE Step 1 2019*. 29th ed. New York, NY: McGraw Hill; 2018.
Le T, Bhushan V. *First Aid for the USMLE Step 2 CK*. 10th ed. New York, NY: McGraw Hill; 2018.

## Pilocytic Astrocytoma
Berkowitz AL. *Clinical Neurology and Neuroanatomy: A Localization-Based Approach*. New York, NY: McGraw Hill; 2017.
Le T, Bhushan V. *First Aid for the USMLE Step 1 2019*. 29th ed. New York, NY: McGraw Hill; 2018.
Le T, Bhushan V. *First Aid for the USMLE Step 2 CK*. 10th ed. New York, NY: McGraw Hill; 2018.

## Secondary Headaches
Berkowitz AL. *Clinical Neurology and Neuroanatomy: A Localization-Based Approach*. New York, NY: McGraw Hill; 2017.
Le T, Bhushan V. *First Aid for the USMLE Step 1 2019*. 29th ed. New York, NY: McGraw Hill; 2018.
Le T, Bhushan V. *First Aid for the USMLE Step 2 CK*. 10th ed. New York, NY: McGraw Hill; 2018.

## Stroke (Ischemic)
Berkowitz AL. *Clinical Neurology and Neuroanatomy: A Localization-Based Approach*. New York, NY: McGraw Hill; 2017.
Le T, Bhushan V. *First Aid for the USMLE Step 1 2019*. 29th ed. New York, NY: McGraw Hill; 2018.
Le T, Bhushan V. *First Aid for the USMLE Step 2 CK*. 10th ed. New York, NY: McGraw Hill; 2018.

## Subdural Hematoma vs Epidural Hematoma
Berkowitz AL. *Clinical Neurology and Neuroanatomy: A Localization-Based Approach*. New York, NY: McGraw Hill; 2017.
Le T, Bhushan V. *First Aid for the USMLE Step 1 2019*. 29th ed. New York, NY: McGraw Hill; 2018.
Le T, Bhushan V. *First Aid for the USMLE Step 2 CK*. 10th ed. New York, NY: McGraw Hill; 2018.

## Tension Headache
Berkowitz AL. *Clinical Neurology and Neuroanatomy: A Localization-Based Approach*. New York, NY: McGraw Hill; 2017.
Le T, Bhushan V. *First Aid for the USMLE Step 1 2019*. 29th ed. New York, NY: McGraw Hill; 2018.
Le T, Bhushan V. *First Aid for the USMLE Step 2 CK*. 10th ed. New York, NY: McGraw Hill; 2018.

## Trigeminal Neuralgia
Berkowitz AL. *Clinical Neurology and Neuroanatomy: A Localization-Based Approach*. New York, NY: McGraw Hill; 2017.
Le T, Bhushan V. *First Aid for the USMLE Step 1 2019*. 29th ed. New York, NY: McGraw Hill; 2018.
Le T, Bhushan V. *First Aid for the USMLE Step 2 CK*. 10th ed. New York, NY: McGraw Hill; 2018.

## Tuberous Sclerosis
Berkowitz AL. *Clinical Neurology and Neuroanatomy: A Localization-Based Approach*. New York, NY: McGraw Hill; 2017.
Le T, Bhushan V. *First Aid for the USMLE Step 1 2019*. 29th ed. New York, NY: McGraw Hill; 2018.
Le T, Bhushan V. *First Aid for the USMLE Step 2 CK*. 10th ed. New York, NY: McGraw Hill; 2018.

Ropper AH, Samuels MA, Klein JP. *Adams and Victor's Principles of Neurology*. 10th ed. New York, NY: McGraw Hill; 2014.

**Vascular Dementia**
Berkowitz AL. *Clinical Neurology and Neuroanatomy: A Localization-Based Approach*. New York, NY: McGraw Hill; 2017.
Le T, Bhushan V. *First Aid for the USMLE Step 1 2019*. 29th ed. New York, NY: McGraw Hill; 2018.
Le T, Bhushan V. *First Aid for the USMLE Step 2 CK*. 10th ed. New York, NY: McGraw Hill; 2018.

**Vestibular Schwannoma**
Berkowitz AL. *Clinical Neurology and Neuroanatomy: A Localization-Based Approach*. New York, NY: McGraw Hill; 2017.
Le T, Bhushan V. *First Aid for the USMLE Step 1 2019*. 29th ed. New York, NY: McGraw Hill; 2018.
Le T, Bhushan V. *First Aid for the USMLE Step 2 CK*. 10th ed. New York, NY: McGraw Hill; 2018.

**Wernicke's Aphasia**
Berkowitz AL. *Clinical Neurology and Neuroanatomy: A Localization-Based Approach*. New York, NY: McGraw Hill; 2017.
Le T, Bhushan V. *First Aid for the USMLE Step 1 2019*. 29th ed. New York, NY: McGraw Hill; 2018.
Le T, Bhushan V. *First Aid for the USMLE Step 2 CK*. 10th ed. New York, NY: McGraw Hill; 2018.

# Obstetrics/Gynecology

*Dana L. Redick, MD*

# Abnormal Uterine Bleeding

 **Structural Causes:**   **Nonstructural Causes:**

## Polyp
Hysteroscopy:  Gross:

Used with permission from Dr. Dana Redick.

## Coagulopathy

Eg: VWF in adolescent
check platelet count, PT/PTT

## Adenomyosis
Endometrial glands in myometrium
*diffusely enlarged uterus*
 US:  Gross:

Reproduced with permission
from Elsayes KM, Oldham SA:
Introduction to Diagnostic
Radiology. New York, NY:
McGraw Hill; 2014.

Reproduced with permission from Creative
Commons. Adenomyosis, Hysterectomy
Specimen by Ed Euthman, MD.
https://commons.wikimedia.org/wiki/File:Ade-
nomyosis._Hysterectomy_Specimen.jpg

## Ovulatory dysfunction

Eg: PCOS

## Endometrial

Eg: Infection

## Leiomyoma (fibroid)
Smooth muscle tumor
*asymmetrically enlarged uterus*
 US:  MRI:

Reproduced with permission from
Cunningham G, Leveno KJ,
Bloom SL, et al: Williams Obstetrics, 25th ed.
New York, NY: McGraw Hill; 2018.

Used with permission from
Dr. Dana Redick.

## Iatrogenic

Eg: Postmenopausal
HRT (prevent with
progestins)

## Malignancy; hyperplasia

(!) Pap smear to r/o cervical cancer;

(!) if >35 years w/ obesity/diabetes *or*
Endometrium 15 mm pre- or >4 mm in
postmenopause, do **endometrial biopsy**

## Not yet classified

Eg: TSH to r/o ↑↓thyroid
Other systemic causes

---

**Evaluation:**
 Hx, PE
Labs (CBC)

 US, +/–Bx

**Treatment:**
 Mild: Medical management
Severe: High-dose IV
estrogen +/– D&C

 *Structural causes:* Surgery

 Rule out PREGNANCY
first check β-hCG

 Postmenopausal: Assess for
endometrial cancer
but most *often vaginal atrophy*

---

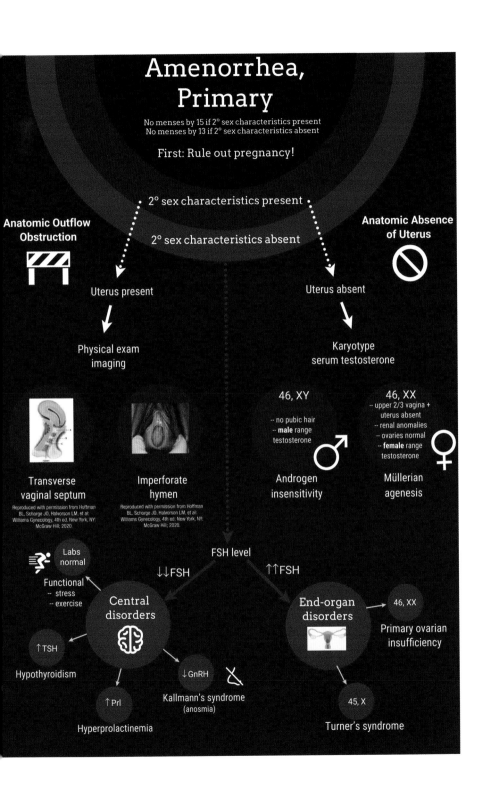

# Amenorrhea, Primary

No menses by 15 if 2° sex characteristics present
No menses by 13 if 2° sex characteristics absent

## First: Rule out pregnancy!

2° sex characteristics present

2° sex characteristics absent

**Anatomic Outflow Obstruction**

**Anatomic Absence of Uterus**

Uterus present

Uterus absent

Physical exam imaging

Karyotype serum testosterone

**46, XY**
-- no pubic hair
-- **male** range testosterone

**46, XX**
-- upper 2/3 vagina + uterus absent
-- renal anomalies
-- ovaries normal
-- **female** range testosterone

Transverse vaginal septum

Reproduced with permission from Hoffman BL, Schorge JO, Halvorson LM, et al: Williams Gynecology, 4th ed. New York, NY: McGraw Hill; 2020.

Imperforate hymen

Reproduced with permission from Hoffman BL, Schorge JO, Halvorson LM, et al: Williams Gynecology, 4th ed. New York, NY: McGraw Hill; 2020.

Androgen insensitivity

Müllerian agenesis

Labs normal

Functional
-- stress
-- exercise

FSH level

↓↓FSH

↑↑FSH

**Central disorders**

**End-organ disorders**

46, XX

↑TSH

Primary ovarian insufficiency

Hypothyroidism

↓GnRH

↑Prl

Kallmann's syndrome (anosmia)

45, X

Hyperprolactinemia

Turner's syndrome

# Amenorrhea, Secondary

*Absence of menses for 6 consecutive months in women who have menstruated previously*

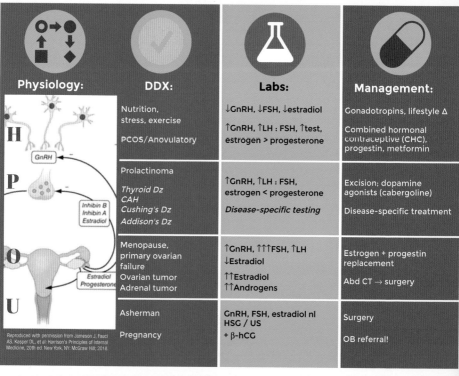

| Physiology: | DDX: | Labs: | Management: |
|---|---|---|---|
| H P O U | Nutrition, stress, exercise | ↓GnRH, ↓FSH, ↓estradiol | Gonadotropins, lifestyle Δ |
| | PCOS/Anovulatory | ↑GnRH, ↑LH : FSH, ↑test, estrogen > progesterone | Combined hormonal contraceptive (CHC), progestin, metformin |
| | Prolactinoma | ↑GnRH, ↑LH : FSH, estrogen < progesterone | Excision; dopamine agonists (cabergoline) |
| | *Thyroid Dz* *CAH* *Cushing's Dz* *Addison's Dz* | *Disease-specific testing* | Disease-specific treatment |
| | Menopause, primary ovarian failure | ↑GnRH, ↑↑↑FSH, ↑LH ↓Estradiol | Estrogen + progestin replacement |
| | Ovarian tumor Adrenal tumor | ↑↑Estradiol ↑↑Androgens | Abd CT → surgery |
| | Asherman | GnRH, FSH, estradiol nl HSG / US | Surgery |
| | Pregnancy | + β-hCG | OB referral! |

Reproduced with permission from Jameson J, Fauci AS, Kasper DL, et al: Harrison's Principles of Internal Medicine, 20th ed. New York, NY: McGraw Hill; 2018.

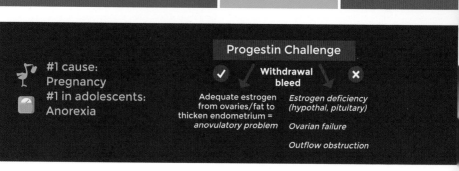

#1 cause:
**Pregnancy**

#1 in adolescents:
**Anorexia**

### Progestin Challenge

✓ Withdrawal bleed

Adequate estrogen from ovaries/fat to thicken endometrium = *anovulatory problem*

✗

*Estrogen deficiency (hypothal, pituitary)*

*Ovarian failure*

*Outflow obstruction*

# Antepartum Hemorrhage
## *3rd Trimester Vaginal Bleeding*

| Abruptio Placentae | | Placenta Previa | Vasa Previa |
|---|---|---|---|

| | **Definition** | | |
|---|---|---|---|
| Premature separation of placenta from uterus **1/100 live births**  Reproduced with permission from Cunningham G, Leveno KJ, Bloom SL, et al: Williams Obstetrics, 25th ed. New York, NY: McGraw Hill; 2018. **PainFUL** dark red bleeding + Uterine CTX **+ Fetal distress** | **Prevalence**  **Presentation** | Placenta overlying internal cervical os **1/200 live births**  Reproduced with permission from DeCherney AH, Nathan L, Laufer N: CURRENT Diagnosis & Treatment: Obstetrics & Gynecology, 11th ed. New York, NY: McGraw Hill; 2013. **PainLESS** bright red bleeding +/− Uterine CTX +/− Fetal distress with bleed, none if early on US | Umbilical cord vessels overlying internal cervical os **1/2,500 live births**  **PainLESS** bright red bleeding @ROM +Uterine CTX **+Fetal distress (bradycardia)** |
| *Clinical:* Sign/symptom based | **Diagnosis**  | 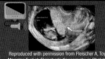 Reproduced with permission from Fleischer A, Toy E, Manning F, et al: Fleischer's Sonography in Obstetrics and Gynecology: Textbook and Teaching Cases, 8th ed. New York, NY: McGraw Hill; 2018. Ultrasound Follow serially, may resolve |  Reproduced with permission from Cunningham G, Leveno KJ, Bloom SL, et al: Williams Obstetrics, 25th ed. New York, NY: McGraw Hill; 2018. US with color Doppler Sinusoidal FHT, if acute bleed |
| Hx abruption HTN disorders Tobacco use Cocaine use Abd/pelvic trauma | **Risk Factors**  | Hx previa Hx C/S AMA Mult gestation | Hx placenta previa IVF Single umbilical artery Mult gestation |
| Mild &/or stabilizes: Expectant mgmt to term Severe: Urgent delivery | **Management**  | Mild: Expectant mgmt C/S @ 35-37 weeks Severe &/or onset labor: Urgent C/S NO MANUAL PELVIC EXAMS! | Schedule delivery @ **35 weeks** C/S ONLY EMERGENT C/S if acute bleed |
| Hemorrhagic shock DIC Fetal hypoxia | **Complications**  | PPH Congenital anomalies IUGR Preterm delivery | Fetal exsanguination  |

# Antepartum    Surveillance

Used in pregnancy when there is an increased risk of **fetal demise**

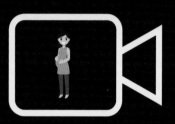

## # of Fetal Movements

Assessed over 1 hour, 10 movements in 2 hours is normal

## Nonstress Test (NST)

"Reactive" = normal: 2 accelerations > or = to 15 bpm lasting at least 15 minutes over a 20 minute period

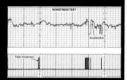

Reproduced with permission from Cunningham FG, Leveno KJ, Bloom SL, et al: Williams Obstetrics, 25th ed. New York, NY: McGraw Hill; 2018.

## Contraction Stress Test (CST)

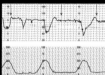

"Positive" CST. Late decelerations following 50% or more contractions in 10 minutes. Consider delivery, if positive.

## High-Risk Conditions Considered for Antepartum Surveillance:

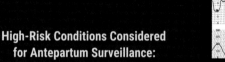

**History of fetal demise**

**Gestational and preexisting diabetes**

## Ultrasound Assessments

## Biophysical Profile (BPP)

Fetal tone, breathing, movement, amniotic fluid index, and NST
- 8-10 = reassuring
- 6 = equivocal
- 0-4 = worrisome

Reproduced with permission from Cunningham G, Leveno KJ, Bloom SL, et al: Williams Obstetrics, 25th ed. New York, NY: McGraw Hill; 2018.

**Hypertensive disorders:**
**Gestational HTN**
**Chronic HTN**
**and preeclampsia**

## Dopplers

Vascular flow assessment (MCA or umbilical) for placental function and fetal neurological and cardiac vessel activity

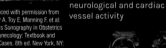

Reproduced with permission from Fleischer A, Toy E, Manning F, et al: Fleischer's Sonography in Obstetrics and Gynecology: Textbook and Teaching Cases, 8th ed. New York, NY: McGraw Hill; 2018.

**Preexisting health conditions (obesity, HIV lupus, AMA, etc.)**

**Multiple gestations**

## Growth

Anatomical survey of the fetus to follow growth, assess placental function, and rule out genetic abnormalities and toxic exposures

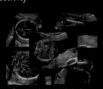

Reproduced with permission from Fleischer A, Toy E, Manning F, et al: Fleischer's Sonography in Obstetrics and Gynecology: Textbook and Teaching Cases, 8th ed. New York, NY: McGraw Hill; 2018.

# Benign Breast Disease

## Fibrocystic Changes

- Age: 30-50s, common
- Cyclic bilateral mastalgia and swelling
- Irregular, bumpy breast tissue
- Associated with trauma, alcohol, caffeine

- Histology is variable. Most are benign.
- Only atypical epithelial hyperplasia subtype is true risk factor for cancer.

- Reassure. Aspirate, if painful
- Caffeine restriction
- OCPs (↓ hormonal fluctuation)

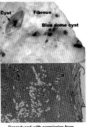

Reproduced with permission from Reisner HM: Pathology: A Modern Case Study. New York, NY: McGraw Hill; 2015.

Cyst    Fibrous
Blue dome cyst

Reproduced with permission from Kemp WL, Burns DK, Brow TG: Pathology: The Big Picture. New York, NY: McGraw Hill; 2008.

## Workup

for palpable breast masses in female <35 years

Return after menses
↓ if unchanged
Ultrasound
↓ if discrete mass
FNA
↓ if bloody or no fluid
Excisional biopsy

## Fibroadenoma

- Most common breast lesion in women <30
- Round, rubbery, discrete, mobile
- ↑ size with ↑ estrogen (eg, pregnancy, premenstrual)

- Reassure. Follow clinically
- If >3-4 cm, excise to rule out phyllodes tumor

Reproduced with permission from Elsayes KM, Oldham SA: Introduction to Diagnostic Radiology. New York, NY: McGraw Hill; 2014.

Reproduced with permission from Reisner H: Pathology: A Modern Case Study, 2nd ed. New York, NY: McGraw Hill; 2020.

## Intraductal Papilloma

- Small papillary tumor within lactiferous ducts beneath areola
- Spontaneous unilateral serosanguinous nipple discharge
- 1.5-2x ↑ risk for cancer

- Excise involved duct

Reproduced with permission from Kuerer HM: Kuerer's Breast Surgical Oncology. New York, NY: McGraw Hill; 2010.

Reproduced with permission from Reisner H. Pathology: A Modern Case Study, 2nd ed. New York, NY: McGraw Hill; 2020.

## Phyllodes Tumor

- Age: 40s
- Resemble fibroadenoma but larger (>4 cm)

- Large mass of connective tissue and cysts
- "Leaf-life" lobulation
- Most are benign but can locally recur
- Some are malignant (grow rapidly)

- Excise with negative margin to avoid recurrence

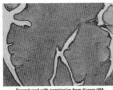

Reproduced with permission from Kuerer HM: Kuerer's Breast Surgical Oncology. New York, NY: McGraw Hill; 2010.

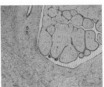

Used with permission from Dr. Kristen Atkins.

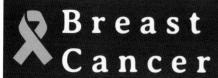 # Breast Cancer

**1** Most common cancer in women (USA)

**2** 2nd leading cause of cancer deaths (USA)

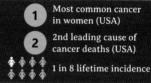 1 in 8 lifetime incidence

## Risk Factors

- ♀ • Female gender
- • Age
- • Genetic (BRCA1/2)
- • Family history
- • Estrogen exposure (early menarche, late menopause, nulliparity)
- • Obesity
- • Alcohol

## Screening

- **Mammography** (frequency & age recommendations differ)
- MRI for high risk
- Tomo/US for dense breasts
- Suspicious lesions requiring biopsy: ↑Density with microcalcifications, irregular borders, spiculated mass

Reproduced with permission from Kuerer HM: Kuerer's Breast Surgical Oncology. New York, NY: McGraw Hill; 2010.

## Diagnosis

- Most found on screening
- *Early:* Nontender, firm, immobile, ill-defined mass
- *Late:* Ulceration, unilateral nipple erosion ± discharge
- Metastatic:
  - Bone (pain)
  - Lung (dyspnea, cough)
  - Liver (nausea, jaundice)

## DCIS

- Microcalcifications on mammography
- Malignant cells fill ducts without invading basement membrane

Reproduced with permission from Karlan BY, Bristow RE, Li AJ: Gynecologic Oncology: Clinical Practice and Surgical Atlas. New York, NY: McGraw Hill; 2012.

## Paget's

- Results from underlying DCIS or invasive cancer
- Eczematous patches on nipple

Reproduced with permission from Usatine RP, Smith MA, Mayeaux EJ, Chumley HS: The Color Atlas and Synopsis of Family Medicine, 3rd ed. New York, NY: McGraw Hill; 2019. Photo contributor: Richard P. Usatine, MD.

## IDC

- Most common (80%)
- Small, glandular duct-like cells
- Skin dimpling 2/2 suspensory ligament deformation

Reproduced with permission from Kuerer HM: Kuerer's Breast Surgical Oncology. New York, NY: McGraw Hill; 2010.

## ILC

- 2nd most common
- Orderly row of cells (↓E-cadherin)
- Often bilateral, multiple lesions

Reproduced with permission from Kemp WL, Burns DK, Brow TG: Pathology: The Big Picture. New York, NY: McGraw Hill; 2008.

## Inflammatory

- Dermal lymphatic invasion
- Peau d'orange
- Poor prognosis (50% 5-year survival rate)

Reproduced with permission from Kantarjian HM, Wolff RA: The MD Anderson Manual of Medical Oncology, 3rd ed. New York, NY: McGraw Hill Education; 2016.

## Treatment

### Early Stage (I, II)

*Mastectomy equivalent*

 Lumpectomy
+
 Radiation

+SLNB

+Adjuvant chemotherapy

+Hormonal therapy, if ER/PR+

+Anti-HER2 trastuzumab, Y if HER2+

### Locally Advanced (III)

Neoadjuvant chemotherapy
↓
Lumpectomy
+
Radiation

+ SLNB

± Adjuvant chemotherapy

+ Hormonal therapy, if ER/PR+

+ Anti-HER2 trastuzumab, Y if HER2+

### Stage IV

Bisphosphonates for bone metastasis

Palliative radiation

Chemotherapy, if rapidly progressive

Hormonal therapy, if ER/PR+

Anti-HER2 trastuzumab, Y if HER2+

## Prognosis

TNM stage is best predictor

ER+ and PR+ are favorable

### Hormonal Therapy

SERM (tamoxifen)
or
Aromatase inhibitor, if postmenopausal

# CERVICAL CANCER

## Presentation

Most common gynecologic cancer worldwide.

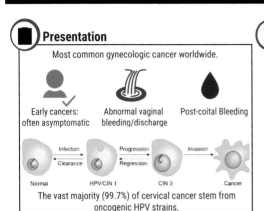

Early cancers: often asymptomatic

Abnormal vaginal bleeding/discharge

Post-coital Bleeding

The vast majority (99.7%) of cervical cancer stem from oncogenic HPV strains.

## Risk Factors

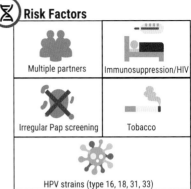

Multiple partners

Immunosuppression/HIV

Irregular Pap screening

Tobacco

HPV strains (type 16, 18, 31, 33)

## Diagnosis

Screening starting at age 21 and until age 65

**Pap Smear Cytology**: Staining helps show cancerous changes in the cells from cervix/endocervix under a microscope.

**HPV Testing**: Test for DNA/RNA from high-risk HPV strains.

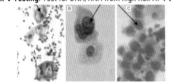

**A:** HPV infection with cytogenic changes (arrow) on a pap smear.
**B/C:** Prominent nucleoli, irregular nuclear membrane, chromatin clumping.

**Colposcopy**: procedure to examine with a magnified view of the cervix for cancerous changes and potential biopsy sites.

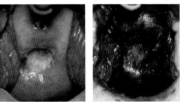

**Left**: High grade lesion posteriorly demonstrating dense white staining following application of 5% acetic acid solution.
**Right**: Same lesion doesn't stain with Lugol's (iodine) so dysplasia lighter in color compared to normal tissue.

## Treatment

Cervical Dysplasia

CIN 1 - Observation; usually recedes spontaneously
CIN 2 and CIN 3 - Surgical excision of cervix (LEEP/CKC)

Cervical Cancer

**Early stage:** Radical hysterectomy with lymph node dissection

**Advanced stage:** Chemotherapy (cisplatin) with pelvic radiation

 +

Radical hysterectomy specimen - In addition to uterus and cervix, the parametrium (arrows) and upper vagina is removed.

## Staging

Cervical cancer is clinically staged before surgery. This includes physical exam, imaging, procedures such as cystoscopy to evaluate disease extent.

| Stage | Location | 5 yr Survival |
|-------|----------|---------------|
| I | Confined to cervix | 88%-100% |
| II | Extension to uterus, upper vagina | 44%-68% |
| III | Extension to lower vagina, pelvic sidewall | 18%-39% |
| IV | Bowel/Bladder involvement, Distant metastases | 18%-34% |

# Contraception

## Permanent Sterilization

Reproduced with permission from Hoffman BL, Schorge JO, Halvorson LM, et al: Williams Gynecology, 4th ed. New York, NY: McGraw Hill; 2020.

Reproduced with permission from Cunningham G, Leveno KJ, Bloom SL, et al: Williams Obstetrics, 25th ed. New York, NY: McGraw Hill; 2018.

**Tubal ligation** — Once

**Vasectomy** — Once

## Long-Acting Reversible Contraception (LARC)

Reproduced with permission from DeCherney AH, Nathan L, Laufer N, et al: CURRENT Diagnosis & Treatment: Obstetrics & Gynecology, 12th ed. New York, NY: McGraw Hill; 2019.

**Progestin implant** — 3 years

**Copper IUD** — 10 years

**Progestin IUD** — 5 years

**MOST EFFECTIVE >99% with both perfect and typical use.**
Permanent and LARCs have low failure rates due to ease of use and minimal steps required by individual.

## Hormonal Methods

Reproduced with permission from DeCherney AH, Nathan L, Laufer N, et al: CURRENT Diagnosis & Treatment: Obstetrics & Gynecology, 12th ed. New York, NY: McGraw Hill; 2019.

Reproduced with permission from Usatine RP, Smith MA, Mayeaux EJ, Chumley HS: The Color Atlas and Synopsis of Family Medicine, 3rd ed. New York, NY: McGraw Hill; 2019. Photo contributor: E. J. Mayeaux, Jr., MD.

**Vaginal ring** — Monthly

**Patch** — Weekly

**Oral contraceptive** — Daily

**Injectable progestin** — 3 months

**VERY EFFECTIVE 90-99%**

<u>Progestins</u> render endometrium atrophic, stimulate thick cervical mucus, and may reduce tubal motility preventing sperm and ovum union.

<u>Estrogen</u> inhibits FSH and additionally improves bleeding profile.

**Contraindications Estrogen:**
Tobacco use >35 years old
Breast cancer
History of blood clot
Migraine with aura
Hypertension

## Barrier Methods

Reproduced with permission from Hoffman BL, Schorge JO, Halvorson LM, et al: Williams Gynecology, 4th ed. New York, NY: McGraw Hill; 2020.

Reproduced with permission from Hoffman BL, Schorge JO, Halvorson LM, et al: Williams Gynecology, 4th ed. New York, NY: McGraw Hill; 2020.

**Diaphragm** — Every time

**Male and female condom** — Every time

## Other Methods

**Natural family planning** — Every time

**Withdrawal method** — Every time

**LESS EFFECTIVE 70-90%**

Condoms are the only method that provides protection against transmission of STIs.

# Diabetes in Pregnancy

Screening, Management, & Complications

## Screening

- At initial visit for preexisting DM
- At 24-28 weeks for gestational DM
  - *1 step or 2 step test*

## Monitoring if Diagnosed

- A1C each trimester
- Cr, TSH, ECG, eye exam

## Maternal Management

- Target glucose <95, A1C <6%
- Insulin, diet, exercise

## Fetal Management

- US + echo at 18 weeks
- US at 38 weeks for weight and delivery (>4500 g → Cesarean)

## Complications

- Macrosomia
- Shoulder dystocia
- Preeclampsia
- Miscarriage
- Malformations

## Primary Dysmenorrhea

**Pain in the ABSENCE of pelvic pathology**
- Caused by excess inflammatory mediators (prostaglandins, leukotrienes)
- Common in adolescents
- Treatment: NSAIDs, OCPs, norethindrone, heat, exercise

# ⁖ Dysmenorrhea ⁖

*Painful menstruation*

## Secondary Dysmenorrhea

**Pain caused by pelvic pathology or medical condition**

**DDX:** **Endometriosis & Adenomyosis (Most Common),** Congenital Abnormalities, Cervical Stenosis, Ovarian Cyst, Uterine Polyp, PID/Pelvic Adhesions

## Endometriosis

- Implantation of endometrial tissue **outside** the endometrial cavity

Ovarian endometrioma (chocolate cyst)

- **Cyclic pain** that peaks **before** menses
- "3 Ds:" Dysmenorrhea, Dyspareunia, Dyschezia
- Definitive diagnosis only by diagnostic laparoscopy

 1st: NSAIDs, OCPs, Progestins
2nd: Danazol, GnRH agonists (leuprolide) or antagonists (elagolix)

 Laparoscopic lysis/resection of lesions
Hysterectomy +/– BSO

## Adenomyosis

- **Direct invasion** of endometrial tissue within the myometrium

"Diffusely enlarged, globular, boggy-feeling uterus"

- Heavy, painful menstrual bleeding
- Definitive diagnosis by pathologic specimen
- Imaging:
  Ultrasound
  (low specificity)
  or MRI

 NSAIDs, OCPs, Progestins

 Hysterectomy

# Early Pregnancy Loss

Loss of POC at GA <20 weeks
Most often from chromosomal abnormalities
1 in 5 pregnancies

Uterus Full    Uterus Empty        Cervix Closed    Cervix Open

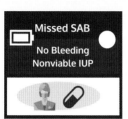

### Missed SAB
No Bleeding
Nonviable IUP

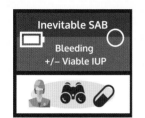

### Inevitable SAB
Bleeding
+/− Viable IUP

### Threatened SAB
Bleeding
Viable IUP *can* --> full term

Observation

### Complete SAB
+/− Bleeding
Nonviable

Follow β-hCG to 0

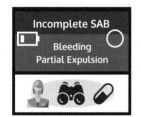

### Incomplete SAB
Bleeding
Partial Expulsion

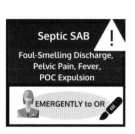

### Septic SAB !
Foul-Smelling Discharge,
Pelvic Pain, Fever,
POC Expulsion

EMERGENTLY to OR

# Elective Termination Methods

(same for SAB treatments)

**Medications: First Trimester Only**

Mifepristone (Progesterone Antagonist)

Misoprostol (PGE1 Agonist)

Methotrexate (DHFR Inhibitor)

 ↑ time, bleeding, pain

**Procedural/Surgical:** *Can* be used in

**2nd Trimester**
Dilation & Curettage
Dilation & Suction
Hysterectomy

Reproduced with
permission from
Hoffman BL,
Schorge JO,
Halvorson LM, et
al: Williams
Gynecology, 4th
ed. New York, NY:
McGraw Hill; 2020

Reproduced with
permission from
Hoffman BL,
Schorge JO,
Halvorson LM, et
al: Williams
Gynecology, 4th
ed. New York, NY:
McGraw Hill; 2020

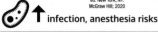 ↑ infection, anesthesia risks

IUP = Intrauterine Pregnancy      SAB = Spontaneous Abortion      POC = Products of Conception

# Ectopic Pregnancy

Embryo implants in location other than the uterus, often fallopian tube

## Presentation
Missed menses &/or (+) home UPT
Pelvic pain/cramping
Vaginal bleeding/spotting

## Diagnosis
No IUP on TVUS
& β-hCG > discriminatory zone

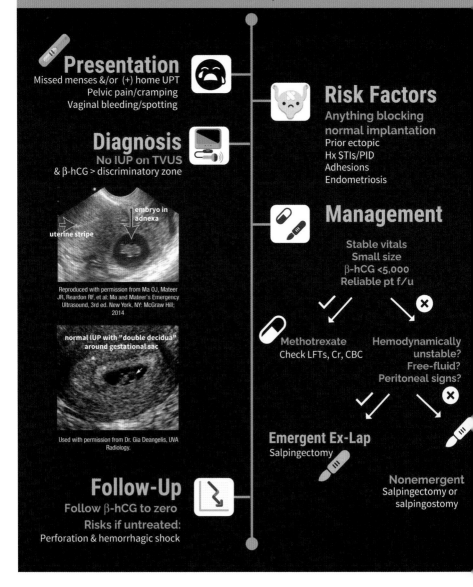

embryo in adnexa

uterine stripe

Reproduced with permission from Ma OJ, Mateer JR, Reardon RF, et al: Ma and Mateer's Emergency Ultrasound, 3rd ed. New York, NY: McGraw Hill; 2014

normal IUP with "double decidua" around gestational sac

Used with permission from Dr. Gia Deangelis, UVA Radiology.

## Follow-Up
Follow β-hCG to zero
Risks if untreated:
Perforation & hemorrhagic shock

## Risk Factors
Anything blocking normal implantation
Prior ectopic
Hx STIs/PID
Adhesions
Endometriosis

## Management
Stable vitals
Small size
β-hCG <5,000
Reliable pt f/u

✓                    ✗

Methotrexate            Hemodynamically
Check LFTs, Cr, CBC              unstable?
                         Free-fluid?
                       Peritoneal signs?

              ✓              ✗

Emergent Ex-Lap
Salpingectomy

                 Nonemergent
              Salpingectomy or
                 salpingostomy

# Endometrial Cancer

## Presentation

Endometrial cancer is the most common gynecologic malignancy in the United States.

Abnormal menstrual bleeding (80%)

Postmenopausal bleeding

## Diagnosis

- Endometrial sampling (Office biopsy, dilation, & curettage, hysterectomy) to make a diagnosis

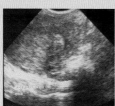

Reproduced with permission from Fleischer A, Toy E, Manning F, et al: Fleischer's Sonography in Obstetrics and Gynecology: Textbook and Teaching Cases, 8th ed. New York, NY: McGraw Hill; 2018.

In a postmenopausal patient, endometrial thickness > 4 mm on ultrasound with vaginal bleeding is concerning for endometrial cancer and requires tissue sampling.

## Risk Factors

Obesity

Older age

Genetic Causes— Lynch syndrome

Chronic anovulation

E2 ↑

Unopposed estrogen

## Treatment

- Total hysterectomy, bilateral salpingo-oophorectomy with lymph node sampling.

- Universal screening for Lynch syndrome.

- In advanced stages, radiation and/or chemotherapy after surgery is used for treatment.

## Endometrial Hyperplasia

Endometrial hyperplasia is the precursor for most cases.

**Simple vs complex**—Presence/absence of abnormalities of endometrial glands: Crowding and complexity.

**Atypia**—Nuclear atypia strongly associated with later development of adenocarcinoma.

## Endometrial Cancer Types

**Type I**—Endometrioid adenocarcinoma comprises most cases. It is estrogen-dependent, typically low grade, and derived from atypical endometrial hyperplasia.

**Type II**—Serous or clear cell histology. Usually more aggressive clinical course.

**80%** of endometrial cancers are endometrioid adenocarcinoma

## Staging

Endometrial cancer is staged surgically.

**Most endometrial cancers are diagnosed with stage I disease**

- Stage I
- Stage II
- Stage III
- Stage IV

| Stage | Location | 5-year Survival Rate |
|---|---|---|
| I | Confined to uterus | 85% |
| II | Extension to cervix | 75% |
| III | Extension to lymph nodes, peritoneal cavity | 45% |
| IV | Spread to bladder, bowel, distant metastasis | 25% |

# Fetal Heart Monitoring

### Baseline HR

Established for a minimum of 2 minutes in any 10-minute segment

Normal fetal heart rate: 110-160 bpm

Any heart rate change that lasts <10 minutes is a new baseline

### Variability

Amplitude range of FHR changes from baseline:

**Absent:** No change

**Minimal:** 1-5 bpm

**Moderate:** 6-25 bpm

**Marked:** >25 bpm

### Accelerations

15 bpm increase from baseline for >15 seconds but <2 minutes

Before 32 weeks GA, 10 bpm or more and lasts >10 seconds but <2 minutes

### Decelerations

**Early:** Nadir at peak of contraction:
 **Head compression**

**Late:** Nadir after peak of contraction:
**Placental insufficiency**

**Variable:** Decrease is 15 bpm or greater and lasts 15 seconds or greater:
**Cord compression**

### Uterine Contractions:

Normal: 5 or less in 10 minutes, averaged over a 30-minute window

Tachysystole: > 5 contractions

Nonstress tests (NSTs) are **reactive** when >2 accelerations in 20 minutes

## Fetal Heart Tracing Categories

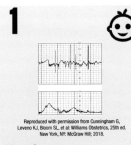

**1**

Reproduced with permission from Cunningham G, Leveno KJ, Bloom SL, et al: Williams Obstetrics, 25th ed. New York, NY: McGraw Hill; 2018.

**Normal**

**Baseline:** Normal

**Variability:** Moderate

**Accelerations:** Absent or present

**Decelerations:** Absent or early

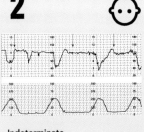

**2**

**Indeterminate**

Everything in between category 1 and 2 tracings

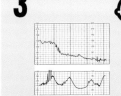

**3**

Reproduced with permission from Cunningham G, Leveno KJ, Bloom SL, et al: Williams Obstetrics, 25th ed. New York, NY: McGraw Hill; 2018.

 Requires urgent attention

**Baseline:** Bradycardia OR

**Variability:** Absent with

**Decelerations:** Recurrent late or variable

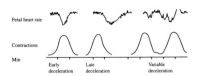

| Fetal heart rate | | | |
| Contractions | | | |
| Min | Early deceleration | Late deceleration | Variable deceleration |

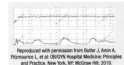

Reproduced with permission from Butler J, Amin A, Fitzmaurice L, et al: OB/GYN Hospital Medicine: Principles and Practice. New York, NY: McGraw Hill; 2019.

### Sinusoidal: Category 3

Smooth, sine wave with regular undulated pattern:
Associated with *fetal anemia*

# Gynecologic Infections

## Vaginitis

Reproduced with permission from Usatine RP, Smith MA, Mayeaux EJ, Chumley HS: The Color Atlas and Synopsis of Family Medicine, 3rd ed. New York, NY: McGraw Hill; 2019. Photo contributor: E. J. Mayeaux, Jr., MD.

Reproduced with permission from Usatine RP, Smith MA, Mayeaux EJ, Chumley HS: The Color Atlas and Synopsis of Family Medicine, 3rd ed. New York, NY: McGraw Hill; 2019. Photo contributor: E. J. Mayeaux, Jr., MD.

Reproduced with permission from Usatine RP, Smith MA, Mayeaux EJ, Chumley HS: The Color Atlas and Synopsis of Family Medicine, 3rd ed. New York, NY: McGraw Hill; 2019. Photo contributor: E. J. Mayeaux, Jr., MD.

| Bacterial Vaginosis | Trichomonas vaginalis | Yeast (eg, Candida albicans) |
|---|---|---|
| Thin, white discharge 🐟 Fishy odor | Frothy, green discharge Foul odor | Thick, white discharge 🧀 Cottage-cheese like |
| Clue cells + Whiff test | Motile trichomonads | Pseudohyphae |
| Vaginal pH >4.5 | Vaginal pH >4.5 | Vaginal pH 3.5-4.5 (normal) |
| Tx: Metronidazole | Tx: Metronidazole (STI testing & treat partners) | Tx: Fluconazole or nystatin |

## Other Infections

Reproduced with permission from Hoffman BL, Schorge JO, Bradshaw KD, et al: Williams Gynecology, 3rd ed. New York, NY: McGraw Hill; 2016.

Reproduced with permission from Hoffman BL, Schorge JO, Bradshaw KD, et al: Williams Gynecology, 3rd ed. New York, NY: McGraw Hill; 2016.

**TSST-1**
*S. aureus* exotoxin

| Bartholin Gland Duct Cyst | Bartholin Gland Duct Abscess | Toxic Shock Syndrome |
|---|---|---|
| Obstructed lubrication ducts | Infection of cyst contents (E. coli, STIs) | Prolonged tampon use / intravaginal contraction |
| Asymptomatic or discomfort with intercourse | Vulvar erythema 😖 Pain | Hypotension, fever rash, desquamation of 🖐 and 🦶 |
| Tx not required | Tx: I&D, marsupialization | Tx: Supportive care Remove object Clindamycin + nafcillin |

⚠️ A Bartholin gland duct cyst or abscess should raise suspicion for malignancy in women over 40. Biopsy/removal required.

# Hypertension in Pregnancy

- **Chronic hypertension:**
  Present before conception or 20 weeks' gestation

- **Gestational hypertension:**
  New-onset BP >140/90 mm Hg after 20 weeks' gestation
  (BP returns to normal after pregnancy)

- **Severe gestational hypertension:**
  New-onset BP >160/110 mm Hg after 20 weeks' gestation
  (BP returns to normal after pregnancy)

**! Absence of end-organ dysfunction**
- Proteinuria
- Increased Cr
- Increased LFTS
- Pulmonary edema
- Cerebral/visual Sx

## Monitoring:

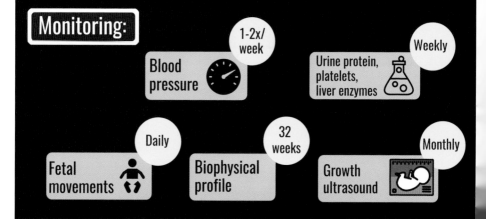

Blood pressure — 1-2x/week

Urine protein, platelets, liver enzymes — Weekly

Fetal movements — Daily

Biophysical profile — 32 weeks

Growth ultrasound — Monthly

## Treatment:

Avoid antihypertensives unless severe

**Safe Medications:** Methyldopa, labetalol, nifedipine

Delivery before 39 weeks

**Medications to avoid:** ACEIs, ARBs, atenolol

# Labor

## Stages:

**1** Onset of labor to **full dilation**

 **0 cm**

*Latent phase*—up to 6 cm

 **6 cm**

*Active phase*—6-10 cm

 **10 cm**

**2** Full dilation to **delivery of baby**

 PUSH! →

**3** Delivery of the baby to **delivery of the placenta**

Assess baby
Delayed cord clamping
Assess for perineal trauma

**4** After delivery of the placenta

Treat PPH (if applicable)
Repair lacerations
Reassess mom and baby

## Failure to Progress:

**Prolonged Latent Phase:**
>20 hours primiparous; >14 hours multiparous

**Prolonged Active Phase:**
<1.2 cm/h primiparous; 1.5 cm/h multiparous

**Arrest of Dilation:**
No change in 4 hours with adequate labor

**Arrest of Descent:**
No change in station (downward descent) with pushing

↓

 ## Operative Delivery:

If >2+ station and adequate pelvis, then can consider vacuum/forceps for operative vaginal delivery

↓

## Cesarean Section:

Consider if:
Breech on presentation/failed ECV
Arrest of dilation/descent
Nonreassuring fetal status
Maternal indications

# Lactation

## Anatomy and Physiology

**The brain reacts to:**

1. Baby's cry
2. Baby suckling

Colostrum secretion:
    5 days to 2 weeks

Mature breast milk:
    Solely by 4-6 weeks

**Hormones involved:**

↑ Prolactin

↑ Oxytocin

↓ PIH

↑ ACTH

**Journey of milk:**

Mammary glands

↳ Lumen of alveoli ducts by myoepithelial cells

↳ Nipple

---

### Benefits to Baby

Protective immunological antibodies for infant

Provides age-specific nutrition

Lower rates of sudden infant death syndrome for infants

### Benefits to Mom

Women who breastfeed have lower risk of breast and reproductive cancers

Cost-effective due to lower morbidity and not needing to buy formula

### Complications

Mastitis: Most common painful inflammatory breast infection

Treat by continuing to breastfeed, pain relievers, and antibiotics if indicated

 Contraindications to breastfeeding:
HIV infection, infant with galactosemia, mother taking cytotoxic drugs such as cyclosporine or doxorubicin

## Physiology

Age-linked follicular resistance to FSH
↓Follicles = ↓ estrogen production

↑androgens to → estrone

## Clinical Presentation

**H**ot flashes
**A**trophic
**V**agina
**O**steoporosis
**C**oronary artery dz
**S**leep disturbances
hirsutism

## Labs

↑↑FSH (40 mg/dL)
↑ LH
↑GnRH
↓ estradiol
TSH unchanged

**Average age
51 years old**

# *Menopause*

### 12 consecutive months of amenorrhea

**<40 years
old =
Premature
ovarian
failure**

## Management

**Vasomotor sx (hot flashes):**
*Hormonal:* Systemic estrogen
*Nonhormonal:* SSRI, SNRI, anti-HTN,
antiepileptics

**Vaginal sx only—**Local estrogen

**Osteoporosis—**Bisphosphonates,
teriparatide, raloxifene

## Complications of ↓ Estradiol

↑LDL & ↓HDL—↑ risk of MI & CAD
↓ urethral tone → dysuria, incontinence
Vaginal atrophy → dyspareunia, ↑risk of UTI
Osteoporosis
Depression

## Contraindications to Estrogen Therapy

Vaginal/uterine bleeding,
Hx thromboembolic dz, MI, CVA,
Endometrial/ovarian Ca, liver dz,
may worsen migraines/HTN

**Risks** Thromboembolic dz,
breast/endometrial Ca

<u>**HRT for Moderate/Severe Symptoms:**</u>
Give lowest effective dose
for shortest duration needed

<u>**Remember:**</u> Progesterone must
be given if uterus present

# Menstrual Cycle

**Menarche** 10-16 years old

**Menopause** avg. 51 years

## Day 1-13
### Follicular Phase
varies between patients

Menses = Cycle day 1

**Normal length** 3-7 days

**Menorrhagia** bleeding >7 days or >80 mL/d

**Dysmenorrhea =** painful

## Day 15-28
### Luteal Phase
always 14 days

**Poly-menorrhea** <21 days

**Normal interval** 21-35 days

**Oligo-menorrhea** <35 days

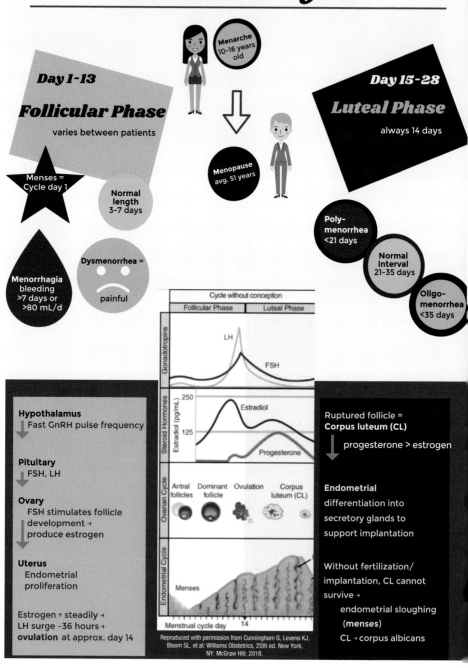

Cycle without conception

Follicular Phase | Luteal Phase

Gonadotropins — LH, FSH

Steroid Hormones (pg/mL) — 250, 125 — Estradiol, Progesterone

Ovarian Cycle — Antral follicles, Dominant follicle, Ovulation, Corpus luteum (CL)

Endometrial Cycle — Menses

Menstrual cycle day — 14

Reproduced with permission from Cunningham G, Leveno KJ, Bloom SL, et al: Williams Obstetrics, 25th ed. New York, NY: McGraw Hill; 2018.

**Hypothalamus**
↓ Fast GnRH pulse frequency

**Pituitary**
↓ FSH, LH

**Ovary**
FSH stimulates follicle development → ↑ produce estrogen

**Uterus**
Endometrial proliferation

Estrogen ↑ steadily →
LH surge ~36 hours →
**ovulation** at approx. day 14

Ruptured follicle = **Corpus luteum (CL)**
↓ progesterone > estrogen

**Endometrial** differentiation into secretory glands to support implantation

Without fertilization/implantation, CL cannot survive →
endometrial sloughing (menses)
CL → corpus albicans

# Multiple Gestations

## Frequency

3% of live births

⬆ due to
Assisted Reproductive
Technologies (ARTs)

## Terminology

Zygotic
(# Fertilizations)

Chorionic
(# Placentas)

Amniotic
(# Amniotic Sacs)

## Diagnosis

First trimester ultrasound

Rapid uterine growth
Excessive maternal weight
gain

Abnormally elevated labs
(β-hCG, HPL, MSAFP)

## Types

### Dizygotic ("Fraternal")
Separate placenta & amnion

### Monozygotic ("Identical")

Dichorionic/Diamniotic

Monochorionic/Diamniotic ····► 

Monochorionic/Monoamniotic ····► 

## Risks

Preterm labor      Need for C/S
Preeclampsia       IUGR
Placenta previa    Congenital malformations

Same risks as above PLUS:

Twin-twin transfusion syndrome

Conjoinment & cord entanglement

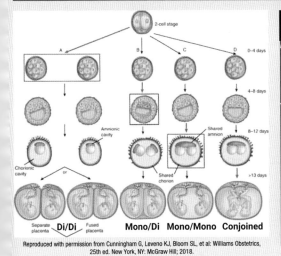

A   B   C   D   0–4 days

4–8 days

Amnionic cavity      Shared amnion      8–12 days

Chorionic cavity      or      Shared chorion      >13 days

Separate placenta   **Di/Di**   Fused placenta      **Mono/Di**   **Mono/Mono**   **Conjoined**

## Management

**with High Risk Specialist**
**Detailed anatomic ultrasound**
**Type/Number**
**Identify Anomalies**

⬆**Antepartum surveillance**
**US, NST, Dopplers**
**Assess for:**
**IUGR**
**Preterm labor**
**Preeclampsia**

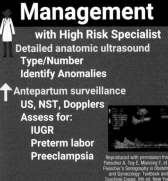

**Delivery based on presentation**
**Increased rate of C/S**

# Nausea & Vomiting in Pregnancy

 **"Morning Sickness"**

Nausea/vomiting in first trimester

Physiology: Hormones + delayed gastric emptying

**Very common**

Treatment: Diet  doxylamine + B$_{12}$

**Progesterone**

**Placenta**

β-hCG

Past 16 weeks GA

 **Hyperemesis Gravidarum**

Persistent nausea/vomiting

Lose >5% prepregnancy body weight

Ketonuria

*Exact cause unclear*

**Rare**

Treatment: Symptom management & fetal monitoring

   Rehydration

      IV fluids +/− enteral nutrition

   Antiemetics

      Promethazine (H1 blocker)

      Ondansetron (5HT3 blocker)

      Prochlorperazine (Dopa blocker)

      Metoclopramide (Dopa blocker/5HT4 agonist)

   +/− Corticosteroids

*Assess fetal growth*

## Normal Weight Gain in Pregnancy
*Never normal to LOSE weight

BMI <18.5

**28-40 lbs**

BMI 18.5-24.9

**25-35 lbs**

BMI 25-29.9

15-25 lbs

BMI >30

11-20 lbs

# OB Anesthesia and Analgesia

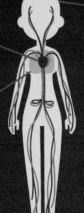

SNS activation in labor can increased plasma catechols, CO, and BP

Unrelieved labor pain can result in depression, decreased maternal-neonatal bonding, & PTSD

Labor pain can cause hyper- and hypoventilation that can induce maternal and fetal hypoxemia

Labor pain origins
T10-L1 uterine CTX

S2-S4 perineal pain

Left uterine tilt essential (keep gravid uterus from compressing vessels)

## Neuraxial Techniques

**Examples**
Spinal, epidural, combined spinal-epidural

**Advantages**
Complete analgesia (visceral and somatic)

No maternal sedation

Minimal to no neonatal sedation

**Contraindications**
Infection, hypovolemia, lumbar spine

pathology, patient refusal

## Nerve Blocks

Low Caudal
Sacral Nerve
Paracervical
Pudendal

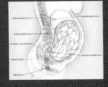

## Systemic Opioid Use

**Examples**
Fentanyl, HYDROmorphone

**Advantages**
Widely available

Anesthesia provider not required

**Disadvantages**
Incomplete analgesia

Crosses placenta–fetal depression

Respiratory depression/hypoxia

Loss of protective airway reflexes

Nausea/vomiting

## Non-pharmacological Methods

Doula, deep breathing, hypnosis, hydrotherapy, acupuncture

# Obstetric Ultrasound

## 1 Trimester

4 weeks = gestational sac
5 weeks = yolk sac
6 weeks = cardiac activity

**Dating and Viability**

Crown rump length can be used until 14 weeks for dating (establish EDD).

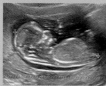 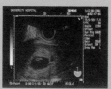

## 2 Trimester

Full fetal anatomy surveys are done between 18 and 22 weeks.

**Anatomy +/– Genetics**

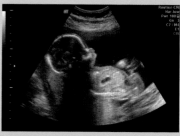

## 3 Trimester

Biophysical Profile (BPP)
    Breathing, movement, AFI
Doppler studies
Amniotic fluid index (AFI)
Placenta: Appearance, size, & location

**Fetal Well-Being**

Common Growth Measurements:
Femur length (FL)
Biparietal diameter (BPD)
Abdominal circumference (AC)

**2 3 Fetal Growth Assessment**

### Polyhydramnios
AFI >25 cm

Etiologies: Maternal DM, Fetal GI, or Pulmonary anomalies, TTTS

### Oligohydramnios
AFI <5 cm

Etiologies: Chronic uteroplacental insufficiency, ROM, and fetal GU anomalies

Doppler studies of umbilical artery assist when IUGR/fetal anemia/ oligohydramnios present.

Absent or reverse end-diastolic flow —Consider delivery

**Macrosomia: EFW >95%**

US imprecise but if EFW >5000 g (or 4500 g in woman with DM) then consider CS as higher risk brachial plexus injury

**IUGR: EFW <10th %**

Asymmetric IUGR (head size preserved)—More likely maternal systemic dz leading to uteroplacental insufficiency

Symmetric IUGR—More likely anomalies, aneuploidy, or infection

EFW: Estimated Fetal Weight     IUGR: Intrauterine Growth Restriction     TTTS: Twin-Twin Transfusion Syndrome

# Ovarian Cancer

**More deaths than all other gynecologic cancers combined.**

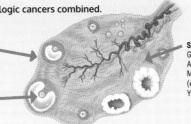

**Epithelial**
Serous, mucinous, endometrioid, clear cell, transitional cell
Accounts for >90% of all ovarian cancers

**Germ Cell**
Dysgerminoma, yolk sac, choriocarcinoma, embryonal, immature teratoma
Younger, prognosis usually excellent

**Sex Cord-Stromal**
Granulosa cell, Sertoli–Leydig cell
Arise from ovarian matrix
May produce hormones (estrogen/testosterone)
Younger and older patients

##  Presentation

Ovarian cancer symptoms often nonspecific making early recognition challenging

- Early satiety
- Bloating
- Increased abdomen size
- Abdominal and pelvic pain
- Nausea
- Fatigue
- Weight loss
- Changes in bowel or bladder habits

##  Risk Factors

- Nulliparity/Infertility
- Increased age
- Endometriosis
- Genetic conditions: *BRCA1, BRCA2, BRIP1, RAD51C, RAD51D*

**Ovarian Cancer Risk Reduction**

Oral contraceptives          Salpingectomy

##  Diagnosis

- CA-125 elevated, but nonspecific
- Imaging with CT and pelvic US
- Tissue diagnosis is definitive

**Ultrasound findings concerning for malignancy:**

Larger size (>10 cm)

Complex cyst
Septations
Papillary projections

Vascularity

Reproduced with permission from Sahdev A: CT in ovarian cancer staging: how to review and report with emphasis on abdominal and pelvic disease for surgical planning, Cancer Imaging 2016 Aug 2;16(1):19.

Metastatic lesions (*arrows*) and ascites (*) are classic hallmarks of advanced ovarian cancer.

## Treatment

Reproduced with permission from Elsayes KM, Oldham SA: Introduction to Diagnostic Radiology. New York, NY: McGraw Hill; 2014.

**TAH, BSO, omentectomy**

**Adjuvant chemotherapy (carboplatin and paclitaxel)**

## Staging

| Stage | Location | 5-year Survival Rate |
|-------|----------|---------------------|
| I | Confined to ovary/tube | 90% |
| II | Extension to uterus, pelvis | 70% |
| III | Extension to lymph nodes, peritoneal cavity | 39% |
| IV | Distant metastases | 17% |

# Pediatric Vaginal Discharge

**Pediatric Gyn Exam:**

- Frog leg position, in parent's lap
- Speculum rarely needed
- Anesthesia for internal exam

## Foreign Objects

Most common: Retained toilet paper
Remove with body temperature saline irrigation

## Infectious Vulvovaginitis

Malodorous, yellow/green, purulent

**Group A Strep**
- Bright "beefy" red vulva
- Dx: Culture
- Rx: Amoxicillin

**Sexually transmitted**
- *N. gonorrhoeae, C. trachomatis, HSV, T. vaginalis, HPV*
- Report abuse to CPS

**Candida**
- Sharp borders, satellite lesions
- Dx: Pseudohyphae on KOH
- Rx: Topical antifungal

**Pinworms**
- Nocturnal pruritus
- Dx: Scotch tape test
- Rx: Albendazole

## Noninfectious Vulvovaginitis

**Allergic & Contact Dermatitis**
- Vesicles, papules on bright red edematous skin
- Offending agents: Soaps, perfume
- Rx: Sitz bath, remove irritant

**Lichen Sclerosus**
- Hypopigmented, atrophic, parchment-like skin in figure of 8 shape
- Not associated with vulvar cancer for pediatric patients
- Rx: Topical corticosteroid

## Sarcoma Botryoides (Embryonal rhabdomyosarcoma)

- Rare malignant tumor of vagina & cervix in girls <3 years old
- Bulges out of vestibule as "bunches of grapes"
- Vaginal bleeding in child, irregular bleeding in pubertal girl
- Rx: Conservative surgery + chemo +/− radiation

# Pelvic Inflammatory Disease (PID)

## CERVICITIS

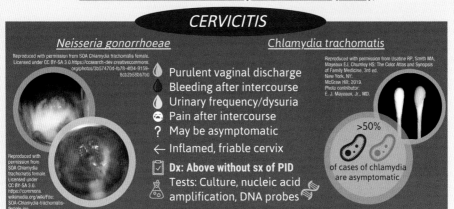

### Neisseria gonorrhoeae

Reproduced with permission from SOA Chlamydia trachomatis female. Licensed under CC BY-SA 3.0. https://ccsearch-dev.creativecommons.org/photos/3b57470d-fb78-4f04-9159-8cb2b58bb7b0

Reproduced with permission from SOA Chlamydia trachomatis female. Licensed under CC-BY-SA 3.0. https://commons.wikimedia.org/wiki/File:SOA-Chlamydia-trachomatis-female.jpg

### Chlamydia trachomatis

Reproduced with permission from Usatine RP, Smith MA, Mayeaux EJ, Chumley HS: The Color Atlas and Synopsis of Family Medicine, 3rd ed. New York, NY: McGraw Hill; 2019. Photo contributor: E. J. Mayeaux, Jr., MD.

💧 Purulent vaginal discharge
💧 Bleeding after intercourse
💧 Urinary frequency/dysuria
😣 Pain after intercourse
? May be asymptomatic
← Inflamed, friable cervix

📋 **Dx: Above without sx of PID**
🧪 Tests: Culture, nucleic acid amplification, DNA probes

>50%
of cases of chlamydia are asymptomatic

## PELVIC INFLAMMATORY DISEASE

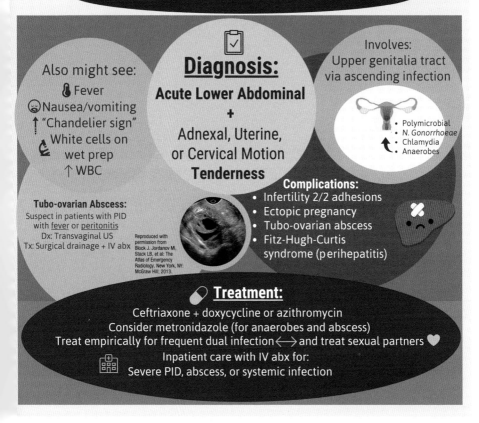

**Also might see:**
🌡 Fever
🤢 Nausea/vomiting
↑ "Chandelier sign"
🔬 White cells on wet prep
↑ WBC

📋 **Diagnosis:**
**Acute Lower Abdominal**
+
**Adnexal, Uterine, or Cervical Motion Tenderness**

Involves:
Upper genitalia tract via ascending infection

• Polymicrobial
• N. Gonorrhoeae
• Chlamydia
• Anaerobes

**Tubo-ovarian Abscess:**
Suspect in patients with PID with fever or peritonitis
Dx: Transvaginal US
Tx: Surgical drainage + IV abx

Reproduced with permission from Block J, Jordanov MI, Stack LB, et al: The Atlas of Emergency Radiology, New York, NY: McGraw Hill; 2013.

**Complications:**
• Infertility 2/2 adhesions
• Ectopic pregnancy
• Tubo-ovarian abscess
• Fitz-Hugh-Curtis syndrome (perihepatitis)

### Treatment:

Ceftriaxone + doxycycline or azithromycin
Consider metronidazole (for anaerobes and abscess)
Treat empirically for frequent dual infection ⟷ and treat sexual partners ♥
Inpatient care with IV abx for:
Severe PID, abscess, or systemic infection

# Pelvic Organ Prolapse (POP)

*When the muscles and connective tissue of the pelvic floor can no longer keep pelvic organs in their proper position*

## Types

| Cystocele (anterior POP) | Rectocele (posterior POP) |
|---|---|

Reproduced with permission from Hoffman BL, Schorge JO, Bradshaw KD, et al: Williams Gynecology, 3rd ed. New York, NY: McGraw Hill; 2016.

| Enterocele | Uterine prolapse |
|---|---|

Reproduced with permission from Hoffman BL, Schorge JO, Bradshaw KD, et al: Williams Gynecology, 3rd ed. New York, NY: McGraw Hill; 2016.

## Risk Factors

Pregnancy, vaginal delivery, aging & menopause, obesity, heavy lifting, chronic coughing, or constipation

## Symptoms

- Pelvic pressure/fullness
- Vaginal bulge
- Difficulty urinating or defecating
- Urinary or fecal incontinence
- "Splinting" (patient applies manual pressure to assist in defecation)
- Lower back pain
- Sexual dysfunction
- Decreased mental health

## Treatment

**Only if symptomatic!**

Lifestyle modifications
 Weight loss
Limit fluid intake
 Timed voids
Kegels/pelvic PT

Vaginal pessaries
Removable device inserted into vagina to support pelvic organs

| Ring Pessary | Gellhorn Pessary |
|---|---|

Surgery
Reconstructive (restores proper organ position) vs obliterative (closes off vagina)

## POP-Q: Standardized Method of Physical Assessment

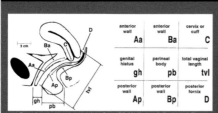

| anterior wall Aa | anterior wall Ba | cervix or cuff C |
|---|---|---|
| genital hiatus gh | perineal body pb | total vaginal length tvl |
| posterior wall Ap | posterior wall Bp | posterior fornix D |

Reproduced with permission from Bump RC, Mattiasson A, Bø K, et al: The standardization of terminology of female pelvic organ prolapse and pelvic floor dysfunction, Am J Obstet Gynecol 1996 Jul;175(1):10-17.

### 6 Defined Points of Measurement

*(all measured in cm)* ABOVE the hymen – NEGATIVE
BELOW the hymen + POSITIVE

- Anterior vaginal wall (Aa, Ba)
- Superior vagina (C, D)
- Posterior vaginal wall (Bp, Ap)

### 3 Additional Measurements

- Total vaginal length (TVL)
- Perineal body (PB)
- Genital hiatus (GH)

### 5 Stages of Pelvic Organ Support

Stage 0: No prolapse
Stage I: >1 cm above level of the hymen
Stage II: <1 cm above or below level of the hymen
Stage III: >1 cm below the hymen, but no further than 2 cm less than the TVL
Stage IV: Complete procidentia or vaginal vault eversion

# Perineal Laceration

Key:　　+/− may or may not need repair　　+ minimal repair　　++ requires repair　　+++ requires extensive repair

### First-Degree Perineal

Involves only perineal skin or vaginal epithelium

+/−

### Second-Degree Perineal

First degree + involves perineal body, most common

+

### Third-Degree Perineal

Extends through perineal body into anal sphincter

++

### Fourth-Degree Perineal

Involves internal and external anal sphincters and through rectal mucosa

+++

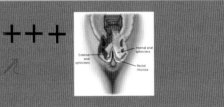

### Episiotomy

Midline or lateral incision to enlarge the opening of the vagina that ends before the external anal sphincter

++

### Cervical and Vaginal

Cervical and vaginal tears more often occur after operative/instrument deliveries

+
−

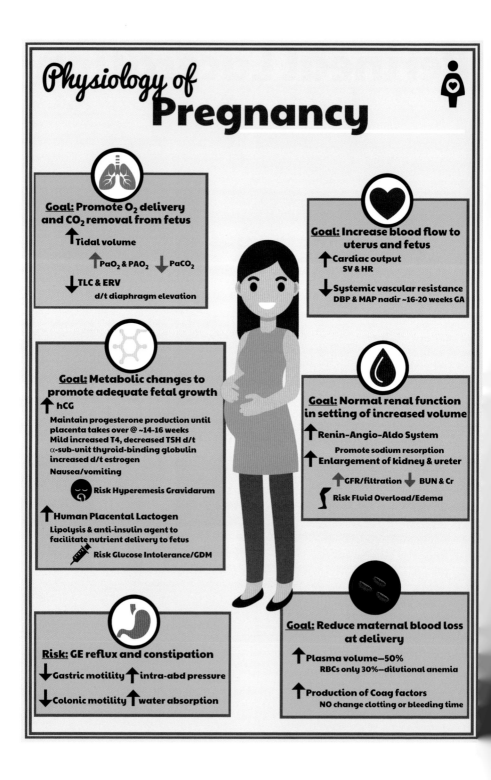

# Physiology of Pregnancy

**Goal: Promote $O_2$ delivery and $CO_2$ removal from fetus**

↑ Tidal volume

↑ $PaO_2$ & $PAO_2$  ↓ $PaCO_2$

↓ TLC & ERV
d/t diaphragm elevation

**Goal: Increase blood flow to uterus and fetus**

↑ Cardiac output
SV & HR

↓ Systemic vascular resistance
DBP & MAP nadir ~16-20 weeks GA

**Goal: Metabolic changes to promote adequate fetal growth**

↑ hCG

Maintain progesterone production until placenta takes over @ ~14-16 weeks

Mild increased T4, decreased TSH d/t α-sub-unit thyroid-binding globulin increased d/t estrogen

Nausea/vomiting

Risk Hyperemesis Gravidarum

↑ Human Placental Lactogen

Lipolysis & anti-insulin agent to facilitate nutrient delivery to fetus

Risk Glucose Intolerance/GDM

**Goal: Normal renal function in setting of increased volume**

↑ Renin–Angio–Aldo System

↑ Promote sodium resorption
Enlargement of kidney & ureter

↑ GFR/filtration ↓ BUN & Cr

Risk Fluid Overload/Edema

**Risk: GE reflux and constipation**

↓ Gastric motility ↑ intra-abd pressure

↓ Colonic motility ↑ water absorption

**Goal: Reduce maternal blood loss at delivery**

↑ Plasma volume—50%
RBCs only 30%—dilutional anemia

↑ Production of Coag factors
NO change clotting or bleeding time

# Polycystic Ovarian Syndrome (PCOS)

## Diagnostic Criteria

Oligomenorrhea ✳
Androgen symptoms ✳
Polycystic ovaries ✳

✳ 2 of the 3

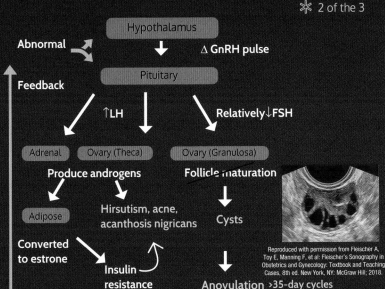

Abnormal ↘

Hypothalamus

↓ Δ GnRH pulse

Feedback

Pituitary

↑LH                    Relatively↓FSH

Adrenal    Ovary (Theca)          Ovary (Granulosa)

**Produce androgens**          **Follicle maturation**

Adipose      Hirsutism, acne,           Cysts
             acanthosis nigricans

**Converted
to estrone**          **Insulin
                      resistance**          **Anovulation** >35-day cycles

Reproduced with permission from Fleischer A,
Toy E, Manning F, et al: Fleischer's Sonography in
Obstetrics and Gynecology: Textbook and Teaching
Cases, 8th ed. New York, NY: McGraw Hill; 2018.

---

↑LH : FSH                    Rule out androgen-secreting ovarian tumor with US
↑Estrogen : Progesterone     Rule out CAH with 17-OH progesterone
↑Free testosterone           Rule out Cushing's, adrenal, thyroid dz with disease-specific tests

---

## 🚑 Complications

Metabolic syndrome (DM II, insulin resistance,
HTN, HLD), especially early onset DM II

Anovulation/oligomenorrhea

Infertility, pregnancy loss

Hyperandrogenism

↑Risk of breast, ovarian, endometrial cancer
from unopposed estrogen release

## 💊 Management

Screening: 2-hour oral GTT, fasting lipid levels
Lifestyle modifications

Combined hormonal contraceptive (CHC),
progestins
Clomiphene, letrozole, metformin , IVF

CHC, spironolactone

CHC, progestins

# Postpartum Hemorrhage

  >1000 mL of blood regardless of mode of delivery

| Risk Factors | Causes | Dx and Tx |
|---|---|---|
| Multiple gestations<br>Rapid or prolonged labor<br>Uterine infection | <br>**Uterine Atony** | **\*Most common cause of PPH\***<br>Dx: Palpation of soft, "boggy" uterus<br>Tx: Bimanual uterine massage, oxytocin, methergine, or PGF2α |
| Precipitous labor<br>Operative vaginal delivery<br>Macrosomia | <br>**Genital Tract Trauma** | Dx: Manual and visual inspection<br>Tx: Surgical repair |
| Uterine leiomyomas<br>Preterm delivery<br>Previous c/s or curettage | <br>**Retained Placental Tissue** | Dx: Manual and visual inspection of placenta and uterine cavity, US<br>Tx: Removal of tissue +/– curettage |
| Prior uterine surgery, c/s, or scar<br>Multiple gestations<br>Prolonged labor | <br>**Uterine Rupture** | Dx: Fetal distress during labor, pain<br>Tx: Surgical repair, hysterectomy |
| von Willebrand's disease<br>Thrombocytopenia | <br>**Coagulopathies** | Dx: Specific blood tests<br>Tx: Address underlying pathology, transfusion |
| Placenta previa<br>Placenta accreta/increta/percreta | <br>**Abnormal Placentation** | Dx: Ultrasound<br>Tx: C/S, resection/removal of placenta; possible hysterectomy |

**Complications**  Fatal blood loss  Anemia  Sheehan's syndrome

PPH: Postpartum hemorrhage        PGF2α: Prostaglandin F2α        C/S: C-section

## Gestational HTN

New-onset HTN
*after* 20 weeks GA
NO proteinuria

## Chronic HTN

Sustained BP
>140/90 *prior*
to 20 weeks GA

**Antihypertensives in Pregnancy**
"Hypertensive Moms Love Nifedipine"
Hydralazine   Labetalol
α-Methyldopa  Nifedipine
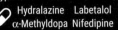 

# Preeclampsia & Eclampsia

End-Organ Damage    Prematurity

## Treatment

**DELIVERY =
ONLY CURE**

 Control BP

Prophylactic Peripartum
IV Mg (seizure ppx)
to all Pre-E/HELLP pts

<34 weeks:
Steroids & IV Mag

34-37 weeks GA:
Maternal−Fetal Monitoring
Expectant Mgmt

>37 weeks:
Immediate Delivery

### Eclampsia
Pre-E + Seizures
IV Mag (sz tx) & Deliver

### Preeclampsia without Severe Features
BP >140/90 on occasions
>4 hours apart
>300 mg/24 hours proteinuria

### Preeclampsia with Severe Features
SBP >160 &/or DBP >110

Proteinuria >5 g/dL; 2x Cr

HA, blurry vision, pulm edema, N/V/Abd pain

### HELLP Syndrome
Hemolysis
Elevated liver enzymes
Low platelets
CBC/CMP

**Magnesium Toxicity
Appx Levels** in mEq/L   ~7-10: Lose DTRs    ~10-13: ↓ RR   ~13+: Cardiotoxic    Reverse with Calcium

# Precocious Puberty

Onset of secondary sexual characteristics <8 years old
Confirm with bone age >2 years above chronologic age

| Central | Peripheral |
|---|---|

## Causes

**Central**
- Constitutional
- Hypothalamic lesions
- CNS infection/trauma
- Hydrocephalus
- Pineal tumor
- Neurofibromatosis
- Tuberous sclerosis

**Peripheral**
- Congenital adrenal hyperplasia
- Adrenal tumors
- McCune–Albright
- Gonadal tumors
- Exogenous estrogen
- Ovarian cysts

## H&P

**Central**
- Sequential maturation of breasts (♀), testicular and penile enlargement (♂), pubic hair
- Accelerated linear growth
- Headache, morning emesis, if intracranial lesion

**Peripheral**

Excess <u>androgen</u> suggests adrenal tumor or CAH →
- Pubic/axillary hair
- Acne
- Enlarged clitoris

Excess <u>estrogen</u> suggests ovarian tumor/cyst →
- Vaginal bleeding
- Breast growth

## Workup

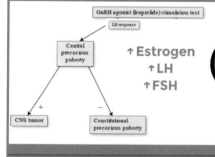

GnRH agonist (leuprolide) stimulation test
LH response

Central precocious puberty

↑ Estrogen
↑ LH
↑ FSH

+ CNS tumor
− Constitutional precocious puberty

GnRH agonist (leuprolide) stimulation test
LH response

↑ Estrogen
↓ LH
↓ FSH

Peripheral precocious puberty

Ultrasonography of ovaries, gonads, and/or adrenals

+ Ovarian cyst / Adrenal tumor / Gonadal tumor
− Exogenous estrogen / CAH

## Treatment

 **Leuprolide**

Continuous stimulation by GnRH agonists desensitizes and suppresses gonadotropin production.

- **CAH:** *steroids*
- **Adrenal/ovarian tumors:** Surgery
- **McCune–Albright:** Antiestrogen

# ✔ Prenatal Care

## Why do prenatal care?

Allows providers to diagnose and treat high-risk pregnancies and potential complications for healthier moms and  and families

Every 4 weeks from GA 0-28

Every 2 weeks from GA 28-36

Every week after GA 36

| At the initial visit | At every visit | Special and repeated tests |
|---|---|---|

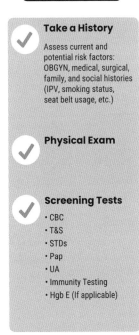

### Take a History

✓ Assess current and potential risk factors: OBGYN, medical, surgical, family, and social histories (IPV, smoking status, seat belt usage, etc.)

### Physical Exam

✓

### Screening Tests

✓
- CBC
- T&S
- STDs
- Pap
- UA
- Immunity Testing
- Hgb E (If applicable)

**At every visit:**

✓  **Weight**

✓  **Blood Pressure**

✓  **Fundal Height and PE**

✓  **Fetal Heart Tones**

✓  **Assess LOF, CTX, Bleeding**

### Genetic Testing

✓ As early as GA 8, includes both noninvasive and invasive measures

### Gestational Diabetes Screen

✓ GA 24-28, perform 1-hour GTT (glucose tolerance test) and if abnormal follow-up with 3-hour GTT

### GBS Swab

✓ GA 35-37, collect at perineum and anus

### Repeat CBC, T&S, and STDs

✓ (If needed)

---

**Continue Anticipatory Counseling Throughout the Pregnancy: What to Expect, How to Prepare, Upcoming Milestones**

---

**36 weeks**

In addition to "every visit" items:

✓ **Ultrasound/ Fetal Monitoring**

✓ **Schedule Induction** For post-dates, GA >40 weeks

✓ **Assess for Presentation** Leopold maneuvers

✓ **Cervical Check** If applicable

### Ultrasound

1st trimester—For dating, viability, or genetic testing

2nd trimester—For anatomy survey, placental location

3rd trimester—For growth, fetal well-being, and presentation

---

T&S: type and screen

Hgb E: Hgb electrophoresis

GA = gestational age

IPV: intimate partner violence

GBS: Group B Streptococcus

LOF: loss of liquid

CTX: contractions

# Prenatal Diagnostic Testing

**Noninvasive** | **Invasive**

## Noninvasive Prenatal Testing
### Starting after 9 weeks

Detects chromosomal abnormalities

Screening for advanced maternal age

PAPP-A + nuchal fold translucency + free β-hCG can detect ~91% cases of Down's syndrome and ~95% of cases of trisomy 18

*PAPP-A: Pregnancy-associated plasma protein A*

## Cell-Free DNA
### Starting after 10 weeks

Can be done as early as 7 weeks but best results 11-12 weeks

Consists of isolation of fetal DNA blood from sample of mother's blood

Detects trisomies 13, 18, and 21 at a high specificity and sensitivity

|  | MSAFP | Estriol | Inhibin A | β-hCG |
|---|---|---|---|---|
| Trisomy 18 | ↓ | ↓ | ↓ | ↓ |
| Trisomy 21 | ↓ | ↓ | ↑ | ↑ |

## Quad Screen
### 15-22 weeks

*MSAFP: Maternal serum alpha-fetoprotein*

Consists of MSAFP, estriol, inhibin A, β-hCG and if elevated, offer chromosomal analysis (+/– invasive procedure with counseling)

Elevated MSAFP associated with neural tube defect

## Chorionic Villus Sampling
### 10-12 weeks

Transcervical or transabdominal aspiration of placental tissue

Risk of fetal loss 1%
Associated with limb defects if done <9 weeks

Reproduced with permission from Yeomans ER, Hoffman BL, Gilstrap LC, et al: Cunningham and Gilstrap's Operative Obstetrics, 3rd ed. New York, NY: McGraw Hill; 2017.

## Amniocentesis
### After 15 weeks

Transabdominal aspiration of amniotic fluid using ultrasound-guided needle

Genetically diagnostic (fetal cells analyzed)

Reproduced with permission from Yeomans ER, Hoffman BL, Gilstrap LC, et al: Cunningham and Gilstrap's Operative Obstetrics, 3rd ed. New York, NY: McGraw Hill; 2017.

Risk/Complications: PROM, chorioamnionitis, or fetal–maternal hemorrhage

Follow-up to abnormal noninvasive testing (or directly when woman is >35 years old)

Other uses: Assess for infection or fetal lung maturity

### Fetal Blood Sampling

Usually reserved for fetal blood karyotyping or platelet alloimmunization

Needle is inserted directly into umbilical vein

1.4% risk of fetal loss

Reproduced with permission from Cunningham G, Leveno KJ, Bloom SL, et al: Williams Obstetrics, 25th ed. New York, NY: McGraw Hill; 2018.

# Preterm Labor & Rupture of Membranes

## Definitions: Preterm Labor

Preterm:
20-37 weeks GA

Labor:
Regular contractions with cervical change

## ROM

ROM: Ruptured amniotic sac
Premature: Prior to onset of labor
Preterm: 20-37 weeks GA
Prolonged: Ruptured >24 hours

## 🔍 Diagnosis

**Confirm Labor:**

Serial cervical exams

Fetal monitoring

Tocometry for contractions

**Rule Out Other Causes:**

Abruption
    Painful bleeding +/– US

Infection (UTI, STI, etc.)
    U/A, GBS Swab, GC/C

**Confirm ROM:**

Sudden gush of fluid

Sterile speculum exam

    +Ferning

    +Pooling

    +Nitrazine Blue

## Management

| Delivery if indicated | Tocolytics | Magnesium for neuroprotection | Steroids for lung maturity | ABX for PPROM, GBS prophylaxis |

STOP

## 😣 Complications

Interventricular hemorrhage

Necrotizing enterocolitis

Retinopathy of prematurity

Low birth weight

Neonatal respiratory distress syndrome

# Sexual Assault

A **nonconsensual** or forced sexual act involving genital, oral, or anal penetration by a part of the body or by an object.

## All persons are susceptible to sexual assault.

*Particularly vulnerable populations:*

A majority of survivors do not report their sexual assault

*The very young*

*The elderly*

**1 in 5**
women have faced sexual assault

*Women in the military*

*The disabled*

The goal of the provider must be supportive, nonjudgmental care for the **physical** and **emotional** consequences of assault.

## Hx

Circumstances of assault:
- Sites of penetration
- Object of penetration (penile, foreign body)
- Condom use
- Activity since assault (changing clothes, urinating, defecating, washing mouth, bathing, cleaning fingernails, douching)

Current contraception use
Last consensual intercourse
Hx of STIs
Depression/anxiety/PTSD
Somatic symptoms of psychological distress

## P.E.

**Detailed whole body exam**
- Injuries—Bruises, lacerations
- Pelvic exam
- Oral exam

**Sexual assault kit**

**Tests to Consider:**
Serum pregnancy test

STD screening:
Gonorrhea/Chlamydia
(**all** sites of penetration)
HIV, syphilis, hepatitis

Toxicology
(to detect date rape drugs
Rohypnol and GHB)

## Tx

STD tx/prophylaxis
- Ceftriaxone 125 mg IM
- Metronidazole 2 g PO
- Azithromycin 1 g PO
- HBIG + Hep B vaccine

HIV postexposure prophylaxis (PEP)
- Within 72 hours

Emergency contraception
- levonorgestrel within 72 hours

Close follow-up:
- Follow-up testing
- Primary care
- Psychological counseling
- Psychiatric care

# Teratogens:

Agents that produce permanent alteration of STRUCTURE or FUNCTION of embryo/fetus

Used with permission from
Dr. Gia Deangelis, UVA Radiology.

| "All or None" Effect | Embryonic Period | Functional Maturation |
|---|---|---|
| 3-4 weeks GA | 5-10 weeks GA | 10+ weeks GA |
| Pregnancy fails or normal development | Organogenesis—Structural problems *Most vulnerable time* | CNS/behavior & functional problems |

## Medications

| | | |
|---|---|---|
| ACE-I/ARB | | Renal Dysgenesis |
| Aminoglycosides | | Hearing Loss |
| Isotretinoin/ Vitamin A | | Intellectual Disability, Microphthalmia, Bone and Heart Defects |
| Lithium | | Ebstein Anomaly |
| Methotrexate, Trimethoprim | | Spontaneous Abortion Neural Tube Defect |
| Tetracyclines | | Dental Discoloration & Hypoplasia |
| Valproate, Phenytoin | | Neural Tube Defect *Consider Increased Folate* |
| Warfarin |  | Nasal Hypoplasia, Bone Stippling, IUGR *"Don't wage a WAR, stay Happy with Heparin!"* |

## Exposures

| | | |
|---|---|---|
| Diethylstilbestrol |  | Uterine/Vaginal Dysgenesis, Clear Cell Carcinoma of Vagina |
| Lead |  | Stillbirth |
| Radiation |  | Microcephaly, Intellectual Disability *<5 Rad okay* |
| TORCH Infections |  | Varies by Pathogen |
| Alcohol |  | Fetal Alcohol Syndrome #1 cause PREVENTABLE Intellectual Disability |
| Cigarettes, Cocaine |  | IUGR, Preterm Birth, Bowel Atresia, Neonatal Abstinence |
| Marijuana |  | Neurocognitive and Behavioral Problems |

| A/B | Generally Safe—Always Check Guidelines |  X | DANGER! NEVER USE IN PREGNANCY! |
|---|---|---|---|

# ToRCHeS Infections

## Infections that pass from mother to fetus

### Toxoplasmosis

- Chorioretinitis
- Hydrocephalus
- Intercranial calcifications

Transplacental

Cat feces, undercooked meat

### HSV-2

- Encephalitis
- Vesicular lesions

Transplacental (rare)
Contact during birth

Skin and mucous membrane contact

### Rubella

- Cataracts
- Deafness
- Congenital heart disease (patent ductus arteriosus)

Transplacental
(first trimester)

Respiratory droplets

### HIV

- Recurrent infections
- Chronic diarrhea

Transplacental
Breastmilk

Sexual contact, needles

### CMV

- Hearing loss
- Seizures
- Petechial rash
- Periventricular calcifications

Transplacental

Sexual contact, organ transplant

### Syphilis

- Stillbirth
- Hydrops fetalis
- Facial abnormalities
- Saber shins
- CN VIII deafness

VDRL/RPR

Transplacental

Sexual contact

Other infections: Parvovirus, varicella, Listeria TB, malaria, fungi

# Urinary Incontinence

## Types of Incontinence

**Stress:** Loss of urine with increased intra-abdominal pressure
**Urge:** Sudden, overwhelming urge to urinate
**Overflow:** Diabetes, neuro/MS, bladder obstruction, post-op
**Mixed:** Features of stress & urge incontinence
**Functional:** Any physical or psychological condition that prevents making it to the toilet on time
**Continuous:** Fistula, urethral diverticulum, ectopic ureter

## Workup

**History:** Precipitating events, # pads used, pregnancy history, UTI symptoms, impact on quality of life, medications taken
**Bladder diary:** Fluid intake, voiding patterns, quantity, leakage
**Physical exam and maneuvers:** POP-Q, cough stress test, cotton swab test, postvoid residual
**Labs/Testing:** UA/urine culture (rule out UTI), urodynamics, & imaging if indicated

| Stress | Urge | Overflow |
|---|---|---|

### 🚨 Symptoms 🚨

| | | |
|---|---|---|
| Leakage with physical exertion, sneezing, coughing, or laughing | Urgency, Frequency, Nocturia | Urinary retention + lack of bladder sensation = overdistension and leakage |

### 🔧 Mechanism 🔧

| | | |
|---|---|---|
| Hypermobile urethra (angle >30° on Q-tip test) | Detrusor overactivity, most commonly idiopathic | Detrusor underactivity or noncontractility |

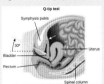

Q-tip test
Symphysis pubis
30°
Uterus
Bladder
Rectum
Spinal column

Insufficient urethral support
Intrinsic sphincteric deficiency (ISD)

**Sympathetic/somatic: INHIBIT urination**
**Parasympathetic: ACTIVATES urination**

**Normal pathway:**
Filling bladder activates stretch receptors →

Inhibition of sympathetic and somatic pathways & activation of parasympathetic pathway →
Detrusor contraction →
Urination

Reproduced with permission from Barrett KE, Barman SM, Brook HL: Ganong's Review of Medical Physiology, 26th ed. New York, NY: McGraw Hill; 2019.

### 📷 Treatment 📷

| | | |
|---|---|---|

- Vaginal pessaries for support
- Intraurethral bulking agents (ISD)
- Surgery: Restore anatomic position, provide structural support (tension-free midurethral sling with mesh)

Incision site on skin
Bladder
Tape (sling)
Vagina
Urethra

- Antimuscarinics (oxybutynin)
- β3 agonist (mirabegron)
- Sacral neuromodulation (stimulates nerves)
- Botulinum toxin injections

- Cholinergic agents (bethanechol)
- Intermittent self-catheterization

| | | |
|---|---|---|
| - Smoking cessation <br>- Weight loss | - Decrease caffeine, alcohol <br>- Decrease fluid intake | - Bladder training (timed voids) <br>- Kegels/pelvic floor PT |

# Uterine Leiomyoma (Fibroids)

 most common pelvic tumor    benign, smooth muscle tumors    hormonally responsive

## Locations

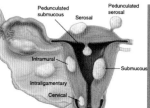

Pedunculated submucous — Serosal — Pedunculated serosal
Intramural — Submucous
Intraligamentary
Cervical

**Subserosal:** Most common
**Intramural:** May distort uterine cavity
**Submucosal:** Most likely to cause bleeding

**+ Parasitic–**
Extrauterine blood supply (omentum)

## Presentation

Majority asymptomatic
*Bleeding:* Heavy, prolonged menses; anemia
*Bulk:* Pelvic pressure, urinary frequency, constipation, pain
Infertility and pregnancy loss
More common in women with FHx or African descent

## Diagnosis

**Physical Exam:** Firm, nontender, irregular-shaped uterus
**Labs:** CBC (assessing for anemia)
**Imaging:** Transvaginal US, saline infusion sonogram (SIS)
**Ultrasound 3D/MRI** (for complex cases)

 *Evaluate bleeding with endometrial biopsy if necessary*

## Medical Management

No symptoms: No treatment! (monitor)
Nonhormonal: NSAIDs, antifibrolytic agents to ↓flow
Hormonal: OCPs, progestins, prog. IUD (if cavity normal)
Hormonal suppression: GnRH agonist or antagonist

## Surgical Management

◌ **Myomectomy:** Remove fibroid(s), can have future pregnancy–
hysteroscopic, laparoscopic, abdominal approaches
**Hysterectomy:** Remove uterus, no future pregnancy–
vaginal, laparoscopic, abdominal approaches
◌ **Uterine artery embolization:** Uterine-preserving
◌ *Risk of recurrence*

## Pregnancy

Usually uncomplicated
↑risk of placental abruption, malpresentation, dysfxn labor, c/s

# UTI and Pyelonephritis in Pregnancy

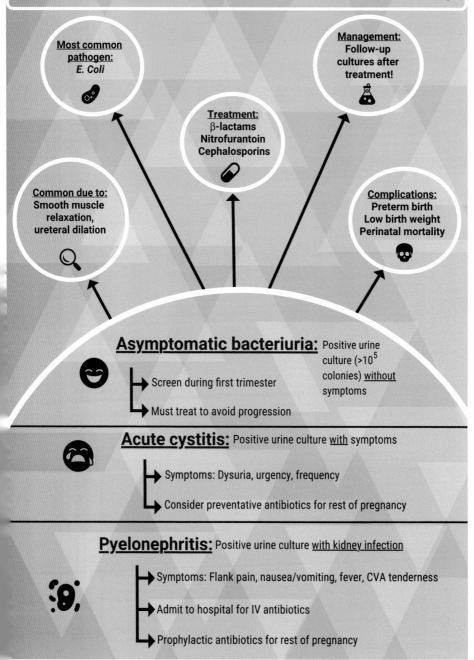

**Most common pathogen:** *E. Coli*

**Management:** Follow-up cultures after treatment!

**Treatment:** β-lactams Nitrofurantoin Cephalosporins

**Common due to:** Smooth muscle relaxation, ureteral dilation

**Complications:** Preterm birth Low birth weight Perinatal mortality

**Asymptomatic bacteriuria:** Positive urine culture (>$10^5$ colonies) <u>without</u> symptoms

- Screen during first trimester
- Must treat to avoid progression

**Acute cystitis:** Positive urine culture <u>with</u> symptoms

- Symptoms: Dysuria, urgency, frequency
- Consider preventative antibiotics for rest of pregnancy

**Pyelonephritis:** Positive urine culture <u>with kidney infection</u>

- Symptoms: Flank pain, nausea/vomiting, fever, CVA tenderness
- Admit to hospital for IV antibiotics
- Prophylactic antibiotics for rest of pregnancy

# Vulvar Cancer

Vulvar cancer accounts for 4% of all gynecologic malignancies.

 ## Presentation

Most cases are diagnosed at an early stage due to uncomfortable symptoms:

- Pruritus
- Discomfort
- Bleeding/ulceration
- Vulvar lump, mass

 Factors such as embarrassment, cultural barriers, and lack of awareness can cause a delay in seeking care.

Reproduced with permission from Hoffman BL, Schorge JO, Bradshaw KD, et al: Williams Gynecology, 3rd ed. New York, NY: McGraw Hill; 2016.

Reproduced with permission from Gadducci A, Carinelli S, Guerrieri ME, et al: Melanoma of the lower genital tract: Prognostic factors and treatment modalities, Gynecol Oncol. 2018 Jul;150(1):180-189.

**Left:** Early-stage vulvar cancer   **Right:** Late-stage vulvar cancer

Overwhelming majority of vulvar cancer cases are squamous cell carcinoma (90%). Vulvar melanoma is next most common (5%).

---

 ## Diagnosis

Biopsy of any abnormal appearing vulvar lesion. Histologic analysis can differentiate between malignant, premalignant, and benign disease.

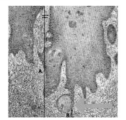

Reproduced with permission from van den Einden LC, Massuger LF, Jonkman JK, et al: An alternative way to measure the depth of invasion of vulvar squamous cell carcinoma in relation to prognosis, Mod Pathol 2015 Feb;28(2):295-302.

Nest of invasive squamous cell carcinoma (*arrow*). Surface epithelium demonstrates high-grade dysplasia.

## Risk Factors

Some risk factors resemble those for cervical cancer:

HPV strains (types 16, 18, 31)   Tobacco use   Immunosuppression

Other risk factors:

Older age

Used with permission from Dr. Dana Redick.

Lichen sclerosus is a benign, chronic inflammatory process with 5% association of subsequent vulvar cancer.

---

 ## Treatment

### Vulvar Intraepithelial Neoplasia (VIN)

VIN is a premalignant lesion strongly associated with HPV.

Wide local excision with 5 mm margin   Laser ablation therapy   Imiquimod cream (immunity modifier)

### Invasive Vulvar Cancer

**Early stages:** Radical vulvectomy with lymph node dissection

**Advanced stages:** Chemoradiation +/− Surgery

## Staging

Early stage: 60-80% survival at 5 years
Advanced stage: 10-40% survival at 5 years

Groin node metastasis status is the most significant prognostic factor in vulvar cancer survival rates.

Reproduced with permission from DeCherney AH, Nathan L, Laufer N, et al: CURRENT Diagnosis & Treatment: Obstetrics & Gynecology, 12th ed. New York, NY: McGraw Hill; 2019.

VIN can transform into invasive vulvar cancer by spreading into the perineum, vagina, urethra, anus. Further invasion to inguinal lymph nodes common.

# References _____

**Abnormal Uterine Bleeding**

Kaufman MS, Holmes JS, Schachel PP, Stead LG. *First Aid for the Obstetrics and Gynecology Clerkship*, 3rd ed. New York, NY: McGraw Hill; 2010.

Le T, Bhushan V. *First Aid for the USMLE Step 2 CK*. 8th ed. New York, NY: McGraw Hill; 2012.

Munro MG, Critchley HOD, Fraser IS, FIGO Menstrual Disorders Committee. The two FIGO systems for normal and abnormal uterine bleeding symptoms and classification of causes of abnormal uterine bleeding in the reproductive years: 2018 revisions. *Int J Gynaecol Obstet*. 2018; 143:393.

**Amenorrhea, Primary**

Le T, Bhushan V. *First Aid for the USMLE Step 2 CK*. 9th ed. New York, NY: McGraw Hill; 2015.

Le T, Bhushan V, Sochat M, et al. *Pediatrics. First Aid for the USMLE Step 1 2017: A Student-to-Student Guide*. New York, NY: McGraw Hill; 2017.

**Amenorrhea, Secondary**

Kaufman M, Stead L, Holmes J, Schachel P. *First Aid for the Obstetrics and Gynecology Clerkship*. 3rd ed. New York, NY: McGraw Hill; 2010.

Le T, Bhushan V. *First Aid for the USMLE Step 2 CK*. 8th ed. New York, NY: McGraw Hill; 2012.

**Antepartum Hemorrhage**

Le T, Bhushan V. *First Aid for the USMLE Step 2 CK*. 9th ed. New York, NY: McGraw Hill; 2015.

Le T, Bhushan V, Sochat M, et al. *Pediatrics. First Aid for the USMLE Step 1 2017: A Student-to-Student Guide*. New York, NY: McGraw Hill; 2017.

**Antepartum Surveillance**

Cunningham F, Leveno KJ, Bloom SL, et al, eds. Prenatal care. *Williams Obstetrics*. 25th ed. New York, NY: McGraw Hill; 2018. http://accessmedicine.mhmedical.com/content.aspx?bookid=1918&sectionid=144148582

Mehta SH, Sokol RJ. Assessment of at-risk pregnancy. *CURRENT Diagnosis & Treatment: Obstetrics & Gynecology*. 12th ed. New York, NY: McGraw Hill; 2019. http://accessmedicine.mhmedical.com/content.aspx?bookid=2559&sectionid=206958883

**Benign Breast Disease**

Le T, Bhushan V. *First Aid for the USMLE Step 2 CK*. 9th ed. New York, NY: McGraw Hill; 2015.

Le T, Bhushan V, Sochat M, et al. *Pediatrics. First Aid for the USMLE Step 1 2017: A Student-to-Student Guide*. New York, NY: McGraw Hill; 2017.

**Breast Cancer**

Breast disease. In: Hoffman BL, Schorge JO, Bradshaw KD, Halvorson LM, Schaffer JI, Corton MM, eds. *Williams Gynecology*. 3rd ed. New York, NY: McGraw-Hill; 2016.

Hayes DF, Lippman ME. Breast cancer. In: Jameson J, Fauci AS, Kasper DL, et al, eds. *Harrison's Principles of Internal Medicine*. 20th ed. New York, NY: McGraw Hill; 2018.

Karuturi M, Valero V, Chavez-MacGregor M. Metastatic breast cancer. In: Kantarjian HM, Wolff RA, eds. *The MD Anderson Manual of Medical Oncology*. 3rd ed. New York, NY: McGraw-Hill; 2016.

**Cervical Cancer**

Hoffman BL, Schorge JO, Bradshaw KD, Halvorson LM, Schaffer JI, Corton MM, eds. *Williams Gynecology*. 3rd ed. New York, NY: McGraw Hill; 2016.

## Contraception
Burkman RT, Brzezinski A. Contraception & family planning. In: DeCherney AH, Nathan L, Laufer N, Roman AS, eds. *CURRENT Diagnosis & Treatment: Obstetrics & Gynecology*. 12th ed. New York, NY: McGraw Hill; 2019.

Cunningham F, Leveno KJ, Bloom SL, et al, eds. Sterilization. *Williams Obstetrics*. 25th ed. New York, NY: McGraw Hill; 2018. http://accessmedicine.mhmedical.com/content.aspx?bookid=1918&sectionid=138823549. Accessed August 18, 2019.

Mayeaux EJ Jr. Family planning. In: Usatine RP, Smith MA, Mayeaux EJ Jr., Chumley HS, eds. *The Color Atlas and Synopsis of Family Medicine*. 3rd ed. New York, NY: McGraw Hill; 2019.

Stuart GS. Contraception and sterilization. In: Hoffman BL, Schorge JO, Bradshaw KD, Halvorson LM, Schaffer JI, Corton MM, eds. *Williams Gynecology*. 3rd ed. New York, NY: McGraw Hill; 2016. http://accessmedicine.mhmedical.com/content.aspx?bookid=1758&sectionid=118167533. Accessed August 18, 2019.

## Diabetes in Pregnancy
Caughey AB. Gestational diabetes mellitus: obstetrical issues and management. In: Werner EF, Barss VA, eds. *UpToDate*. Waltham, MA: UpToDate Inc. https://www.uptodate.com. Accessed June 06, 2019.

Durnwald C. Diabetes mellitus in pregnancy: screening and diagnosis. In: Nathan DM, Werner EF, Barss, VA, eds. *UpToDate*. Waltham, MA: UpToDate Inc. https://www.uptodate.com. Accessed June 06, 2019.

Durnwald C. Gestational diabetes mellitus: glycemic control and maternal prognosis. In: Nathan DM, Werner EF, Barss, VA, eds. *UpToDate*. Waltham, MA: UpToDate Inc. https://www.uptodate.com. Accessed June 06, 2019.

## Dysmenorrhea
ACOG Committee Opinion No. 760: Dysmenorrhea and Endometriosis in the Adolescent. *Obstet Gynecol*. 2018;132(6):e249-e258.

Hoffman BL. Endometriosis. In: Hoffman BL, Schorge JO, Bradshaw KD, Halvorson LM, Schaffer JI, Corton MM, eds. *Williams Gynecology*. 3rd ed. New York, NY: McGraw Hill, 2016. https://accessmedicine.mhmedical.com/content.aspx?bookid=1758&sectionid=118168644

Hoffman BL. Pelvic mass. In: Hoffman BL, Schorge JO, Bradshaw KD, Halvorson LM, Schaffer JI, Corton MM, eds. *Williams Gynecology*. 3rd ed. New York, NY: McGraw Hill, 2016. https://accessmedicine.mhmedical.com/content.aspx?bookid=1758&sectionid=118168387

## Early Pregnancy Loss
Cunningham F, Leveno KJ, Bloom SL, et al, eds. Abortion. *Williams Obstetrics*. 25th ed. New York, NY: McGraw Hill; 2018. https://accessmedicine.mhmedical.com/content.aspx?bookid=1918&sectionid=166439017

## Ectopic Pregnancy
Le T, Bhushan V. *First Aid for the USMLE Step 2 CK*. 9th ed. New York, NY: McGraw Hill; 2015.

Le T, Bhushan V, Sochat M, et al. *Pediatrics. First Aid for the USMLE Step 1 2017: A Student-to-Student Guide*. New York, NY: McGraw Hill; 2017.

Cunningham F, Leveno KJ, Bloom SL, et al, eds. Ectopic pregnancy. *Williams Obstetrics*. 25th ed. New York, NY: McGraw Hill; 2018.

## Endometrial Cancer
Schorge JO, Kehoe SM, Miller DS. Endometrial cancer. In: Hoffman BL, Schorge JO, Bradshaw KD, Halvorson LM, Schaffer JI, Corton MM, eds. *Williams Gynecology*. 3rd ed. New York, NY: McGraw Hill; 2016.

## Fetal Heart Monitoring
Cunningham F, Leveno KJ, Bloom SL, et al, eds. Intrapartum assessment. Williams Obstetrics. 25th ed. New York, NY: McGraw Hill; 2018. http://accessmedicine.mhmedical.com/content.aspx?bookid=1918&sectionid=185051515

Sholapurkar S. Categorization of fetal heart rate decelerations in American and European practice: importance and imperative of avoiding framing and confirmation biases. *J Clin Med Res*. 2015 Sep;7(9):672-680.

## Gynecologic Infections

Griffith WF, Werner CL. Benign disorders of the lower genital tract. In: Hoffman BL, Schorge JO, Bradshaw KD, Halvorson LM, Schaffer JI, Corton MM, eds. *Williams Gynecology*. 3rd ed. New York, NY: McGraw Hill; 2016. https://accessmedicine.mhmedical.com/content.aspx?bookid=1758&sectionid=118167322&jumpsectionid=118167460

Hoffman BL, Corton MM. Surgeries for benign gynecologic disorders. In: Hoffman BL, Schorge JO, Bradshaw KD, Halvorson LM, Schaffer JI, Corton MM, eds. *Williams Gynecology*. 3rd ed. New York, NY: McGraw Hill; 2016. http://accessmedicine.mhmedical.com/content.aspx?bookid=1758&sectionid=118174996.

Mayeaux EJ Jr. Candida vulvovaginitis. In: Usatine RP, Smith MA, Mayeaux EJ Jr., Chumley HS, eds. *The Color Atlas and Synopsis of Family Medicine*. 3rd ed. New York, NY: McGraw Hill; 2019. https://accessmedicine.mhmedical.com/content.aspx?bookid=2547&sectionid=206784429&jumpsectionid=206784433

Mayeaux EJ Jr., Usatine RP. Trichomonas vaginitis. In: Usatine RP, Smith MA, Mayeaux EJ Jr., Chumley HS. *The Color Atlas and Synopsis of Family Medicine*. 3rd ed. New York, NY: McGraw Hill; 2019. https://accessmedicine.mhmedical.com/content.aspx?sectionid=206784479&bookid=2547&Resultclick=2

Mayeaux EJ Jr., Usatine RP, Davis TJ, Weiner-Johnson C. Bacterial vaginosis. In: Usatine RP, Smith MA, Mayeaux EJ Jr., Chumley HS, eds. *The Color Atlas and Synopsis of Family Medicine*. 3rd ed. New York, NY: McGraw Hill; 2019. https://accessmedicine.mhmedical.com/content.aspx?bookid=2547&sectionid=206784386&jumpsectionid=206784406

## Hypertension in Pregnancy

August P. Management of hypertension in pregnant and postpartum women. *UpToDate*. Waltham, MA: UpToDate Inc. https://www.uptodate.com. Accessed June 06, 2019.

Magloire L, Funai EF. Gestational hypertension. *UpToDate*. Waltham, MA: UpToDate Inc. https://www.uptodate.com. Accessed June 06, 2019.

U.S Preventive Services Task Force. Preeclampsia: screening. *United States Preventive Services Taskforce*. https://www.uspreventiveservicestaskforce.org/uspstf/recommendation/preeclampsia-screening. Accessed July 23, 2019.

## Labor

Archie CL, Roman AS. Normal & abnormal labor & delivery. In: DeCherney AH, Nathan L, Laufer N, Roman AS, eds. *CURRENT Diagnosis & Treatment: Obstetrics & Gynecology*. 11th ed. New York, NY: McGraw Hill, 2013. http://accessmedicine.mhmedical.com/content.aspx?bookid=498&sectionid=41008596

Cunningham F, Leveno KJ, Bloom SL, et al, eds. Abnormal labor. *Williams Obstetrics*. 25th ed. New York, NY: McGraw Hill; 2018. http://accessmedicine.mhmedical.com/content.aspx?bookid=1918&sectionid=185051261

Incerpi MH. Operative delivery. In: DeCherney AH, Nathan L, Laufer N, Roman AS, eds. *CURRENT Diagnosis & Treatment: Obstetrics & Gynecology*. 12th ed. New York, NY: McGraw Hill; 2019. http://accessmedicine.mhmedical.com/content.aspx?bookid=2559&sectionid=206960294

## Lactation

Cunningham F, Leveno KJ, Bloom SL, et al, eds. The puerperium. *Williams Obstetrics*. 25th ed. New York, NY: McGraw Hill; 2018. http://accessmedicine.mhmedical.com/content.aspx?bookid=1918&sectionid=138823398

## Menopause

ACOG Practice Bulletin No. 141: management of menopausal symptoms. *Obstet Gynecol*. 2014;123(1):202–216. doi: 10.1097/01.AOG.0000441353.20693.78.

Kaufman M, Stead L, Holmes J, Schachel P. *First Aid for the Obstetrics and Gynecology Clerkship*. 3rd ed. New York, NY: McGraw Hill; 2010.

Le T, Bhushan V, Matthew S, Mehboob K, Chavda Y. *First Aid for the USMLE Step 1 2016*. 12th ed. New York, NY: McGraw Hill; 2016.

## Menstrual Cycle

Le T, Bhushan V. *First Aid for the USMLE Step 2 CK*. 8th ed. New York, NY: McGraw Hill; 2012.

Le T, Bhushan V, Matthew S, Mehboob K, Chavda Y. *First Aid for the USMLE Step 1 2016*. 12th ed. New York, NY: McGraw Hill; 2016.

**Multiple Gestations**
Cunningham F, Leveno KJ, Bloom SL, et al, eds. Multifetal pregnancy. *Williams Obstetrics*. 25th ed. New York, NY: McGraw Hill; 2018.

**Nausea & Vomiting in Pregnancy**
Le T, Bhushan V. *First Aid for the USMLE Step 2 CK*. 9th ed. New York, NY: McGraw Hill; 2015.

Le T, Bhushan V, Sochat M, et al. *Pediatrics. First Aid for the USMLE Step 1 2017: A Student-to-Student Guide*. New York, NY: McGraw Hill; 2017.

Cunningham F, Leveno KJ, Bloom SL, et al, eds. Gastrointestinal disorders. *Williams Obstetrics*. 25th ed. New York, NY: McGraw Hill; 2018.

**OB Anesthesia and Analgesia**
Butterworth IV JF, Mackey DC, Wasnick JD, eds. Spinal, epidural, & caudal blocks. *Morgan & Mikhail's Clinical Anesthesiology*. 6th ed. New York, NY: McGraw Hill; 2018. http://accessmedicine.mhmedical.com/content.aspx?bookid=2444&sectionid=193555666

Eltzschig HK, Lieberman ES, Camann WR. Regional anesthesia and analgesia for labor and delivery. *N Engl J Med*. 2003 Jan 23;348(4):319-332. doi: 10.1056/NEJMra021276. PMID: 12540646.

Hawkins JL. Epidural analgesia for labor and delivery. *N Engl J Med*. 2010 Apr 22;362(16):1503-1510. doi: 10.1056/NEJMct0909254.

McDonald JS, Chen B, Kwan W. Obstetric analgesia & anesthesia. In: DeCherney AH, Nathan L, Laufer N, Roman AS, eds. *CURRENT Diagnosis & Treatment: Obstetrics & Gynecology*. 12th ed. New York, NY: McGraw Hill; 2019. http://accessmedicine.mhmedical.com/content.aspx?bookid=2559&sectionid=206961144.

**Obstetric Ultrasound**
Bernstein HB. Normal pregnancy & prenatal care. In: DeCherney AH, Nathan L, Laufer N, Roman AS, eds. *CURRENT Diagnosis & Treatment: Obstetrics & Gynecology*. 12th ed. New York, NY: McGraw Hill; 2019. http://accessmedicine.mhmedical.com/content.aspx?bookid=2559&sectionid=206957929

Cunningham F, Leveno KJ, Bloom SL, et al. Amnionic fluid. In: Cunningham F, Leveno KJ, Bloom SL, et al. *Williams Obstetrics*. 25th ed. New York, NY: McGraw Hill; 2018. http://accessmedicine.mhmedical.com/content.aspx?bookid=1918&sectionid=185048302

Rahimian J. Disproportionate fetal growth. In: DeCherney AH, Nathan L, Laufer N, Roman AS, eds. *CURRENT Diagnosis & Treatment: Obstetrics & Gynecology*. 12th ed. New York, NY: McGraw Hill; 2019. http://accessmedicine.mhmedical.com/content.aspx?bookid=2559&sectionid=206959761

Usatine RP, Smith MA, Chumley HS, Mayeaux EJ Jr., eds. Second trimester obstetrical ultrasound. In: *The Color Atlas of Family Medicine*. 2nd ed. New York, NY: McGraw Hill; 2013. http://accessmedicine.mhmedical.com/content.aspx?bookid=685&sectionid=45361126

**Ovarian Cancer**
Elsamaloty H, Al-Natour M, Haswah N, Holz S, Elsayes KM. Introduction to women's imaging. In: Elsayes KM, Oldham SA, eds. *Introduction to Diagnostic Radiology*. New York, NY: McGraw Hill; 2014.

Schorge JO. Epithelial ovarian cancer. In: Hoffman BL, Schorge JO, Bradshaw KD, Halvorson LM, Schaffer JI, Corton MM, eds. *Williams Gynecology*. 3rd ed. New York, NY: McGraw Hill; 2016.

Schorge JO. Ovarian germ cell and sex cord-stromal tumors. In: Hoffman BL, Schorge JO, Bradshaw KD, Halvorson LM, Schaffer JI, Corton MM, eds. *Williams Gynecology*. 3rd ed. New York, NY: McGraw Hill; 2016.

**Pediatric Vaginal Discharge**
Le T, Bhushan V. *First Aid for the USMLE Step 2 CK*. 9th ed. New York, NY: McGraw Hill; 2015.

## Pelvic Inflammatory Disease (PID)

Mayeaux EJ Jr., Usatine RP. Chlamydia cervicitis. In: Usatine RP, Smith MA, Mayeaux Jr. EJ, Chumley HS, eds. *The Color Atlas and Synopsis of Family Medicine*. 3rd ed. New York, NY: McGraw Hill; 2019. https://accessmedicine.mhmedical.com/content.aspx?bookid=2547&sectionid=206784522&jumpsectionid=206784537

Ram S, Rice PA. Gonococcal infections. In: Jameson J, Fauci AS, Kasper DL, Hauser SL, Longo DL, Loscalzo J, eds. *Harrison's Principles of Internal Medicine*. 20th ed. New York, NY: McGraw Hill; 2018. https://accessmedicine.mhmedical.com/content.aspx?bookid=2129&sectionid=192021881&jumpsectionid=192021918

Woo J, Scott, RK. Gynecologic disorders. In: Papadakis MA, McPhee SJ, Rabow MW, eds. *Current Medical Diagnosis & Treatment 2019*. New York, NY: McGraw Hill; 2019. https://accessmedicine.mhmedical.com/content.aspx?bookid=2449&sectionid=194441864&jumpsectionid=194442219

## Pelvic Organ Prolapse (POP)

Bump RC, Mattiasson A, Bø K, et al. The standardization of terminology of female pelvic organ prolapse and pelvic floor dysfunction. *Am J Obset Gynecol*. 1996;175(1):10-17.

Committee on Practice Bulletins-Gynecology, American Urogynecologic Society. Practice Bulletin No. 185: Pelvic Organ Prolapse. *Obsetet Gynecol*. 2017 Nov;130(5):e234-e250.

Schaffer JI. Pelvic organ prolapse. In: Hoffman BL, Schorge JO, Bradshaw KD, Halvorson LM, Schaffer JI, Corton MM, eds. *Williams Gynecology*. 3rd ed. New York, NY: McGraw Hill, 2016. https://accessmedicine.mhmedical.com/content.aspx?bookid=1758&sectionid=118171360

## Perineal Laceration

Cunningham F, Leveno KJ, Bloom SL, et al, eds. Vaginal delivery. *Williams Obstetrics*. 25th ed. New York, NY: McGraw Hill; 2018. http://accessmedicine.mhmedical.com/content.aspx?bookid=1918&sectionid=150960110

Hamilton C, Stany M, Gregory W, Kohn EC. Gynecology. In: Brunicardi F, Andersen DK, Billiar TR, et al, eds. *Schwartz's Principles of Surgery*. 10th ed. New York, NY: McGraw Hill; 2015. http://accessmedicine.mhmedical.com/content.aspx?bookid=980&sectionid=59610883

## Physiology of Pregnancy

Le T, Hwang W, Muralidhar V, White JA. *First Aid for Basic Sciences: Organ Systems*. 3rd ed. New York, NY: McGraw Hill; 2017.

## Polycystic Ovarian Syndrome (PCOS)

Beckmann CRB, Ling FW, Barzansky BM, Herbert WNP, Laube DW, Smith RP, eds. *Obstetrics and Gynecology*. 6th ed. Baltimore, MD: Wolters Kluwer Health/Lippincott Williams & Wilkins; 2010.

Le T, Bhushan V. *First Aid for the USMLE Step 2 CK*. 8th ed. New York, NY: McGraw Hill; 2012.

McCartney CR, Marshall JC. CLINICAL PRACTICE. Polycystic Ovary Syndrome. *N Engl J Med*. 2016;375(1):54-64. doi:10.1056/NEJMcp1514916

## Postpartum Hemorrhage

Poggi SH. Postpartum hemorrhage & the abnormal puerperium. In: DeCherney AH, Nathan L, Laufer N, Roman AS, eds. *CURRENT Diagnosis & Treatment: Obstetrics & Gynecology*. 12th ed. New York, NY: McGraw Hill; 2019. http://accessmedicine.mhmedical.com/content.aspx?bookid=2559&sectionid=206960406

## Preeclampsia & Eclampsia

Cunningham F, Leveno KJ, Bloom SL, et al, eds. Hypertensive disorders. In: *Williams Obstetrics*, 25th ed. New York, NY: McGraw Hill; 2018.

Le T, Bhushan V. *First Aid for the USMLE Step 2 CK*. 9th ed. New York, NY: McGraw Hill; 2015.

Le T, Bhushan V, Sochat M, et al. *Pediatrics. First Aid for the USMLE Step 1 2017: A Student-to-Student Guide*. New York, NY: McGraw Hill; 2017.

**Precocious Puberty**

Le T, Bhushan V. *First Aid for the USMLE Step 2 CK*. 9th ed. New York, NY: McGraw Hill; 2015.

Styne D. Puberty. In: Gardner DG, Shoback D, eds. *Greenspan's Basic & Clinical Endocrinology*. 10th ed. New York, NY: McGraw Hill; 2017.

**Prenatal Care**

Bernstein HB. Normal pregnancy & prenatal care. In: DeCherney AH, Nathan L, Laufer N, Roman AS, eds. *CURRENT Diagnosis & Treatment: Obstetrics & Gynecology*. 12th ed. New York, NY: McGraw Hill; 2019. http://accessmedicine.mhmedical.com/content.aspx?bookid=2559&sectionid=206957929

**Prenatal Diagnostic Testing**

Cunningham F, Leveno KJ, Bloom SL, et al, eds. Prenatal diagnosis. *Williams Obstetrics*. 25th ed. New York, NY: McGraw Hill; 2018. http://accessmedicine.mhmedical.com/content.aspx?bookid=1918&sectionid=155911338

McCarthy JJ, Mendelsohn BA, eds. Pregnancy. *Precision Medicine: A Guide to Genomics in Clinical Practice*. New York, NY: McGraw Hill; 2016. http://accessmedicine.mhmedical.com/content.aspx?bookid=1930&sectionid=140197086

**Preterm Labor and Rupture of Membranes**

Le T, Bhushan V. *First Aid for the USMLE Step 2 CK*. 9th ed. New York, NY: McGraw Hill; 2015.

Le T, Bhushan V, Sochat M, et al. *Pediatrics. First Aid for the USMLE Step 1 2017: A Student-to-Student Guide*. New York, NY: McGraw Hill; 2017.Cunningham F, Leveno KJ, Bloom SL, et al, eds. Preterm birth. *Williams Obstetrics*. 25th ed. McGraw Hill; 2018.

**Sexual Assault**

Lu MC Lu JS, Halfin VP, Hsu JY. Domestic Violence & Sexual Assault. In: DeCherney AH, Nathan L, Laufer N, Roman AS, eds. *CURRENT Diagnosis & Treatment: Obstetrics & Gynecology*. 12th ed. New York, NY: McGraw Hill; 2019. https://accessmedicine.mhmedical.com/content.aspx?sectionid=207399735&bookid=2559. Accessed July 23, 2019.

**Teratogens**

Le T, Bhushan V. *First Aid for the USMLE Step 2 CK*. 9th ed. New York, NY: McGraw Hill; 2015.

Le T, Bhushan V, Sochat M, et al. *Pediatrics. First Aid for the USMLE Step 1 2017: A Student-to-Student Guide*. New York, NY: McGraw Hill; 2017.

**ToRCHeS Infections**

Le T, Bhushan V. *First Aid for the USMLE Step 1 2016: A Student-to-Student Guide*. New York, NY: McGraw Hill; 2016.

**Urinary Incontinence**

ACOG Practice Bulletin 155: Urinary incontinence in women. *Obstet Gynecol*. 2015;126(5):e66-81.

Callahan T, Caughey AB. Urinary incontinence. *Blueprints Obstetrics & Gynecology*. 7th ed. Philadelphia, PA: Wolters Kluwer Health, 2018.

Rahn DD, Wai CY. Urinary incontinence. In: Hoffman BL, Schorge JO, Bradshaw KD, Halvorson LM, Schaffer JI, Corton MM, eds. *Williams Gynecology*. 3rd ed. New York, NY: McGraw Hill, 2016. https://accessmedicine.mhmedical.com/content.aspx?bookid=1758&sectionid=118171153

**Uterine Leiomyoma (Fibroids)**

Kaufman M, Stead L, Holmes J, Schachel P. *First Aid for the Obstetrics and Gynecology Clerkship*. 3rd ed. New York, NY: McGraw Hill; 2010.

Le T, Bhushan V. *First Aid for the USMLE Step 2 CK*. 8th ed. New York, NY: McGraw Hill; 2012.

## UTI and Pyelonephritis in Pregnancy

Hooton TM, Gupta K. Urinary tract infections and asymptomatic bacteriuria in pregnancy. *UpToDate*. Waltham, MA: UpToDate Inc. https://www.uptodate.com. Accessed June 06, 2019.

US Preventive Services Task Force, Owens DK, Davidson KW, et al. Screening for asymptomatic bacteriuria in adults: US preventive services task force recommendation statement. *JAMA*. 2019;322(12):1188-1194. doi:10.1001/jama.2019.13069

## Vulvar Cancer

Dooley-Hash S, Lisse SA, Knoop KJ. Gynecologic and obstetric conditions. In: Knoop KJ, Stack LB, Storrow AB, Thurman R, eds. *The Atlas of Emergency Medicine*. 4th ed. New York, NY: McGraw Hill; 2016.

Lea JS. Vulvar cancer. In: Hoffman BL, Schorge JO, Bradshaw KD, Halvorson LM, Schaffer JI, Corton MM, eds. *Williams Gynecology*. 3rd ed. New York, NY: McGraw Hill; 2016.

Richardson DL. Vaginal cancer. In: Hoffman BL, Schorge JO, Bradshaw KD, Halvorson LM, Schaffer JI, Corton MM, eds. *Williams Gynecology*. 3rd ed. New York, NY: McGraw Hill; 2016.

# Pediatrics

*Amy D. Thompson, MD*

# APGAR Score

## Assessment of Newborn Vital Signs Following Birth on a 10-Point Scale

### Appearance

**2 points**: Pink

**1 point**: Extremities blue

**0 points**: Pale or blue

Scores are determined at **1 minute** and **5 minutes** after birth

### Pulse

**2 points**: >100 bpm

**1 point**: <100 bpm

**0 points**: No pulse

Apgar scores help physicians determine the level of post delivery care

### Grimace

**2 points**: Cries and pulls away

**1 point**: Grimaces or weak cry

**0 points**: No response to stimulation

Scores < 7 need further evaluation

### Activity

**2 points**: Active movement

**1 point**: Arms, legs flexed

**0 points**: No movement

Scores < 4 may need life-saving efforts

### Respiration

**2 points**: Strong cry

**1 point**: Slow, irregular

**0 points**: No breathing

Prolonged low scores increase risk for long-term neurological damage

# Atrial & Ventricular Septal Defects

## ASD

- Most commonly ostium secundum defects
- Leads to dilated right ventricle

**⚠ Can lead to paradoxical emboli**

### Murmur
Systolic at LUSB
Loud S1
Split fixed S2

### Associations
 Down's syndrome

 Alcohol exposure in utero

## VSD

- Most common congenital heart defect
- Occurs most commonly in muscular septum

### Murmur
Holosystolic at LLSB

### Associations
🧬 Down's syndrome & other trisomies

🍷 Alcohol exposure

🦠 TORCH Infection

## Presentation

Asymptomatic at birth

Failure to thrive

Frequent URIs

Can develop heart failure & Eisenmenger's syndrome

## Management

### Workup
Echo for definitive diagnosis
Chest X-ray will show increased pulmonary markings

### Treatment
Surgical correction for large, unchanging, or symptomatic defects

**⚠ Smaller defects can self-resolve**

# B-Cell Immunodeficiencies
## Primary Immunodeficiency Disorders

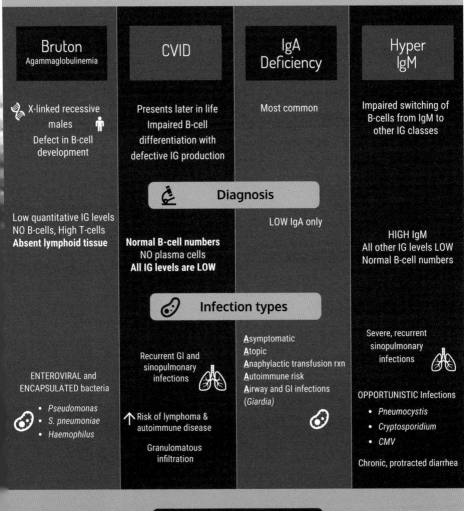

### Bruton
Agammaglobulinemia

X-linked recessive males

Defect in B-cell development

Low quantitative IG levels
NO B-cells, High T-cells
**Absent lymphoid tissue**

ENTEROVIRAL and ENCAPSULATED bacteria
- *Pseudomonas*
- *S. pneumoniae*
- *Haemophilus*

### CVID

Presents later in life
Impaired B-cell differentiation with defective IG production

**Normal B-cell numbers**
NO plasma cells
**All IG levels are LOW**

Recurrent GI and sinopulmonary infections

↑ Risk of lymphoma & autoimmune disease

Granulomatous infiltration

### IgA Deficiency

Most common

LOW IgA only

**A**symptomatic
**A**topic
**A**naphylactic transfusion rxn
**A**utoimmune risk
**A**irway and GI infections
(*Giardia*)

### Hyper IgM

Impaired switching of B-cells from IgM to other IG classes

HIGH IgM
All other IG levels LOW
Normal B-cell numbers

Severe, recurrent sinopulmonary infections

OPPORTUNISTIC Infections
- *Pneumocystis*
- *Cryptosporidium*
- CMV

Chronic, protracted diarrhea

### Diagnosis

### Infection types

### Treatment
Immunization with killed vaccines
Prophylactic antibiotics
IVIG in all <u>except</u> IgA deficiency

# Bone Disorders

## Osteosarcoma

 Tumor of **mesenchyme** origin (osteoblasts) presents with intractable bone pain at night, constitutional symptoms occasionally, and sometimes enlargement at site

 Elevated alkaline phosphatase

 Cellular atypia and lacey osteoid

 Get chest CT for lung metastasis and staging

 **Metaphysis** of long bones most common: Around knee Lytic lesion with **sunburst** pattern or Codman's triangle

 Surgical resection and chemotherapy

 Associated with retinoblastoma, Li–Fraumeni syndrome, and Paget's disease

Reproduced with permission from Brunicardi FC, Andersen DK, Billiar TR, et al: Schwartz's Principles of Surgery, 10th ed. New York, NY: McGraw Hill; 2015.

Reproduced with permission from Tehranzadeh J: Basic Musculoskeletal Imaging. New York, NY: McGraw Hill; 2014.

## Ewing's Sarcoma

 Tumor of **neuroectoderm** origin presents with **local pain and swelling**, systemic symptoms commonly

 Elevated ESR and leukocytosis

 Small, round blue cells, pseudorosettes

 Midshaft of long bones lytic lesion with **onion skinning**

 Surgical resection and chemotherapy +/– radiation

 Associated with **11;22 translocation**

Reproduced with permission from Brunicardi FC, Andersen DK, Billiar TR, et al: Schwartz's Principles of Surgery, 10th ed. New York, NY: McGraw Hill; 2015.

Reproduced with permission from Tehranzadeh J: Basic Musculoskeletal Imaging. New York, NY: McGraw Hill; 2014.

## Langerhans Cell Histiocytosis

 Proliferative disorders of **dendritic (Langerhans) cells:** Multiple subtypes can present in children, usually **toddlers**, with **skin rash** (diaper dermatitis) and skeletal abnormalities

 **Birbeck granules:** Tennis racket or rod shaped under electron microscope

 **Lytic bone lesions** (especially skull and long bones)

 Chemotherapy (prednisone +/– vinblastine)

https://en.wikipedia.org/wiki/Birbeck_granules

Reproduced with permission from Wells RG: Diagnostic Imaging of Infants and Children. New York, NY: McGraw Hill; 2013.

 Cells express S100 and CD1a

# Bronchiolitis

## Etiology

- Typically respiratory syncytial virus (**RSV**) infection
- Respiratory symptoms due to obstructive edema of submucosa
- Especially affects **children <2 years old** during the **winter**

**Other viral causes**
Rhinovirus
Parainfluenza virus
Metapneumovirus
Influenza virus
Coronavirus

## Clinical Presentation

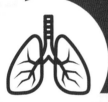

- Cough, rhinorrhea, and fever followed by **wheezing, dyspnea, and tachypnea**
- Symptoms peak at day 3-4

## Diagnosis

 Clinical diagnosis

 CXR to rule out pneumonia, rapid antigen testing of nasopharyngeal aspirate

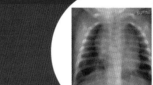

Reproduced with permission from Bronchiolitis. Radiopaedia. Case contributed by Dr Jeremy Jones. April 2, 2015 https://radiopaedia.org/cases/bronchiolitis-2

## Treatment

**Palivizumab for Prophylaxis**
Pre-term infant
Chronic lung disease
Acyanotic heart disease
Immunodeficiency

 Symptomatic management, suctioning, and supplemental oxygen

! Watch out for **apnea**, hypoxemic respiratory failure, ARDS

# Cerebral Palsy

- Group of nonhereditary, nonprogressive, permanent disorders of muscle tone, movement, and posture
- Due to cerebral insult or injury during early brain development

**Majority born full term with uncomplicated labor and delivery**

Risk factors include:
- Prematurity (<28 weeks are at increased risk)
- Intraventricular hemorrhage
- Intrapartum or neonatal infection
- Perinatal asphyxia
- Trauma
- Brain malformations
- Genetic syndromes

## 0.2%
of all live births result in cerebral palsy

- Abnormal tone
- Persistence of primitive reflexes after 1 year of age
- Toe walking and scissor gait
- Hand preference before 1 year of age
- Associated conditions: Intellectual disability, growth failure, vision and hearing impairment, seizure disorders

- Monoplegia = 1 limb affected
- Diplegia = both legs affected, arms mildly affected
- Quadriplegia = arms and legs equally affected
- Hemiplegia = arm and leg on the same side of body affected, arm more affected than leg

## Classification

**Spastic**
- Increased muscle tone
- Accounts for 75% of cases

**Nonspastic**
- Decreased and/or fluctuating muscle tone; involuntary movements
- Subtypes include hypotonic, ataxic, choreoathetoid, and dystonic

## Treatment

- Maximize function using PT, OT, and speech therapy
- Drug treatment --> baclofen, dantrolene, diazepam, tizanidine, botox, and carbidopa-levodopa (for dystonia)
- Selective dorsal rhizotomy if severe
- Orthopedic follow-up due to complications arising from spasticity—scoliosis and hip dislocations

# Chediak–Higashi Syndrome

## Description

- Autosomal **recessive** disorder that leads to **defective neutrophil chemotaxis and microtubule polymerization**

## Presentation

Oculocutaneous Albinism          Neuropathy          Neutropenia

## Diagnosis

Giant Granules in Neutrophils

## Infectious Agents

S. pneumo

S. aureus          Pseudomonas

## Treatment

 **Bone Marrow Transplant**

**Antibiotic Therapy**

# Child Abuse

**Suspect if:**
- History discordant with physical findings or developmental age
- Delay in obtaining appropriate medical care
- Specific injury patterns or exam findings consistent with abuse

**Risk Factors:**
- Children with complex medical problems
- Infants with colic
- Repeat hospitalizations

## Bruises
- Most common finding
- Head/torso
- May reflect implement (hand, belt)

Reproduced with permission from Tintinalli J, Ma O, Yealy DM, et al: Tintinalli's Emergency Medicine: A Comprehensive Study Guide. 9th ed. New York, NY: McGraw Hill; 2020.

## Burns
Contact: Cigarette, curling iron
Immersion: Hot water
- Buttock, spares flexor surfaces
- Glove-stocking distribution

Reproduced with permission from Knoop KJ, Stack LB, Storrow AB, et al: The Atlas of Emergency Medicine, 4th ed. New York, NY: McGraw Hill; 2016. Photo contributor: Cincinnati Children's Hospital Medical Center.

## Sexual Abuse
- Genital bleeding, trauma, or discharge

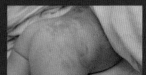

Reproduced with permission from Tintinalli J, Ma O, Yealy DM, et al: Tintinalli's Emergency Medicine: A Comprehensive Study Guide. 9th ed. New York, NY: McGraw Hill; 2020.

## Fractures

Posterior rib fractures (squeezing)

Reproduced with permission from Knoop KJ, Stack LB, Storrow AB, et al: The Atlas of Emergency Medicine, 4th ed. New York, NY: McGraw Hill; 2016. Photo contributor: Cincinnati Children's Hospital Medical Center.

Epiphyseal-metaphyseal "bucket" fractures

Reproduced with permission from Tintinalli J, Ma O, Yealy DM, et al: Tintinalli's Emergency Medicine: A Comprehensive Study Guide. 9th ed. New York, NY: McGraw Hill; 2020.

Spiral fractures (humerus/femur)

Reproduced with permission from Elsayes KM, Oldham SA: Introduction to Diagnostic Radiology. New York, NY: McGraw Hill; 2014.

## Abusive Head Trauma
- Symptoms include lethargy, feeding difficulty, vomiting, apnea, and seizures

Retinal hemorrhage

Reproduced with permission from Knoop KJ, Stack LB, Storrow AB, et al: The Atlas of Emergency Medicine, 4th ed. New York, NY: McGraw Hill; 2016. Photo contributor: Rees W. Sheppard, MD.

Subdural hematoma

Reproduced with permission from Knoop KJ, Stack LB, Storrow AB, et al: The Atlas of Emergency Medicine, 4th ed. New York, NY: McGraw Hill; 2016. Photo contributor: Cincinnati Children's Hospital Medical Center.

## Diagnosis:
- Skeletal survey
- Ophthalmological exam for retinal hemorrhages
- Noncontrast CT
- STI testing

Reproduced with permission from Knoop KJ, Stack LB, Storrow AB, et al: The Atlas of Emergency Medicine, 4th ed. New York, NY: McGraw Hill; 2016. Photo contributor: Kathi L. Makoroff, MD.

## Treatment:
- Document injuries
- Notify Child Protective Services
- Consider hospitalization

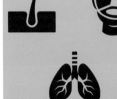 

# Chronic Granulomatous Disease

## Description

- X-linked (2/3 patients) or recessive (1/3 patients) disease marked by deficient superoxide production by PMNs and macrophages

## Presentation (Chronic Infections)

Skin

Pulmonary

GI

UTI

## Diagnosis

Nitroblue tetrazolium test

## Infectious Agents

Catalase + Organisms

## Treatment

 **Bone marrow transplant**

**Antibiotic therapy TMP-SMX / IFN-γ**

# Clavicular Fracture/Osgood-Schlatter Disease

| Clavicular Fracture | Osgood-Schlatter Disease |
|---|---|

## Clinical Presentation

| Etiology: Birth trauma and fall on shoulder | Etiology: Overuse apophysitis of tibial tubercle |
|---|---|
|  Pain, exacerbated by arm movement |  Knee pain worsened by trauma/activity |
|  Crepitus |  Pain worst with quadriceps contraction |
|  Swelling |  Limp or impaired activity |
|  Visible bulge and bruising |  Adolescents with recent growth spurt |

## Imaging

Midshaft clavicular fracture in a 15-year-old girl who slipped on ice

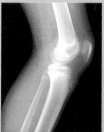

Reproduced with permission from Sherman SC: Emergency Orthopedics: The Extremities, 8th ed. New York, NY: McGraw Hill; 2019.

Plain radiographs can show sclerosis and fragmentation of the tibial tubercle (arrow) with soft tissue swelling

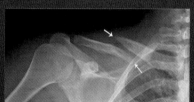

Reproduced with permission from Tehranzadeh J: Basic Musculoskeletal Imaging. New York, NY: McGraw Hill; 2014.

**!** Most patients do not require imaging for diagnosis. Used to exclude other conditions (fracture, tumor, osteomyelitis)

## Treatment

| | |
|---|---|
|  Nondisplaced/minimally displaced fracture: Sling and analgesics |  Decreased activity for 2-3 months or until asymptomatic |
|  Completely displaced fracture (>1 bone width): Possible surgical repair |  Ice and NSAIDs for pain/swelling control |
|  Open fracture or neurovascular compromise: Emergent orthopedic referral |  Physical therapy that involves stretching and strengthening of quadriceps muscles |
|  Displaced fractures can cause brachial plexus/subclavian vein injury | Neoprene brace for symptomatic relief |

# Coarctation of the Aorta

## Pathophysiology

Aortic narrowing near the ductus arteriosus

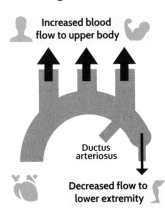

**Increased blood flow to upper body**

Ductus arteriosus

**Decreased flow to lower extremity**

## Associations

 Bicuspid aortic valve

Turner's syndrome

Berry aneurysms

## Sequelae

 Heart failure

Cerebral hemorrhage (Berry aneurysms)

Aortic rupture

## Presentation

 **Upper extremity**
High BP
**Lower extremity**
Delayed pulses
and lower BP

Lower extremity claudication, syncope, epistaxis, and headache may be present

 **Rib notching on chest film**
With age, intercostal arteries enlarge for collateral circulation and erode ribs

## Management

 PGEs to maintain PDA

Surgical repair

Monitoring for sequelae

# Combined Immunodeficiencies
## Disorders of B- and T-cell function

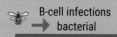 B-cell infections → bacterial

T-cell infections → fungal and viral

## Ataxia-Telangiectasia

- Defective *ATM* gene—Codes for DNA repair enzymes
- Autosomal recessive

## SCID
**S**evere **C**ombined **I**mmuno**d**eficiency

- Lack of B- and T-cells caused by a defect in stem cell maturation and adenosine deaminase deficiency
- Autosomal recessive or x-linked recessive

## Wiskott–Aldrich Syndrome

- Defective *WAS* gene—Relays signals to the actin cytoskeleton
- X-linked recessive

### Diagnosis

↓ **LOW** IgA
Lymphopenia predominantly affecting T lymphocytes

↑ **HIGH** AFP

↓ **LOW** absolute lymphocyte count
**LOW** CD3+ T-cells
**LOW** or absent T-cell proliferative response to mitogens
Hypogammaglobulinemia

↑ **HIGH** IgE and IgA

↓ **LOW** IgM
**LOW** number and function of T-cells
Thrombocytopenia with small platelet volume

### Clinical findings

Ig**A** deficiency (recurrent sinopulmonary infections)

Spider **A**ngioma (telangiectasia)

Cerebellar **A**taxia

- Severe, recurrent infections
- Chronic mucocutaneous candidiasis
- Persistent diarrhea
- Absent thymic shadow and discernible peripheral lymphoid tissue

**T**hrombocytopenic Purpura

**E**czema

**TIE**

**I**nfections (encapsulated organisms and opportunistic infections)

- Increased incidence of lymphoreticular malignancies and adenocarcinoma

- Increased incidence of EBV-associated malignancies

### Treatment

- IVIG and antimicrobials as needed
- Limit radiation exposure

- IVIG and antimicrobials as needed
- Transplantation

- IVIG, platelet transfusions, and antimicrobials as needed
- Transplantation

**LIVE vaccines contraindicated! (MMR, varicella, rotavirus, oral polio, BCG, intranasal influenza)**

# Congenital Adrenal Hyperplasia

(The hat of the kidney)

## ⌛ Physiology

**Mutations:**

**95%** 21-hydroxylase deficiency
- 17-OHP —| 11-deoxycortisol

**~5%** { 11β-hydroxylase
17α-hydroxylase

**Pathologic Outcome**

⬇ Cortisol synthesis

↓

⬆ ACTH synthesis

↓

⬆ Adrenal stimulation

↓

⬆ Androgens

## 👤 Presentation

Genitalia:
- Females: Clitoral enlargement, labial fusion, formation of urogenital sinus
- Males: Normal appearing

Salt-Losing Adrenal Crisis:
- Usually at 10-20 days of life
- Hyponatremia, hyperkalemia, failure to thrive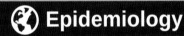

## 🌍 Epidemiology

- Prevalence: 1 in 15,000
- 2/3: "salt-wasting"
- 1/3: "nonsalt wasting" AKA "simple virilizing"

## ☑ Diagnosis

- Newborn screening for 21-OHD showing elevated serum concentration of 17-OHP (usually >3500 ng/dL)
- False-positive possible in premature and sick infants
- Adrenal ultrasound (>4 mm)

## 🧰 Treatment

Adrenal Crisis:
- Treat hypotension, hypoglycemia, and electrolyte abnormalities
- Stress doses of hydrocortisone until patient is stable and feeding normally

Chronic Treatment:
- Glucocorticoid (Hydrocortisone)
- Mineralocorticoid (Fludrocortisone)
- Sodium chloride supplements

# Congenital Malformations

## Congenital Diaphragmatic Hernia

Defect of the pleuroperitoneal membrane leading to pulmonary hypoplasia

| **Presentation** | **Management** |
|---|---|
| Respiratory distress | CXR shows bowel in thorax |
| Bowel sounds in chest | Surgical repair ~3-4 days of life |

## Tracheoesophageal Fistula & Esophageal Atresia

Most commonly EA with distal TE fistula (85%)

### Presentation

| | |
|---|---|
|  Laryngospasm and cyanosis |  Drooling/emesis with feeds |
| Poly-hydramnios | NG tube curls in esophagus |

 **Initiate VACTERL Workup**

## Duodenal Atresia

**Presentation**
Bilious vomiting
Double Bubble sign
1. Duodenum
2. Stomach
**Associations**
Down's syndrome

Reproduced with permission from Brunicardi FC, Andersen DK, Billiar TR, et al: Schwartz's Principles of Surgery, 10th ed. New York, NY; McGraw Hill; 2015.

## Jejunal & Ileal Atresia

### Presentation
Bilious vomiting

### Pathophysiology

 >>  >>

| Disruption of mesenteric vessels | Ischemic necrosis | Segmental resorption "apple peel" |

## Anal Atresia

**Diagnosis**
Failure to stool in 24 hours
No anus noted on exam

 **Initiate VACTERL Workup**

## VACTERL Syndrome

Vertebral anomalies
Anal atresia
Cardiac defects
TracheoEsophageal fistula
Renal anomalies
Limb deformities

# Croup
## Viral Laryngotracheobronchitis

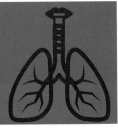

## Etiology

- Viral infection of upper airway
- Most common causes are parainfluenza viruses, esp. paramyxovirus
- Occurs in children aged 6 months to 3 years
- Peaks at age 1-2 years and in the fall/winter months ❄

## Presentation

Often begins with mild URI symptoms such as congestion and cough

Progresses to include:
1. **Inspiratory stridor**
2. **Harsh, "seal-like," barking cough**
3. Hoarse voice

*Clinical Hints*:
→ Onset is 1-3 days
→ Symptoms worse at night
→ Symptoms improve with cold air

## Diagnosis

**Croup is a clinical diagnosis**

Look for the above patient presentation and characteristics

AP CXR can help if uncertain
→ Subglottic tracheal narrowing ie, the **"steeple sign"**

*Clinical Hint*: Look for signs of respiratory distress, such as sternal retractions

Reproduced with permission from Knoop KJ, Stack LB, Storrow AB, et al: The Atlas of Emergency Medicine, 4th ed. New York, NY: McGraw Hill; 2016. Photo contributor: Stephen W. Corbett, MD.

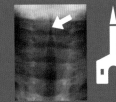

Reproduced with permission from Tintinalli J, Ma O, Yealy DM, et al: Tintinalli's Emergency Medicine: A Comprehensive Study Guide. 9th ed. New York, NY: McGraw Hill; 2020. Photo contributor: W. McAlister, MD, Washington University School of Medicine, St. Louis, MO.

## Treatment

**Based on severity of illness, escalating**

**Mild-Moderate:**

 Corticosteroids

**Severe:** Plus treatment with

🔲 Nebulized racemic epinephrine
🔲 Supplemental oxygen

**Severe, Refractory:** Plus treatment with

📅 Inpatient admission
🔆 Possible intubation

# Cryptorchidism

## Definition

Abdominal - ● - Inguinal
Suprascrotal - ● - Normal

- Undescended testis
- Can be located in:
  - abdomen
  - inguinal canal
  - high scrotum
- Affects 2-4% of male infants

## Risk factors

- Prematurity
- Low birth weight
- Presence of other genital abnormalities
  - eg, hypospadias
- Family history of cryptorchidism

## Associations

- Impaired spermatogenesis
  - sperm develops best at cooler temps
- Increased risk of germ cell tumors
- Low inhibin B, high FSH, high LH

## Treatment

- Many resolve on own by 6 months
- Surgery to permanently fix testes to scrotum
- Goal to perform surgery in first 6-12 months of life to optimize fertility
- Still at increased risk for germ cell tumor after surgery, but reduced risk if surgery completed prior to 1 year of life

# Developmental Dysplasia of the Hip

## Etiology

- Shallow, poorly developed acetabulum due to excessive uterine packing
- Leads to dysplasia, subluxation, and possible dislocation of the hip
- Seen in newborns, especially **females**

**Risk Factors**
First born
Breech presentation
Oligohydramnios
Large for gestational age
Multiple gestation
Family history

## Clinical Presentation

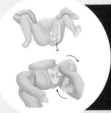

 Found with **Barlow (dislocation)** and **Ortolani (reduction)** maneuvers during newborn screening

 **Left sided** most common, followed by bilateral, then right sided

## Diagnosis

 Galeazzi test: Leg length discrepancy with both knees and hips flexed
Asymmetric inguinal folds

 **Hip ultrasound if <4 months old**
X-rays if >4 months old

 Screening ultrasound for breech babies when 4-6 weeks old

Reproduced with permission from Hay WW, Levin MJ, Absug MJ, et al: Current Diagnosis & Treatment: Pediatrics, 25th ed. New York, NY: McGraw Hill; 2020.

## Treatment

 **Pavlik harness** if <6 months old (abduction bracing)

 Spica cast if 6-15 months old, open reduction then spica cast if >15 months old

 Watch out for joint contractures and a**vascular necrosis** of femoral head

# Developmental Milestones
## 2 to 15 months

🏃 **Gross Motor**   ✏️ **Fine Motor**
👤 **Language**   ✋ **Social/Self-Care**

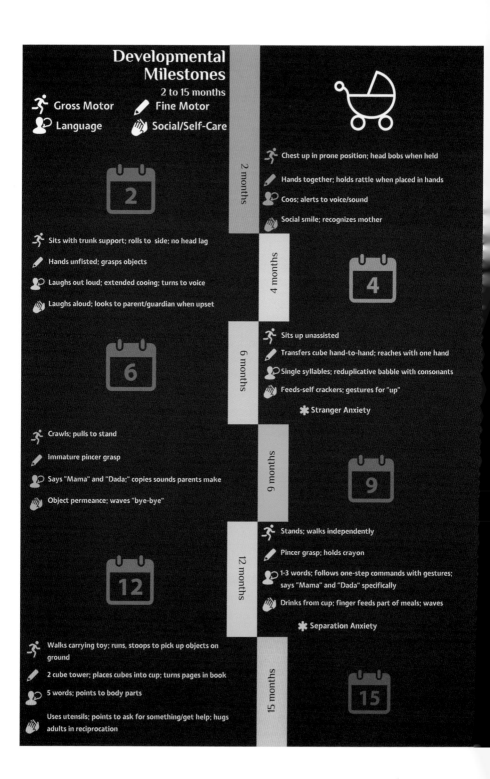

**2 months**

🏃 Chest up in prone position; head bobs when held

✏️ Hands together; holds rattle when placed in hands

👤 Coos; alerts to voice/sound

✋ Social smile; recognizes mother

**4 months**

🏃 Sits with trunk support; rolls to side; no head lag

✏️ Hands unfisted; grasps objects

👤 Laughs out loud; extended cooing; turns to voice

✋ Laughs aloud; looks to parent/guardian when upset

**6 months**

🏃 Sits up unassisted

✏️ Transfers cube hand-to-hand; reaches with one hand

👤 Single syllables; reduplicative babble with consonants

✋ Feeds-self crackers; gestures for "up"

✱ **Stranger Anxiety**

**9 months**

🏃 Crawls; pulls to stand

✏️ Immature pincer grasp

👤 Says "Mama" and "Dada;" copies sounds parents make

✋ Object permeance; waves "bye-bye"

**12 months**

🏃 Stands; walks independently

✏️ Pincer grasp; holds crayon

👤 1-3 words; follows one-step commands with gestures; says "Mama" and "Dada" specifically

✋ Drinks from cup; finger feeds part of meals; waves

✱ **Separation Anxiety**

**15 months**

🏃 Walks carrying toy; runs, stoops to pick up objects on ground

✏️ 2 cube tower; places cubes into cup; turns pages in book

👤 5 words; points to body parts

✋ Uses utensils; points to ask for something/get help; hugs adults in reciprocation

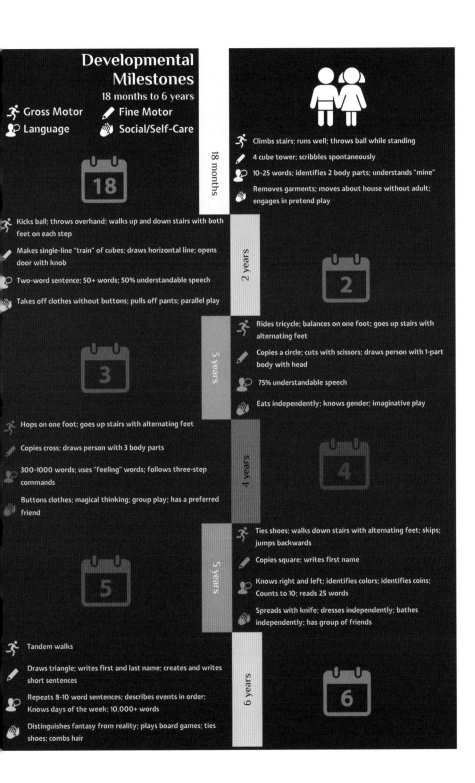

# Developmental Milestones
## 18 months to 6 years

🏃 **Gross Motor**  ✏️ **Fine Motor**
👤 **Language**  👏 **Social/Self-Care**

**18 months**
- 🏃 Climbs stairs; runs well; throws ball while standing
- ✏️ 4 cube tower; scribbles spontaneously
- 👤 10-25 words; identifies 2 body parts; understands "mine"
- 👏 Removes garments; moves about house without adult; engages in pretend play

**2 years**
- 🏃 Kicks ball; throws overhand; walks up and down stairs with both feet on each step
- ✏️ Makes single-line "train" of cubes; draws horizontal line; opens door with knob
- 👤 Two-word sentence; 50+ words; 50% understandable speech
- 👏 Takes off clothes without buttons; pulls off pants; parallel play

**3 years**
- 🏃 Rides tricycle; balances on one foot; goes up stairs with alternating feet
- ✏️ Copies a circle; cuts with scissors; draws person with 1-part body with head
- 👤 75% understandable speech
- 👏 Eats independently; knows gender; imaginative play

**4 years**
- 🏃 Hops on one foot; goes up stairs with alternating feet
- ✏️ Copies cross; draws person with 3 body parts
- 👤 300-1000 words; uses "feeling" words; follows three-step commands
- 👏 Buttons clothes; magical thinking; group play; has a preferred friend

**5 years**
- 🏃 Ties shoes; walks down stairs with alternating feet; skips; jumps backwards
- ✏️ Copies square; writes first name
- 👤 Knows right and left; identifies colors; identifies coins; Counts to 10; reads 25 words
- 👏 Spreads with knife; dresses independently; bathes independently; has group of friends

**6 years**
- 🏃 Tandem walks
- ✏️ Draws triangle; writes first and last name; creates and writes short sentences
- 👤 Repeats 8-10 word sentences; describes events in order; Knows days of the week; 10,000+ words
- 👏 Distinguishes fantasy from reality; plays board games; ties shoes; combs hair

# Epiglottitis

## Etiology

 Cellulitis of the epiglottis, aryepiglottic folds, and other tissues

 Prior to immunizations, *H. influenzae* Type B most common cause

 Common causes now *Strep* species, nontypeable *H. influenzae,* and viral agents

 In immunocompromised hosts, caused by *Pseudomonas, Serratia* spp, *Enterobacter* spp, and *Candida* species

 Other causes: Thermal injury, foreign body ingestion, caustic ingestion, and post transplant lymphoproliferative disorder

## Clinical Manifestations

 Acute-onset high fever (102-104°F)

 Dysphagia

 Muffled voice

 Cyanosis

 Drooling

 Leaning forward in tripod position with neck hyperextended and chin protruding

## Diagnosis

 Diagnosed by clinical impression. DDx includes croup, tracheitis, retropharyngeal abscess, and peritonsillar abscess

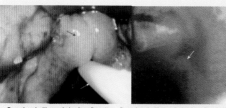

Reproduced with permission from Brunette DD: Extraordinary Cases in Emergency Medicine. New York, NY: McGraw Hill; 2019.

Reproduced with permission from Zaoutis LB, Chiang VW: Comprehensive Pediatric Hospital Medicine, 2nd ed. New York, NY: McGraw Hill; 2018.

Definitive diagnosis made via direct fiberoptic visualization of a cherry-red swollen epiglottis and arytenoids

Lateral film shows "thumbprint sign," swollen epiglottis obliterating the valleculae

 **Need to secure airway. DO NOT examine the throat without anesthesia or ENT present**

## Treatment

 With signs of near-total airway obstruction, airway control should PRECEDE diagnostic evaluation

 Start with bag mask ventilation with 100% oxygen

 Intubation or tracheostomy if needed for further airway control

 IV antibiotics (ceftriaxone or cefuroxime)

 Complications: Epiglottic abscess, delayed airway obstruction, sepsis, and cervical adenitis

# Failure to Thrive

## Background

- Infants may lose 5-10% of birth weight over the first few days of life
- Should return to birth weight by 14 days
- Infants should be 2x birth weight by 4-5 months, 3x by 1 year, 4x by 2 years

## Clinical Manifestations

- Fall off weight curve → fall of height curve → fall of head circumference curve
- Bony deformities (Rickets)
- Drooling
- Delayed closure of fontanelle
- Sparse hair
- Candidiasis
- Delayed tooth eruption
- Chronic diaper rash
- Hypotension
- Oral motor dysfunction

## Etiology

### Organic

 Cystic fibrosis

 Congenital heart disease

 Celiac sprue

 Pyloric stenosis

 Chronic infection (HIV)

 Severe GERD

### Inorganic

Poverty

 Inaccurate mixing of formula

Maternal depression

Neglect/Abuse

## Diagnosis/Treatment

- Careful/dietary history and close observation of mother–infant interactions
- CBC, CRP, ESR, UA, CMP, blood and urine cultures
- Chest X-ray to assess for cardiopulmonary disease
- Hospitalization if evidence of neglect or severe malnourishment

## Growth Chart

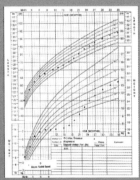

Reproduced with permission from Centers for Disease Control and Prevention, National Center for Health Statistics.

Defined as persistent weight <5th percentile for age or falling off the curve (ie, crossing 2 major percentile lines)

# Febrile Seizures

## ☑ Criteria

- A convulsion associated with temperature greater than 38°C
- A child between 6 months and 6 years (majority 12-18 months)
- Not due to other causes such as CNS infection or inflammation or acute systemic abnormality
- No history of previous afebrile seizures

## ☼ Pearls

- More common with viral infections than bacterial
- HHV-6 and influenza are most common
-  Febrile status epilepticus: 30+ minutes of continuous or intermittent seizures without neurologic recovery

## Simple    vs    Complex

**Simple**

- Generalized tonic-clonic is most common
- <15 minutes (median duration is 3-4 minutes)
- Does not recur in 24 hours
- Return to baseline quickly
- Facial and respiratory muscle commonly involved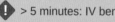

**Complex**

- Focal onset
- Prolonged (>15 minutes)

OR
- Recurrent within 24 hours

Children are often...
- Younger
- More likely to have abnormal development

## 🔋 Treatment

- Supportive
- Treat fever with antipyretics and reassurance for parents
- ⚠ > 5 minutes: IV benzos to abort seizure
- Most children do not require hospital admission once they return to baseline
- Current management does not recommend labs, imaging, or EEG for a simple febrile seizure

# Genetic Disorders

| Fragile X | Prader–Willi | Friedreich Ataxia |
|---|---|---|

## Clinical Features

| Fragile X | Prader–Willi | Friedreich Ataxia |
|---|---|---|
| • Intellectual disability<br>• Autism spectrum disorder<br>• Mitral valve prolapse<br>• **Macroorchidism**<br>• **Large everted ears**<br>• Long and narrow face with prominent forehead and chin **(prognathism)** | • Failure to thrive in infancy<br>• Intellectual disability<br>• Behavior problems<br>• Short stature with small hands and feet<br>• **Hyperphagia with obesity;** onset 6 months to 6 years<br>• **Hypotonia**<br>• **Hypogonadism** | • Diabetes mellitus<br>• Kyphoscoliosis<br>• **Hypertrophic cardiomyopathy**<br>• Neurologic dysfunction— dysarthric speech, nystagmus, weakness, sensory loss **ataxia** |

## Genetics

| Fragile X | Prader–Willi | Friedreich Ataxia |
|---|---|---|
| • X-linked dominant<br>• Trinucleotide repeat disorder (CGG) affecting the methylation & expression of the *FMR1* gene | • Mutation or deletion at 15q11-q13<br>• Paternal chromosome<br>• Imprinting disorder | • Autosomal recessive<br>• Trinucleotide repeat expansion (GAA) causing abnormal frataxin protein |

 Images

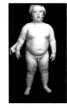

# Group A *Streptococcus* and Rheumatic Fever

## Strep Throat

### ☼ Physiology:
- Infection of the oropharynx with Group A *Streptococcus* (*Streptococcus pyogenes*)
- Gram-positive *cocci* in chains
- β-hemolytic on sheep blood agar (complete clearing)

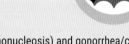

### 🔬 Clinical Features & Diagnosis:
- Sore throat and painful swallowing with fever
- Centor criteria (1 point for each)
  - Fever >38°C
  - Tender anterior cervical lymphadenopathy
  - Lack of cough
  - Tonsillar exudates
- Differential includes viral pharyngitis (including mononucleosis) and gonorrhea/chlamydia
- Diagnosis via rapid strep antigen test and throat culture

### 💊 Treatment:
- Penicillin or amoxicillin (erythromycin or azithromycin if penicillin allergy)

Untreated *streptococcal* pharyngitis

## Rheumatic Fever

### ☼ Physiology:
- Molecular mimicry causing autoantibodies to cardiac valvular tissue
- Genetic predisposition

### 🔬 Clinical Features & Major Diagnostic Criteria:

**J** oints Inflammatory polyarthritis

**♥** heart Carditis and mitral valve disease

**N** odes Painless subcutaneous nodules

**E** rythema marginatum Pink macules & central clearing

**S** ydenham's chorea Dance-like movements—head & arms

### 💊 Treatment:
- Penicillin or amoxicillin to treat the underlying infection
- Aspirin to reduce inflammation
- Long-term penicillin prophylaxis to prevent recurrence

# Hirschsprung's Disease
## Congenital Megacolon

## Etiology

- Failure of migration of inhibitory neural plexus in distal colon

- Rectum with increased sphincter tone

### Associations
Males>Females
Waardenburg syndrome
Down's syndrome
MEN 2

## Clinical Presentation

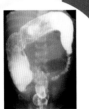

 **Failure to pass meconium** in newborn presentation, chronic constipation in childhood presentation

 Distended abdomen

 10% present with diarrhea from chronic constipation

## Diagnosis

- **Squirt sign:** Explosive diarrhea on DRE

- X-ray/barium enema: Dilation of normal colon with transition point

- **Rectal suction biopsy:** Aganglionic

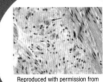

## Treatment

 Surgical resection of denervated colon

 Watch out for enterocolitis, diarrhea, constipation, obstruction, or perforation

Enlarged colon
Nerves
No nerves
Collapsed rectum

# _Infant Hypotonia_

| Botulism  | Spinal Muscular Atrophy | Myotonic Dystrophy |
|---|---|---|

## Clinical Presentation

| Classic triad: (1) afebrile; (2) symmetrical, flaccid, descending paralysis with prominent bulbar palsies; (3) clear sensorium | Bilateral proximal muscle weakness due to degeneration of anterior horn cells | Muscle weakness, myotonia, hypogonadism, cardiac conduction abnormalities, and cataracts |
|---|---|---|

 Potential progression to respiratory failure

##  Diagnosis and Workup

| Clinical signs in infant less than 12 months old | Genetic testing  | Genetic testing  |
|---|---|---|

## Management

Supportive care and potential ventilator use

IV human botulism immunoglobulin

 **Contraindication in Botulism** — Aminoglycosides and clindamycin may exacerbate neuromuscular blockade

# Inherited Metabolic Disorders
## Lysosomal Storage Diseases:

| Fabry | Gaucher | Krabbe |
|---|---|---|

### Clinical Features

| Fabry | Gaucher | Krabbe |
|---|---|---|
| • Early disease—**Peripheral neuropathy, angiokeratomas, hypohidrosis**<br><br>• Late disease—Renal failure, cardiovascular events (stroke, MI) | • **Pancytopenia**<br>• Hepatosplenomegaly<br>• Avascular necrosis of femur, osteoporosis, **bone crisis**<br>• **"Crinkled tissue paper"** macrophages<br><br>• Infantile form—Early rapid neurological decline<br>• Adult—Normal life span, no brain involvement | • Developmental delay<br>• **Optic atrophy**<br>• Spasticity<br>• Peripheral neuropathy<br>• **Globoid cells**<br>• Destruction of oligodendrocytes |

### Deficient Enzyme

| Fabry | Gaucher | Krabbe |
|---|---|---|
| • α-Galactosidase A | • β-Glucocerebrosidase | • Galactosylceramidase |

### Accumulated Substrate

| Fabry | Gaucher | Krabbe |
|---|---|---|
| • Ceramide trihexoside | • Glucocerebroside | • Galactocerebroside |

### Inheritance

| Fabry | Gaucher | Krabbe |
|---|---|---|
| • X-linked recessive | • Autosomal recessive | • Autosomal recessive |

 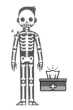

# Inherited Metabolic Disorders

 ## Lysosomal Storage Diseases:

## Hurler Syndrome          Hunter Syndrome

###  Clinical Features

| | |
|---|---|
| • Coarse facies | • Shared features of Hurler syndrome; milder symptoms |
| • Umbilical and inguinal hernias | |
| • Hepatosplenomegaly | • **No corneal clouding** |
| • Skeletal and cardiac abnormalities | • **Aggressive hyperactive behavior** |
| • Cognitive decline and hydrocephalus | |
| • Recurrent respiratory infections and airway obstruction | • **Pearly skin papules** |
| • **Corneal clouding** | |

Reproduced with permission from Schaefer GB, Thompson JN: Medical Genetics: An Integrated Approach. New York, NY: McGraw Hill; 2014.

###  Deficient Enzyme

| | |
|---|---|
| • α-L-iduronidase | • Iduronidase-2-sulfate |

###  Accumulated Substrate

| | |
|---|---|
| • Heparan sulfate | • Heparan sulfate |
| • Dermatan sulfate | • Dermatan sulfate |

###  Inheritance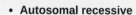

| | |
|---|---|
| • **Autosomal recessive** | • **X-linked** recessive |

  A **HUrLEr** with **cloudy vision** can't see where he's throwing

 A **HUNTER** has **clear sight** to **aggressively** aim for the **X**

# Inherited Metabolic Disorders
## Lysosomal Storage Diseases:

## Tay–Sachs

## Niemann–Pick

###  Clinical Features

- Progressive neurodegeneration
- **"Onion skin"** lysosomes
- Hyperreflexia
- Hyperacusis
- Seizures
- **NO hepatomegaly**
- **Cherry red macula**

- Progressive neurodegeneration
- **Foam cells** (lipid-laden macrophages)
- **Hepatomegaly**
- **Cherry red macula**

Reproduced with permission from
Lueder G: Pediatric Practice Ophthalmology.
New York, NY: McGraw Hill; 2011.

###  Deficient Enzyme

- Hexosaminidase A

- Sphingomyelinase

###  Accumulated Substrate

- GM2 ganglioside

- Sphingomyelin cholesterol

###  Inheritance

- Autosomal recessive

- Autosomal recessive

Tay-Sa**X** lacks
He**X**osaminidase A

**No man picks** (**Niemann–Pick**)
his nose with a
**finger** (**Sphing**omyelinase)

# Inherited Metabolic Disorders: PKU, Homocystinuria, MLD

| Homocystinuria | Phenylketonuria | Metachromatic Leukodystrophy |
|---|---|---|
| **Clinical Features** | | |
| • Intellectual disability<br>• Osteoporosis<br>• Fair complexion<br>• Marfanoid body habitus<br>• **Hypercoagulability**<br>• **Lens subluxation**<br>• Dietary supplement with B6, B12, folate | • Intellectual disability<br>• Vomiting and growth retardation<br>• Seizures and athetosis<br>• Fair complexion<br>• Eczema<br>• **Musty body odor**<br>• **Avoid aspartame** | • **Progressive ataxia—** Muscle weakness, difficulty walking<br>• Dementia |
| **Deficient Enzyme** | | |
| • Cystathionine synthase | • Phenylalanine hydroxylase | • Arylsulfatase A |
| **Accumulated Substrate** | | |
| • Homocysteine | • Phenylalanine | • Cerebroside sulfate |
| **Inheritance** | | |
| • Autosomal recessive | • Autosomal recessive | • Autosomal recessive |

Homocysteine in urine
Osteoporosis
Marfanoid habitus
Ocular changes
CV effects
kYphosis
-stinuria

Pale
Krazy (neurological abnormalities)
Unpleasant smell

Muscle
Loss
Dementia

# Intoeing

## Metatarsus Adductus

- Inward torsion of mid- or forefoot; hindfoot unaffected
- Most common cause age ≤1 year
- **Flexible**: Able to adduct forefoot to midline, observation
- **Rigid**: Corrective casting

## Talipes Equinovarus

- Also known as clubfoot
- Forefoot adduction and varus of calcaneus, talus, and midfoot
- May be congenital, positional, or syndromic
- Immediate serial casting and surgery if unresolved

## Internal Tibial Torsion

- Medial rotation of tibia
- Most common cause age 1-3 years
- Measure with thigh/foot angle
- No treatment, resolves with normal growth

## Internal Femoral Torsion

- Also known as femoral anteversion
- Increased internal rotation of hip
- Most common cause age ≥3 years
- Associated with W-sitting
- Observation, rarely requires surgical correction

# Intussusception

Telescoping of proximal bowel segment into distal segment

## Pathophysiology

A pathologic lead point causes telescoping of proximal bowel segment into distal segment

Leads to vascular compromise of the bowel

## Associations

Viral enteritis & hypertrophy of Peyer's patches

Lymphoma

Henoch–Schönlein purpura

Meckel's diverticulum

## Presentation

Intermittent abdominal pain with knees drawn to abdomen

Currant jelly stools

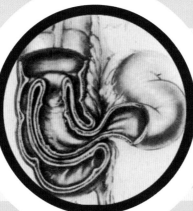

Reproduced with permission from Doherty GM: Current Diagnosis & Treatment Surgery, 15th ed. New York, NY: McGraw Hill; 2020.

## Physical Exam

Palpable mass, typically in right upper quadrant

## Abdominal Ultrasound

Bowel within bowel creates a target-like mass on ultrasound

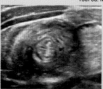

Reproduced with permission from Elsayes KM, Oldham SA: Introduction to Diagnostic Radiology. New York, NY: McGraw Hill; 2014.

## Management

Contrast enema (air or barium) for reduction

Surgical intervention indicated if enema reduction fails or for signs of peritonitis/bowel perforation

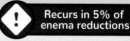

**!** Recurs in 5% of enema reductions

Most common cause of intestinal obstruction in children ages 6 months to 2 years old

# Job Syndrome
# (Hyper-IgE)

## Description

 Defect in the chemotaxis of neutrophils

## F.A.T.E.D.

Coarse
**F**acies

**A**bscesses
(*S. aureus*)

Retained
Baby **T**eeth

Hyper-Ig**E**
(Eosinophilia)

**D**ermatitis

## Genetics

Autosomal **Dominant** (70%)

Autosomal Recessive (30%)

## Treatment

 **IVIG**

 **Penicillinase-Resistant Antibiotics**

# Juvenile Idiopathic Arthritis

## Clinical Features

- Joint pain, swelling, warmth, and decreased motion
- Salmon-colored macular rash
- Daily fever
- Morning stiffness

## Subtypes

### Pauciarticular
- 1-4 joints
- Peak age <6 years
- Uveitis is common

### Systemic Onset
- 1 to >5 joints
- Peak age 2-4 years
- Fever, rash, lymphadenopathy, hepatosplenomegaly, serositis

### RF+ Polyarticular
- ≥5 joints
- Peak age 9-12 years
- 10% with rheumatoid nodules

### RF– Polyarticular
- ≥5 joints
- Peak age 6-7 years

## Diagnosis

- <u>NO</u> 1 lab test to confirm or exclude
- Rule out other causes (infection, malignancy)
- Lab findings: Elevation of acute-phase reactants and anemia of chronic disease
- Elevated ANA in 40-85%; mostly with polyarticular RF- and pauciarticular disease
- RF+ typically in polyarticular disease and when onset of disease occurs in older children

## Treatment

NSAIDs
Glucocorticosteroids
DMARDs (Disease-Modifying Antirheumatic Drugs)
Ophthalmology follow-up

## Complications

- Uveitis
- Pericarditis/pleuritis/peritonitis
- Poor weight gain and growth
- Rheumatoid nodules
- Macrophage activation syndrome

**BUZZWORDS:** Salmon-colored, macular, evanescent rash + fever + morning joint pain

Reproduced with permission from Kane KS, Nambudiri VE, Stratigos AJ: Color Atlas & Synopsis of Pediatric Dermatology, 3rd ed. New York, NY: McGraw Hill; 2017.

# Kawasaki Disease

Multisystemic, acute vasculitis

## 🔗 Associations

Age <5
Asian & Pacific
Islander descent

## 📋 Diagnostic

More than 5 days of fever and at least
4 of the following:

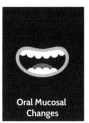
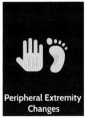
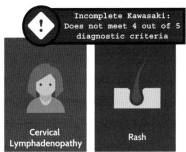

| Conjunctivitis | Oral Mucosal Changes | Peripheral Extremity Changes | Cervical Lymphadenopathy | Rash |
|---|---|---|---|---|
| Bilateral Nonexudative | Strawberry tongue Cracked lips | Edema & induration Red & desquamating palms/soles | >1.5 cm Tender Unilateral | Primarily truncal Polymorphous |

**Incomplete Kawasaki:** Does not meet 4 out of 5 diagnostic criteria

## Lab Findings 🧪

Anemia
Leukocytosis
ESR and CRP elevated
Thrombocytosis
Elevated transaminases
Sterile pyuria

## ⚠️ Complications

Coronary artery
aneurysms &
myocardial infarction

- Monitor with echocardiograms at presentation
- If present, anticoagulate

## Treatment 💉

High-dose aspirin
Intravenous
immunoglobulin (IVIG)

# Lead Poisoning

## Neurobehavioral Symptoms

 Irritability

 Hyperactivity or apathy

 Difficulty concentrating

## Neurologic Symptoms

 Peripheral neuropathy (wrist/foot drop)

 Tremor

 Paresthesias

## GI Symptoms

 Intermittent abdominal pain

 Vomiting

 Constipation

## Systemic Symptoms

 Fatigue

 Weight loss

 Arthralgias

 **Acute encephalopathy (usually levels >70 μg/dL): ↑ ICP, vomiting, confusion, seizures, and coma**

## Diagnosis

 Initial screen with fingerstick test at age 1-2

 Obtain serum lead level if abnormal

Basophilic stippling (arrows) seen on peripheral smear

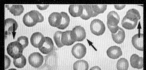

Reproduced with permission from van Dijk HA, Fred HL: Images of memorable cases: case 81. Connexions Web site. December 3, 2008. Available at https://cnx.org/contents/MZa_Ph4e@4/Images-of-Memorable-Cases-Case

 **Impaired intelligence and neurodevelopmental outcomes can be present at levels as low as 10 μg/dL**

## Treatment 💊

 <45 μg/dL and asymptomatic: Retest; Remove sources of lead exposure (most commonly lead paint from houses pre-1950)

 45-69 μg/dL: Chelation therapy (inpatient EDTA or outpatient DMSA)

 ≥70 μg/dL: Chelation therapy (inpatient EDTA + British anti-Lewisite)

# Legg-Calvé-Perthes Disease

Idiopathic avascular necrosis of the proximal femoral epiphysis

## Clinical Presentation

- Presents between 3 and 12 years of age; peak ages 5-7
- 4:1 male predominance
- Insidious pain and/or limp and activity-related pain
- Referred pain to anterolateral thigh or knee
- Trendelenburg gait
- Decreased hip abduction & internal rotation

## Diagnosis

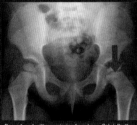

Reproduced with permission from Legg-Calvé-Perthes disease. Case contributed by Assoc Prof Frank Gaillard. December 25, 2009. https://radiopaedia.org/cases/legg-calv-perthes-disease-1

- X-ray
- May be _normal_ initially
- Progression shows joint space widening, femoral head flattening
- Can be detected earlier on bone scan and MRI

## Complications

- Premature arthritis
- Prognosis depends on:
  1. Child's age at onset (younger, better)
  2. Percentage of affected femoral head

## Management

- Nonsurgical
  - Observation
  - NSAIDs
  - Limited activity
  - Physical therapy
  - Casts and bracing
- Surgical
  - Osteotomy

# Leukocyte Adhesion Deficiency

## Description

Defect in the chemotaxis of leukocytes → Impaired phagocytosis

## Common Infections

Skin

Mucosal

Pulmonary

## Features

Nonpurulent skin infections
Poor wound healing
High WBCs in blood

## Presentation

Newborn with delayed
separation of the umbilical cord

## Treatment

**Bone Marrow Transplant**

# Malrotation with Volvulus

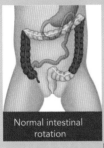

Normal intestinal rotation

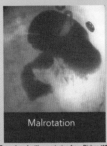

Malrotation

Reproduced with permission from Bishop WP: Pediatric Practice: Gastroenterology. New York, NY: McGraw Hill; 2010.

## Description

- Anomaly of midgut rotation occurring during fetal development

- Malpositioning of bowel (small bowel clumped on the right)

- Formation of fibrous bands (Ladd bands) between cecum and duodenum can cause obstruction

- Twisting of portion of bowel around its mesentery (volvulus) can lead to obstruction and infarction

## Clinical Presentation

- Often presents in 1st month of life
- Abdominal pain and distention
- Bilious emesis
- Blood or mucus in stool

## Diagnosis

- Upper GI series
- Barium contrast enema

## Treatment

- Nasogastric tube placement

- IV fluids for electrolyte replacement

- Emergent surgical correction

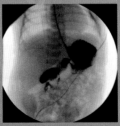

Reproduced with permission from Rozenfeld RA: The PICU Handbook. New York, NY: McGraw Hill; 2018.

- Abnormal location of the ligament of Treitz

- Corkscrew configuration

- Bird's beak sign

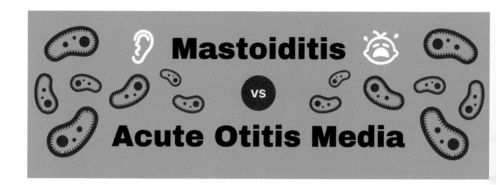

| Mastoiditis | Acute Otitis Media |
|---|---|

 **Presentation**

| Mastoiditis | Acute Otitis Media |
|---|---|
| • Postauricular tenderness, erythema, swelling<br>• Protrusion of the auricle<br>• Otalgia<br>• Fever<br>• Abnormal tympanic membrane (TM)<br>• Otorrhea | • Otalgia/ear-related complaints<br>• Abnormal tympanic membrane<br>• Fever<br>• Irritability<br>• Headache<br>• Nausea/vomiting |

📋 **Diagnosis** 📋

| Mastoiditis | Acute Otitis Media |
|---|---|
| 1. Physical exam findings<br>  ↳ tender, red, edematous mastoid process<br>  ↳ displaced pinna<br><br>2. Elevated WBC count<br>3. CT-A of the temporal bone | 1. Physical exam findings<br>  ↳ purulent middle ear effusion<br>  ↳ bulging, red TM |

🩹 **Treatment** 🩹

| Mastoiditis | Acute Otitis Media |
|---|---|
| 1. IV antibiotics<br>2. Myringotomy drainage<br>3. ENT referral | 1. Oral antibiotics<br>2. Symptom relief (analgesics and antipyretics as needed)<br>3. Recurrent AOM may require tympanostomy tubes |

# Meckel's Diverticulum

## Etiology

- Remnant of vitelline duct (omphalomesenteric duct)
- **True** diverticulum
- Most common congenital anomaly of the small intestine

## Clinical Presentation

 **Painless**, intermittent, bright red blood per rectum (hematochezia)

 Can also cause abdominal pain and mimic appendicitis

Reproduced with permission from Zinner MJ, Ashley SW, Hines OJ: Maingot's Abdominal Operations, 13th ed. New York, NY: McGraw Hill; 2019.

## Rule of 2s

- <2 years old
- <2% of the population
- 2 times more common in males
- 2 inches long
- 2 types of tissue (pancreatic, gastric)
- 2 feet from ileocecal valve

## Diagnosis and Treatment

 Technetium-99 scan

 Treat with **surgical resection**

 Watch out for obstruction (if untreated)

Reproduced with permission from Block J. Jordanov MI, Stack LB, et al: The Atlas of Emergency Radiology. New York, NY: McGraw Hill; 2013.

# Meningitis

## Overview

- Infection of the meninges of the CNS
- Neonates: Group B *streptococcus*, *Escherichia coli*, Listeria
- Infants/children: *Streptococcus pneumoniae*, *Neisseria meningitidis*, *Haemophilus influenzae*
- Adolescents: *Neisseria meningitidis*, *Streptococcus pneumoniae*

## Diagnosis

- Imaging first if concern for potential herniation (coma, papilledema, focal neurologic abnormalities)
- Lumbar puncture for CSF testing: culture, Gram stain, cell count, glucose, protein

## Physical

- Altered mental status
- Focal neurological deficit
- Bulging or full fontanel
- Papilledema
- Petechiae or purpura
- Nuchal rigidity

Kernig sign: Reluctance of knee extension when the hip is flexed
Brudzinski sign: Hips are flexed in response to forced flexion of the neck

## Presentation

Infants:
- Fever or hypothermia
- Lethargy and irritability
- Respiratory distress and apnea
- Poor feeding and vomiting
- Seizure

Older children:
- Fever
- Headache
- Confusion and irritability
- Vomiting
- Neck stiffness and back pain
- Photophobia

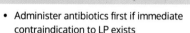

## Treatment

- Administer antibiotics first if immediate contraindication to LP exists
- Neonates <28 days old: Cefotaxime or gentamycin plus ampicillin
- All others: Ceftriaxone and vancomycin
- Consider acyclovir if concern for HSV
- For children with Hib meningitis, adjunctive treatment with dexamethasone may reduce hearing loss
- *Neisseria meningitidis* prophylaxis for close contacts: Rifampin, ciprofloxacin, or ceftriaxone

# Muscular Dystrophy

| Duchenne | Becker | Myotonic |
|---|---|---|

 ## Genetics

| Duchenne | Becker | Myotonic |
|---|---|---|
| • X-linked recessive<br>• Frameshift deletion in dystrophin gene | • X-linked recessive<br>• Nonframeshift deletion in dystrophin gene | • Autosomal dominant<br>• CTG trinucleotide expansion in the *DMPK* gene |

 ## Symptoms

| Duchenne | Becker | Myotonic |
|---|---|---|
| • Age of onset: 2-6 years<br>• Weakness: Proximal → distal limbs and lower limbs → upper limbs<br>• Hip waddling gait, lumbar lordosis, leg pain<br>• Pseudohypertrophy = Calf hypertrophy from fatty infiltration of muscles<br>• Gower maneuver = Use of arms to push into upright position | • Age of onset: 6 years-adulthood<br>• Similar symptoms to Duchenne but milder<br><br><br>**Gower Manuever**<br>Reproduced with permission from Zaoutis LB, Chiang VW: Comprehensive Pediatric Hospital Medicine, 2nd ed. New York, NY: McGraw Hill; 2018. | • Age of onset: Infancy-adulthood<br>• Progressive weakness<br>• Muscle pain<br>• Slowed relaxation of muscles after contraction (myotonia)—Abnormally long handshake<br><br> |

 ## Diagnosis

| Duchenne | Becker | Myotonic |
|---|---|---|
| • Muscle biopsy: <u>Absent</u> dystrophin protein<br>• CK: **Severely** elevated<br>• EMG: Myopathic | • Muscle biopsy: <u>Abnormal</u> dystrophin protein<br>• CK: **Moderately** elevated<br>• EMG: Myopathic | • CK: **Normal-mildly** elevated<br>• EMG: Myotonic |

 ## Complications

| Duchenne | Becker | Myotonic |
|---|---|---|
| • Wheelchair bound by age 12; death in early adulthood<br><br><br>Reproduced with permission from Reisner H. Pathology: A Modern Case Study, 2nd ed. New York, NY: McGraw Hill; 2020. | • Near-normal life expectancy<br><br>Both Duchenne and Becker:<br>• Cardiomyopathy<br>• Scoliosis<br>• Osteoporosis and fractures<br>• Intellectual impairment<br>• Pharyngeal weakness<br>• Respiratory insufficiency | • Dysrhythmia<br>• Dysphagia<br>• Cataracts<br>• Intellectual impairment<br>• Testicular atrophy<br>• Frontal baldness |

# Necrotizing Enterocolitis

## History

- Inflammation and necrosis of the bowel
- Seen in **preterm infants** and rarely full term infants
- Days to weeks after birth
- **Formula-fed** infants are at highest risk
- Change in feeding tolerance, abdominal distension, tenderness, bilious emesis/gastric residuals, bloody stool

## Diagnosis

**Abdominal X-ray**

- **Pneumatosis intestinalis**, portal venous air, free intraperitoneal air

**Lab findings**

- Thrombocytopenia
- Hyponatremia
- Lactic acidosis

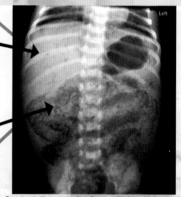

Portal venous air

Pneumatosis intestinalis

Reproduced with permission from Stevenson DK, Cohen RS, Sunshine P: Neonatology: Clinical Practice and Procedures. New York, NY: McGraw Hill; 2015.

## Treatment

- Stop all enteral feeding, gastric decompression
- Broad-spectrum **antibiotics**, cover anaerobes and aerobes
- **Surgery** may be necessary if intestinal perforation or not improving with medical management

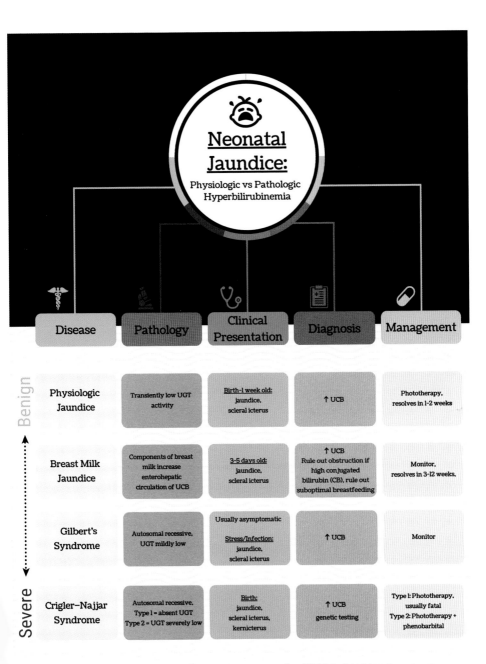

# Neonatal Jaundice:
## Physiologic vs Pathologic Hyperbilirubinemia

| | Disease | Pathology | Clinical Presentation | Diagnosis | Management |
|---|---|---|---|---|---|
| **Benign** | Physiologic Jaundice | Transiently low UGT activity | Birth-1 week old: jaundice, scleral icterus | ↑ UCB | Phototherapy, resolves in 1-2 weeks |
| | Breast Milk Jaundice | Components of breast milk increase enterohepatic circulation of UCB | 3-5 days old: jaundice, scleral icterus | ↑ UCB Rule out obstruction if high conjugated bilirubin (CB), rule out suboptimal breastfeeding | Monitor, resolves in 3-12 weeks. |
| | Gilbert's Syndrome | Autosomal recessive, UGT mildly low | Usually asymptomatic. Stress/Infection: jaundice, scleral icterus | ↑ UCB | Monitor |
| **Severe** | Crigler-Najjar Syndrome | Autosomal recessive, Type 1 = absent UGT Type 2 = UGT severely low | Birth: jaundice, scleral icterus, kernicterus | ↑ UCB genetic testing | Type 1: Phototherapy, usually fatal Type 2: Phototherapy + phenobarbital |

 Total bilirubin (TB) varies by ethnicity in neonates:

Caucasian/African American:
- Peak TB: 48-96 hours old
- Mean: 7-9 mg/dL

East Asian:
- Peak TB: 72-120 hours old
- Mean: 10-14 mg/dL

 Watch for kernicterus!
Unconjugated bilirubin (UCB) is fat soluble and can deposit in the basal ganglia
→ neurological deficits
→ death

# Neonatal Respiratory Distress Syndrome

## Key Facts

- Most common cause of respiratory failure in preterm infants
- Deficiency of surfactant leads to alveolar collapse and diffuse atelectasis

## Clinical Signs

- Tachypnea
- Nasal flaring
- Grunting
- Retractions
- Cyanosis

## Risk Factors

- Prematurity
- Maternal diabetes mellitus
- Male gender

## Diagnosis

- Chest radiograph shows ground-glass appearance, atelectasis, air bronchograms

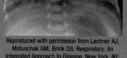

Reproduced with permission from Lechner AJ, Matuschak GM, Brink DS: Respiratory: An Integrated Approach to Disease. New York, NY: McGraw Hill; 2012.

## Treatment

- Antenatal corticosteroids
- Exogenous surfactant
- Supplemental oxygen
- Assisted ventilation
- Fluid management

## Differential

- Pneumonia
- Congenital heart disease
- Transient tachypnea of the newborn (TTN)
- Diaphragmatic hernia
- Pneumothorax

## Complications

- Bronchopulmonary dysplasia (BPD)
- Pulmonary air leak
- Persistent PDA

# Neuroblastoma

The adrenal gland is the most common primary site

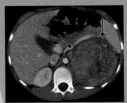

Reproduced with permission from Elsayes KM, Oldham SA: Introduction to Diagnostic Radiology. New York, NY: McGraw Hill; 2014.

### Third most common childhood cancer and most common neoplasm in infants

More than 50% of patients are <2 years of age at diagnosis

**Associated syndromes:**

Opsoclonus-myoclonus syndrome (Dancing eyes-dancing feet)

Horner's syndrome (Miosis, ptosis, anhidrosis)

**Presentation:**
- Abdominal mass that **may cross midline**
- Abdominal pain or constipation
- Proptosis
- Periorbital ecchymoses
- Back pain, weakness
- Palpable subcutaneous nodules
- Hypertension
- Weight loss, anemia, fever

HVA and VMA (catecholamine metabolites)

Originates from neural crest cells

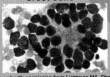

Reproduced with permission from Lichtman MA, Shafer MS, Felgar RE, et al: Lichtman's Atlas of Hematology 2016. New York, NY: McGraw Hill; 2017.

Small, round, blue tumor cells with rosette pattern

# Fifth Disease - Parvovirus B19

 Erythema infectiosum lacy, reticular, macular, **slapped cheek** rash

 Supportive treatment

 Arthritis in adults
**Aplastic anemia** in sickle cell patients
fetal hydrops fetalis if pregnant

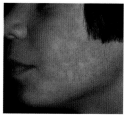

Reproduced with permission from Soutor C, Hordinsky MK: Clinical Dermatology. New York, NY: McGraw Hill; 2013.

# Hand-Foot-Mouth - Coxsackie A virus

 Painful oral ulcers and maculopapular or vesicular rash on hands, feet, face, and sometimes buttocks

 Supportive treatment

 Does not spare palms or soles

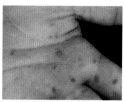

Reproduced with permission from Shah B, Lucchesi M: Atlas of Pediatric Emergency Medicine, 3rd ed. New York, NY: McGraw Hill; 2019. Photo contributor: Binita R. Shah, MD.

# Roseola - HHV-6

 Exanthem subitum, sixth disease
**High fever** for 3-4 days then maculopapular rash

 Supportive treatment

 **Febrile seizures**

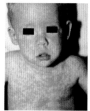

Reproduced with permission from Knoop KJ, Stack LB, Storrow AB, et al: The Atlas of Emergency Medicine, 4th ed. New York, NY: McGraw Hill; 2016. Photo contributor: Raymond C. Baker, MD.

# Ocular Infections

## Bacterial Conjunctivitis

| Common | *N. gonorrhoeae* | *C. trachomatis* |
|---|---|---|
| S. aureus, S. pneumoniae, H. flu, Pseudomonas, Moraxella | Emergency<br>Corneal involvement may → blindness | Recurrent epithelial keratitis leading cause of preventable blindness |
| Gram stain & culture if necessary | Gram stain showing Gram − *Diplococci* | Giemsa stain |
| Antibiotic drops/ointment  | IM ceftriaxone<br>PO ciprofloxacin/ofloxacin | Azithromycin<br>Tetracycline<br>Erythromycin 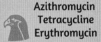 |

## Orbital Cellulitis

Streptococcus, MRSA, H. flu

Infection of the soft tissues of the orbit

Admit + IV antibiotics

## Viral Conjunctivitis

Adenovirus

Conjunctival injection

Watery discharge

Contagious

# Patent Ductus Arteriosus

## Pathophysiology

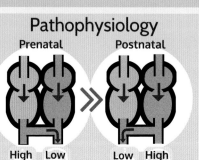

**Prenatal**

**Postnatal**

| High PVR | Low SVR | Low PVR | High SVR |
|----------|---------|---------|----------|

Normal right to left shunting due to high pulmonary resistance

Pathologic left to right shunting if remains patent after first few days of life

Can maintain perfusion in other cardiac defects

PGE keeps the duct patent

**Murmur**
Continuous & machine-like at LUSB

### Associations

Rubella first-trimester infection

Prematurity

Female gender

## Presentation

Acyanotic & pink at birth

Bounding peripheral pulses

Failure to thrive

Frequent URIs

Heart failure & Eisenmenger's syndrome

## Management

### Workup

Echo for definitive diagnosis
Chest X-ray will show increased pulmonary markings

### Treatment

Duct closure via:
Indomethacin (NSAID)
Surgical Treatment

 # Eisenmenger's Syndrome

Can occur in any left to right shunt

Uncorrected left to right shunt » Increased pulmonary blood flow » Pulmonary arterial hypertension » Right ventricular hypertrophy » Shunt becomes right to left

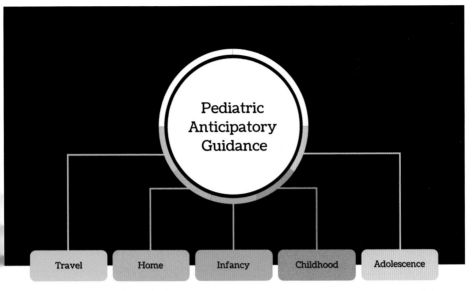

# Pediatric Anticipatory Guidance

| Travel | Home | Infancy | Childhood | Adolescence |
|---|---|---|---|---|
|  Rear-facing car seat until 2 years of age |  Set home water temperature to ‹120°F |  Feed child only breast milk or iron fortified formula until 4-6 months of age |  Recommend screen time ‹2 hours a day | Discuss avoidance of tobacco/alcohol/drugs |
|  Forward-facing car seat until they outgrow it |  Remove guns from home. If necessary, store locked and unloaded separate from ammo |  Cereal/small foods can be started when developmentally ready (~6 months) |  Children should read for 15-30 minutes every day |  Promote healthy sexual behavior: abstinence, condom usage, and birth control |
|  Booster seat until 4 ft 9 in, usually 8-12 years old |  Call poison control if ingestion is suspected (1-800-222-1222) |  Avoid use of infant walkers due to risk of injury |  Sunscreen SPF ›15 on exposed skin. Reapply every 2 hours |  Consider locking away liquor and prescription medication |
|  When old enough, always use lap and shoulder seat belts |  Never induce vomiting w/ syrup of ipecac |  Sleep on back on firm surface in separate bed from parents |  Healthy diet and 60 minutes of physical activity per day |  Praise activities and achievements not appearance to promote good self-image |
|  Kids younger than 13 should remain in rear seat of car |  Keep house/vehicle smoke free to avoid secondhand exposure |  Never leave an infant alone on an elevated surface or when in the bath |  Explain that private parts are private |  Limit night driving, driving with multiple passengers. Avoid distractions |
|  All children of any age should wear a fitted bike helmet |  Check home for sources of lead (paint if built before 1978) |  Ensure fluoride source (tap water and toothpaste) to prevent caries |  Visit dentist twice a year, brush twice a day, floss once |  Monitor for signs of depression: crying, isolation, weight change, insomnia, etc. |

# Pediatric Elbow Injuries

## Supracondylar Fracture    Nursemaid's Elbow

## Clinical Presentation

- Fracture of the distal humerus
- Etiology: Fall onto an outstretched hand (FOOSH)
- Associated with bony tenderness, deformity, and swelling
- Child will refuse to use arm or flex the elbow due to pain
- Dx: X-ray
- Assess for:

  - **!** Arterial injury: Radial/brachial pulses and capillary refill
  - **!** Nerve injury (median, radial, ulnar)
  - **!** Compartment syndrome

- Radial head subluxation
- Etiology: Occurs secondary to being pulled or lifted by hand (ie, swung by arms while playing)
- **NOT** associated with bony tenderness, deformity, or swelling
- Child will refuse to use arm or flex the elbow due to pain
- Dx: Clinical diagnosis

## Imaging

Lateral radiograph of an elbow with a supracondylar humeral fracture and an elevated posterior fat pad

Reproduced with permission from Tenenbein M, Macias CG, Sharieff GQ, et al: Strange and Schafermeyer's Pediatric Emergency Medicine, 5th ed. New York, NY: McGraw Hill; 2019.

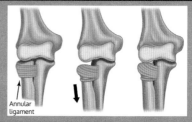

Annular ligament

**!** Imaging NOT recommended unless mechanism unclear/concern for fracture

## Treatment

- Type I Fx: Nondisplaced. Cast
- Type II Fx: Moderately displaced. Ortho consult
- Type III Fx: Severely displaced. Ortho consult
- Prognosis: Good if treated promptly
- **!** Complications: Volkmann's contracture 2/2 compartment syndrome

A — Flexion, Supination
B — Hyperpronation

- Manual reduction with any above method
- Results in immediate pain relief and ability to move arm
- Prognosis: Excellent

# Pediatric Forearm Fracture

## Clinical Presentation

- Fall onto an outstretched hand (FOOSH) or accidental trauma
- Swelling, bony pain, and/or deformity of the forearm present on exam
- ❗ Assess for vascular compromise/compartment syndrome
- ❗ Assess for nonaccidental trauma (abuse)

## Imaging

### Greenstick Fx

Reproduced with permission from Randsborg PH, Sivertsen EA: Distal radius fractures in children: substantial difference in stability between buckle and greenstick fractures, Acta Orthop 2009 Oct;80(5): 585-589.

Reproduced with permission from Rowland D, Baird E: Common upper limb injuries in childhood, Surgery 2014;32(1): 9-16.

**Incomplete fracture extending partway through width of bone following bending stress**

### Torus Fx

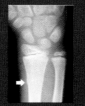 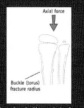

Reproduced with permission from Schwartz DT: Emergency Radiology: Case Studies. New York, NY: McGraw Hill; 2008.

Reproduced with permission from Rowland D, Baird E: Common upper limb injuries in childhood, Surgery 2014;32(1): 9-16.

**Axial force applied to immature bone leads to a simple buckle fracture of cortex**

## Treatment

### Greenstick Fx

- Nondisplaced: Splinting and casting within 3-5 days
- Mild displacement: Possible reduction prior to casting depending on degree of angulation
- Severe displacement: Prompt reduction prior to casting

### Torus Fx

- Treatment centered on pain relief and splinting only

❗ Need to distinguish via XR from nondisplaced greenstick fracture which requires casting

# Pediatric Leukemia

## Clinical Presentation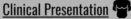

 Anorexia

 Fatigue

 Bone pain

 Fever

 Lymphadenopathy

 Ecchymosis/petechiae

Hepatosplenomegaly

**Childhood Leukemias**

AML- 15%

ALL- 85%

**❗**ALL is the most common childhood malignancy

### Risk Factors

 Trisomy 21

 Fanconi anemia

 Prior radiation

 SCID

Congenital bone marrow failure

## Diagnosis

 CBC and coagulation studies

 Peripheral smear (right)

 Bone marrow aspirate and biopsy for immunophenotyping

 CXR to rule out a mediastinal mass

 Mediastinal mass can present with SVC-like syndrome

**❗** WBC can be low, normal, or high

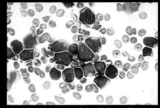

Reproduced with permission from Culligan D, Watson HG: Underwood's Pathology: a clinical approach. 7th ed. St. Louis, MO: Elsevier; 2019.

Peripheral smear showing blasts (seen in 90% of cases)

## Treatment

 Chemotherapy (induction, consolidation, maintenance)

 CNS-specific chemotherapy via lumbar puncture

 Broad-spectrum antibiotics for neutropenic fever

 Fluids, diuretics, and allopurinol for tumor lysis syndrome

Tumor lysis syndrome

Lysis of neoplastic cells

Release of cell contents into bloodstream

High $K^+$, high $PO_4$, high uric acid, low $Ca^{2+}$

**❗ Corticosteroids may precipitate TLS**

# Pertussis

## Whooping Cough

### Bacteria

- *Bordetella pertussis;* Gram-negative *coccobacillus*
- Prevented by Tdap and DTaP vaccines
- Transmitted through aerosol droplets; average incubation period is 7-10 days

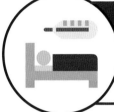

### Clinical Stages

- Catarrhal: Mild cough, coryza (1-2 weeks)
- Paroxysmal: Paroxysms of intense cough with inspiratory "whoop" and posttussive emesis (2-8 weeks)
- Convalescent: Cough subsides (weeks-months)

### Diagnosis

- Leukocytosis and lymphocytosis on CBC
- Culture or PCR of nasopharyngeal secretions, serology (ELISA) blood
- Reportable to public health authorities

### Treatment

- Hospitalization for infants <4 months
- Azithromycin
- Close contacts and exposed individuals at high risk require prophylaxis

# Pyloric Stenosis

Thickening of pylorus muscle leading to gastric outlet obstruction

## Presentation

2-6 weeks old

Nonbilious & projectile vomiting
2-6 weeks old

Continues to be hungry and feed

## Physical Exam

Palpable olive-shaped mass in epigastric region

Visible peristaltic waves

## Associations

First-born males

Exposure to macrolides

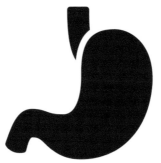

## Labs

Hypokalemic
Hypochloremic
Metabolic alkalosis

## Abdominal Ultrasound

Thickened & elongated hypoechoic pyloric—typo muscle

## Treatment

Rehydration & correction of acidosis

Surgical correction (pyloromyotomy)

Most common cause of gastric outlet obstruction in infants

# SCFE
## Slipped Capital Femoral Epiphysis

### Demographics

 Obese children (BMI 25-30 kg/m$^2$)

 Most common in 12- to 13-year-olds who need to have open growth plates

 More common in Polynesian, Black, and Hispanic children

 Occurs in 1-30/100,000 children

### Presentation/Physical Exam

 Obese child with hip, groin, thigh, or knee pain

 Change in gait with out-turning foot on affected side

 Obligatory external rotation with hip flexion

 Cannot internally rotate hip

### X-Ray Findings

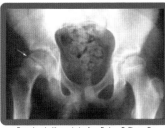

Reproduced with permission from Brukner P, Clarsen B, Cook J, et al: Brukner & Khan's Clinical Sports Medicine: Injuries, Volume 1, 5th ed. New York, NY: McGraw Hill; 2017.

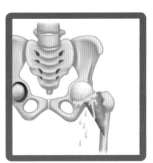

✔ Physeal widening or an indistinct metaphyseal border

✔ Posterior displacement of epiphysis

✔ Looks like slipped ice cream cone

### Treatment

Need referral to orthopedic surgery for in situ fixation

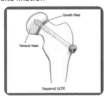

### Complications

➖ Osteonecrosis of femoral head

➖ Narrowing of the joint space and loss of articular cartilage

➖ Femoroacetabular impingement

# Scoliosis

## Etiology

 Most commonly idiopathic

 Some genetic contribution

 Evidence that environmental factors like hypoxia at birth may also play a role

 7:1 female to male ratio

## Clinical Manifestation

 Truncal asymmetry

 Vertebral and rib deformities

 Findings accentuated by Adam's forward-bending test

 Severe curves usually have onset before age 10

## Diagnosis

 Radiographs of the spine (posterior, anterior, and full-length views)

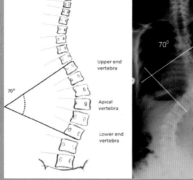

Reproduced with permission from Haleem S, Nnadi C: Scoliosis: a review, Paediatrics and Child Health May;2018;28(5):209-217.

 Cobb angle: The two "end" vertebrae are the last vertebrae whose end plates are tilted into the concavity. Cobb angle is measured between a line drawn from the upper end plate of the superior vertebrae and another along the lower end plate of the inferior vertebrae

## Treatment

 Close observation for <20°

 Spinal bracing for 20°-49° in patients with remaining growth

 Surgical correction for >50° of curvature

## Complications

 Curvature may progress even with bracing

 Severe scoliosis can lead to restrictive lung disease

 Spinal deformity can be a presenting sign of other conditions such as heritable collagen disease, neurologic conditions, and skeletal dysplasia

# Sex Chromosomes

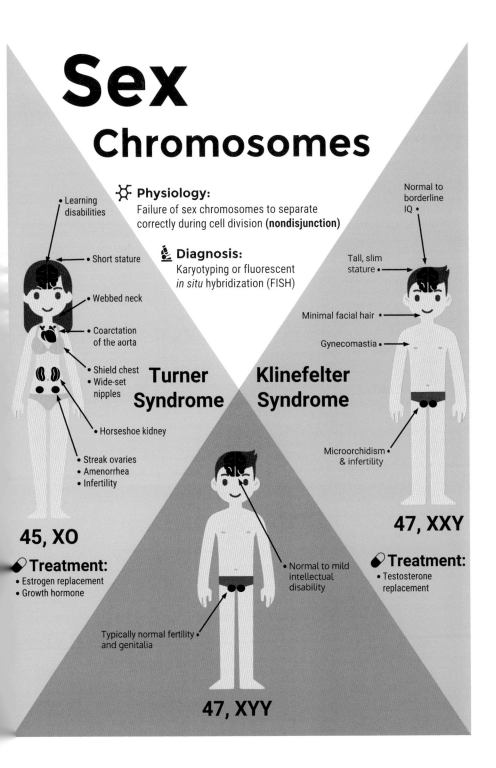

☼ **Physiology:**
Failure of sex chromosomes to separate correctly during cell division (**nondisjunction**)

🔬 **Diagnosis:**
Karyotyping or fluorescent *in situ* hybridization (FISH)

## Turner Syndrome

- Learning disabilities
- Short stature
- Webbed neck
- Coarctation of the aorta
- Shield chest
- Wide-set nipples
- Horseshoe kidney
- Streak ovaries
- Amenorrhea
- Infertility

**45, XO**

💊 **Treatment:**
- Estrogen replacement
- Growth hormone

## Klinefelter Syndrome

- Normal to borderline IQ
- Tall, slim stature
- Minimal facial hair
- Gynecomastia
- Microorchidism & infertility

**47, XXY**

💊 **Treatment:**
- Testosterone replacement

- Normal to mild intellectual disability
- Typically normal fertility and genitalia

**47, XYY**

# Sexual Development
### Classified Based on Tanner Stages 1-5

- <u>Gonadarche:</u> Activation of the gonads by pituitary hormones
- <u>Adrenarche:</u> Increase in production of androgens by adrenal cortex, causes pubarche and adult body odor
- <u>Pubarche:</u> Appearance of pubic hair, primarily due to effects of androgens
- <u>Thelarche:</u> Appearance of breast tissue, primarily due to action of estradiol from the ovaries
- <u>Menarche:</u> Time of first menstrual bleed
- <u>Spermarche:</u> Time of first sperm production, seen with nocturnal sperm emissions and sperm in urine

| Stage | Age (years) | Description | Image |
|---|---|---|---|
| 1 | | Prepubertal and no hair | |
| 2 | 10.5-12.9 | Breast buds and slightly pigmented long downy hair | |
| 3 | 11.3-13.5 | Enlargement of areola and curly, pigmented, coarser hair | |
| 4 | 11.8-14 | Secondary mound forms and hair covers pubic area | |
| 5 | 13.3-15.5 | Mature stage and hair spreads to medial thighs | |

*Puberty in Females*

| Stage | Age (years) | Description | Image |
|---|---|---|---|
| 1 | | Prepubertal and no hair | |
| 2 | 12.4-14.5 | Enlargement of scrotum and testes and sparse pubic hair | |
| 3 | 12.9-14.9 | Enlargement of penis and curly, pigmented, coarser hair | |
| 4 | 13.3-15.4 | Continued enlargement of the penis and hair covers pubic area | |
| 5 | 14.1-16.3 | Mature stage and hair spreads to medial thighs | |

*Puberty in Males*

## Pinworm - *Enterobius vermicularis*

 Parasitic infection with thin, white worms (1-2 mm long), leading to nocturnal **perianal pruritus**

 Scotch tape test

 Albendazole or pyrantel pamoate

1-2 mm
Nocturnal
Scotch Tape
Test

## Ringworm - *Tinea corporis*

 Fungal skin infection with itchy, scaly plaques, and **central clearing**

 KOH scrapings and fungal culture

 Topical azoles use **oral griseofulvin** for *Tinea capitus*

Reproduced with permission from Knoop KJ, Stack LB, Storrow AB, et al: The Atlas of Emergency Medicine, 4th ed. New York, NY: McGraw Hill; 2016. Photo contributor: Department of Dermatology, Wilford Hall USAF Medical Center and Brooke Army Medical Center, San Antonio, TX.

## Scabies - *Sarcoptes scabiei*

 Burrowing mites lead to itching of fingers, **webs** of hands, and intertriginous area

Reproduced with permission from Kelly AP, Taylor SC, Lom HW, et al: Taylor and Kelly's Dermatology for Skin of Color, 2nd ed. New York, NY: McGraw Hill; 2016.

 Skin scrapings for mites

 **Permethrin** for patients and all contacts

Reproduced with permission from Usatine RP, Sabella C, Smith MA, et al: The Color Atlas of Pediatrics. New York, NY: McGraw Hill; 2015. Photo contributor: Richard P. Usatine, MD.

# T-Cell Immunodeficiencies
## Primary Immunodeficiency Disorders

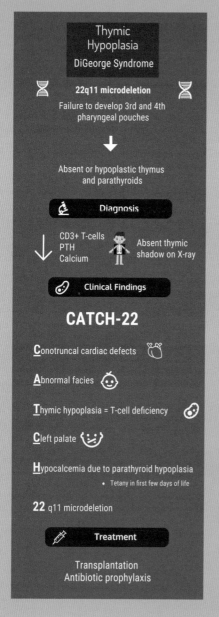

### Thymic Hypoplasia
#### DiGeorge Syndrome

**22q11 microdeletion**
Failure to develop 3rd and 4th pharyngeal pouches

↓

Absent or hypoplastic thymus and parathyroids

**Diagnosis**

↓ CD3+ T-cells
PTH
Calcium

Absent thymic shadow on X-ray

**Clinical Findings**

## CATCH-22

**C**onotruncal cardiac defects

**A**bnormal facies

**T**hymic hypoplasia = T-cell deficiency

**C**left palate

**H**ypocalcemia due to parathyroid hypoplasia
- Tetany in first few days of life

**22** q11 microdeletion

**Treatment**

Transplantation
Antibiotic prophylaxis

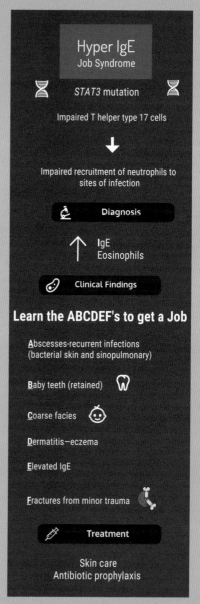

### Hyper IgE
#### Job Syndrome

*STAT3* mutation

Impaired T helper type 17 cells

↓

Impaired recruitment of neutrophils to sites of infection

**Diagnosis**

↑ IgE
Eosinophils

**Clinical Findings**

## Learn the ABCDEF's to get a Job

**A**bscesses-recurrent infections (bacterial skin and sinopulmonary)

**B**aby teeth (retained)

**C**oarse facies

**D**ermatitis—eczema

**E**levated IgE

**F**ractures from minor trauma

**Treatment**

Skin care
Antibiotic prophylaxis

# Tetralogy of Fallot

## Pathophysiology

1. Pulmonary stenosis
2. Right ventricular hypertrophy
3. Overriding aorta
4. Ventricular septal defect

### Associations

- DiGeorge syndrome
- Fetal alcohol syndrome

## "Tet Spells"

| Decreased oxygen saturation (crying/feeding) | **or** | Decreased SVR (playing/kicking legs) | ≫ | R-to-L shunting across VSD | ≫ | Decreased arterial PaO$_2$ | ≫ | Profound cyanosis + hypoxia | ≫ | Syncope + death |

 Compensation = squatting  ↑ SVR  ≫  ↓ R-to-L shunt  ≫  ↓ Cyanosis

## Presentation

Cyanotic at birth

Heart murmur

Poor weight gain

Shortness of breath

## Management

### Workup

Echo for definitive diagnosis

Chest X-ray will show "boot-shaped" heart

Reproduced with permission from Brunicardi FC, Andersen DK, Billiar TR, et al: Schwartz's Principles of Surgery, 11th ed. New York, NY: McGraw Hill; 2019.

### Treatment

Early surgical correction

# TORCH Infections

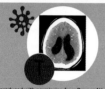

## Toxoplasmosis
Diffuse CNS calcifications
Chorioretinitis
Hydrocephalus
Jaundice

## Other

### Varicella
Limb hypoplasia
Chorioretinitis
Microcephaly
Cutaneous scars

### Syphilis
Early—Snuffles, osteitis, rash of palms/soles
Late—Hutchinson teeth, saber shins, saddle nose

### Parvovirus
Hydrops fetalis
Cardiomegaly

## Rubella
Deafness
Cataracts
Congenital heart disease (PDA or pulmonary artery stenosis)
Blueberry muffin rash (extramedullary hematopoiesis)

## Cytomegalovirus (CMV)
Periventricular calcifications
Hearing loss
Seizures
Chorioretinitis
Jaundice

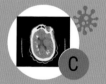

## HSV
Microcephaly
Meningoencephalitis
Vesicular rash
Keratoconjunctivitis

## HIV
Failure to thrive
Interstitial pneumonia
Recurrent infections
Protracted diarrhea
Oral thrush

Nonspecific signs common to all TORCH infections: Hepatosplenomegaly, rash, growth retardation, thrombocytopenia

# Transposition of the Great Arteries

## Pathophysiology

Aorticopulmonary septum fails to spiral leading to parallel circulation

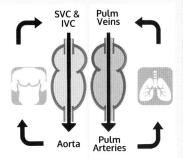

Most common cyanotic congenital cardiac lesion in newborns

Not compatible with life unless a shunt is present (ASD, VSD, PDA)

### Associations

 Infant of a diabetic mother

 DiGeorge (rarely)

## Presentation

Early cyanosis "Blue Baby"

Diagnosed prenatally or evident shortly after birth

No murmur (unless associated with a shunt)

## Management

PGEs to maintain PDA

Balloon atrial septostomy

Surgical repair

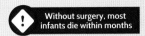 Without surgery, most infants die within months

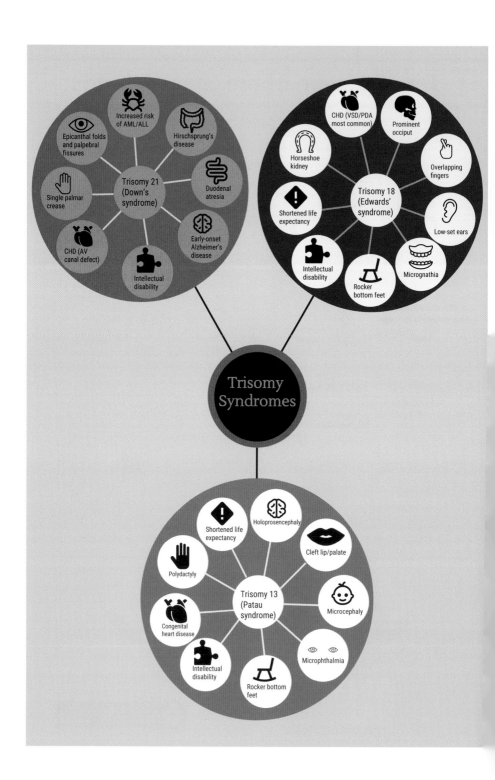

# Vaccinations

## Vaccination Schedule
### Birth to 18 years

**Birth**
- Hepatitis B

**2 months**
- Hepatitis B
- DTaP
- Polio
- PCV13
- HiB
- Rotavirus

**4 months**
- Hepatitis B
- DTaP
- Polio
- PCV13
- HiB
- Rotavirus

**6 months**
- Hepatitis B
- DTaP
- Polio
- PCV13
- HiB
- Rotavirus

**1 year**
- MMR
- Varicella
- Hepatitis A

**15 months**
- DTaP
- PCV13
- HiB

**18 months**
- Hepatitis A

**2 years**
- Hepatitis A (If not given at 18 months)

**4-6 years**
- MMR
- Varicella
- DTaP
- Polio

**11-12 years**
- MCV4
- Tdap
- HPV (2nd dose in 6 months)

**16-17 years**
- MCV4
- Meningitis B

**6 months to 18 years given influenza each year. If first time receiving vaccine, given 2 doses at least 4 weeks apart.**

# Viral Exanthems

## Measles - Paramyxovirus

Fever and cephalocaudal maculopapular rash
**4 Cs: Cough, coryza, conjunctivitis, Koplik's spots**

Supportive treatment
Vitamin A

Airborne spread
Subacute sclerosing panencephalitis years later

Reproduced with permission from Usatine RP, Sabella C, Smith MA, et al: The Color Atlas of Pediatrics. New York, NY: McGraw Hill; 2015. Photo contributor: Richard P. Usatine, MD.

## Rubella - German measles

Cephalocaudal maculopapular rash
Posterior auricular **lymphadenopathy**

Supportive treatment

**Congenital rubella:** Patent
ductus arteriosus, deafness,
cataracts, blueberry muffin rash

Reproduced with permission from the Centers for Disease Control and Prevention.

## Varicella - Chicken pox

Prodrome of fever and malaise, then rash with
diffuse **itching**
**Vesicles** on erythematous base with "teardrop on
rose" appearance

Supportive treatment
Acyclovir

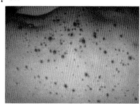

**Shingles** in adults from
reactivation in dorsal ganglia

Lesions in different stages of healing
Contagious until lesions crust over

Reproduced with permission from Ryan K, Ahmad N, Alspaugh JA, et al: Sherris Medical Microbiology, 7th ed. New York, NY: McGraw Hill; 2018.

# VACTERL/CHARGE

 **V** Vertebral Defects

 **C** Coloboma/CNS Anomalies

 **A** Anal Atresia

 **H** Heart Defects

 **C** Cardiac Defects

 **A** Atresia Choanae

 **T** Tracheoesophageal Fistula

 **R** Retardation of Growth/Development

 **E** Esophageal Atresia

 **G** Genitourinary Abnormalities

 **R** Renal Defects

 **E** Ear Anomalies and/or Deafness

 **L** Limb Defects

# Vesicoureteral Reflux Disease

## Description

- Retrograde passage of urine from bladder into ureter and kidney from inadequate closure of the ureterovesical junction
- Most commonly caused by a congenitally short intravesical ureter

## Grading

- I) Reflux into ureter without dilation
- II) Reflux into ureter AND kidney without dilation
- III) Reflux into ureter and kidney with MILD dilation
- IV) Reflux into ureter and kidney with MODERATE dilation and blunting of calyces
- V) Reflux into ureter and kidney with SEVERE dilation and loss of papillar impressions

## Symptoms

- Prenatal: Hydronephrosis on prenatal ultrasound
- Postnatal: Febrile UTI
- Complications: Recurrent UTIs, renal scarring, end-stage renal disease

## Diagnosis

- Voiding cystourethrogram (VCUG)
- High rates of spontaneous resolution for grades I-III

## Management

- Prophylactic antibiotics
- Strict bladder and bowel training
- Surgical correction if medical therapy fails or reflux persists with age; reimplantation of ureter vs endoscopic injection of a periurethral bulking agent

# *Vision and Hearing Screening*

 **Vision**        **Hearing**

## Incidence

| | |
|---|---|
| Refractive errors, amblyopia, and/or strabismus occur in 5-10% of preschoolers | Bilateral hearing deficit present in 1-3 per 1000 well neonates |
| | ⓘ May present as inattention |

## 🗓 Test Schedule

| | |
|---|---|
| • At birth screen for: Red reflex | • At birth screen for: Otoacoustic emissions or auditory brainstem responses |
| • 3 months: Alignment and conjugate gaze | |
| • 6 months: Tracking 180° | • Assessment of speech development at checkups |
| • 3 years: Stereopsis/alignment, track moving object with both eyes, participate in formal testing with tumbling E/Allen picture chart, and corneal light reflex | • Hand raising test starting at age 4 with screening at 5, 6, 8, and 10 years of age |

## 🕐 When to Refer ❗

| | |
|---|---|
| Refer to ophthalmologist: Unable to cooperate with testing, 2 line chart discrepancy between eyes, preterm infants, family history, or Down's syndrome at 6 months of age | Refer to audiologist: Speech impediment or parent concerns (more predictive than informal testing) |

# Wilms Tumor

## The most common renal malignancy in children

### Typical Presentation:

- Firm, nontender, smooth abdominal mass
- Most often unilateral, may be bilateral
- Rarely crosses midline

Typically children 2-5 years of age

### Associated Syndromes:

1. WAGR: Wilms tumor, aniridia, genitourinary malformations, mental retardation

2. Beckwith–Wiedemann: Hemihypertrophy, visceromegaly, macroglossia, omphalocele

### Symptoms:

- Often asymptomatic
- Abdominal pain
- Hematuria
- Fever
- Hypertension
- Vomiting

### Treatment:

Total nephrectomy

**+**

Chemotherapy & radiation

### Diagnostic Evaluation:

1. Ultrasonography (screening)

2. Contrast-CT (confirmation)

# References _____

**APGAR Score**
Raab EL, Kelly LK. Normal newborn assessment & care. In: DeCherney AH, Nathan L, Laufer N, Roman AS, eds. *CURRENT Diagnosis & Treatment: Obstetrics & Gynecology*. 12th ed. New York, NY: McGraw Hill; 2019.

**Atrial & Ventricular Septal Defects**
Jone P, VonAlvensleben J, Burkett D, Darst JR, Collins KK, Miyamoto SD. Cardiovascular diseases. In: Hay WW Jr., Levin MJ, Deterding RR, Abzug MJ, eds. *Current Diagnosis & Treatment: Pediatrics*. 24th ed. New York, NY: McGraw-Hill; 2018. http://accessmedicine.mhmedical.com/content.aspx?bookid=2390&sectionid=189078621. Accessed August 26, 2021.

Le T, Bhushan V, Sochat M, et al. Cardiovascular. In: *First Aid for the USMLE Step 1 2017: A Student-to-Student Guide*. New York,NY: McGraw Hill; 2017.

Le T, Bhushan V, Sochat M, et al. Pediatrics. In: *First Aid for the USMLE Step 1 2017: A Student-to-Student Guide*. New York, NY: McGraw Hill; 2017.

**B-Cell Immunodeficiencies**
Le T. Bhushan V. *First Aid for the USMLE Step 2 CK*. 10th ed. New York, NY: McGraw Hill; 2018.
Le T, Bhushan V, Sochat M, et al. *First Aid for the USMLE Step 1 2018*. New York, NY: McGraw Hill; 2017.

**Bone disorders**
Le T. Bhushan V. *First Aid for the USMLE Step 2 CK*. 10th ed. New York, NY: McGraw Hill; 2018.
Le T, Bhushan V, Sochat M, et al. *First Aid for the USMLE Step 1 2018*. New York: McGraw Hill; 2017.

**Bronchiolitis**
Le T. Bhushan V. *First Aid for the USMLE Step 2 CK*. 10th ed. New York, NY: McGraw Hill; 2018.
Le T, Bhushan V, Sochat M, et al. *First Aid for the USMLE Step 1 2018*. New York, NY: McGraw Hill; 2017.

**Cerebral Palsy**
Le T. Bhushan V. *First Aid for the USMLE Step 2 CK*. 10th ed. New York, NY: McGraw Hill; 2018.
Le T, Bhushan V, Sochat M, et al. *First Aid for the USMLE Step 1 2018*. New York, NY: McGraw Hill; 2017.

**Chediak–Higashi Syndrome**
Le T, Bhushan V, Skelley N. *First Aid for the USMLE Step 1*. 27th ed. New York, NY: McGraw Hill; 2017.
Le T, Bushan V, Skelley N. *First Aid for the USMLE Step 2 CK*. 8th ed. New York, NY: McGraw Hill; 2012.

**Child Abuse**
Colbourne M, Clarke MS. Child abuse and neglect. In: Tintinalli JE, Stapczynski J, Ma O, et al, eds. *Tintinalli's Emergency Medicine: A Comprehensive Study Guide*. 8th ed. New York, NY: McGraw Hill; 2016.

Makoroff KL, Lindberg DM, Care MM. Child abuse. In: Knoop KJ, Stack LB, Storrow AB, Thurman R, eds. *The Atlas of Emergency Medicine*. 4th ed. New York, NY: McGraw Hill; 2016.

Speer M, Mahlmann M, Caero J, Morani AC. Pediatric radiology. In: Elsayes KM, Oldham SA, eds. *Introduction to Diagnostic Radiology*. New York, NY: McGraw Hill; 2014.

**Chronic Granulomatous Disease**
Le T, Bhushan V, Skelley N. *First Aid for the USMLE Step 1*. 27th ed. New York, NY: McGraw Hill; 2017.
Le T, Bushan V, Skelley N. *First Aid for the USMLE Step 2 CK*. 8th ed. New York, NY: McGraw Hill; 2012.

### Clavicular Fracture/Osgood-Schlatter Disease

Chumley H, Scott E. Clavicular fracture. In: Usatine RP, Sabella C, Smith M, Mayeaux EJ Jr., Chumley HS, Appachi E, eds. *The Color Atlas of Pediatrics*. New York, NY: McGraw Hill; 2015.

Hatch RL, Clugston JR, Taffe J. Clavicle fractures. In: Eiff P, Asplund CA, Grayzel J, eds. *UpToDate*. Waltham, MA: UpToDate Inc. https://www.uptodate.com

Indiran V, Jagnnathan D. Osgood-Schlatter disease. *N Engl J Med*. 2018;378(11)e15. doi:10.1056/NEJMicm1711831.

Kienstra AJ, Macias CG. Osgood-Schlatter disease (tibial tuberosity avulsion). In: Phillips WA, Singer JI, Wiley JF, eds. *UpToDate*. Waltham, MA: UpToDate Inc. https://www.uptodate.com

Le T, Bhushan V. *First Aid for USMLE Step 2 CK*. 9th ed. New York, NY: McGraw Hill; 2015.

### Coarctation of the Aorta

Le T, Bhushan V, Sochat M, et al. Pediatrics. In: *First Aid for the USMLE Step 1 2017: A Student-to-Student Guide*. New York, NY: McGraw Hill; 2017.

Murthy R, Moe TG, Van Arsdell GS, Nigro JJ, Karamlou T. Congenital heart disease. In: Brunicardi F, Andersen DK, Billiar TR, et al, eds. *Schwartz's Principles of Surgery*. 11th ed. New York, NY: McGraw Hill; 2019.

### Combined Immunodeficiencies

Le T. Bhushan V. *First Aid for the USMLE Step 2 CK*. 10th ed. New York, NY: McGraw Hill; 2018.

Le T, Bhushan V, Sochat M, et al. *First Aid for the USMLE Step 1 2018*. New York, NY: McGraw Hill; 2017.

### Congenital Adrenal Hyperplasia

Merke DP. Treatment of classic congenital adrenal hyperplasia due to 21-hydroxylase deficiency in infants and children. In: Geffner ME, Hoppin AG, eds. *UpToDate*. Waltham, MA: UpToDate Inc. https://www.uptodate.com

Merke DP, Auchus RJ. Diagnosis of classic congenital adrenal hyperplasia due to 21-hydroxylase deficiency in infants and children. In: Geffner ME, Martin KA, eds. *UpToDate*. Waltham, MA: UpToDate Inc. https://www.uptodate.com

### Congenital Malformations

Le T, Bhushan V, Sochat M, et al. Pediatrics. *In: First Aid for the USMLE Step 1 2017: A Student-to-Student Guide*. New York, NY: McGraw Hill; 2017.

TEF Image: Wall J, Albanese CT. Pediatric surgery. In: Doherty GM, ed. *CURRENT Diagnosis & Treatment: Surgery*, 14th ed. New York, NY: McGraw Hill; 2014. Figure 43-8.

Hackam DJ, Upperman J, Grikscheit T, Wang K, Ford HR. Pediatric surgery. In: Brunicardi F, Andersen DK, Billiar TR, et al, eds. *Schwartz's Principles of Surgery*. 11th ed. New York, NY: McGraw-Hill. Figure 39-13. http://accessmedicine.mhmedical.com/content.aspx?bookid=2576&sectionid=216211209. Accessed August 24, 2021.

### Croup

Corbett SW, Stack LB, Knoop KJ. Chest and abdomen. In: Knoop KJ, Stack LB, Storrow AB, Thurman R, eds. *The Atlas of Emergency Medicine*. 4th ed. New York, NY: McGraw Hill; 2016.

Le T, Bhushan V, Sochat M, et al. Pediatrics. In: *First Aid for the USMLE Step 1 2017: A Student-to-Student Guide*. New York, NY: McGraw Hill; 2017.

Mapelli E, Sabhaney V. Stridor and drooling in infants and children. In: Tintinalli JE, Stapczynski J, Ma O, Yealy DM, Meckler GD, Cline DM, eds. *Tintinalli's Emergency Medicine: A Comprehensive Study Guide*. 8th ed. New York, NY: McGraw Hill; 2016.

### Cryptorchidism

Le T, Bhushan V, Sochat M, et al. *First Aid for the USMLE Step 1 2018*. New York, NY: McGraw Hill; 2017.

## Developmental Dysplasia of the Hip
Le T, Bhushan V. *First Aid for the USMLE Step 2 CK*. 10th ed. New York, NY: McGraw Hill; 2018.

Le T, Bhushan V, Sochat M, et al. *First Aid for the USMLE Step 1 2018*. New York, NY: McGraw Hill; 2017.

## Developmental Milestones 2 months to 15 months
Scharf RJ, Scharf GJ, Stroustrup A. Developmental milestones. [published correction appears in *Pediatr Rev*. 2016 Jun;37(6):266]. *Pediatr Rev*. 2016;37(1):25-47.

## Developmental Milestones 18 months to 6 years
Scharf RJ, Scharf GJ, Stroustrup A. Developmental milestones. [published correction appears in *Pediatr Rev*. 2016 Jun;37(6):266]. *Pediatr Rev*. 2016;37(1):25-47.

## Epiglottitis
Gonzalez C, Gartner JC, Casselbrant ML, Kenna MA. Complication of acute epiglottitis. *Int J Pediatr Otorhinolaryngol*. 1986;11(1):67-71. doi:10.1016/s0165-5876(86)80029-5

Le T, Bhushan V. *First Aid for the USMLE Step 2 CK*. 9th ed. New York, NY: McGraw Hill; 2015.

Woods CR. Epiglottitis (supraglottitis): clinical features and diagnosis. In: Edwards MS, Isaacson GC, Fleisher GR, Wiley JF, eds. *UpToDate*. Waltham, MA: UpToDate Inc. https://www.uptodate.com

Woods CR. Epiglottitis (supraglottitis): management. In: Edwards MS, Isaacson GC, Fleisher GR, Wiley JF, eds. *UpToDate*. Waltham, MA: UpToDate Inc. https://www.uptodate.com

## Failure to Thrive
Le T, Bhushan V. *First Aid: USMLE Step 2 CK*. Ninth Edition. 9th ed. New York, NY: McGraw Hill; 2016.

Poor weight gain in children younger than two years: etiology and evaluation. -*Uptodate*.: "Poor weight gain in children younger than two years: Etiology and evaluation" https://www.uptodate.com/contents/poor-weight-gain-in-children-younger-than-two-years-in-resource-abundant-countries-etiology-and-evaluation?search=poor-weight-gain-in-infants-and-children. Accessed December 3, 2019.

## Febrile Seizures
Clinical features and evaluation of febrile seizures as well as Treatment and prognosis of febrile seizures. *UpToDate*. https://www.uptodate.com/contents/clinical-features-and-evaluation-of-febrile-seizures. Accessed December 17, 2019.

## Genetic Disorders
Acquired diseases of the heart and pericardium. In: Wells RG, ed. *Diagnostic Imaging of Infants and Children*. New York, NY: McGraw Hill; 2015. https://accesspediatrics.mhmedical.com/content.aspx?bookid=1429&sectionid=84704354&jumpsectionid=84704362. Accessed November 11, 2019.

Disorders of growth. In: Sarafoglou K, Hoffmann GF, Roth KS, eds. *Pediatric Endocrinology and Inborn Errors of Metabolism*. 2nd ed. 2017. https://accesspediatrics.mhmedical.com/content.aspx?bookid=2042&sectionid=154114052&jumpsectionid=154114317. Accessed November 11, 2019. Copyright © 2019 McGraw-Hill Education. All rights reserved.

Chapter 21. Genetic testing for neurological disorders. In: Carney PR, Geyer JD, eds. *Pediatric Practice: Neurology*. 2010. https://accesspediatrics.mhmedical.com/content.aspx?bookid=459&sectionid=41027649&jumpsectionid=41031814. Accessed November 11, 2019. Copyright © 2019 McGraw-Hill Education. All rights reserved.

## Group A Streptococcus and Rheumatic Fever
Lustig LR, Schindler JS. Pharyngitis & tonsillitis. In: Papadakis MA, McPhee SJ, Rabow MW, eds. *Current Medical Diagnosis and Treatment 2020*. New York, NY: McGraw Hill; 2020.

Papadakis MA, McPhee SJ, Bernstein J, eds. Rheumatic fever & rheumatic heart disease. *Quick Medical Diagnosis & Treatment 2020*. New York, NY: McGraw Hill; 2020.

Riedel S, Hobden JA, Miller S, et al, eds. The streptococci, enterococci, and related genera. *Jawetz, Melnick, & Adelberg's Medical Microbiology*. 28th ed. New York, NY: McGraw Hill; 2019.

### Hirschsprung's Disease
Le T, Bhushan V. *First Aid for the USMLE Step 2 CK*. 10th ed. New York, NY: McGraw Hill; 2018.

Le T, Bhushan V, Sochat M, et al. *First Aid for the USMLE Step 1 2018*. New York, NY: McGraw Hill; 2017.

### Infant Hypotonia
Gaensbauer J, Nomura Y, Ogle JW, Anderson MS. Infections: bacterial & spirochetal. In: Hay WW Jr., Levin MJ, Deterding RR, Abzug MJ, eds. *Current Diagnosis & Treatment: Pediatrics*. 24th ed. New York, NY: McGraw-Hill; 2018. https://nam03.safelinks.protection.outlook.com/?url=http%3A%2F%2Faccessmedicine.mhmedical. com.elibrary.amc.edu%2Fcontent.aspx%3Fbookid%3D2390%26sectionid%3D189086581&data=02 %7C01%7Clangn%40amc.edu%7C1e5f08e134e3484bece108d784358681%7Cc04845f042244637aed29 beea8319b5b%7C0%7C0%7C637123237741714573&sdata=tz0pwbv1YdF8wNo1HJxx4CXPO0EUc 8OyElf27yF4qmc%3D&reserved=0. Accessed December 14, 2019.

Kim H, Shoval H, Kim N. Pediatric neurologic disorders. In: Mitra R, ed. *Principles of Rehabilitation Medicine*. New York, NY: McGraw-Hill; 2018. https://nam03.safelinks.protection.outlook.com/?url=http%3A%2F%2Facc essmedicine.mhmedical.com.elibrary.amc.edu%2Fcontent.aspx%3Fbookid%3D2550%26sectionid%3D2067 64693&data=02%7C01%7Clangn%40amc.edu%7C1e5f08e134e3484bece108d784358681%7Cc04845f 042244637aed29beea8319b5b%7C0%7C0%7C637123237741704615&sdata=CEhPnhDA8wh6iz%2FVh 40pakleYZRegDjlPC0qRJtDWTs%3D&reserved=0. Accessed December 14, 2019.

Meeks NL, Saenz M, Tsai A, Elias FR. Genetics & dysmorphology. In: Hay WW Jr., Levin MJ, Deterding RR, Abzug MJ, eds. *Current Diagnosis & Treatment: Pediatrics*. 24th ed. New York, NY: McGraw-Hill; 2018. https:// nam03.safelinks.protection.outlook.com/?url=http%3A%2F%2Faccessmedicine.mhmedical.com.elibrary. amc.edu%2Fcontent.aspx%3Fbookid%3D2390%26sectionid%3D189084922&data=02%7C01%7Clang n%40amc.edu%7C1e5f08e134e3484bece108d784358681%7Cc04845f042244637aed29beea8319b5b%7C0 %7C0%7C637123237741714573&sdata=m1c3bOg1z7MUlAoZrEz02vvf7giwyO0uFTPy59HsU%2F0%3D &reserved=0. Accessed December 14, 2019.

### Inherited Metabolic Disorders: Fabry, Gaucher, Krabbe
Le T. Bhushan V. *First Aid for the USMLE Step 2 CK*. 10th ed. New York, NY: McGraw Hill; 2018.

Le T, Bhushan V, Sochat M, et al. *First Aid for the USMLE Step 1 2018*. New York, NY: McGraw Hill; 2017.

### Inherited Metabolic Disorders: Hurler Syndrome and Hunter Syndrome
Giugliani R, Vairo F, Beck M, Wraith E, Cowan T, Grabowski G. Lysosomal disorders. In: Sarafoglou K, Hoffmann GF, Roth KS, eds. *Pediatric Endocrinology and Inborn Errors of Metabolism*. 2nd ed. New York, NY: McGraw-Hill; 2017. http://accesspediatrics.mhmedical.com/content.aspx?bookid=2042§ionid=154117568. Accessed May 20, 2019.

### Inherited Metabolic Disorders: Tay–Sachs and Niemann–Pick disease
Le T. Bhushan V. *First Aid for the USMLE Step 2 CK*. 10th ed. New York, NY: McGraw Hill; 2018.

Le T, Bhushan V, Sochat M, et al. *First Aid for the USMLE Step 1 2018*. New York, NY: McGraw Hill; 2017.

### Inherited Metabolic Disorders: PKU, Homocystinuria, MLD
Le T. Bhushan V. *First Aid for the USMLE Step 2 CK*. 10th ed. New York, NY: McGraw Hill; 2018.

Le T, Bhushan V, Sochat M, et al. *First Aid for the USMLE Step 1 2018*. New York, NY: McGraw Hill; 2017.

### Intoeing
Epps HR, Rathjen KE. Torsional and angular deformities. In: Kline MW, ed. *Rudolph's Pediatrics*, 23rd ed. New York, NY: McGraw Hill; 2018. https://accesspediatrics.mhmedical.com/content.aspx?bookid=2126&sectionid=176094147&jumpsectionid=191276202. Accessed July 16, 2019

Hill JF, Johnston CE. Disorders of the foot. In: Kline MW, ed. *Rudolph's Pediatrics*. 23rd ed. New York, NY: McGraw Hill; 2018. https://accesspediatrics.mhmedical.com/content.aspx?bookid=2126&sectionid=178132686&jumpsectionid=191276224. Accessed July 16, 2019.

Rab GT. Pediatric orthopedic surgery. In: Skinner HB, McMahon PJ, eds. *Current Diagnosis & Treatment in Orthopedics*. 5th ed. New York, NY: McGraw Hill; 2014. https://accessmedicine.mhmedical.com/content.aspx?bookid=675&sectionid=45451716&jumpsectionid=45457727. Accessed July 16, 2019.

### Intussusception
Le T. Bhushan V. *First Aid for the USMLE Step 2 CK*. 10th ed. New York, NY: McGraw Hill; 2018.

Le T, Bhushan V, Sochat M, et al. *First Aid for the USMLE Step 1 2018*. New York, NY: McGraw Hill; 2017.

### Job Syndrome (Hyper-IgE)
Le T, Bhushan V, Skelley N. *First Aid for the USMLE Step 1*. 27th ed. New York, NY: McGraw Hill; 2017.

Le T, Bushan V, Skelley N. *First Aid for the USMLE Step 2 CK*. 8th ed. New York, NY: McGraw Hill; 2012.

### Juvenile Idiopathic Arthritis
Akoghlanian S, Zeft A. Juvenile idiopathic arthritis. In: Usatine RP, Sabella C, Smith M, Mayeaux EJ Jr., Chumley HS, Appachi E, eds. *The Color Atlas of Pediatrics*. New York, NY: McGraw Hill; 2015. https://accesspediatrics.mhmedical.com/content.aspx?bookid=1443&sectionid=79847651&jumpsectionid=94716271. Accessed July 22, 2019.

### Kawasaki Disease
Le T, Bhushan V, Sochat M, et al. Pediatrics. In: *First Aid for the USMLE Step 1 2017: A Student-to-Student Guide*. New York, NY: McGraw Hill; 2017.

Shandera WX, Clark E. Kawasaki disease. In: Papadakis MA, McPhee SJ, Rabow MW, eds. *Current Medical Diagnosis and Treatment 2020*. New York, NY: McGraw Hill; 2020. http://accessmedicine.mhmedical.com/content.aspx?bookid=2683&sectionid=225055423

### Lead Poisoning
Le T, Bhushan V. *First Aid for the USMLE Step 2 CK*. 9th ed. New York, NY: McGraw Hill; 2015.

Sample JA. Childhood lead poisoning: clinical manifestations and diagnosis. In: Mahoney DH Jr., Burns MM, Drutz JE, Wiley JF, eds. *UpToDate*. Waltham, MA: UpToDate Inc. https://www.uptodate.com

### Legg-Calvé-Perthes Disease
Bachmann K, Goodwin RC. Legg-Calvé-Perthes. In: Usatine RP, Sabella C, Smith M, Mayeaux EJ Jr., Chumley HS, Appachi E, eds. *The Color Atlas of Pediatrics*. New York, NY: McGraw-Hill. http://accesspediatrics.mhmedical.com/content.aspx?bookid=1443&sectionid=79843411. Accessed May 22, 2019.

### Leukocyte Adhesion Deficiency
Le T, Bhushan V, Skelley N. *First Aid for the USMLE Step 1*. 27th ed. New York, NY: McGraw Hill; 2017.

Le T, Bushan V, Skelley N. *First Aid for the USMLE Step 2 CK*. 8th ed. New York, NY: McGraw Hill; 2012.

### Malrotation with Volvulus
GI emergencies. In: Rozenfeld RA, ed. *The PICU Handbook*. New York, NY: McGraw Hill; 2018. https://accesspediatrics.mhmedical.com/content.aspx?bookid=2388&sectionid=186994467. Accessed May 31, 2019. Copyright © 2019 McGraw-Hill Education.

## Mastoiditis vs Acute Otitis Media

Pelton S. Acute otitis media in children: treatment. In: Edwards MS, Isaacson GC, Torchia MM, eds. *UpToDate*. Waltham, MA: UpToDate Inc. https://www.uptodate.com/contents/acute-otitis-media-in-children-treatment?search=acute%20otitis%20media%20children&source=search_result&selectedTitle=1~150&usage_type=default&display_rank=1#H49926436

Wald ER. Acute mastoiditis in children: clinical features and diagnosis. In: Edwards MS, Messner AH, Armsby C, eds. *UpToDate*. Waltham, MA: UpToDate Inc. https://www.uptodate.com/contents/acute-mastoiditis-in-children-clinical-features-and-diagnosis?search=mastoiditis%20children&source=search_result&selectedTitle=1~44&usage_type=default&display_rank=1#H13

Wald ER. Acute mastoiditis in children: treatment and prevention. In: Edwards MS, Messner AH, Armsby C, eds. *UpToDate*. Waltham, MA: UpToDate Inc. https://www.uptodate.com/contents/acute-mastoiditis-in-children-treatment-and-prevention?search=acute%20mastoiditis%20treatment&source=search_result&selectedTitle=1~150&usage_type=default&display_rank=1

Wald ER. Acute otitis media in children: epidemiology, microbiology, clinical manifestations, and complications. In: Kaplan SL, Messner AH, Armsby C, eds. *UpToDate*. Waltham, MA: UpToDate Inc. https://www.uptodate.com/contents/acute-otitis-media-in-children-epidemiology-microbiology-clinical-manifestations-and-complications?search=acute%20otitis%20media%20children&source=search_result&selectedTitle=3~150&usage_type=default&display_rank=3#H26

## Meckel's Diverticulum

Le T, Bhushan V. *First Aid for the USMLE Step 2 CK*. 10th ed. New York, NY: McGraw Hill; 2018.

Le T, Bhushan V, Sochat M, et al. *First Aid for the USMLE Step 1 2018*. New York, NY: McGraw Hill; 2017.

## Meningitis

Le T. Bhushan V. *First Aid for the USMLE Step 2 CK*. 10th ed. New York, NY: McGraw Hill; 2018.

Le T, Bhushan V, Sochat M, et al. *First Aid for the USMLE Step 1 2018*. New York, NY: McGraw Hill; 2017.

## Muscular Dystrophy

Friedman N. Duchenne muscular dystrophy. In: Usatine RP, Sabella C, Smith M, Mayeaux EJ Jr., Chumley HS, Appachi E, eds. *The Color Atlas of Pediatrics*. New York, NY: McGraw Hill; 2015.

## Necrotizing Enterocolitis

Slaughter JL, Moss RL. Necrotizing enterocolitis and spontaneous intestinal perforation. In: Stevenson DK, Cohen RS, Sunshine P, eds. *Neonatology: Clinical Practice and Procedures*. 2015. https://accesspediatrics.mhmedical.com/ViewLarge.aspx?figid=85592478&gbosContainerID=0&gbosid=0&groupID=0. Accessed April 30, 2019.

## Neonatal Jaundice

Le T, Bhushan V. *First Aid for the USMLE Step 1 2019*. 29th ed. New York: McGraw Hill; 2018.

Sattar HA. *Fundamentals of Pathology*. Pathoma; 2011. https://www.pathoma.com/fundamentals-of-pathology

Wong RJ, Bhutani VK. Unconjugated hyperbilirubinemia in the newborn: pathogenesis and etiology. In: Abrams SA, Rand EB, Kim MS., eds. *UpToDate*. Waltham, MA: UpToDate Inc. https://www.uptodate.com/contents/unconjugated-hyperbilirubinemia-in-the-newborn-pathogenesis-and-etiology?search=neonatal%20jaundice&source=search_result&selectedTitle=1~97&usage_type=default&display_rank=1#H21

## Neonatal Respiratory Distress Syndrome

Fleming RE, Panneton W, Lechner AJ. Neonatal respiratory distress syndrome and sudden infant death syndrome. In: Lechner AJ, Matuschak GM, Brink DS, eds. *Respiratory: An Integrated Approach to Disease*. New York, NY: McGraw Hill; 2012. http://accessmedicine.mhmedical.com/content.aspx?bookid=1623&sectionid=105765587. Accessed June 27, 2019.

**Neuroblastoma**
Elsayes KM, Oldham SA. *Introduction to Diagnostic Radiology*. New York, NY: McGraw-Hill; 2014. Copyright McGraw-Hill education.

**Nonvaccine Preventable Viral Exanthems**
Le T. Bhushan V. *First Aid for the USMLE Step 2 CK*. 10th ed. New York, NY: McGraw Hill; 2018.

Le T, Bhushan V, Sochat M, et al. *First Aid for the USMLE Step 1 2018*. New York, NY: McGraw Hill; 2017.

**Ocular Infections**
Le T, Bhushan V, Skelley N. *First Aid for the USMLE Step 1*. 27th ed. New York, NY: McGraw Hill; 2017.

Le T, Bushan V, Skelley N. *First Aid for the USMLE Step 2 CK*. 8th ed. New York, NY: McGraw Hill; 2012.

**Patent Ductus Arteriosus**
Jone P, Von Alvensleben J, Burkett D, et al. Cardiovascular diseases. In: Hay WW Jr., Levin MJ, Deterding RR, Abzug MJ, eds. *Current Diagnosis & Treatment: Pediatrics*. 24th ed. New York, NY: McGraw Hill; 2018. http://accessmedicine.mhmedical.com/content.aspx?bookid=2390&sectionid=189078621.

Le T, Bhushan V, Sochat M, et al. Pediatrics. In: *First Aid for the USMLE Step 1 2017: A Student-to-Student Guide*. New York, NY: McGraw Hill; 2017.

**Pediatric Anticipatory Guidance**
American Academy of Pediatrics. AAP Updates Recommendations on Car Seats for Children. AAP.org. https://www.aap.org/en-us/about-the-aap/aap-press-room/Pages/AAP-Updates-Recommendations-on-Car-Seats-for-Children.aspx. Published August 30, 2018. Accessed October 11, 2019.

American Academy of Pediatrics. Pacifiers. AAP.org. https://www.aap.org/en-us/about-the-aap/aap-press-room/aap-press-room-media-center/Pages/Pacifiers.aspx. Accessed October 11, 2019.

American Academy of Pediatrics, Committee on Injury and Poison Prevention. Bicycle helmets. *Pediatrics*. 2001;108(4):1030-1032. doi:10.1542/peds.108.4.1030.

Committee on Injury and Poison Prevention; American Academy of Pediatrics. Selecting and using the most appropriate car safety seats for growing children: guidelines for counseling parents. *Pediatrics*. 2002;109(3):550-553. doi:10.1542/peds.109.3.550.

Hagan JF, Shaw JS, Duncan PM, eds. *Bright Futures: Guidelines for Health Supervision of Infants, Children, and Adolescents* [pocket guide]. 4th ed. Elk Grove Village, IL: American Academy of Pediatrics; 2017.

Jenco M. Study: Infant walker injuries support AAP's call for a ban. AAP Gateway. https://www.aappublications.org/news/2018/09/17/babywalkers091718. Published September 17, 2018. Accessed October 11, 2019.

Wyckoff AS. Thermometer use 101. AAP Gateway. https://www.aappublications.org/content/30/11/29.2. Published November 1, 2009. Accessed October 11, 2019.

**Pediatric Elbow Injuries**
Baratz M, Micucci C, Sangimino M. Pediatric supracondylar humerus fractures. *Hand Clin*. 2006;22(1):69-75. doi:10.1016/j.hcl.2005.11.002.

Frumkin K. Nursemaids elbow: a radiographic demonstration. *Ann Emerg Med*. 1985;14(7):690-693. doi:10.1016/s0196-0644(85)80890-8.

Moore BR, Bothner J. Radial head subluxation (nursemaid's elbow). In: Stack AM, Wiley JF, eds. *UpToDate*. Waltham, MA: UpToDate Inc. https://www.uptodate.com

Ryan ML. Evaluation and management of supracondylar fractures in children. In: Boutis K, Wiley JF, eds. *UpToDate*. Waltham, MA: UpToDate Inc. https://www.uptodate.com

Wu J, Perron AD, Miller MD, Powell SM, Brady WJ. Orthopedic pitfalls in the ED: pediatric supracondylar humerus fractures. *Am J Emerg Med*. 2002;20(6):544-550. doi:10.1053/ajem.2002.34850.

**Pediatric Forearm Fractures**
Atanelov Z, Bentley TP. *Greenstick fracture*. StatPearls [Internet]. Treasure Island, FL: StatPearls Publishing; 2020. https://www.ncbi.nlm.nih.gov/books/NBK513279/. Last updated August 26, 2020.

Schweich P. Distal forearm fractures in children: initial management. In: Boutis K, Wiley JF, eds. *UpToDate*. Waltham, MA: UpToDate Inc. https://www.uptodate.com

Solan M, Rees R, Daly K. Current management of torus fractures of the distal radius. *Injury*. 2002;33(6):503-505. doi:10.1016/s0020-1383(01)00198-x

**Pediatric Leukemia**
Culligan D, Watson HG. Blood and bone marrow. In: Cross S, ed. *Underwood's Pathology*. Philadelphia, PA: Elsevier; 2019.

Horton TM, Steuber CP. Overview of the treatment of acute lymphoblastic leukemia/lymphoma in children and adolescents. In: Park JR, Rosmarin AG, eds. *UpToDate*. Waltham, MA: UpToDate Inc. https://www.upto-date.com

Horton TM, Steuber CP, Aster JC. Overview of the clinical presentation and diagnosis of acute lymphoblastic leukemia/lymphoma in children. In: Park JR, Rosmarin AG, eds. *UpToDate*. Waltham, MA: UpToDate Inc. https://www.uptodate.com

Le T, Bhushan V. *First Aid for the USMLE Step 2 CK*. 9th ed. New York, NY: McGraw Hill; 2015.

Le T, Bhushan V, Sochat M, et al. Pediatrics. In: *First Aid for the USMLE Step 1 2017: A Student-to-Student Guide*. New York, NY: McGraw Hill; 2017.

Tarlock K, Cooper TM. Acute myeloid leukemia in children and adolescents. In: Park JR, Rosmarin AG, eds. *UpToDate*. Waltham, MA: UpToDate Inc. https://www.uptodate.com

**Pertussis**
Le T. Bhushan V. *First Aid for the USMLE Step 2 CK*. 10th ed. New York, NY: McGraw Hill; 2018.

Le T, Bhushan V, Sochat M, et al. *First Aid for the USMLE Step 1 2018*. New York, NY: McGraw Hill; 2017.

**Pyloric Stenosis**
Le T, Bhushan V, Sochat M, et al. Pediatrics. In: *First Aid for the USMLE Step 1 2017: A Student-to-Student Guide*. New York, NY: McGraw Hill; 2017.

Wall J, Albanese CT. Pediatric surgery. In: Doherty GM, ed. *CURRENT Diagnosis & Treatment: Surgery*, 14th ed. New York, NY: McGraw Hill; 2014. http://accessmedicine.mhmedical.com/content.aspx?bookid=1202&sectionid=71529153. Accessed September 25, 2019.

**SCFE: Slipped Capital Femoral Epiphysis**
Wylie JD, Eduardo NN. Evolving understanding of and treatment approaches to slipped capital femoral epiphysis. *Curr Rev Musculoskelet Med*. 2019;12(2):213-219.

**Scoliosis**
Le T, Bhushan V. *First Aid for the USMLE Step 2 CK*. 9th ed. New York, NY: McGraw Hill; 2015.

Scherl SA. Adolescent idiopathic scoliosis: clinical features, evaluation, and diagnosis. In: Phillips WA, Torchia MM, eds. *UpToDate*. Waltham, MA: UpToDate Inc. https://www.uptodate.com

Scherl SA. Adolescent idiopathic scoliosis: management and prognosis. In: Phillips WA, Torchia MM, eds. *UpToDate*. Waltham, MA: UpToDate Inc. https://www.uptodate.com

Sparrow DB, Chapman G, Smith AJ, et al. A mechanism for gene-environment interaction in the etiology of congenital scoliosis. *Cell*. 2012;149(2):295-306. doi:10.1016/j.cell.2012.02.054

**Sex Chromosomes**
Fitzgerald PA. Turner syndrome (gonadal dysgenesis). In: Papadakis MA, McPhee SJ, Rabow MW, eds. *Current Medical Diagnosis and Treatment 2020*. New York, NY: McGraw Hill; 2020.

Meeks NL, Saenz M, Tsai A, Elias ER. Genetics & dysmorphology. In: Hay WW Jr., Levin MJ, Deterding RR, Abzug MJ, eds. *Current Diagnosis & Treatment: Pediatrics*. 24th ed. New York, NY: McGraw Hill; 2018.

**Sexual Development**

Marshall WA, Tanner JM. Variations in pattern of pubertal changes in girls. *Arch Dis Child*. 1969;44:291.

Tanner JM. *Growth at Adolescence*. Oxford: Blackwell Scientific Publications; 1962.

**Skin Infections and Infestations**

Le T, Bhushan V. *First Aid for the USMLE Step 2 CK*. 10th ed. New York, NY: McGraw Hill; 2018.

Le T, Bhushan V, Sochat M, et al. *First Aid for the USMLE Step 1 2018*. New York, NY: McGraw Hill; 2017.

**T-Cell Immunodeficiencies**

Le T. Bhushan V. *First Aid for the USMLE Step 2 CK*. 10th ed. New York, NY: McGraw Hill; 2018.

Le T, Bhushan V, Sochat M, et al. *First Aid for the USMLE Step 1 2018*. New York, NY: McGraw Hill; 2017.

**Tetralogy of Fallot**

Le T, Bhushan V, Sochat M, et al. *First Aid for the USMLE Step 1 2018*. New York, NY: McGraw Hill; 2017.

Murthy R, Moe TG, Van Arsdell GS, Nigro JJ, Karamlou T. Congenital heart disease. In: Brunicardi F, Andersen DK, Billiar TR, et al, eds. *Schwartz's Principles of Surgery*. 11th ed. New York, NY: McGraw Hill; 2019.

**TORCH Infections**

Mayeaux EJ Jr., Usatine RP. Herpes simplex. In: Usatine RP, Sabella C, Smith M, Mayeaux EJ Jr., Chumley HS, Appachi E, eds. *The Color Atlas of Pediatrics*. New York, NY: McGraw Hill; 2015. https://accesspediatrics mhmedical.com/content.aspx?bookid=1443&sectionid=79844582

Sabella C. Congenital and Perinatal Infections. In: Usatine RP, Sabella C, Smith M, Mayeaux EJ Jr., Chumley HS, Appachi E, eds. *The Color Atlas of Pediatrics*. New York, NY: McGraw Hill; 2015. https://accesspediatrics mhmedical.com/content.aspx?bookid=1443&sectionid=79849573

Usatine RP, Chumley H. Syphilis. In: Usatine RP, Sabella C, Smith M, Mayeaux EJ Jr., Chumley HS, Appachi E, eds. *The Color Atlas of Pediatrics*. McGraw Hill; 2015. https://accesspediatrics.mhmedical.com/content.aspx?bookid=1443&sectionid=79848788

**Transposition of the Great Arteries**

Le T, Bhushan V, Sochat M, et al. Pediatrics. In: *First Aid for the USMLE Step 1 2017: A Student-to-Student Guide*. New York, NY: McGraw Hill; 2017.

**Trisomy Syndromes**

Biersch BS. Congenitalc abnormalities. In: Lockwood CJ, Wilkins-Haug L, Firth HV, TePas E, eds. *UpToDate*. Waltham, MA: UpToDate Inc. https://www.uptodate.com

Le T, Bhushan V. *First Aid for the USMLE Step 2 CK*. 9th ed. New York, NY: McGraw Hill; 2015.

**Vaccinations**

Daley MF, O'Leary ST, Nyquist A. Immunization. In: Hay WW Jr., Levin MJ, Deterding RR, Abzug MJ, eds. *Current Diagnosis & Treatment: Pediatrics*. 24th ed. New York, NY: McGraw Hill; 2018.

**Vaccine Preventable Viral Exanthems**

Le T, Bhushan V. *First Aid for the USMLE Step 2 CK*. 10th ed. New York, NY: McGraw Hill; 2018.

Le T, Bhushan, V. Sochat M. et al. *First Aid for the USMLE Step 1 2018*. New York, NY: McGraw Hill; 2017.

**VACTERL/CHARGE**

Le T. Bhushan V. *First Aid for the USMLE Step 2 CK*. 10th ed. New York, NY: McGraw Hill; 2018.

Le T, Bhushan V, Sochat M, et al. *First Aid for the USMLE Step 1 2018*. New York, NY: McGraw Hill; 2017.

**Vesicoureteral Reflux Disease**

Le T. Bhushan V. *First Aid for the USMLE Step 2 CK*. 10th ed. New York, NY: McGraw Hill; 2018.

Le T, Bhushan V, Sochat M, et al. *First Aid for the USMLE Step 1 2018*. New York, NY: McGraw Hill; 2017.

**Vision and Hearing Screening**

Treitz M, Nicklas D, Bunik M, Fox D. Ambulatory & Office Pediatrics. In: Hay WW Jr., Levin MJ, Deterding RR, Abzug MJ, eds. *Current Diagnosis & Treatment: Pediatrics*. 24th ed. New York, NY: McGraw-Hill; 2018. https://accessmedicine.mhmedical.com/content.aspx?bookid=2390&sectionid=189074222. Accessed December 13, 2019.

**Wilms Tumor**

Le T. Bhushan V. *First Aid for the USMLE Step 2 CK*. 10th ed. New York, NY: McGraw Hill; 2018.

Le T, Bhushan V, Sochat M, et al. *First Aid for the USMLE Step 1 2018*. New York, NY: McGraw Hill; 2017.

# Psychiatry
*Neeral Shah, MD*

# ADHD
## Attention-Deficit Hyperactivity Disorder

- Persistent and marked pattern of **inattention** and/or **hyperactive** and **impulsive** behavior
- Most commonly presents between ages 3 and 13
- Can present as predominantly **inattentive**, predominantly **hyperactive**, or **combined**

## DSM-5 Criteria

Symptoms must:
Be present ≥**6 months** in at least **2 settings** (school, home, etc.)
Be present **before age 12**
Interfere with social, academic, or extracurricular functioning
Not happen only during the course of schizophrenia or another psychotic disorder
Not be better explained by another mental disorder

 **6+** symptoms for children **up to age 16**
**5+** for adolescents **17 and older** adults

| Inattention | Hyperactivity-Impulsivity |
|---|---|
| <ul><li>Fails to give close attention to details</li><li>Has trouble holding attention on tasks</li><li>Does not seem to listen when spoken to directly</li><li>Does not follow through on instructions</li><li>Has trouble organizing tasks and activities</li><li>Avoids, dislikes tasks that require mental effort over a long period of time</li><li>Loses things necessary for tasks and activities</li><li>Easily distracted</li><li>Forgetful in daily activities</li></ul> | <ul><li>Fidgets with or taps hands or feet, or squirms in seat</li><li>Frequently leaves seat</li><li>Runs about or climbs inappropriately</li><li>Unable to play quietly</li><li>"On the go" acting as if "driven by a motor"</li><li>Talks excessively</li><li>Blurts out answers</li><li>Has trouble waiting his/her turn</li><li>Interrupts or intrudes on others</li></ul> |

## Treatment

Cognitive Behavioral Therapy (CBT)

**Nonstimulants:**
Atomoxetine,
Clonidine/Guanfacine,
Bupropion, TCAs

 **CNS Stimulants:**
Methylphenidate (Ritalin)
Dextroamphetamine/Amphetamine
Salts (Adderall, Vyvanse)

 **Exercise & Meditation**

# Adjustment Disorder

## DSM-5 Diagnosis

- Symptoms develop within 3 months of identifiable stressful life event and resolve within 6 months of stressor termination.

- Symptoms produce either marked distress in excess of what would be expected after such an event OR significant impairment in daily functioning.
- Symptoms are NOT those of normal bereavement.

## Subtypes

| Depressed mood | Anxiety | Conduct disturbance | Mixed |

## Adjustment Disorder

### Versus Bereavement

Like AD, bereavement is a reaction to major loss (usually of a loved one)

Like AD, symptoms are self-limited and only last several months

### Versus PTSD

In AD, the event is *not* life-threatening

In PTSD, the event *is* life-threatening

### TREATMENT

Bereavement is not a mental illness

Does not include gross psychotic symptoms or active suicidality

CBT (most effective), group therapy

Pharmacotherapy (ie, SSRIs); time-limited

# Alcohol Use Disorder

## Epidemiology

Lifetime prevalence:
- 17.8% alcohol abuse
- 12.5% alcohol dependence

Demographics:
- Highest in age 18-29, lowest in >65
- Men > women
- Highest in native Americans, lowest in Asians

## Clinical features

Screening:
- CAGE ≥ 2 points
- AUDIT-C ≥4 points in men, 2 in women

DSM-5 criteria

- Drank more/longer than intended
- Wanted/tried to reduce/stop but failed
- Spent extensive time drinking & dealing with its effects
- Intense craving for alcohol
- Drinking interfered with family/job/school
- Continued drinking despite social/interpersonal effects
- Continued drinking despite health/memory effects
- Drinking led to unsafe behaviors
- Gave up other activities for drinking
- Developed tolerance to alcohol
- Experienced withdrawal:
Nausea/vomiting, diaphoresis, restlessness, hallucinations, seizures, etc.

## Diagnosis

DSM-5 diagnostic criteria:
- Mild: 2-3 symptoms, moderate: 4-5, severe: 6 or more

Labs can show:
- Megalocytosis
- AST >2 ALT

## Treatment

Withdrawal:
- CIWA (<8: mild, 8-15: moderate, >15: severe)
- Mild-mod: Outpatient ± meds
- Severe (or history of delirium tremens/seizures): Inpatient + benzodiazepines

Replete thiamine, folate, B12 if needed

Rehab & maintenance:
- Disulfiram        - Naltrexone
- Acamprosate       - Topiramate
- 12 Steps & Alcoholics Anonymous
- Cognitive behavioral therapy
- Motivational enhancement therapy

## Complications

- Wernicke
- Korsakoff

- Hypertension
- CV disease

- Cirrhosis
- Gastritis
- GI cancers
- Malnutrition

- Poverty
- Social isolation
- Mood disorder
- Drug use disorder

# Anorexia Nervosa

## Etiology

Biological susceptibility

- Norepinephrine transporter, serotonin transporter, MAO-A genes
- Norepinephrine, serotonin disturbances

Cultural pressure

Determines degree of phenotypic expression

## Clinical Features

  BMI <18.5

**DSM-5 criteria**

- Restriction of energy intake → significantly low weight
- Intense fear of gaining weight/behavior that interferes with weight gain
- Body image distortion with undue influence on self-evaluation; lack of recognition of seriousness

- Lanugo (downy body hairs)
- ↓ bone density + stress fractures
- Amenorrhea/delayed menarche
- Anemia + electrolyte disturbances

## Diagnosis

- DSM-5 diagnostic criteria
- Eating disorders inventory
- Eating attitudes test

Labs can show:
- Malnutrition, dehydration
- Metabolic alkalosis if vomiting
- Low FSH/LH

## Treatment

Nutritional rehabilitation
- Weight restoration
- Correct fluid/electrolytes

Beware of refeeding syndrome

Psychotherapy
- Cognitive behavioral therapy
- Interpersonal therapy

Pharmacotherapy
- SSRI
- 2nd-generation antipsychotics

## Complications

Malnutrition
Osteoporosis
Delayed growth

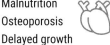
Hypotension
Arrhythmias
Anemia

Dehydration
↓ Renal function
Hypokalemia

Depression
Obsessive compulsive disorder

# Antisocial Personality Disorder

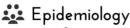 

## 👥 Epidemiology

Occurrence:

♂ Men: 2-4%    ♀ Women 0.5-1.0%

Correlation with conduct disorder and later development of antisocial personality disorder

## ⊗ Risk Factors

Family history
Family dysfunction
History of conduct problems
Family with adult criminal offenses
Lack of affection and emotional support during childhood

## Features

Often associated with:

 Poor job performance

 Unstable relationships

 Substance abuse

 Impulsivity

 Exploitation of others

## Diagnosis

 Recurrent criminal and delinquent behavior

 Diagnosed in those 18 years & older

 Disregard for others

 Patients often have history of similar behaviors during childhood

## 💊 Treatment

- Psychopharmacologic agents for symptoms, not underlying etiology
- Family psychotherapy for relationships
- Group therapy with other antisocial personality disorder patients for sense of belonging
- Individual therapy not as effective & most patients discontinue therapy
- CBT may have increased effects by challenging patients' self-serving thoughts

**Cluster A B C**

# Autism Spectrum Disorder

## Epidemiology

Developmental disorder characterized by:
- Impairments in social interaction & communication
- Repetitive/restricted behavior, interests, or activities

Prevalence: 1.7% (1 in 59)
Female < Male predominance

## DSM-5 Criteria

- Deficits in **language development**
- **Difficulty using language** to communicate
- **Restrictive, repetitive patterns** of behavior, interests, or activities
- Symptoms must **impair function** in school, work, and other areas of life
- Symptoms must be present in the **early developmental period** (<3 years)

### Social Interaction & Communication

- Reduced interest in socialization
- Reduced empathy
- Inability to form relationships
- Impaired language development
- Inability to understand social cues
- Poor eye contact

### Repetitive/Restrictive Patterns

- Highly fixated or restricted interests
- Inflexibility to change
- Hand flapping
- Hyper/hyporeactive response to sensations (sensory overload)
- Stereotyped or repetitive motor movements, use of objects, or speech
- Ritualized patterns of behavior

## Treatment

 Early Intervention Services

Behavioral Management Therapy

 Nutritional Management

Cognitive Behavioral Therapy (CBT)

# Borderline Personality Disorder

##  Epidemiology

**Occurrence:**
General: 1-2%
Psychiatry inpatients: 20-30%
♀ > ♂   Women > Men
Young adults

## Risk Factors

 History of abuse

 Family history

## Features

**Often associated with:**

 Inappropriate anger

 Repeated suicidal gestures or self-injury

 Fear of abandonment

 Use of splitting defense mechanism

## Diagnosis

**Pattern of:**

 Mood instability

 Unstable relationships

 Impulsivity

Persistent feeling of emptiness

 Lack of identity or self-image

##  Treatment

- Psychopharmacologic agents for symptoms, not underlying etiology
- Group therapy and family therapy for interpersonal issues
- Dialectical behavior therapy (DBT) to recognize patterns of self-destruction
- Mentalization-based therapy to create an alliance with the patient

**Cluster A B C**

# Thought Disorders
# Brief Psychotic Disorder

##  Features

 Commonly in response to a stressor

 Acute onset with previous normal functioning

## Diagnosis

 Classic positive symptoms:
- Hallucinations
- Delusions

 Also possible:
- Confusion
- Catatonia
- Agitation
- Mood changes

##  Treatment

 Hospitalization often required

Rule out other disorders

 Antipsychotics

 Address underlying disorders

Improve coping skills

##  Prognosis

 Symptoms last less than 1 month

 Continue antipsychotics for 1-3 months
( longer if recurrent )

 Recurrence is common

##  Epidemiology

 Prevalence: Higher in populations with increased stressors

 Postpartum: Occurrence within 4 weeks of delivery

# Bulimia Nervosa

## Etiology

 Cultural pressure
- Idealization of thinness

 Biological changes
- Aberrant CNS monoamine metabolism
- Possible genetic component

## Clinical features

  ANY BMI

**DSM-5 criteria**

- Recurrent binge eating:
  1. Eating more than what most would in a discrete period of time (2 hours)
  2. Lack of control over eating
- Recurrent inappropriate compensatory behaviors to prevent weight gain:
  Purging type: Self-induced vomiting, laxative/diuretics/emetics abuse
  Nonpurging type: Fasting, excessive exercise, medication/substance abuse
- Binge & compensation occur ≥1x/week for 3 months
- Overemphasis on body shape & weight
- Disturbance not exclusively during episodes of anorexia nervosa

- Consumption of high-calorie foods with typically normal BMI
- Usually preserved menstruation

## Diagnosis

- DSM-5 diagnostic criteria
- Eating disorders examination

 Labs can show:
- If vomiting: ↓Cl, ↓K, ↓Mg, metabolic alkalosis, mildly ↑amylase
- If abusing laxatives: ↓phos, ↓Na, metabolic acidosis

## Treatment

 Hospitalize if:
- Has major electrolyte disturbance
- Has depression with suicidal ideation
- Failed outpatient management

 Psychotherapy
- Cognitive behavioral or interpersonal
- Group therapy

 Pharmacotherapy
- SSRI

## Complications

 - Dental caries
- Enamel loss
- Salivary gland hypertrophy

 - Esophageal/ gastric perf
- Esophagitis/ gastritis

- Dehydration
- Electrolyte/pH disturbance

 - Russell sign (abrasions)
- Petechiae

Uncommonly: Seizure, arrhythmias, amenorrhea

# Conduct Disorder

## DSM-5 Criteria

- A **repetitive and persistent pattern** of behavior in which the basic rights of others, societal norms, or rules are violated
- **Behavioral disturbances** causing clinically significant impairment in social, academic, or occupational functioning
- **<18 years old** | If >18—Antisocial Personality Disorder

| Aggression | Destruction of Property | Deceit/Theft | Rule Violations |
|---|---|---|---|
| <ul><li>Bullies, threatens, or intimidates others</li><li>Initiates physical fights</li><li>Uses weapons</li><li>Physical cruelty</li><li>Forced sexual activity</li></ul> | <ul><li>Fire setting with the intention of causing serious damage</li><li>Deliberate destruction of others' property</li></ul> | <ul><li>Breaking & entering</li><li>Lying to obtain goods/favors or to avoid obligations</li><li>Stealing items of nontrivial value</li></ul> | <ul><li>Stays out at night despite parental prohibitions</li><li>Runs away from home overnight at least twice or once without returning</li><li>Truancy from school</li></ul> |

## Treatment

Cognitive Behavioral Therapy
**CBT**

# Conversion Disorder

At least one neurological symptom that can't be explained by a medical disorder—normally preceded by a psychological stressor

## Epidemiology

**20-25%**

 >

20-25% incidence in a general hospital setting

2-5x more common in women

Onset at any age, but *most common* in adolescence and early adulthood

# DSM-5 Criteria

## Symptoms

**All of the following criteria:**

 At least one symptom of altered voluntary motor or sensory function.

 Clinical findings provide evidence of incompatibility between the symptoms and recognized medical conditions.

 The symptom is not better explained by another medical or mental disorder.

 The symptom or deficit causes clinically significant distress or impairment in social, occupational, or other important areas of functioning or warrants medical evaluation.

Blindness

Mutism

Paresthesias

Shifting paralysis

## Management

Most patients recover spontaneously without treatment

Some patients may need insight-oriented psychotherapy

# Delirium

A state in which patients become acutely agitated, disoriented, and are unable to sustain attention

## Epidemiology

**10-30%**

10-30% prevalence in all hospitalized patients

Increased incidence with post-surgical and terminal disease patients

Age is the most identified risk factor

## DSM-5 Criteria

Delirium is classified by its presumed etiology:

 **1. Systemic disease**

 **3. Exogenous toxic agents**

 **2. Primary intracranial disease**

 **4. Substance withdrawal**

## Clinical Features

 • **Disturbed consciousness and cognition**

 • **"Sundowning"**

 • **Fluctuation of symptoms**

 • **Sleep disturbance**

## Management

**Look for all possible causes of delirium through labs and physical exam**

**Review the patient's medication list for unnecessary drugs**

**Diagnose and treat psychiatric comorbidities**

# Thought Disorders
# Delusional Disorder

## Features

Types:
- Persecutory
- Jealous
- Erotomanic
- Grandiose
- Somatic
- Mixed
- Unspecified

Persistent and fixed

## Diagnosis

Does not meet schizophrenia criteria

Otherwise patients are functional

Possible comorbid mood disorder, but delusions also present without mood symptoms

## Treatment

Pharmacologic agents*

Psychotherapy

*High risk of noncompliance due to persistence of delusions

## Prognosis

67%

2/3 of patients recover or improve

20% persist with treatment-resistant delusions

## Epidemiology

Occurs in mid-late adulthood

Men: 40-49 years
Women: 60-69 years

Lifetime prevalence is ~ 0.2%

# Dependent Personality Disorder

## Epidemiology

Occurrence:

General: 0.5-3%

♀ > ♂  Women > Men

More common in psychiatric settings

## Risk Factors

 History of success with dependent behavior in childhood

 Older individuals

## Features

Reliance on others

 Fear of abandonment

Attempt to appease others

 Panic disorder and agoraphobia common

## Diagnosis

Persistent pattern of:

 Submissiveness in relation to others

 Low self-esteem

 Feeling inadequate

## Treatment

- Psychopharmacologic treatment with SSRIs or TCAs for associated fatigue and anxiety
- Group therapy for patients to develop relationships and autonomy
- Family and individual psychotherapy to achieve a state of independence

**Cluster A B C**

# Factitious Disorder

Patients intentionally produce illness for primary gain (no obvious external reward)

## Epidemiology

**Unknown**

Unknown incidence and prevelance in the general public

Common factitious disorder more common in females

Increased incidence in healthcare workers

# DSM-5 Criteria

Falls under criteria for somatic symptom disorder:

 One or more somatic symptoms that are distressing or result in significant disruption of daily life

 Excessive thoughts, feelings, behaviors related to somatic symptoms or health concerns of at least **one** of the following:
- Persistent thoughts about the seriousness of the symptoms
- Persistently high anxiety levels about health or symptoms
- Excessive time and energy devoted to these symptoms or health concerns

 Although the somatic symptom may not be present, the state of being symptomatic is persistent

## Common Presentations

Hypoglycemia

Blood dyscrasia

Dermatologic conditions

Infections

## Management

Avoid any unnecessary procedures

Patients should be managed by one physician and have a close relationship

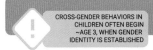 CROSS-GENDER BEHAVIORS IN CHILDREN OFTEN BEGIN ~AGE 3, WHEN GENDER IDENTITY IS ESTABLISHED

# Gender Dysphoria

## DSM-5 Criteria

 ≥6 months of:
Incongruence between one's experienced/expressed gender and assigned gender
Significant distress/impairment in social, school, or other important functions

### In Children

≥**6** of the following:

 Desire to be another gender or insistence that one is the other gender

 Prefers playmates of other gender

Prefers cross-gender roles in make-believe play

 Prefers dressing in attire typical of opposite gender

 Prefers toys/activities stereotypically engaged by other gender

 Rejects toys/activities stereotypically engaged by one's assigned gender

 Strong dislike of one's sexual anatomy

 Strong desire for the sex characteristics that match one's experienced gender

### In Adults

≥**2** of the following:

 Desire to be another gender

Desire to be treated as another gender

 Incongruence between one's expressed gender & primary or secondary sex characteristics

 Desire for primary or secondary sex characteristics of another gender

 Desire to be rid of or prevent development of one's primary or secondary sex characteristics

 Conviction that one has typical feelings and reactions of another gender

##  Diagnosis vs Stigma

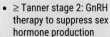

The DSM-5 replaced "disorder" with "dysphoria" in the diagnostic label to remove the stigma & connotation that the patient is disordered. However, persons experiencing gender dysphoria still need a diagnostic label that protects their access to care, helps direct treatment, and facilitates insurance coverage.

## 🛏 Psychiatric Care

- Therapies directed toward altering gender identity are NOT effective
- May benefit from psychotherapy, peer support groups, and parent education

## 💊 Medical Care

- ≥ Tanner stage 2: GnRH therapy to suppress sex hormone production
- At ~ 16: Cross-sex hormone therapy to promote secondary sex characteristics
- Treatment has beneficial effects on behavioral and emotional problems

## ✏ Surgical Options

- ≥ 18 years old
- 1 year hormone therapy recommended before gonadectomy
- 1 year living as gender identity recommended before genital reconstruction
- Rates of suicide fall significantly after surgery

# Generalized Anxiety Disorder

## Epidemiology

 Don't confuse with adjustment disorder: Anxiety that develops within 3 months of an identifiable stressor and lasts no longer than 6 months after stressor stops

1/3 of risk for developing GAD is genetic

Symptoms of worry usually begin in childhood

2:1 female:male
Median age of onset in 20s

## DSM-5 Criteria

 Excessive anxiety/worry about various daily events/activities (ie, school, family, finances, health)

 ≥6 months

Difficulty controlling worry

 Symptoms not caused by direct effects of a substance, other mental disorder, or mental condition

 Significant social or occupational dysfunction

**≥ 3 Somatic symptoms**

Restlessness
Fatigue
Impaired concentration
Irritability
Muscle tension
Insomnia

## Management

 GAD is highly comorbid with other anxiety and depressive disorders

CBT (most effective when combined with pharmacotherapy)

SSRI (sertraline, citalopram)
SNRI (venlafaxine)
*Rarely*, TCAs or MAOIs

Can consider short-term course of benzodiazepines or augment with buspirone

# Histrionic Personality Disorder

##  Epidemiology

<u>Occurrence:</u>
General: 1-3%
Women up to 12%
More common in psychiatric settings

##  Risk Factors

 Low self-esteem

Family history

##  Features

 Attention-seeking

Provocative demeanor

 Somatization & conversion disorders are common

 Extraverted personality style

##  Diagnosis

 Increased sexuality & emotionality for gains (attention, control, etc.)

 Labile emotions

 Preoccupation with physical appearance

 Superficial relationships

##  Treatment

- Psychopharmacologic agents usually not effective but may treat comorbid depression/anxiety
- Group therapy with similar patients to mirror behavior to others
- Psychotherapy may be difficult due to superficiality

**Cluster A B C**

# Intellectual Disability Disorder

## DSM-5 Criteria

- Deficits in **intellectual functioning**
- Deficits in **adaptive functioning**
- Results in substantial functional limitations in **3+ areas of life activity**
- Onset **before age 18**

### Intellectual Functioning

- Reading
- Learning
- Problem solving
- Judgment
- Memory

### Life Activity

- Ability to self-care
- Receptive and expressive language
- Mobility
- Self-direction
- Capacity for independent learning
- Economic self-sufficiency

### Adaptive Functioning

- Social skills
- Empathy
- Ability to follow rules
- Writing
- Knowledge
- Reasoning

## Treatment

 **Early intervention**

**Family therapy**

# Mood Disorders:
# Bipolar

## Epidemiology

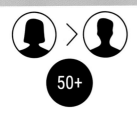

Increased prevalence in females and people over age 50

## Etiology

**Biological**

 Neurotransmitter fluctuations

**Genetics**

 Twin studies show strong genetic component to bipolar disorder

## Clinical Features

**Mania**

 Euphoria and irritability

 Sleep disruption

 Racing thoughts

 Excessive spending and acting out

**Depression**

 Lowered mood
Feelings of worthlessness

 Decreased concentration
Loss of energy and interest

## Diagnosis

**Bipolar 1**
Recurrent major depressive episodes with *manic* episodes that last *at least* 1 week

**Bipolar 2**
Recurrent major depressive episodes with *hypomanic* episodes that last more than 4 days but less than 7

## Treatment

Pharmacotherapy

Lithium, lamotrigine, and atypical antipsychotics

Other Modalities

Electroconvulsive therapy (ECT)

Hospitalize if:

Patient is exhibiting suicidal ideation with an active plan or with uncontrollable mania

# *Mood Disorders:*
# Major Depressive Disorder

## Epidemiology

Increased incidence and prevalence in females after puberty

## Etiology

**Life Events**

 Death or loss of a loved one can precede depressive episode

**Biological**

 Neurotransmitter deficiencies

## Clinical Features

Depressed mood or the loss of interest or pleasure for at least **2 weeks** and *4 of the following:*

 Changes in:
Appetite
 Sleep
Body activity

Loss of energy
Feelings of worthlessness
Decreased concentration
Suicidal ideation

## Diagnosis

Clinical features must cause *significant impairment*

Features can't be:

 Due to the effects of a substance or medical condition

 Part of a mixed episode (such as bipolar)

 Better accounted for by bereavement

## Treatment

Pharmacotherapy

SSRIs, MAOIs, and TCAs can be used

Other Modalities

Electroconvulsive therapy (ECT and CBT)

Hospitalize if:

Patient is exhibiting suicidal ideation with an active plan

# Narcissistic Personality Disorder

##  Epidemiology

Occurrence:
<1% of general population
2-16% of psychiatric patients

♂    ♀
Men > Women

## ⊗ Risk Factors

Lack of clear, appropriate parental appreciation of child's accomplishments:
over- or under-reaction

##  Features

 Grandiosity with exaggerated sense of entitlement or uniqueness

 Lack of empathy

 Manipulative

 Hypersensitivity to evaluation with envy of others

 Injury to self-image → depression, social withdrawal

## ☰ Diagnosis

  Clinical diagnosis based on features, especially pervasive pattern of grandiosity, need for admiration, lack of empathy

  Differential diagnosis include hypomania, antisocial personality disorder, borderline personality disorder

##  Treatment

**Psychopharmacotherapy** is only for comorbid conditions: Depression & anxiety
**Group therapy** with other narcissistic personality patients can help increase insight
**Couples therapy** with role-playing and role-reversal especially helpful
**Individual therapy** may be challenging; should provide support and empathy while confronting patient on their distorted self-image

### Cluster A B C

# Obsessive-Compulsive Disorder

## DSM-5 Diagnosis

Obsessions and/or compulsions that are time-consuming (eg, >1 hour/day) or cause significant distress or dysfunction

**Obsessions**: Recurrent, intrusive, anxiety-provoking thoughts, images, or urges that the patient attempts to ignore or suppress by some other thought or action

**Compulsions**: Repetitive behaviors or mental acts performed in response to an obsession or a rule aimed at stress reduction

---

### Epidemiology

- Significant genetic component
- Similar rates of male:female
- Neurologic abnormalities of fine motor coordination & involuntary movements are common

### OCD Spectrum

- Spectrum includes tics, trichotillomania (hair pulling), excoriation disorder (skin picking), hoarding, body dysmorphia
- Highly comorbid with other anxiety disorders, depressive or bipolar disorder, tic disorder, & OCPD

### OCD vs OCPD

- **OCPD**: Obsession with details, control, and perfectionism; no unwanted compulsions. Tend not to be distressed by their symptoms (*ego-syntonic*)
- **OCD**: Distressed by their symptoms (*ego-dystonic*)

---

  Under extreme stress, these patients sometimes exhibit paranoid and delusional behaviors, which can mimic schizophrenia.

---

### Pharmacologic Treatment

- **First-line: SSRIs** (ie, sertraline, fluoxetine), usually at higher doses
- Clomipramine (most serotonin selective TCA)
- For tx-resistant cases: Antipsychotics, topiramate
- Usually requires a longer time to response than depression (up to 12 weeks)

### Behavioral Treatment

- **CBT**: Focuses on *exposure and response prevention* (prolonged, graded exposure to ritual-eliciting stimulus and prevention of performing the compulsion)

### Psychological Treatment

- Family education
- Transcranial magnetic stimulation
- Deep brain stimulation
- For severely debilitating, treatment-resistant OCD: Psychosurgery (ie, cingulotomy), or ECT

---

  Plasma levels of clomipramine and its metabolite should be checked q2–3 weeks to avoid toxicity

### Prognosis

- Chronic, with waxing and waning course
- <20% remission rate without treatment
- ~60% respond to pharmacologic treatment
- Suicidal *ideation* in 50% of patients
- Suicide *attempts* in 25% of patients

# Oppositional Defiance Disorder

## DSM-5 Criteria

- A pattern of **angry/irritable mood, argumentative/defiant behavior**, or **vindictiveness** lasting at least 6 months.
- The **disturbance in behavior is associated with distress** in the individual or others, or it **impacts negatively on social, educational, occupational, or other important areas of functioning**.
- The behaviors do not occur exclusively during the course of a psychotic, substance use, depressive, or bipolar disorder.

### Angry/ Irritable Mood

- Loses temper often
- Often easily annoyed
- Often angry and resentful

### Argumentative/ Defiant Behavior

- Argues with authority figures
- Actively defies or refuses to comply with rules or authority figures
- Deliberately annoys others
- Blames others for their mistakes or misbehavior

### Vindictiveness

- Has been spiteful or vindictive at least twice within the past 6 months

## Treatment

 **CBT**

**Family Therapy**

# Panic Disorder

## Epidemiology

Onset usually <25 years

Affects 3-5% of population

Tends to be familial

2:1 female:male

## DSM-5 Diagnosis

≥ 1 month of:

- ☐ Recurrent unexpected panic attacks
- ☐ Persistent worry about additional attacks OR a significant maladaptive change in behavior related to the attacks
- ☐ Not related to another medical condition (hyperthyroid, cardiopulmonary disorder, pheochromocytoma, drug intoxication/withdrawal)
- ☐ Not better explained by another mental disorder (social anxiety, phobic)

## Panic Attacks

Abrupt surge of intense fear that peaks in minutes & has 4 of the following:

Dyspnea, sensation of choking or smothering

Paresthesias, heat/chills

Tachycardia, palpitations, chest pain

Derealization, depersonal-ization

Feeling of impending doom, losing control, dying

Headache, dizziness

Nausea, vomiting, diarrhea

## Treatment

First-line: SSRI (fluoxetine, paroxetine, sertraline)

First-line: SNRI (venlafaxine)

Long-acting benzodiazepines (clonazepam, alprazolam)

Propranolol for resistant cases

! Taper BDZs after 4 weeks when SSRIs have begun to take effect

! Side effects of benzodiazepines include disinhibition, ataxia, dysarthria, nystagmus, and delirium. Abrupt withdrawal may cause convulsive seizures. Flumazenil is a BDZ antagonist effective in overdose.

# Paranoid Personality Disorder

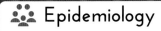 

## Epidemiology

Prevalence:
~0.5-4.5% of general population
Common among psychiatric inpatients

♀ ♂
Women > men

## Risk Factors

Family history of schizophrenia and delusional disorder

Parents exhibited irrational outbursts of anger in patient's childhood

## Features

 Generalized distrust or suspiciousness

 Feel mistreated and bear grudges

 Can be hostile to others if autonomy threatened

 Poor or fixated eye contact

 Externalization of emotions and blame

## Diagnosis

 Clinical diagnosis based on features, especially generalized distrust, feeling of unfair treatment, unsuccessful intimate relationships, underlying hostility and resentment

 Differential diagnosis and comorbid conditions include other cluster A, narcissistic and borderline disorders, delusional disorder, schizophrenia

## Treatment

**Psychopharmacotherapy** has little evidence; antipsychotics for decompensation
**Group therapy** is difficult due to suspicious nature; DO NOT see family members without patient present
**Individual therapy** is difficult, and no technique has been proven efficacious
**Cognitive techniques** to correct overgeneralizations, and splitting can be useful

### Cluster A B C

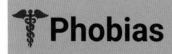 # Phobias

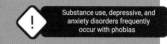
**Substance use, depressive, and anxiety disorders frequently occur with phobias**

| Agoraphobia | Social Phobia | Specific Phobia |
|---|---|---|

## DSM-5 Criteria

**Agoraphobia**
- Intense fear/anxiety about **>2 situations** (ie, outside the home alone, public transport, crowds) due to concern of difficulty escaping or obtaining help in case of panic or humiliating symptoms
- Situation is avoided when possible, tolerated with intense anxiety, or requires a companion (even if the patient suffers from potentially embarrassing medical condition)

**Social Phobia**
- Persistent, excessive fear of **scrutiny, or rejection** by others or fear of acting in a humiliating or embarrassing way (ie, speaking in public, eating in public, using public restrooms)
- Exposure triggers *immediate* fear response
- Situation is avoided when possible or tolerated with intense anxiety

**Specific Phobia**
- Persistent, irrational fear of a **specific object or situation** (ie, the phobic stimulus, which is commonly an animal, environmental condition, situation [elevator, airplane, closed space], blood, injection, or injury)
- Exposure triggers *immediate* fear response
- Situation is avoided when possible or tolerated with intense anxiety

## Criteria Common to All 3 Diagnoses

Fear out of proportion to threat
Significant social or occupational dysfunction
Symptoms ≥ 6 months
Not better explained by another medical disorder

## Etiology & Epidemiology

**Agoraphobia**
Strongly genetic
Onset frequently follows trauma
Mean age of onset: <35

**Social Phobia**
♀ = ♂
Mean age of onset: 13

**Specific Phobia**
2♀:1♂
Mean age of onset: 10

## Management

**Agoraphobia**
- Cognitive behavior therapy (CBT)
- SSRIs (sertraline, fluoxetine)

**Social Phobia**
- CBT
- SSRIs or SNRI (venlafaxine) for debilitating symptoms
- β-blockers (atenolol, propranolol) for performance anxiety

**Specific Phobia**
- CBT

**Start SSRIs or SNRIs at low doses and ↑ slowly because side effects may initially worsen the anxiety**

# PTSD

### Exposure to Trauma Followed by Intrusive Symptoms

- Nightmares, flashbacks
- Avoidance negative alterations in thoughts and mood
- Increased arousal

May occur immediately after the trauma or with delayed expression

### PTSD
- Trauma occurred *any* time in the past
- Symptoms last >1 month

### Acute Stress Disorder
- Trauma occurred <1 month ago
- Symptoms last <1 month

### Epidemiology & Prognosis
- Higher prevalence in women
- 50% recover in 3 months
- Symptoms tend to ↓with age
- 80% of patients have another mental disorder (MDD, bipolar, anxiety, & substance use disorders)

### Treatment
- SSRIs, SNRIs (venlafaxine)
- Prazosin (selective α1-blocker) to ↓nightmares
- CBT

### DSM-5 Criteria
- Exposure to actual or threatened death, serious injury, or sexual violence by directly experiencing or witnessing the trauma
- Recurrent intrusions of reexperiencing the event via memories, nightmares; intense distress or physiological reactions to cues relating to the trauma
- Active avoidance of triggering stimuli associated with the trauma
- Significant impairment in social or occupational functioning

### At least 2 of the following:
- Dissociative amnesia
- Negative feelings of self/others/world
  - Self-blame
  - Fear, horror, anger, guilt
  - Detachment, anhedonia

### And 2 of:
- Hypervigilance
- Exaggerated startle response
- Irritability/angry outbursts
- Impaired concentration
- Insomnia

\+

!  Addictive medications such as benzodiazepines should be avoided in the treatment of PTSD because of the high rate of comorbid substance use disorders.

# Schizoaffective Disorder

## Features

 Chronic psychotic disorder

 Prominent mood symptoms
- Mania
- Depression
- Bipolar

## Diagnosis

Patients meet criteria for schizophrenia + mood episodes

Psychosis must be present for at least 2 weeks without mood symptoms

## Treatment

 Goals:
- Manage both mood and psychotic symptoms

 Antipsychotics

 Antidepressants or mood stabilizers

Psychotherapy/support programs

## Prognosis

Chronic

Intermediate prognosis between those of mood disorders & schizophrenia

## Epidemiology

 Lifetime prevalence: <1%

# Schizoid Personality Disorder

##  Epidemiology

Prevalence:
0.5-7% of general population
Rare in treatment settings due to general withdrawal

♂  ♀
Men > Women

## Risk Factors

Deficient emotional nurturing
Famine
Family history of schizophrenia
Possible relationship to autism

## Features

 Preference to be alone

 No or few intimate relationships

Little interest in people

 Idiosyncratic interpretation of social transactions

 Restricted affect

 Intact reality testing

## Diagnosis

 Clinical diagnosis based on features, especially profound inability to develop personal relationships and respond to people meaningfully

 Differential diagnosis includes: Avoidant and schizotypal personality disorders, autism spectrum disorder

##  Treatment

**Psychopharmacotherapy** is only for comorbid conditions: Anxiety and depression
**Family therapy** for clarifying family's expectations and correcting their invasive or intolerant behaviors
**Group therapy** for acquisition of social skills and directed feedback
**Individual therapy** is challenging due to low perceived distress and low regard for relationships; cognitive approach can help explore distorted relationship views

### Cluster A B C

# Thought Disorders

# Schizophrenia

 > 6 months

## Features

 Symptoms >6 months

 Not caused by a substance or medical condition

 Results in life dysfunction

## Diagnosis

 Two or more of the following:
- Delusions
- Hallucinations
- Disorganized behavior or speech

 - Negative symptoms (Avolition, alogia, asociality, anhedonia, flat affect)

## Treatment

 Goals:
- Reduce symptoms
- Maximize functioning

 Hospitalization during acute episodes

Antipsychotics

 Psychotherapy/support programs

## Prognosis

 Chronic

 Relapsing with incomplete remissions

 Often with significant impairment

## Epidemiology

 Lifetime prevalence: 4/1000

 Onset
- Males: Adolescence/early adulthood
- Females: Bimodal in 20s and >45 years

# Schizophreniform Disorder

##  Features

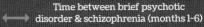

Time between brief psychotic disorder & schizophrenia (months 1-6)

Not caused by a substance or medical condition

 Cognitive impairment not usually present

##  Diagnosis

Symptoms of schizophrenia:
- Delusions
- Hallucinations
- Disorganized behavior or speech
- Negative symptoms

##  Treatment

 Goals:
- Reduce symptoms
- Maximize functioning

 Hospitalization during acute episodes

 Antipsychotics

 Psychotherapy/support programs

##  Prognosis

Most go on to display schizophrenia
- Small number recover

Those most likely to recover:
- Good premorbid function
- Acute onset
- Little to no psychosocial deficits

##  Epidemiology

Small percentage who recover

Typically follows that of schizophrenia

# Schizotypal Personality Disorder

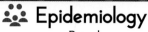 

##  Epidemiology

Prevalence:
~3-5% of general population
Up to 30% of psychiatric patients have
≥1 schizotypal traits

♂ ♀
Men > Women

## Risk Factors

Family history of schizophrenia

Schizotypal is on the schizophrenia spectrum

## Features

 Peculiar behavior, odd thoughts, odd speech, unusual perception, magical beliefs

 Social dysfunction, social anxiety, lack of motivation

 Underachieving in career

 High rates of anxiety and depression

## Diagnosis

 Clinical diagnosis based on features, especially odd behavior and perception, as well as social dysfunction

 Differential diagnosis includes other cluster A personality disorders, schizophrenia

 Comorbid conditions include mood disorder, anxiety, substance use disorder

##  Treatment

**Psychopharmacotherapy** involves antipsychotics for mod-severe symptoms and mild transient psychotic episodes, possible role of lithium in mood stabilization
**Group therapy** for social skills training; patients with severe symptoms can be disruptive
**Individual therapy** focuses on directed, supportive approach for reality testing, interpersonal boundaries, and problematic behavior. Cognitive focus for distorted thinking

### Cluster A B C

# Somatic Symptom Disorder

## DSM-5 Criteria

One or more somatic symptoms (may be predominantly pain) that are distressing or result in significant disruption

Excessive thoughts, feelings, or behaviors related to the symptoms or associated health concerns

Lasts at least 6 months

## Risk Factors

Female > male

Fewer years of education, lower SES unemployment

Childhood sexual abuse

Older age

## Treatment

Regular visits with one primary care physician

Patients often resist referral to mental health professional

Minimize unnecessary medical workups and treatments

Address psychological issues slowly

## Somatic Symptom **VS** Conversion Disorder

Express *lots of concern* about symptoms

Often do not appear concerned about symptoms

*Chronically* perseverate over symptoms

Symptoms tend to come on *abruptly*

Symptoms usually *somatic* in nature

Psychologic stress "converted" to *neurologic* symptoms

## Somatic Symptom **VS** Illness Anxiety Disorder

Somatic symptoms present

Somatic symptoms *not* present or are mild

### Both

Treat with regularly scheduled visits with one PCP. Use CBT and SSRIs for comorbid anxiety & depression

Preoccupation with *acquiring* or having a serious illness

Excessive health-related or maladaptive behavior

# Stimulant Use Disorder

## Epidemiology

 Used in the past month (2013):
- Cocaine: 1.5 million
- Methamphetamine (meth): 600,000

 Demographics:
- Highest in age 18-25
- Men > women

Cocaine implicated in ~40% of drug-related ED visits in 2011

## Clinical features

Intoxication: Euphoria, ↑energy, hyper-vigilance, psychosis; ↑BP/HR, mydriasis

 **DSM-5 criteria**

- Used more/longer than intended
- Wanted/tried to reduce/stop but failed
- Spent extensive time obtaining, using & recovering
- Intense craving for stimulant
- Use interfered with family/job/school
- Continued use despite social/interpersonal effects
- Continued use despite physical/mental health effects
- Gave up other activities due to stimulant use
- Use in physically hazardous context
- Developed tolerance
- Experienced withdrawal: Fatigue, anxiety, anhedonia, depression, ↑appetite/sleep

## Diagnosis

 DSM-5 diagnostic criteria
- Mild: 2-3 symptoms, moderate: 4-5, severe: 6 or more

 Labs can show
- Urine drug screen positive for cocaine/amphetamines

## Treatment

 Acute intoxication
- Benzodiazepines (BZD) for intense agitation
- Monitor & treat chest pain, seizures

 Withdrawal  β-Blockers alone → unopposed α activity
- BZD for agitation/insomnia
- Monitor & treat for depression/SI

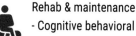 Rehab & maintenance
- Cognitive behavioral therapy
- 12 Steps
- Contingency management

## Complications

 - Myocardial infarction
- Cardiomyo-pathy
 - Stroke
- Seizures
- Cognitive impairment

 - Delayed gastric emptying
- Weight loss
 - Meth: Tooth decay, skin abrasions
- Nasal septal perforation

# Suicidality

 Suicide is the 10th and 14th leading cause of death in the United States and worldwide, respectively.

 In the United States, nearly half of completed suicides involve firearms.

## Risk Factors "Sad Persons"

 Sex—Male

 Age—Greater than 60 years

 Depression (and other psychiatric disorders)

Previous suicide attempts

Ethanol (and other substances)

(Loss of) Rational thinking

 Suicide in family

 Organized plan and access

 No social support

 Sickness

 In the United States, white, elderly males exhibit the highest rates of completed suicides

 A prior suicide attempt is the single most important risk factor for completed suicide

## Other Significant Risk Factors

 Childhood adversity

 Low educational attainment and socioeconomic status

 Military service

 Rural residence

 LGBTQ

 Single, divorced, and widowed marital status

## Protective Factors

 Social support

 Religiosity

 Pregnancy and parenthood

## Management

 A patient contemplating or actively planning suicide requires hospitalization, either voluntary or involuntary

 Pharmacotherapy

 Safety planning

 Psychotherapy

 Electroconvulsive therapy

# Tourette's Disorder
## Chronic Tic Disorder

### Tourette's Disorder

- **2+ motor and 1+ verbal tics**

### Chronic Tic Disorder

- **Either motor or verbal tics**

### DSM-5 Criteria

- Tics must be present for **1+ year**
- Tics must be **recurrent**
- Age of onset **<18 years**
- Must not be due to the direct physiologic effects of a substance or another general medical condition

## What Are Tics?

**Motor Tics**

- Rapid and repetitive **involuntary** muscle contractions resulting in **movements** or **vocalization**
- Prompted by **premonitory urges** that are relieved when the behavior is performed

- **Echophenomena:** Imitation of movements or sounds
- **Paliphenomena:** Repetition of actions or sounds
- **Coprophenomena:** Obscene gestures or vocalizations that occur without intent

**Vocal Tics**

## Treatment

α-1 Agonists
Clonidine, Guanfacine

Antipsychotics
First-generation antipsychotics (Haloperidol)
Atypical antipsychotics (Quetiapine)

Cognitive Behavioral Therapy (CBT)

# References _____

**ADHD**

Le T, Bhushan, V. *First Aid for the USMLE Step 2 CK*. 9th ed. New York, NY: McGraw Hill; 2015.

Le T, Bhushan V, Sochat M, Chavda Y. *First Aid for the USMLE Step 1 2017*. New York, NY: McGraw Hill; 2017.

Sadock BJ, Ahmad S, Sadock VA. *Kaplan & Sadock's Pocket Handbook of Clinical Psychiatry*. 6th ed. Lippincott Williams & Wilkins; 2018.

**Adjustment Disorder**

Ganti L, Kaufman MS, Blitzstein SM. *First Aid for the Psychiatry Clerkship*. 4th ed. New York, NY: McGraw Hill; 2016.

**Alcohol Use Disorder**

Ebert MH, Leckman JF, Petrakis IL, eds. *Current Diagnosis & Treatment: Psychiatry*. 3rd ed. New York, NY: McGraw Hill; 2019.

National Institute on Alcohol Abuse and Alcoholism. Alcohol Use Disorder: A Comparison Between DSM -IV and DSM -5. https://www.niaaa.nih.gov/publications/brochures-and-fact-sheets/alcohol-use-disorder-comparison-between-dsm

Papadakis MA, McPhee SJ, Bernstein J, eds. *Quick Medical Diagnosis & Treatment 2019*. New York, NY: McGraw Hill; 2019.

Toy E, Klamen D. *Case Files: Psychiatry*. 5th ed. New York, NY: McGraw Hill; 2015.

**Anorexia Nervosa**

Call C, Walsh BT, Attia E. From DSM-IV to DSM-5: changes to eating disorder diagnoses. *Curr Opin Psychiatry*. 2013;26(6):532-536. doi:10.1097/YCO.0b013e328365a321

Ebert MH, Leckman JF, Petrakis IL, eds. *Current Diagnosis & Treatment: Psychiatry*. 3rd ed. New York, NY: McGraw Hill; 2019.

Papadakis MA, McPhee SJ, Bernstein J, eds. *Quick Medical Diagnosis & Treatment 2019*. New York, NY: McGraw Hill; 2019.

**Antisocial Personality Disorder**

Weissman SH. Personality disorders. In: Ebert MH, Leckman JF, Petrakis IL, eds. *Current Diagnosis & Treatment: Psychiatry*. 3rd ed. New York, NY: McGraw Hill; 2019. http://accessmedicine.mhmedical.com/content.aspx?bookid=2509&sectionid=200806589.

**Autism Spectrum Disorder**

Le T, Bhushan, V. *First Aid for the USMLE Step 2 CK*. 9th ed. New York, NY: McGraw Hill; 2015.

Le T, Bhushan V, Sochat M, Chavda Y. *First Aid for the USMLE Step 1 2017*. New York, NY: McGraw Hill; 2017.

Sadock BJ, Ahmad S, Sadock VA. *Kaplan & Sadock's Pocket Handbook of Clinical Psychiatry*. 6th ed. Philadelphia, PA: Lippincott Williams & Wilkins; 2018.

**Borderline Personality Disorder**

Weissman SH. Personality disorders. In: Ebert MH, Leckman JF, Petrakis IL, eds. *Current Diagnosis & Treatment: Psychiatry*. 3rd ed. New York, NY: McGraw Hill; 2019. https://accessmedicine.mhmedical.com/content.aspx? bookid=2509&sectionid=20080658.

### Brief Psychotic Disorder

Shelton RC. Other psychotic disorders. In: Ebert MH, Leckman JF, Petrakis IL, eds. *Current Diagnosis & Treatment: Psychiatry*. 3rd ed. New York, NY: McGraw Hill; 2019. http://accessmedicine.mhmedical.com/content .aspx?bookid=2509&sectionid=200804045.

### Bulimia Nervosa

Call C, Walsh BT, Attia E. DSM-IV to DSM-5: changes to eating disorder diagnoses. *Curr Opin Psychiatry*. 2013;26(6):532-536. doi:10.1097/YCO.0b013e328365a321

Ebert MH, Leckman JF, Petrakis IL, eds. *Current Diagnosis & Treatment: Psychiatry*. 3rd ed. New York, NY: McGraw Hill; 2019.

Papadakis MA, McPhee SJ, Bernstein J, eds. *Quick Medical Diagnosis & Treatment 2019*. New York, NY: McGraw Hill; 2019.

### Conduct Disorder

Le T, Bhushan, V. *First Aid for the USMLE Step 2 CK*. 9th ed. New York, NY: McGraw Hill; 2015.

Le T, Bhushan V, Sochat M, Chavda Y. *First Aid for the USMLE Step 1 2017*. New York, NY: McGraw Hill; 2017.

Sadock BJ, Ahmad S, Sadock VA. *Kaplan & Sadock's Pocket Handbook of Clinical Psychiatry*. 6th ed. Lippincott Williams & Wilkins; 2018.

### Conversion Disorder

Ebert MH, Leckman JF, Petrakis IL, eds. *Current Diagnosis & Treatment: Psychiatry*. 3rd ed. New York, NY: McGraw Hill; 2019.

Papadakis MA, McPhee SJ, Bernstein J, eds. *Quick Medical Diagnosis & Treatment 2019*. New York, NY: McGraw Hill; 2019.

### Delirium

Ebert MH, Leckman JF, Petrakis IL, eds. *Current Diagnosis & Treatment: Psychiatry*. 3rd ed. New York, NY: McGraw Hill; 2019.

Papadakis MA, McPhee SJ, Bernstein J, eds. *Quick Medical Diagnosis & Treatment 2019*. New York, NY: McGraw Hill; 2019.

### Delusional Disorder

Shelton RC. Other psychotic disorders. In: Ebert MH, Leckman JF, Petrakis IL, eds. *Current Diagnosis & Treatment: Psychiatry*. 3rd ed. New York, NY: McGraw Hill; 2019. http://accessmedicine.mhmedical.com/content .aspx?bookid=2509&sectionid=200804045.

Sewell DD, Koh S, Maglione J, Greytak R, Marrone L, Jeste DV. General topics in geriatric psychiatry. In: Halter JB, Ouslander JG, Studenski S, et al., eds. *Hazzard's Geriatric Medicine and Gerontology*, 7th ed. New York, NY: McGraw Hill; 2017. http://accessmedicine.mhmedical.com/content.aspx?bookid=1923& sectionid=144524420.

### Dependent Personality Disorder

Weissman SH. Personality disorders. In: Ebert MH, Leckman JF, Petrakis IL, eds. *Current Diagnosis & Treatment: Psychiatry*. 3rd ed. New York, NY: McGraw Hill; 2019. https://accessmedicine.mhmedical.com/content.aspx? bookid=2509&sectionid=200806589.

### Factitious Disorder

Ebert MH, Leckman JF, Petrakis IL, eds. *Current Diagnosis & Treatment: Psychiatry*. 3rd ed. New York, NY: McGraw Hill; 2019.

Papadakis MA, McPhee SJ, Bernstein J, eds. *Quick Medical Diagnosis & Treatment 2019*. New York, NY: McGraw Hill; 2019.

## Gender Dysphoria

American Psychiatric Association. *Diagnostic and Statistical Manual of Mental Disorders (The DSM-5)*. 5th ed. Washington, D: American Psychiatric Association; 2013.

Raj KS, Williams N, DeBattista C. Psychiatric disorders. In: Papadakis MA, McPhee SJ, Rabow MW, eds. *Current Medical Diagnosis & Treatment 2019*. New York, NY: McGraw Hill; 2019. https://accessmedicine.mhmedical.com/content.aspx?bookid=2449&sectionid=1945769917. Accessed August 10, 2019.

VanderLaan DP, Zucker KJ. Gender dysphoria in children and adolescents. In: Ebert MH, Leckman JF, Petrakis IL, eds. *Current Diagnosis & Treatment: Psychiatry*. 3rd ed. New York, NY: McGraw Hill; 2019. https://accessmedicine.mhmedical.com/content.aspx?bookid=2509&sectionid=200808639. Accessed August 10, 2019.

## Generalized Anxiety Disorder

Ganti L, Kaufman MS, Blitzstein SM. *First Aid for the Psychiatry Clerkship*. 4th ed. New York, NY: McGraw Hill; 2016.

Le T, Bhushan, V. *First Aid for the USMLE Step 2 CK*. 9th ed. New York, NY: McGraw Hill; 2015.

## Histrionic Personality Disorder

Weissman SH. Personality disorders. In: Ebert MH, Leckman JF, Petrakis IL, eds. *Current Diagnosis & Treatment: Psychiatry*. 3rd ed. New York, NY: McGraw Hill; 2019. https://accessmedicine.mhmedical.com/content.aspx?bookid=2509&sectionid=200806589.

## Intellectual Disability Disorder

Le T, Bhushan, V. *First Aid for the USMLE Step 2 CK*. 9th ed. New York, NY: McGraw Hill; 2015.

Le T, Bhushan V, Sochat M, Chavda Y. *First Aid for the USMLE Step 1 2017*. New York, NY: McGraw Hill; 2017.

Sadock BJ, Ahmad S, Sadock VA. *Kaplan & Sadock's Pocket Handbook of Clinical Psychiatry*. 6th ed. Lippincott Williams & Wilkins; 2018.

## Mood Disorders: Bipolar

Ebert MH, Leckman JF, Petrakis IL, eds. *Current Diagnosis & Treatment: Psychiatry*. 3rd ed. New York, NY: McGraw Hill; 2019.

Papadakis MA, McPhee SJ, Bernstein J, eds. *Quick Medical Diagnosis & Treatment 2019*. New York, NY: McGraw Hill; 2019.

## Mood Disorders: Major Depressive Disorder

Ebert MH, Leckman JF, Petrakis IL, eds. *Current Diagnosis & Treatment: Psychiatry*. 3rd ed. New York, NY: McGraw Hill; 2019.

Papadakis MA, McPhee SJ, Bernstein J, eds. *Quick Medical Diagnosis & Treatment 2019*. New York, NY: McGraw Hill; 2019.

## Narcissistic Personality Disorder

Ebert MH, Leckman JF, Petrakis IL, eds. *Current Diagnosis & Treatment: Psychiatry*. 3rd ed. New York, NY: McGraw Hill; 2019.

Papadakis MA, McPhee SJ, Bernstein J, eds. *Quick Medical Diagnosis & Treatment 2019*. New York, NY: McGraw Hill; 2019.

## Obsessive-Compulsive Disorder

Ganti L, Kaufman MS, Blitzstein SM. *First Aid for the Psychiatry Clerkship*. 4th ed. New York, NY: McGraw Hill; 2016.

Raj KS, Williams N, DeBattista C. Obsessive-compulsive disorder & related disorders. In: Papadakis MA, McPhee SJ, Rabow MW, eds. *Current Medical Diagnosis and Treatment 2020*. New York, NY: McGraw Hill; 2020. http://accessmedicine.mhmedical.com/content.aspx?bookid=2683&sectionid=225133048. Accessed December 19, 2019.

**Oppositional Defiance Disorder**
Le T, Bhushan, V. *First Aid for the USMLE Step 2 CK*. 9th ed. New York, NY: McGraw Hill; 2015.

Le T, Bhushan V, Sochat M, Chavda Y. *First Aid for the USMLE Step 1 2017*. New York, NY: McGraw Hill; 2017.

Sadock BJ, Ahmad S, Sadock VA. *Kaplan & Sadock's Pocket Handbook of Clinical Psychiatry*. 6th ed. Lippincott Williams & Wilkins; 2018.

**Panic Disorder**
Ganti L, Kaufman MS, Blitzstein SM. *First Aid for the Psychiatry Clerkship*. 4th ed. New York, NY: McGraw Hill; 2016.

**Paranoid Personality Disorder**
Ebert MH, Leckman JF, Petrakis IL, eds. *Current Diagnosis & Treatment: Psychiatry*. 3rd ed. New York, NY: McGraw Hill; 2019.

Papadakis MA, McPhee SJ, Bernstein J, eds. *Quick Medical Diagnosis & Treatment 2019*. New York, NY: McGraw Hill; 2019.

**Phobias**
Ganti L, Kaufman MS, Blitzstein SM. *First Aid for the Psychiatry Clerkship*. 4th ed. New York, NY: McGraw Hill; 2016.

**PTSD**
Ganti L, Kaufman MS, Blitzstein SM. *First Aid for the Psychiatry Clerkship*. 4th ed. New York, NY: McGraw Hill; 2016.

**Schizoaffective Disorder**
Shelton RC. Other psychotic disorders. In: Ebert MH, Leckman JF, Petrakis IL, eds. *Current Diagnosis & Treatment: Psychiatry*. 3rd ed. New York, NY: McGraw Hill; 2019. http://accessmedicine.mhmedical.com/content.aspx?bookid=2509&sectionid=200804045.

**Schizoid Personality Disorder**
Ebert MH, Leckman JF, Petrakis IL, eds. *Current Diagnosis & Treatment: Psychiatry*. 3rd ed. New York, NY: McGraw Hill; 2019.

Papadakis MA, McPhee SJ, Bernstein J, eds. *Quick Medical Diagnosis & Treatment 2019*. New York, NY: McGraw Hill; 2019.

**Schizophrenia**
Radhakrishnan R, Ganesh S, Meltzer HY, et al. In: Ebert MH, Leckman JF, Petrakis IL, eds. *Current Diagnosis & Treatment: Psychiatry*. 3rd ed. New York, NY: McGraw Hill; 2019. http://accessmedicine.mhmedical.com/content.aspx?bookid=2509&sectionid=200803785.

**Schizophreniform Disorder**
Shelton RC. Other psychotic disorders. In: Ebert MH, Leckman JF, Petrakis IL, eds. *Current Diagnosis & Treatment: Psychiatry*. 3rd ed. New York, NY: McGraw Hill; 2019. http://accessmedicine.mhmedical.com/content.aspx?bookid=2509&sectionid=200804045.

**Schizotypal Personality Disorder**
Ebert MH, Leckman JF, Petrakis IL, eds. *Current Diagnosis & Treatment: Psychiatry*. 3rd ed. New York, NY: McGraw Hill; 2019.

Papadakis MA, McPhee SJ, Bernstein J, eds. *Quick Medical Diagnosis & Treatment 2019*. New York, NY: McGraw Hill; 2019.

**Somatic Symptom Disorder**
Ganti L, Kaufman MS, Blitzstein SM. *First Aid for the Psychiatry Clerkship*. 4th ed. New York, NY: McGraw Hill; 2016.

**Stimulant Use Disorder**

Ebert MH, Leckman JF, Petrakis IL, eds. *Current Diagnosis & Treatment: Psychiatry*. 3rd ed. New York, NY: McGraw Hill; 2019.

Papadakis MA, McPhee SJ, Bernstein J, eds. *Quick Medical Diagnosis & Treatment 2019*. New York, NY: McGraw Hill; 2019.

**Suicidality**

Ganti L, Kaufman MS, Blitzstein SM. *First Aid for the Psychiatry Clerkship*. 5th ed. New York, NY: McGraw Hill; 2018

Schreiber J, Culpepper L. Suicidal ideation and behavior in adults. In: Roy-Byrne PP, Solomon D, eds. *Up-To-Date*. Waltham, MA: UpToDate Inc. https://www.uptodate.com. Accessed September 17, 2019.

**Tourette's Disorder**

Le T, Bhushan, V. *First Aid for the USMLE Step 2 CK*. 9th ed. New York, NY: McGraw Hill; 2015.

Le T, Bhushan V, Sochat M, Chavda Y. *First Aid for the USMLE Step 1 2017*. New York, NY: McGraw Hill; 2017.

Sadock BJ, Ahmad S, Sadock VA. *Kaplan & Sadock's Pocket Handbook of Clinical Psychiatry*. 6th ed. Lippincott Williams & Wilkins; 2018.

# Pulmonology

*Neeral Shah, MD*

# Acute Respiratory Distress Syndrome (ARDS)

**Definition:** Clinical syndrome of rapid-onset dyspnea and hypoxemia characterized by diffuse alveolar damage (DAD). Multiple etiologies; suspect in patients with new oxygen needs

**Risk Factors:** Older age, chronic alcohol use, metabolic acidosis, pancreatitis, severity of associated illness

## Causes

- Pneumonia
- Gastric acid aspiration
- Pulmonary contusion
- Toxin inhalation
- Near-drowning

**Direct Lung Injury**

- Sepsis
- Severe trauma
- Pancreatitis
- Drug overdose
- Burns

**Indirect Lung Injury**

## Diagnosis

**Chest X-ray:** Bilateral opacities
**BNP:** Normal
**Echo:** Normal, unless other heart pathology present

**Notable Diagnostic Tests**

**$PaO_2/FiO_2$ ratio:**
Mild: >200-300
Moderate: >100-200
Severe: ≤100

**Severity**

## Phases

**Exudative:** Day 1-7
DAD from alveolar edema, neutrophil-rich infiltration, hyaline membrane formation

**Proliferative:** Day 7-21
Interstitial inflammation, early fibrotic changes

**Fibrotic:** Day 21+
Major fibrosis, bullae, only in some patients

## Rule Out

Cardiogenic Pulmonary Edema

Alveolar Hemorrhage

Bilateral Pneumonia

## Treatment

**Ventilator Support:**
**Tidal Volume:** 6 mL/kg predicted body weight
**PEEP:** Titrate to optimize $PaO_2$ and minimize $FiO_2$

**Fluids:** Limit to avoid pulmonary edema

**Treat underlying condition!**

# Asthma

## Clinical Features

**Mild/Moderate Symptoms**
Dry cough
End-expiratory wheezing
Chest tightness

**Severe Symptoms**
Dyspnea
Hypoxemia
Pulsus paradoxus

## Precipitating Factors

Viral URI
Allergens
Stress

**Atopic Triad-Associated Risks** !
1. Asthma
2. Eczema
3. Allergic rhinitis

## Diagnosis

Pulmonary Function Test: $FEV_1$/FVC ratio ⬇

Methacholine Challenge: $FEV_1$ ⬇

CXR: Normal; possible hyperinflation with diaphragm flattening

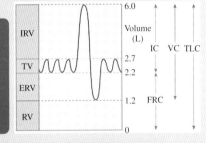

## Treatment/Management

**Acute Symptoms:**
Short-acting $\beta_2$-agonist
Inhaled corticosteroid
Anticholinergic

**For Severe Symptoms:**
Systemic corticosteroids
Magnesium

# Bronchiectasis
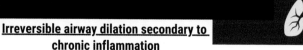

**Irreversible airway dilation secondary to chronic inflammation**

## Clinical Presentation

**History:**

Productive cough—Yellow/Green sputum
Dyspnea
Hemoptysis

**Physical Findings:**

Rales/Rhonchi
Wheezing
Clubbed digits

## Diagnosis

**Gold Standard—High-Resolution CT Scan**
**Findings:**
Airway dilation **(Tram-Track Sign)**
Lack of bronchial tapering
Bronchial wall thickening

**Spirometry:**
Decreased $FEV_1$/FVC

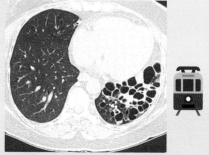
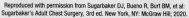

Reproduced with permission from Sugarbaker DJ, Bueno R, Burt BM, et al: Sugarbaker's Adult Chest Surgery, 3rd ed. New York, NY: McGraw Hill; 2020.

## Treatment

**Antibiotics:** (For Acute Exacerbations)
**Common Bugs:**
*H. influenzae*
*P. aeruginosa*

**Bronchial Hygiene:**
Hydration
Hypertonic saline
Chest physiotherapy
Exercise

**Anti-inflammatories:**
Inhaled/systemic glucocorticoids

# COPD

## Clinical Presentation:

| Emphysema |  VS | Chronic Bronchitis |
|---|---|---|
| "Pink Puffer"—Late hypercarbia + hypoxia | | "Blue Bloater"—Early hypercarbia + hypoxia |
| Thin with muscle wasting and pursed lips | | Overweight and edematous |
| Productive cough >3 months for 2 years | | Terminal airway destruction + dilation |

## Diagnosis:

**Pulmonary Function Tests (PFTs)**

**Gold Standard:**

| $FEV_1/FVC$ | FVC | $FEV_1$ | TLC | Diffusing Capacity |
|---|---|---|---|---|
| Decreased | Decreased-Normal | Decreased | Normal-Increased | Decreased |

**Chest X-Ray:**
Hyperinflated lungs, flat diaphragm with reduced lung markings

**Arterial Blood Gas:**
Hypoxemia with acute/chronic respiratory acidosis

  $O_2 \downarrow$

## Treatment:

| Acute Exacerbation |  VS | Chronic COPD |
|---|---|---|
| Inhaled β-2 agonists<br>Anticholinergics<br>IV/Inhaled corticosteroids<br>Antibiotics<br>Supplemental oxygen<br>BiPAP<br>INTUBATION if severe<br>hypoxemia/hypercapnia | | Inhaled β-2 agonists<br>Anticholinergics<br>Inhaled corticosteroids<br>Supplemental oxygen only<br>if hypoxemic,<br>right heart failure, or<br>polycythemia<br>Encourage smoking cessation +<br>pneumococcal + flu vaccine |

# Cystic Fibrosis

Autosomal recessive mutations in the gene for CFTR, a cell-surface chloride ion channel, cause chronic pulmonary and pancreatic disease

Pathophysiology: Nonfunctional, incorrectly transported, or improperly folded CFTR protein, causing buildup of exocrine secretions

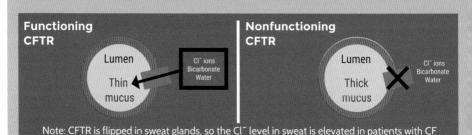

**Functioning CFTR**

Lumen — Thin mucus — Cl⁻ ions, Bicarbonate, Water

**Nonfunctioning CFTR**

Lumen — Thick mucus — Cl⁻ ions, Bicarbonate, Water

Note: CFTR is flipped in sweat glands, so the Cl⁻ level in sweat is elevated in patients with CF

Diagnosis: Typically found during newborn screen. Confirmed in patients of all ages by genetic testing (most common mutation = deletion of F508) and skin chloride sweat test

## Manifestations

**Pulmonary**
- Acute exacerbations
- Infections: *Pseudomonas*, *S. aureus*, *Burkholderia*, *Mycobacteria*, *Aspergillus*
- Chronic inflammation
- Lung failure

**Pancreatic**
- Malabsorption
- Steatorrhea
- Vitamin deficiency
- CF-related diabetes mellitus
- Failure to thrive

**Other**
- Osteopenia/Osteoporosis
- Liver steatosis/cirrhosis
- Meconium ileus (neonates)
- Distal intestinal obstruction syndrome (DIOS)
- Vas deferens agenesis

## Treatment

**Medical**
- Pancreatic enzyme replacement
- Bronchodilators, steroids
- Oral/nebulized/IV antibiotics
- Mucus clearance: Nebulized DNAse, nebulized hypertonic saline, and chest physiotherapy

**Molecular**
- Target-specific mutations
- Ivacaftor: Promotes CFTR channel opening; targets G551D CFTR
- Lumacaftor: Promotes cell surface localization of delF508 CFTR

**Transplant**
- Bilateral lung transplant
- Median survival >8 years
- Eligibility based on PFTs, exacerbation frequency, and oxygen requirements

# Environmental Exposures

**Asbestosis**  **Silicosis**

**Berylliosis** **Coal Miners Pneumoconiosis**

## The Disease

**Asbestosis:** Fibrotic lung disease; >20 years post-exposure

**Berylliosis:** Chronic granulomatous lung disease; months to >30 years post-exposure

**Silicosis:** Inflammatory and scarring lung disease; 10-30 years post-exposure

**Coal miners pneumoconiosis:** Chronic lung disease with parenchymal infiltration; >10 years post-exposure

## Exposure

**Asbestos:** Widely used in construction materials

**Beryllium:** Industrial applications (metal alloy manufacturing, ceramics, electronics, aerospace)

**Silica:** Blasting agent in mining, masonry, stone cutting, glass manufacturing

**Coal miners pneumoconiosis:** Coal dust, urban industrial smoke

## Symptoms

 Cough and dyspnea common to all 4 diseases

**Asbestosis:** Clubbing, cor pulmonale

Reproduced with permission from Simel DL, Rennie D: The Rational Clinical Examination: Evidence-Based Clinical Diagnosis. New York, NY: McGraw Hill; 2009.

**Berylliosis:** Fevers, night sweats, weight loss, cutaneous nodules

**Silicosis:** Fevers, weight loss, fatigue, chest pain

**Coal miners pneumoconiosis:** Black sputum, cor pulmonale

## Diagnosis

 Chest CT and PFTs for all 4 diseases

**Asbestosis:** Lung biopsy; PFTs with reduced volumes & compliance in restrictive pattern

**Berylliosis:** PFTs with restrictive pattern and decreased DLCO; bronchial biopsy shows noncaseating granulomas

**Silicosis:** Chest X-ray with nodules, hilar calcification, lymphadenopathy; bronchoalveolar lavage to exclude other causes

**Coal miners pneumoconiosis:** Chest CT with lung fibrosis, lung mass

## Management

 Avoidance of further exposure

 Smoking cessation

 Steroids and bronchodilators for symptomatic treatment

 Pneumococcal and influenza vaccination

 Lung transplant for advanced disease

# Eosinophilic Pulmonary Syndromes

**Definition:** Diverse group of disorders, typically presenting with eosinophilic pulmonary infiltrates, dyspnea, cough, and fever

## Extrinsic Causes

 **Medications**

Phenytoin
Acetaminophen
Nitrofurantoin
Ampicillin
Ranitidine

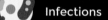 **Infections**

Helminths
*Ascaris,* Hookworms, *Strongyloides*
Filariae
*W. bancrofti, B. malayi,*
Tropical pulmonary eosinophilia

## Intrinsic Causes

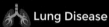 **Lung Disease**

-ABPA
-Eosinophilic granuloma of the lung
-ILD

 **Systemic Disease**

-Eosinophilic granulomatosis with polyangiitis
-Various systemic hypereosinophilic syndromes
-Neoplasm

### Diagnosis:
Workup extrinsic and intrinsic causes based on patient history

### Treatment:
Stop offending medication, start antimicrobials, or manage lung/systemic disease

## Idiopathic

One-third of all cases are idiopathic
Treat with steroids

### Acute
Sudden symptom onset
Non-specific chest X-ray findings
BAL shows eosinophilia
Peripheral blood eosinophilia rare

### Chronic
Systemic symptoms and asthma
Peripheral infiltrates on chest X-ray
BAL shows eosinophilia
Peripheral blood eosinophilia common

# Hypoxia & Hypoxemia

## Mechanisms of oxygen deprivation

### Hypoxia

Reduced oxygen delivery to tissues

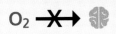

Decreased cardiac output

Hypoxemia

Anemia

Carbon monoxide poisoning

### Hypoxemia

Reduced partial pressure of oxygen in blood

$O_2$ ⇥ ◦

**Normal A-a gradient:**
- Low $FiO_2$ (high altitudes)
- Hypoventilation

**Increased A-a gradient:**
- V/Q mismatch
- Right-to-left shunt
- Diffusion limitation

! $PaO_2$ does NOT correct with oxygen in shunt

### Ischemia

Reduced blood flow to tissues

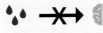

Impaired arterial flow

Decreased venous drainage

---

## Oxygen–Hemoglobin Dissociation Curve

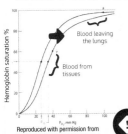

Reproduced with permission from Levitzky MG: Pulmonary Physiology, 9th ed. New York, NY: McGraw Hill; 2017.

**Rightward shift:**
- ↓affinity of Hb for oxygen
- Facilitates oxygen unloading to tissues

**Causes of right shift:**
- ↓ pH (↑[H+])
- ↑$CO_2$
- Exercise (↑temperature)
- 2,3-BPG
- Altitude

! Sigmoid shape is from positive cooperativity of Hb tetramer

$O_2$ Content of blood = (1.34 x [Hb] x $SaO_2$) + (0.003 x $PaO_2$)

**Anemia** - ↓[Hb]
- Decreased hemoglobin level
- Reduced $O_2$ carrying capacity

**Carbon monoxide** - ↓$SaO_2$
- CO has greater Hb affinity than $O_2$
- Causes left shift in Hb curve & impaired $O_2$ offloading to tissues
- Reduced $O_2$ saturation of Hb
- Normal pulse oximetry reading

**Hypoxemia** - ↓$PaO_2$
- Less dissolved $O_2$ for binding Hb

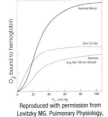

Reproduced with permission from Levitzky MG. Pulmonary Physiology, 9th ed. New York, NY: McGraw Hill; 2017.

## Alveolar Gas Equation

$$PAO_2 = PIO_2 - PaCO_2/R$$

$PIO_2 = FiO_2 \times Pb$

On room air at sea level:
$PIO_2 = 0.21 \times 760$ mm Hg
$PIO_2 = \sim150$ mm Hg

$PAO_2$ - alveolar $PO_2$
$PaO_2$ - arteriolar $PO_2$
R - respiratory quotient (0.8)
$PIO_2$ - $PO_2$ of inspired air
$FiO_2$ - $O_2$ fraction of air
Pb - barometric pressure

$$PAO_2 = 150 \text{ mm Hg} - PaCO_2/0.8$$

### A-a Gradient = $PAO_2 - PaCO_2$

Normal A-a gradient increases with age (< age/4 + 4)

### V/Q Mismatch

Ventilation (V) & perfusion (Q) are not matched (ideal V/Q = 1)

V/Q = 0
- Perfusion without ventilation (**shunt**)
- ie, alveolar obstruction

V/Q = ∞
- Ventilation without perfusion
- ie, pulmonary embolism

# Interstitial Lung Disease

Class of 200+ typically chronic diseases characterized by diffuse parenchymal abnormalities. Broadly divided into diseases with predominant fibrosis vs predominant granulomatous reaction.

## Presentation: Typically Chronic

Dyspnea       Cough       Fatigue

## Risk Factors

Advanced Age       Exposures

Smoking       Family History

## Workup

- Exam: Bibasilar crackles, clubbing
- Imaging: Honeycombing on CT
- PFTs: Restrictive pattern, decreased total lung capacity
- Lung Biopsy: Gives specific diagnosis

## Treatment

- Remove causative agent
- Lung transplant
- Smoking cessation
- Glucocorticoids
- Oxygen support

# Differential Diagnosis

## Idiopathic Pulmonary Fibrosis
- Common type, shows typical ILD story
- CT: Lower lobe opacities, honeycombing
- Acute exacerbations carry high mortality
- Treat with antifibrotic agents, not steroids

## Cryptogenic Organizing Pneumonia
- Pathologic pattern that is either idiopathic or due to another condition
- Can present as subacute and flu-like
- CT: Recurrent & migratory consolidations and ground glass opacities

## Hypersensitivity Pneumonitis
- Inflammatory, rather than fibrotic, process
- Caused by repeated inhalation of antigen by a susceptible person
- Avoid exposure (animals, mold, chemicals), treat with glucocorticoids

## Other Important Causes
- Sarcoidosis
- Pulmonary vasculitides
- Connective tissue diseases: Scleroderma, rheumatoid arthritis, and lupus
- Acute interstitial pneumonia

# Interstitial Lung Disease, Drug-Induced

## Etiologies

Over 450 drugs can cause ILD:

**Antimicrobials**
Nitrofurantoin, Amphotericin B

**Anti-inflammatories**
NSAIDs

**Biologics**
Infliximab, Rituximab

**Cardiovascular**
Amiodarone, Statins

**Chemotherapy**
Bleomycin, Methotrexate

Mechanisms include:

**Direct damage**

**Hypersensitivity**
Drug haptens

**Phospholipidosis**
eg, amiodarone

## Presentation

Post-exposure onset is variable
Days to even years
**Acute**: Fever, rash, wheeze
**Chronic**: Progressive dyspnea
May present as **pulmonary hemorrhage** with **hemoptysis**

Acute injury → Chronic injury → Fibrosis → Poor gas exchange

## Diagnosis

**4 key steps to diagnosis:**
History of drug exposure
Clinical/imaging/histological findings of ILD
Rule out other causes of ILD
Improvement with removal of drug

**Histopathological patterns are variable:**
- Hypersensitivity pneumonitis
- Granulomatous pneumonitis
- Bronchiolitis obliterans organizing pneumonia (BOOP)
- Pulmonary hemorrhage

**PFTs:**
Most often—**Restrictive** pattern
Low TLC, RV, DLCO
Bronchospasm or BOOP can be **obstructive**
Low $FEV_1$/FVC ratio

**Bronchoalveolar lavage (BAL) patterns:**
- BOOP—Increased lymphocytes
- Chemotherapy—Increased neutrophils
- Amiodarone—**Foamy macrophages**

## Management

Initial management—**Remove offending agent**

If severe or unresponsive—**Glucocorticoids**

Time to resolution depends on chronicity of injury

# Mechanical Ventilation & Noninvasive Positive Pressure Ventilation (NIPPV)

## Mechanical Ventilation

Positive inspiratory pressure delivered to a patient through an endotracheal tube

### Indications for Ventilation:

Hypoxemia or hypercarbia due to lung pathology

Inability to protect the airway
- Decreased consciousness (low GCS)
- Impending airway obstruction

Impending respiratory failure due to excessively increased work of breathing

### $O_2$ Goals

**Oxygenation ($\uparrow PaO_2$)**
- Increase $FiO_2$
- Increase PEEP

**Ventilation ($\downarrow PaCO_2$)**
- Increase RR
- Increase TV

### Ventilator Modes

**Volume Control**
- TV is preset
- Paw varies

**Pressure Control**
- Paw is preset
- TV varies

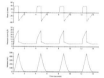

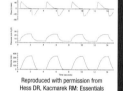

Reproduced with permission from Hess DR, Kacmarek RM: Essentials of Mechanical Ventilation, 4th ed. New York, NY: McGraw Hill; 2019.

Reproduced with permission from Hess DR, Kacmarek RM: Essentials of Mechanical Ventilation, 4th ed. New York, NY: McGraw Hill; 2019.

Setting to allow patient to trigger breaths (arrows)

### Vent Parameters:

**Tidal Volume (TV)**
- Volume of air delivered per breath

**Respiratory Rate (RR)**
- Number of breaths delivered per minute

**$O_2$ Fraction of Oxygen in Inspired Air ($FiO_2$)**

**Positive End-Expiratory Pressure (PEEP)**
- Pressure to keep alveoli open at the end of expiration

**Peak Airway Pressure Delivered (Paw)**

**Pressure Support**
- Pressure to assist a patient's breathing
- Used for weaning patients from the vent

---

## Noninvasive Positive Pressure Ventilation

Assisted ventilation without the use of an endotracheal tube

### CPAP vs BiPAP

### Benefits

Intubation is not necessary
- No indwelling ET tube
- Lower risk of vocal cord injury
- Lower rate of infection

No sedation or neuromuscular paralysis is needed

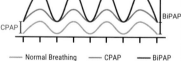

Continuous positive pressure at one level

Two levels of positive pressure

CPAP

BiPAP

— Normal Breathing  — CPAP  — BiPAP

CPAP promotes oxygenation by keeping airways open (OSA)

BiPAP assists ventilation and removal of $CO_2$ (COPD exacerbation)

### Contraindications

Comatose state

Inability to clear secretions

Upper airway obstruction

Respiratory arrest

Mask intolerance & patient noncompliance

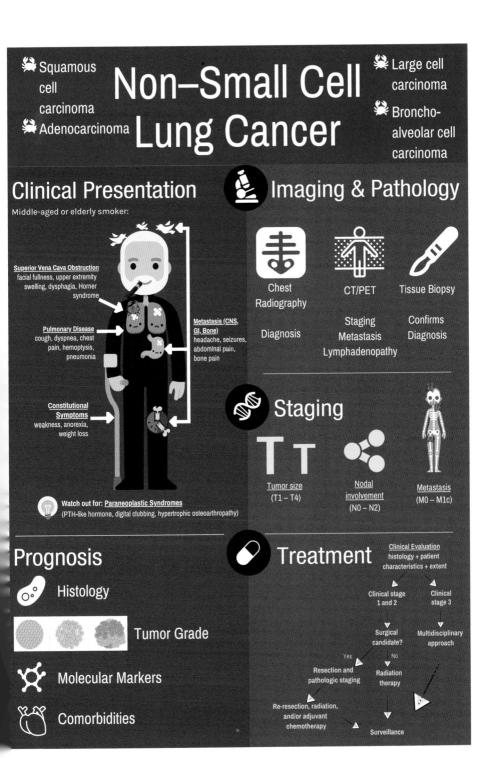

# Non–Small Cell Lung Cancer

🦀 Squamous cell carcinoma
🦀 Adenocarcinoma
🦀 Large cell carcinoma
🦀 Broncho-alveolar cell carcinoma

## Clinical Presentation

Middle-aged or elderly smoker:

**Superior Vena Cava Obstruction**
facial fullness, upper extremity swelling, dysphagia, Horner syndrome

**Pulmonary Disease**
cough, dyspnea, chest pain, hemoptysis, pneumonia

**Metastasis (CNS, GI, Bone)**
headache, seizures, abdominal pain, bone pain

**Constitutional Symptoms**
weakness, anorexia, weight loss

💡 Watch out for: **Paraneoplastic Syndromes**
(PTH-like hormone, digital clubbing, hypertrophic osteoarthropathy)

## Imaging & Pathology

**Chest Radiography**
Diagnosis

**CT/PET**
Staging
Metastasis
Lymphadenopathy

**Tissue Biopsy**
Confirms Diagnosis

## Staging

T  T
Tumor size (T1 – T4)

Nodal involvement (N0 – N2)

Metastasis (M0 – M1c)

## Prognosis

🔬 Histology

Tumor Grade

Molecular Markers

Comorbidities

## Treatment

**Clinical Evaluation**
histology + patient characteristics + extent

Clinical stage 1 and 2 → Surgical candidate?
- Yes → Resection and pathologic staging → Re-resection, radiation, and/or adjuvant chemotherapy
- No → Radiation therapy → Surveillance

Clinical stage 3 → Multidisciplinary approach

# PFTs and Pulmonary Physical Exam

## Pulmonary Function Tests

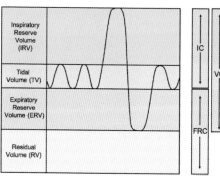

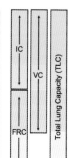

**Inspiratory Capacity (IC):** Air that can be taken in after normal exhalation

**Functional Residual Capacity (FRC):** Volume of gas in lungs after normal expiration

**Vital Capacity (VC):** Maximum volume expired after a maximal inspiration

**Forced Expiratory Volume (FEV$_1$):** Volume that can be expelled from lungs in 1 second

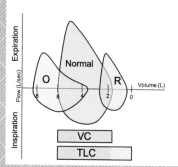

| **Obstructive (O):** Air trapping in lungs | **Restrictive (R):** Decreased lung volumes |
|---|---|
| ↓ FEV$_1$/FVC | ↑ FEV$_1$/FVC (≥80%) |
| ↑ TLC, ↑ FRC, ↑ RV | ↓ TLC, ↓ FVC |
| Includes: COPD, asthma, chronic bronchitis | Includes: Interstitial lung diseases, diseases of poor breathing mechanics |

## Pulmonary Physical Exam

### Inspection

Cyanosis/clubbing

Scars/discoloration

Respiratory rate

### Examination

Percussion & auscultation of the lung fields

Tactile fremitus (99)

Egophony

Chest wall expansion

### Locations of auscultation and percussion

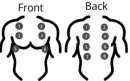

Front    Back

---

**Inspiratory Stridor:** Upper airway obstruction

**Abnormal Breath Sounds**

**Wheeze:** Asthma & COPD

**Coarse Crackles:** Pneumonia & Pulmonary edema

**Fine Crackles:** Pulmonary fibrosis

# ✚ Pleural Effusions

**Etiology:** ↑Pleural fluid formation or ↓removal

## Diagnosis

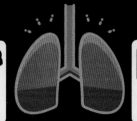

**Clinical Presentation**
Dyspnea
Decreased breath sounds
Dullness to percussion
Symptoms of underlying cause

**Imaging**
<u>Noninvasive:</u>
X-ray, CT scan
<u>Invasive:</u>
US-guided thoracentesis

**Fluid Analysis: Light's Criteria**
Pleural fluid **protein**/serum **protein** >0.5?
Pleural fluid **LDH**/serum **LDH** >0.6?
Pleural fluid **LDH** >2/3 upper normal serum limit?

Yes to 1+ ✓                    No to all ✗

### Exudate

 **Extra Labs:** Glucose, Cytology, Diff, Culture/Stain, TB Assay

Glucose <60                          Glucose >60

 **Bacterial Pneumonia**      **Viral/TB Infection**

 **Malignancy**           **Chylothorax**

 **Rheumatic Disease**      **Pulmonary Embolism**

### Transudate
↑Hydrostatic Pressure

**Left Heart Failure**

↓ Oncotic Pressure

                    **Cirrhosis**

**Nephrotic Syndrome**

## Treatment

Thoracentesis for symptomatic relief
Cure: Treat underlying condition

## Complications

Empyema, Pleural scarring
Iatrogenic: Pneumothorax

# Pneumothorax

__Definition__: Accumulation of air in the pleural cavity
__Symptoms__: Dyspnea, uneven chest expansion, chest pain
__Physical Exam__: Hyperresonance, diminished breath sounds on affected side
__Imaging__: Confirmed on chest X-ray

## Primary Spontaneous

__Etiology__: Spontaneous rupture of apical pleural blebs
__Risk Factors__: Smoking; tall, thin, young men
__Treatment__: Oxygen, simple needle aspiration (2nd intercostal space, midclavicular line)
__Refractory__: Thoracoscopy—bleb stapling or pleural abrasion

## Secondary

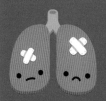

__Etiology__: Rupture of blebs associated with lung disease
__Risk Factors__: COPD, occasionally other lung disease
__Treatment__: Chest tube (4th/5th intercostal space, mid-axillary line). May need thoracoscopy/thoracotomy for bleb stapling or abrasion
__Alternative__: Pleurodesis—Use a sclerosing agent, like doxycycline

## Traumatic

__Etiology__: Non/penetrating trauma (rib fracture/gunshot)
__Treatment__: Chest tube to remove air if hemopneumothorax present, place one inferiorly to drain blood
__Iatrogenic__: Think thoracentesis, central line placement. Treat with oxygen and simple aspiration, chest tube if needed

## Tension

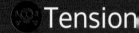

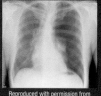

__Etiology__: All of the above, ventilator barotrauma, CPR: creates one-way valve, trapping air in pleural space & causing mediastinal shift
__Caution__: Decreases venous return to heart and cardiac output
__Special Exam Findings:__ Tracheal deviation, hemodynamic instability
__Treatment__: Immediate needle aspiration, followed by chest tube

# Pulmonary Hypertension

## Background

- Pulmonary HTN: Mean pulmonary arterial pressure of >25 mm Hg (normal = 15)
- Cor Pulmonale: Right-sided heart failure due to pulmonary HTN

## Classification

| Group 1 | Pulmonary arterial HTN (see below) |
|---------|-------------------------------------|
| Group 2 | PH from left-sided heart disease |
| Group 3 | PH from chronic hypoxic lung disease |
| Group 4 | PH from chronic thromboembolic disease |
| Group 5 | PH with unclear, multifactorial etiology |

## Clinical Manifestations

 Dyspnea on Exertion

 Fatigue

 Syncope

 Chest Pain

 JVD

 Abdominal Distention

 Edema

2° to right ventricular failure

## Group 1 Etiologies

 Congenital heart disease

 Drug/toxin induced

 Connective tissue disease

 HIV infection

Portal HTN

## Diagnosis

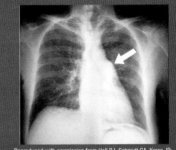

Reproduced with permission from Hall BJ, Schmidt GA, Kress JP: Principles of Critical Care, 4th ed. New York, NY: McGraw Hill; 2015.

 CXR shows enlargement of pulmonary arteries (above)

 ECG shows RVH

 Echo shows right ventricular overload

## Treatment

 Supplemental O$_2$

 Anticoagulation

 Diuretics

 Vasodilators

 Prostanoids, endothelin receptor antagonists, and PDE inhibitors

# Pulmonary Thromboembolism

## Clinical Presentation:

| History: | Physical Exam: |
|----------|----------------|
| Dyspnea | Tachypnea |
| Cough | Rales |
| Hemoptysis | Tachycardia |

### Risk Factors

Prior DVT

Malignancy

Age >60 years

Pregnancy

Hypercoagulability (Factor V Leiden, Protein C Deficiency)

## Diagnosis:

**First-Line Imaging—CT Angiography**
- Sensitive and specific test
- Renal insufficiency potential contraindication

**Gold Standard**—Pulmonary angiogram
- Definitive, but highly invasive

**Venous Duplex of Lower Extremities**
- Assess for DVT

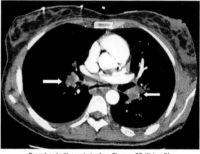

Reproduced with permission from Sherman SC, Weber JM, Schindlbeck MA, et al: Clinical Emergency Medicine. New York, NY: McGraw Hill; 2014.

## Treatment:

### Anticoagulation
- Therapeutic heparin + warfarin (INR goal of 2-3)/direct oral anti-coagulants (DOACs)
- Start before studies if high clinical suspicion

### IVC Filter
- Anticoagulation contraindicated
- Recurrent failure of sufficient anticoagulation

### Surgical Thrombectomy
- Last resort for life-threatening hemodynamic instability
- Large proximal thrombus on imaging

# Respiratory Physiology

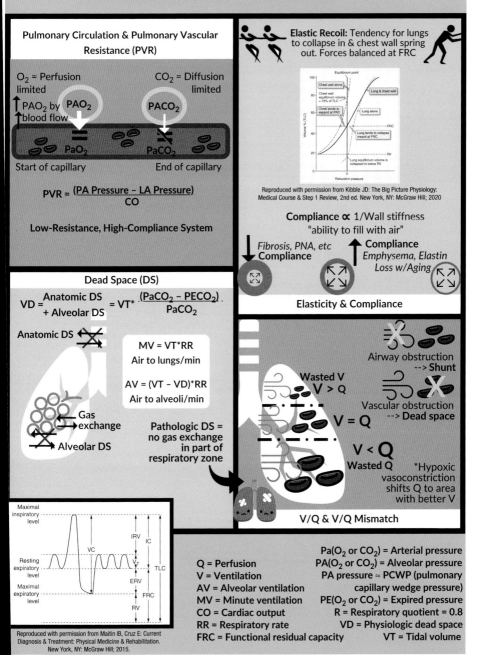

## Pulmonary Circulation & Pulmonary Vascular Resistance (PVR)

$O_2$ = Perfusion limited

↑ $PAO_2$ by blood flow

$CO_2$ = Diffusion limited

$PAO_2$    $PACO_2$

$PaO_2$    $PaCO_2$

Start of capillary    End of capillary

$$PVR = \frac{(PA\ Pressure - LA\ Pressure)}{CO}$$

Low-Resistance, High-Compliance System

## Elastic Recoil: Tendency for lungs to collapse in & chest wall spring out. Forces balanced at FRC

Equilibrium point
Chest wall alone
Chest wall equilibrium volume = 75% of TLC
Chest tends to expand at FRC
Lung & chest wall
Lung alone
FRC
Lung tends to collapse inward at FRC
RV
Lung equilibrium volume is collapsed to below RV
Relaxation pressure

Reproduced with permission from Kibble JD: The Big Picture Physiology: Medical Course & Step 1 Review, 2nd ed. New York, NY: McGraw Hill; 2020

Compliance ∝ 1/Wall stiffness
"ability to fill with air"

↓ Fibrosis, PNA, etc Compliance

↑ Compliance Emphysema, Elastin Loss w/Aging

### Elasticity & Compliance

## Dead Space (DS)

$$VD = \frac{Anatomic\ DS}{+\ Alveolar\ DS} = VT^* \cdot \frac{(PaCO_2 - PECO_2)}{PaCO_2}$$

Anatomic DS

MV = VT*RR
Air to lungs/min

AV = (VT – VD)*RR
Air to alveoli/min

Gas exchange

Alveolar DS

Pathologic DS = no gas exchange in part of respiratory zone

Airway obstruction --> Shunt

Wasted V
V > Q

Vascular obstruction --> Dead space

V = Q

V < Q
Wasted Q

*Hypoxic vasoconstriction shifts Q to area with better V

### V/Q & V/Q Mismatch

Maximal inspiratory level

IRV
IC
VC
VT
TLC
Resting expiratory level
ERV
Maximal expiratory level
FRC
RV

Reproduced with permission from Maitin IB, Cruz E: Current Diagnosis & Treatment: Physical Medicine & Rehabilitation. New York, NY: McGraw Hill; 2015.

Q = Perfusion
V = Ventilation
AV = Alveolar ventilation
MV = Minute ventilation
CO = Cardiac output
RR = Respiratory rate
FRC = Functional residual capacity

$Pa(O_2$ or $CO_2)$ = Arterial pressure
$PA(O_2$ or $CO_2)$ = Alveolar pressure
PA pressure ≈ PCWP (pulmonary capillary wedge pressure)
$PE(O_2$ or $CO_2)$ = Expired pressure
R = Respiratory quotient = 0.8
VD = Physiologic dead space
VT = Tidal volume

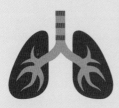

# Sarcoidosis

## A pathological chameleon, characterized by noncaseating granulomas

## Etiology

-Poorly understood growth of granulomas made of epithelioid histiocytes
-USA: Most common in African-American women

## Workup and Diagnosis

-Chest X-ray for lung staging
-Biopsy: Need clinical and pathological correlation!
-PET scan to find occult granulomas
-Rule out mimics, like TB, fungi, and cancer

## Lofgren Syndrome

-A common presentation - erythema nodosum, uveitis, hilar adenopathy
-Has a good prognosis!

## Complications

-Blindness, paraplegia, renal failure, cardiac arrest, cirrhosis, lung fibrosis

## Treatment

-First line, based on clinical picture: Monitoring, topical steroids, systemic glucocorticoids

## Systemic manifestations: Fatigue, night sweats, fever, weight loss

### Lung

- Bilateral hilar and paratracheal adenopathy
- Restrictive or obstructive lung disease

### Ocular

- Anterior uveitis
- Retinitis
- Pars planitis
- Sicca

### Skin

- Erythema nodosum
- Maculopapular lesions
- Pigmentation changes
- Keloids
- Subcutaneous nodules

### Liver

- Obstruction (with elevated alk phos and total bilirubin)
- Portal hypertension

### Renal

- Nephritis
- Renal stones
- Acute renal failure from hypercalcemia

### Calcium Metabolism

Ca

- Increased 1,25 dihydroxyvitamin D production
- Hypercalcemia
- Hypercalciuria

### Nervous System

- Cranial nerve palsy
- Optic neuritis
- Central diabetes insipidus

### Bone Marrow/Spleen

- Lymphopenia due to sequestration
- Anemia

### Cardiac

- Congestive heart failure
- Arrhythmias

### MSK

- Myalgias
- Arthralgias

# Sleep-Disordered Breathing

**Obstructive Sleep Apnea/Hypopnea Syndrome (OSA/OSAHS):** Impaired ventilation during sleep due to respiratory tract obstruction with intact respiratory drive

## Symptoms

 Snoring, Gasping, Breathing Pauses

 Daytime Sleepiness, Fatigue

 Mood Disturbances, Irritability

## Major Risk Factors

 Obesity

 Craniofacial Abnormalities

 Male Sex

 Family History, Genetic Syndromes

Cause: Pharyngeal airway collapse due to the negative pressure generated during inspiration overcoming the pharyngeal dilator muscles

## Complications

 HTN, CAD, Heart Failure, Arrhythmias

 Diabetes

 Stroke

 Depression, Sleepiness

Diagnosis: Overnight polysomnogram monitors breathing, blood oxygen levels, body position, cardiac rhythms, and sleep patterns

## Obesity Hypoventilation Syndrome (OHS)

-Similar symptoms and complications as OSA

-Diagnosis: BMI of 30+ and chronic daytime alveolar hypoventilation ($PaCO_2$: 45 mm Hg+) with no other explanation

-Typically caused by combination of OSA, increased work of breathing, and VQ mismatch

**OSA and OHS Treatment** First line: CPAP, weight loss, optimize treatment for other lung disease
Alternative: Oral appliances, pharyngeal surgery, hypoglossal nerve stimulation

# Small Cell Lung Cancer

## Clinical Presentation

Middle-aged or elderly smoker:

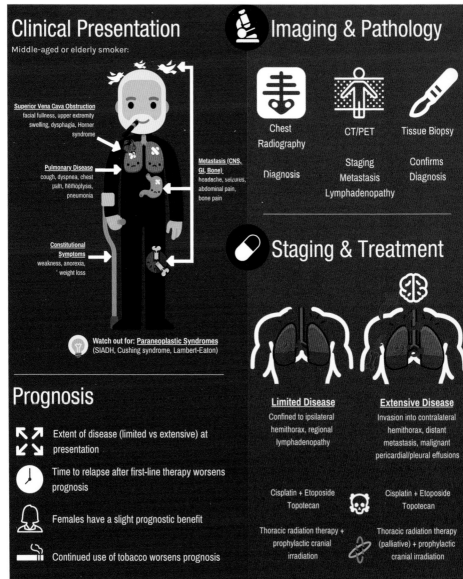

**Superior Vena Cava Obstruction**
facial fullness, upper extremity swelling, dysphagia, Horner syndrome

**Pulmonary Disease**
cough, dyspnea, chest pain, hemoptysis, pneumonia

**Metastasis (CNS, GI, Bone)**
headache, seizures, abdominal pain, bone pain

**Constitutional Symptoms**
weakness, anorexia, weight loss

Watch out for: **Paraneoplastic Syndromes**
(SIADH, Cushing syndrome, Lambert-Eaton)

## Imaging & Pathology

**Chest Radiography**
Diagnosis

**CT/PET**
Staging
Metastasis
Lymphadenopathy

**Tissue Biopsy**
Confirms
Diagnosis

## Staging & Treatment

**Limited Disease**
Confined to ipsilateral hemithorax, regional lymphadenopathy

**Extensive Disease**
Invasion into contralateral hemithorax, distant metastasis, malignant pericardial/pleural effusions

Cisplatin + Etoposide
Topotecan

Cisplatin + Etoposide
Topotecan

Thoracic radiation therapy + prophylactic cranial irradiation

Thoracic radiation therapy (palliative) + prophylactic cranial irradiation

## Prognosis

- Extent of disease (limited vs extensive) at presentation
- Time to relapse after first-line therapy worsens prognosis
- Females have a slight prognostic benefit
- Continued use of tobacco worsens prognosis

# Solitary Pulmonary Nodules

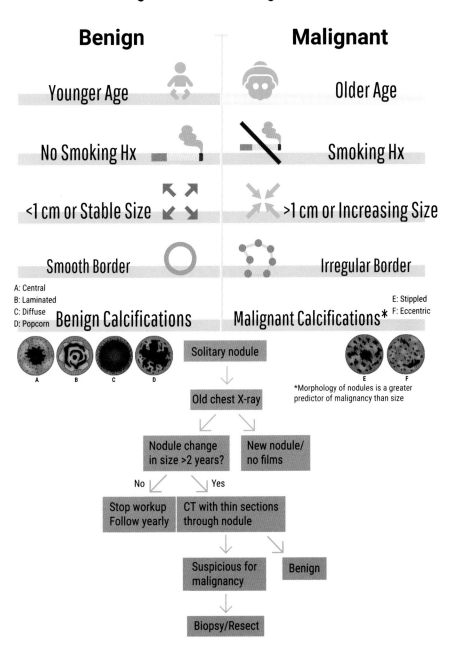

**Benign** | **Malignant**

Younger Age | Older Age

No Smoking Hx | Smoking Hx

<1 cm or Stable Size | >1 cm or Increasing Size

Smooth Border | Irregular Border

A: Central
B: Laminated
C: Diffuse
D: Popcorn

E: Stippled
F: Eccentric

Benign Calcifications | Malignant Calcifications *

A  B  C  D

E  F

*Morphology of nodules is a greater predictor of malignancy than size

Solitary nodule

Old chest X-ray

Nodule change in size >2 years? | New nodule/ no films

No — Stop workup Follow yearly

Yes — CT with thin sections through nodule

Suspicious for malignancy | Benign

Biopsy/Resect

**Cerebral edema**
- Headaches, confusion, visual, and auditory changes

## Clinical Features

**Facial swelling or head fullness**
- Exacerbated by bending forward, lying down, or arm swelling
- Can lead to dyspnea, stridor, cough, respiratory distress

**Superficial venous distention of the neck and chest wall**

# Superior Vena Cava Syndrome

## Grading

| Grade | Findings |
|-------|----------|
| 0 | Asymptomatic with radiographic evidence |
| 1 | Mild—Vascular distention, facial swelling |
| 2 | Moderate—Facial swelling w/ functional impairment (cough, dysphagia) |
| 3 | Severe—Mild/moderate cerebral edema (headache), mild/moderate laryngeal edema |
| 4 | Life-threatening—Severe cerebral edema, significant laryngeal edema, HD unstable |
| 5 | Fatal—Death |

### Pathophysiology

Obstruction of vascular flow through the SVC by direct invasion or external compression of a pathological process (majority due to lung cancer)

## Imaging
- CT with contrast or MRI for patients with grade 0-2 to define extent of blockage and map collateral vasculature
- CT venograph for grade 3-4 for both diagnostic and therapeutic approach

## Treatment

Stenting
Radiation therapy
Medical management
Supportive care

# Thoracic Tumors

## Lab Tests

- Anti-acetylcholine receptor antibodies
- α-fetoprotein (AFP)
- β-hCG
- Lactate dehydrogenase (LDH)

## Imaging

Chest film

Chest CT w/ contrast

## Tissue Diagnosis

Percutaneous biopsy

Surgical biopsy

Endobronchial biopsy

## Mediastinal Segments

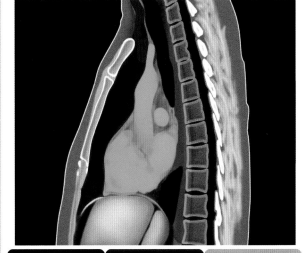

| Anterior Mediastinum (4Ts) | Middle Mediastinum | Posterior Mediastinum |
|---|---|---|
| - Thyroid tumors | - Lung cancer | - Neurogenic tumors |
| - Teratogenic tumors | - Lymphoma | - Esophageal mass |
| - Thymoma | - Cardiovascular aneurysm | - Meningocele |
| - Terrible lymphoma | - Bronchogenic cyst | - Thoracic spine lesion |

## Symptoms

### Mediastinal mass effect:

Stridor

Venous distention

Horner syndrome

Facial swelling

Hemoptysis

Cough

### Systemic effects:

Fever

Weight loss

Night sweats

Paraneoplastic syndrome

# References _____

**Acute Respiratory Distress Syndrome (ARDS)**
Baron RM, Levy BD. Acute respiratory distress syndrome. In: Jameson J, Fauci AS, Kasper DL, Hauser SL, Longo DL, Loscalzo J, eds. *Harrison's Principles of Internal Medicine*. 20th ed. New York, NY: McGraw Hill; 2018.

**Asthma**
Le T, Bhushan V. *First Aid for the USMLE Step 2 CK*. 9th ed. New York, NY: McGraw Hill; 2015.
Le T, Bhushan V, Sochat M, et al. *First Aid for the USMLE Step 1 2018*. New York, NY: McGraw Hill; 2017.

**Bronchiectasis**
Agabegi SS, Agabegi ED. *Step-Up to Medicine*. 4th ed. Philadelphia, PA: Wolters Kluwer; 2016.
Le T, Bhushan V. *First Aid for the USMLE Step 2 CK*. 9th ed. New York, NY: McGraw Hill; 2015.
Le T, Bhushan V, Sochat M, et al. *First Aid for the USMLE Step 1 2018*. New York, NY: McGraw Hill; 2017.

**COPD**
Le T, Bhushan V. *First Aid for the USMLE Step 2 CK*. 9th ed. New York, NY: McGraw Hill; 2015.
Le T, Bhushan V, Sochat M, et al. *First Aid for the USMLE Step 1 2018*. New York, NY: McGraw Hill; 2017.

**Cystic Fibrosis**
Sorscher EJ. Cystic fibrosis. In: Jameson J, Fauci AS, Kasper DL, Hauser SL, Longo DL, Loscalzo J, eds. *Harrison's Principles of Internal Medicine*. 20th ed. New York, NY: McGraw Hill; 2018.

**Environmental Exposures**
Jameson J, Fauci AS, Kasper DL, Hauser SL, Longo DL, Loscalzo J, eds. *Harrison's Manual of Medicine*. 20th ed. New York, NY: McGraw Hill; 2018.
Usatine RP, Smith MA, Mayeaux Jr. EJ, Chumley HS, eds. *The Color Atlas and Synopsis of Family Medicine*. 3rd ed. New York, NY: McGraw Hill; 2019.

**Eosinophilic Pulmonary Syndromes**
Chesnutt AN, Chesnutt MS, Prendergast NT, Prendergast TJ. Eosinophilic pulmonary syndromes. In: Papadakis MA, McPhee SJ, Rabow MW, eds. *Current Medical Diagnosis and Treatment 2020*. New York, NY: McGraw Hill; 2020.

**Hypoxia & Hypoxemia**
Le T, Bhushan V, Chen V, King M. *First Aid for the USMLE Step 2 CK*. 9th ed. New York, NY: McGraw Hill; 2016.
Le T, Bhushan V, Sochat M, et al. *First Aid for the USMLE Step 1 2017*. New York, NY: McGraw Hill; 2017.

**Interstitial Lung Disease**
Hunninghake GM, Rosas IO. Interstitial lung disease. In: Jameson J, Fauci AS, Kasper DL, Hauser SL, Longo DL, Loscalzo J, eds. *Harrison's Principles of Internal Medicine*. 20th ed. New York, NY: McGraw Hill; 2018.

**Interstitial Lung Disease, Drug-Induced**
Schwaiblmair M, Behr W, Haeckel T, Märkl B, Foerg W, Berghaus T. Drug induced interstitial lung disease. *Open Respir Med J*. 2012;6:63-74. doi:10.2174/1874306401206010063

**Mechanical Ventilation & Noninvasive Positive Pressure Ventilation (NIPPV)**
Dmello D, Matuschak GM. Principles and goals of mechanical ventilation. In: Lechner AJ, Matuschak GM, Brink DS, eds. *Respiratory: An Integrated Approach to Disease.* New York, NY: McGraw Hill; 2012.

**Non-Small Cell Lung Cancer**
Biswas T, Machtay M. Treatment of non-small-cell lung cancer: radiation therapy. In: Grippi MA, Elias JA, Fishman JA, et al, eds. *Fishman's Pulmonary Diseases and Disorders.* 5th ed. New York, NY: McGraw Hill; 2015.

Carr LL, Jett JR. Treatment of non-small-cell lung cancer: chemotherapy. In: Grippi MA, Elias JA, Fishman JA, et al, eds. *Fishman's Pulmonary Diseases and Disorders.* 5th ed. New York, NY: McGraw Hill; 2015.

Chang L, Rivera M. Clinical evaluation, diagnosis, and staging of lung cancer. In: Grippi MA, Elias JA, Fishman JA, et al, eds. *Fishman's Pulmonary Diseases and Disorders.* 5th ed. New York, NY: McGraw Hill; 2015.

Kelly K. Extensive-stage small cell lung cancer: initial management. In: Lilenbaum RC, Schild SE, Vora SR, eds. *UpToDate.* Waltham, MA: UpToDate Inc. https://www.uptodate.com/contents/image?imageKey= ONC%2F100459&topicKey=ONC%2F4639&search=non%20small%20cell%20lung%20cancer&rank=1~150& source=see_link

Lilenbaum RC. Overview of the initial treatment of advanced non-small cell lung cancer. In: West (Jack) H, Vora SR, eds. *UpToDate.* Waltham, MA: UpToDate Inc. https://www.uptodate.com

Midthun DE. Overview of the initial treatment and prognosis of lung cancer. In: Lilenbaum RC, Schild SE, Vora SR, eds. *UpToDate.* Waltham, MA: UpToDate Inc. https://www.uptodate.com

Reznik SI, Smythe W. Treatment of non-small-cell lung cancer: surgery. In: Grippi MA, Elias JA, Fishman JA, et al, eds. *Fishman's Pulmonary Diseases and Disorders.* 5th ed. New York, NY: McGraw Hill; 2015.

**PFTs and Pulmonary Physical Exam**
Le T, Bhushan V, Sochat M. *First Aid for the USMLE Step 1 2021.* 31st ed. New York, NY: McGraw Hill; 2021.
UVA OSCE physical exam notes

**Pleural Effusions**
Light RW. Disorders of the pleura. In: Jameson J, Fauci AS, Kasper DL, Hauser SL, Longo DL, Loscalzo J, eds. *Harrison's Principles of Internal Medicine.* 20th ed. New York, NY: McGraw Hill; 2018.

**Pneumothorax**
Ahern G, Brygel M, eds. Pleural cavity. In: *Exploring Essential Radiology.* New York, NY: McGraw Hill; 2014.

Silverman EK. Diseases of the pleura. In: Jameson J, Fauci AS, Kasper DL, Hauser SL, Longo DL, Loscalzo J, eds. *Harrison's Manual of Medicine.* 20th ed. New York, NY: McGraw Hill; 2018.

**Pulmonary Hypertension**
Connolly MJ, Kovacs G. Pulmonary hypertension: a guide for GPs. *Br J Gen Pract.* 2012;62(604):e795-e797. doi:10.3399/bjgp12x658467.

Le T, Bhushan V. *First Aid for the USMLE Step 2 CK.* 9th ed. New York, NY: McGraw Hill; 2015.

Rubin LJ, Hopkins W. Clinical features and diagnosis of pulmonary hypertension of unclear etiology in adults. In: Mandel J, Finlay G, eds. *UpToDate.* Waltham, MA: UpToDate Inc. https://www.uptodate.com

**Pulmonary Thromboembolism**
Agabegi SS, Agabegi ED. *Step-Up to Medicine.* 4th ed. Philadelphia, PA: Wolters Kluwer; 2016.

Le T, Bhushan V. *First Aid for the USMLE Step 2 CK.* 9th ed. New York, NY: McGraw Hill; 2015.

Le T, Bhushan V, Sochat M, et al. *First Aid for the USMLE Step 1 2018.* New York, NY: McGraw Hill; 2017.

**Respiratory Physiology**
Le Tao, Bhushan Vikas, Sochat Matthew, C et al. *First Aid for the USMLE Step 1 2018.* New York, NY: McGraw Hill; 2017.

## Sarcoidosis

Baughman RP, Lower EE. Sarcoidosis. In: Jameson J, Fauci AS, Kasper DL, Hauser SL, Longo DL, Loscalzo J, eds. *Harrison's Principles of Internal Medicine*. 20th ed. New York, NY: McGraw Hill; 2018.

## Sleep-Disordered Breathing

McConville JF, Solway J, Mokhlesi B. Disorders of ventilation: obesity hypoventilation syndrome. In: Jameson J, Fauci AS, Kasper DL, Hauser SL, Longo DL, Loscalzo J, eds. *Harrison's Principles of Internal Medicine*. 20th ed. New York, NY: McGraw Hill; 2018.

Wellman A, Redline S. Sleep apnea. In: Jameson J, Fauci AS, Kasper DL, Hauser SL, Longo DL, Loscalzo J, eds. *Harrison's Principles of Internal Medicine*. 20th ed. New York, NY: McGraw Hill; 2018.

## Small Cell Lung Cancer

Baldini EH, Kalemkerian GP. Limited-stage small cell lung cancer. In: Lilenbaum RC, Schild SE, Vora SR, eds. *UpToDate*. Waltham, MA: UpToDate Inc. https://www.uptodate.com

Dowell JE, Gerber DE, Johnson DH. Small cell lung cancer: diagnosis, treatment, and natural history. In: Grippi MA, Elias JA, Fishman JA, et al, eds. *Fishman's Pulmonary Diseases and Disorders*. 5th ed. New York, NY: McGraw Hill; 2015.

Glisson BS, Byers LA. Pathobiology and staging of small cell carcinoma of the lung. In: Lilenbaum RC, Nicholson A, Vora SR, eds. *UpToDate*. Waltham, MA: UpToDate Inc. https://www.uptodate.com

Kelly K. Extensive-stage small cell lung cancer: initial management. In: Lilenbaum RC, Schild SE, Vora SR, eds. *UpToDate*. Waltham, MA: UpToDate Inc. https://www.uptodate.com

## Solitary Pulmonary Nodules

Ost D. Approach to the patient with pulmonary nodules. In: Grippi MA, Elias JA, Fishman JA, et al, eds. *Fishman's Pulmonary Diseases and Disorders*. 5th ed. New York, NY: McGraw Hill; 2015.

Weinberger SE, McDermott S. Diagnostic evaluation of the incidental pulmonary nodule. In: Muller NL, King Jr. TE, Midthun DE, Finlay G, eds. *UpToDate*. Waltham, MA: UpToDate Inc. https://www.uptodate.com

## Superior Vena Cava Syndrome

Drews RE, Rabkin DJ. Malignancy-related superior vena cava syndrome. In: Bruera E, Eidt JF, Mills JL, Sr, Savarese DMF, Collins KA, eds. *UpToDate*. Waltham, MA: UpToDate Inc. https://www.uptodate.com

Grading table adapted from https://www.uptodate.com/contents/image?imageKey=SURG%2F117725&topicKey=ONC%2F2832&search=SVC%20Syndrome&rank=1~150&source=see_link

## Thoracic Tumors

Berry MF. Approach to the adult patient with a mediastinal mass. In: Muller NL, Friedberg JS, Midthun DE, Collins KA, Vora SR, eds. *UpToDate*. Waltham, MA: UpToDate Inc. https://www.uptodate.com

Chesnutt AN, Chesnutt MS, Prendergast NT, Prendergast TJ. Mediastinal masses. In: Papadakis MA, McPhee SJ, Rabow MW, eds. *Current Medical Diagnosis and Treatment 2020*. New York, NY: McGraw Hill; 2020.

# Rheumatology

*Geeta Nayyar, MD, MBA*

# Fibromyalgia

Most common in **women** 20-50 years old

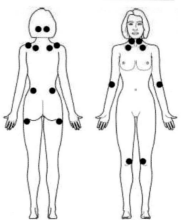

Reproduced with permission from LeBlond RF, Brown DD, Suneja M, et al: DeGowin's Diagnostic Examination, 10th ed. New York, NY: McGraw Hill; 2015.

**Neuropsychiatric Symptoms**:
Poor sleep, fatigue, cognitive disturbance, anxiety, depression

"Fibro Fog"

**Tender Points**
Stiffness, Increased pain sensitivity, Chronic, widespread musculoskeletal pain

## Etiology

**Unknown**

**?**

Associated with other pain and fatigue syndromes

## Diagnosis/Workup

**Clinical Diagnosis of Exclusion**
Normal CRP, ESR

 Pain for most of the day, on most days, for at least 3 months

## Treatment

**Quality of Life Focus**

Regular exercise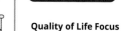

 Antidepressant therapy

Sleep

# Gout

## Etiology: Joint Deposition of Monosodium Urate Crystals

**Demographics**

 >

Middle age— Elderly    Postmenopausal

**Dietary Risk Factors**

**↑ Urate Production**
- Obesity
- Increased cell turnover
  - Tumor lysis
  - Hemolytic anemia
  - Myeloproliferative dz
- Lesch–Nyhan syndrome

**↓ Urate Excretion**
- Diuretics
- Salicylates
- CKD
- Pb toxicity

## Acute Gouty Arthritis
### Sudden-Onset, Monoarticular

- Erythema
- Tenderness
- Swelling

Commonly involves **1st MTP** (podagra)

Subsides in 10-14 days

Reproduced with permission from Suneja M, Szot JF, LeBlond RF, et al: DeGowin's Diagnostic Examination, 11th ed. New York, NY: McGraw Hill; 2020.

**Increased:**
- Attack frequency
- # Joints involved

## Chronic Gouty Arthritis
### Continuous Joint Pain + Acute Attacks

**Complications**
- **Tophi**
- Secondary OA
- Urate kidney stones

(L): Reproduced with permission from Kang S, Amagai M, Bruckner AL, et al: Fitzpatrick's Dermatology, 9th ed. New York, NY: McGraw Hill; 2019.
(R): Reproduced with permission from Sherman SC: Simon's Emergency Orthopedics, 8th ed. New York, NY: McGraw Hill; 2019.

## Diagnosis

**Arthrocentesis**

- **Negatively birefringent needle-shaped crystals**
- Chalky/cloudy aspirate
- 15-20k WBC
- No bacteria

birefringence axis

Serum urate **NOT** helpful for diagnosis

Reproduced with permission from Mitra R: Principles of Rehabilitation Medicine. New York, NY: McGraw Hill; 2019.

## Acute Treatment
### Pain Relief + Resolution of Acute Attack

**1. High-dose NSAIDs**
(indomethacin, naproxen, ibuprofen)

**2. Colchicine**

if NSAIDs + colchicine ineffective, not tolerated, or contraindicated

**3. Steroids**

Monoarticular → Intra-articular triamcinolone
Polyarticular → PO prednisone

## Chronic Workup

**Joint Radiograph**
- "Rat-bite" erosions = chronic disease

**24-Hour Urine Urate Excretion**
- If <800 mg, treat to increase excretion

Reproduced with permission from Elsayes KM, Oldham SA: Introduction to Diagnostic Radiology. New York, NY: McGraw Hill; 2014.

## Chronic Treatment
### Slow/Prevent Progression to Chronic Gout

**1. Avoid dietary triggers**

**Indications for medical therapy:** ≥2 Attacks **OR** serum urate >550 **OR** tophi or urate kidney stones

Do **NOT** initiate during acute attack

**↓ Urate Production**

**2. Xanthine oxidase inhibitors**
(allopurinol, febuxostat)

**↑ Urate Excretion**

**2. Urate reuptake inhibitor**
(probenecid)

# Inclusion Body Myositis

## Clinical Presentation

Asymmetric progressive muscle weakness + atrophy

50+ years

♂ > ♀

Finger flexors

Wrist flexors
Triceps

Quadriceps
Ankle dorsiflexors

## Workup

Labs

- Elevated or normal CK
- Normal ESR

Serology

⊙ Anti-cN-1A

🕸 Nonspecific

⊙ Specific

Muscle biopsy

🕸 Endomysial inflammation

⊙ Inclusion bodies ( β-amyloid )

## Treatment

PT/OT/speech therapy

NOT responsive to steroids or immunomodulators

## Complications

Require mobility assistance within 10-15 years

NO change in life expectancy

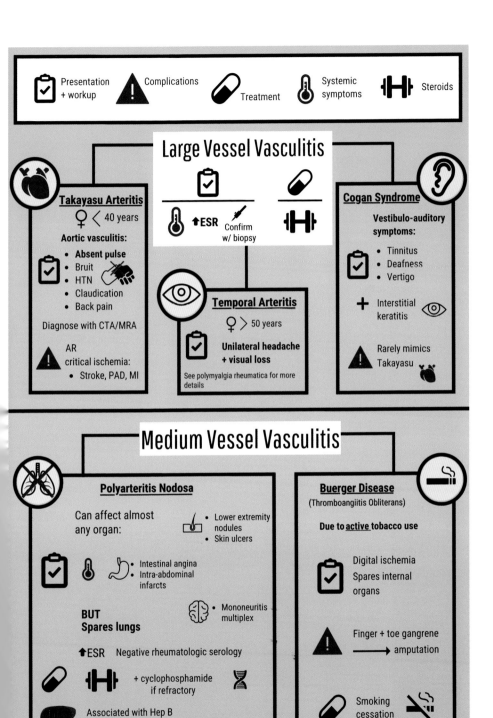

**Presentation + workup**

**Complications**

**Treatment**

**Systemic symptoms**

**Steroids**

# Large Vessel Vasculitis

↑ESR · Confirm w/ biopsy

## Takayasu Arteritis

♀ < 40 years

**Aortic vasculitis:**

- **Absent pulse**
- Bruit
- HTN
- Claudication
- Back pain

Diagnose with CTA/MRA

AR critical ischemia:
- Stroke, PAD, MI

## Temporal Arteritis

♀ > 50 years

**Unilateral headache + visual loss**

See polymyalgia rheumatica for more details

## Cogan Syndrome

**Vestibulo-auditory symptoms:**

- Tinnitus
- Deafness
- Vertigo

+ Interstitial keratitis

Rarely mimics Takayasu

# Medium Vessel Vasculitis

## Polyarteritis Nodosa

Can affect almost any organ:

- Lower extremity nodules
- Skin ulcers

- Intestinal angina
- Intra-abdominal infarcts

**BUT Spares lungs**

- Mononeuritis multiplex

↑ESR   Negative rheumatologic serology

+ cyclophosphamide if refractory

Associated with Hep B
Obtain serology and treat if positive

## Buerger Disease
(Thromboangiitis Obliterans)

**Due to active tobacco use**

Digital ischemia
Spares internal organs

Finger + toe gangrene → amputation

Smoking cessation

# Lupus

## Inflammatory Autoimmune Disorder

### Presentation

♀ Young women

Systemic symptoms
(fever, malaise)

**Malar
(butterfly)
rash**

**Cytopenias**

 **Photosensitivity**

Reproduced with permission from Kang S, Amagai M, Bruckner AL, et al: Fitzpatrick's Dermatology, 9th ed. New York, NY: McGraw Hill; 2019.

### Antibodies

**Sensitive, not specific**
Antinuclear antibody

**Specific**
Anti-dsDNA
Anti-Smith

**Drug-Induced Lupus**
Antihistone

### Treatment

**NSAIDs**

**Corticosteroids**

**Immunosuppressants**

**Hydroxychloroquine**

---

## ⚠ Complications

 **Other
Autoimmune
Disorders**
(eg, Antiphospholipid
syndrome)

 **Carditis**
Libman–Sacks
endocarditis
Pericarditis

 **Arthritis**

 **Nephritis**

 **Pneumonitis**

 **Vasculitis**

# Polymyalgia Rheumatica

 ♀ > ♂  ☑ Age >50

## Presentation

- Pain + stiffness in proximal muscles
- Difficulty combing hair + rising from chairs
- Normal strength

### Associated with
## Giant Cell Arteritis
### (temporal)

Unilateral:
- ☑ New/different headache
- ☑ Temporal scalp tenderness
- Jaw claudication
- Blurred vision

± fever, malaise, weight loss

## Diagnosis/Workup

**Clinical Diagnosis**

 PMR ESR >30

☑ ESR >50

☑ Temporal artery biopsy

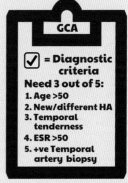

GCA

☑ = Diagnostic criteria

**Need 3 out of 5:**
1. Age >50
2. New/different HA
3. Temporal tenderness
4. ESR >50
5. +ve Temporal artery biopsy

## Treatment

 Prednisone
10-20 mg/day

**Complications**
- Blindness
- Subclavian/carotid stenosis ♥
- Aortic aneurysms
- Aortic regurgitation

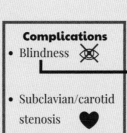

**prevent** → prednisone
20-40 mg/day

**treat** (any visual loss) → methyl-prednisolone
1000 mg/day
**URGENT**

**prevent** → 81 mg ASA
**81**

# Polymyositis
# +
# Dermatomyositis

## Clinical Presentation

### Dermatological manifestations = dermatomyositis

**Proximal symmetric muscle weakness**

**Manifests as difficulty:**
- Rising from chairs
- Climbing stairs
- Combing/washing hair

Gottron papules

Reproduced with permission from Kang S, Amagai M, Bruckner AL, et al: Fitzpatrick's Dermatology, 9th ed. New York, NY: McGraw Hill; 2019.

Heliotrope rash

Reproduced with permission from Kang S, Amagai M, Bruckner AL, et al: Fitzpatrick's Dermatology, 9th ed. New York, NY: McGraw Hill; 2019.

V-neck sign

Reproduced with permission from Jameson J, Fauci AS, Kasper DL, et al: Harrison's Principles of Internal Medicine, 20th ed. New York, NY: McGraw Hill; 2018.

Shawl sign

Reproduced with permission from Kang S, Amagai M, Bruckner AL, et al: Fitzpatrick's Dermatology, 9th ed. New York, NY: McGraw Hill; 2019.

## Workup

**Labs**    **Serology**    **MRI** —— guides ——▶ **Muscle biopsy**

- ⬆ CK
- ⬆ AST/ALT
- ⬆ ESR

🕸 ANA
⊛ Anti-Jo-1
⊛ Anti-SRP
⊛ Anti-Mi2

🕸 Nonspecific   ⊛ Specific

**Edema in affected muscles**

Reproduced with permission from Jameson J, Fauci AS, Kasper DL, et al: Harrison's Principles of Internal Medicine, 20th ed. New York, NY: McGraw Hill; 2018.

**Endomysial inflammation**

Reproduced with permission from Jameson J, Fauci AS, Kasper DL, et al: Harrison's Principles of Internal Medicine, 20th ed. New York, NY: McGraw Hill; 2018.

**Perifascicular atrophy = dermatomyositis**

Reproduced with permission from Amato AA, Russell JA: Neuromuscular Disorders, 2nd ed. New York, NY: McGraw Hill; 2016.

## Treatment

 ➡
- Methotrexate
- Azathioprine

**Steroids**    **Immunomodulators**

## Associated Pathology

**Cancer**    **Myocarditis**    **ILD**

# Pseudogout
(Calcium Pyrophosphate Deposition Disease)

---

## Etiology: Joint Deposition of Calcium Pyrophosphate Crystals

### Risk Factors

- Age >60 years
- Preexisting joint disease (OA, RA, etc.)

### Secondary Causes
- Hemochromatosis
- Orthopedic trauma
- Hyperparathyroidism
- Hypothyroidism
- Thiazide diuretics

---

## Acute Attack

Often Presents Like **Gout**

**BUT** more likely to:
- Involve **knees** + **wrists**
- Be polyarticular

Subsides in 1 week to 1 month

**Increased:**
- Attack frequency
- # Joints involved

## Chronic Degenerative Arthritis

Progressive Joint Pain + Acute Attacks

### Complications
- Joint degeneration
- Charcot-like joint
- Axial disease

---

## Diagnosis

### Arthrocentesis
- **Positively birefringent rhomboid crystals**
- 5-15k WBC
- No bacteria

birefringence axis

Reproduced with permission from Nicoll D, Lu CM, McPhee SJ: Guide to Diagnostic Tests, 7th ed. New York, NY: McGraw Hill; 2017.

### Joint Radiography
- **Chondrocalcinosis**
- Subchondral cysts

Reproduced with permission from Chen MYM, Pope TL, Ott DJ: Basic Radiology, 2nd ed. New York, NY: McGraw Hill; 2011.

---

## Acute Treatment
Pain Relief + Resolution of Acute Attack

1. **High-dose NSAIDs**
   (indomethacin, naproxen, ibuprofen)
2. **Colchicine**
   if NSAIDs + colchicine ineffective, not tolerated, or contraindicated

3. **Steroids**
   Monoarticular → Intra-articular triamcinolone

## Chronic Treatment
Prevent and Manage Complications

1. **Treat secondary causes if present**

Indications for surgical therapy:
Progressive + destructive arthropathy

2. Joint replacement

---

# Rheumatoid Arthritis

| | ETIOLOGY | |
|---|---|---|
| **Autoimmune** joint destruction | | Inflammation induces formation of <u>pannus</u> (proliferative granulation tissue) which erodes cartilage and bone |

| | PRESENTATION | |
|---|---|---|
| Pain, swelling, and morning stiffness lasting > 1 hour Symmetric polyarthritis | | Improves with physical activity Systemic symptoms: Fever, fatigue, weight loss |

## JOINT FINDINGS

**Joints Involved**

(UL): Reproduced with permission from Elsayes KM, Oldham SA: Introduction to Diagnostic Radiology. New York, NY: McGraw Hill; 2014.
(R, LL): Reproduced with permission from Imboden JB, Hellmann DB, Stone JH: Current Diagnosis & Treatment: Rheumatology, 3rd ed. New York, NY: McGraw Hill; 2013.

**Cervical Involvement**
Reproduced with permission from Mitra R: Principles of Rehabilitation Medicine. New York, NY: McGraw Hill; 2019.

**Swan-neck Deformity**
Reproduced with permission from Imboden JB, Hellmann DB, Stone JH: Current Diagnosis & Treatment: Rheumatology, 3rd ed. New York, NY: McGraw Hill; 2013.

**Ulnar Deviation**
Reproduced with permission from Mitra R: Principles of Rehabilitation Medicine. New York, NY: McGraw Hill; 2019.

| | LABS | |
|---|---|---|
| Cyclic citrullinated peptide antibodies (Higher specificity!) | | Rheumatoid Factor |

| | TREATMENT | |
|---|---|---|
| NSAIDs Glucocorticoids Biologics | | DMARDs Disease-modifying antirheumatic drugs (ie, Methotrexate) |

## COMPLICATIONS

**Rheumatoid Nodule**
Reproduced with permission from Imboden JB, Hellmann DB, Stone JH: Current Diagnosis & Treatment: Rheumatology, 3rd ed. New York, NY: McGraw Hill; 2013.

**Pyoderma Gangrenosum**
Reproduced with permission from Usatine RP, Smith MA, Mayeaux EJ, Chumley HS: The Color Atlas and Synopsis of Family Medicine, 3rd ed. New York, NY: McGraw Hill; 2019. Photo contributor: Richard P, Usatine, MD.

Secondary Sjögren's Syndrome
Felty Syndrome

**Lungs** (eg, ILD)    **Eyes**    **Cardiac**

# Sjögren's Syndrome

Autoimmune Destruction of Exocrine Glands (Especially Lacrimal and Salivary) by Lymphocytic Infiltration

Females 40-60 years old
Both a primary and a
secondary process

Inflammatory joint
pain,
Bilateral parotid
enlargement

Keratoconjunctivitis
sicca—decreased tear
production, dry eye,
gritty feeling in the eye

Xerostomia—Dry mouth,
decreased
saliva production

## Diagnosis and Workup

ANA antibodies
Rheumatoid factor
SSA (anti-Ro)
SSB (anti-La)
Labial salivary gland biopsy

\* Sjögren's can be primary or
secondary to other autoimmune
diseases

## Complications

Dental Caries

Mucosa-associated lymphoid
tissue (MALT) lymphoma

Extraglandular manifestations:
Raynaud's
Renal tubular acidosis
Vasculitis

## Treatment

Focused on
symptoms!

Avoid triggers,
lubrication with
artificial tears,
pilocarpine

Oral hygiene,
maintaining hydration,
cholinergic agonists

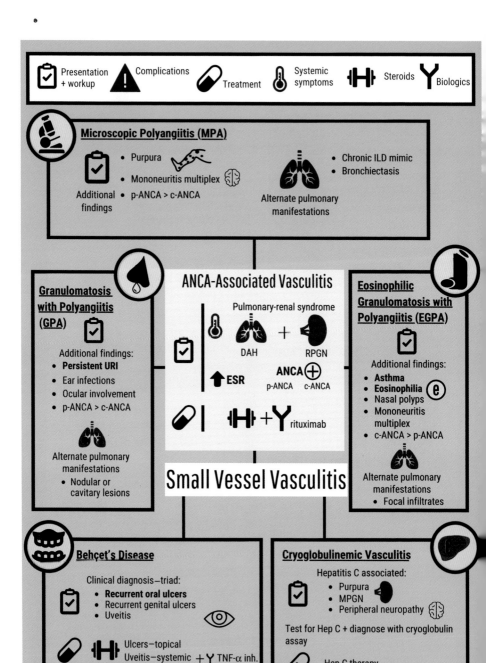

**Presentation + workup** | **Complications** | **Treatment** | **Systemic symptoms** | **Steroids** | **Biologics**

## Microscopic Polyangiitis (MPA)

Additional findings
- Purpura
- Mononeuritis multiplex
- p-ANCA > c-ANCA

Alternate pulmonary manifestations
- Chronic ILD mimic
- Bronchiectasis

## ANCA-Associated Vasculitis

Pulmonary-renal syndrome

DAH + RPGN

↑ESR

ANCA ⊕
p-ANCA   c-ANCA

**I**H**I** + **Y**rituximab

## Small Vessel Vasculitis

## Granulomatosis with Polyangiitis (GPA)

Additional findings:
- **Persistent URI**
- Ear infections
- Ocular involvement
- p-ANCA > c-ANCA

Alternate pulmonary manifestations
- Nodular or cavitary lesions

## Eosinophilic Granulomatosis with Polyangiitis (EGPA)

Additional findings:
- **Asthma**
- **Eosinophilia** ⓔ
- Nasal polyps
- Mononeuritis multiplex
- c-ANCA > p-ANCA

Alternate pulmonary manifestations
- Focal infiltrates

## Behçet's Disease

Clinical diagnosis—triad:
- **Recurrent oral ulcers**
- Recurrent genital ulcers
- Uveitis

Ulcers—topical
Uveitis—systemic + **Y** TNF-α inh.

Blindness
Large vessel + CNS involvement
GI bleed—small bowel + cecal ulcers

## Cryoglobulinemic Vasculitis

Hepatitis C associated:
- Purpura
- MPGN
- Peripheral neuropathy

Test for Hep C + diagnose with cryoglobulin assay

Hep C therapy

Evolution to malignant B-cell lymphoma

# Systemic Sclerosis

- Inflammation and autoimmunity leading to visceral and vascular fibrosis in the skin and many other organs
- Chronic and progressive course
- Wide variability in patient's extent of organ involvement

## Diffuse Scleroderma Presentation

**Sclerotic, thickened skin**

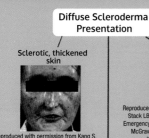

Reproduced with permission from Kang S, Amagai M, Bruckner AL, et al: Fitzpatrick's Dermatology, 9th ed. New York, NY: McGraw Hill; 2019.

**Raynaud's**

Reproduced with permission from Knoop KJ, Stack LB, Storrow AB, et al: The Atlas of Emergency Medicine, 4th ed. New York, NY: McGraw Hill; 2016. Photo contributor: Kevin J. Knoop, MD, MS.

**Fingertip pitting**

Reproduced with permission from Kang S, Amagai M, Bruckner AL, et al: Fitzpatrick's Dermatology, 9th ed. New York, NY: McGraw Hill; 2019.

## Limited Scleroderma (CREST Syndrome)

Reproduced with permission from Usatine RP, Smith MA, Mayeaux EJ, Chumley HS: The Color Atlas and Synopsis of Family Medicine, 3rd ed. New York, NY: McGraw Hill; 2019. Photo contributor: Richard P. Usatine, MD.

Reproduced with permission from McKean S, Ross JJ, Dressler DD, et al. Principles and Practice of Hospital Medicine, 2nd ed. New York NY: McGraw Hill; 2017.

Reproduced with permission from Wolff K, Johnson RA, Saavedra AP, et al: Fitzpatrick's Color Atlas and Synopsis of Clinical Dermatology, 8th ed. New York, NY: McGraw Hill; 2017.

| | |
|---|---|
| C | Calcinosis |
| R | Raynaud's |
| E | Esophageal Dysmotility |
| S | Sclerodactyly |
| T | Telangiectasia |

## Antibodies

**Diffuse Scleroderma**
Anti-Scl-70
(Anti-DNA topoisomerase I)

**Diffuse Scleroderma Hypertensive Renal Crisis**
Anti-RNAP III (RNA polymerase III)

**Limited Scleroderma**
Anti-centromere

## Treatment
No good treatment

**Immunosuppression:** Cyclophosphamide Mycophenolate Rituximab

**Symptom based** Eg: Keeping warm for Raynaud's, PPI for reflux

**Physical therapy and patient education**

## Complications
Level of involvement of internal organs determines the prognosis

**Pulmonary HTN Pulmonary fibrosis**

**Hypertensive scleroderma renal crisis**

# References

**Fibromyalgia**
Le T, Bhushan V. *First Aid for the USMLE Step 2 CK*. 10th ed. New York, NY: McGraw Hill Education; 2019.

Richard FL, Donald DB, Manish S, Joseph F. *Szot: DeGowin's Diagnostic Examination*. 10th ed. McGraw-Hill Education. www.accessmedicine.com. Accessed August 19, 2021.

**Gout**
Burns C, Wortmann RL. Gout. In: Imboden JB, Hellmann DB, Stone JH, eds. *CURRENT Diagnosis & Treatment: Rheumatology*. 3rd ed. New York, NY: McGraw Hill; 2013.

Le T, Bhushan V. *First Aid for USMLE Step 2 CK*. 9th ed. New York, NY: McGraw Hill; 2015.

Schumacher H, Chen LX. Gout and other crystal-associated arthropathies. In: Jameson J, Fauci AS, Kasper DL, Hauser SL, Longo DL, Loscalzo J, eds. *Harrison's Principles of Internal Medicine*. 20th ed. New York, NY: McGraw Hill; 2018.

**Inclusion Body Myositis**
Greenberg SA, Amato AA. Inflammatory myopathies. In: Jameson J, Fauci AS, Kasper DL, Hauser SL, Longo DL, Loscalzo J, eds. *Harrison's Principles of Internal Medicine*. 20th ed. New York, NY: McGraw Hill; 2018:chap 358.

Mammen AL, Truong A, Christopher-Stine L. Dermatomyositis, polymyositis, & immune-mediated necrotizing myopathy. In: Imboden JB, Hellmann DB, Stone JH, eds. *CURRENT Diagnosis and Treatment: Rheumatology*. 3rd ed. New York, NY: McGraw Hill; 2013.

**Large and Medium Vessel Vasculitis**
Hellmann DB. Giant cell arteritis & polymyalgia rheumatica. In: Imboden JB, Hellmann DB, Stone JH, eds. *CURRENT Diagnosis & Treatment: Rheumatology*. 3rd ed. New York, NY: McGraw Hill; 2013.

Hellmann DB. Takayasu arteritis. In: Imboden JB, Hellmann DB, Stone JH, eds. *CURRENT Diagnosis & Treatment: Rheumatology*. 3rd ed. New York, NY: McGraw Hill; 2013.

Langford CA, Fauci AS. The vasculitis syndromes. In: Jameson J, Fauci AS, Kasper DL, Hauser SL, Longo DL, Loscalzo J, eds. *Harrison's Principles of Internal Medicine*. 20th ed. New York, NY: McGraw Hill; 2018.

Stone JH. Buerger disease. In: Imboden JB, Hellmann DB, Stone JH, eds. *CURRENT Diagnosis & Treatment: Rheumatology*. 3rd ed. New York, NY: McGraw Hill; 2013.

**Lupus**
Kang S, Amagai M, Bruckner AL, et al. *Fitzpatrick's Dermatology*. 9th ed. McGraw-Hill Education. www.accessmedicine.com. Accessed August 19, 2021.

Le T, Bhushan V. *First Aid for the USMLE Step 2 CK*. 10th ed. New York, NY: McGraw Hill Education; 2019.

**Polymyalgia Rheumatica**
Hellmann DB. Giant cell arteritis & polymyalgia rheumatica. In: Imboden JB, Hellmann DB, Stone JH, eds. *CURRENT Diagnosis & Treatment: Rheumatology*. 3rd ed. New York, NY: McGraw Hill; 2013.

Langford CA, Fauci AS. The vasculitis syndromes. In: Jameson J, Fauci AS, Kasper DL, Hauser SL, Longo DL, Loscalzo J, eds. *Harrison's Principles of Internal Medicine*. 20th ed. New York, NY: McGraw Hill; 2018.

Le T, Bhushan V. *First Aid for USMLE Step 2 CK*. 9th ed. New York, NY: McGraw Hill; 2015.

### Polymyositis + Dermatomyositis

Greenberg SA, Amato AA. Inflammatory myopathies. In: Jameson J, Fauci AS, Kasper DL, Hauser SL, Longo DL, Loscalzo J, eds. *Harrison's Internal Medicine*. 20th ed. New York, NY: McGraw Hill; 2018:chap 358.

Le T, Bhushan V. *First Aid for USMLE Step 2 CK*. 9th ed. New York, NY: McGraw Hill; 2015.

Mammen AL, Truong A, Christopher-Stine L. Dermatomyositis, polymyositis, & immune-mediated necrotizing myopathy. In: Imboden JB, Hellmann DB, Stone JH, eds. *CURRENT Diagnosis and Treatment: Rheumatology*. 3rd ed. New York, NY: McGraw Hill; 2013.

### Pseudogout

Le T, Bhushan V. *First Aid for USMLE Step 2 CK*. 9th ed. New York, NY: McGraw Hill; 2015.

Schumacher H, Chen LX. Gout and other crystal-associated arthropathies. In: Jameson J, Fauci AS, Kasper DL, Hauser SL, Longo DL, Loscalzo J, eds. *Harrison's Principles of Internal Medicine*. 20th ed. New York, NY: McGraw Hill; 2018.

### Rheumatoid Arthritis

Le T, Bhushan V. *First Aid for the USMLE Step 2 CK*. 10th ed. New York, NY: McGraw Hill Education; 2019.

### Sjögren's Syndrome

Le T, Bhushan V. *First Aid for the USMLE Step 2 CK*. 10th ed. New York, NY: McGraw Hill Education; 2019.

### Small Vessel Vasculitis

Duvuru G, Stone JH. Microscopic polyangiitis. In: Imboden JB, Hellmann DB, Stone JH, eds. *CURRENT Diagnosis & Treatment: Rheumatology*. 3rd ed. New York, NY: McGraw Hill; 2013.

Langford CA, Fauci AS. The vasculitis syndromes. In: Jameson J, Fauci AS, Kasper DL, Hauser SL, Longo DL, Loscalzo J, eds. *Harrison's Principles of Internal Medicine*. 20th ed. New York, NY: McGraw Hill; 2018.

Hellmann DB. Behçet Disease. In: Imboden JB, Hellmann DB, Stone JH, eds. *CURRENT Diagnosis & Treatment: Rheumatology*. 3rd ed. New York, NY: McGraw Hill; 2013.

Moutsopoulos HM. Behçet's syndrome. In: Jameson J, Fauci AS, Kasper DL, Hauser SL, Longo DL, Loscalzo J, eds. *Harrison's Principles of Internal Medicine*. 20th ed. New York, NY: McGraw Hill; 2018.

Seo P, Stone JH. Eosinophilic granulomatosis with polyangiitis (Churg-Strauss syndrome). In: Imboden JB, Hellmann DB, Stone JH, eds. *CURRENT Diagnosis & Treatment: Rheumatology*. 3rd ed. New York, NY: McGraw Hill; 2013.

Stone JH. Granulomatosis with polyangiitis (Wegener granulomatosis). In: Imboden JB, Hellmann DB, Stone JH, eds. *CURRENT Diagnosis & Treatment: Rheumatology*. 3rd ed. New York, NY: McGraw Hill; 2013.

Stone JH. Mixed cryoglobulinemia. In: Imboden JB, Hellmann DB, Stone JH, eds. *CURRENT Diagnosis & Treatment: Rheumatology*. 3rd ed. New York, NY: McGraw Hill; 2013.

### Systemic Sclerosis

Le T, Bhushan V. *First Aid for the USMLE Step 2 CK*. 10th ed. New York, NY: McGraw Hill Education; 2019.

# Urology
*Ryan P. Smith, MD*

# Benign Prostatic Hyperplasia

- Prevalence increases with age
- Affects 70% of US men 60-69 years of age, and 80% over 70 years of age

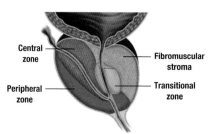

Central zone
Fibromuscular stroma
Peripheral zone
Transitional zone

## Pathophysiology

- Increase in prostatic stromal and epithelial cells
- Formation of large, discrete nodules in transition zone of the prostate
- Large nodules can cause urethral compression leading to bladder outlet obstruction
- Bladder outlet obstruction can lead to lower urinary tract symptoms

## Evaluation and Diagnosis

- Exclude other causes of lower urinary tract symptoms
- Digital rectal exam
- PSA testing
- International Prostate Symptom Score (I-PSS)
- Flow rate
- Post-void residual

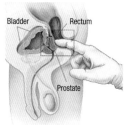

Bladder        Rectum

Prostate

Reproduced with permission from National Cancer Institute at the National Institutes of Health.
https://www.cancer.gov/publications/dictionaries/cancer-terms/def/benign-prostatic-hyperplasia

### α-blockers

Improve symptoms and increase urinary flow rate by relaxing prostatic and bladder-neck smooth muscle through sympathetic activity blockade

### 5α-reductase inhibitors

Improve symptoms, increase urinary flow rate, and prevent BPH outcomes by reducing prostate enlargement through hormonal mechanisms

## Medical Treatment

- α-adrenergic receptor blockers (eg, tamsulosin, alfuzosin)
- 5α-reductase inhibitors (eg, finasteride, dutasteride)
- Combination therapy

## Surgical Treatment

- Transurethral resection of the prostate (TURP)
- Transurethral laser surgery
- Prostatectomy

## Minimally Invasive Therapy

- Transurethral microwave procedures
- Transurethral needle ablation
- Water-induced thermotherapy
- High-intensity focused ultrasound
- Prostatic urethral lift
- Prostatic stents
- Intraprostatic injection

### Transurethral Resection of the Prostate (TURP)

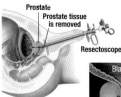

Prostate
Prostate tissue is removed
Resectoscope

Bladder
Prostate
Preprocedure

Postprocedure

Reproduced with permission from National Cancer Institute at the National Institutes of Health.
https://www.cancer.gov/publications/dictionaries/cancer-terms/def/turp

Nitinol Capsular Tab
Permanent Suture
< 1 cm
Stainless Steel Urethral End Piece

# Bladder Cancer

## Epidemiology

- Most common site of cancer in the urinary system
- More common in males
- Average age of diagnosis is 65

## Types

- **Urothelial carcinoma**—90% of cases
  - 75% are low grade and noninvasive or invading subepithelial connective tissue
  - 40% of muscle-invasive bladder cancer progresses from noninvasive tumor
  - 95% are positive on urine cytology
- **Squamous cell carcinoma**—5% of cases
  - Less responsive to chemo and radiation, treated with radical cystectomy
- **Adenocarcinoma**—1% of cases
  - Serum CEA may be elevated

## Risk Factors

- **Smoking**—Most common cause of bladder cancer due to aromatic amines in tobacco smoke
- **Chronic cystitis**—Continued bladder inflammation increases risk of squamous cell bladder cancer
  - Chronic UTIs
  - Chronic indwelling urinary catheter
  - Chronic bladder stones
- **Chemical exposure**—Most bladder carcinogens are aromatic amines
  - Consider occupational exposure to aniline dyes
- **Cyclophosphamide**—The metabolite acrolein causes hemorrhagic cystitis and increased risk of bladder cancer
  - Mesna administration binds acrolein in the urine to reduce the risk of cancer

## Presentation

- Painless hematuria is the most common symptom
- Advanced cases may have flank pain from ureteral obstruction or bone pain from metastasis

Reproduced with permission from Shah B, Lucchesi M: Atlas of Pediatric Emergency Medicine, 3rd ed. New York, NY: McGraw Hill; 2019. Photo contributor: Binita R. Shah, MD.

## Work Up

- Cystoscopy with biopsy is gold standard
- Urine cytology
- CT urogram to rule out upper tract cancer

Reproduced with permission from Muñoz DI, Martinez IQ, Militino AF, et al: Virtual cystoscopy, computed tomography urography and optical cystoscopy for the detection and follow-up for bladder cancer, Radiologia Sep-Oct 2017;59(5):422-430.

Reproduced with permission from McAninch JW, Lue TF: Smith & Tanagho's General Urology, 19th ed. New York, NY: McGraw Hill; 2020.

## Management

**Non–Muscle Invasive:**

- Transurethral resection of the bladder tumor—Confirm depth of invasion
- Likely to recur, recommend intravesical chemotherapy or immunotherapy
- Follow-up cystoscopy and urine tumor markers for surveillance

**Muscle Invasive:**

- Gold standard—Radical cystectomy, urinary diversion, and pelvic lymphadenectomy
- Neoadjuvant chemotherapy preferred over adjuvant therapies
- Systemic cisplatin is most effective against urothelial carcinoma
- Follow-up chest imaging, CT urogram, and urine cytology for surveillance

# Epididymitis

## Etiology

- <35 years: Sexually transmitted chlamydia or gonococcal infection
- Older men: Gram-negative bacteria (*E. coli*, *Pseudomonas*) from ascending urinary infection

Noninfectious
- Adverse effect of medications
- Urinary reflux within ejaculatory ducts
- Sperm and fluid extravasation postvasectomy

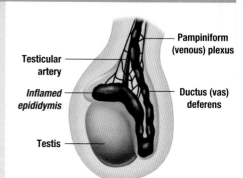

## Clinical Presentation

- Irritative voiding symptoms
- Gradual, progressive onset of pain
- Tenderness posterior and lateral to the testis
- Scrotal ultrasound: Enlarged, hypervascular epididymis
- Pain alleviated by lifting the scrotum (Prehn sign)
- Normal cremasteric reflex

Adapted with permission from Lee JC, Bhatt S, Dogra VS. Imaging of the epididymis, Ultrasound Q 2008 Mar;24(1):3-16.

## Management

- Broad-spectrum antibiotics with narrowing based on urine cultures
- Analgesics
- Rest
- Scrotal elevation

### Antibiotic Management

| Age | <35 | >35 |
|---|---|---|
| Common organisms | Chlamydia, gonorrhea | E. coli, Pseudomonas |
| Antibiotic regimen | Azithromycin or doxycycline and ceftriaxone | Fluoroquinolone |

Epididymo-orchitis

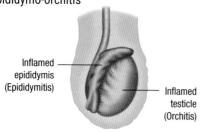

Inflamed epididymis (Epididymitis)

Inflamed testicle (Orchitis)

## Complications

- Epididymo-orchitis
- Abscess formation
- Testicular vasculature compression
- Orchiectomy

# Erectile Dysfunction

Inability to sustain an erection sufficient in rigidity or duration for sexual intercourse for at least 6 months

## Etiology

### Trauma

Pelvic fracture
Penile fracture
Spinal cord injury
Urethral injury

### Psychiatric

+ Nighttime erections
Depression
Anxiety (performance)
Stress

### Vascular

History of HTN, DM, dyslipidemia,
or presence of risk factors of CAD
Absent nighttime erections

### Neurological

Diabetic neuropathy
Multiple sclerosis

### Endocrine

Hyperprolactinemia
Thyroid derangements
Hypogonadism with low serum testosterone

### Iatrogenic

Medications: antidepressants,
antipsychotics, antihypertensives
Surgery: radical prostatectomy

## Evaluation

Medical, sexual, psychosocial, and medication review
Physical exam targeting cardiovascular and genital assessment
Validated questionnaires

Serum testosterone level
Intracavernosal injection to test for functionality of erectile mechanism +/–
ultrasound

## Treatment

Identify and correct underlying etiology with general lifestyle recommendations, including avoiding smoking and alcohol, maintaining ideal body weight, and exercising regularly

Psychogenic ED may benefit from counseling +/– medication

Oral phosphodiesterase-5 inhibitors—ie, sildenafil
Intracavernosal injections (ie, prostaglandin E1, papaverine, phentolamine)
Penile prosthesis

# Hydrocele

- A hydrocele is a collection of fluid surrounding the testis and spermatic cord

- Arise from imbalance between secretion and reabsorption of fluid in the parietal and visceral layers of the tunica vaginalis

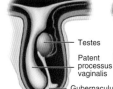

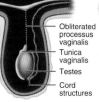
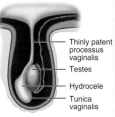

**Normal testicular development: Inguinoscrotal descent (third trimester)**

Peritoneal cavity

Scrotum — Testes — Patent processus vaginalis — Gubernaculum

**Normal testes**

Obliterated processus vaginalis — Tunica vaginalis — Testes — Cord structures

**Hydrocele**

Thinly patent processus vaginalis — Testes — Hydrocele — Tunica vaginalis

- Testis descends during gestation through a peritoneal channel known as the processus vaginalis

- Processus vaginalis then involutes to form the tunica vaginalis

## Presentation

**Communicating Hydrocele:**

- Patent processus vaginalis filled with peritoneal fluid
- Expands with rising abdominal pressure (valsalva)

*Pediatric:*

- Delayed closure or fluid trapping during testicular descent
- A majority resolve by the second birthday

**Noncommunicating Hydrocele:**

- No peritoneal fluid, but rather mesothelial lining secretions
- Independent of intra-abdominal pressure

*Adult:*

- Frequently idiopathic hydrocele from chronic accumulation of fluid
- Acute hydroceles form with scrotal inflammation but resolve with treating underlying condition

## Diagnosis

- *Physical exam* to rule out varicocele, epididymal cyst, torsion
- Ultrasound can confirm diagnosis

Transillumination demonstrating fluid in the scrotum

## Management

*Surgery* if:

- A communicating hydrocele persists beyond 2 years of age
- Idiopathic noncommunicating hydrocele is symptomatic or compromising to skin integrity

# Prostate Cancer

## Epidemiology

- Most common solid organ cancer in men
- Second leading cause of cancer death in men
- Vast majority of prostatic carcinoma arises in the peripheral zone of the prostate
- About 70% of men deceased in their seventies have prostate cancer present on autopsy
- Incidence is highest in African Americans, intermediate in Caucasians, and least in Asians

## Screening

Decision to biopsy should take into account:
- DRE results
- Age
- Ethnicity
- Comorbidities
- Prior biopsy history
- Serum PSA level

AUA suggests that an interpretation of PSA should be individualized to each patient.

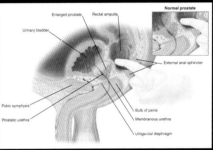

Reproduced with permission from Hankin MH, Morese DE, Bennett-Clarke CA: Clinical Anatomy: A Case Study Approach. New York, NY: McGraw Hill; 2013.

## Treatment & Staging

- Diagnosed by prostate biopsy
- TNM staging is used for clinical staging
- Gleason score is used for pathological staging
- Localized cancer treatment: Radiation therapy, surgery (prostatectomy), active surveillance
- Younger and healthier men with more aggressive cancers should undergo radiation or surgery
- Low-grade and low-volume disease can undergo active surveillance
- Nonlocalized cancer treatment: Anti-androgen therapy
- No definitive cure for metastatic disease

### Gleason's Pattern Scale

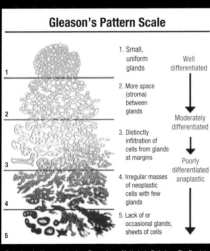

1. Small, uniform glands — Well differentiated
2. More space (stroma) between glands — Moderately differentiated
3. Distinctly infiltration of cells from glands at margins — Poorly differentiated anaplastic
4. Irregular masses of neoplastic cells with few glands
5. Lack of or occasional glands, sheets of cells

Reproduced with permission from Tannenbaum M: Urologic Pathology: The Prostate. Philadelphia, PA: Lea and Febiger, 1977.

# Renal Cell Carcinoma
## ── Malignant Subtypes ──

### Clear Cell RCC

**Pathophysiology**
- Most common subtype
- Proximal tubule origin
- Inactivating mutation on VHL gene (3p)
- Worst prognosis

**Presentation**
- Asymptomatic
- One-third of patients present with abdominal mass, flank pain, and hematuria

**Histology**
- Microscopic clear cells filled with glycogen around a "chicken wire" vessel pattern

Reproduced with permission from Reisner H. Pathology: A Modern Case Study, 2nd ed. New York, NY: McGraw Hill; 2020.

### Papillary RCC

**Pathophysiology**
- Second most common subtype
- Proximal tubule origin
- More likely multifocal or bilateral
- Type 1: Low grade
- Type 2: High grade

**Presentation**
- Most common renal cancer with acquired cystic kidney disease from renal failure
- Most common neoplasm on dialysis

**Histology**

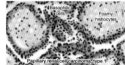

Type I: Basophilic cytoplasm

### Chromophobe RCC

**Pathophysiology**
- Third most common subtype
- Collecting duct origin
- Abundant mitochondria like oncocytoma
- Best prognosis (5 years >90%)

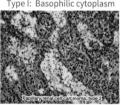

Type II: Eosinophilic cytoplasm

Reproduced with permission from Abrahams NA, Tamboli P: Practical Renal Pathology, A Diagnostic Approach. St. Louis, MO: Elsevier; 2013.

## Benign Subtypes

### Oncocytoma

**Pathophysiology**
- Collecting duct origin

**Presentation & Management**
- Asymptomatic and detected radiographically
- Imaging cannot distinguish from RCC, thus frequently surgically excised

**Histology**
- Cells in nests with an eosinophilic granular cytoplasm and abundant mitochondria
- Grossly, a tan mass with a central scar and fibrous capsule

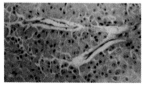

Reproduced with permission from McAninch JW, Lue TF: Smith & Tanagho's General Urology, 19th ed. New York, NY: McGraw Hill; 2020.

### Angiomyolipoma

**Pathophysiology**
- Mass composed of blood vessels (angio), smooth muscle (myo), and fat (lipo)

**Presentation & Management**
- Most frequent among females between 40 and 60, and those with tuberous sclerosis
- Surgical intervention recommended for tumors >4 cm to prevent retroperitoneal hemorrhage

**For all renal tumors...**
- *Prevention:* Avoid smoking and obesity.
- *Diagnosis:* Radiographic mass characterization preferred. Biopsy is not required before excision because most lesions are malignant.
- *Paraneoplastic syndromes:* Seen in 20-30% of masses. Include elevated ESR, anemia, hypercalcemia (from PTH-rp), and polycythemia (from EPO).
- *Treatment:* Surgery (partial or total nephrectomy) recommended for resectable primary tumors.

# Testicular Cancer

Most lesions are derived from the germinal tissue; the remainder arise from nongerminal or stromal cells. May be associated with a history of undescended testes.

## Germ-Cell Tumors

### Seminoma
- Most common germ-cell tumor
- Extremely chemo- and radiosensitive

### Nonseminoma
- Embryonal
- Teratoma
- Choriocarcinoma (increase in hCG)
- Yolk sac (increase in AFP)
- Schiller-Duval bodies: Resemble primitive glomeruli

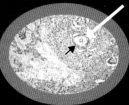

Reproduced with permission from Reisner H. Pathology: A Modern Case Study, 2nd ed. New York, NY: McGraw Hill; 2020.

## Stromal Tumors

### Leydig Cell
- Reinke's crystals (rod-like cytoplasmic inclusions) can be seen on histology
- May be associated with gynecomastia
- Usually secretes testosterone, can produce other hormones

Reproduced with permission from Reisner H: Pathology: A Modern Case Study, 2nd ed. New York, NY: McGraw Hill; 2020.

### Sertoli Cell
- Rare, comprises <1% of testis tumors
- Most tumors have benign behavior, 10% are malignant

 **Evaluation**

Painless testicular mass
Palpation with ultrasound confirmation
Diagnostic staging: Abdominopelvic and chest CT or CXR and determination of serologic tumor markers (AFP, hCG, LDH)
Do *not* perform transscrotal biopsy
Mixed tumors contain >1 germ-cell components

**Treatment**

Sperm preservation prior to treatment
Radical inguinal orchiectomy of the affected side
Surveillance, retroperitoneal radiotherapy, retroperitoneal lymph node dissection, and platinum-based chemotherapy may be recommended after orchiectomy
Overall prognosis of testicular tumors is excellent

# Testicular Torsion

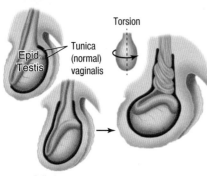

Epid.
Testis
Tunica (normal) vaginalis
Torsion

Bell-clapper deformity

## Risk Factors

- Bell-clapper deformity
- Inappropriately high attachment of tunica vaginalis causing transverse lie of testicle
- Allows for free rotation of testicle on the spermatic cord within the tunica vaginalis

## Clinical Presentation

- Most often occurs in children and adolescents
- Rapid onset of severe pain and swelling
- Tender testicle
- High, horizontal lie
- Cremaster reflex absent
- Pain is not alleviated with scrotal elevation (negative Prehn sign)
- Early: Torsed cord and testis palpable
- Later (12-24 hours): Hemiscrotum appears as confluent mass without identifiable landmarks

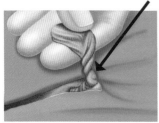

Torsed spermatic cord

Dark, cyanotic color suggesting nonviability of testis after detorsion

## Evaluation

- History
- Physical exam
- Urinalysis
- Doppler ultrasonography: Absent arterial flow
- Surgical scrotal exploration if high degree of suspicion

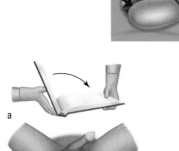

a

b

## Management

- Urgent detorsion within 4-6 hours. Either surgical or manual
- Orchiopexy* bilaterally to prevent recurrence
- Orchiectomy if testis nonsalvageable

*Orchiopexy: Anchoring tunica albuginea of testis to the overlying parietal tunica vaginalis and scrotal dartos muscle

# Varicocele

## Clinical Presentation

 Incidental/asymptomatic

 Infertility

 Pain

 Palpable scrotal "bag of worms"

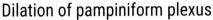
Dilation of pampiniform plexus

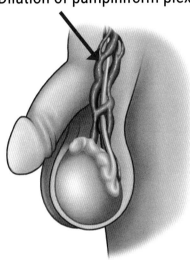

## Evaluation

 Physical exam

 More common on left side

 Semen analysis to evaluate fertility

 Increase with Valsalva and standing

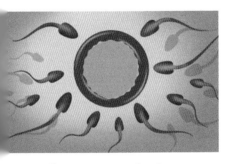

Semen analysis

# References _____

**Benign Prostatic Hyperplasia**
American Urological Association. Medical BPH. https://university.auanet.org/modules/webapps/core/index.cfm#/corecontent/72. Updated January 31, 2020.

American Urological Association. https://www.auanet.org/education/auauniversity/for-medical-students/medical-student-curriculum. Accessed January 31, 2019.

American Urological Association. Surgical BPH. https://university.auanet.org/modules/webapps/core/index.cfm#/corecontent/73. Updated 31 January, 2020.

Canada Pharmacy. Benign prostatic hypertrophy drugs recommended by our specialists. Mycanadianpharmacypro.com. https://www.mycanadianpharmacypro.com/alpha-blockers-for-bph-treatment. Accessed January 31, 2019.

National Cancer Institute at the National Institutes of Health. TURP. https://www.cancer.gov/publications/dictionaries/cancer-terms/def/turp. Accessed January 31, 2019.

Sukin S. Urolift for BPH. http://www.drstevensukinurology.com/bph-urolift.shtml. Accessed January 31, 2019.

TeachMe Anatomy. The prostate gland. https://teachmeanatomy.info/pelvis/the-male-reproductive-system/prostate-gland/. Updated December 4, 2019.

**Bladder Cancer**
Lotan Y, Choueiri TK. Clinical presentation, diagnosis, and staging of bladder cancer. In: Lerner S, ed. *UpToDate.* 2019. www.uptodate.com/contents/clinical-presentation-diagnosis-and-staging-of-bladdercancer?search=bladder%2Btumor&source=search_result&selectedTitle=1~150&usage_type=default&display_rank=1.

Miller J. Urinary tract imaging. In: Lee S, ed. *Radiology Rounds November 2003 – Urinary Tract Imaging.* 2003. www.massgeneral.org/imaging/news/radrounds/november_2003/.

Smith K. What causes blood in urine (hematuria)? Everyday Health. *EverydayHealth.com.* www.everydayhealth.com/urine/what-causes-blood-urine-hematuria/. September 24, 2018.

Wieder JA, ed. Bladder tumors. In: *Pocket Guide to Urology.* J. Oakland, CA: Wieder Medical; 2010:40-58.

Williams S, Jorda M, Manoharan M, et al. Bladder cancer. In: *Urology: An Atlas of Investigation and Diagnosis.* Clinical Publishing; 2009.

**Epididymitis**
American Urological Association. https://www.auanet.org/education/auauniversity/for-medical-students/medical-students-curriculum. Accessed August 19, 2020.

Harvard Health Publishing. Epididymitis and orchitis. https://www.health.harvard.edu/a_to_z/epididymitis-and-orchitis-a-to-z. Published January 2019.

SlideShare. Doppler ultrasound of acute scrotum. https://www.slideshare.net/shaffar75/doppler-ultrasound-of-acute-scrotum-23607822

Smith Y. What is epididymitis? News-Medical.Net. https://www.news-medical.net/health/What-is-Epididymitis.aspx.Last Updated August 23, 2018.

**Erectile Dysfunction**
Aday C. Erectile dysfunction. In: Chisholm-Burns MA, Schwinghammer TL, Malone PM, et al, eds. *Pharmacotherapy Principles and Practice.* 5th ed. New York, NY: McGraw Hill; 2018. https://ppp.mhmedical.com/content.aspx?bookid=2440&sectionid=196188960. Accessed June 18, 2019.

## Hydrocele

Bowling K, Hart N, Cox P, et al. Management of paediatric hernia. *BMJ*. 2017;359:j4484. doi:10.1136/bmj.j4484.

Brenner J, Ojo A. Causes of painless scrotal swelling in children and adolescents. In: Middleman A, et al, eds. *UpToDate*. www.uptodate.com/contents/causes-of-painless-scrotal-swelling-in-children-and -adolescents?search=hydrocele&source=search_result&selectedTitle=2~31 &usage_type=default&display_rank=2. February 2019.

Bryson D. Transillumination of testicular hydrocele. *Clin Med Img Lib*. 2017;3(3). doi:10.23937/2474-3682/1510075.

Eyre R, Givens J. Evaluation of nonacute scrotal conditions in adults. In: O'Leary M, ed. *UpToDate*. 2019. www.uptodate.com/contents/evaluation-of-nonacute-scrotal-conditions-in-adults?search=hydrocele&source=search_result&selectedTitle=1~31&usage_type=default&display_rank=1#H2795396049.

## Prostate Cancer

American Urological Association. https://www.auanet.org/education/auauniversity/for-medical-students/medical-student-curriculum

Prostate Conditions Education Council. Gleason score. https://www.prostateconditions.org/about-prostate-conditions/prostate-cancer/newly-diagnosed/gleason-score

UCSF Health. Prostate cancer. https://www.ucsfhealth.org/conditions/prostate_cancer/. Accessed August 14, 2016.

## Renal Cell Carcinoma

American Urological Association. Clear cell renal cell carcinoma. www.auanet.org/education/auauniversity/education-products-and-resources/pathology-for-urologists/kidney/renal-cell-carcinomas/clear-cell-renal-cell-carcinoma

American Urological Association. Chromophobe renal cell carcinoma. www.auanet.org/education/auauniversity/education-products-and-resources/pathology-for-urologists/kidney/renal-cell-carcinomas/chromophobe-renal-cell-carcinoma

American Urological Association. Papillary renal cell carcinoma. www.auanet.org/education/auauniversity/education-products-and-resources/pathology-for-urologists/kidney/renal-cell-carcinomas/papillary-renal-cell-carcinoma

American Urological Association. Renal angiomyolipoma. www.auanet.org/education/auauniversity/education-products-and-resources/pathology-for-urologists/kidney/mesenchymal-and-other-tumors/renal-angiomyolipoma

American Urological Association. Renal oncocytoma. www.auanet.org/education/auauniversity/education-products-and-resources/pathology-for-urologists/kidney/benign-epithelial-tumors/renal-oncocytoma

Wieder JA, ed. Renal tumors. In: *Pocket Guide to Urology*. J. Wieder Medical; 2010:1-24.

## Testicular Cancer

Harano K, Ando M, Sasajima Y, et al. Primary yolk sac tumor of the omentum: a case report and literature review. *Case Rep Oncol*. 2012;5(3):671-675. doi:10.1159/000337281

Leydig cells. In: Takisawa P, ed. *Histology @ Yale* [online histology atlas]. New Haven, CT: Takisawa, Peter; [date unknown].

## Testicular Torsion

American Urological Association. https://www.auanet.org/education/auauniversity/for-medical-students/medical-student-curriculum

Perron CE, Bin SS. Pain: Scrotal. Anesthesia Key. https://aneskey.com/pain-scrotal/

## Varicocele

[Author unknown]. Varicocele. University of Miami Health System. http://urology.med.miami.edu/specialtie male-urologic-health/varicocele. Accessed May 15, 2019.

Spitzer S. Microsurgery varicocelectomy. In: Baazeem, A, ed. *British Journal of Urology* [Online Surgical Atlas]. Oxford, United Kingdoms: BJUI; 2009.

Varicocele embolization. Azura Vascular Care. https://www.azuravascularcare.com/medical-services/varicocele-embolization/. Accessed May 15, 2019.

BK p/n MHID 1-260-45398-7  ISBN 978-1-260-45398